P9-BHW-127

AMERICAN LAW YEARBOOK 2006

AN ANNUAL SOURCE PUBLISHED BY THOMSON GALE AS A SUPPLEMENT TO WEST'S ENCYCLOPEDIA OF AMERICAN LAW

ISSN 1521-0901

AMERICAN LAW YEARBOOK 2006

AN ANNUAL SOURCE PUBLISHED BY THOMSON GALE AS A SUPPLEMENT TO WEST'S ENCYCLOPEDIA OF AMERICAN LAW

Detroit • New York • San Francisco • New Haven, Conn. • Waterville, Maine • London

American Law Yearbook 2006

Project Editor
Jeffrey Wilson

Editorial
Laurie Fundukian, Jeffrey Lehman

Editorial Support Services
Selwa Petrus, Mike Lesniak, Luann Brennan

Permissions
Margaret Chamberlain, Jacqueline Key, Margaret Abendroth

Imaging and Multimedia
Randy Bassett, Dean Dauphinais, Lezlie Light

Composition and Electronic Capture
Evi Seoud

Manufacturing
Rhonda Dover

For more information, contact
Thomson Gale
27500 Drake Rd.
Farmington Hills, MI 48331-3535
Or you can visit our Internet site at
http://www.gale.com

ISBN-13: 978-0-7876-9029-8
ISBN-10: 0-7876-9029-5
ISSN: 1521-0901

Printed in the United States of America
10 9 8 7 6 5 4 3 2 1

CONTENTS

Preface . . . . *vii*

Acknowledgments . . . . *xi*

Abortion 1
Aliens. 6
Alito, Jr., Samuel Anthony. 7
Americans With Disabilities Act. 8
Antitrust Law 9
Arbitration 13
Assisted Suicide 14
Attorney 16
Bankruptcy 19
Birth Control 22
Capital Punishment 25
Census. 32
Civil Procedure 33
Civil Rights. 35
Class Action 37
Clean Water Act 40
Commerce Clause 42
Conspiracy 44
Consuls 46
Corporate fraud 48
Cox, Christopher 52
Criminal Procedure 52
DNA 55
Drugs and Narcotics 56
Due Process 58
Education 61
Elections 65
Eleventh Amendment 66
Eminent domain. 67
Environmental Law 69
ERISA. 70
Establishment Clause. 71
Exhaustion of Remedies. 73
Fair Labor Standards Act. 75
Federal Tort Claims Act 76
First Amendment 77
Fourth Amendment 81
Fraud. 86
Freedom of Religion 89
Freedom of Speech 91
Gas 93
Gay and Lesbian Rights. 95
Geneva Convention 97
Gun Control. 98
Habeas Corpus 101
Hate Crime. 106
Hurricane Katrina 107
Identity Theft. 111
Immigration 112
Immunity 113
Insanity Defense. 114
Internet. 116
Jurisdiction 119
Labor Law 125
Malpractice 127
Manslaughter 129
Medicaid 130
Mexico and the United States. 131
Miranda Rights. 133
Murder 134
Native American Rights. 137
Obscenity 139
Organized Crime 140
Patent 143
Perjury 147
Piracy 148
Privacy 149
Probate 151

Property Law 152
Rehnquist, William Hubbs 155
Religion. 157
RICO 159
Search and Seizure. 165
Sentencing 167
Sex Offenses 169
Sexual Harassment 170
Sixth Amendment. 171
Social Security 174
Sovereign Immunity. 176
Sports Law 178
Supreme Court. 179
Taxation 181
Terrorism 182
Tobacco/RICO 187
Voting. 189
Waiver 193
Whistleblowing 194
Wiretapping 195

Bibliography *199*

Appendix (documents):
Abortion:
South Dakota 2006 Anti-Abortion Law 215
Drugs and Narcotics:
Denver's Alcohol-Marijuana Equalization Initiative 216
Internet:
Child Online Protection Act 217
Privacy:
Wisconsin's Anti-Cloning Law 218

Glossary of Legal Terms *221*

Abbreviations *237*

Table of Cases Cited *257*

Index by Name and Subject *261*

PREFACE

The need for a layperson's comprehensive, understandable guide to terms, concepts, and historical developments in U.S. law has been well met by *West's Encyclopedia of American Law* (*WEAL*). Published in a second edition in 2004 by Thomson Gale, *WEAL* has proved itself a valuable successor to West's 1983 publication, *The Guide to American Law: Everyone's Legal Encyclopedia*, and the 1997 first edition of WEAL.

Since 1998, Thomson Gale, a premier reference publisher, has extended the value of *WEAL* with the publication of *American Law Yearbook* (*ALY*). This supplement adds entries on emerging topics not covered in the main set. A legal reference must be current to be authoritative, so *ALY* is a vital companion to a key reference source. Uniform organization by *WEAL* term and cross-referencing make it easy to use the titles together, while inclusion of key definitions and summaries of earlier rulings in supplement entries—whether new or continuations—make it unnecessary to refer to the main set constantly.

Understanding the American Legal System

The U.S. legal system is admired around the world for the freedoms it allows the individual and the fairness with which it attempts to treat all persons. On the surface, it may seem simple, yet those who have delved into it know that this system of federal and state constitutions, statutes, regulations, and common-law decisions is elaborate and complex. It derives from the English common law, but includes principles older than England, along with some principles from other lands. The U.S. legal system, like many others, has a language all its own, but too often it is an unfamiliar language: many concepts are still phrased in Latin. *WEAL* explains legal terms and concepts in everyday language, however. It covers a wide variety of persons, entities, and events that have shaped the U.S. legal system and influenced public perceptions of it.

FEATURES OF THIS SUPPLEMENT

Entries

ALY 2006 contains 136 entries covering individuals, cases, laws, and concepts significant to U.S. law. Entries are arranged alphabetically and use the same entry title as in *WEAL* or *ALY*—when introduced in an earlier *Yearbook* (e.g., September 11th Attacks). There may be several cases discussed under a given topic.

Profiles of individuals cover interesting and influential people from the world of law, government, and public life, both historic and contemporary. All have contributed to U.S. law as a whole. Each short biography includes a timeline highlighting important moments in the subject's life. Persons whose lives were detailed in *WEAL*, but who have died since publication of that work, receive obituary entries in *ALY*.

Definitions

Each entry on a legal term is preceded by a definition, which is easily distinguished by its sans serif typeface. The back of the book includes a Glossary of Legal Terms containing the definitions for a selection of the most important terms **bolded** in the text of the essays and biographies. Terms bolded but not included in the Glossary of Legal Terms in ALY can be found in the Dictionary volume of WEAL.

Cross References

To facilitate research, *ALY 2006* provides two types of cross-references: within and following entries. Within the entries, terms are set in small capital letters (e.g., FIRST AMENDMENT) to indicate that they have their own entry in *WEAL*. At the end of each entry, additional relevant topics in *ALY 2006* are listed alphabetically by title.

In Focus Pieces

In Focus pieces present additional facts, details, and arguments on particularly interesting, important, or controversial issues. These pieces are set apart from the main entries with boxed edges and their own logo.

Appendix

This section follows the Glossary of Legal Terms and features the text of documents complementary to the main entries, such as excerpts from the Geneva Conventions and the Department of Justice's so-called "torture memo."

Table of Cases Cited and Index by Name and Subject

These features make it quick and easy for users to locate references to cases, people, statutes, events, and other subjects. The Table of Cases Cited traces the influences of legal precedents by identifying cases mentioned throughout the text. In a departure from *WEAL*, references to individuals have been folded into the general index to simplify searches. Litigants, justices, historical and contemporary figures, as well as topical references are included in the Index by Name and Subject.

Citations

Wherever possible, *ALY* includes citations to cases and statutes for readers wishing to do further research. They refer to one or more series, called "reporters," which publish court opinions and related information. Each citation includes a volume number, an abbreviation for the reporter, and the starting page reference. Underscores in a citation indicate that a court opinion has not been officially reported as of *ALY*'s publication. Two sample citations, with explanations, are presented below.

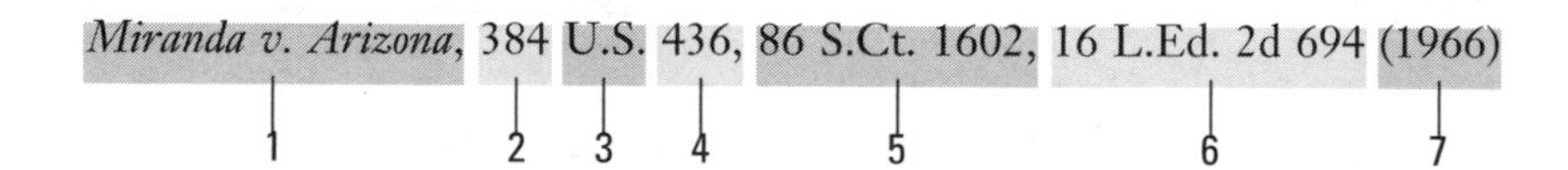

1. *Case title.* The title of the case is set in i and indicates the names of the parties. The suit in this sample citation was between Ernesto A. Miranda and the state of Arizona.
2. *Reporter volume number.* The number preceding the reporter abbreviation indicates the reporter volume containing the case. The volume number appears on the spine of the reporter, along with the reporter abbreviation.
3. *Reporter abbreviation.* The suit in the sample citation is from the reporter, or series of books, called *U.S. Reports,* which contains cases from the U.S. Supreme Court. Numerous reporters publish cases from the federal and state courts; consult the Abbreviations list at the back of this volume for full titles.
4. *Reporter page.* The number following the reporter abbreviation indicates the reporter page on which the case begins.
5. *Additional reporter citation.* Many cases may be found in more than one reporter. The suit in the sample citation also appears in volume 86 of the *Supreme Court Reporter,* beginning on page 1602.
6. *Additional reporter citation.* The suit in the sample citation is also reported in volume 16 of the *Lawyer's Edition,* second series, beginning on page 694.
7. *Year of decision.* The year the court issued its decision in the case appears in parentheses at the end of the cite.

Brady Handgun Violence Prevention Act, Pub. L. No. 103-159, 107 Stat. 1536 (18 U.S.C.A. § § 921-925A)

1 2 3 4 5 6 7 8

1. *Statute title.*
2. *Public law number.* In the sample citation, the number 103 indicates this law was passed by the 103d Congress, and the number 159 indicates it was the 159th law passed by that Congress.
3. *Reporter volume number.* The number preceding the reporter abbreviation indicates the reporter volume containing the statute.
4. *Reporter abbreviation.* The name of the reporter is abbreviated. The statute in the sample citation is from *Statutes at Large.*
5. *Reporter page.* The number following the reporter abbreviation indicates the reporter page on which the statute begins.
6. *Title number.* Federal laws are divided into major sections with specific titles. The number preceding a reference to the U.S. Code stands for the section called Crimes and Criminal Procedure.
7. *Additional reporter.* The statute in the sample citation may also be found in the *U.S. Code Annotated.*
8. *Section numbers.* The section numbers following a reference to the *U.S. Code Annotated* indicate where the statute appears in that reporter.

COMMENTS WELCOME

Considerable efforts were expended at the time of publication to ensure the accuracy of the information presented in *American Law Yearbook 2006.* The editor welcomes your comments and suggestions for enhancing and improving future editions of this supplement to *West's Encyclopedia of American Law.* Send comments and suggestions to:

American Law Yearbook
Thomson Gale
27500 Drake Rd.
Farmington Hills, MI 48331-3535

ACKNOWLEDGMENTS

SPECIAL THANKS

The editor wishes to acknowledge the contributions of the writers and copyeditors who aided in the compilation of *American Law Yearbook*. The editor gratefully thanks Matthew Cordon, Frederick K. Grittner, Lauri R. Harding, David R. Johnstone, Mary Hertz Scarbrough, and Heidi Splete. Furthermore, valuable content review of entries came from: Matthew Cordon, Frederick K. Grittner, and Lauri R. Harding.

PHOTOGRAPHIC CREDITS

The editor wishes to thank the permission managers of the companies that assisted in securing reprint rights. The following list—in order of appearance—acknowledges the copyright holders who have granted us permission to reprint material in this edition of *American Law Yearbook*:

Accused millennium bomber Ahmed Ressam, 122299 mug shot. Corbis Sygma. -**Alabama Gov. Bob Riley discusses eminent domain bill**, August 2005, photograph. AP Images. -**Attorney Michael Piuze speaks to media** June 2001, photograph. AP Images. -**Bronfman, Jeffrey, president of the US chapter of Espirita Beneficente Uniao Do Vegetal, speaks outside US Supreme Court**, November, 2005, photograph. AP Images. -**Carabell, Keith**, photograph. AP Images. -**Congressman Tom Delay speaks to his attorney in court**, 21 October, 2005, photograph. Jay Janner Pool/Corbis. -**Cox, Christopher**, photograph. Win McNamee/Corbis. -**eBay offices in San Jose CA**, photograph. AP Images. -**Enron founder Kenneth Lay**, 27 April 2006, photograph. AP Images. -**Executives from six major oil companies are sworn in before testimony before Congress on rising gas prices**, 14 March 2006, photograph. Jason Reed/Reuters/Corbis. -**Flooded neighborhoods in Louisiana after Hurricane Katrina**, photograph. AP Images. -**Florida parents and students protest education bill**, February, 2006, photograph. AP Images. -**Former Worldcom CEO Bernard Ebbers leaves Federal Court**, 30 January, 2006, photograph. AP Images. -**Georgia prison photo of Tony Goodman**, November, 2005, photograph. AP Images. -**Gotti, John Jr**, photograph. Mike Segar/ Reuters/Corbis. -**hands holding a Blackberry device**, photograph. Justin Laneepa/Corbis. -**Illinois Gov Rod Blagojevich speaks in his office**, January, 2005, photograph. AP Images. -**Katyal, Neal**, photograph. AP Images. -**Libby, Lewis Scooter leaves federal court in Washington DC**, 3 February, 2006, photograph. Jim Young/Reuters/Corbis. -**Mastromarino, Michael**, photograph. Aristide Economopoulos Star Ledger/Corbis. -**Military solider with detainee at Guantanamo Bay naval base prison**, photograph. AP Images. -**Mitchell, George and baseball commissioner Bud Selig discuss baseball steroid investigation**, March 2006, photograph. AP Images. -**New Hampshire Attorney General Kelly Ayotte speaks to press outside US Supreme Court**, photograph. AP Images. -**Plaintiffs in Wal-Mart emergency contraceptives lawsuit speak to press**, February, 2006, photograph. AP Images. -**Powell, Charles Jr., leaves federal court in East St Louis, IL after sentencing on vote fraud**

charges, photograph. AP Images. -**Pro-assisted suicide picketers outside US Supreme Court** October 2005, photograph. AP Images. -**Sanders, Ronald California prison photo**. AP Images. -**Smith, Anna Nicole arrives at the Supreme Court for her hearing in her probate case**, 28 Feb 2006, photograph. Chris Kleponis/Reuters/Corbis. -**South Dakota Governor Mike Rounds sign abortion bill**, March 2006, photograph. AP Images. -**Terry and Dave Clark outside Arizona home**, April 2006, photograph. AP Images. -**Toledo Jeep plant**, February, 2006, photograph. AP Images. -**Tuscaloosa City Sheriff Ted Sexton speaks to press after arrests in Alabama church burnings**, March 2006, photograph. AP Images. -**US Supreme Court Justice Samuel Alito**, photograph. Yuri Gripas/Reuters/Corbis. -**Whitbread, Ed**, photograph. Andrew Holbrook/ Corbis. -**Anonymous, "2005 Assembly Bill 499," Wisconsin State Legislature**, June 16, 2005. -**Anonymous, "Alcohol-Marijuana Equalization Initiative," www.saferchoice .org**, July 12, 2006. Reproduced by permission. -**Anonymous, "House Bill No. 1215," South Dakota Legislature**, 2006. -**Anonymous, "Title XIV—Child Online Protection Act," www.epic.org**, 1998.

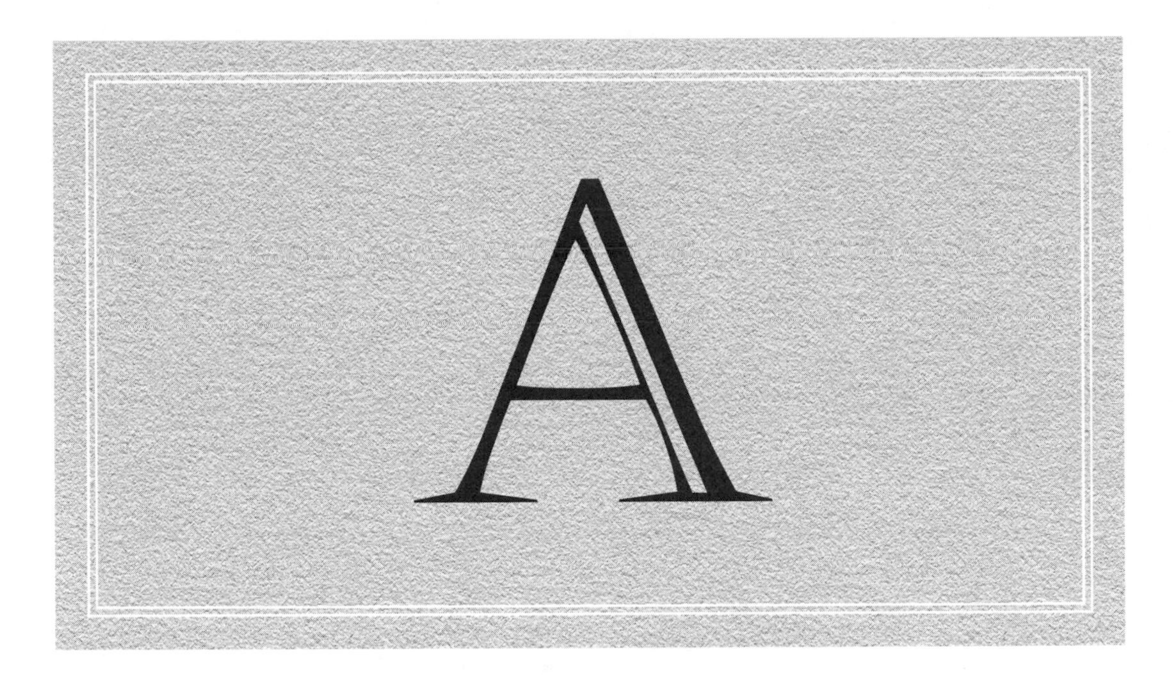

ABORTION

The spontaneous or artificially induced expulsion of an embryo or fetus. As used in legal context, the term usually refers to induced abortion.

Ayotte v. Planned Parenthood of Northern New England

Though the Supreme Court has consistently upheld a woman's right to have an abortion, it has allowed states to impose parental notification requirements on minors who wish to have an abortion. In *Ayotte v. Planned Parenthood of Northern New England*, __U.S.__, 126 S.Ct. 961, 163 L.Ed.2d 812 (2006), the Court examined how lower **federal courts** should treat abortion notification statutes that may contain some provisions that are constitutionally suspect. Lower courts had generally invalidated the entire **statute**, but the Supreme Court ruled that this response is not always necessary or justified. Federal courts might be able to issue narrower decisions that preserve the remainder of such statutes.

In 2003, New Hampshire passed the Parental Notification Prior to Abortion Act, which prohibited doctors from performing an abortion on a pregnant minor until 48 hours after written notice of the pending abortion had been given to the parent or **guardian**. Persons who violated the act were subject to criminal and civil penalties. The act made three exceptions to this notice requirement: (1) a parent or guardian may certify that they have already been notified; (2) the abortion is needed to prevent the minor's death and there is insufficient time for notice; and (3) the minor petitions a judge to authorize the abortion without parental notification. The law did not explicitly permit a doctor to perform an abortion in a medical emergency without parental notification.

Planned Parenthood of Northern New England, a doctor, and two other abortion providers filed a federal lawsuit, challenging the constitutionality of the act because the law failed to permit a prompt abortion to a minor whose health would be endangered by the delays built into the notification statute. The federal **district court** agreed with the plaintiffs and issued an injunction permanently forbidding the enforcement of the statute. The judge ruled that the law should have included a health exception and found that the judicial bypass proceedings would not have worked quickly enough when a medical emergency was present. The First **Circuit Court** of Appeals upheld the district court decision, adopting much of the lower court's legal reasoning for the act's unconstitutionality.

The Supreme Court, in a unanimous decision, ruled that the lower courts had not adequately considered whether the notification statute needed to be invalidated in its entirety. Justice SANDRA DAY O'CONNOR, writing for the Court, noted that the states have the right to require parental involvement when a minor is considering ending a pregnancy. However, O'Connor also pointed to prior Court rulings that prohibit states from restricting access to abortions that are necessary for preserving the life or health of the mother. New Hampshire contended that in most situations the judicial bypass proceeding would move quickly enough to prevent medical harm to the minor seeking an abortion. In addition, a state "competing harms" law would permit a doctor to perform an

New Hampshire Attorney General Kelly Ayotte speaks to press outside U.S. SUPREME COURT.
AP IMAGES

abortion without following the notifications statute if avoiding harm to the mother outweighed allegiance to the notification provisions. However, the lower courts had rejected these claims because the two provisions did not protect the minors' health reliably in all emergencies.

Justice O'Connor focused on the judicial remedy, stating that "when confronting a constitutional flaw in a statute, we try to limit the solution to the problem," preferring to enjoin only the "unconstitutional applications of a statute while leaving other applications in force." Another option was for a court to "sever the problematic portions while leaving the remainder intact." These considerations were based on respect for the legislature's work. This sensitivity to the work of the legislative branch led to another principle: it was not appropriate for a court to rewrite the law to conform to constitutional requirements as a way to "salvage" a law. Where there is a "murky constitutional context" or "line-drawing is inherently complex," the courts must not invade the legislative domain and rewrite a statute. A final principle governing remedy barred courts from circumventing the intent of the legislature. If a portion of a law is held to be unconstitutional, courts must ask whether the legislature would have "preferred what is left of its statute to no statute at all?"

As to the New Hampshire statute, Justice O'Connor concluded that the lower courts had favored the "blunt" remedy of invalidating the entire law. This approach was not unusual, for the Supreme Court itself had struck down in its entirety a Nebraska law prohibiting partial birth abortions that did not contain a provision that allowed the procedure to save the life of the pregnant woman. However, in the Nebraska case the state did not ask for narrower relief that would have saved the rest of the law. In the case of New Hampshire, the state had argued against invalidating the entire notification statute. O'Connor found that only a few applications of the statute would present constitutional difficulties; as long as the lower courts were faithful to legislative intent, they could issue an injunction that prohibited the law's unconstitutional application.

The Court declined to make a definitive ruling because of a dispute as to whether the state legislature preferred no notification law rather than one with a "health of the mother" exception. Though the statute contained a severability clause that provided that if any provision was ruled invalid the remainder of the statute continued in effect, Planned Parenthood argued that the legislature would have wanted the law at all if modified by the courts. Therefore, the Court remanded the case to the lower courts to determine whether the law should be modified or struck down in its entirety.

Indiana, Missouri Supreme Courts Uphold Waiting Periods for Abortions

In 2005 and 2006, high courts in both Indiana and Missouri upheld laws that require women to wait certain periods of time before undergoing abortions. The state laws in question also require women to consent to abortions after being informed of the dangers associated with and alternatives to abortion procedures. Neither court, however, addressed the question of whether a woman has a constitutional right to have an abortion.

In *Planned Parenthood v. Casey*, 505 U.S. 833, 112 S. Ct. 2791, 120 L. Ed. 2d 674 (1992), the U.S. SUPREME COURT upheld a Pennsylvania **statute** that required a woman to give **informed consent** before undergoing an abortion procedure and specified that a doctor must give information to the woman at least 24 hours prior to the procedure. Those opposed to the informed consent requirement have continued to argue that the mandate violates *Roe v. Wade*, 410 U.S. 113, 93 S. Ct. 705, 35 L. Ed. 2d 147 (1973).

In 1995, the Indiana Legislature passed a statute that included provisions nearly identical to those found in the Pennsylvania statute. Under the Indiana statute, an abortion is considered to be voluntary and informed only if the physician who performs the abortion (or a person to whom the physician has delegated this responsibility) provides information specified in the statute. This information includes, among other items, the risks and alternatives to the procedure, the probable gestational age of the fetus, the medical risks associated with carrying the fetus to term, and the availability of medical assistance benefits and adoption alternatives. The woman must receive this information at least 18 hours prior to undergoing the procedure, and the physician must provide the information in the presence of the woman. Although the majority of states require abortion counseling, Indiana is one of only six states that requires the counseling sessions to be conducted in person.

Shortly after the enactment of the Indiana statute, a group of health care facilities and a physician who performs abortions brought suit in federal court, arguing that the state law was unconstitutional. The U.S. **District Court** for the Southern District of Indiana ruled in 2001 that requiring a physician to provide information to the woman in the woman's presence placed an undue burden on the woman's constitutional right to receive the abortion. *A Woman's Choice-East Side Women's Clinic v. Newman*, 132 F. Supp. 2d 1150 (S.D. Ind. 2001). After its ruling, the district court permanently enjoined the enforcement of the statute. The Seventh **Circuit Court** of Appeals, however, determined that the district court abused its discretion and reversed the ruling. *A Woman's Choice-East Side Women's Clinic v. Newman*, 305 F.3d 684 (7th Cir. 2002). The U.S. Supreme Court denied **certiorari** to review the case in February 2003.

Some of the same plaintiffs from the federal litigation filed suit in Indiana state court in 2003, arguing that the **statutory** provisions violated the Indiana Constitution. The Marion County Superior Court dismissed the suit without explanation. The Court of Appeals in 2004 affirmed part of the trial court's decision, but reversed other parts of the decision and remanded the case to the trial court in order for the trial court to determine whether the statute imposed a material burden on a woman seeking an abortion. *Clinic for Women, Inc. v. Brizzi*, 814 N.E.2d 1042 (Ind. Ct. App. 2004).

The Indiana Supreme Court, in a 4–1 decision, vacated the **appellate** court's decision and affirmed the decision of the Superior Court. *Clinic for Women, Inc. v. Brizzi*, 837 N.E.2d 973 (Ind. 2005). Relying on *Casey* and several prior Indiana state court decisions, the court ruled that the provisions of the statute do not impinge upon a woman's right to privacy under the state constitution. Because the case concerned an application of state law, the decision probably concludes this lengthy litigation.

In 2003, the Missouri Legislature passed a law requiring physicians to mention any "physical, psychological, or situational" risk associated with an abortion. The law also requires a woman to wait 24 hours before having the abortion. Bob Holden, then governor of Missouri, vetoed the bill, but the Missouri Legislature later overrode the veto.

Similar to the Indiana litigation, the Missouri statute was challenged in both state and federal court. The U.S. District Court for the Western District of Missouri in 2004 granted a **preliminary injunction**, preventing enforcement of the statute until the state courts could resolve the issue. Judge Scott O. Wright allowed enforcement of the 24-hour waiting period. The Eighth Circuit Court of Appeals vacated the injunction in November 2005. *Reproductive Health Services of Planned Parenthood of the St. Louis Region v. Nixon*, 428 F.3d 1139 (8th Cir. 2005).

The Circuit Court of Boone County in Missouri determined that the statute was constitutional under state law. A unanimous Missouri Supreme Court agreed, finding that the law was not unconstitutionally vague and that the law did not violate the due process, liberty, or privacy rights of women. Like the Indiana court, the Missouri Supreme Court cited *Casey* in support of its conclusion that the waiting period was constitutional.

Pro-choice groups expressed disappointment in both the Indiana and the Missouri cases. According to these groups, the waiting periods hinder the ability of women to get abortions, especially because these laws require the women to make two trips to abortion clinics. Pro-life groups have countered that waiting periods and information provided by physicians allow for greater protection for the health of the women who might seek an abortion.

Courts Strike Down Partial Birth Abortion Ban Act

Several federal courts in 2005 and 2006 struck down the Partial Birth Abortion Ban Act of 2003, Pub. L. No. 108-105, 117 Stat. 1201. The Supreme Court agreed to hear one of the cases, decided by the Eighth Circuit Court of Appeals, during its 2005 term. However, the Court concluded its session while the case was still pending.

During the 1990s, about 30 states enacted statutes that banned a procedure known as a partial birth abortion. In this procedure, the person performing the abortion partially delivers a living fetus, kills the fetus, and then completes the delivery. Congress also attempted to pass such a statute on the federal level, but President BILL CLINTON vetoed those bills. In 2000, a splintered Supreme Court struck down a Nebraska partial birth abortion statute in a case that featured three concurrences and three dissents. *Stenberg v. Carhart*, 530 U.S. 914, 120 S.Ct. 2597, 147 L.Ed.2d 743 (2000). The reason for the Court's decision was twofold. First, the law was unconstitutional because it did not include an exception to protect the health of the mother. Second, the statute was worded so broadly that the Court thought that it banned most late-term abortions.

Three years later, Congress enacted the Partial Birth Abortion Ban Act of 2003, which rendered the procedure a federal crime. Under the statute, a partial birth abortion occurs when the person performing the procedure "deliberately and intentionally vaginally delivers a living fetus until, in the case of a head first presentation, the entire fetal head is outside the body of the mother, or, in the case of a breech presentation, any part of the fetal trunk past the naval is outside the body of the mother, for the purpose of performing an overt act that the person knows will kill the partially delivered living fetus." Although the statute contains an exception that applies when the life of the mother is at risk, the statute does not contain an exception for when the health of the mother is at risk.

Parties in California, New York, and Nebraska challenged the new law in federal courts. Several doctors, representing both themselves and the patients that they serve, brought suit in the U.S. District Court for the District of Nebraska. In 2004, District Judge Richard G. Kopf held that the statute was unconstitutional for the same reasons that the Supreme Court had struck down the Nebraska state law in *Stenberg v. Carhart*. *Carhart v. Ashcroft*, 331 F. Supp. 2d 805 (D. Neb. 2004). Attorney General Alberto Gonzales appealed the decision to the Eighth Circuit Court of Appeals. The Eighth Circuit in July 2005 affirmed the lower court's ruling, deciding that the statute was unconstitutional because it did not contain an exception that would protect the health of the mother. *Carhart v. Gonzales*, 413 F.3d 791 (8th Cir. 2005).

In California, Judge Phyllis J. Hamilton of the U.S. District Court for the Northern District of California ruled that the statute was unconstitutional because it was vague, it unduly burdened a woman's right to an abortion, and it failed to contain an exception to protect the health of the mother. *Planned Parenthood Federation of America v. Ashcroft*, 320 F. Supp. 2d 957 (N.D. Cal. 2004). The Ninth Circuit Court of Appeals in January 2006 affirmed the district court's decision. *Planned Parenthood Federation of America v. Gonzales*,435 F.3d 1163 (9th Cir. 2006). In New York, the Second Circuit Court of Appeals affirmed a trial court's ruling that the statute was unconstitutional because it violated the due process rights of both physicians and patients. *National Abortion Federation v. Gonzales*,437 F.3d 278 (2d Cir. 2006).

Gonzales filed a petition for writ of certiorari on September 23, 2005, asking the Court to review *Carhart v. Gonzales*. Less than a week later, John G. Roberts was sworn in as the new Chief Justice of the Supreme Court. Four months after the petition was filed, Samuel Alito joined the Court. During confirmation hearings for both Roberts and Alito, the nominees were grilled about their beliefs on abortion rights. This was particularly true of Alito, who replaced SANDRA DAY O'CONNOR, who had long held the swing vote in abortion cases.

On February 21, 2006, the Court granted the petition to hear *Carhart*. The case immediately garnered attention from both pro-life and pro-choice groups. The American Center for Law and Justice, a group opposed to partial-birth abortions, called upon the Court to "put an end to this barbaric procedure." The government submitted its briefs on the merits on May 22, 2006. The respondents were required to submit their briefs by August 10.

South Dakota Law Bans Most Abortions

The South Dakota Legislature in March 2006 approved a bill that prohibits doctors from performing abortions in the state. Although the bill provides for an exception where a woman's life is at risk, the bill does not allow abortions in cases involving rape or incest. Pro-choice activists immediately announced that they would challenge the law. Supporters of the legislation acknowledged that they want to spark a challenge of the U.S. SUPREME COURT's landmark decision in *Roe v. Wade*, 410 U.S. 113, 93 S. Ct. 705, 35 L. Ed. 2d 147 (1973).

In February 2005, the legislature held a public hearing to discuss possible amendments to the state's **informed consent** abortion **statute**. This hearing led to the creation of the South Dakota Task Force to Study Abortion. The Task Force was charged with studying a number of different aspects of abortion, including the practice of abortion; technological advances since the Supreme Court's decision in *Roe*; the societal, ethical, and economic effects of abortion; the effect of abortions on pregnant

South Dakota Governor Mike Rounds signs abortion bill, March 2006.
AP IMAGES

women; the relationship between a woman and an unborn child; and other items. The Task Force released its report in December 2005.

Among several other findings in its 71-page report, the Task Force took aim at the *Roe* decision and the decision's underlying bases. The report asserted that the Court's decision was flawed in numerous ways and was based on several incorrect assumptions. The Task Force asserted that each of the following of the Court's assumptions were incorrect: (1) that the Court could not determine when human life begins; (2) that a normal physician-patient relationship would exist, where the doctor would provide pertinent information about the abortion to the woman; (3) that motherhood and child-rearing forced the woman to life a distressful life, and thus the option of abortion was necessary to save a woman from this distress; (4) that an abortion would be truly voluntary and informed; (5) that the abortion procedure was less risky to the health of the mother than the process of childbirth; and (6) that women face a cultural stigma associated with unwed motherhood. The report concluded that between 43 and 45 million abortions had taken place in the U.S. since *Roe* was decided. About 800 abortions per year are performed in South Dakota.

In addition to the creation of the Task Force in 2005, the South Dakota Legislature passed legislation stating that all abortions resulted in the termination of a living human being. The Task Force's finding reiterated this conclusion. According to one of the experts who testified before the Task Force, developments in the area of molecular biology between the 1970s and the 1990s proved that a separate and unique human being is created at conception, rather than at birth. Other experts who testified concurred with this assessment.

The Task Force made four conclusions based on its study. First, it concluded that an "abortion terminates the life of a unique, whole, living human being." Second, it concluded that a physician who performs an abortion terminates the life of a separate patient. Third, it concluded that "the authority for the physician to terminate the life of his or her patient rests exclusively upon the written consent of the pregnant mother. . . ." Fourth, it concluded that "the mother has an existing and important and beneficial relationship with her child that is irrevocably terminated by an abortion procedure."

The Legislature accepted and concurred with the Task Force's findings. It also found that protecting the life of the unborn child was mandated under the state's constitution. According to the legislation that eventually passed, "the Legislature finds that the guarantee of **due process of law** under the Constitution of South Dakota applies equally to born and unborn human beings, and that under the Constitution of South Dakota, a pregnant mother and her unborn child, each possess a natural and inalienable right to life."

Under the statute, no person in the state may cause or **abet** the termination of the life of an unborn human being. The statute also prohibits the sale, use, prescription, or administration of a contraceptive that could be used to abort a pregnancy. The only exception to the statute allows a doctor to perform an abortion that is "designed or intended to prevent the death of a pregnant mother," though the statute also requires the physician to "make reasonable medical efforts" to save the lives of both the mother and the unborn child. Efforts to amend the bill to create exceptions in cases of rape or incest or for the woman's health failed.

The South Dakota Senate passed the provision on February 23, 2005, and shortly thereafter, Governor Mike Rounds acknowledged that he favored the bill. He signed the bill, known as the Women's Health and Human Life Protection Act, on March 6. Its provisions become effective on July 1, though court challenges will likely postpone the application of the statute.

Prior efforts on the part of pro-life advocates have attempted to erode the effects of *Roe* rather than call for the Supreme Court to overturn the decision. Some pro-choice advocates expressed surprise that the state of South Dakota would lead a "frontal assault" on *Roe*, noting that the pro-life camp has acted "emboldened."

The appointments of Chief Justice JOHN ROBERTS and Associate Justice SAMUEL ALITO by President GEORGE W. BUSH were partially responsible for the passage of the legislation (though similar legislation was introduced in 2004, prior to these appointments). By April 2006, at least five other states were considering similar bans. A challenge of this law could take several years to reach the Supreme Court.

Opponents of the legislation announced that they would attempt to have this issue placed on a ballot to put the matter to a popular vote. Even some pro-life advocates have questioned the legislation because it blatantly violates requirements under both *Roe* and another landmark abortion case, *Planned Parenthood v. Casey*, 505 U.S. 833, 112 S. Ct. 2791, 120 L. Ed. 2d 674 (1992). A pro-choice supporter noted that the fight over this statute would be "very ugly and divisive." The petition for a referendum on the law was successful and it will go on the November 2006 ballot.

ALIENS

Foreign-born persons who have not been naturalized to become U.S. citizens under federal law and the Constitution.

Fernandez-Vargas v. Gonzales

The Illegal Immigration Reform and Immigrant Responsibility Act of 1996 (IIRIRA), P.L. 104-208, made amendments to the longstanding Immigration and Nationality Act (INA). Existing immigration law had already provided that an order to deport an illegal immigrant could be reinstated if that person left and unlawfully reentered the United States again. However, provisions under the IIRIRA expanded the class of illegal reentrants whose prior orders for deportation (now referred to as removal) could be reinstated. Moreover, the IIRIRA provisions bar reentrants from seeking relief under the INA.

In a decidedly important case during a politically-tense time over immigration issues, the U.S. SUPREME COURT, in *Fernandez-Vargas v. Gonzales*, No. 04-1376, 548 U.S. ___ (2006) considered whether IIRIRA's new provisions could be applied to illegal immigrants who reentered the United States before its enactment. Humberto Fernandez-Vargas, an illegal reentrant, argued that such application would be impermissibly retroactive. The Supreme Court disagreed, finding no retroactive effect or burden upon a "continuing violator" who had no vested rights under the act.

Fernandez-Vargas, a citizen of Mexico, first came to the United States in 1970, but was deported for immigration violations. He reentered illegally several times, without detection, and from 1982 to the present, essentially resided illegally in the United States. In 1989, Fernandez-Vargas fathered a son, who is a United States citizen. He also married the boy's mother in 2001. Shortly thereafter, she filed a relative-visa petition on behalf of her husband, and he filed a separate application for adjustment of status to lawful permanent resident. The filings caught the attention of authorities, who, under the auspices of the §241(a)(5) of the amended INA, reinstated his 1981 deportation order. He was detained for ten months, then removed to Juarez, Mexico in 2004.

On appeal to the Tenth Circuit Court of Appeals, Fernandez-Vargas argued that because he illegally reentered the United States prior to the effective date of the IIRIRA, the controlling reinstatement provision (of prior deportation orders) was that of the old INA §242(f). The old provision would have permitted Fernandez-Vargas to apply for an adjustment of status as a spouse of a U.S. citizen. He further argued that the new provision would be impermissibly retroactive because he would lose his eligibility to apply for adjustment of status.

The appellate court agreed that new §241(a)(5) did bar Fernandez-Vargas's application and eligibility. However, the appellate court also found that under *Landgraf v. USI Film Products*, 511 U.S. 244 (1994), the new provision had no impermissibly retroactive effect on Fernandez-Vargas. The U.S. Supreme Court granted review based on a split among the circuit courts of appeal over the application of §241(a)(5) of the INA to aliens who illegally reentered prior to IIRIRA's effective date.

Justice Souter, writing the majority opinion for eight justices, first noted that statutes are disfavored as retroactive when their application "would impair rights a party possessed when he acted, increase a party's liability for past conduct, or impose new duties with respect to transactions already completed." (quoting *Landgraf*, above).The Court went on to state that modern law follows Justice Story's definition of a retroactive statute, as "tak[ing] away or impair[ing] vested rights acquired under existing laws, or creat[ing] a new obligation, impos[ing] a new duty, or attach[ing] a new disability, in respect to transactions or consideration already past." (The Court quoted from *Society for the Propagation of the Gospel v. Wheeler*, 22. F.Cas. 756.)

The Court next noted that §241(a)(5) of the subject statute neither expressly includes nor excludes aliens who illegally entered the country before the IIRIRA's effective date. The Court reasoned that to apply §241(a)(5) only to deportations or departures after IIRIRA's effective date would exempt anyone who left prior to that date but reentered after it. This would produce a "strange result," since the statute was revised to *expand* the scope of the reinstatement authority, and fortify it with something close to finality.

The Court further found that Fernandez-Vargas caused his own predicament because he had plenty of notice that the new provisions would take effect in 1997. He could have left for Mexico and applied for legal admission from there. Instead, he chose to stay in the United States illegally. Therefore, §241(a)(5) of the INA had no impermissibly retroactive effect on him, because it did not deprive him (or others similarly situated) of any rights he was lawfully or legitimately entitled to.

Justice Stevens was the lone dissenter, citing "harsh consequences" on "thousands of individuals." He disagreed with both conclusions drawn by the majority, that the statute applied to pre-enactment reentries, and that the statute had no retroactive effect.

ALITO, JR., SAMUEL ANTHONY

Samuel Alito

YURI GRIPAS/REUTERS/CORBIS

On October 31, 2005, United States Court of Appeals Judge Samuel A. Alito Jr. was nominated to a seat on the U.S. SUPREME COURT. His nomination followed the withdrawal of former nominee Harriet E. Miers and promised a battle in an increasingly contentious and partisan Senate.

Alito was born on April 1, 1950 in Trenton, New Jersey. His father had emigrated from Italy as a boy and become a high school teacher before changing careers in the 1950s to work as the research director of a nonpartisan agency that analyzed legislation for state legislators. His mother was an elementary school principal. Alito excelled as a student, deciding on a legal career after discovering a special affinity for in-depth research and finely-honed argument on the high school debate team. He graduated as valedictorian of his class and headed off to Princeton University in 1968.

After receiving his undergraduate degree in 1972, Alito pursued a law degree at Yale Law School (1975). There, he quickly became known as a traditionalist with a quick intellect. It was a reputation that he was to carry with him throughout his working life. In 1976, Alito was hired as a law clerk by Third Circuit Court of Appeals Judge Leonard I. Garth (who eventually became a colleague when Alito was named to the same bench). After clerking for Garth, Alito spent 1977 to 1981 as an assistant U.S. attorney in New Jersey. He then went to Washington, DC to work for the Department of Justice, first as an assistant to the solicitor general from 1981 to 1985 and then as a deputy assistant attorney general from 1985 to 1987. In the former position, he argued several cases before the U.S. Supreme Court. 1987 saw Alito's return to New Jersey as United States attorney, where he handled cases from organized crime to child pornography.

Alito took a seat on the U.S. Court of Appeals for the Third Circuit in 1990. While his time there undisputedly marked him as a solidly conservative jurist, it is also showed a man unwilling to parade his political views in public. He was widely respected by Democrats and Republicans alike, and few saw him as either rigid or an ideologue. Still, Alito's controversial opinions included his lone dissent in a 1991 case that felled a Pennsylvania law requiring married women seeking abortions to inform their husbands and his 1998 holding that a holiday display that included secular symbols along with religious ones did not violate the FIRST AMEND-

SAMUEL A. ALITO, JR.

1975 Earned law degree from Yale Law School
1985 Deputy Assistant U.S. Attorney General
1987 U.S. Attorney for New Jersey
1990 Took seat on U.S Court of Appeals for Third Circuit
2006 Sworn into U.S. Supreme Court

MENT. On the other hand, Alito voted with the majority to find a ban on late-term abortions unconstitutional where there was no exception considering the health of the mother. These, and the broad array of other published opinions stemming from 15 years on the bench, were to come under intense scrutiny when Alito was nominated to replace retiring U.S. Supreme Court Justice SANDRA DAY O'CONNOR in October of 2005.

Alito's nomination came in the wake of the withdrawal of previous nominee Harriet E. Miers. It also came at a time when President GEORGE W. BUSH was lagging in the polls and there was increasing acrimony between parties in the Senate. The situation was further sharpened by O'Connor's pivotal role as a centrist justice on a fairly divided Court, thus making the stakes particularly high for both parties in finding a suitable replacement. In short, there was little doubt that Alito's confirmation hearings were destined to be difficult and time-consuming, with conservative and liberal agendas likely to take precedence.

As expected the ideological battle between the parties caused great friction and talk of filibustering Alito's nomination. Despite Democratic attempts to block a vote on the nomination by filibustering, a Senate closure motion ended debate by a 72-25 vote. The closure motion forced a vote on the nomination, and Alito was confirmed by a 58-42 vote, the smallest margin since CLARENCE THOMAS's 1991 confirmation. Alito was sworn in on January 31, 2006.

AMERICANS WITH DISABILITIES ACT

U.S. v. Georgia

Title II of the Americans with Disabilities Act (ADA), 42 U.S.C.A. § 12131 *et seq.*, prohibits disabled persons from being denied the benefits of the "services, programs, or activities of a public **entity**, or to be subjected to discrimination by any such entity." A public entity includes any state or local government. Title II authorizes lawsuits by private citizens for money damages against public entities who violate Title II provisions. However, since the late 1990s the U.S. SUPREME COURT has issued decisions that have limited the ability to Congress to revoke state **sovereign immunity** and permit lawsuits under civil rights statutes for money damages. The Court shifted course in *U.S. v. Georgia*, __U.S.__, 126 S.Ct. 877, 163 L.Ed.2d 650 (2006), ruling that a Georgia state prison inmate who is paraplegic can pursue a Title II damages lawsuit against the state of Georgia for the conditions of his confinement.

Tony Goodman was confined to the Georgia State Prison at Reidsville. Goodman filed administrative complaints with the prison system and then filed a complaint in federal **district court** in which he challenged the conditions of his confinement. He named the State of Georgia and the Georgia Department of Corrections as defendants. He sought money damages and injunctive relief. In the list of allegations submitted to the court, Goodman claimed that he was confined almost 24 hours per day in his 12-by-3 foot cell. He could not turn his wheelchair around and he could not use toilet and shower facilities without assistance. Sometimes, he alleged, the guards denied him this assistance. He also alleged that he had injured himself many times when he tried to use the toilet or shower on his own and on several occasions he had been forced to sit in his own feces and urine. Other allegations included denial of physical therapy and medical treatment, and denial of access to almost all prison programs because of his disability.

The federal district court ruled that Goodman's allegations were vague and dismissed his complaint without allowing Goodman the chance to amend his pleadings and provide more detail. The judge dismissed the prisoner's Title II claims because the Supreme Court had ruled that states could not be sued for damages under Title II, as the law violated state sovereign immunity. Goodman appealed to the Eleventh **Circuit Court** of Appeals and at that point the United Sates government intervened on his behalf, arguing that in this case Title II had constitutionally abrogated the state's immunity. The court of appeals concluded that Goodman had alleged sufficient facts to support a civil rights lawsuit based on violations of the EIGHTH AMENDMENT's Cruel and Unusual Punishments Clause. The court ordered the district court to allow Goodman to amend his complaint relating to the conditions of his confinement. As to the Title II claims, the Eleventh Circuit upheld the district court, finding that these claims were barred by sovereign immunity. The Supreme Court agreed to hear the federal government's appeal to consider this sovereign immunity question.

The Court, in a unanimous decision, ruled that Title II validly abrogated state sovereign immunity when it created a private **cause of action** for damages against the states for conduct that actually violated the FOURTEENTH AMENDMENT. Justice ANTONIN SCALIA, writing for the Court, made clear that it was not reviewing the Eighth Amendment claims. The state had not contested the Eleventh Circuit ruling, so the Supreme Court would not consider the merits of those claims. However, Goodman had also argued that this same conduct also violated Title II. Justice Scalia found it plausible that the alleged deliberate refusal of prison officials to accommodate Goodman's disability-related mobility, hygiene, medical care and other prison programs constituted a denial of Title II discrimination. This was important because the Fourteenth Amendment's Due Process Clause incorporates the Eighth Amendment's **Cruel and Unusual Punishment** into its protections, making the Eighth Amendment applicable to state governments. Section 1 of the Fourteenth Amendment, which includes the Due Process Clause, the **Equal Protection** Clause, and the **Privileges and Immunities** Clauses, sets out these powerful substantive guarantees. Section 5 authorizes Congress to pass laws to enforce Section 1 and that power extends to the **abrogation** of state sovereign immunity.

Justice Scalia concluded that Title II created a private cause of action for damages against the state for acts that "*actually*" violate the Fourteenth Amendment. Prior Title II cases that refused to abrogate sovereign immunity dealt with actions that did not violate a person's constitutional rights. Therefore, Goodman was entitled to pursue the Title II cause of action as well as the Fourteenth/Eighth Amendment claim. The Court directed that the lawsuit be sent back to the district court, where Goodman could attempt to sort out these claims. Once he files an amended complaint the court can decide (1) which aspects of the state's alleged misconduct violated Title II, (2) which misconduct violated the Fourteenth Amendment, and (3) which misconduct violated Title II but not the Fourteenth Amendment. As to the third category, the lower courts would have to decide if the "purported **abrogation** of sovereign immunity as to that class of conduct is nevertheless valid."

Georgia prison photo of Tony Goodman, November 2005.
AP IMAGES

ANTITRUST LAW

Legislation enacted by the federal and various state governments to regulate trade and commerce by preventing unlawful restraints, price-fixing, and monopolies, to promote competition, and to encourage the production of quality goods and services at the lowest prices, with the primary goal of safeguarding public welfare by ensuring that consumer demands will be met by the manufacture and sale of goods at reasonable prices.

Illinois Tool Works Inc. v. Independent Ink, Inc.

The United States government awards patents to the inventors of new products and technologies, giving patent holders exclusive rights to control these inventions for a certain number of years. The courts have historically viewed a patent as giving the owner a **monopoly**, which is an exception to federal antitrust laws. However, the courts used the Sherman Act antitrust provisions (15 U.S.C.A. §§ 1 and 2) to prohibit "tying arrangements," in which patent holders require purchasers of their product to also buy some other product. The U.S. SUPREME COURT presumed that the patent holder had market power, a prerequisite for an antitrust violation, merely having the patent. In *Illinois Tool Works Inc. v. Independent Ink, Inc.*, __U.S.__, 126 S.Ct. 1281, 164 L.Ed.2d 26 (2006), the Court reversed course and abandoned this presumption. In future antitrust litigation the patent holder must be shown to dominate the market in order to be held liable for an antitrust violation.

Illinois Tool Works, Inc. (ITW), through its Trident Industrial Inkjet unit, held the patent on an inkjet printhead. Trident sold this printhead technology to printer manufacturers who produced printers that were sold to companies that placed barcodes on cartons during assembly line production. Under the licensing agreement, the printer manufacturers and their customers could use the printheads if they agreed to only use ink and ink systems supplied by Trident. Independent Ink Inc. (Independent) reverse engineered Trident's ink and sought to market it at a cheaper price. However, the **tying arrangement** (Trident printheads and Trident ink) prevented Independent from competing with Trident. Even if companies wanted to purchase the cheaper ink, the licensing agreement barred them from **doing business** with Independent.

Independent filed a federal lawsuit against ITW, contending that the tying arrangement was presumptively illegal under the Sherman Act. The federal **district court** ruled against Independent, concluding that Independent had failed to provide any evidence of market power over the tying product (the printhead). The Court of Appeals for the Federal Circuit reversed the district court ruling, finding that "a **rebuttable presumption** of market power arises from the possession of a patent over a tying product." In so ruling the Federal Circuit followed Supreme Court precedents. The Supreme Court agreed to hear ITW's appeal to reconsider whether this presumptive finding of market power for a patented product still made sense.

In a unanimous decision the Court reversed the Federal Circuit decision and the Court's prior holdings on the issue. Justice JOHN PAUL STEVENS, writing for the Court, noted that disapproval of tying arrangements began in court and legislative actions in the early Twentieth Century. Since that time four different rules of law have supported challenges to tying arrangements. These arrangements have been attacked as improper extensions of the patent monopoly (patent misuse doctrine), as unfair methods of competition under the FEDERAL TRADE COMMISSION Act (15 U.S.C.A. § 45), as contracts tending to create a monopoly under the CLAYTON ACT (15 U.S.C.A. § 13a), and as contracts in **restraint of trade** under the Sherman Act. All four rules were based on the either the assumption or direct proof that the defendant's market power for the tying product was used to restrain competition for the tied product.

Although the courts had endorsed the four rules of law, Justice Stevens found that the Supreme Court's "strong disapproval of tying arrangements has substantially diminished." More recent opinions showed the Court moving away from the presumption of market power, requiring the plaintiff to prove market power in the tying product. Since 1977 the Court had not endorsed the assumption that the purpose of tying arrangements was only to suppress competition. The intertwining of patent and **antitrust law** that led to the condemnation of tying arrangements began to wither in the 1980s, when Congress codified the patent laws for the first time. One provision excluded tying arrangements from the patent misuse doctrine when the sale of the patented product was tied to an "essential" product that had no use except as part of the patented product or method. In a 1988 amendment to the Patent Code, Congress eliminated the presumption of market power in a patent misuse claim. Therefore, Congress made clear that it "did not intend the mere existence of a patent to constitute 'market power.'"

Justice Stevens admitted that the 1998 amendment did not expressly refer to federal antitrust laws but it "certainly invited" the court to reexamine its precedents in this area. Accepting the invitation, the Court found that it should follow this congressional lead and abandon the presumption of market power in tying arrangements. Justice Stevens noted that some arrangements were still unlawful, "such as those that are the product of a true monopoly or a marketwide conspiracy," but these conclusions must be "supported by proof of power in the relevant market rather than by a mere presumption thereof."

Justice Stevens rejected Independent's contention that the Court should create a rebuttable presumption of market power. This would have required ITW to prove that it did not have market power. The Court looked at academic literature in the antitrust field and discovered that most scholars found that a patent did not necessarily confer market power. Moreover, many tying arrangements were "fully consistent with a free, competitive market." Therefore, the Court rejected the call for a rebuttable presumption and held that in all tying arrangement cases "the plaintiff must prove that the defendant has market power in the tying product."

Texaco Inc.v. Dagher

The federal Sherman Act (15 U.S.C.A. § 1) governs antitrust regulation in the United States. Enacted in the late Nineteenth Century, the act sought to prevent the growth of monopolies and other anti-competitive activities. One such activity is known as horizontal price fixing, where two or more companies agree to set prices for their competing goods or services. The Supreme Court has recognized horizontal price fixing as a *per se* violation of the Sherman Act's prohibition against "contracts, combinations, or conspiracies_in the restraint of trade." A *per se* violation means that the price fixing agreement is illegal on its own terms, without regard to any legitimate business justifications that the companies might offer. The Supreme Court, in *Texaco Inc. v. Dagher*, 126 S.Ct. 1276, 164 L.Ed.2d 1 (2006), narrowed the *per se* rule, holding that it did not apply to joint ventures entered into by business competitors.

In 1998, the Texaco and Shell Oil companies formed a **joint venture** called Equilon Industries. Equilon refined and sold gasoline in the western United States under the original Texaco and Shell Oil brand names. In their non-competition agreements, Texaco and Shell were prohibited from competing with Equilon in the western marketer. In effect, the two companies ended competing against each other in the refining and sale of gasoline. The two companies pooled their resources and appointed representatives to the Equilon board of directors. The joint venture was approved by the FEDERAL TRADE COMMISSION and by the state attorneys general of the four states where Equilon sold its gasoline. Outside of Equilon market the two companies continued to refine and sell their gasoline independently. Though the two companies believed the joint venture was good for their businesses, a group of 23,000 Texaco and Shell service station owners were not pleased. Under the joint venture agreement, Equilon set a fixed price for gasoline that was sold to these stations.

The station owners filed a **class action** lawsuit in California federal **district court**, alleging that Texaco and Shell had conspired to fix gasoline prices by creating Equilon. The plaintiffs contended that the joint venture amounted to horizontal price fixing barred as a *per se* Sherman Act violation. The district court ruled in favor of Texaco and Shell, finding that the station owners could not use the *per se* because the joint venture was not the same as horizontal price fixing between two independent companies. Instead, the plaintiffs were required to apply the "rule of reason" to claim. The rule of reason in **antitrust law** refers to whether or not the particular contract or combination was unreasonable and anticompetitive. Because the plaintiffs failed to use the rule of reason, there were no triable facts and the case was dismissed. The Ninth **Circuit Court** of Appeals reversed the district court decision, holding that an exception to the *per se* could not be made in this case. The Supreme Court granted review to determine whether the *per se* rule applied to joint business ventures.

The Supreme Court, in a unanimous decision, overturned the Ninth Circuit. Justice CLARENCE THOMAS, writing for the Court, reemphasized prior **case law** which stated that Congress, in passing the Sherman Act, meant to outlaw only unreasonable restraints on competition. The rule of reason addressed this approach, while *per se* liability was reserved only for agreements that were "so plainly anticompetitive that no elaborate study of the industry is needed to establish their illegality." The *per se* rule was not to be applied to practices that the economic impact was not "immediately obvious."

Justice Thomas agreed that horizontal price fixing agreements are *per se* unlawful. However, the Equilon joint venture did not fit the standard horizontal arrangement. Texaco and Shell did not compete against each other in the western United States market in the sale of gasoline to service stations. Instead, the companies participated in the market as joint investors. Therefore, the challenged pricing policy amounted to "little more than price setting by a single entity" and not an agreement between competing entities. Texaco and Shell shared in Equilon's profits as investors rather than as competitors. Viewed this way, Equilon's pricing policy may have been price fixing "in the literal sense," but it was "not price fixing in the antitrust sense."

This reasoning was reinforced by the station owners concession that if Equilon had sold the gasoline under a single brand it would not have been a *per se* violation. Justice Thomas saw no reason to treat Equilon differently because it sold two brands of gas at a single price. A joint venture was entitled to have the discretion to determine prices for its products, "including the discretion to sell a product under two different brands at a single unified price." If Equilon's pricing was uncompetitive the station owners should have challenged it using the rule of reason.

Volvo Trucks North America, Inc. v. Reeder-Simco GMC, Inc.

The Robinson-Patman Price Discrimination Act of 1936, 15 U.S.C.A. § 13, sought to stop the anticompetitive practice of allowing chain stores to purchase wholesale goods at lower prices than other retailers. Since its enactment the act has been used by other businesses to attack alleged anticompetitive pricing policies. In *Volvo Trucks North America, Inc. v. Reeder-Simco GMC, Inc.*, __U.S.__, 126 S.Ct. 860, 163 L.Ed.2d 663 (2006), the U.S. SUPREME COURT reviewed a case involving a major heavy-duty truck manufacturer and one of its authorized dealers. The dealer claimed that the manufacturer offered better prices to other dealerships as a way to disqualify the dealer as an authorized reseller. The Court disagreed, finding that the manufacturer had not violated the act because the trucks were sold through a customer-specific bidding process.

Reeder-Simco GMC Inc., based in Arkansas signed a five-year contract with Volvo Trucks North America Inc. in 1995, agreeing to become an authorized dealer of Volvo heavy-duty trucks. Reeder failed to meet sale goals set by Volvo during the first two years of the contract and was placed on probationary status. By 1997 Volvo had rethought its dealership structure and wanted to prune its authorized dealers by half. Reeder feared that it would lose its dealership and suspected that Volvo was offering better prices to other dealerships with the goal of severing its ties with Reeder.

The industry-wide practice of selling heavy-duty trucks by manufacturers to retailers like Reeder is much different than the way cars and light trucks are sold. Dealers purchase cars and light trucks using set price lists provided by the manufacturers. For heavy-duty trucks, potential end users contact a dealer and ask for a bid on a particular kind of truck. The dealer in turn contacts the manufacturer and asks for a discounted wholesale price, known as a concession, on the particular model. Volvo, like other manufacturers, requires bids from several authorized dealers. Volvo then offers different price concessions to each dealer, in effect make a discount on the wholesale price on a case-by-case basis. Volvo took into account a number of factors, including industry-wide demand and whether the retail customer had historically purchased a different brand of truck. In Reeder's case it alleged that Volvo was giving more favorable concessions to other dealers. For example, in one case Reeder asked for a 12 percent concession on a sale of a fleet of trucks and Volvo countered with a 7.5 percent concession. In the end another dealer got the contract with an 8.5 percent concession.

In 2000, Reeder filed a lawsuit against Volvo in federal **district court**, alleging that the pricing concessions made by Volvo were discriminatory, anticompetitive, and violated the ROBINSON-PATMAN ACT. Reeder presented evidence that Volvo had failed to follow a policy of offering equal concessions to competing Volvo dealerships. A jury awarded Reeder $1.3 million of **compensatory damages**, which under the antitrust **statute** was tripled to $4.1 million. Volvo appealed the verdict to the Eighth **Circuit Court** of Appeals, which upheld the decision. The appeals court found that Reeder's profits had fallen precipitously during the life of the Volvo contract, while other authorized dealers had continued to have strong sales. The jury could have concluded that the reason for the disparity was that Volvo had discriminated against Reeder in its price concessions. Volvo then appealed to the Supreme Court.

The Supreme Court, in a 7–2 decision, reversed the Eighth Circuit. Justice RUTH BADER GINSBURG, in her majority opinion, made clear that the Robinson-Patman Act does not apply "when a product subject to special order is sold through a customer-specific competitive bidding process." The act was designed to address price discrimination in cases involving "competition between different purchasers for resale of the purchased product." Because Reeder's claim fit the special order, customer-specific bidding model, the act did not apply.

Justice Ginsburg noted that the Act does not ban all price differences but only price discrimination that threatens to injure competition. The key issues were whether Volvo had discriminated in price between Reeder and other dealers of Volvo trucks and whether Reeder had suffered a competitive injury. Reeder had to show the "diversion of sales or profits from a disfavored purchaser to a favored purchaser." If Reeder could not show actual competition with another Volvo dealer for the same sale, it could not establish the competitive injury required by the act. The evidence Reeder presented failed to meet this requirement. One category of evidence compared concessions Reeder received for four successful bids against non-Volvo dealers. Another category compared unsuccessful bids against non-Volvo dealers. A third category of evidence showed just two instances in which Reeder competed directly with another Volvo dealer. However, in these cases Reeder and the other Volvo dealership were bidding for the business of the same retail customer. Only one dealer would win the business and thereafter purchase Volvo's truck. Because the act prohibits only discrimination between different purchasers, Robinson-Patman did not "reach markets characterized by competitive bidding and special order sales, as opposed to sales from inventory." Even if the Court were to apply the act to the facts in the case, there appeared to be minimal impact on competition between Reeder and the "favored" Volvo dealer.

Justice JOHN PAUL STEVENS, in a dissenting opinion joined by Justice CLARENCE THOMAS, argued that the Court's decision eliminated "that **statutory** protection in all but those rare situations in which a prospective purchaser is negotiating with two Volvo dealers at the same time."

ARBITRATION

The submission of a dispute to an unbiased third person designated by the parties to the controversy, who agree in advance to comply with the award—a decision to be issued after a hearing at which both parties have an opportunity to be heard.

Buckeye Check Cashing, Inc. v. Cardegna

Commercial lenders, like many other businesses, typically require borrowers to sign an agreement that includes a provision mandating arbitration if there is a dispute. The question has arisen whether an unhappy borrower may go to court and seek to void the entire contract or whether the legality of the contract must be submitted to the arbitrator for resolution. The U.S. SUPREME COURT, in *Buckeye Check Cashing, Inc. v. Cardegna*, __U.S.__, 126 S.Ct. 1204, 163 L.Ed.2d 1038 (2006), ruled that in a state court proceeding, the Federal Arbitration Act (FAA) mandates that the arbitrator consider whether the contract is void for illegality.

John Cardegna and another Florida plaintiff entered into deferred-payment transactions with Buckeye Check Cashing. Buckeye operates what is known as a "fast money service." Cardegna borrowed $337 from Buckeye, which required him to write a check for the sum of the borrowed money plus a processing fee. The check would be cashed after Cardegna's next payday, giving him the opportunity to have the money on hand. Cardegna kept renewing his loan each time it came due. By the time he filed suit, Cardegna owed Buckeye around $1000. Cardegna's state lawsuit alleged that the processing fee amounted to criminal **usury** and that the lending agreement he signed was criminal on its face and should be voided.

Buckeye filed a motion to compel arbitration, submitting a copy of the lending agreement to the court that contained two pertinent provisions. The first provision stated that Cardegna agreed to submit to binding arbitration if "a dispute of any kind arises out of this Agreement." The second provision stated that if there was a dispute about the "validity, enforceability, or scope of this Arbitration Provision or the entire Agreement," the parties agreed to settle it through arbitration. This section also provided that the arbitration agreement was governed by the FAA. The Florida trial court denied Buckeye's motion, finding that a court of law rather than an arbitrator should determine whether the contract was illegal and void. The Florida Court of Appeals reversed this decision, ruling that because Cardegna had not challenged the arbitration provision itself, claiming instead that the entire contract was void, the agreement to arbitrate was enforceable. The arbitrator would decide the legality of the contract. The Florida Supreme Court reversed the appeals court, concluding that to allow the arbitration to go forward in an allegedly unlawful contract "could breathe life into a contract that not only violates state law, but is also criminal in nature."

The U.S. Supreme Court, in a 7–1 decision (newly confirmed Justice SAMUEL ALITO did not participate in the case), overturned the Florida Supreme Court ruling. Justice ANTONIN SCALIA, writing for the majority, noted that Congress had passed the FAA to "overcome judicial resistance to arbitration." The act placed arbitration agreements on equal footing with other contracts. Arbitration agreements have been challenged in two ways. The first challenges the validity of the agreement to arbitrate, while the second challenges the contract as a whole. Attacks on the contract are based either on a claim that affects the entire agreement or on a claim that the illegality of one contract provision makes the entire contract invalid. In the present case the entire contract was challenged as invalid because of the **usurious finance charge**.

Justice Scalia cited an earlier case, *Prima Paint Corp. v. Flood & Conklin Mfg. Co.*, 388 U.S.

395, 87 S.Ct. 1801, 18 L.Ed.2d 1270 (1967), as precedent. That case involved a federal lawsuit claiming that a contract was induced by **fraud** and whether a federal judge or an arbitrator should resolve the issue. The Court held that if the claim is fraud in the inducement of the arbitration provision itself, then the federal court must handle the matter. However, the FAA did not permit the **federal courts** to consider claims of fraud in the inducement of the contract generally. In addition, an arbitration provision was severable from other provisions of a contract, meaning that it could remain in effect even if other provisions were ruled invalid. In a 1984 case the Court went further and stated that the FAA created a body of law that applies to both federal and state courts, rejecting the possibility of a state court barring the enforcement of FAA provisions. Based on these rulings, Justice Scalia found that Cardegna's challenge of the entire agreement meant that an arbitrator would have to consider this claim.

The Court rejected Cardegna's argument that the severability rule did not apply to state court cases because the FAA provisions involved in *Prima Paint* applied only to federal courts. Justice Scalia interpreted that decision to be based on another section of the act that states that arbitration agreements must be treated like all other contracts, whether in state or federal court. *Prima Paint's* holding relied on "Congress' broad power to fashion substantive rules under the Commerce Clause." Therefore, the FAA was not limited only to federal court jurisdiction. Whether a "challenge is brought in federal or state court, a challenge to the validity of the contract as a whole, and not specifically to the arbitration clause, must go to the arbitrator."

Justice CLARENCE THOMAS, in a dissenting opinion, contended that the FAA does not apply to state court proceedings. Therefore, the FAA could not "be the basis for displacing a state law that prohibits enforcement of an arbitration clause contained in a contract that is unenforceable under state law."

ASSISTED SUICIDE

Gonzales v. Oregon

The U.S. Supreme Court on January 17, 2006 determined that the U.S. Attorney General's office did not have the authority to issue a ruling that prohibited the use of controlled substances for the purpose of physician-assisted suicide. The ruling, which affirmed the judgment of the Ninth **Circuit Court** of Appeals, allows a 1997 Oregon assisted suicide **statute** to remain in effect.

Voters in Oregon passed the Oregon Death with Dignity Act, Or. Rev. Stat. §§ 127.800 **et seq.**, in 1994. The statute exempts state-licensed physicians from civil or criminal liability for dispensing or prescribing lethal doses of drugs to terminally ill patients. The physicians must adhere to the statute's requirements in order to be exempt from liability. The statute did not become effective for nearly four years after its enactment due to a series of legal and voter challenges. Between 1998 and 2006, a total of 246 Oregon patients died as a result of assisted suicide.

The Supreme Court visited the issue of assisted suicide in 1997. In *Washington v. Glucksberg*, 521 U.S. 702, 117 S. Ct. 2258, 138 L. Ed. 2d 772 (1997), the Court upheld a Washington state statute that proscribed assisted suicide. A group of terminally-ill patients and other groups sought a ruling that would declare the Washington statute unconstitutional. In rejecting the challenge, the Court noted that it would have to strike down policy choices in nearly every state in order to invalidate the Washington statute.

On November 6, 2001, former U.S. Attorney General JOHN ASHCROFT issued a ruling that declared that the use of controlled substances for the purpose of assisted suicide violated the Controlled Substances Act (CSA), 21 U.S.C. §§ 801 et seq. This ruling, known as the "Ashcroft Directive," reversed the position taken by former Attorney General Janet Reno in 1998. Two days after the publication of the directive, the state of Oregon filed suit in federal court against Ashcroft and other federal officers and agencies. The U.S. **District Court** for the District of Oregon on November 8, 2001 enjoined the enforcement of the directive.

The CSA includes a schedule of controlled substances that are available only through written prescription. In 1971, Attorney General John N. Mitchell issued a regulation that requires such a prescription to be used "for a legitimate medical purpose by an individual practitioner acting in the usual course of his professional practice." 21 C.F.R. § 1306.04 (2005). Under the CSA, physicians are required to register with the Attorney General, and the Attorney General may deny, revoke, or suspend a registration when the registration would be "inconsistent with the public interest." 21 U.S.C. §§ 822, 824 (2000).

In issuing the directive, Ashcroft determined that use of controlled substances for assis-

Pro-assisted suicide picketers outside U.S. SUPREME COURT, October 2005.
AP IMAGES

ted suicide was not a "legitimate medical purpose." U.S. District Judge Robert E. Jones reviewed the CSA to determine whether Ashcroft had exceeded his authority in issuing the directive. According to Jones, Congress did not intend for the CSA to override a state's decision regarding what constitutes the practice of medicine. Since Ashcroft had acted pursuant to power that he did not possess, the court determined that his directive was invalid. Accordingly, the court entered a permanent injunction that prevented the directive from taking effect. *Oregon v. Ashcroft*, 192 F. Supp. 2d 1077 (D. Or. 2002).

The federal government appealed the decision to the U.S. Court of Appeals for the Ninth Circuit. In an opinion issued on May 26, 2004, the Ninth Circuit upheld the district court's decision. According to Judge Richard C. Tallman, who wrote the opinion, not only had Ashcroft exceeded his authority in issuing the directive, but also the directive had exercised control over an area of law that was traditionally reserved to the states. Unless Congress is "unmistakably clear," a unit of federal government may not exercise this type of control. The Ninth Circuit thus let the injunction remain in force. *Prima Paint Corp. v. Flood & Conklin Mfg. Co., Oregon v. Ashcroft*, 368 F.3d 1118 (9th Cir. 2004).

The U.S. Supreme Court granted CERTIORARI in 2005 and rendered its decision on January 17, 2006. In an opinion written by Justice ANTHONY KENNEDY, the majority affirmed the Ninth Circuit's decision. Kennedy wrote that Ashcroft's interpretation of the CSA was not entitled to deference by the Court because the CSA only extended limited power to the Attorney General's office. Moreover, the Court noted that Ashcroft did not have sufficient expertise for his rule to be entitled to deference. According to Kennedy, "[t]he deference here is tempered by the Attorney General's lack of expertise in this area and the apparent absence of any consultation with anyone outside the Department of Justice who might aid in a reasoned judgment."

The federal government continued to argue that its power extended to this area through the provisions of the CSA. Kennedy disagreed entirely. "The Government, in the end, maintains that the prescription requirement delegates to a single Executive officer the power to effect a radical shift of authority from the States to the Federal Government to define general standards of medical practice in every locality," Kennedy wrote. "The text and structure of the CSA show that Congress did not have this far-reaching intent to alter the federal-state balance and the congressional role in maintaining it." Accordingly, the Court affirmed the Ninth Circuit's judgment. *Gonzales v. Oregon*, ___ U.S. ___, 126 S. Ct. 904, 163 L. Ed. 2d 748 (2006).

Justice ANTONIN SCALIA, joined by two other justices, dissented. According to his dissent, the Attorney General's decision was entitled to some deference by the courts. Because it was entitled to deference, Scalia argued that the Court should have allowed the directive to stand. In a second dissent, Justice CLARENCE THOMAS asserted that the CSA was broad enough in application that it extended authority to the Attorney General.

Since the decision, six other states have considered proposals for assisted suicide statutes. According to a report issued by the Oregon Department of Human Services, the median age of a person who chooses assisted suicide in the state is 70. The majority of these people suffered from cancer, while others had Lou Gehrig's Disease or AIDS.

ATTORNEY

A person admitted to practice law in at least one jurisdiction and authorized to perform criminal and civil legal functions on behalf of clients. These functions include providing legal counsel, drafting legal documents, and representing clients before courts, administrative agencies, and other tribunals.

Rise in Internet Legal Services Raises Questions

The field of law has embraced the INTERNET in many ways, though the incorporation of this technology has given rise to numerous issues as well. In some instances, operators of web sites that promote free legal advice may be guilty of practicing law without a license. Similarly, an attorney who is licensed in one state may commit the unauthorized practice of law by soliciting clients from other states through use of advertisements on the Internet. Rules of ethics as well as ethics opinions have attempted to clarify some questions in recent years, though issues related to Internet legal services remain.

A growing number of web sites attract visitors by advertising free legal advice, often by offering answers to general legal questions. Examples of such sites include FreeAdvice (http://freeadvice.com), 911 Law Network (http://www.911law.net), and Legal Advice Line (http://www.legaladviceline.com/default_1024.htm). Several online bulletin boards also provide legal information to those who pose questions. A number of these web sites double as lawyer referral systems, allowing users to find names and contact information for lawyers who specialize in certain areas of the law. Some sites, such as LegalMatch (http://www.legalmatch.com), focus more exclusively on the latter service.

Definitions of the practice of law vary widely from one state to another. The Rules of the Supreme Court of Arizona provide a representative example. Under these rules, the "'practice of law' means providing legal advice or services to or for another by: (A) Preparing any document in any medium intended to affect or secure legal rights for a specific person or **entity**; (B) Preparing or expressing legal opinions; (C) Representing another in a judicial, **quasi-judicial**, or administrative proceeding, or other formal dispute resolution process such as arbitrations and mediations; (D) Preparing any document through any medium for filing in any court, **administrative agency** or **tribunal** for a specific person or entity; or (E) Negotiating legal rights or responsibilities for a specific person or entity." Other states also include employment as a judge and certain official as the practice of law.

In 2003, the AMERICAN BAR ASSOCIATION (ABA) established the Task Force on the Model Definition of the Practice of Law. In the years prior to the formation of the Task Force, the ABA had adopted policies that were dependent on the definition of the practice of law, but the organization never formally adopted a definition of this phrase. The Task Force released a 14-page report in August 2003. This report did not provide a short, concise definition of the practice of law, but rather discussed the basic premises for such a definition. The starting point for such a definition is the provision of legal advice, the report noted. According to the Task Force, "the application of legal principles and judgment to the circumstances or objectives of another person or entity is implicit in the giving of legal advice" and thus the ABA used this notion "as the broad basic premise for creating a definition of the practice of law."

An Illinois **appellate court** in 2002 determined that a law firm could bring an action against an Internet business that was allegedly engaged in the unauthorized practice of law. *Richard F. Mallen & Assoc., Ltd. v. Myinjuryclaim.com, Corp.*, 769 N.E.2d 74 (Ill. App. 2002). An individual who was injured in an automobile accident could seek and obtain legal advice from the business, which did not have a license to practice law. In some instances, the person seeking the advice was charged a fee for the advice. Although the decision hinged on whether the law firm that brought the suit had STANDING to do so, this case suggests that businesses that run these web sites could be liable for giving legal advice without a license.

On the other hand, some commentators have noted that few states actively prosecute instances where a business or individual has engaged in the unauthorized practice of law, except in the most egregious cases. Laws governing the unauthorized practice of law are often enforced by state bar associations, although in some states, such as California, a county prosecutor may bring an action. A person who engages in unauthorized practice is more likely to be subject to a cease-and-desist order than criminal prosecution, even though in many states this practice constitutes a crime.

In addition to a non-lawyer who improperly provides legal advice, an attorney licensed in one state may engage in the unauthorized practice of law by soliciting business from and representing clients in another state where the attorney is not licensed. In a 1998 decision, the California Supreme Court recognized that an out-of-state attorney may engage in unauthorized practice "by advising a California client on California law in connection with a California legal dispute by telephone, fax, computer, or other modern technological means." *Birbrower, Montalbano, Condon, & Frank, P.C. v. Superior Court*, 949 P.2d 1 (Cal. 1998).

Even where attorneys communicate through the Internet in states where they are licensed, this communication can give rise to other issues. Where an attorney offers legal advice to another person concerning a legal dispute or a legal question, the nature of the communication could give rise to an attorney-client relationship. For this reason, commentators generally recommend that lawyers do not provide advice via email, web sites, message boards, or in chat rooms. Communication through email, a web site, or other means could also compromise a client's confidential information. For this reason, lawyers prefer to send encrypted emails. If encryption is not available and the lawyer believes that a certain communication is highly sensitive, the lawyer should consult with the client regarding how that information should be communicated.

BANKRUPTCY

A federally authorized procedure by which a debtor—an individual, corporation, or municipality—is relieved of total liability for its debts by making court-approved arrangements for their partial repayment.

Central Virginia Community College v. Katz

Since the early 1990s the Supreme Court has reexamined the scope of congressional authority to override the **sovereign immunity** of state governments. In a series of cases the Court has nullified various federal laws that sought to allow private parties to file civil lawsuits for damages against state governments. However, in *Central Virginia Community College v. Katz*, __U.S.__, 126 S.Ct. 990, __L.Ed.2d__ (2006), the Court reversed course and ruled that the Constitution's Bankruptcy Clause abrogated state sovereign immunity. In so ruling, the Court allowed a federal bankruptcy **trustee** to seek return of assets from state colleges so they could be redistributed to creditors.

Bernard Katz was appointed by a federal bankruptcy judge in Kentucky as the liquidating supervisor for Wallace Bookstores, Inc. The corporation had filed for Chapter 11 reorganization. Katz discovered that four Virginia publicly funded educational institutions, including Central Virginia Community College, had received rental payments from Wallace Bookstores early in the bankruptcy process. Under the Bankruptcy Code Katz had the authority to seek recovery of these payments as "preferential transfers" prohibited by law. Such transfers include those made on or within 90 days before the filing of the bankruptcy. The purpose of the provision is to create an asset pool that will give more creditors the opportunity to recover at least some of their debt. Katz filed a proceeding in Kentucky Bankruptcy Court, demanding that the four educational institutions return a total of $400,000 to the bankruptcy estate. The schools moved to dismiss the action, arguing that state sovereignty prevented them form being sued for the money. The **district court** disagreed and allowed the case to proceed. The decision was upheld by the Sixth **Circuit Court** of Appeals, concluding that Congress had abrogated the state's sovereign immunity when it enacted the Bankruptcy Code provision 11 U.S.C.A. § 106(a). The Supreme Court agreed to hear the state's appeal to resolve the sovereign immunity issue.

The Supreme Court, in a 5–4 decision, upheld the lower courts but found that the enactment of § 106(a) had not been necessary to authorize the Bankruptcy Code's jurisdiction over the preferential transfer proceedings. Justice John Paul Stevens, in his majority opinion, noted that Article I, § 8, cl. 4 of the Constitution provides that Congress shall have the power to establish "uniform Laws on the subject of Bankruptcies throughout the United States." The Court had made clear in previous cases that bankruptcy jurisdiction is *in rem*. Generally, *in rem* actions involve a proceeding where property, rather than a person, is a party, with the bankruptcy court's jurisdiction premised on the debtor and his estate, and not on the creditors. As such, Justice Stevens concluded that it did not implicate state sovereign immunity "to nearly the same degree as other kinds of jurisdiction."

Justice Stevens placed heavy emphasis on the early history of American bankruptcy law, the drafting of the Constitution, and the first federal bankruptcy law enacted in 1800. Stevens pointed out that before the Constitution American bankruptcy law was very similar to that found in England. Debtors were imprisoned and treated harshly. Moreover, each state administered its own bankruptcy law and a discharge granted in one state was not honored in another state where a person owed money. The substantive provisions varied from state-to-state created legal uncertainties that the framers of the Constitution addressed with the Bankruptcy Clause. Justice Stevens interpreted the lack of debate over the clause to mean that there was "general agreement on the importance of authorizing a uniform federal response to the problems presented" in the state courts.

The Court dispensed with the need to interpret the scope of the bankruptcy preferential transfer provisions. Justice Stevens reasoned that framers of the Bankruptcy Clause "would have understood it to give Congress the power to authorize courts to avoid preferential transfers and to recover the transferred property." Turning to early bankruptcy law, he noted that Congress passed the first Bankruptcy Act in 1800. It gave the **federal courts** the power to use the **writ** of **habeas corpus** to free debtors from state prison. This "remarkable" grant of power came in the aftermath of the passage of the ELEVENTH AMENDMENT, which barred citizens from one state suing another state for damages. The states at that time were sensitive to any efforts that would abrogate their sovereignty, yet the habeas provision was accepted without objection. Justice Stevens concluded that the Bankruptcy Clause gave Congress "the power to **redress** the rampant injustice resulting from States' refusal to respect one another's discharge orders." Therefore, the "ineluctable conclusion" was that the states agreed at the Constitutional Convention to "not assert any sovereign immunity defense" involving federal bankruptcy laws. Congress had never "abrogated" state sovereign immunity, it had merely acted within the scope of its powers when it declared that states are not immune to preferential transfer lawsuits.

Justice CLARENCE THOMAS, in a dissenting opinion joined by Chief Justice John Roberts and Justices ANTONIN SCALIA and ANTHONY KENNEDY, disagreed with the majority's reading of constitutional history. Moreover, the Court had made clear in its recent opinions on sovereign immunity and the Eleventh Amendment that Article I provisions did not waive state sovereign immunity. The passage of the Bankruptcy Clause "merely established federal power to legislate in the area of bankruptcy law."

Howard Delivery Service v. Zurich

In *Howard Delivery Service v. Zurich American Insurance Co.*, No.05–128, 547 U.S. ___ (2006), the U.S. SUPREME COURT ruled that claims from insurance companies for unpaid worker's compensation insurance premiums were not entitled to priority status in bankruptcy proceedings. The 6–3 decision resolved a split among the circuit courts of appeal, specifically reversing rulings of the Fourth and Ninth Circuits. The case turned on **statutory** construction of the U.S. Bankruptcy Code, Section 507(a)(5).

Howard Delivery Service (Howard), an over-the-road freight carrier based in West Virginia, self-insured its employees through a workers' compensation policy issued by Zurich American Insurance (Zurich) rather than participate in the state workers' compensation program. In January 2002, Howard cancelled its policy with Zurich. Eight days later, Howard filed for bankruptcy, seeking protection through a Chapter 11 reorganization scheme.

Section §507(a)(4) of the Bankruptcy Code prioritizes payment for unpaid "wages, salaries, [and] commissions." Later, Congress added a new priority to the list, §507(a)(5) (one step lower than the wage priority), for "unpaid contributions to an employee benefit plan . . . arising from services rendered." Under this statutory scheme, because §507(a)(4) has a higher priority status, all claims for unpaid wages are paid first (up to the statutory maximum of $10,000), followed by any outstanding claims under §507(a)(5) for benefit plan contributions.

In May 2002, Zurich filed an unsecured creditor's claim seeking priority status under §507(a)(5) for unpaid premiums to "an employee benefit plan," i.e., characterizing workers compensation benefits as employee benefits. In July 2003, the bankruptcy court denied Zurich's claim, reasoning that the unpaid premiums were not bargained-for, wage-substitute-type benefits furnished in lieu of higher wages. The federal **district court** affirmed, similarly concluding that unpaid workers' compensation premiums do not share the priority afforded unpaid contributions to **pension** and health plans.

A divided Fourth **Circuit Court** of appeals reversed, but failed to agree on a rationale. Essentially, the **appellate court** found that a contribution to an employee benefit plan need not be made voluntarily to qualify for priority status under the Bankruptcy Code. The court noted that the statutory language was plain in that it did not require that compensation received by an employee be a wage substitute (in order to qualify for priority status).

But the U.S. Supreme Court was more precise in its ruling. Writing for the majority, Justice RUTH BADER GINSBURG concluded that insurance carriers' claims for unpaid workers' compensation premiums fell outside the **purview** of §507(a)(5) of the Bankruptcy Code.

Congress did not define §507(a)(5)terms. This fact contributed to Zurich's argument urging the Supreme Court to adopt the encompassing definition of "employee benefit plan" as used in the EMPLOYEE RETIREMENT INCOME SECURITY ACT of 1979 (ERISA): "[A]ny plan, fund, or program [that provides] its participants . . . , through the purchase of insurance or otherwise, . . . benefits in the event of sickness, accident, disability, [or] death." 29 USC 1002(1).

But the majority opinion rejected this argument. Instead, the Court relied on one of its earlier decisions, *United States v. Reorganized CF&I Fabricators of Utah, Inc.*, 518 U.S. 213, quoting that "[h]ere and there in the Bankruptcy Code Congress has included specific directions that establish the significance for bankruptcy law of a term used elsewhere in the federal statutes." But no such directions are included in the text of §507(a)(5), and the Court refused to write them into the text.

The Supreme Court also agreed with the lower courts' reasoning relating to the essential character of workers' compensation. Unlike pension plans or group insurance—negotiated or granted to supplement or substitute for wages—workers' compensation programs substitute for liability of employers for work-related accidents.

Zurich also argued that according its claims a §507(a)(5) status would give workers' compensation **carriers** an incentive to continue coverage of a failing enterprise. The Court found this argument too speculative. More convincing is the Bankruptcy Code's objective of securing fair and equal distribution among creditors. The Code therefore limits the priority status of claims to ensure that some creditors (such as insurance companies) do not come out better than the workers themselves.

Justice Kennedy filed a dissenting opinion, joined by Justices Alito and Souter. He noted that the majority opinion relied on the premise that statutorily prescribed workers' compensation regimes did not run exclusively to the employees' benefit. That, in itself, did not justify the Court's holding; neither did it comport with the text or purpose of the Bankruptcy Code's prioritization under §507(a)(5).

Uniform Debt Management Services Act

In November 2005, the National Conference of Commissions on Uniform State Laws (NCCUSL) approved the final draft of the Uniform Debt-Management Services Act (UDMSA), addressing rising problems in the credit/debt counseling industry. The AMERICAN BAR ASSOCIATION's (ABA) House of Delegates endorsed the Act in February 2006. Adoption by states is not mandatory but encouraged to effect the purpose of uniformity among states, as comparable to the Uniform **Probate** Code, the **Uniform COMMERCIAL CODE** (UCC), and others. As of early 2006, adoption of the UDMSA was already pending in Colorado, Illinois, Nebraska, and Utah.

The UDMSA provides guidance to, and regulation of, two separate industries: credit counseling and debt management services. **Consumer credit** counseling services assist consumers with budgeting skills and help them pay off their debts. Credit counseling agencies are generally supported by fair share payments made to them by creditors, usually in the form of a percentage of the total payment made by a consumer/debtor. Because many states prohibit debt adjustment but have exemptions in their laws for nonprofit or tax-exempt organizations, most of the existing credit counseling agencies are organized as tax-exempt non-profit entities under INTERNAL REVENUE CODE 501(C).

Debt management service providers, on the other hand, function as negotiators who persuade creditors to settle for less than the full amount owed by individual consumer/debtors. Such entities may or may not directly control consumers' funds, but most are organized as taxable entities that are supported by incentive-based percentages of collections and/or contract amounts.

The need for regulation and oversight of these entities is undisputed. There is no comprehensive federal law that regulates credit counseling or debt management organizations. (The federal Credit Repair Organization Act regulates entities claiming to offer "credit repair services," but the majority of credit counselors do not offer credit repair services, and are accordingly not subject to the CROA.) The 2005 amendments to the U.S. Bankruptcy Code (**U.S. Code**, Title 11), especially under the Bankruptcy Abuse Prevention and Consumer Protection Act of 2005, added a requirement that debtors seek credit counseling assistance prior to Chapter 7 filings [§ 109(h)]. Additionally, many state laws require credit-counseling services in conjunction with high-cost mortgages and short-term payday loans. The industry goes largely unregulated, at least with respect to some of the issues addressed by the UDMSA.

Starting around 2003,several high-level investigations and reports focusing on the industry surfaced, including those from the National Consumer Law Center, Consumer Federal of America, INTERNAL REVENUE SERVICE, FEDERAL TRADE COMMISSION, and the Permanent Subcommittee on Investigations of the Committee on Homeland Security. The latter **entity** published its findings in its 2005 report, *Profiteering in a Non-Profit Industry: Abusive Practices in Credit Counseling*. As a result of the escalating incidence of alleged unfair and deceptive trade practices and other reported abuses, the Internal Revenue Service, by 2005, was in the process of revoking the tax exempt status of over 50 percent of the industry, based on the number of debt management plans.

The UDMSA is constructed to regulate both nonprofit/tax-exempt and for-profit organizations. For those organizations entering into agreements with consumers, the UDMSA requires certain important disclosures and terms of the agreement. A number of consumer protections are required. There is a provision specifying maximum fees. Consumer funds must be held in a trust account. With respect to consumer relations, the UDMSA requires service providers to act in **good faith**, to maintain toll-free communications that permit clients to speak with credit counselors during regular business hours; and to render determinations as to whether debt management plans are suitable for particular consumers. The Act provides for both private and public enforcement, and provides for the recovery of minimum, actual, and **punitive damages**.

To offer debt management services in a state adopting UDMSA, a provider must be registered or licensed within that state. Registration requires the applicant to provide state regulatory authorities with comprehensive background information. Additionally, applicants must show proof of liability insurance, proof of surety bond, and evidence that they meet industry competency standards.

The Consumer Federation of America (CFA), on behalf of low-income consumer clients, has opposed the UDMSA. Its chief concerns are: (1) that the Act regulates debt settlement as a valid type of debt management service, thereby legitimizing a business deemed dangerous to some consumers; and (3) the Act gives states the option of allowing for-profit firms to offer debt management and debt settlement services. This could undermine IRS efforts to weed out abuses in the industry. CFA urged states to choose the non-profit option to improve consumer protections.

The National Conference of Commissioners on Uniform State Laws (NCCUSL) drafted the text of the NDMSA. The Act's text can be found at that organization's web site, http://www.nccusl.org.

BIRTH CONTROL

A measure or measures undertaken to prevent conception.

Wal-Mart Sued for Failing to Stock Emergency Contraceptives

In February 2006, three women from Massachusetts sued Wal-Mart for failing to stock the emergency contraceptive Plan B, also known as the "morning after pill." Several pro-choice groups backed the filing of the suit, which took place a few months after the State of Massachusetts passed legislation requiring pharmacies to fill prescriptions for the pills. Wal-Mart announced in March 2006 that it would stock the pill in each of its more than 3700 pharmacies nationwide.

The FOOD AND DRUG ADMINISTRATION first approved the morning after pill in 1999. If taken within 72 hours after a woman engages in intercourse, then the chance of the woman becoming pregnant is 0.4 percent. In the first five years of its availability, about 2.4 million doses were administered. The pill blocks ovulation and prevents egg fertilization or implantation, thus acting much like a birth control pill. The pill is an ineffective contraceptive for a woman who is already pregnant.

Some groups, including the Catholic Church and other pro-life groups, oppose the pill, equating its use with an abortion procedure. According to a survey taken in Massachusetts in 2004 by pro-choice groups, nearly 17 percent of the state's 71 hospitals did not provide the morning after pill. Advocates for this pill focused on its use for rape victims, noting that it could be the only option to

Plaintiffs in Wal-Mart emergency contraceptives lawsuit speak to press, February 2006; left to right: Julie Battel, Katrina McCarty, Rebekah Gee
AP IMAGES

prevent an unwanted pregnancy in the event of a sexual assault. Efforts to make the pill more easily accessible failed in the Massachusetts General Assembly in 2004.

The debate over use of this drug continued in 2005. Stories emerged that some pharmacists refused to fill prescriptions for the pill based on moral objections. Some of these pharmacists organized the group Pharmacists for Life, and its membership included the chief pharmacist for **Medicaid** in the state of North Carolina. Various states handled this issue differently. The state of Illinois issued emergency rules that require pharmacists to fill prescriptions for the pill, and states such as Arizona and California considered similar proposals. On the other hand, legislation introduced in North Carolina in April 2005 would have allowed pharmacists to refuse to fill prescriptions based on the pharmacist's moral or religious objection to abortion.

In July 2005, the Massachusetts legislature passed a bill that would require hospitals to offer the pill to rape victims and would allow special pharmacists to dispense the pill without a prescription from a doctor. Governor Mitt Romney, however, vetoed the bill in a move that many viewed as political, based on Romney's potential candidacy for president in 2008. Romney claimed that because the pill could prevent an embryo that has already been formed from implanting in the womb, the pill was not merely a contraceptive. He instead referred to it as an "abortion pill."

By overwhelming majorities, both chambers of the state legislature in September voted to override Romney's veto. The new law could not take effect until the state's Department of Public Health could draft new rules to implement the legislation. The action in Massachusetts occurred at a time when the issue had heated up considerably in other states. Four pharmacists in Illinois lost their jobs when they refused to fill prescriptions for the pill, and the attorney general for the state of Wisconsin announced plans to file a lawsuit against the FDA to require the agency to allow sales of the pill without a prescription. Throughout much of 2005, the FDA delayed a decision about over-the-counter sales of the pill.

Arkansas-based Wal-Mart had maintained a policy that it would not stock the morning after pill, even after the Massachusetts law came into effect. Three Massachusetts women filed suit against Wal-Mart on February 1, 2006, seeking to compel the company to stock the drug in its 44 Wal-Mart and four Sam's Club pharmacies in the state. The women's lawsuit was backed by Planned Parenthood of Massachusetts, NARAL Pro-Choice Massachusetts, and Jane Doe, Inc.

Wal-Mart claimed that it did not carry the pill for undisclosed business reasons. In another statement, a company spokesperson claimed that the pill was not "commonly prescribed" or within the "usual needs of the community." The company adhered to a policy whereby it would refer a customer to a competitor that does stock the drug. Although other pharmacies in Massachusetts generally stock the pill, the state law that was passed in 2005 does not require pharmacies to fill prescriptions for the drug.

Just days after the women filed the lawsuit against the company, a coalition of women's and family planning groups urged Wal-Mart to stock the drug. According to a joint statement issued by the groups, "Wal-Mart's actions are clearly an outrageous intrusion into the health and privacy of all U.S. women. When a doctor prescribes emergency contraception for a woman, Wal-Mart does not have the right to overrule that decision." Among the organizations in this group were the NATIONAL ORGANIZATION OF WOMEN and the National Council of Women's Organizations.

In early March, the company announced that it would stock the pill. A company spokesperson noted that Wal-Mart expected "more states to require us to sell emergency contraceptives in the months ahead. Because of this and the fact that this is an FDA-approved product, we feel it is difficult to justify being the country's only major pharmacy chain not selling it."

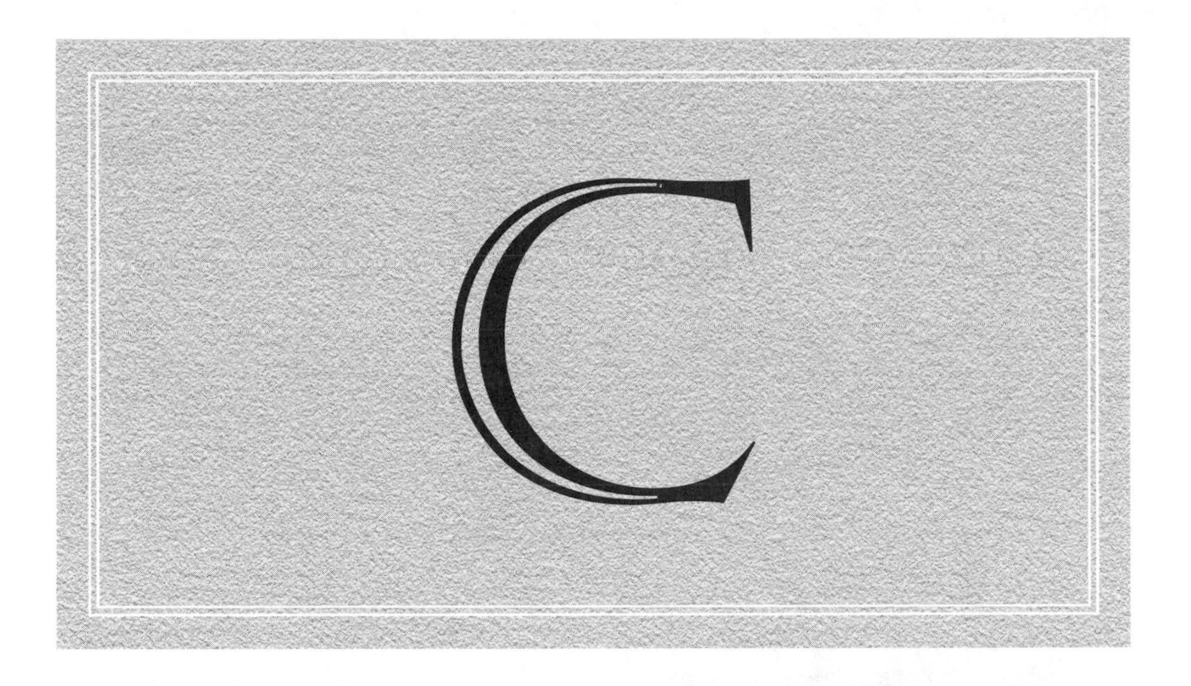

CAPITAL PUNISHMENT

The lawful infliction of death as a punishment; the death penalty.

Brown v. Sanders

The U.S. Supreme Court requires states to limit the class of murderers to which the death penalty may be applied. This "narrowing requirement" is met when the jury finds at least one eligibility factor defined in the capital punishment **statute** applies to a defendant. This finding can be made during the guilt or penalty phase of a trial. Once a jury finds the defendant eligible for the death penalty it must then determine if the defendant should receive it. State laws list aggravating factors which must be weighed against mitigating factors when deciding a defendant's fate. The aggravating factors may be similar or identical to the eligibility factors, which has led the Court to review the relationship of these factors in certain circumstances. In *Brown v. Sanders*, __U.S.__, 126 S.Ct. 884, __L.Ed.2d__ (2006), the Court examined a California case where a jury imposed a death penalty after finding four eligibility factors, two of which were later declared invalid. The Court held that the two remaining factors sustained the death penalty because the facts and circumstances in the invalidated factors were admissible under an aggravating factor that dealt with the "circumstances of the crime."

In 1981, Ronald Sanders and an accomplice broke into the Bakersfield, California home of Dale Boender and his girlfriend, Janice Allen, seeking to rob Boender of his stash of cocaine. Sanders struck the victims on the head with a blunt object, injuring Boender and killing Allen. Sanders was convicted of first-degree murder, attempted murder, **robbery**, **burglary**, and attempted robbery. The jury found four factors, called "special circumstances" in California, which made Sanders eligible for the death penalty. The circumstances included committing murder during the course of a robbery, the killing of a witness to a crime, committing murder during the course of a burglary, and committing a murder that was "especially heinous, atrocious, or cruel." The jury then considered a list of sentencing factors during the penalty phase, one of which was the circumstances of the crimes Sanders committed. The jury sentenced Sanders to death.

Sanders appealed to the California Supreme Court, which ruled invalid the burglary and "heinous, atrocious, and cruel" special circumstances. However, the court found that the surviving special circumstances were sufficient to sustain capital punishment. Sanders then filed a petition for a **writ** of **habeas corpus** in federal **district court**, arguing that the invalidity of the two special circumstances considered by the jury made the death sentence unconstitutional. The district court denied relief but the Ninth **Circuit Court** of Appeals reversed. The appeals court concluded that the California Supreme Court had erroneously applied a U.S. Supreme Court precedent. The California court could only uphold the death sentence if it found the jury's use of the invalid special circumstances had been **harmless error** or it had independently reweighed the sentencing factors as applied to Sanders. The state then appealed to the U.S. Supreme Court.

The Court, in a 5–4 decision, reversed the Ninth Circuit ruling. Justice ANTONIN SCALIA,

Ronald Sanders, California prison photo.
AP IMAGES

in his majority opinion, reviewed the Court's capital punishment **jurisprudence** and noted that it had divided state death penalty processes into "weighing" and "non-weighing" categories. In weighing states, the jury could only consider aggravating factors that were specified eligibility factors. Therefore, when an eligibility factor was ruled invalid the death penalty sentence must be reversed unless the error was harmless or the court reweighed the mitigating evidence against the valid aggravating factors. In non-weighing states the jury could consider aggravating factors different from, or in addition to, the eligibility factors. An invalid eligibility factor in a non-weighing state would be constitutional error if the jury drew conclusions from evidence it should not have heard based on this factor. Justice Scalia acknowledged that the use of this "weighing/non-weighing scheme is accurate as far as it goes, but it now seems to us needlessly complex and incapable of providing for the full range of possible variations." The Court then invoked a new rule: "an invalidated sentencing factor (whether an eligibility factor or not)" will make a death sentence unconstitutional "*unless* one of the other sentencing factors enables the sentencer to give aggravating weight to the same facts and conclusions."

Justice Scalia disagreed with the Ninth Circuit's conclusion that California was a weighing state. In fact, the "circumstances of the crime" aggravating factor had the effect of turning California into a non-weighing state. The act of burglary and the facts and circumstances of how the crime was committed had been removed as eligibility factors but this evidence was properly used when the jury considered the aggravated circumstances of the crime. In Scalia's view the erroneous factors could not have "skewed" the sentence and made it unconstitutional. Whether California was a weighing or non-weighing state, the special circumstances of the crime aggravating factor was a proper channel for the jury to consider the evidence of Sanders' crimes. Therefore, the death penalty sentence was correct.

Justice JOHN PAUL STEVENS, in a dissenting opinion joined by Justice DAVID SOUTER, chastised the court for modifying the law regarding weighing and non-weighing states. Justice STEPHEN BREYER, in a dissenting opinion joined by Justice RUTH BADER GINSBURG, contended that the real issue was whether a court must find that "the jury's consideration of an invalid aggravator was harmless **beyond a reasonable doubt**, regardless of the form a State's death penalty law takes." The Court should have remanded the case to the Ninth Circuit for a full review based on the Court's new rule.

ABA Recommends Moratorium on Death Penalty in Georgia

A group of legal experts sponsored by the AMERICAN BAR ASSOCIATION (ABA) issued a report in January 2006 urging the state of Georgia to place a moratorium on the death penalty in the state. The group concluded that the state could not ensure fairness in conducting trials and appeals. The recommended moratorium would remain in place until the state could guarantee fairness and accuracy in every case.

The ABA has expressed concern about the nation's death penalty system in the past. In 1997, the ABA called for the suspension of capital punishment throughout the U.S. until serious flaws in the system could be eliminated. More specifically, the organization urged states that allow capital punishment to ensure that death penalty cases are administered fairly and impartially and that the procedures employed by the states minimize risks that innocent persons may be executed.

The ABA's Section of Individual Rights and Responsibilities established the Death Penalty Moratorium Implementation Project in 2001. Two years later, the Project initiated an examination of death penalty systems in 16 states to determine whether those states achieved fairness and due process. The states included Alabama, Arizona, Arkansas, Florida, Georgia, Indiana, Louisiana, Mississippi, Nevada, Ohio, Oklahoma, Pennsylvania, Tennessee, South Carolina, Texas, and Virginia. Assessment teams in each of these states consisted of judges, legislators, prosecutors, defense attorneys, law professors, bar association leaders, and others.

State assessment teams collected data in thirteen categories, which were established in an assessment guide created by the Project. These categories include the following: (1) death row demographics, DNA testing, and the location, testing, and preservation of biological evidence; (2) evolution of the state death penalty **statute**; (3) law enforcement tools and techniques; (4) crime laboratories and medical examiners; (5) prosecutors; (6) defense services during trial, appeal, and state post-conviction relief proceedings; (7) direct appeal and the unitary appeal process; (8) state post-conviction relief proceedings; (9) **clemency**; (10) jury instructions; (11) judicial independence; (12) the treatment of racial and ethnic minorities; and (13) mental retardation and mental illness.

The team that assessed the implementation of the death penalty in Georgia released a 323-page report in January 2006 that found seven distinct problems with the system in that state. The assessment team was made up of ten prominent Georgia lawyers and political figures. Nine of the ten members recommended the moratorium, with a former U.S. attorney dissenting from this recommendation.

The report identified that Georgia provides inadequate funding for defense counsel. According to the report, the state's capital defender office has a budget for a total of 49 capital cases per year, fewer than the total number of pending capital cases by the end of 2005. Likewise, the report criticized Georgia for not providing defense counsel for state HABEAS CORPUS proceedings. Georgia is one of only two states, along with Alabama, that does not provide counsel for this purpose.

Race plays a significant factor in capital sentencing in Georgia, which was a major cause for concern for the assessment team. Statistics indicate that a person who is suspected of killing a white victim is 4.56 times as likely to be given the death sentence as a person who kills a black victim. Thus, according to the report, race is not only important with respect to the identity of the suspect, but also the identity of the victim.

The report also discovered problems with the treatment of mentally retarded suspects. Georgia is among 26 states that have enacted statutes prohibiting the execution of mentally retarded persons. However, of these states, Georgia is the only one that requires a suspect to prove retardation **beyond a reasonable doubt**. The ABA recommends that this burden of proof should be by a preponderance of the evidence.

The final two areas of concern in the report focused on procedural issues and statewide review of capital punishment. The report found that jurors in capital cases were given inadequate instructions about mitigating factors presented by the defense. In fact, 41 percent of jurors interviewed for the study said that they were not aware that they could consider any mitigating evidence, while 62.2 percent thought that the defense had to prove **mitigating circumstances** beyond a reasonable doubt. In addition to inadequate jury instructions, the assessment team determined that the Georgia Supreme Court failed to conduct an adequate review of death penalty cases so as to ensure that sentencing is not arbitrary.

Top officials in Georgia disagreed with the report. Spokespersons for both Governor Sonny Perdue and Attorney General Thurbert Baker indicated that the state would not consider a moratorium. According to Ken Hodges, vice chairman of the Prosecuting Attorneys Council of Georgia, "Georgia is very careful and very deliberate in its imposition of the death penalty. The defendant in a capital case is given every right afforded him or her under the U.S. and Georgia constitutions. They get a heck of a lot more constitutional protections than the victims, who are heinously, brutally raped and murdered."

Hill v. McDonough

In *Hill v. McDonough*, 547 U.S. ___, 126 S.Ct. 2096 (2006), the U.S. SUPREME COURT unanimously held that a death-row inmate who had exhausted all appeals and habeas relief could nonetheless file a **civil action** under 42 U.S.C. §1983 challenging the constitutionality of a state's method of execution. The **district court** and Eleventh **Circuit Court** of Appeals had dismissed the inmate's action on the rationale that it was the functional equivalent of a habeas petition, thus barring the claim as a successive petition. The Supreme Court disagreed. It did not rule on the constitutionality of the intended execution by lethal injection (as "cruel and unusual punishment under the EIGHTH AMENDMENT to the U.S. Constitution), but merely allowed the inmate to proceed with his civil suit in lower court.

Section 1983 claims prohibit persons who, under the **color of law** or custom, subject other persons to the deprivation of any right, privilege, or immunity secured by the Constitution or other laws. It is commonly invoked in lawsuits against police and public officials not otherwise protected by **sovereign immunity**.

In 1983, Clarence Hill was convicted of murder and sentenced to death in a Florida state court. From the time of his conviction and sentence to the time of his intended execution, Florida law had changed the method of prescribed execution from electrocution to lethal injection. In 2000, the Florida Supreme Court rejected another inmate's Eighth Amendment challenge to the protocol three-drug sequence (constituting lethal injection) as too speculative. In that case, the inmate claimed that the sequential injection of three different drugs could cause great pain *if administered improperly*. *Sims v. State*, 754 So.2d 657.

More than 20 years after Hill's conviction and sentence, and after all his state and federal appeals were exhausted, Florida's governor signed his **death warrant** in November 2005, scheduling his execution for January 24, 2006. Hill then challenged, for the first time, Florida's lethal injection protocol. In December 2005, he filed a successive postconviction petition in state court, which was dismissed as procedurally barred. The Florida Supreme Court affirmed on January 17, 2006. *Hill v. State*, 921 So.2d 579, cert. den., 546 U.S. ___ (2006).

Just four days before execution, Hill brought a civil rights action in federal district court under §1983, alleging that the scheduled lethal execution violated the Eighth Amendment as **cruel and unusual punishment**. He alleged that the substance used in the first of three injections, sodium pentothal, would not be a sufficient anesthetic to render painless the administration of the other two substances. This could potentially leave a person conscious and suffering from severe pain as the other two drugs are administered. Hill asked for an injunction barring the state from executing him in the intended (protocol) manner. On the same day, he filed with the Eleventh Circuit Court of Appeals a petition for leave to file a second habeas action.

The federal district court found that Eleventh Circuit precedent viewed such claims as the functional equivalents of petitions for writs of **habeas corpus**. As Hill had already exhausted his habeas corpus relief in an earlier action, the district court deemed his new claim "successive" and thus barred, for failure to obtain leave to file from the Court of Appeals, as required by 28 USC § 2244(b).

The Eleventh Circuit affirmed both the decision and the grounds on January 24, 2006, the day of scheduled execution. The Supreme Court, however, issued a temporary stay of execution, and then granted **certiorari**.

In its decision, the high court first distinguished between the purpose of habeas actions (to challenge the *lawfulness* of a confinement or sentence) versus a §1983 action, generally brought to challenge the *conditions* or *circumstances* of a confinement or sentence.

Next, the Court summarized its previous holdings in *Nelson v. Campbell*, 541 U.S. 637, 124 S.Ct. 2117, 158 L.Ed.2d 924 (2004). In *Nelson*, the Court addressed whether a challenge to the *procedure* used to administer lethal injection must proceed as a habeas corpus action. The Court then concluded that *Nelson* was controlling in the present case. If the challenge was to the method of carrying out a sentence, rather than the lawfulness of the sentence itself, the challenge was distinct from a habeas petition and was not barred. In the present case, Hill did not claim that the execution itself was unlawful, but rather, that he should not be forced into painful execution. This left the state free to use an alternative lethal injection procedure.

The Court noted that filing a §1983 action did not entitle the complainant to an automatic stay of execution. A stay is an equitable remedy not available by right, and matters of equity must be sensitive to the State's strong interest in enforcing its criminal judgments without undue interference from **federal courts**. One of the requirements that inmates must satisfy when seeking time to challenge the manner of their execution is a significant possibility of success on the merits. A court must also apply a strong equitable presumption against granting relief where the claim could have been brought at an earlier time that would have allowed consideration of the merits without the necessity of a stay. Indeed, since *Nelson*, many federal courts have invoked their equitable powers to dismiss claims deemed speculative or untimely.

Writing for a unanimous Court, Justice ANTHONY KENNEDY reversed the Eleventh Circuit's decision and remanded Hill's case back for consideration on the merits.

Kansas v. Marsh

Constitutional challenges to capital punishment occur in state courts as well as the **federal courts**. The state of Kansas enacted a death penalty **statute** that established a presumption in favor of death by directing imposition of the death penalty when aggravating and **mitigating circumstances** were in equipoise (i.e., equal). A defendant convicted and sentenced to death under the statute challenged the constitutionality of this presumption and the Kansas Supreme Court found that the law violated the EIGHTH AMENDMENT. However, the U.S. SUPREME COURT agreed to hear Kansas' appeal and reversed the state court decision, ruling in *Kansas v. Marsh*, __U.S.__, 126 S.Ct., __L.Ed.2d __ 2006 WL 1725515 (2006) that the presumption was not unconstitutional. In essence, the ruling meant that a tie requires a jury to sentence a defendant to death.

In 1996, Michael Marsh broke into the home of Marry Ane Pusch and waited for her to return. He intended to hold Pusch and her 19-month-old daughter hostage and to extort money from her husband. Pusch came home earlier than expected and surprised Marsh. He shot and stabbed Pusch and then slit her throat. He set the house on fire and left the infant to die in the fire. Marsh was convicted by a jury of the capital murder of the infant, the first-degree premeditated murder of Marry Ane, aggravated arson, and aggravated **burglary**. During the penalty phase of the trial, the jury found there were three aggravating circumstances that justified the death penalty and that those circumstances outweighed the mitigating circumstances offered by Marsh. Marsh was sentenced to death for the murder of the child and to a life sentence for the killing of Marry Ane Pusch.

Marsh appealed his convictions and his death penalty sentence to the Kansas Supreme Court. He challenged the Kansas death penalty statute that stated a jury must sentence a defendant to death if the "existence of such aggravating circumstances is not outweighed by any mitigating circumstances which are found to exist." The Kansas Supreme Court agreed with him that the statute created an unconstitutional presumption in favor of the death penalty when aggravating and mitigating circumstances had equal weight. The statute violated the Eighth Amendment's prohibition against **cruel and unusual punishment**, as applied by the FOURTEENTH AMENDMENT to the states. The state appealed the decision to the U.S. Supreme Court, contending the Court had jurisdiction to hear a state law case because the decision had been based on the federal constitutional amendment.

The Supreme Court agreed to hear the case. The Court heard oral argument while Justice SANDRA DAY O'CONNOR was a member. With the confirmation of Justice Samuel Alito and the retirement of Justice O'Connor, the Court ordered reargument of the case. In a 5–4 decision the Court reversed the Kansas Supreme Court ruling. Justice CLARENCE THOMAS, writing for the majority, first addressed the issue of jurisdiction. He concluded that although the Kansas court had vacated the capital murder conviction and ordered a retrial the case was sufficiently "final" to allow review. In addition, he found that the Kansas decision was not supported by adequate and independent state grounds that would bar review by the Supreme Court.

Turning to the substantive issues of the case, Justice Thomas pointed to a 1990 decision, *Walton v. Arizona*, 497 U.S. 639, 110 S.Ct. 3047, 111 L.Ed.2d 511 (1990), that involved a Arizona death penalty statute similar to Kansas's. The statutes had two things in common. First, both laws permitted the imposition of capital punishment where the jury found that the aggravating circumstances were not outweighed by the mitigating circumstances. Second, the two laws required the prosecutor to carry the burden of proving aggravating circumstances. With the burden of proof placed on the prosecutor, the defendant was required to offer mitigating evidence. However, the Arizona law differed from the Kansas law in one significant respect. Under the Arizona law, once the state had met its burden, the defendant had the burden of proving sufficient mitigating circumstances to overcome the aggravating circumstances and that a sentence less than death was warranted. In contrast, the Kansas law was more favorable to the defendant. The prosecutor was required to bear the burden of proving **beyond a reasonable doubt** that the aggravating circumstances were not outweighed by the mitigating circumstances. There was no "additional evidentiary burden on the capital defendant." Based on the similarities of the statutes, Justice Thomas concluded that the *Walton* precedent and reasoning, which sustained the constitutionality of the Arizona statute, should be applied to the Kansas statute.

Justice Thomas also relied on the Court's general death penalty principles. He found that the Kansas law rationally narrowed the pool of death-penalty eligible defendants by permitting the death penalty only if the prosecutor could prove aggravating circumstances. In addition, the Kansas law authorized a jury to consider any relevant mitigating evidence offered by the defendant. He rejected Marsh's argument that a jury could not make a reasoned decision, citing Kansas jury instructions that explicitly stated that a tie would result in the death penalty. A jury would be aware of the consequences if it found the mitigating and aggravating circumstances were in equipoise.

Justice DAVID SOUTER, in a dissenting opinion joined by Justices JOHN PAUL STEVENS, RUTH BADER GINSBURG, and STEPHEN BREYER, argued that in the Kansas scheme a finding of equipoise meant that the nature of the crime and the characteristics of the defendant were ignored in favor of a presumption of death. Therefore, such a tie breaker was "morally absurd." In addition, he contended that "the Court's holding that the Constitution tolerates this moral irrationality defies decades of precedent aimed at eliminating freakish capital sentencing in the United States." Pointing to the use of DNA testing and the state of Illinois's death penalty moratorium, Souter believed that the number of false verdicts was "disproportionately high in capital cases."

Justice ANTONIN SCALIA, in a concurring opinion, attacked the dissenters for inserting their personal beliefs against capital punishment into the decision-making process. He also sought to discredit the scholarly articles cited by Justice Souter in his dissent.

New Jersey Suspends Executions, Pending Study

The New Jersey Legislature in January 2006 approved a bill that suspended executions in the state. The bill also established the New Jersey Death Penalty Study Commission, charged with examining the state's capital punishment system, including aspects of fairness and costs. The commission is expected to release its report in November.

New Jersey performed its last execution in 1963. The U.S. SUPREME COURT invalidated most federal and state death penalty laws in *Furman v. Georgia*, 408 U.S. 153, 92 S. Ct. 2726, 33 L. Ed. 2d 346 (1972), due primarily to the procedures used in death penalty cases. The case effectively placed a moratorium on the death penalty in the nation for four years. In a series of cases decided in 1976, though, the Court upheld several state death penalty laws, thus reestablishing capital punishment in the U.S.

New Jersey reinstated the death penalty in 1982, though no prisoners have been executed since that time. Between 1982 and 2006, the state has brought 197 capital cases, with 60 people sentenced to death. Most of these sentences were later overturned, however, and those who had been convicted were later sentenced to life terms. According an advocate from New Jerseyans for Alternatives to the Death Penalty, "By any measure, the death penalty has failed the people of New Jersey who have come to know that it risks executing innocent people and wastes millions of taxpayer dollars." One group estimated that the New Jersey death penalty **statute** has cost the state about $253 million.

Prior to the New Jersey Legislature's action, the states of Illinois and Maryland suspended capital punishment by way of a governor's order. Moreover, the New York Court of Appeals in June 2004 ruled that the New York's death penalty statute was unconstitutional. *People v. LaValle*, 817 N.E.2d 341 (N.Y. 2004). About 12 other states are reportedly re-examining the death penalty laws.

Between 1994 and 2005, public support for capital punishment dropped from 80 percent to 64 percent. Sixty executions were performed in 2005, reduced from 98 that were performed in 1999. Public interest groups have continued to actively campaign against executions. These groups often point to statistics regarding the number of innocent people that have been wrongly sentenced to death. Since 1973, more than 120 people have been freed from death row due to the discovery of exculpatory evidence.

The New Jersey Legislature concurred with many of these opinions. The bill recognized that the state's experience with capital punishment caused significant expenditures of money and time, but these costs may not be justified as compared with other needs of the state. The legislation additionally recognized that the state lacked a procedure to ensure uniform application of capital punishment. Moreover, the legislature acknowledged public concern regarding the roles of race and socio-economic factors in the death penalty as well as the public awareness that individuals across the nation had been wrongly convicted of murder. According to the bill, "The execution of an innocent person by the State of New Jersey would be a grave and irreversible injustice."

Under the legislation, the New Jersey Death Penalty Study Commission was charged with considering seven issues. These include the following: (1) whether the death penalty rationally serves a legitimate penological intent, such as deterrence; (2) whether there is a significant difference between the cost of the death penalty from indictment to execution and the cost of life in prison without parole; (3) whether the death penalty is consistent with evolving standards of decency; (4) whether the selection of defendants in New Jersey for capital trials is arbitrary, unfair or discriminatory and if there is unfair, arbitrary, or discriminatory variability in the sentencing phase or at any stage of the process; (5) whether there is a significant difference in the crimes of those selected for the punishment of death as opposed to those who receive life in prison; (6) whether the penological interest in executing certain persons found guilty of murder is sufficiently compelling that the risk of an irreversible mistake is acceptable; and (7) whether alternatives to the death penalty exist that would sufficiently ensure public safety and address other legitimate social and penological interests, including the interests of victims' families.

Eight members of the New Jersey Senate introduced the bill on January 26, 2004. The Senate approved the legislation by a wide margin in December 2005. The State Assembly's Judiciary Committee voted 4–2 in favor of the bill, which led to its presentation before the full State Assembly. The bill passed by a vote of 55 to 21. Acting Governor Richard Codey, a Democrat, signed the bill into law. The legislation requires the commission to issue its report no later than November 15, 2006. The commission may introduce new legislation at that time. Under this legislation, anyone in the state who has been sentenced to death cannot be executed prior to 60 days after the commission issues its report.

Several members of the New Jersey Legislature said that they still supported the death penalty, even though they voted for the moratorium. Their greatest concern was that the state should have a better policy and better procedures in place.

Oregon v. Guzek

A criminal defendants accused of a capital crime must undergo a two-phase trial. During the guilt phase the jury hears evidence on whether the defendant committed the crime. If the jury issues a guilty verdict, the trial enters the sentencing phase. In this phase the prosecution attempts to prove a number of aggravating factors that justify the death penalty, while the defense presents mitigating factors that may convince the jury to refrain from recommending capital punishment. The U.S. SUPREME COURT has reviewed many decisions of state supreme courts concerning the constitutionality of various procedural rules governing death penalty juries. In *Oregon v. Guzek*, __U.S.__, 126 S.Ct. 1226, __L.Ed.2d__ (2006), the Court ruled that a defendant is not entitled to present new alibi evidence during the sentencing phase that is inconsistent with the finding of guilt.

Randy Lee Guzek was convicted in 1988 for capital murder in the state of Oregon. In 1987 Guzek and two associates killed a **husband and wife** during the course of a **burglary**; Guzek knew the murdered couple and had a grudge against them. The police found out about Guzek's relationship with the victims and arrested the trio. Guzek's two associates confessed to participating in the crimes and said Guzek was the ringleader. At trial Guzek's defense relied on two alibi witnesses, his mother and grandfather, who testified that he had been with both of them at different times during the evening when the crime was committed. The jury convicted Guzek of murder and sentenced him to death. In 1990 the Oregon Supreme Court upheld the conviction but reversed Guzek's death sentencing because his defense was not able to present mitigating evidence. A second jury sentenced Guzek to death in 1991 but in 1995 the Oregon Supreme Court again threw out the death sentence. This time the court ruled that the victims' family should not have been allowed to testify as to the impact of the crimes on their lives. In 1998 a third jury sentenced Guzek to death and in 2004 the state supreme court again overturned it. The court held that the jury should have been instructed to consider a sentence of life without parole. In addition, the trial court had erred by refusing to admit new alibi evidence from Guzek's mother and grandfather that cast doubt on whether he committed the crime. The supreme court relied on U.S. Supreme Court cases that seemed to indicate that alibi evidence must be admitted during the sentencing phase. The state of Oregon petitioned the U.S. Supreme Court, challenging this interpretation of **case law**.

The Supreme Court, in a 8–0 decision (newly confirmed Justice SAMUEL ALITO did not participate in the consideration of the case), reversed the Oregon Supreme Court holding. Justice STEPHEN BREYER, writing for the Court, framed the question narrowly: Did the Eighth and Fourteenth Amendments give Guzek the right to introduce new evidence that he was not at the scene of the crime? This evidence would be inconsistent with his conviction for murder. More importantly, the evidence would not try to explain the manner in which he committed his crime and it was not unavailable to Guzek at the time of the original trial. These elements, plus the fact that Guzek could introduce transcripts of his relatives' testimony during the guilt phase of his first trial, undercut his claims. As to the constitutional argument, Breyer found nothing in the amendments "that provides a right to introduce new evidence of this kind at sentencing."

Breyer examined three U.S. Supreme Court cases relied on by the Oregon Supreme Court. In the first case the Court permitted a defendant to introduce evidence at the sentencing stage that she had played a small role in the crime. Such a mitigating factor was allowable because the defendant did not dispute that she had participated in the crime but rather sought to explain the circumstances of the offense. The key was that the defendant introduced evidence "that tended to show the defendant committed the crime." In addition, the evidence was not "directly inconsistent with the jury's finding of guilt." The Oregon Supreme Court had mistakenly concluded that it did not matter if the alibi evidence was inconsistent rather than consistent with the underlying conviction.

In *Franklin v. Lynaugh*, 487 U.S.164, 108 S.Ct. 2320, 101 L.Ed.2d 155 (1988), a **plurality** of the Court held that a capital defendant did not have an EIGHTH AMENDMENT right to introduce evidence at sentencing that was designed to throw "residual doubt" on his guilt of the underlying crime. A later decision reinforced this holding, finding that residual doubt was not a mitigating factor in capital sentencing proceedings. Justice Breyer acknowledged the precedents did not resolve all the issues surrounding this topic. However, three circumstances convinced the Court to uphold Oregon's bar on allowing in the alibi evidence. First, the sentencing phase concerns itself with the how, not the whether of the crime. Second, the state and Guzek had litigated whether the defendant had committed the crime and the alibi evidence had been relevant in that phase. The law usually discourages the relitigation of cases that have been fully and fairly heard. The Court saw no reason to give defendants an opportunity to challenge their guilt during the sentencing phase. Finally, Justice Breyer noted that Guzek could introduce transcripts of the prior testimony at the resentencing; this would have a "minimal adverse impact" on Guzek's ability to present his alibi claim.

Justice ANTONIN SCALIA, in a concurring opinion joined by Justice CLARENCE THOMAS, agreed with the result of the case but was vexed by the majority's failure to clearly state that the Eighth Amendment does not give a convicted capital defendant in any circumstances the right to present evidence concerning residual doubts about guilt at his sentencing hearing. The third reason offered by Breyer, that Oregon would allow enough evidence into the record through trial transcripts, suggested that future defendants might argue that the amount of "residual-doubt evidence carried over from the guilt phase" was insufficient to satisfy the court's ruling in this case. He believed it would have been better for the Court to say all such claims were meritless.

CENSUS

An official count of the population of a particular area, such as a district, state, or nation.

League of United Latin American Citizens v. Perry

The 132-page **plurality** opinion in *League of United Latin American Citizens v. Perry*, No.05–204, 548 U.S. ___ (2006) was delivered at the end of the U.S. SUPREME COURT's 2005–2006 session. Three other related cases, on appeal from the same court (the U.S. **District Court** for the Eastern District of Texas) were consolidated and decided together with this one. The subject matter of the cases involved congressional redistricting plans and allegations of impermissible political gerrymandering in Texas. Precisely, the high court ruled that only one of the challenged new voting districts created by the 2003 Texas Redistricting Plan violated the VOTING RIGHTS ACT OF 1965 because it amounted to vote dilution. The Supreme Court further ruled that the plaintiffs failed to state a claim of actionable partisan gerrymandering.

As background, Texas had been a Democratic stronghold for years, but began to shift after the 1960s. By the 1990s, the Republicans had won every statewide race, although they did not gain a majority in the state's legislature until the 2002 elections.

A census taken every ten years helps to redistrict states by accounting for population changes. Following the 1990 census, Texas was allotted three additional seats for its congressional delegation. Additionally, the REPUBLICAN PARTY had received 47 percent of the 1990 statewide vote. Sensing a change in the air, the Democratic-controlled state legislature attempted to draw a new congressional redistricting plan that would favor Democratic candidates. A Republican challenge on constitutional grounds failed.

By the time of the 2000 census, the Republicans controlled the governorship (GEORGE W. BUSH) and the state senate. The 2000 census authorized two additional seats for the Texas congressional delegation. The Texas legislature could not agree on a new redistricting plan and requested a federal court to devise a plan. The three-judge federal district court drew Plan

1151C, creating two new seats in high-growth areas, following county and voting precinct lines, and avoiding the pairing of incumbents. Under this independent plan, the 2002 congressional elections resulted in a 17–15 Democratic majority in the Texas congressional delegation. This, however, did not reflect the 59 percent to 40 percent wins by Republicans for statewide offices.

However, by 2003, Texas Republicans had gained control of both legislative houses and, after contentious partisan struggle, the legislature enacted a new congressional districting map, Plan 1374C. The 2004 elections resulted in Republicans winning 21 of the 32 congressional seats and holding 58 percent of statewide offices.

The LEAGUE OF UNITED LATIN AMERICAN CITIZENS (LULAC), along with a group of Democrats challenged Plan 1374C, filed suit claiming that the Plan violated the **Equal Protection** Clause of the U.S. Constitution, in its guarantee that "no state shall deny to any person within its jurisdiction the equal protection of the law." Since some forms of *partisan* gerrymandering are legal, the GI Forum of Texas, an advocate for the Hispanic community, filed a separate suit alleging that the Plan served to dilute minority voices and discriminate against Hispanics, making it illegal under §2 of the Voting Rights Act. Several other **statutory** and constitutional violations were alleged, in four separate suits. The suits were consolidated by the federal district court.

In 2004, the district court entered judgment for the state, but the Supreme Court ultimately vacated and remanded for consideration under *Vieth v. Jubelirer*, 541 U.S.267. (In that case, the Court held that a Pennsylvania redistricting need not be set aside simply because it constituted political gerrymandering.) On remand, the district court, perceiving its review on remand limited to questions of political gerrymandering, again rejected plaintiffs' claims and found for the state.

On direct appeal from that court, plaintiffs argued to the U.S. Supreme Court that they had raised more issues than mere partisan gerrymandering. Several of the newly-created voting districts were challenged as violative of §2 of the Voting Rights Act. States potentially violate §2 "if, based on the totality of circumstances, it is shown that the political processes leading to nomination or election . . . are not [as] equally open to . . . members of [a racial group as they are to] other members of the electorate." 42 USC 1973(b). A subsequent Court decision, *Thornburg v. Gingles*, 478 U.S. 30, identified three threshold conditions for establishing §2 violations: (1) the racial group must be "sufficiently large and geographically compact to constitute a majority in a single-member district"; (2) the group must be "politically cohesive"; and (3) the white majority must "vot[e] sufficiently as a bloc to enable it . . . usually to defeat the minority's preferred candidate." The legislative history identified other factors to consider, once all three threshold requirements were met, when reviewing the Act's "totality of circumstances" standard.

Applying established precedent to the present case(s), the Supreme Court found that only District 23 satisfied all three *Gingles* requirements. The Court's analysis was lengthy and convoluted.

Other findings and holdings of the Court constituted plurality opinions extracted from the separate justices. A 7–2 majority held that mid-decade redistricting did not create an inference of an unconstitutional partisan **gerrymander**, thereby demanding less other proof of unconstitutionality than would be required in a conventional decade (census) redistricting. But an unanimous Court ruled that mid-decade redistricting was not a violation of the one-person, one-vote principle. At least seven justices held that decennial census figures used in mid-decade redistricting did not violate the one-person, one-vote principle.

Six justices found that District 23, involving Latino voters in Laredo, was invalid under the Voting Rights Act. A 5–3 split (one justice not addressing the issue) found that District 24, involving African-American voters in Dallas-Fort Worth, was not invalid under the Voting Rights Act.

There was no clear majority, and the Court was well-divided, on the question of whether there is now a judicially manageable standard for evaluating claims of partisan gerrymandering. Four justices believe there is; two justices thought not; Justice Kennedy thought not yet, maybe never; two justices did not address this question.

CIVIL PROCEDURE

The methods, procedures, and practices used in civil cases.

Unitherm Food Systems, Inc. v. Swift-Eckrich, Inc.

The Federal Rules of **Civil Procedure** provide lawyers and parties with guidance on how they must proceed in a lawsuit. Under Rule 50(a) a party in a civil jury trial may file a motion before the case is submitted to the jury, arguing that the evidence presented is legally insufficient to support a jury verdict adverse to the party. If the judge denies the motion and the jury decides against that party, the party may then file a Rule 50(b) motion. In this motion the party may renew its request for judgment as a matter of law and may alternatively request a new trial. In *Unitherm Food Systems, Inc. v. Swift-Eckrich, Inc.*, __U.S.__, 126 S.Ct. 980, 163 L.Ed.2d 974 (2006), the Supreme Court was confronted with a case where the party lost its Rule 50(a) motion, was found liable by the jury, but then failed to file a Rule 50(b) motion. The Supreme Court held that the failure to file the Rule 50(b) motion deprived the **appellate** courts from ordering a new trial based on insufficient evidence.

The substance of the lawsuit in question dealt with patent infringement and antitrust claims. Unitherm Food Systems, Inc., a manufacturer of commercial cooking equipment, sued Swift-Eckrich, Inc., which does business as ConAgra. Unitherm alleged that ConAgra did not have a valid patent on a cooking process that Unitherm had patented several years before. In addition, Unitherm claimed that ConAgra violated federal antitrust laws when it attempted to enforce a patent it had obtained by committing **fraud** on the PATENT AND TRADEMARK OFFICE. The federal **district court** ruled that the ConAgra patent was invalid and then allowed the parties to go to trial before a jury on the antitrust claims. Right before the judge submitted the case to the jury, ConAgra moved for a **directed verdict** under Rule 50(a), arguing that Unitherm had failed to meet the evidentiary burden required by the antitrust provisions. The judge denied the motion and the jury returned a verdict in favor of Unitherm, awarding the company $22 million. ConAgra did not file a Rule 50(b) motion renewing its request for a judgment as a matter of law.

ConAgra appealed the verdict to the Federal **Circuit Court** of Appeals, which handles all patent-related cases. It contended that there was insufficient evidence to uphold the jury's verdict. The Federal Circuit, which sits in Washington, D.C., applies the legal precedents from the circuit court of appeals in which the federal litigation took place to non-patent issues on appeal. In this case it applied the Tenth Circuit Court of Appeals precedents. It believed that it could not address ConAgra's insufficiency of the evidence claim because it had not filed the post-trial motion under Rule 50(b). However, the Federal Circuit was bound to apply Tenth Circuit law on this issue and that circuit said ConAgra's appeal was proper because the filing of a Rule 50(a) motion was sufficient. However, the relief granted by an appeals court under this precedent could not be a decision in favor of ConAgra on the merits but only the granting of a new trial. The Federal Circuit then ruled in favor of ConAgra on the antitrust claim, vacated the jury verdict, and remanded the case for a new trial. Unitherm then appealed to the Supreme Court.

The Supreme Court, in a 7–2 decision, reversed the Federal Circuit decision and the Tenth Circuit's interpretation of the rules of procedure. Justice CLARENCE THOMAS, writing for the majority, pointed out that the Court had previously addressed the implications of a party's failure to file Rule 50(b) motion in a number of procedural contexts. In a 1947 case, *Cone v. West Virginia Pulp & Paper Co.*, 330 U.S.212, 67 S.Ct. 752, 91 L.Ed.2d 849 (1947), the Court ruled that without the filing of a post-trial motion an "appellate court [is] without power to direct the District Court to enter judgment contrary to the one it had permitted to stand." Other cases in 1948 and 1952 reinforced this holding, which was based on the belief that a Rule 50(b) motion "calls for the judgment in the **first instance** of the judge who saw and heard the witnesses and has the feel of the case which no appellate printed transcript can impart." Justice Thomas concluded that the requirement was based on principles of fairness.

ConAgra had argued these precedents did not apply because they involved cases where the **appellate court** sought to direct judgment in the absence of a postverdict motion; the Federal Circuit had only ordered a new trial. Justice Thomas rejected this approach, finding the distinction "immaterial." The principles set out in *Cone* and the other cases applied with "equal force whether a party is seeking judgment as a matter of law or simply a new trial." The trial judge's postverdict review was essential in determining whether a new trial should be granted. Without a Rule 50(b) motion "a party is not entitled to pursue a new trial on appeal" based on the insufficiency of the evidence. Addressing the Tenth Circuit precedent, Justice Thomas noted that the rules of procedure foreclosed appealing an unsuccessful Rule 50(a) motion unless that motion was renewed through the Rule 50(b) motion. In ConAgra's case the issue it raised on the Rule 50(a) motion-a directed verdict as a matter of law—was not the issue it appealed to the Federal Circuit, which was a new trial. Because ConAgra did not seek a new trial before the district court "forfeited its right to do so on appeal."

Justice JOHN PAUL STEVENS, in a dissenting opinion joined by Justice ANTHONY KENNEDY, contended that despite the mistake made by ConAgra's lawyers in not filing a Rule 50(b) motion, the federal appeals courts were not limited "by an explicit **statute** or controlling rule" to disallow consideration of the appeal.

CIVIL RIGHTS

Personal liberties that belong to an individual owing to his or her status as a citizen or resident of a particular country or community.

Burlington Northern & Santa Fe Railway Co. v. White

In an important civil rights case addressing actionable conduct and plaintiff burden, the U.S. SUPREME COURT, in *Burlington Northern & Santa Fe Railway Co. v. White*, No. 05–259, 548 U.S. ___ (2006), distinguished the scope and meaning of substantive discrimination from retaliatory discrimination under Title VII of the Civil Rights Act of 1964. Under its anti-retaliatory provision, the Act prohibits discrimination against an employee or job applicant who has "opposed" a practice that Title VII forbids, or who has "made a charge, testified, assisted, or participated in_" a Title VII proceeding or investigation. 42 USC 2000e-3(a). The Court found that the anti-retaliation provision under the Act does not confine the actions and harms it prohibits to those that are related to employment or that occur at the workplace. However, the provision covers only those employer actions that would have been materially adverse to a reasonable employee or applicant.

The Tennessee Yard of Burlington Northern & Santa Fe Railway (Burlington) maintained railroad track and cleared litter and cargo spillage from the track right-of-way in the area. In June 1997, Burlington's roadmaster, Marvin Brown, interviewed Sheila White and expressed interest in her previous experience operating forklifts. White was hired as a general track laborer, but when another worker assumed other job responsibilities, White was assigned to operate the forklift as her primary responsibility.

In September 1997, White complained to Burlington officials that her immediate supervisor, Bill Joiner, had repeatedly told her that women should not be working in her department. She also complained that Joiner had made insulting and inappropriate remarks to her in front of male coworkers. Burlington investigated the complaint and suspended Joiner for ten days. When roadmaster Brown advised White of the disciplinary action taken against her supervisor, he also advised that he was reassigning her from the forklift duties to standard track labor duties. He explained that the reassignment addressed coworkers' complaints that, in all fairness, a "more senior man" should have the less strenuous and cleaner job of forklift operaton.

By October, White had filed a complaint with the EQUAL EMPLOYMENT OPPORTUNITY COMMISSION (EEOC), claiming that the reassignment was in reality a gender-based discriminatory action as well as retaliation for her earlier complaint against her supervisor. In December, she filed a second EEOC complaint that Roadmaster Brown had placed her under surveillance and was monitoring all her activities. A few days after this, White and her immediate supervisor, Percy Sharkey, disagreed over which truck should transport White from one location to another. Later that afternoon, Sharkey informed Roadmaster Brown that White had been insubordinate. Brown immediately suspended her without pay. White filed an internal grievance, and management's responsive investigation showed that White had not been insubordinate. Burlington reinstated her and awarded her 37 days' backpay. White then filed her third EEOC charge based on this suspension.

After exhausting administrative remedies, White filed a Title VII action in federal court. She alleged unlawful retaliation under §2000e-3(a) on the part of Burlington officials by (1) changing her job duties, and (2) suspending her for 37 days without pay. The jury returned a verdict in her favor for both claims. Burlington appealed. A divided Sixth **Circuit Court** of Appeals initially found in favor of Burlington and reversed the judgment, but an **en banc** court voted to affirm the district court's judgment. Notwithstanding, they differed internally as to the proper standard to use. Other **appellate** circuits also had struggled (and came to different conclusions) in determining whether an allegedly discriminatory action had to be employment- or work-related, and in determining the degree of harmfulness that an action must reach to constitute a prohibited retaliatory action. The U.S. Supreme Court granted **certiorari** to resolve this confusion.

Justice Breyer delivered the opinion of the Court. First, the high court noted that the language of the substantive discrimination and the anti-retaliation provisions differed to reflect their respective purposes. Explicit language (e.g., "hire," "discharge," "compensation, terms, conditions, or privileges of employment," etc.) limited the substantive provision's scope to actions that affect employment or alter workplace conditions. No such limiting words are found in the anti-retaliatory provision. This reflects the fact that the substantive anti-discrimination provision seeks a workplace free of discrimination based on status, while the anti-retaliation provision seeks to prevent employers from interfering with an employee's efforts to secure the discrimination-free guarantees protected by Title VII. The Court presumes that, where words differ, Congress intended the difference. Therefore, concluded the Court, the anti-retaliatory provision does not confine prohibited harms and actions to only those related to employment or that occur at the workplace.

Next, the Court reviewed the differing standards of interpretation among the various circuit appellate courts as to the threshold of harmfulness needed for a challenged action to constitute a retaliatory one. The Court explained that the anti-retaliatory provision covers only those employer actions that would have been materially adverse to a reasonable employee or applicant. But what is the threshold for "materially adverse?" The Court referred to "material" adversity to distinguish significant from trivial harm. The Court referred to a "reasonable" employee or applicant to remind that the standard for judging harm is an objective, not subjective one.

Ultimately, the high court agreed with and accepted the standard used by the Seventh and DISTRICT OF COLUMBIA Circuits. Those circuits require a plaintiff alleging retaliation to show that the challenged action "well might have 'dissuaded a reasonable worker from making or supporting a charge of discrimination,'" (quoting from *Rochon v. Gonzales*, 438 F.3d 1211).

Applying the standard to the facts in White's case, the Court found sufficient evidence to support the jury's verdict for White. A reassignment of duties can constitute retaliatory discrimination where both the former and the present job duties fall within the same job description. Since almost every job category involves at least some less desirable tasks or duties, this is presumably why the EEOC has consistently recognized retaliatory job reassignments as prohibited retaliation.

Burlington also argued that White's suspension was moot because she was made whole again, i.e., she was reinstated with backpay. But the Court rejected this, noting that Congress intended both compensatory and **punitive damages** as recoverable in order to make a wronged plaintiff "whole" again; otherwise, employers could avoid liability by simply responding in a manner similar to that used by Burlington.

All nine justices concurred in the judgment, but eight justices comprised the majority opinion. Justice Alito filed a separate opinion concurring in the judgment. However, he disagreed with the majority's interpretation of the anti-retaliatory provision as having no basis in the **statutory** language, potentially leading to "practical problems."

Domino's Pizza, Inc. v. McDonald

The federal civil rights law that governs racial discrimination in the making and enforcing of contracts, 42 U.S.C.A. § 1981, was enacted in 1866 and amended as recently as 1991. A person may sue for damages under the law. Section 2 of the **statute** defines "make and enforce contracts" to include the "making, performance, modification, and termination of contracts, and the enjoyment of all benefits, privileges, terms, and conditions of the contractual relationship." In *Domino's Pizza, Inc. v. McDonald*, __U.S.__, 126 S.Ct. 1246, 163 L.Ed.2d 1069 (2006), the U.S. SUPREME COURT made clear that only a person who was party to a contract could sue under § 1981. A shareholder of a corporation did not have standing to sue for discriminatory acts allegedly committed against the corporation.

John W. McDonald, a black man, was the sole shareholder and president of JWM Investments, Inc. (JWM), a Nevada corporation. JWM and Domino's Pizza entered into contracts in which JWM would build four restaurants in the Las Vegas area and then lease them to Domino's. Problems occurred after JWM completed the first building. Debbie Pear, Domino's agent, refused to cooperate with bank financing paperwork for JWM and persuaded the local water district to change its records to reflect that Domino's owned the real estate that JWM had acquired for construction of the four restaurants. McDonald had this action rescinded but tensions increased. Pear told him he risked serious consequences if he didn't agree to end the contractual relationship. Pear allegedly told

McDonald that "I don't like dealing with you people anyway." She refused to explain what she meant by "you people." The contracts remained uncompleted and JWM filed for Chapter 11 bankruptcy. The bankruptcy **trustee** pursued an action for breach of contract against Domino's but did not make a § 1981 claim alleging racial discrimination in the making and enforcing of JWM's contracts. Domino's settled with the trustee and paid $45,000; in turn, JWM gave Domino's a complete release against further claims. However, McDonald filed a § 1981 federal lawsuit against Domino's in his personal capacity while the bankruptcy proceedings were still active. He claimed that Domino's had broken the contracts with JWM because of racial **animus** against McDonald and that the contract breach had caused him severe financial and emotional injury. McDonald sought compensatory and **punitive damages**.

Domino's filed a motion with the court asking it to dismiss the case because McDonald was not a party to the contract. The **district court** agreed, noting that it is fundamental proposition that "a corporation is a separate legal **entity** from its stockholders and officers." Therefore, JWM would have had standing to file a § 1981 lawsuit but for its signed release of claims but McDonald, as sole shareholder and president, could not "step into the shoes of the corporation and assert that claim personally." The Ninth **Circuit Court** of Appeals reversed the district court, relying on a circuit case that held when there are "injuries distinct from that of the corporation," a nonparty like McDonald may sue under § 1981. The court did acknowledge that other circuit courts of appeals did not agree with this holding. The Supreme Court agreed to hear Domino's appeal to resolve the issue.

The Supreme Court, in an 8–0 decision (newly confirmed Justice SAMUEL ALITO did not participate in the case), reversed the Ninth Circuit decision. Justice ANTONIN SCALIA, writing for the Court, pointed out that § 1981 was enacted following the CIVIL WAR to give African Americans the right "to give and receive *contractual rights* on one's own behalf." A claim brought under § 1981 must identify a contractual relationship under which the plaintiff has rights. Moreover, the statute can apply even when no contractual relationship exists. If racial animus prevents the creation of a contractual relationship, a plaintiff would have the right to sue as long as the plaintiff would have rights under the proposed contract. On its face, § 1981 clearly required that the person suing must have rights under the contractual relationship. To ignore the plain meaning would turn § 1981 into a "strange remedial provision designed to fight racial animus in all of its noxious forms, but only if the animus and the hurt it produced were somehow connected to *somebody's* contract." Justice Scalia concluded that the Court had never read the statute in this "*peculiarly* bounded way."

Justice Scalia also looked to the 1991 congressional amendments to § 1981 for additional support. Congress overturned a Supreme Court ruling and reinstated the interpretation that applied the statute to postformation conduct, but it inserted the reference to a "contractual relationship" in the definition section. Scalia saw this as reinforcing the need for a plaintiff to have contractual rights to sue under § 1981. With these factors in tow, Justice Scalia concluded that McDonald did not have a contractual relationship with Domino's. The JWM corporation was a separate legal entity, a "person" recognized as such in **civil law**. Scalia noted that McDonald had benefited from this separate legal status-Domino's had made a claim in bankruptcy against JWM, not McDonald personally. McDonald's personal assets were protected even though he had negotiated and signed contracts for JWM. The Court refused to alter settle corporation and agency law to allow McDonald to proceed personally against Domino's.

CLASS ACTION

A lawsuit that allows a large number of people with a common interest in a matter to sue or be sued as a group.

Kircher v. Putnam Funds Trust

In *Kircher v. Putnam Funds Trust*, No. 547 U.S. ___, 126 S.Ct. 2145, ___ L.Ed.2d ___ (2006), the U.S. SUPREME COURT unanimously held that a district court's remand of a case to state court, pursuant to the Securities Litigation Uniform Standards Act of 1998 (SLUSA), was not subject to **appellate** review. This decision resolved a split between the Second and Seventh Circuit Courts of Appeal on the issue.

The SLUSA provides that private state-law "covered" class actions that allege untruth or manipulation "in connection with the purchase or sale" of a "covered" security could not "be maintained in any State or Federal Court." 15 U.S.C. § 77p(b). In other words, SLUSA generally precludes bringing a securities **class action** based on state law into a state court. The Act authorizes removal to federal **district court** of "[a]ny covered class action brought in any State court involving a covered security, as set forth in subsection (b)." 15 U.S.C. § 77p(c). A "covered class action" is a lawsuit seeking damages on behalf of more than 50 people. A "covered security" is one traded nationally and listed on a regulated national exchange.

In 2003, plaintiffs Kircher and Brockway filed suit in an Illinois state court against several mutual funds, including defendant Putnam Funds Trust (Putnam). The complaint alleged misconduct that resulted in devalued shares owned by plaintiffs, who comprised eight groups of investors holding mutual funds shares. Each group had filed a separate action in Illinois state courts, and all of them alleged only state-law claims, such as negligence and breach of **fiduciary** duty.

Although the defendants filed notices of removal to federal district court in each case, stating that SLUSA precluded state actions and authorized such removals, the separate plaintiffs resisted. They argued that SLUSA only covered injuries relating to "the purchase or sale" of covered securities (see above) and that their claims were premised upon injuries as "holders" of **mutual fund** shares, not involving purchase or sale. Therefore, SLUSA did not preclude their actions in state court. The federal District Court for the Southern District of Illinois agreed, and in separate orders remanded each case back to state court, citing lack of **subject matter jurisdiction**.

The defendant funds then appealed to the Seventh **Circuit Court** of Appeals, but plaintiffs next argued that any appeal was barred by 28 U.S.C. § 1447(d), which provides that a district court's order to remand a case to state court is not appealable.

The Seventh Circuit disagreed with plaintiffs, holding that remand was not affected by 28 U.S.C. § 1447(d), which only affected lawsuits in which removal was not proper. In this case, the court held, removal was proper because the securities were regulated by federal securities laws, giving federal court jurisdiction. This decision was consistent with similar decisions in the Third and 11th Circuit Courts of Appeal.

Title 28 USC §1447(d) bars review of district court orders remanding removed cases for lack of subject matter jurisdiction. But the Seventh Circuit reasoned that §1447(d) was not applicable because the district court had rendered a substantive decision of no preclusion (under SLUSA), rather than a procedural decision of no subject matter jurisdiction, thus making the decision appealable. Defendants were permitted to remove the case to federal district court for a determination on whether the case was preempted by **statute**. If it were, the district court would have to dismiss the case. If not, the district court would have to remand back to state court.

In an opinion delivered by Justice DAVID SOUTER, the U.S. Supreme Court reversed. The Court noted that under SLUSA's text, removal and jurisdiction to deal with removed cases was limited to those precluded by the statute. Any motion to remand which claims the action is not precluded contemplates a jurisdictional issue. Therefore, a federal district court's exercise of its adjudicative power is jurisdictional, so a remand decision under these circumstances is not appealable.

The Supreme Court also noted that the Seventh Circuit's rationale was in part motivated by an erroneous assumption that SLUSA gave **federal courts** exclusive jurisdiction to decide preclusion issues. Nothing in SLUSA created this exclusive jurisdiction, and on remand, the state court would be "perfectly free to reject the remanding court's reasoning" and render its own determination as to preclusion. The Court vacated the judgment of the Seventh Circuit and remanded the case with instructions to dismiss the appeal for lack of jurisdiction.

The Court's decision was nearly unanimous. Justice ANTONIN SCALIA filed a separate opinion concurring in part and concurring in the judgment. Said Justice Scalia, "I disagree with the Court's reasoning in Part II, however, because it holds only that the Court of Appeals' recharacterization was incorrect, and not (as I believe) that recharacterization—being a form of review—is categorically forbidden."

Merrill Lynch, Pierce, Fenner & Smith v. Dabit

Since the disastrous collapse of the stock market in 1929 and the Great Depression that continued through the 1930s, the federal government has asserted **primary authority** over the regulation of stocks and other publicly traded securities. The Securities Act of 1993, 48 Stat. 74, and the SECURITIES AND EXCHANGE COMMISSION Act of 1934, 48 Stat. 881, remain the central laws governing securities regulation in the United States. However, in the 1990s **class action** lawsuits involving securities **fraud** and misrepresentation began to be filed that were based on state regulatory laws. Congress responded by passing the Securities Litigation Uniform Standards Act of 1998 (SLUSA), 112 Stat. 3227, which prohibited the filing of class actions based on state laws and alleging "a misrepresentation or omission of a material fact in connection with the purchase or sale of a covered security" in any state or federal court by any private party. The Supreme Court, in *Merrill Lynch, Pierce, Fenner & Smith v. Dabit*, __U.S.__, 126 S.Ct. 1503, __L.Ed.2d __ (2006), was called upon to decide whether a class action under state law could proceed if the plaintiffs alleged they were holders of securities rather than purchasers or sellers. The Court concluded that Congress intended to cut off all class action suits based on state law when it enacted SLUSA.

Shadi Dabit was a broker for Merrill Lynch, Pierce, Fenner & Smith, a prominent investment banking firm that offers research and brokerage services to investors. In 2002 Eliot Spitzer, New York Attorney General, began an investigation into Merrill Lynch's business practices, raising questions about the objectivity and truthfulness of the reports produced by the firm's investment analysts concerning the value of certain stocks. Though Merrill Lynch settled the dispute with Spitzer, a number of class action lawsuits were filed alleging financial losses because of the firm's practices. Dabit, who lived in Oklahoma, filed a class action suit against his former employer in Oklahoma federal **district court** based on violations of Oklahoma state laws rather than on federal securities laws. Dabit argued that Merrill Lynch had breached its **fiduciary** duty and covenant of fair dealing and **good faith** that it owed its stock brokers. He alleged that the firm's analysts had fed the brokers misleading and overoptimistic research as a way to manipulate stock prices. Because of this false information brokers and their customers held onto stock long past the time they would have sold the stock, if they had known the truth. When the truth was revealed, the stock prices dropped precipitously. Dabit alleged the brokers had been injured by this behavior and by the loss of commission fees when their disgruntled customers took their business elsewhere.

Merrill Lynch moved the district court to dismiss the case, arguing that SLUSA barred this type of class action. The court agreed that Dabit's allegations involving the purchase of securities were prohibited under SLUSA but that "holding" claims might not be pre-empted by the federal law. The court dismissed Dabit's complaint but gave him the opportunity to re-file the case with only the holding claims. Dabit complied, listing as members of his class Merrill Lynch brokers who "owned and continued to own" the subject securities. During this same period dozens of similar lawsuits were filed around the United States, leading to a consolidation of all the cases in New York federal district court. Merrill Lynch renewed its motion to dismiss with this court and the court agreed that SLUSA barred holding claims as well. Dabit appealed to the Second **Circuit Court** of Appeals, which reversed the district court. The appeals court concluded that Congress intended to limit SLUSA to the purchase and sale of stocks; allegations that brokers were fraudulently induced to retain or delay the sale of their securities was outside the language of SLUSA. Merrill Lynch then took its case to the Supreme Court.

The Court, in an 8-0 ruling (newly confirmed Justice Samuel Alito did not participate in the consideration of the case), overturned the Second Circuit decision. Justice JOHN PAUL STEVENS, writing for the Court, noted that the Court had established in a 1975 case a limitation on private class action suits filed under federal securities law. The Court permitted such suits only in cases where the class members were purchasers or sellers of securities. This limitation was justified on policy grounds, specifically the need to prevent lawsuits that could, even in weak cases, lead to substantial settlements that would hurt brokerage firms. Congress had adopted this same stance when it passed the Private Securities Litigation Reform Act of 1995, 109 Stat. 737, pointing to nuisance filings, complicated discovery requests and the manipulation by class action lawyers of their clients. The 1995 Reform Act placed limits on the amount of recoverable damages and attorney's fees.

The 1995 act produced the unintended consequence of encouraging lawyers to file class actions using state rather than federal laws and to try these cases in state courts. This shift was a dramatic change, for state-court class actions involving national securities firms had been rare. Justice Stevens pointed out that this was the context for Congress's passage of SLUSA and for the current dispute over the breadth of the phrase "in connection with the purchase or sale" of securities. Stevens concluded that the policy considerations that led to the Court's 1975 decision involving federal law class action suits were applicable to state law actions. That fact that Dabit's lawsuit was brought by holders rather than purchasers or sellers was, for SLUSA purposes, "irrelevant; the identity of the plaintiffs does not determine whether the complaint alleges fraud 'in connection with the purchase or sale' of securities." The misconduct at issue was the "fraudulent manipulation of stock prices," which qualified "in connection with the purchase or sale' of securities." Therefore, Dabit could not pursue his class action suit under state law.

CLEAN WATER ACT

Rapanos v. United States

When Congress enacted the Clean Water Act (CWA), 86 Stat. 816, in 1972, it gave the U.S. Army Corps of Engineers the authority to regulate the discharge of any pollutants into "navigable waters." The Corps has given a broad reading to the term "navigable waters," which has led to lawsuits by land developers and property owners who believe their property is not linked to navigable waters. The Corps extended its control by regulating wetlands in the United States (approximately 300 million acres) which drain into tributaries of navigable waters. The Supreme Court has approved the regulation of wetlands that are adjacent to navigable waters but the regulation of more remote wetlands remained unresolved. In *Rapanos v. United States/Carabell v. Army Corps of Engineers*, __U.S.__, 126 S.Ct., __L.Ed.2d __ 2006 WL 1667087 (2006), the Court failed to deliver a clear ruling on how courts and the Corps are to deal with wetlands. In the **plurality** decision, Justice ANTHONY KENNEDY announced a "significant nexus" test that appeared to give the federal government continuing control over the management of wetlands.

John Rapanos, a Michigan real estate developer, owned three parcels of land about 20 miles from Lake Huron which he wanted to use for a shopping center. The state of Michigan classified the parcels as wetlands because after a heavy rain the water from these fields flowed into a drainage ditch, then into a small stream that emptied into Lake Huron. Under the CWA a permit is required before a landowner may drain or fill a wetland. When it became clear that Rapanos would not receive a permit, he had the land filled in with sand. He was convicted of criminal charges for his actions and a **civil action** was filed by the federal government seeking multimillion dollar fines. Rapanos claimed that his property was not a wetland but a federal **district court** concluded otherwise. On appeal, the Sixth **Circuit Court** of Appeals upheld the lower court ruling that the Corps had not exceeded its authority under the CWA.

The Supreme Court could not reach a majority conclusion. Four justices held that the Corps had exceeded its authority and that a new definition of wetlands was required. Four justices dissented, arguing that prior Court precedents and deference to the Corps justified the lower court rulings. Justice Anthony Kennedy, in a separate opinion, announced a new test for determining whether land could be classified as a wetland under the CWA. Because of this splintered decision, Kennedy's opinion appeared to give the most guidance to the lower courts and the Corps. However, Chief Justice Roberts, in a concurring opinion, lamented the fact that the Court had failed to reach a majority conclusion "on precisely how to read Congress' limits on the reach of the Clean Water Act." Because of this failure lower courts "and regulated entities will now have to feel their way on a case-by-case basis."

Four conservative justices (Chief Justice JOHN ROBERTS and Justices ANTONIN SCALIA, CLARENCE THOMAS, and SAMUEL ALITO) voted to restrict the definition of wetlands. Justice Scalia, writing for the four justices, argued that the Corps of Engineers had exceeded its authority "beyond parody" by regulating land that contained nothing but drainage ditches, storm sewers and "dry arroyos in the middle of the desert." The federal **encroachment** on local lands had diminished the ability of the states to manage land and made the Corps look like "a local **zoning** board." Scalia proposed that the only wetlands subject to the CWA were those "with a continuous surface connection" to actual waterways, "so that there is no clear demarcation between 'waters' and wetlands." The linkage between a wetland and a waterway also had to be defined more restrictively. He contended that the waters adjacent to the wetlands must be "relatively permanent, standing, or flowing."

Justice Kennedy disagreed with this interpretation. He argued that the current regulations gave the Corps too much discretion to classify land as wetlands but there was no need to establish a restrictive bright-line rule advocated by Scalia and the other three justices. Instead, Kennedy proposed the adoption of a "significant nexus test" that would be applied on a case-by-case basis. Under this test the wetlands must have a significant nexus to a body of water that is actually navigable. This meant that even temporary channels could qualify as a tributary to navigable waters. He pointed out that the Los Angeles River in California is dry for much of the year, yet it can send "torrents thundering" down its steel and concrete protected waterway for short periods of time. Kennedy believed the Corps needed to rewrite its regulations to identify "categories of tributaries" that were "significant enough that wetlands adjacent to them are likely, in the majority of cases, to perform important functions for an aquatic system incorporating navigable waters." Though he voted to vacate the lower court ruling so the district court could conduct hearing based on his significant nexus test, Kennedy believed the federal government could make its case for the Rapanos wetlands. The wetlands drained into a stream that flowed into Lake Huron.

Justice JOHN PAUL STEVENS, in a dissenting opinion joined by Justice DAVID SOUTER, RUTH BADER GINSBURG, and STEPHEN BREYER, contended that the Kennedy test "will probably not do much to diminish the number of wetlands covered by the act in the long run." However, in the short term the test "will have the effect of creating additional work for all concerned parties." Stevens believed the Court should have paid more deference to the Corps's regulations, which attempt to manage a complicated system of water management. He also accused Justice Scalia and the conservatives of judicial activism in attempting to rewrite the CWA.

S.D. Warren Company v. Maine Board of Environmental Protection

The federal Clean Water Act, 86 Stat. 877, sets standards and review processes for industries that discharge material into navigable waters. Under § 401 of the act a federal license will be issued to a business if the state certifies that water protection laws will not be violated. A Maine company that operated a number of hydroelectric dams sought to renew its federal power licenses and questioned the need to submit to the water certification as part of the renewal process, arguing that it did not discharge into the river any pollutants when it returned the water used to generate electricity. The Supreme Court, in *S.D. Warren Company v. Maine Board of Environmental Protection*, __U.S.__, 126 S.Ct. 1843, __L.Ed.2d __ (2006), rejected this argument and held that the government did not need to show that something was added to the water before it was returned to the river to trigger this Clean Water Act provision.

The S.D. Warren company operated a series of dams on a 25-mile span of the Presumpscot River in Southern Maine to generate electricity for its paper mills. Each dam created a pond, where water was funneled into a canal, sent through turbines, and then returned to the river. The company had operated the dams since 1935 and had a license to do so from the Federal Energy Regulatory Commission (FERC). In 1999, the company sought renewal of its licenses for five of its dams. It applied for water quality certification from the Maine Board of Environmental Protection, which was assigned the job of enforcing this Clean Water Act requirement. However, Warren filed its application under protest, contending its dams did not discharge into the river any materials, thus making it exempt from the Clean Water Act. The Maine agency certified the dams but required Warren to maintain a minimum stream flow and to allow passage of migratory fish and eels. FERC then issued new licenses to the dams. Despite winning renewal of the licenses, Warren pursued legal action against Maine's clean water certification process. The case eventually made its way to the Maine Supreme Judicial Court, which ruled that Warren's dams did discharge into navigable waters for Clean Water Act purposes.

Keith Carabell in the woods. Carabell's suit against the Army Corps of Engineers was argued in conjunction with John Rapanos.
AP IMAGES

The U.S. SUPREME COURT, in a unanimous decision, upheld this interpretation of the Clean Water Act. Justice DAVID SOUTER, writing for the Court, noted that the dispute turned on the meaning of the word "discharge." The Clean Water Act did not define this term but it provided that the "term 'discharge' when used without qualification includes a discharge of a pollutant, and a discharge of pollutants." The act did define pollutants to mean "any addition of any pollutant to navigable waters from any point source." Justice Souter rejected the claim that "discharge" was limited to this definition, opting instead to construe the word in its ordinary or natural meaning. When applied to water, the word 'discharge' meant a "flowing or issuing out." The Court had adopted this definition in prior water cases, including a 1994 case involving the Clean Water Act that involved hydroelectric dams. Though the Court's opinion did not discuss whether the dam had added anything to the water, even the dissenting justices agreed that the discharge of water from the dam was within the sphere of the Clean Water Act. In addition, Justice Souter pointed out that the federal ENVIRONMENTAL PROTECTION AGENCY and FERC had read "discharge" to include releases from hydroelectric dams.

Warren presented three arguments as to why the ordinary meaning of "discharge" should not be used. He first argued that a proper reading of the act's provision demonstrated that "discharge" was linked to a requirement that an "addition" of pollutants to water be made for Clean Water Act coverage. The company contended that because the release of the water from the dams added nothing to the river, "the water flowing out of the turbines cannot be a discharge into the river." Justice Souter discounted this claim, finding that the company had improperly sought to "convert express inclusion into restrictive equation." Warren also argued that the Court's recent decision in *South Florida Water Management District v. Miccosukee Tribe of Indians*, 541 U.S.95, 124 S.Ct. 1537, 158 L.Ed.2d 264 (2004), required it to find no discharge under the act. Justice Souter concluded that this case was not on point because it involved a different section of the Clean Water Act, § 402. The two sections were "not interchangeable, as they serve different purposes and use different language to reach them." Section 402 had a more specific focus, requiring a permit for the "discharge of any pollutant" in the navigable waters of the United States. The triggering **statutory** term was not "discharge" alone but the "discharge of a pollutant." This term was narrower than the language of § 401 because it defined this phrase to require an "addition" of a pollutant to the water. Section 401 did not require that something be added to the water before triggering the coverage of the act. Finally, Warren tried to use legislative history to show that Congress had inadvertently let the word "includes" in the definition of "discharge" after an unsuccessful attempt to deal with "thermal discharges" in § 402. Warren contended that Congress carelessly retained the word "includes" in § 401 when it really meant to limit the term "discharges" to the discharge of pollutants. Justice Souter rejected this claim as well, finding that Congress "probably distinguished the terms 'discharge' and 'discharge of pollutants' deliberately, in order to use them in separate places and to separate ends." The Court generally presumed that when Congress used particular language in one section but omitted it in another section of the same law, it acted "intentionally and purposely."

Justice Souter also found that the discharge of the dam water back into the river did alter water quality by limiting river flow and by modifying the chemical balance of water in ways that can affect aquatic organisms. These changes justified the use by the states of the Clean Water Act to protect against "the broad range of pollution."

COMMERCE CLAUSE

The provision of the U.S. Constitution that gives Congress exclusive power over trade activities between the states and with foreign countries and Indian tribes.

DaimlerChrysler Corp. v. Cuno

The U.S. SUPREME COURT on May 15, 2006 ruled that a group of taxpayers did not have STANDING to challenge local property tax abatements and state franchise tax credit that was extended to automobile manufacturer DaimlerChrysler Corporation by the city of Toledo and the state of Ohio. The Court vacated a decision of the Sixth **Circuit Court** of Appeals, which had ruled that the state franchise tax credit violated the **Commerce Clause** of the U.S. Constitution.

In 1998, both Toledo and the state of Ohio wanted to encourage DaimlerChrysler to expand its facility in Toledo. The manufacturer agreed to construct the expansion, expecting the project to cost $1.2 billion. In exchange, the city of Toledo and two local school districts agreed to a 10-year personal property tax exemption as well as credit that could be applied to the state corporate franchise tax. The franchise tax credit and property tax exemption were both authorized by state statutes in Ohio.

Under the Constitution, Congress has the power to "regulate Commerce with foreign Nations, and among the several States." The courts have interpreted this provision to include a "negative" or "dormant" aspect, which restricts a state from imposing a tax on interstate commerce. A tax is constitutional under the Commerce Clause if it satisfies four requirements, including the following: (1) the activity that is taxed has a substantial nexus with the

Toledo, Ohio, Jeep plant, February 2006.
AP IMAGES

taxing state; (2) the tax is fairly apportioned to the activity that occurs in the state; (3) the tax does not discriminate against interstate commerce; and (4) the tax is fairly related to benefits offered by the state. *Complete Auto Transit, Inc. v. Brady*, 430 U.S. 274, 97 S. Ct. 1076, 51 L. Ed. 2d 326 (1977).

A group of residents in Toledo sued the state, the city of Toledo, and DaimlerChrysler in state court in Ohio. These taxpayers claimed that the tax breaks extended to the manufacturer placed a "disproportionate burden" on the plaintiffs because these tax breaks diminished the funds that were available to the city and the state. The plaintiffs claimed that due to this burden, the tax benefits violated the Commerce Clause.

The case was removed to the U.S. **District Court** for the Northern District Court in Ohio because it involved a **federal question**. The plaintiffs argued that the case should be REMANDED to state court because they had "substantial doubts about their ability to satisfy either the constitutional or the prudential limitations on standing in the federal court." U.S. District Judge David A. Katz declined to remand the case and later dismissed the claim, finding that neither of the tax benefits violated the Commerce Clause. *Cuno v. DaimlerChrysler, Inc.* 154 F. Supp. 2d 1196 (N.D. Ohio 2001).

The plaintiffs appealed the decision to the U.S. Court of Appeals for the Sixth Circuit. The court reviewed the constitutionality of both the investment tax credit and the personal property tax exemption under Commerce Clause **jurisprudence**. With respect to the personal property tax exemption, the plaintiffs argued that it was unconstitutional because it subjected similarly situated business owners in the state to differential tax rates. In other words, those businesses that met eligibility requirements, including a specified level of employment and investment in the state, were exempt, while businesses that were not eligible paid higher tax rates.

The **appellate court**, per an opinion by Judge Martha Craig Daughtrey, rejected the plaintiff's arguments with respect to the property tax exemption. According to the court, the conditions that the manufacturer had to meet in order to qualify for the exemption were "minor **collateral** requirements" and were "directly linked to the use of the exempted personal property." Because of this, the court concluded that the exemption does not independently burden interstate commerce such that the exemption violated the Commerce Clause. *Cuno v. DaimlerChrysler*, 386 F.3d 738 (6th Cir. 2004).

The plaintiffs also argued that the investment tax credit was unconstitutional. The plaintiffs relied on Supreme Court decisions that invalidated tax schemes that encouraged the development of local industry by imposing burdens on economic activities that take place outside of the state. According to the plaintiffs, allowing a tax credit for in-state business operations hindered free trade among the states because the operations must take place in the home state in order for the credit to apply.

The Sixth Circuit agreed with the plaintiffs, holding that the investment tax credit indeed violated the Commerce Clause. The court reviewed a number of holdings from prior Supreme Court cases and determined that the Ohio tax credit did not differ materially from other tax schemes that the Supreme Court had ruled unconstitutional. The Sixth Circuit noted that though it was "sympathetic to efforts by the City of Toledo to attract industry into its economically depressed areas," it could not uphold the credit under the Commerce Clause.

The defendants appealed the Sixth Circuit's decision to the U.S. Supreme Court, which rendered a decision on May 15, 2006. Chief Justice John Roberts, writing for the majority, avoided the Commerce Clause arguments and instead focused on whether the plaintiffs had standing to bring the suit. The plaintiffs argued that as taxpayers, they should be proper parties because the franchise tax credit depletes money from Ohio to which the plaintiffs contribute through their tax payments.

The Court reiterated a long-standing principle that in order for a plaintiff to have standing, the plaintiff must allege an injury that is concrete and particularized. In the case of a taxpayer who does not allege a particular injury other than a burden on taxpayers in general, the alleged injury is merely hypothetical. Since the plaintiffs in this case had not established a particular injury, the Court ruled that the lower courts had erred in considering their Commerce Clause arguments in the first place. *DaimlerChrysler v. Cuno*, ___ U.S. ___, ___ S. Ct. ___, ___ L. Ed. 2d ___ (May 15, 2006).

Even though the Court did not address the argument on the merits, officials in Ohio expressed their approval of the decision. According to Ohio Lieutenant Governor Bruce Johnson, "With its ruling, the Supreme Court has enabled states to pursue economic development projects by offering incentives to companies without the lingering concern that they may be found to be unconstitutional."

CONSPIRACY

An agreement between two or more persons to engage jointly in an unlawful or criminal act, or an act that is innocent in itself but becomes unlawful when done by the combination of actors.

Tom DeLay Indicted, Resigns Seat in Congress

Representative Tom DeLay (R.-Tex.) was forced to resign his position as House Majority Leader in 2005 when he was indicted on charges that he violated a Texas political fundraising law. The charges stem from DeLay's alleged role in a conspiracy to inject illegal contributions into the 2002 state elections in Texas. The scandal later led to his announcement that he would not seek reelection in 2006, ending an 11-term run in Congress. DeLay resigned from Congress on June 9, 2006.

DeLay was first elected to Congress in 1984 as a representative of the 22nd District of Texas. Ten years later he was elected as House Majority Whip. As one of the more vocal members of Congress, he played a public role in several controversies during the 1990s. He was part of a group in 1997 that tried to remove former House Speaker NEWT GINGRICH. During the following year, DeLay helped lead calls for the IMPEACHMENT of President BILL CLINTON. After the retirement of Dick Armey in 2002, DeLay was elected as majority leader without opposition. His hard-nosed approach to politics earned him the nickname, "The Hammer." He describes himself as a champion of free enterprise and deregulation.

According to allegations, DeLay's legal problems began in 2002, when he helped found Texans for a Republican Majority PAC (TRMPAC). This political action committee allegedly sent a check for $190,000 to the Republican National State Elections Committee (RNSEC), which in turn sent money to Texas House candidates. The Texas Elections Code forbids corporations from contributing to election campaigns. This law has existed for more than a century. After the 2002 elections, Texas Republicans took control of its state legislature for the first time in 130 years. In order to be convicted of violating the state election law, prosecutors would have to prove that DeLay knew about and approved the transaction between TRMPAC and RNSEC.

In September 2004, grand jurors indicted three of DeLay's associates, including Jim Ellis, John Colyandro, and Warren RoBold, in an investigation of these corporate contributions. If DeLay were indicted as well, he would be forced to resign his position as House Majority Leader because REPUBLICAN PARTY rules forbid a person facing a criminal indictment from serving in a leadership position. In November 2004, party members adopted a rule change that would allow DeLay to keep his post. Two months later, however, the party reversed this rule after facing pressure from Democrats and members of the public. The House of Representatives also rejected changes in ethics rules that would have made an investigation of ethical violations more difficult. House Democrats claimed that these proposed changes were designed to protect DeLay.

On September 28, 2005, a **grand jury** in Travis County, Texas (which includes state capital Austin) indicted DeLay, Ellis, and Colyandro. Within hours, House Republicans named Representative Roy Blunt (R.-Mo.) as a temporary replacement for majority leader. DeLay attacked the prosecutor, Ronnie Earle, calling him a "partisan fanatic." According to DeLay, he violated no laws and said that he would prevail. He would face up to two years in prison if he were convicted of violating state campaign laws.

DeLay, Ellis, and Colyandro faced additional charges when a grand jury on October 3 indicted the three for **money laundering** and conspiracy to launder money. These charges were more serious than the previous ones and surprised commentators. According to the indictment, DeLay orchestrated an effort to launder the $190,000 through an arm of the Republican National Committee in Washington and then send the money back to Texas Republicans. DeLay turned himself in later that month, smiling broadly in his mug shot.

A squabble ensued regarding the judge that would preside over DeLay's case. The first judge, Bob Perkins, was removed in November due to an allegedly liberal bias, despite protests by the prosecution. On November 4, the chief justice of the Texas Supreme Court, Wallace B. Jefferson, appointed retired judge Pat Priest to preside over the case. Even this choice was not without controversy, since Priest had reportedly contributed small amounts to state Democratic candidates in 2004.

DeLay and the other defendants sought to have the court dismiss the charges. In December, Priest dismissed the charge that the three had conspired to violate the election law. However, the judge refused to dismiss the money laundering charges, which carry long prison terms and fines. An **appellate court** in Texas upheld the judge's ruling in April 2006.

DeLay's reputation was further tarnished by his relationship with lobbyist Jack Abramoff. In November 2005, Michael Scanlon, a former aide of DeLay, pleaded guilty to conspiracy to bribe public officials. This charge stemmed from a government investigation of work that Scanlon performed with Abramoff in an Indian gaming scandal. Abramoff pleaded guilty in January 2006 to charges of conspiracy, tax evasion, and tax **fraud**. He was later sentenced to six years in prison but has been allowed to remain free while he assists in an investigation of corruption in Congress.

Congressman Tom DeLay (l) speaks to his attorney in court, October 21, 2005.
JAY JANNER/POOL/CORBIS

The controversies surrounding DeLay and Abramoff led in part to an effort to reform ethics rules in Congress. House Speaker Dennis Hastert (R.-Ill.) led calls to restrict members of Congress from receiving free gifts and travel through outside groups. However, these proposals met with resistance, even within the Republican Party. Some lawmakers argued that instead of restricting meals and gifts paid by lobbyists, the rules should require more complete disclosure.

DeLay won the Republican primary for his House seat on March 7, but polls indicated that he would face stiff challenges in the November elections. The investigation into Abramoff's activities also led to speculation that DeLay could face additional legal problems. Moreover, DeLay expressed dissatisfaction with not being a leader in the House. These factors led DeLay to announced his decision to resign his seat.

Conviction of Former Alabama Governor Don Siegelman

After a six-week trial, 11 days of jury deliberations, and two jury deadlocks, a federal **district court** jury convicted former Alabama Governor Don E. Siegelman on seven counts of conspiracy, bribery, **mail fraud**, and obstruction of justice. The July 2006 verdict concerned crimes committed from 1994 (when Siegelman was running for lieutenant governor), to January 2003, when Siegelman's term as governor ended. The charges centered on illegal activity in conjunction with Siegelman's official acts and duties while in public office.

On the day that Siegelman was convicted, FBI Director Robert Mueller reported there had been 1,700 public corruption-related convictions nationwide in the previous two years. In Alabama alone, two governors had been convicted in the last 13 years.

In October 2005, the U.S. Department of Justice (DOJ) released a public announcement that a 30-count superceding indictment had been returned by a federal **grand jury** in Montgomery, Alabama, charging Siegelman and his former chief of staff Paul Michael Hamrick with various federal crimes, including violations under the Racketeer Influenced and Corrupt Organizations (RICO) **statute**.

The indictments were the result of a joint federal and state investigation starting in 2001 into numerous improprieties in the Siegelman administration. They directly followed the entering of guilty pleas from three other individuals in connection with the alleged scheme involving Siegelman. Alabama businessman Clayton Young, former director of Alabama's Department of Economic and Community Affairs Nick Bailey, and architect William Curtis Kirsch all pleaded guilty to public corruption charges, including bribery. The indictment of Siegelman included a charge that he and Paul Hamrick accepted hundreds of thousands of dollars in bribes from Young in return for favorable government treatment of Young's business interests, including the awarding of contracts to companies controlled by Young. Both Young and Bailey were key prosecution witnesses at Siegelman's trial.

The five-year investigation leading up to the indictment began in May 2001, following a local newspaper story reporting irregularities connected with the building of two state warehouses. The story reported that G.H. Construction Company had been awarded the contract to build the warehouses. The company was secretly owned by Young, a major contributor and friend of Siegelman's, and a close associate of Hamrick and Bailey. Allegedly, the initials "G.H." stood for "Goat Hill," the nickname for the area of downtown Montgomery where key state offices are located. Young, Bailey, and a Montgomery architect pleaded guilty to bribery and other associated crimes involving the warehouse deal, and agreed to cooperate with prosecutors in the Siegelman probe.

Perhaps the most visible and reported charges against Siegelman focused on his relationship with then-HealthSouth CEO Richard M. Scrushy, who was also indicted along with Siegelman. (Prosecutors suffered a defeat in 2005 in the widely-reported acquittal of Scrushy on charges that he had participated in a $2.7 billion Enron-style accounting **fraud** at HealthSouth, the corporation of local hospitals that he founded.)

One of the more egregious charges of criminal enterprise stemmed from Siegelman's alleged acceptance of bribes from Scrushy in return for official actions. To wit, the indictment charged that Scrushy made two disguised payments totaling $500,000 to Siegelman in exchange for an appointment to Alabama's hospital-regulatory review board. Siegelman also allegedly demanded $100,000 and accepted $40,000 from another person after threatening to harm that person's business with the Alabama Department of Transportation, and demanded $250,000 from still another individual under the same threat.

Ultimately, Siegelman was acquitted of RICO charges, but convicted of bribery and conspiracy charges relating to the $500,000 from Scrushy for the board seat. (Scrushy was also convicted.) In conjunction with this, Siegelman was convicted of separate counts of mail fraud regarding letters of appointment and reappointment of Scrushy to the state hospital board.

Siegelman had been targeted once before for state **Medicaid** fraud in connection with the alleged aiding of a Tuscaloosa physician seeking to rig bids for Medicaid contracts. A federal district judge dismissed the charges in 2004. Two years prior, in 2002, the state Ethics Commission, following a closed-door hearing, cleared then-governor Siegelman of accusations that he had used his official position for personal benefit. The complaint alleged that Siegelman had been paid $800,000 by a law firm that benefited from a settlement he arranged in a lawsuit by the University of South Alabama against cigarette makers.

CONSULS

Public officials stationed in a foreign country who are responsible for developing and securing the economic interests of their government and safeguarding the welfare of their government's citizens who might be traveling or residing within their jurisdiction.

Sanchez-Llamas v. Oregon

In a closely-watched case of international import, a divided U.S. SUPREME COURT held, in *Sanchez-Llamas v. Oregon*, No.04–10566, 548 U.S. ___ (2006), that a defendant Mexican national could not have incriminating statements suppressed, simply because arresting police did not notify him of his right (under Article 36 the Vienna Convention) to access the Mexican consulate. In a companion, consolidated case, *Bustillo v. Johnson, Virginia Department of Corrections*, No.05–51, the high court also denied a foreign defendant a reversal of conviction based on the same alleged failure of authorities to advise him of his right to notify the Honduran Consulate. He had raised this argument for the first time under a habeas petition filed after his conviction and prison sentence.

In deciding these cases, the majority opinion relied on the language of the treaty itself to find (in the first case) that suppression of evidence was not an appropriate remedy for an alleged violation. The Court held, in the second case, that states may subject Vienna Convention Article 36 claims to the same procedural default rules that generally apply to other federal-law claims.

Article 36(1)(b) of the Vienna Convention on Consular Relations (the Vienna Convention), (ratified in 1969, and to which 170 countries, including the United States and Mexico, are signatories), states, in relevant part, that if a person being detained by a foreign country "so requests, the competent authorities of the receiving State shall, without delay, inform the consular post of the sending State" of such a detention, and "inform the [detainee] of his rights under this sub-paragraph." This provision is followed by Article 36(2), which specifies that the above rights "shall be exercised in conformity with the laws and regulations of the receiving State, subject to the proviso . . . that the said laws . . . must enable full effect to be given to the purposes for which the rights accorded under this Article are intended."

In Sanchez-Llamas's case, police responded to a call that an intoxicated man was threatening two women with a handgun. When police arrived and ordered him to drop the gun, the man shot at the officers, wounding one. He then ran behind a building and put the gun and another handgun on the ground. He was arrested, and an interpreter advised him of his Miranda rights. He waived his rights and agreed to talk to the police. During questioning, he made several incriminating statements, later used as evidence at his trial. However, prior to trial, defense counsel for Sanchez-Llamas notified the Mexican consulate of his arrest and pending charges. At trial, Sanchez-Llamas moved to suppress his statements, claiming that because his consulate was notified after he made incriminating statements, they must be suppressed. Moreover, Sanchez-Llamas claimed his Miranda waiver was involuntary. The trial court denied both claims, and he was convicted and sentenced to prison. Both the Oregon Court of Appeals and the state supreme court affirmed the conviction, the latter court specifically concluding that Article 36 did not create rights that a detained individual could enforce in a judicial proceeding.

In the second case, Mario Bustillo, a Honduran national, was arrested, tried, and convicted of murder in Virginia. His conviction and sentence were upheld on appeal. He then filed a habeas petition in state court, arguing for the first time that authorities had violated his Article 36 rights to consular notification. The court denied his claim as procedurally barred because he had failed to raise this issue at either trial or upon appeal. The Virginia Supreme Court found no reversible error.

Now before the U.S. Supreme Court, both cases were consolidated. Chief Justice Roberts, writing for the 6-justice majority, clarified the three questions before the Court as: (1) whether Article 36 created rights that defendants could invoke against the detaining authorities in a criminal trial or in a post-conviction hearing; (2) did a violation of Article 36 require suppression of a defendant's statements to police; and (3) whether a State, in a post-conviction hearing, treat a defendant's Article 36 claim as procedurally defaulted for failure to raise that claim at trial.

The Court concluded that, even assuming the Convention created judicially-enforceable rights, suppression of evidence is not an appropriate remedy for a violation of Article 36 (Sanchez-Llamas), and further, that a State may apply its regular rules of procedural default to Article 36 claims (Bustillo). Because both defendants were not entitled to relief, the Court concluded that it need not resolve whether the Vienna Convention even granted individuals enforceable rights; however, the Court assumed so in resolving the cases before it. In so holding, the Supreme Court affirmed the decisions below.

As to Sanchez-Llamas, the Court noted that the Vienna Convention did not mandate suppression or any other specific remedy, and it is not for the **federal courts** to impose a remedy on the States through lawmaking of their own. Even if Article 36 were read to require a judicial remedy in order "to give full effect" to its purpose, the **exclusionary rule** would not be an appropriate remedy. Used primarily for Fourth and FIFTH AMENDMENT violations, the exclusionary rule has nothing to do with Article 36; neither does the Article guarantee defendants any assistance at all. Therefore, the suppression remedy sought by Sanchez-Llamas for his asserted right had nothing to do with the gathering of evidence. Other remedies, including diplomatic avenues (the primary means of enforcing the treaty) remain open.

In Bustillo's case, the Court found *Breard v. Greene*, 523 U.S. 371, controlling. In that case, the petitioner's failure to raise an Article 36 claim in state court prevented him from later attempting to raise it at a subsequent federal habeas proceeding.

Justice Breyer, joined by Justices Stevens, Souter, and (in Part II) Ginsburg, dissented. The dissent concluded that a criminal defendant may raise Article 36 claims at trial or at post-conviction hearings. Further, *sometimes* state procedural default rules must yield to the Convention's proviso that domestic law "enable full effect to be given to the purposes for which" Article 36's rights were intended. And *sometimes*, suppression of evidence may be an appropriate remedy. After answering the three questions in this manner, the dissent would have remanded the cases, permitting States to apply their own procedural and remedial laws.

CORPORATE FRAUD

Top Enron Executives Convicted

More than four years after Houston-based Enron had collapsed, federal prosecutors finally brought two of the company's former top executives to trial in Houston. The trial of former chairman Kenneth Lay and former chief executive officer Jeffrey Skilling began in January 2006 and concluded with their conviction on a number of charges on May 25. The cases against both men were strengthened by the testimony of other former Enron executives who pleaded guilty to corporate crimes.

Once the sixth-largest energy company in the world, Enron suffered a historic collapse in 2001. For years the company used a complex web of partnerships to hide company debt and misrepresent company revenue. By the end of 2001, the company's stock sank to "junk" status, and Enron filed the largest bankruptcy in U.S. history at that time. The company's auditor, Arthur Anderson, was convicted in June 2002 of obstructing justice for its role in destroying Enron documents. In 2005, however, the U.S. SUPREME COURT vacated the conviction due to faulty jury instructions given in the trial. *Arthur Anderson, L.L.P. v. United States*, 544 U.S. 696, 125 S. Ct. 2129, 161 L. Ed. 2d 1008 (2005). However, the company went out of business due to the scandal.

In the years leading up to the trial of Lay and Skilling, several top executives agreed to plea bargains. Former treasurer Ben Glisan pleaded guilty in September 2003 to a charge of conspiracy. He was sentenced to five years in prison. About four months later, former chief financial officer Andrew Fastow entered into a plea agreement and received a 10-year prison sentence on charges of conspiracy to commit wire **fraud** and conspiracy to commit securities fraud. Fastow's wife and former Enron assistant treasurer, Lea Fastow, later pleaded guilty to a count of filing false tax forms.

In February 2004, Skilling pleaded not guilty to 40 federal charges ranging from making false statements to auditors to insider trading. In July of that year, Lay was charged on 11 counts, including making false statements and securities and wire fraud. Shortly after Lay was formally charged, a New York judge approved Enron's bankruptcy plan, which called for the company to pay $12 billion of the $63 billion it owed to creditors. The company, as well as Skilling and Lay, also faced civil lawsuits.

On July 15, 2005, Enron announced that it had settled a case involving allegations of price gouging during an energy shortage in California in 2000 and 2001. As part of the settlement, the state of California received $47 million. It also became an unsecured creditor, along with the states of Oregon and Washington, in Enron's bankruptcy case.

In December 2005, former chief accountant Richard Causey, who faced trial with Lay and Skilling, agreed to plead guilty on a single charge of securities fraud in exchange for his testimony against the pair. Causey had originally pleaded not guilty in 2004 to 34 counts of **money laundering**, fraud, insider trading, making false statements to auditors, and conspiracy. His sentence was reportedly set at seven years, though it could be reduced if prosecutors were satisfied with his cooperation in the Lay and Skilling prosecution.

Jury selection in the Lay and Skilling trial began at the U.S. **District Court** for the Southern District of Texas in Houston on January 30, 2006. The prosecution's case lasted most of February and March. The prosecution sought to establish that both men lied to analysts, shareholders, and the SECURITIES AND EXCHANGE COMMISSION about the financial health of the company. The prosecution also alleged that the men participated in the company's manipulation of financial statements as well as in a conspiracy to inflate the value of Enron's stock.

The prosecution rested at the end of the trial's ninth week. At the conclusion of the prosecution's case, U.S. District Judge Sim Lake dismissed three charges against Skilling and one count against Lay. Each of these charges was based on alleged actions that were taken during the first quarter of 2000. However, the judge determined that prosecutors had failed to present any evidence of criminal activity during that period of time.

Skilling testified in April. He told jurors that he was "absolutely innocent" and that he would "fight these charges until the day I die." During the prosecution's case, Fastow testified that Skilling knew that Fastow had used partnerships to artificially boost company's earnings. Skilling denied this allegation and said that he thought that the company was in good financial shape when he resigned in August 2001.

Lay, who began to give his testimony in late April, similarly said that he thought that the company was in good financial shape in September 2001, a time when he informed employees that the Enron should see continued growth. He denied known that Enron officials had lied to auditors, investors, and employees. He gave a detailed account of the events during the fall of 2001, when allegations of financial wrongdoing began to surface. He said that he never envisioned that the company was headed for bankruptcy.

The prosecution began cross-examination by questioning Lay about his contact with witnesses and about ignoring Enron's code of ethics. Lay began to become loud and angry when responding to the questioning by prosecutor John Hueston. On the third day of cross-examination, Hueston asked Lay about the latter's lavish lifestyle and several questionable withdrawals from Enron at a time when the company appeared to be in decline. Lay said that Hueston was being "unfair" and "mischaracterizing."

Enron founder Kenneth Lay, April 27, 2006.
AP IMAGES

Lay's testimony concluded on May 2. Even on the final day of testimony, Lay continued to spar with Hueston. Commentators and observers said that Lay's demeanor came across as abrasive. One former prosecutor, Michael Wynne, said that "Lay was arrogant and defiant" in the fact of the prosecutor's questions. Moreover, Lay appeared to be grouchy during questioning by his own attorney, George "Mac" Secrest. Following the government's rebuttal presentation, the case proceeded to final arguments. The jury spent six days deliberating before returning its verdicts on May 25. Lay was convicted on all six counts against him, while Skilling was convicted on 19 of the 28 counts against him, including one count of insider trading.

Lay also faced additional charges in a separate trial that involved four counts of bank fraud and making false statements. Lay elected to have Judge Lake decide the case rather than a jury. Judge Lake found him guilty on all charges. The judge set September 11, 2006 for sentencing. Under federal sentencing guidelines, Lay and Skilling faced long prison terms and enormous fines. However, on July 5 Lay suffered a fatal heart attack at his vacation house in Aspen, Colorado. Because Lay had not been sentenced, his criminal case had not become final. Under federal law a criminal defendant convicted of a crime who dies before exhausting his appeals will have his conviction erased. Therefore, it was expected that the court would dismiss the charges against Lay, making him legally innocent despite the verdicts. Skilling will face sentencing alone.

Ronald Perelman leaves court, May 12, 2005.
AP IMAGES

Morgan Stanley Muddles E-mail

The largest monetary verdict of 2005, of $1.6 billion in damages including pre-judgment interest, was paid to financier Ronald Perelman by Morgan Stanley & Co., Inc., after a jury found the company guilty of defrauding Perelman, a billionaire businessman, with regard to the financial viability of Sunbeam Corporation in a deal that Morgan Stanley had managed.

The lawsuit stemmed from a botched deal in 1998, when Perelman relied on misleading statements from Morgan Stanley that the financially troubled Sunbeam could in fact afford to buy Coleman Holdings, Inc., his camping equipment company Sunbeam filed for bankruptcy in 2001, and both Perelman and Morgan Stanley claimed to have lost money as a resut.

Prior to the start of the trial, Perelman won a judge's ruling that allowed the jury to accept the fact that Morgan Stanley was helping Sunbeam to disguise its fragile financial state while advising Perelman to acquire the failing company.

A close look at the case revealed that Morgan Stanley's legal team was involved in discovery misconduct with regard to incorrect and ineffective e-mail searches that they have been unable to successfully defend.

Morgan Stanley executive Arthur Riel said in a deposition that more than 1000 backup tapes had not been searched for relevant e-mails prior to the trial. Consequently, Judge Elizabeth Maass told the jury members that they should assume that Morgan Stanley helped to defraud Mr. Perelman.

The logistics of handing over documents in legal battles have become increasingly complicated in the age of e-mail. "Lawsuits these days require companies to comb through electronic archives and are sometimes won or lost based on how the litigants perform these tasks," noted *Wall Street Journal* reporter Susanne Craig.

During the legal discovery process in 2003, Morgan Stanley resisted some of the judge's requests for documents. The company said that handing over personnel files of employees who had worked on the Sunbeam account would be an invasion of privacy. Judge Maass limited her request to documents relating to the relevant employees' "truthfulness, veracity, or moral turpitude."

William Strong, the top Morgan Stanley banker on the Sunbeam account, had been tried on bribery charges in Italy in the 1990s in connection with a previous job. Although Strong was acquitted, no information about the charges existed in his personnel file; Mr. Perelman's lawyers learned of the charges when they found a news clipping during the course of their research. Judge Maass determined that Morgan Stanley had deliberately withheld this relevant information.

Mr. Perelman's legal team requested e-mails dating back to 1998, and Morgan Stanley's legal team objected, saying that a search for the older documents would require "a massive safari into the remote corners" of backup computer files, which would cost several hundred thousand dollars and take months to complete. In April 2004, Judge Maass ordered Morgan Stanley to produce relevant documents from its oldest full backup, and Arthur Riel, the company technology executive, reported that the oldest records dated from 2000.

However, in May 2004, Morgan Stanley employees found additional tapes from the 1990s that had not been searched for information relevant to the Perelman case. Subsequently, Riel was placed on administrative leave for reasons not related to the Perelman case, and his successor, Allison Nachtigal, was finally brought up to date on the case by early 2005.

Morgan Stanley continued to turn over e-mail in the first few months of 2005, but the company also continued to report software problems, and offered to pay the court to delay the trial. However, by March 2005, Judge Maass was determined to move forward with the case, and employed an extreme legal tactic—an adverse inference order—at the request of the Perelman legal team. This order cited the "willful and gross abuse of its discovery obligations" and put the pressure on Morgan Stanley to prove its innocence as a result.

This discovery misconduct turned a case that could have been settled quietly into a "monstrous legal liability," wrote Susan Beck in the April 2006 issue of *The American Lawyer*. "To what extent these acts were deliberate deceptions, **good faith** mistakes, or errors of incompetence—or some combination of all three—is still not entirely clear," Beck noted.

Morgan Stanley plans to appeal the verdict.

Former Worldcom CEO Bernard Ebbers leaves Federal Court, January 30, 2006.
AP IMAGES

WorldCom CEO Convicted of Corporate Fraud

Bernard Ebbers, the founder and CEO of WorldCom Corp., was convicted by a federal jury on March 15, 2005 of **fraud**, conspiracy, and filing false documents with regulators as part of the largest bankruptcy in U.S. history. Ebber was sentenced to 25 years in prison on July 13, 2005. At age 63, Ebbers would not be eligible for release, assuming good behavior, until he was 85. The sentence was the toughest handed down in a string of corporate scandals that included the energy company Enron and the cable television company Adelphia. The court granted Ebbers bail, allowing him to remain a free man while awaiting the decision on his appeal to U.S. Second **Circuit Court** of Appeals.

Ebbers entered the telecom business in 1983 with a diverse background that included work as a milkman, basketball coach, and hotel owner. He devised the business plan for WorldCom himself, and acquired many other communications companies throughout the 1980s and 1990s. WorldCom's inflated projections of Internet growth included a statement that Internet traffic was doubling every 100 days, which increased the demand for Internet and telecommunications stock. Even when Internet growth slowed significantly in the late 1990s, WorldCom executives continued to cite rapid exponential growth, which left competitors such as AT&T cutting costs and laying off workers in attempts to match the fictitious growth rates of WorldCom.

WorldCom declared bankruptcy in 2002 in conjunction with charges of committing nearly $11 billion worth of accounting fraud. Many employees lost their jobs, and many stockholders lost significant savings as a result. In addition, WorldCom investors filed a securities fraud suit against the auditor and former directors of WorldCom, and against several banks including Bank of America, Citigroup, and Deutsche Bank. After declaring bankruptcy, WorldCom re-emerged as MCI, which was purchased by Verizon in 2006.

Ebbers was indicted in 2004. The charges included conspiracy to commit securities fraud, securities fraud, and filing false financial reports with the SECURITIES AND EXCHANGE COMMISSION. Prosecutors alleged that he had initiated the **fraudulent** activities in 2000, when the company began to cut spending on telecom products and services. Prosecutors accused Ebbers of acting out of a desire to protect his personal assets, many of which were invested in WorldCom stock. Although Ebbers took the stand in his own defense and denied knowledge of the fraudulent accounting at WorldCom, he was not able to win over the jury. The jury heard damaging evidence from his former right-hand man and chief financial officer, Scott Sullivan, who said that Ebbers had played an active rile in the fraud. They falsified statements of the company, adjusting revenue to meet the expectations of financial analysts. An example of the fraudulent activity was a "close the gap" process, in which the company found one-time revenue sources, such as selling something, during each **fiscal** quarter that allowed the company to meet the target revenues that it had predicted. Sullivan, along with several other former WorldCom executives pleaded guilty to securities fraud charges and cooperated with the prosecution.

In his appeal, Ebbers claimed that the trial was unfair because several high-level WorldCom executives were prohibited from testifying on his behalf. One of his lawyers was quoted as saying that the jury received incorrect information; they were told that Ebbers could be convicted based on "conscious avoidance" of the fraudulent accounting practices at WorldCom. The appeals court, which heard oral argument on the case in January 2006, had not issued a decision as of early July 2006.

COX, CHRISTOPHER

Christopher Cox
WIN MCNAMEE/POOL/POOL/EPA/CORBIS

On August 3, 2005, Christopher Cox was sworn in as the chairman of the SECURITIES AND EXCHANGE COMMISSION after a unanimous confirmation vote by the U.S. Senate. Cox was born October 16, 1952, in St. Paul, Minnesota. He graduated magna cum laude from the University of Southern California in 1973, after completing a three-year accelerated course.

In 1976, Cox graduated simultaneously from Harvard Business School and the Harvard Law School, with honors, where for two years he served as an Editor of the Harvard Law Review. He graduated magna cum laude from the University of Southern California in 1973, after completing a three-year accelerated course.

Cox, along with his father, a retired publisher, founded a company that provided a complete English translation of the former Soviet Union's leading daily paper, Pravda. From 1978 to 1986, he specialized in venture capital and corporate finance with the international law firm of Latham and Watkins, where he was the partner in charge of the Corporate Department in Orange County and a member of the firm's national management. In 1982-83, Rep. Cox took a leave of absence from Latham and Watkins to teach federal income tax at Harvard Business School. In 1977 to 1978, he was law clerk to U.S. Court of Appeals Judge Herbert Choy, the first Asian-American federal appellate judge in America.

Each year since he was first elected, he has earned the prestigious "Golden Bulldog Award" from the Watchdogs of the Treasury for his consistent votes to stop runaway government spending. He has regularly been named a "Hero to the Taxpayer" by the 500,000-member grassroots lobbying group Citizens Against Government Waste. In addition, the National Taxpayers Union has consistently honored him with the "Taxpayer's Friend Award" for his work to promote free enterprise and limit the scope of government; the National Federation of Independent Business has each year given him the "Friend of Small Business" Award; and the citizen watchdog group Consumer Alert has twice presented him with their "Friend of the Consumer" Award, most recently in 1996, when this exclusive honor was conferred on a total of only 26 members in both the House and Senate.

CHRISTOPHER COX

1976	Graduated from Harvard Business School and Law School simultaneously
1977	Served as clerk to Judge Herbert Choy
1982	Taught at Harvard Business School
1988	Elected to U.S. House of Representatives
2005	Confirmed as SEC Chairman

Cox served on several committees in the House of Representatives, holding positions as Chairman of the House Policy Committee, Chairman of the Committee on Homeland Security; Chairman of the Select Committee on U.S. National Security; Chairman of the Select Committee on Homeland Security (the predecessor to the permanent House Committee); Chairman of the Task Force on Capital Markets; and Chairman of the Task Force on Budget Process Reform.

As SEC chairman, he has emphasized securities law enforcement and providing investors with comprehensible information minus confusing jargon. At his swearing in, he commented that "It is an honor to lead the Securities and Exchange Commission, and to be sworn in by so wise and able a champion of America's capital markets," referring to outgoing chairman Alan Greenspan.

CRIMINAL PROCEDURE

The framework of laws and rules that govern the administration of justice in cases involving an individual who has been accused of a crime, beginning with the initial investigation of the crime and concluding either with the unconditional release of the accused by virture of acquittal (a judgment of not guilty) or by the imposition of a term of punishment pursuant to a conviction for the crime.

Medina v. People of the State of Colorado

The relatively newer practice of permitting jurors to submit their own questions to witnesses during civil or criminal trials has already withstood federal court challenge that the practice fell outside the **purview** of the jury or that it interfered with jurors' duties as neutral factfinders. In recent years, a majority of states has adopted the practice by passing laws designed to overcome similar challenges. For example, most jurisdictions now require that jury questions be submitted through the court/judge, at which point counsels' concerns regarding admissibility, prejudice, fairness, etc. are addressed.

Colorado's courts had successfully phased-in jury questioning over the past decade, starting with civil trials and progressing to criminal trials involving less serious offenses. In 2004, Colorado Rule 24(g) of its Rules of **Criminal Procedure** went into effect, empowering jurors with the right to ask questions in all trials, including criminal **felony** trials.

But in a pair of 2005 consolidated cases referentially cited as *Medina v. People*, No. 04SC167, and *Moses v. People*, No. 04SC334, Colorado's Supreme Court addressed the constitutionality of jury questioning as to whether it violated a defendant's right to a fair trial. Each of the cases was fact-specific. However, both cases articulated the court's central holding that the practice of allowing jurors to question witnesses through the court did not violate a defendant's right to a fair trial, due process, or impartial jury. If a trial court errs and asks an otherwise impermissible question over counsel's objection, such error will be reviewed for **harmless error**.

As background for both cases, the Colorado Jury Reform Pilot Project Subcommittee provided a list of policies and procedures for district courts to follow when allowing jurors to submit questions for witnesses. Courts were instructed that the purpose behind the project was to clarify testimony and to assist jurors in understanding the evidence. Courts were not required to ask all questions submitted by jurors. (This pilot project culminated in the adoption of subject Rule 24(g).) The two cases in the consolidated opinion were randomly selected at the trial level to be included in the pilot project.

In the *Medina* case, subject Yvonne Medina was convicted by a jury of second degree assault, criminal mischief, first degree criminal trespass, menacing, and criminal violence. The facts surrounding the crimes involved Medina's attack on an ex-boyfriend and his new girlfriend at his apartment. At the beginning of trial, defense counsel objected to any procedure allowing the submission of jury questions to witnesses but was overruled.

The jury ended up asking only one question throughout the trial. Medina's defense theory was that the boyfriend and new girlfriend had concocted the whole story, and had made several inconsistent pre-trial statements to investigators. The sole juror question asked how frequently witnesses modified or made inconsistent statements. The court overruled defense counsel's objection and asked the question, and an investigator witness responded to the jury.

A state **appellate court** followed other jurisdictions in concluding that juror questions do not violate a defendant's right to a fair trial. Moreover, noted the **appellate** court, in this case, the resulting witness testimony actually helped Medina's defense and hardly prejudiced it (even though she was ultimately convicted).

Likewise, the Colorado Supreme Court affirmed that juror questioning of witnesses did not create a *per se* violation of a defendant's right to a fair trial. This was true even if the court erred in permitting the particular question at issue (which should not have been permitted because the testifying witness was not qualified as an expert). Said the court,

> When the applicable rules of law and evidence are applied and after consulting with counsel, the decision of whether to ask a juror's question is committed to the sound discretion of the court. Like other instances where a trial court errs in admitting otherwise inadmissible evidence, improper juror questions which are asked by the court will be reviewed for harmless error.

In this case, held the court, there was no prejudice to the defendant.

In *Moses*, the companion case, the record contained 17 written questions from the jury, four of which were denied by the court, although defense counsel had objected to any and all. There was also a question of whether the jury had heard any of the bench conferences between counsel and the court regarding the admission of these questions. However, the court found no evidence that the jury overheard the bench conversation or that Moses was prejudiced by any of the objections or comments **of counsel**. The jury acquitted Moses of first-degree assault but convicted him of **felonious** menacing, resisting arrest and reckless driving. The convictions were upheld on appeal, despite the arguments that Moses had been prejudiced by the bench discussion over whether a question could be submitted to a witness.

Again, the Colorado Supreme Court found no prejudice: "No statements about testimony not already admitted were made. . . . [W]e decline to find an error simply because the jury may have overheard a bench conference where no prejudicial statements were made."

As of the date of the Colorado decision, two states' highest courts (in Mississippi and Nebraska) had ruled against juror questioning in all cases. Minnesota and Texas prohibited juror questioning in criminal trials, but their highest courts had not yet ruled on the issue in a civil context. Two other state supreme court cases provide in-depth discussion, *State v. Doleszny*, 2004 VT 9; 844 A2d. 773 (Vermont), and *Cathcart v. State Farm Insurance* , 2005 WY 154 (Wyoming).

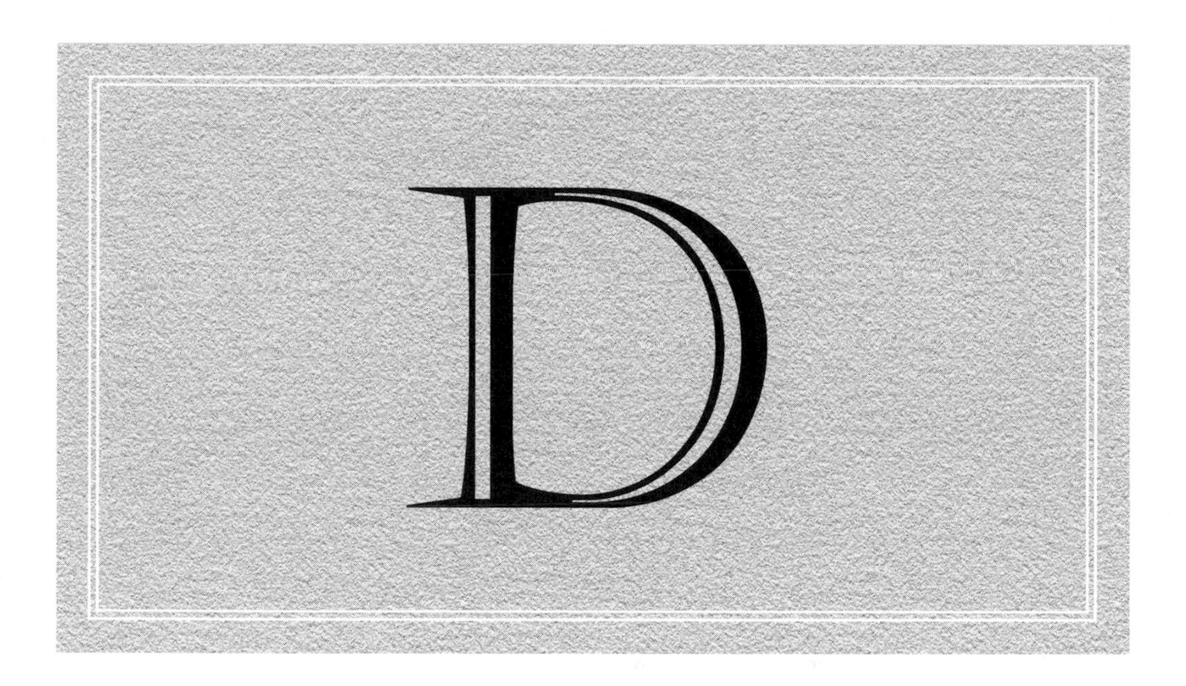

DNA

Kohler v. Englade

The use of widespread DNA testing to search for criminals remains a contentious issue, especially when it is widespread enough to include people who live and work near a crime scene but for whom there is no evidence of motive or opportunity. A Louisiana DNA dragnet led one man to fight a request that he give a DNA sample, fearing that his sample would be included in a government database despite the fact he had not been implicated in the crime.

In 2002, Shannon F. Kohler was asked to voluntarily contribute a DNA sample as part of a DNA dragnet in search of a serial killer in southern Louisiana. He refused the request, as did a number of other men contacted by law enforcement, leading the police to obtain a search warrant to force Kohler to provide a DNA sample. During this period Kohler was identified as a suspect by the police and news. After Mr. Kohler gave his DNA to police he filed a federal civil rights suit under 42 U.S.C.A § 1983, alleging that the police had violated his right to privacy and the security of his person, as guaranteed by the Louisiana Constitution and the Fourth and Fourteenth Amendments of the U.S. Constitution.

In *Kohler v. Englade*, 365 F. Supp.2d 751 (2005), the **district court** dismissed Kohler's lawsuit. The court concluded that the police had **probable cause** to support the warrant that compelled the production of the DNA sample. The task force working on the serial killings had received two anonymous tips implicating Kohler and discovered he had been convicted of **burglary** in 1982. In addition, the property of one of the victims had been found near Kohler's former place of employment. These facts, along with an FBI profile of the suspect that Kohler fit in some areas, were sufficient to support a finding of probable cause to justify the warrant. Therefore, the court ruled that the police officers and the local government were immune from the civil damages lawsuit.

The case drew more attention to the collection and retention of DNA samples.The federal government's existing DNA database includes only DNA material taken from crime scenes and from convicted criminals. At the state level, some states maintain DNA databases of people arrested for rape, murder, and other violent crimes, and other states extend the DNA collection to include people arrested for burglary and other lesser charges.

"Some experts fear that, with DNA **forensic** databanks now authorized nationwide, practices for evidence collection are evolving in a vacuum, with little precedent or supervision," wrote Glynn Wilson in an editorial to the *Christian Science Monitor*. The existence of DNA databases raises more issues, including whether employers, acquaintances, or even strangers gain access to the genetic profiles of individuals and use the information to avoid hiring someone with a medical condition, for instance.

State lawmakers are grappling with legislating the collection of DNA from not only rapists and murderers, but from all felons and youth offenders. The rationale behind increasing the number of samples in DNA databases is to increase the odds that law enforcement officers will find a match, and a subsequent criminal prosecution. Many felons are repeat offenders, and a DNA database arguably serves a similar function to checking fingerprints found at a crime scene against law enforcement fingerprint files. However, mass collection of fingerprints in criminal cases is rare because of the high probability that fingerprints from a crime scene will be those of someone other than the criminal. DNA evidence, such as semen in a rape case, is less likely to have been innocently left at the scene of the crime.

In addition to identifying the guilty, DNA evidence can exonerate the innocent. Several men who had been convicted in the 1989 rape of the woman known as the Central Park Jogger were eventually cleared of the crime based on DNA evidence. In addition, the Innocence Project, a non-profit legal center sponsored by New York University Law School, continues to free convicted felons based on post-conviction DNA evidence.

If convicted felons have a reduced right to privacy, the question remains whether citizens who are compelled to submit DNA samples as part of a dragnet should automatically have their information expunged from state records if they are eliminated as suspects, or if they are arrested but not indicted or later acquitted. "The price to clear your name shouldn't be surrendering your personal biological information to the government for any and all purposes," reporter Jane Black wrote in *Business Week*.The AMERICAN CIVIL LIBERTIES UNION supported Kohler's lawsuit and has raised concerns about the widespread collection of DNA as part of criminal dragnets, and the issue continues to evolve.

DRUGS AND NARCOTICS

Drugs are articles intended for use in the diagnosis, cure, mitigation, treatment, or prevention of disease in humans or animals, and any articles other than food intended to affect the mental or body function of humans or animals. *Narcotics* are any drugs that dull the senses and commonly become addictive after prolonged use.

FDA Approves Vaccine for Human Papilloma Virus

The FDA announced on June 8, 2006, that it would approve a vaccine to combat human papillomavirus (HPV). The FDA granted a license to Gardasil, made by Merck and Co. The FDA licensed the vaccine for use in females ages 9 to 26. The vaccine will be available by the end of June. It will cost around $350 for a series of three shots over a six-month period.

Experts estimate that 70 percent of cervical cancer cases are caused by two strains of HPV. Clinical trials indicated that the vaccine prevented 100 percent of cervical cancer for the two strains of cancer-causing HPV in women who had not been infected with the virus before. The vaccine also protects against two other types of HPV that are responsible for 90 percent of genital wart cases. There are more than 30 strains of HPV.

The HPV virus is sexually transmitted. More than 50 percent of sexually active adults are affected by it at some point in their lives. It most commonly strikes men and women who are in their late teens and early 20s, and 6.2 million people are infected in the U.S. each year. Most people who contract it have no symptoms, and the virus goes away on its own. While HPV is present, a woman's cervical cells are changed, which may result in an abnormal pap. Once the virus goes away, the cervical cells return to normal.

Cervical cancer ranks second as the cancer killer in women. It kills about 290,000 worldwide each year. In the U.S., the annual number of deaths is around 3,700; 9,700 women will be diagnosed with cervical cancer in the U.S. each year. The U.S. number is influenced by the incidence of regular pap smears, which can detect precancerous lesions and early cancer. About one million women per year in the U.S. have an abnormal pap result. Women will still need to be screened for cervical cancer, as the vaccine does not provide protection against all types of HPV viruses that cause cancer. Thirty percent of cervical cancers would not be prevented by the vaccine.

Merck says the vaccine could cut worldwide deaths by two-thirds. Merck plans to seek licenses for the vaccine in more than 50 countries. The company says the vaccine is most effective when given to girls before they have sex. The vaccine is designed for both males and females. Although rare, males can contract anal or penile cancer from HPV.

Some questions remain unanswered. Longer studies are needed to determine how long the vaccine will work. Thus far, studies have followed subjects for up to 4.5 years and found the vaccine to be effective. Moreover, it's uncertain the effect the vaccine will have on women who have had persistent HPV infections, or who have been exposed to HPV and may have developed some form of immunity. Women are not routinely tested for HPV, partly because there is no way to know which strain someone has.

Initially, some conservative groups opposed an HPV vaccine, arguing that it would encourage sexual activity in young people. However, the opposition faded in light of the drug's potential in reducing cancer. Focus on the Family, a conservative Christian organization, has announced it supports universal availability of the vaccine, but opposes mandatory vaccination for entry to school. Conservative groups now generally seem to view the vaccine as an opportunity to discuss sexual health issues with young people.

The Advisory Committee on Immunization Practices will decide whether to endorse routine vaccination. It is already studying the Gardasil vaccine, and another proposed vaccine.

Gardasil could result in sales of more than $1 billion for Merck, market analysts predict. Drug manufacturer GlaxoSmithKline has announced plans to apply for FDA approval of Cervarix, its HPV vaccine, later in 2006.

Cities, States Debate Legalizing Marijuana

Despite a U.S. SUPREME COURT ruling in 2005 that allowed the federal government to forbid the use of marijuana, several cities and states continued to allow use of the drug for medical purposes. The state of Rhode Island in 2006 became the 11th state to allow medical cannabis. Moreover, the city of Denver in 2005 became the first major city to legalize adult use of the drug in small quantities.

Prior to June 2005, California was one of nine states that had legalized use of marijuana for medical purposes. Under the authority of the Compassionate Use Act of 1996, Cal. Health & Safety Code § 11362.5 (West 2005), an estimated 100,000 chronically ill patients in the state legally used cannabis for medicinal reasons. The federal government, however, contended that since the Controlled Substances Act, 21 U.S.C. § 802 (2000) did not recognize a legitimate medical use for marijuana, the federal government could prosecute those who took the drug pursuant to state law. Beginning in 2002, agents with the DRUG ENFORCEMENT ADMINISTRATION began to conduct raids of homes of those using cannabis.

Two California residents brought suit in federal court in California, seeking to enjoin the federal government from prosecuting possession and use of medical cannabis. Although the plaintiffs, Angel McClary Raich and Diane Monson, lost at the **district court** level, they prevailed before the Ninth **Circuit Court** of Appeals, which held that the Controlled Substances Act was unconstitutional. *Raich v. Ashcroft*, 352 F.3d 1222 (9th Cir. 2003). The Supreme Court issued a **writ** of **certiorari** to review the case. In a 6–3 decision, the Court reversed the Ninth Circuit, holding that the federal government could legally forbid use of this drug for any purpose. *Gonzales v. Raich*, ___ 125 S. Ct. 2195, ___ L. Ed. 2d ___ (2005).

The effect of the Court's decision was not clear. One of official in California said that the decision had no effect other than mere "semantics." California Attorney General Bill Lochyer echoed this belief, telling California residents that nothing had changed with respect to the California law. "People shouldn't panic," Lockyer said. "There aren't going to be many changes."

Operators of cannabis clubs, which provide marijuana to the chronically ill that seek it, were not quite as sure. Advocates for medical cannabis had sought for cities to draft regulations that would control how marijuana was distributed. After the case, however, many cities put those efforts on hold. Some cities maintained that the activities of the cannabis clubs were illegal after the decision in *Raich*.

The state of Rhode Island in January 2006 became the 11th state to allow medical cannabis. However, it was not clear how chronically ill patients would be able to obtain the drug. Unlike California, which has about 175 dispensaries that grow and distribute marijuana for the patients, Rhode Island's law allows for no such system. Many users reportedly could be forced to grow the drug themselves or buy it on the streets.

Although much of the focus on the legalization of marijuana has been on its medical uses, some advocates have pushed for laws that would allow use of the drug for any purpose. Voters in Seattle, Washington approved an initiative in 2003 that eased enforcement of marijuana laws for those possessing 40 grams or less of the drug. In 2004, voters in Oakland, California approved an initiative that would require the city to tax and regulate marijuana, much like it regulates alcohol. However, because this law conflicts with California state law, it has not become effective.

Voters in Denver, Colorado in November 2005 approved a similar regulation. The group Safer Alternative for Enjoyable Recreation collected more than 12,000 signatures to place an initiative on the city's ballot that would make it legal for adults age 21 or older to possess less than one ounce of the drug. Denver City Council members objected to the initiative but could not prevent it from being placed on the ballot due to the number of signatures. According to one council member, the discussion of legalizing the drug "has no place in the public dialogue."

Although Colorado law prohibits possession of marijuana, the state is one of about 12 where possession is not a crime but rather results in a fine. It is also one of the states that allows use of marijuana for medical purposes. Advocates in other cities, such as Tallahassee, Florida and Columbia, Missouri, have pushed similar measures. However, another Colorado town, Telluride, with a population of 2300, defeated an effort in 2005 to make marijuana possession a low police priority.

In 2006, the conviction of one of the more public activists for medical marijuana was overturned by a federal appeals court. Ed Rosenthal grew pot at his home and in a warehouse in Oakland, and supplied a medical marijuana club in San Francisco. Federal agents raided the sites were he grew the drug in 2002, leading to his conviction in 2003 on three **felony** counts related to his growing of the cannabis. The Ninth Circuit Court of Appeals determined that Rosenthal's right to a fair trial had been compromised due to a juror's communications with an attorney during the criminal case.

Rosenthal's supporters have supported a bill that was introduced in the House of Representatives that would allow defendants charged with possession of marijuana to plead an **affirmative defense** that marijuana possession was legal for medical purposes in the state where the possession occurred. The Steve McWilliams Truth in Trials Act, H.R. 4272, 109th Cong., 1st Sess. (2005), would amend the Controlled Substances Act to allow for this defense. However, a similar proposal died in committee during the previous Congressional session.

DUE PROCESS

A fundamental, constitutional guarantee that all legal proceedings will be fair and that one will be given notice of the proceedings and an opportunity to be heard before the government acts to take away one's life, liberty, or property. Also, a constitutional guarantee that a law shall not be unreasonable, arbitrary, or capricious.

Jones v. Flowers

A fundamental principle of due process is that notice be given to a person when legal action is initiated against that person. Notice may be given by personally serving a copy of the legal documents to the person or by mailing the documents. If the person cannot be served in person or by mail, a legal notice may be published in a local newspaper. In the case of tax **forfeiture** proceedings by state and local governments, questions have arisen over how far the government must go to notify a property owner who stands to lose the property for failing to pay taxes. The Supreme Court, in *Jones v. Flowers*, __U.S.__, 126 S.Ct. 1708, __L.Ed.2d __ (2006), ruled that a state must do more than serve a tax forfeiture sale notice by certified mail when the certified letters are returned as unclaimed. The Court held that a state must take "additional reasonable steps" to provide notice before taking the owner's property.

Gary Jones purchased a house in Little Rock, Arkansas in 1967, living there with his wife until they separated in 1993. He moved into an apartment in Little Rock but kept paying the mortgage on the house until it was paid off in 1997. Local property tax payments were included in the monthly mortgage payments. When the mortgage ended, Jones did not pay the property taxes. In April 2000 his tax delinquency triggered a letter from the Arkansas Commissioner of State Lands, informing Jones that he needed to redeem his property by paying back taxes and penalties. The letter, which was sent by certified mail, notified Jones that failure to redeem the property by April 2002 would lead to the public sale of his house. The certified letter did not reach Jones, as there was no one home to sign for the letter and no one appeared at the post office to claim it within 15 days. The letter was returned to the commissioner's office and marked "unclaimed." In April 2002 the commissioner published a notice of public sale in the Little Rock newspaper on the Jones property. Linda Flowers submitted the winning offer on the property, offering $21,000 for a house with a **fair market value** of $80,000. The commissioner sent another letter to Jones by certified mail, informing him that the house would be sold to Flowers if he did not pay his taxes. As with the prior letter, this notice was returned as unclaimed. The commissioner then closed the deal with Flowers, who served an eviction notice on the property. This notice was personally served on Jones' daughter, who contacted her father and told him of the **tax sale**.

Jones filed a lawsuit in state court against the commissioner and Flowers, contending that he had not been provided notice of the tax sale and his right to redeem. He argued that the lack of notice resulted in the taking of his property without **due process of law**. The defendants replied that the two unclaimed certified letters were constitutionally adequate attempts at notice and that the lawsuit should be dismissed. The trial court agreed to the dismissal, finding that the state tax forfeiture statute's notice provisions met due process requirements. The Arkansas Supreme Court upheld the trial court, citing U.S. SUPREME COURT precedent that due process does not require **actual notice**; the attempt to notify Jones by certified mail satisfied process. The U.S. Supreme Court agreed to hear Jones' appeal because state supreme courts and federal circuit courts of appeals were divided over whether the government must take additional reasonable steps to notify a property owner when notice of a tax sale is returned undelivered.

The Court, in a 5–3 decision (newly confirmed Justice Samuel Alito did not participate in the consideration of the case), reversed the Arkansas Supreme Court. Chief Justice John Roberts, writing for the majority, held that when certified letters containing notice of a tax sale are returned, the government must take "additional reasonable steps to attempt to provide notice to the property owner before selling his property, if it is practicable to do so." Roberts acknowledged that a property owner does not need to receive actual notice before the government can take his property and that the property owner was obligated under Arkansas law to keeping his mailing address up to date. Arkansas also pointed to the use of certified mail as a way to insure that a property owner receives notification and that such notice is documented through postal records. Roberts noted that this case contained a new "wrinkle:" the state became aware before the tax sale that its attempts at notifying Jones had failed. Under these "circumstances and conditions" the Court needed to determine if due process had been met.

Chief Justice Roberts concluded that in these circumstances the government needed to do something more before selling property for back taxes. In this case the Court determined that Arkansas could have taken several reasonable steps. Once the certified letter was returned, the commissioner should have sent out the notice using regular mail, so that a signature was not required. If Jones had moved, Roberts believed that the new occupant might have written the forwarding address on the envelope or contacted Jones directly. Other reasonable steps included posting the notice on Jones' apartment door or addressing the mail to "occupant." The Chief Justice suggested that "[o]ccupants who might disregard a certified mail slip not addressed to them are less likely to ignore posted notice, and a letter addressed to them might be opened and read." However, Roberts rejected Jones' contention that the state should have searched for his new address in the Little Rock phonebook. Such an "open-ended search" would impose burdens on the state "significantly greater than the several relatively easy options outlined above."

Justice CLARENCE THOMAS, in a dissenting opinion joined by Justices ANTONIN SCALIA and ANTHONY KENNEDY, argued that Arkansas had met its due process requirements. The reasonableness of government notice requirements must be made assessed at the time the state sends the notice, not afterwards. As to the Court's suggested additional reasonable steps, Justice Thomas characterized them as "burdensome, impractical, and no more likely to effect notice than the methods actually employed by the State."

EDUCATION

Arlington Central School District Board of Education v. Murphy

In *Arlington Central School District Board of Education v. Murphy*, No. 05-18, 548 U.S. ___ (2006), a very divided U.S. SUPREME COURT held that "fee-shifting" provisions under the Individuals with Disabilities Education Act (IDEA) (the Act) did not cover fees paid by parents to an educational consultant in conjunction with litigation over their disabled son's private education. Specifically, 20 USC 1415(i)(3)(B) of the Act provides for an award (recovery) of "reasonable attorneys' fees as part of the costs" to prevailing parents (prevailing parties) who sue under the Act on behalf of their child. In this particular case, the educational consultant had served as an expert witness during court proceedings. The high court's majority opinion upheld both **district court** and **appellate court** decisions holding that the Act would not be read to permit recovery of expert fees without explicit **statutory** authority. Justice Samuel Alito delivered the lengthy opinion of the court. Justice Breyer filed a multiple-paged and very detailed dissenting opinion, in which he was joined by three other justices. Justice Ginsburg wrote a separate opinion, concurring in part and concurring in the judgment.

In 1999, parents Pearl and Theodore Murphy filed a complaint on behalf of their dyslexic son, who suffered several other cognitive disabilities, claiming that the Arlington Central School District (Arlington) failed to provide a proper Individualized Education Program (IEP) for their son. Under the Act, local school systems are required to develop such an educational development plan specifically designed to address the needs of any or each child in the school system who suffers a disability. The Murphys petitioned for an order requiring Arlington to pay for their son's private school tuition for specified school years. The federal district court (Southern District of New York) agreed with the parents, and the Court of Appeals for the Second Circuit affirmed.

Section 1415(i)(3)(B) of the Act allows for the award of "reasonable attorneys fees" incurred in an "action or proceeding" brought under the Act, but makes no mention of awarding "expert fees." Notwithstanding, as "prevailing" parents in the IDEA litigation, the Murphys then sought to recover more than $29,000 in fees for the services of an educational consultant who had assisted them throughout the proceedings.

For its part, Arlington argued that the educational expert was not eligible to receive attorneys' fees because she was not a licensed attorney. Neither was she eligible to receive expert fees because they were not recoverable under the Act. (In a separate action, the Delaware Supreme Court ruled in 2000 that the educational consultant had engaged in the unauthorized practice of law by representing families of children with disabilities in due process hearings).

The district court had actually permitted the limited recovery of the expert's fees for her "expert consulting services," (e.g., observing a student in class, interviewing teachers, attending IEP meetings, preparing reports, advising parents, etc.) that were provided between the time of the hearing request and the ruling, which amounted to about $8,000 of the requested $29,000. However, the district court ruled that the expert could not be awarded any fees for time that could be characterized as legal representation. The court further found that all of the time spent during the relevant period in this case could be characterized as falling within the compensable category, and awarded $8,650.

The Second Circuit affirmed. It had first relied on two previous U.S. Supreme Court cases holding that expert fees were not recoverable as taxed costs under particular cost- or fee-shifting provisions of other acts or statutes. (See *Crawford Fitting Co. v. J.T. Gibbons*, 482 U.S. 437, interpreting Fed. Rule Civ. Proc. 54(d); and *West Virginia Univ. Hospitals v. Casey*, interpreting 42 USC 1988.) Ultimately, however, the Second Circuit was persuaded by statements found in a Conference Committee Report relating to the relevant provision in the IDEA, 1415(i)(3)(B) and a footnote in *Casey*, above. Based on these considerations, the **appellate** court affirmed the district court's award of costs (including experts' fees) incurred by prevailing parents. The Supreme Court granted **certiorari** based on the conflict among circuits regarding the compensation of expert fees to prevailing parents under the IDEA.

The high court first noted that it was guided in this case by the fact that Congress had enacted IDEA pursuant to the Spending Clause of the U.S. Constitution (Article I, Section 8). While Congress has broad power to set the terms on which it disburses money to states, any conditions it attaches to a state's acceptance of such funds must be expressed unambiguously. Accordingly, noted the Court, the question here was whether IDEA provided clear notice regarding experts fees. There is no such provision in the text of the Act that even hints toward acceptance of IDEA funds making states responsible for reimbursing prevailing parents for the services of experts. The express language only provides for adding reasonable attorneys' fees "as part of the costs."

The majority opinion also noted that the Second Circuit's initial reliance on *Crawford* and *Casey*, above, was correct, as these cases, though involving other statutes, nonetheless reinforce that IDEA does not unambiguously authorize prevailing parents to recover such expert fees. Moreover, Arlington's other arguments were unpersuasive, including that regarding legislative history. The arguments that IDEA's purpose was to ensure that all children have available to them a free education, and that parents' rights to challenge adverse school decisions must be safeguarded, were too general in nature to support a conclusion that states must reimburse parents for experts' fees. The Supreme Court then reversed the Second Circuit and remanded the case.

Justice Ginsburg agreed with the Court's resolution of the case, but did not agree with the Court's repeated reference to a "clear notice" requirement derived from the Spending Clause.

Justice Breyer's strong dissent focused on an interpretation of the word "costs" within the Act itself (see above). "The word 'costs' does not define its own scope," the dissenting opinion stated. ". . . But members of Congress did make clear their intent by . . . approving a Conference Report that specified that 'the term attorneys fees as part of the costs include[s] reasonable expenses of expert witnesses and reasonable costs of any test or evaluation which is found to be necessary for the preparation of the parent or guardian's case in the action or proceeding." The dissent concluded that the use of the word "costs" in the Act's text thereby included and authorized payment of costs for experts. Justices Stevens and Souter joined in the dissent.

Bush v. Holmes

The legal controversy over the constitutionality of school **voucher** programs that directed public education funds into private secular and religious schools was resolved at the federal level in *Zelman v. Simmons-Harris*, 536 U.S. 639, 122 S.Ct. 2460, 153 L.Ed.2d 604 (2002). The Supreme Court ruled that an Ohio voucher program did not violate the FIRST AMENDMENT's Establishment Clause. However, opponents of voucher programs sought to challenge these state laws on state constitutional grounds. A number of states have constitutional provisions that ban the funding of private and religious schools, while others include language that suggests voucher programs are precluded. The Florida Supreme Court, in *Bush v. Holmes*, 919 So.2d 392 (2006), struck down a state law that authorized a voucher program, finding that the state constitution barred the program on several grounds. The decision was a setback for Governor Jeb Bush, who had based much of his educational reform efforts on this program.

The Florida legislature enacted the Opportunity Scholarship Program (OSP) in 1999. The OSP authorized a system of school vouchers that was intended to give students in poorly performing ("failing") schools the chance to use public education funds as a scholarship to pay for private school tuition. Under the law private schools, whether secular or religious, were eligible to receive students and their scholarships if they met a set of criteria. Parents of OSP scholarship students were to comply with the private school's parental involvement requirements and to make sure that students take all required statewide assessments. Once a student was admitted to a private school under OSP, the student did not have to transfer back to the public school if that school's performance had improved. The maximum amount of the scholarship was equivalent to the per-pupil **allocation** granted to the public school district. The school district's amount of funds was reduced for each student who left to take an OSP placement. The scholarship was paid directly to the parent, who endorsed the check over to the private school.

Florida parents and students protest education bill, February 2006.

AP IMAGES

A group of plaintiffs filed suit to prevent the implementation of OSP, arguing that it violated the Establishment Clause and the Florida Constitution. After the *Zelman* decision was announced, the plaintiffs voluntarily dismissed the Establishment Clause challenge and proceeded only on state constitutional grounds. The lower Florida courts ruled in favor of the plaintiffs, striking down OSP as unconstitutional. The Florida Supreme Court then addressed this controversial issue.

The court, in a 5–2 decision, ruled OSP unconstitutional. Chief Justice Barbara Pariente, writing for the majority, looked to Art. IX, § 1(a) of the Florida Constitution, which declared that it was "a paramount duty of the state to make adequate provision for the education of all children residing within its borders" and to provide "by law for a uniform, efficient, safe, secure, and high quality system of free public schools that allow students to obtain a high quality education." Pariente reviewed the constitutional history of the education article, which reached back to 1838. The adoption of a revised constitution in 1968 included the "adequate provision" language and a 1998 amendment inserted the "paramount duty of the state" phrase. By inserting this language the court concluded that Florida's education article imposed "a maximum duty on the state to provide for public education that is uniform and of high quality."

The court found that OSP was in direct conflict with the state's "paramount duty" to make adequate provision for education and to maintain a "high quality system of free public schools." The OPS violated the education article because it devoted "the state's resources to the education of children within our state through means other than a system of free public schools. Paying tuition to have children attend private schools was a substantially different manner of meeting this obligation and one which did not pass constitutional muster. Chief Justice Pariente rejected the claim tat OPS supplemented the public school system because the tax money transferred to private schools went to pay for the "same service—basic primary education." Though these scholarships had not been widely used since 1999, the potential scale of this program was in the court's view "unlimited." As the OSP grew it would take more and more money away from the public schools and would undermine the system of "high quality" schools mandated by the constitution.

Another problem with the scholarship program was that it did not comply with the constitution's mandate to provide a "uniform" system of public education. Private schools were not required under OSP eligibility requirements to hire teachers with undergraduate degrees and state teaching certifications. In addition, private schools were not obligated to teach the subjects mandated by the state board of education nor meet uniform curriculum standards. By failing to meet the uniformity standard in the constitution, OSP was constitutionally deficient.

The court emphasized that OSP was distinguishable from other programs that allowed exceptional students to attend private schools because of the lack of special services in their school district. These programs were tailored for physically disabled students who needed special facilities or instructional personnel. They were "structurally different from the OSP, which provides a systematic private school alternative to the public school system mandated by our constitution."

Justice Kenneth Bell, in a dissenting opinion joined by Justice Raoul Cantero, contended that nothing in the constitution prohibited the legislature from enacting the OSP. Unlike other state constitutions, Florida's did not clearly preclude the funding of private schools from public funds. Justice Bell found no "language of exclusion" in the education article that required that "public schools be the sole means by which the State fulfills its duty to provide for the education of children."

Schaffer v. Weast

The Individuals with Disabilities in Education Act (IDEA), 20 U.S.C.A. § 1400 *et seq.*, seeks to ensure that all children with disabilities have the right to a "free appropriate public education." School districts are required by the **statute** to develop an "individualized education program" (IIEP) for each disabled child. Parents may challenge an IEP if they believe it is not appropriate through an administrative hearing. An administrative law judge then decides the issue. Though the IDEA is a detailed law, it does not state which party bears the **burden of persuasion** at an administrative hearing. Normally the party that requests a hearing bears this burden, but there are some exceptions. In the IDEA arena parents have argued that the school district should bear this burden, even if the parent requests the hearing. The U.S. SUPREME COURT, in *Schaffer v. Weast*, __U.S.__, 126 S.Ct. 528, 163 L.Ed.2d 387 (2005), rejected this argument. The Court held that the party seeking relief bears the burden of persuasion.

In 1997, the parents of seventh-grader Brian Schaffer were told by the administrator of the private school Brian attended that he must leave because of his poor academic record. His parents contacted the local Maryland public school district, Montgomery County Public Schools System (MCPS), which evaluated Brian's needs and convened an IEP team. The committee offered Brian a place in either of two middle schools but the parents objected, believing he needed to be placed in smaller classes and provided more intensive services. Ultimately, the parents placed Brian in another private school and asked for an administrative hearing challenging the IEP. They also asked that the school district pay for Brian's private school tuition.

An administrative law judge (ALJ) conducted a three-day hearing, concluding that the evidence was close. He held that the parents bore the burden of persuasion. Because the parents could not provide enough evidence to tip the balance, the ALJ ruled in favor of the school district. The parents then filed a lawsuit in federal **district court**, which reversed and remanded the case. The district court ruled that the school board carried the burden of persuasion. At about the same time as this decision the parents accepted an offer from the school district to place Brian in a high school with a special learning center. The lawsuit continued because the parents sought compensation for the two years of private middle-school tuition and other educational expenses. The school district appealed the burden of persuasion ruling but the ALJ used that ruling to reconsider the case. Again he found that the evidence was in "equipoise" but because the school district now had the burden of persuasion it was the losing party. The Fourth **Circuit Court** of Appeals then considered the matter, reversing the district court and ruling that the party seeking relief has the burden of proof.

The Supreme Court, in a 6–2 decision (newly confirmed Chief Justice John Roberts did not take part in the case), upheld the Fourth Circuit ruling. Justice SANDRA DAY O'CONNOR, writing for the majority, reviewed the legislative mission and history of the IDEA, emphasizing that the "core of the statute" is the "cooperative process that it establishes between parents and schools." Though Congress set out minimal due process requirements for the IEP review hearings, it did give all parties the right to have legal counsel and to present evidence and confront, cross-examine and compel the attendance of witnesses. Parents who prevail in this proceeding may also recover their attorney's fees. However, as to which party should bear the burden of proof, Congress was silent. Justice O'Connor noted that the term "burden of proof" referred to two separate and distinct burdens: the "burden of persuasion" and the "burden of production." The burden of persuasion refers to which party will lose if the evidence is closely balanced. The burden of production refers to which party bears the responsibility of producing evidence at different points in a proceeding. In this case only the burden of persuasion was at issue.

With the absence of congressional direction on the burden of persuasion, the Court first looked at the "ordinary default rule that plaintiffs bear the risk of failing to prove their claims." Justice O'Connor pointed out that other federal laws authorizing lawsuits did not define who carried the burden of proof and the Supreme Court has presumed that the default rule applied. Exceptions to the rule have been made in civil rights trials, where the defendant is obligated to present affirmative defenses or exemptions, but these exceptions were few and limited. The Schaffer's argued that Congress had been guided by two lower court opinions when it drafted the IDEA and that in these two cases the courts had placed the burden of persuasion on the school districts. Justice O'Connor rejected this claim because it was not permissible for the Court to conclude Congress intended to adopt ideas not written into the law.

Justice O'Connor also disputed the parents' contention that placing the burden on the school district would help ensure that children receive what they are entitled to under the IDEA. Very few cases "will be in evidentiary equipoise" and shifting the burden to the school district might force them to spend more funds on litigation costs than educational services. The Court refused to shift the burden because that implied that every IEP was invalid "until the school district says it is not. The Act does not support that conclusion." Moreover, the IDEA includes a "stay-put" provision which requires the student to remain in his or her current educational placement until the IEP dispute is resolved. Congress could have required that the child be given the educational placement required by the parents during the dispute, but it did not. This suggested that Congress presumed "parents will prevail when they have legitimate grievances." Finally, the IDEA provided parents with many tools to prepare for the IEP hearing, including the right to review all school records, to have an independent evaluation of their child, and to receive from the school district written reasons for the disputed actions. Therefore, the party who files the complaint challenging an IEP must carry the burden of persuasion."

Justice RUTH BADER GINSBURG dissented, arguing that school districts have been charged with fulfilling the needs of a disabled child with an IEP and therefore they should be "called upon to demonstrate its adequacy." School districts were in a better position to prove the adequacy of an IEP than the parents of a disabled child are to show the inadequacy of the program. In a separate dissent, Justice Stephen Beyer contended that the absence of a congressional provision on the burden of proof meant that the issue should be left to each state to decide.

ELECTIONS

The processes of voting to decide a public question or to select one person from a designated group to perform certain obligations in a government, corporation, or society.

Wisconsin Right to Life v. Federal Election Commission

The Bipartisan Campaign Reform Act of 2002 (BCRA), Pub. L. No. 107-155, 116 Stat. 91 (also known as the McCain-Feingold Act for its bipartisan sponsors), was ostensibly created to assuage the general public's growing wariness and distrust of "special interest groups," in particular, their perceived exertion of influence and control over political election processes. Various provisions of the Act address these and related issues. The Act is enforced by the Federal Election Commission (FEC).

Section 203 of the Act prohibits corporations and labor unions from using their corporate or general funds to pay for political "electioneering communications," including certain paid political advertisements. Technically, Section 201 of the BCRA defines "electioneering communications" as any broadcast, cable, or satellite communication that refers to a candidate for federal office and that is broadcast within 30 days of a federal primary election or 60 days of a federal general election in the jurisdiction in which that candidate is running for office. 2 U.S.C. § 434(f)(3). In *Wisconsin Right to Life v. FEC*, 546 U.S. ___; 163 L.Ed.2d 990 (2006), the Wisconsin Right to Life (WRTL) challenged the BCRA, as applied to a series of WRTL's political advertisements. The U.S. SUPREME COURT, in a 9–0 **per curiam** opinion, agreed with the organization. The high court vacated the opinion of the **district court** dismissing the challenge, then remanded the matter back to that court for consideration on the merits.

Back in July 2004, WRTL paid for and aired a series of television advertisements. These ads encouraged viewers to contact Wisconsin's two Democratic senators (expressly identified by name in the advertisements) for the purpose of urging them to oppose efforts in Congress (mostly by Democrats) to **filibuster** President George Bush's federal judicial nominees. The advertisements were intended to run for several weeks, up to and including the weeks preceding the November 2004 general elections. One of the senators was running for reelection in November (less than 60 days away).

As a preemptive move, the WRTL sought a **preliminary injunction** barring the FEC from enforcing the BCRA against the pending television advertisements. Its legal argument urged the court to find the BCRA unconstitutional *as applied* to the advertisements. The organization did not dispute that the advertisements were covered by the BCRA's definition of prohibited "electioneering communications," which had previously withstood constitutional challenge in *McConnell v. Federal Election Commission*, 124 S.Ct. 619, 157 L.Ed.2d 491, (2003). Instead, the WRTL argued that the BCRA could not be applied to its advertisements because they constituted "grassroots lobbying advertisements" not related to electoral campaigning. The communications merely encouraged citizens to contact Congress to influence legislation, and not to influence the electoral process.

The U.S. District Court for the DISTRICT OF COLUMBIA denied the motion for preliminary injunction and later dismissed the WTRL's complaint in an unpublished opinion.

The U.S. Supreme Court, noting probable jurisdiction after the D.C. **appellate court** ruled that it lacked jurisdiction, later issued a short opinion vacating the district court's judgment and instructing it to consider WTRL's arguments on the merits following remand.

The significant holding in the high court's opinion was in noting that the district court had misinterpreted the relevance of (i.e., had incorrectly read) a footnote in *McConnell* as barring any "as-applied" challenges to the BCRA's prohibition on electioneering communications. Said the Supreme Court in its opinion,

> "Contrary to the understanding of the District Court, that footnote merely notes that because we found BCRA's primary definition of 'electioneering communication' facially valid when used with regard to BCRA's disclosure and funding requirements, it was unnecessary to consider the constitutionality of the backup definition Congress provided. *Ibid.* In upholding § 203 against a facial challenge, we did not purport to resolve future as-applied challenges."

For its part, the FEC argued that the district court had rested its decision on the ground that the facts of this case "suggest that WRTL's advertisements may fit the very type of activity *McConnell* found Congress had a compelling interest in regulating." But the Supreme Court could not conclude that the district court intended its opinion to also rest on this ground, noting that the district court had used the word "may." Further, the district court had expressly found that WRTL's 'as-applied' challenge to BCRA was foreclosed by the *McConnell* decision. Therefore, given this ambiguity, the Supreme Court could not now "say with certainty that the District Court's dismissal was based on this alternative ground."

ELEVENTH AMENDMENT

Northern Insurance Company of New York v. Chatham County, Georgia

The ELEVENTH AMENDMENT bars individuals from suing state governments unless a state consents to such a lawsuit. In addition, the U.S. SUPREME COURT has recognized that states possess **sovereign immunity**, which bars damages suits against state governments unless they consent to be sued. However, the Supreme Court has made clear that only states and "arms of the state" possess sovereign immunity from suits authorized by federal law. Sovereign immunity has not been extended to municipalities, regional governing councils, and counties. Despite this demarcation between state and local government, a federal appeals court held that a county was entitled to sovereign immunity where the county exercised powers delegated from the state. The Supreme Court, in *Northern Insurance Company of New York v. Chatham County, Georgia*, __U.S.__, 126 S.Ct. 1689, __L.Ed.2d __ (2006), reversed the appeals court, reaffirming the limitation on state sovereign immunity.

The case arose from James Ludwig's sailing trip down Georgia's Wilmington River in 2002. Ludwig was sailing his yacht towards a drawbridge owned and operated by Chatham County, Georgia. He radioed the bridge operator, requesting that the bridge be raised so he could pass underneath. As Ludwig proceeded under the span a section of the bridge moved downward. The yacht hit the span and sustained substantial damage. Ludwig filed a claim with his insurance company, Northern Insurance Company of New York, which paid $138,000. Northern then filed suit in Georgia federal **district court** against Chatham County, alleging negligence in the operation and maintenance of the drawbridge and seeking recovery of its costs. Chatham County filed a motion to dismiss the lawsuit, claiming sovereign immunity. The county did not claim Eleventh Amendment immunity. The district court, relying on precedent by the Eleventh **Circuit Court** of Appeals, agreed that the county as immune because it exercised power delegated by the state of Georgia. The Eleventh Circuit upheld this ruling but acknowledged the county could not claim Eleventh Amendment immunity because it did not qualify as an "arm of the state." However, the appeals court reasoned that the **common law** had established a "residual immunity" which protected the county from the lawsuit.

The Supreme Court, in a unanimous decision, overturned the ruling and the reasoning behind it. Justice CLARENCE THOMAS, writing for the Court, reaffirmed the validity of state sovereign immunity as a component of sovereignty recognized before the **ratification** of the Constitution. Sovereign immunity has been limited by constitutional amendments, primarily the Fourteenth. As for the Eleventh Amendment, Thomas admitted that this form of immunity had become misleading "shorthand" for state sovereign immunity, which was not derived from or limited by the amendment. The Court, in recognizing state sovereign immunity, had limited it to states and arms of the state, rejecting extension of it to local government units. In this case Chatham County claimed that there was a residual immunity that permitted the use of a broader test than the Court's Eleventh Amendment precedents in determining "whether an **entity** is acting as an arm of the State and is accordingly entitled to immunity." Thomas rejected this argument, finding that the county could not claim immunity based upon its identity as a county or an expansive arm-of-the-state test. The only way it could prevail was to show that it was acting as an arm of the state under prior Court rulings. The county's task was made more difficult because it had conceded in the lower courts that it had failed to qualify for Eleventh Amendment immunity because it did not qualify as an arm of the state. Justice Thomas concluded that this same disqualification applied to a state sovereign immunity claim, making Chatham County amenable to the federal lawsuit.

The county argued in the alternative that it should be granted immunity because in cases involving ships, which is known as admiralty law, the county's "exercise of core state functions with regard to navigable waters" barred civil lawsuits. Justice Thomas was not persuaded by this argument, finding that Court precedents in admiralty had not created a special category governing sovereign immunity. The Court applied general principles of immunity and had found in prior cases that sovereign immunity did not bar an admiralty suit against a city. Therefore, the county could not avoid litigation on the damages claim.

EMINENT DOMAIN

The power to take private property for public use by a state, municipality, or private person or corporation authorized to exercise functions of public character, following the payment of just compensation to the owner of that property.

Supreme Court's Eminent Domain Case Leads to Fallout

In *Kelo v. City of New London*, ___ U.S. ___, 125 S. Ct. 2655, 162 L. Ed. 2d 439 (2005), the U.S. SUPREME COURT issued a controversial ruling that allows governmental units to seize private property for the purpose of economic development. The decision led the vast majority of states and hundreds of local governmental entities to consider laws that would restrict use of **eminent domain**.

The case that gave rise to this controversy began when the city council of New London, Connecticut approved a development plan near the Thames River. The development plan called for the acquisition of several parcels of private property. Where owners were unwilling to sell the property, the city voted to use eminent domain in order to acquire the property. The development was expected to increase tax revenue and jobs in the area, but some of the property that would be condemned would not be open to the general public.

Several residents objected to the condemnation and sued the city of New London. The case reached the Connecticut Supreme Court, which ruled that the city's plans were primarily intended to benefit the public, and this use was sufficient to establish a "public use" of the property. *Kelo v. City of New London*, 843 A.2d 500 (Conn. 2004). The Supreme Court granted **certiorari** in 2004, and a fractured Supreme Court affirmed the Connecticut court's decision. The opinion noted that the Court had historically defined the term "public purpose" broadly, and so public use could encompass an economic development plan.

Both conservatives and liberals sharply criticized the decision. Former House Majority Leader Tom DeLay (R.-Tex.) said he hoped that a major backlash would result from the case. "The only silver lining to the decision is the possibility that this time the court has finally gone

Alabama Governor Bob Riley discusses eminent domain bill, August 2005.
AP IMAGES

too far and that the American people are ready to reassert their constitutional authority," he said.

Representative Scott Garrett (R.-N.J.) introduced a clause in an appropriations bill that would prevent federal transportation funds from being used for improvements on lands that are seized through eminent domain for anything other than a public use. Under the **statute**, "public use shall not be construed to include economic development that primarily benefits private entities. . . ." Thus, a private developer who obtains land through eminent domain cannot receive transportation funds. The House approved the bill in June 2005, and the Senate approved the legislation in November. President GEORGE W. BUSH signed the bill on November 30. Pub. L. No. 109–115, 119 Stat. 2396 (2005).

Prior to the decision, eight states forbid the taking of private property for economic development through the employment of eminent domain. These states include Arkansas, Florida, Illinois, Kentucky, Maine, Montana, South Carolina, and Washington. Within two months of the decision, an estimated 16 states were considering bills that would either ban or restrict the use of eminent domain for private economic development. On August 3, Alabama became the first state to enact this type of prohibition.

Attorneys for the Institute for Justice, based in Arlington, Virginia, represented the plaintiffs in *Kelo*. This **public policy** organization has led a grass-roots effort to urge states to enact provisions that would limit the use of eminent domain. One of the senior attorneys for the Institute said that Alabama had taken an important first step by enacting its legislation, but she said that the statute contained a loophole that could be used by government entities to condemn land for private use.

Public opinion in many areas appeared to support the limitation on eminent domain. According to a poll conducted by Quinnipiac University, 89 percent of Connecticut voters wanted the state legislature to restrict eminent domain. Similarly, a University of New Hampshire poll showed that 93 percent of residents in that state opposed use of eminent domain for economic development.

New Hampshire became the center of one of the more unusual actions in the eminent domain debate. In Weare, New Hampshire, a town warrant was introduced that would have required the city to condemn a farmhouse owned by Justice DAVID SOUTER, who wrote the lead opinion in *Kelo*. According to reports, the farmhouse would be converted into a hotel and named the "Lost Liberty Hotel." Residents of Weare rejected the proposal by a vote of 94 to 59, choosing instead to ask the New Hampshire legislature to strengthen its eminent domain law.

The mayor of the City of New London proposed a compromise with several of the residents that were scheduled to be evicted. Under this proposal, the city would own the homes of four people whose homes were seized, and those people would pay the city to live there. Susette Kelo, who brought the suit against the city, rejected the offer, saying that she did not engage in the litigation so that she could pay rent to the city.

By April 2006, lawmakers in 47 states had introduced more than 325 measures that are designed to protect private property from seizure through eminent domain. According to a land-use specialist with the National Conference of State Legislatures, "I have never seen a response to a Supreme Court decision this dramatic." As many Democrats have introduced legislation as have Republicans. Commentators have noted that because Americans view ownership of their land as something of a sacred right, they have taken this decision more personally. Moreover, the case has increased public knowledge about what governmental entities can do with the power of eminent domain. Several experts have agreed that changes to eminent domain laws will continue to take place.

Supporters of the use of eminent domain for development note that many sites that are condemned are blighted areas that serve no purpose. Moreover, these supporters note that the homeowners who may lose their land are compensated for their loss, and that the condemnation is generally done for the greater good.

ENVIRONMENTAL LAW

An amalgam of state and federal statutes, regulations, and common-law principles covering air pollution, water pollution, hazardous waste, the wilderness, and endangered wildlife.

States of California, New Mexico, and Oregon Sue Bush Administration for Dismantling Environmental Restrictions

In September 2005, the people of the states of California, New Mexico, and Oregon filed suit against the U.S. DEPARTMENT OF AGRICULTURE, represented by Secretary of the Department of Agriculture Mike Johanns and Under Secretary for Natural Resources and Environment of the Department of Agriculture Mark Rey, and the U.S. Forest Service, represented by Chief Dale Bosworth. California Attorney General Bill Lockyer, New Mexico Attorney General Patricia A. Madrid, and Oregon Governor Theodore Kulongoski filed the complaint through the U.S. **District Court** for the Northern District of California, challenging the Forest Service's May 2005 decision to **rescind** a nationwide resources-protection rule as a violation of the National Environmental Policy Act (NEPA) procedures and the Administrative Procedure Act (APA) prohibition on arbitrary and capricious action. The policy change dismantles road-building and logging restrictions in the United State's nearly 60 million acres of backcountry and undeveloped forests, a decision that allegedly constitutes an abuse of agency discretion.

The Forest Service conducted a comprehensive survey of roadless areas in the 1970s, cataloging areas larger than 5000 acres within the National Forest System. Approximately 2.8 million acres of these Inventoried Roadless Areas (IRAs) have since been developed by the Forest Service. Under the Clinton Administration, the agency announced an 18-month suspension of road construction or reconstruction in National Forest IRAs beginning in February 1999, pending investigation and potential policy revision designed to protect remaining roadless areas from degradation.

A draft Environmental Impact Statement (EIS) for a nationwide policy—titled "Forest Service Roadless Area Conservation"—was released in May 2000, detailing various conservation alternatives, including restrictions on road construction, road reconstruction, and timber harvesting, for the roadless areas in question. The Final Environmental Impact Statement (FEIS), released in November 2000, identified the Roadless Rule as the agency's preferred method of conservation. Its stated purpose was to halt all activities that posed great risk to the social and ecological values of the inventoried areas. The FEIS affected an identified 58.5 million acres nationwide.

The Forest Service issued the final Roadless Rule in January 2001, prohibiting road construction, reconstruction, and timber harvesting in the IRAs in order to guard against altering and fragmenting the landscapes. The study concluded that additional development of the acreage would be unwise in light of the size of the existing road system and budget constraints that would hamper appropriate management to maintain safety and environmental standards. The two-volume document analyzed alternatives and provided the Forest Service's rationale for selecting the Roadless Rule under the NEPA. Nine lawsuits relating to the Roadless Rule were filed in federal district courts in Idaho, Utah, North Dakota, Wyoming, Alaska, and the DISTRICT OF COLUMBIA. However, more than 95 percent of 1.2 million public commenters in the public involvement process supported the rule.

On July 16, 2004, the Forest Service published "Special Areas: State Petitions for Inventoried Roadless Area Management", which proposed revoking the Roadless Rule in favor of a petition process that would give state governors an 18-month window to seek or decline to seek changes in the **disposition** of roadless areas in National Forests within their states. Such petitions would be reviewed by a National Advisory Committee, yet to be established, and the Secretary of Agriculture was given responsibility to accept, reject, or revise petitions, in effect having the authority to determine the disposition of the roadless lands.

Called the Roadless Repeal, this proposal was finalized in May 2005. The complaint filed by California, New Mexico, and Oregon contends that the defendant agencies failed to conduct a new environmental analysis, a public involvement process, offer an explanation for reversing policy, or an explanation for their lack of concern about the inability to finance the maintenance of National Forest roads. This failure allegedly violates the NEPA and the APA, harming the procedural interests of the plaintiff states and the broader public. Lockyer et al. argue that the Roadless Repeal will compromise their states' **proprietary** interests in protecting natural resources on state lands adjacent to or affected by policies on National Forest roadless areas; protection of state public trust wildlife, including rare and endangered species; and protection of state waterways, water quality and quantity.

The defendant agencies have stated that the Roadless Repeal is procedural rather than a NEPA document, therefore it is not necessary to pass it through the NEPA process. They also maintain that the original FEIS analysis that established the Roadless Rule as the preferred method adequately describes the effect of the repeal, so a new analysis would be redundant. The agencies call the repeal environmentally neutral, claiming it will have no identifiable resource outcomes.

The plaintiffs contest this, listing some of the species potentially effected by the policy change, including state and federally protected animals and plants. California currently has 2.5 million roadless acres and such rare and endangered species as the California condor and the Coho salmon. The latter has habitat designated under the ENDANGERED SPECIES ACT as critical to species survival and recovery within or affected by the roadless areas of California.

New Mexico's 1.6 million roadless acres of National Forest are home to American bald eagles and the Mexican spotted owl, both of which are federally threatened species, as well as gray wolves and other species to whom the habitat is considered critical.

Approximately one quarter of Oregon's land mass, or 15.6 million acres, consists of National Forest land. Nearly 2 million are IRAs, and 1.2 million of those would be vulnerable to road-building under the Roadless Repeal. The American bald eagle, brown pelican, northern spotted owl, and Coho and Chinook salmon are among the potentially effected species. The viability of salmon in Oregon would be affected by habitat changes within Oregon, as well as in the surrounding states, including California. The Forest Service in Oregon has already begun taking action, such as moving to approve timber sales, that would have been impermissible under the Roadless Rule.

The complaint also indicates that the Roadless Repeal would affect water quality and quantity, specifically in California and Oregon. In California, concerns about water tie into issues of erosion, while Oregon's state-owned waterways are the stated concern.

The plaintiff states are asking the court to declare the repeal in violation of NEPA and the APA, vacate the repeal, and require the defendants to create a NEPA-compliant Roadless Repeal or withdraw the rule. They also are seeking cost and expense compensation, along with whatever relief the court deems appropriate.

ERISA

The name of federal legislation, popularly abbreviated as ERISA (29 U.S.C.A. § 1001 et seq. [1974]), which regulates the financing, vesting, and administration of pension plans for workers in private business and industry.

Sereboff v. Mid Atlantic Medical Services., Inc.

Insurance companies that write health and medical insurance policies routinely include in their contracts the right to be reimbursed for benefits from a beneficiary who receives money from a **third party** for an injury. This typically means that when a person is injured in an accident and recovers a tort award, the person must pay back the insurance company for the medical benefits already provided. In recent years a number of cases have been litigated under the federal EMPLOYEE RETIREMENT INCOME SECURITY ACT of 1974 (ERISA), 88 Stat. 829, to determine how insurance companies may enforce their right to recovery when a beneficiary does not make reimbursement of the benefits. In *Sereboff v. Mid Atlantic Medical Services., Inc.*, __U.S.__, 126 S.Ct. 1869, __L.Ed.2d __ (2006), the Supreme Court ruled that an insurance company could obtain an injunction ordering the beneficiary to payback the company of out of the proceeds of a damages award. The use of equitable relief, which is given to insurance companies under ERISA, was extended to the use of injunctions for such recoveries.

Marlene and Joel Sereboff, **husband and wife**, were injured in an automobile accident in California. Marlene Sereboff's employer sponsored a health insurance plan that was administered by Mid Atlantic Medical Services and was covered by ERISA. Sereboff's benefit plan included an "Acts of Third Parties" provision that required beneficiaries who were injured by third parties and who recovered damages from third parties by way of lawsuits or settlements to reimburse Mid Atlantic for the medical benefits provided. The Sereboffs filed a tort lawsuit against several third parties. Mid Atlantic became aware of the lawsuit and sent a letter to their lawyer asserting a **lien** on the anticipated proceeds of the suit for the benefits paid on their behalf. Over the next two year Mid Atlantic sent similar letters to the lawyer with updated information on the amount of medical expenses provided. The Sereboffs settled their case and received $750,000 but neither they nor their lawyer paid Mid Atlantic the lien, which was valued at almost $76,000. Mid Atlantic then filed suit in California federal **district court** under a provision of ERISA that gave the company the right to "enjoin any act or practice which violates any provision of the benefit plan. The company asked the court for an injunction that required the Sereboffs to retain and set aside $76,000 from the settlement while the lawsuit was pending. It also asked for a permanent injunction that directed the Sereboffs to pay them the amount in question. The district court granted the injunction and the Sereboffs placed the amount in an investment account. It rejected the Sereboffs' claim that this was a contract dispute that could not be settled in equity. The district ultimately ruled in favor of Mid Atlantic and ordered the Sereboffs to pay the $76,000, plus interest, to Mid Atlantic. The court did allow the couple to deduct a share of the attorney's fees and court costs they had incurred during the tort litigation. Although the Fourth **Circuit Court** of Appeals upheld the payment to Mid Atlantic, it noted that the circuit courts of appeals were divided on whether the ERISA provision dealing with equitable relief authorized such recoveries. The Supreme Court agreed to hear the Sereboffs' appeal to resolve the issue.

The Court, in a unanimous decision, upheld the Fourth Circuit ruling as consistent with the ERISA provision. Chief Justice John Roberts, writing for the Court, concluded that the only question to resolves was whether the relief Mid Atlantic requested was "equitable" under ERISA. Roberts pointed out that a recent ERISA decision, *Great-West Life & Annuity Insurance Company v. Knudson*, 534 U.S. 204, 122 S.Ct. 708, 151 L.Ed.2d 635 (2002), involved similar facts involving an "Acts of Third Parties" clause. The Court in that case concluded that ERISA only provided equitable remedies, such as an injunction. The insurance company, in asking for money, asked for a legal remedy that was not provided in **statute**. Great-West also contended its suit could be viewed as a request for **restitution**, which is a form of equitable relief. Roberts noted that Great-West's claim for restitution failed because the funds it sought were not in possession of the defendant but had been placed in a special needs trust. However, in the current dispute "That impediment to characterizing the relief in *Knudson* is not present here." Mid Atlantic sought "specially identifiable" funds that the Sereboffs possessed and controlled. Though Mid Atlantic alleged a breach of contract it did not ask for damages, which is a legal remedy. Instead, it sought an equitable lien on the settlement money. Because ERISA provided for such an equitable remedy to enforce plan terms, the equitable remedy in this case was justified.

Chief Justice Roberts found that Mid Atlantic had established that the basis for its claim was equitable. Longstanding Court precedents demonstrated that Mid Atlantic had identified a particular fund (settlement money) distinct from the Sereboffs general assets and a particular share that it was entitled to for reimbursement. The company could "follow" or trace a portion of the recovery into the hands of the couple as soon as the settlement funds were identified and then assert an equitable lien. Roberts rejected the Sereboffs' contention that the fund over which a lien is asserted must be in existence when the contract containing the lien provision is executed.

ESTABLISHMENT CLAUSE

Federal Judge Strikes Down Iowa Faith-Based Prison Program

Judge Robert W. Pratt of the U.S. **District Court** for the Southern District of Iowa in June

2006 struck down a faith-based prison program established in Iowa prisons. Similar programs exist in six other states. The case has been viewed as part of a larger challenge to proposed religious-based government programs.

InnerChange Freedom Initiative is a non-profit **entity** associated with the Prison Fellowship Ministries, a group founded by Charles W. Colson. Colson, a well-known evangelist who once spent time in prison for a role in the WATERGATE cover-up (he was special counsel to President RICHARD NIXON), is reportedly a close ally of President GEORGE W. BUSH. Colson also had a close working relationship with Walter "Kip" Kautzky, the former director of the Iowa Department of Corrections.

InnerChange attempts to rehabilitate inmates through the teachings of Christianity. The program has proven to be successful in terms of its relatively high rates of **recidivism**. InnerChange began its program in the Iowa prison system in 1999 through a contract with the Department of Corrections. The state of Iowa paid a significant portion of the contract with InnerChange, which also has programs in Texas, Minnesota, Kansas, Tennessee, Arkansas, and Missouri.

The organization has an overtly religious mission. According to the group's mission statement, its goal is "to exhort, equip, and assist the Church in its ministry to prisoners, ex-prisoners, victims, and their families, and in its promotion of biblical standards of justice in the criminal justice system." The organization produces numerous publications that it uses in its program, and much of the content of these publications is based explicitly on Christian teachings.

Critics challenged the program, arguing that because it received state funds, the existence of the program at the prisons violated the principle of separation of church and state. In 2003, Americans United for Separation of Church and State, a Washington D.C.-based advocacy group, brought suit against the Iowa Department of Corrections. The group sought injunctive relief as well as a declaration that the program was unconstitutional. Regarding the injunctive relief, the group wanted the court to ban InnerChange from operating at all within the Iowa correctional system. Pratt held hearings for two weeks in October and November 2005.

Pratt issued his ruling on June 2, 2006. In a lengthy opinion, Pratt summarized the history of the InnerChange program in the Iowa system, as well as the instruction and goals of the organization. The judge determined that Christianity lied at the heart of the program. According to the opinion, "The overtly religious atmosphere of the InnerChange program is not simply an overlay or secondary effect of the program—it is the program."

Moreover, Pratt determined that inmates who voluntarily entered into the program received significant benefits, including better living conditions. The prisons did not offer a non-Christian alternative. Pratt determined that the program practically requires inmates to convert to Christianity. "Though an inmate could, theoretically, graduate from InnerChange without converting to Christianity, the coercive nature of the program demands obedience to its dogmas and doctrine," he said in the opinion.

A series of cases in the U.S. SUPREME COURT has established the basic principles of **jurisprudence** regarding the Establishment Clause of the FIRST AMENDMENT. Under the case of *Lemon v. Kurtzman*, 411 U.S. 192, 93 S. Ct. 1463, 36 L. Ed. 2d 151 (1973) and its progeny, the Court looks to a series of factors to determine whether a state's involvement with religion violates the constitution. Among the questions that the court asks is whether the program in question has a secular purpose; whether the primary effect of the program is to **advance** a religious purpose; whether the program is pervasively sectarian; whether the sectarian aspect of the program may be separated from the secular aspects of the program; and whether the program excessively entangles the state with religion.

After reviewing the Iowa program in light of these questions, Pratt determined that the Iowa program was indeed unconstitutional. He ordered the discontinuation of the program within 60 days, and also ordered the Prison Fellowship ministries to pay back $1.5 million that it had received from the state since 1999. These orders were stayed pending a likely appeal by the state department of corrections. *Americans United for Separation of Church & State v. Prison Fellowship Ministries*, 2006 WL 1523092 (S.D. Iowa June 2, 2006).

Representatives of Americans United for the Separation of Church and State applauded the decision. Barry Lynn, the executive director of the organization, said that the decision may lead to the end of other religious-based programs. "If the reasoning of this decision is held to apply in future cases, there is no way you can use government funds for so-called 'transformational' programs that are really saying, 'To deal with your sins you have to embrace

Jesus,'" he said. "In the distance, one can hear the bells tolling deep trouble for the faith-based initiative."

Supporters of the program, on the other hand, expressed obvious disappointment. Mark Earley, former attorney general of Virginia who is president of Prison Fellowship, said that he expects an appeal. "I think it is an extreme decision that if allowed to stand strikes a pretty serious blow at the religious freedom of prisoners," he said. "And it strikes an equally destructive blow to rehabilitation efforts in the prisons of America."

EXHAUSTION OF REMEDIES

The exhaustion-of-remedies doctrine requires that procedures established by statute, common law, contract, or custom must be initiated and followed in certain cases before an aggrieved party may seek relief from the courts. After all other available remedies have been exhausted, a lawsuit may be filed.

Woodford v. Ngo

The Prison Litigation Reform Act of 1995(PLRA), 42 USC 1997e *et seq.*, requires inmates to exhaust any available administrative remedies before challenging their prison conditions in federal court. In *Woodford v. Ngo*, No. 05-416, 548 U.S. ___ (2006), the U.S. SUPREME COURT was faced with the question of whether a prisoner satisfied the "exhaustion of administrative remedies" requirement by filing an untimely or otherwise defective administrative grievance or appeal that is dismissed or rejected. The high court held that the PLRA required a "proper" exhaustion of administrative remedies. The effect of the Court's holding was to dismiss prisoner Ngo's civil rights action in federal court because he had not "properly exhausted" his administrative appeals when he filed an untimely prison grievance. His failure to file a timely grievance cost him the right to have his claim adjudicated on the merits.

Prisoner Viet Mike Ngo was serving a life sentence for murder in a California state prison. In October 2000, Ngo was placed in administrative segregation for allegedly engaging in inappropriate sexual misconduct in the prison chapel. Two months later, he was returned to the general prison population, but still prohibited from participating in "special programs," which included a variety of religious activities.

Not until approximately six months later did Ngo file a grievance with prison officials challenging that action. California has a grievance system for prisoners which requires the completion of a simple Form 602 "readily available to all inmates" which requires a staff member to sign, verifying that the prisoner first attempted informal resolution with the staff member. Following this, a dissatisfied prisoner may pursue a three-step administrative review process, commenced by the filing of the same Form 602, and any supporting documents within 15 working days (three weeks) of the action taken. Ngo's grievance was rejected as untimely because he did not file it within 15 working days of the action challenged. He appealed that decision internally, without success.

He then filed suit against prison officials in federal **district court** under 42 USC § 1983. The district court dismissed the claim, finding that Ngo had not fully exhausted his administrative remedies as required by the PLRA. The court reasoned that if Ngo had filed a timely grievance, the other appeals within the prison system would have been "available." The Ninth **Circuit Court** of Appeals reversed. It held that Ngo had "exhausted" his remedies because none remained available to him (even though this was caused by his own failure to timely file a grievance).

In its petition for **writ** of **certiorari** to the U.S. Supreme Court, the State of California noted the sharp disagreement among federal circuits over whether procedural failures in grievance filing (resulting in dismissal with no **adjudication** on the merits) constituted an "exhaustion of remedies" in the administrative forum, thus allowing prisoners to proceed to court. The Sixth and Ninth Circuits had so held, but the Third, Seventh, Tenth, and Eleventh Circuits came to the opposite conclusion and barred prisoners from habeas relief in **federal courts**. The U.S. Supreme Court granted certiorari.

The Court ruled 6–3 against prisoner Ngo, holding that the PLRA required "proper exhaustion" of administrative remedies to gain access to federal court. To hold otherwise would have the effect of allowing prisoners to disregard administrative rules and requirements, garner defaults, and start yet another **appellate** process in federal district court.

Writing for the Court, new Justice Alito first reviewed the PLRA, enacted "in the wake of a sharp rise in prisoner litigation in the federal courts_The PLRA contains a variety of provisions designed to bring this litigation under control." According to the Court, a centerpiece of the PLRA's efforts was an "invigorated" exhaustion provision considerably more restrictive than that required by other legislation prior to the PLRA.

The Court then reviewed California's prison grievance system. The majority opinion disagreed with Ngo's argument that the state prison system was harsh for prisoners, who were generally untrained in the law and/or poorly educated. Justice Alito noted the relative informality and simplicity of California's system. The Court otherwise dismissed Ngo's arguments that the PLRA exhaustion requirement was patterned on habeas law or similar to §14(b) of the Age Discrimination in Employment Act (ADA) or §706(e) of Title VII of the Civil Rights Act, stating that neither provision was in any way an exhaustion provision. Further, said the Court, no **statute** or case purports to require exhaustion while at the same time allows a person to deliberately bypass the administrative process with no risk of sanction.

Justice Stevens was joined in his dissent by Justices Souter and Ginsburg. He argued the absence of textual support for the conclusion drawn by the majority, stating "[t]he plain text of the PLRA simply requires that 'such administrative remedies as are available' be exhausted." The three justices wrote that the Constitution guaranteed prisoners, like all citizens, a reasonably adequate opportunity to raise constitutional concerns before impartial judges.

FAIR LABOR STANDARDS ACT

Federal legislation enacted in 1938 by Congress, pursuant to its power under the Commerce Clause, that mandated a minimum wage and forty-hour work week for employees of those businesses engaged in interstate commerce.

IBP, Inc. v. Alvarez

The FAIR LABOR STANDARDS ACT (FLSA), 29 U.S.C.A. § 201 *et seq.*, was passed in 1938, giving U.S. hourly workers a 40-hour workweek (unless the workers gets overtime pay) and setting a minimum wage. However, FLSA does not define "work" or "workweek," which has pushed definitional questions into the judicial system. A series of Supreme Court decisions in the 1940s that were favorable to employees caused Congress to pass the Portal-to-Portal Act, 29 U.S.C.A. § 252(a), a 1949 amendment to FLSA. This act narrowed FLSA coverage by treating two activities as not compensable: walking on the employer's premises to and from the actual place of performance of the principal activity of the employees, and activities that are "preliminary or postliminary" to that principal activity. Despite DEPARTMENT OF LABOR regulations on when the workday starts and ends, there have been controversies about whether the time it takes for workers to put on and take off special work gear, and to walk to and from the changing room is compensable work time. The U.S. SUPREME COURT, in *IBP, Inc. v. Alvarez*, __U.S.__, 126 S.Ct. 514, 163 L.Ed.2d 288 (2005), resolved most of these matters in favor of employees.

The case consolidated two disputes from Washington state and Maine. In the Washington case, a group of workers at an IBP, Inc. meat-packing plant filed a **class action** lawsuit. Production workers are required to wear hardhats, hairnets, ear plugs, gloves, sleeve, aprons, leggings, and boots. Those workers who use knives must also wear heavier gear, including chain link metal aprons and plexiglass armguards. These workers were "on the clock" when the first piece of meat processed and the compensable workday ended with the last piece of meat processed. In 1998 the company began paying the workers an extra four minutes for clothes-changing time but the workers' lawsuit asked for additional pay for the time spent putting on and removing protective gear and walking between the locker room to the production floor before and after each shift. The Maine case involved a class action lawsuit by workers at a poultry processing plant operated by Barber Foods, Inc. These meat processing workers also wore heavy protective gear and were not paid for the time it took to put on and remove the gear. They also wanted to be paid for the time spent waiting to don and doff the protective gear.

The Washington federal **district court** ruled in favor of the IBP employees, finding that the donning and doffing of protective gear for these particular jobs were compensable under FLSA because they were "integral and indispensable to the work of the employees who wore such equipment." In addition, the time spent walking between the locker room and the production was also compensable because it occurred during the workday. Based on these conclusions the judge ruled that workers who used knives were entitled to pay for between 12 and 14 minutes of work, including about 4 minutes of walking time. The

Ninth **Circuit Court** of Appeals upheld the district court's ruling but employed different reasoning. The appeals court distinguished between workers who donned hardhats and safety goggles, who were not entitled to additional work time and pay, with the IBP workers who were required to wear elaborate and burdensome gear.

In the Maine lawsuit, the federal district court ruled that workers were entitled to be compensated for the time spent donning and doffing protective gear but not for the time walking to and from the production floor. In addition, the court ruled against the employees' request that they be paid for the time they spent waiting to pick up their gear and equipment at the beginning of their workday. The First Circuit Court of Appeals upheld the lower court. The Supreme Court agreed to hear the consolidated case to resolve this split in the circuits.

The Supreme Court, in a unanimous decision, upheld the Ninth Circuit's decision. However, the Court agreed with the First Circuit that the waiting time for picking up protective gear at the beginning of a shift was not compensable. Justice JOHN PAUL STEVENS, writing for the Court, reviewed the history of the statutes, regulations, and court rulings that dealt with defining work and the parameters of the workday. A 1955 Supreme Court decision had ruled in favor of workers at a **battery** plant who had to change clothes and shower because of their work with caustic and toxic materials. The Court found that the employees had a right to be paid for the time it took to change clothes at the beginning and end of the shift, and for the time it took to clean up. The key to the decision was language in the Portal-to-Portal Act that principal work activities include all activities which are an "integral and indispensable part of the principal activities."

Justice Stevens concluded that the donning and doffing of protective gear in both plants were an integral and indispensable part of the work of meat processing. These activities signaled the start and end of the workday. Therefore, walking to and from the production was compensable time as well. As to the First Circuit ruling that waiting time was not compensable, Justice Stevens concurred. Under FLSA, waiting for the issuance of protective gear was a "preliminary" rather than a "principal" activity and should not be counted as part of the workday. Stevens noted that walking from the time clock near the factory entrance to a workstation was necessary for employees to begin work but the Portal-to-Portal Act ruled that it was not compensable under the FLSA. Therefore, the waiting in this case was "two steps removed from the productive activity on the assembly line" and was not integral and indispensable to a principal activity.

FEDERAL TORT CLAIMS ACT

A federal statute enacted in 1946 that removed the inherent immunity of the federal government from most tort actions brought against it and established the conditions for the commencement of such suits.

Will v. Hallock

The FEDERAL TORT CLAIMS ACT (FTCA), 28 U.S.C.A. § 1346 waives the federal government's **sovereign immunity** in certain circumstances to permit persons to sue it for damages. However, there are exceptions and limitations. In *Will v. Hallock*, __U.S.__, 126 S.Ct. 952, 163 L.Ed.2d 836 (2006), a married couple sued under the FTCA claiming that government agents had destroyed the wife's computerized business records during an investigation into child pornography. It later was revealed that the husband had been the victim of identity theft and no criminal charges were brought. Under an exception to the FTCA, the court dismissed the claim but the couple had also filed a civil rights lawsuit against the government agents in their personal capacity. The court refused to dismiss this lawsuit after the FTCA was thrown out, triggering an appeal from the agents. The Supreme Court did not address the merits of the agents' claims, ruling that they had no right to appeal this issue until the a **final decision** had been made in the **district court**.

Susan Hallock owned a computer software business that she operated from home with her husband Richard. Richard's credit card information was stolen and used to pay for a child pornography web site subscription. Agents of the U.S. Custom Service traced the payment to Hallock's credit card account and obtained a search warrant for the Hallocks' home. The agents took all the computer equipment, software, and disk drives from the home. When Richard proved that he was a victim of identity theft the investigation was dropped and the seized property was returned. However, several of the disk drives were damaged and all the data on the drives was lost. As a result the Hallocks were forced to close the business.

They sued the federal government under the FTCA, alleging that the agents had been negligent in searching their property. However, the Hallocks did not get a chance to a hearing on the merits of their case. The district court agreed with the government that the suit must be dismissed because of an FTCA detention-of-goods exception: when agents' activities occur during the course of detaining goods the government does not surrender its sovereign immunity. While the FTCA claim was pending, Susan Hallock filed a federal civil rights suit for damages against the Custom Service agents, alleging that they had deprived her of her property, including business income, in violation of the FIFTH AMENDMENT's Due Process Clause. After the FTCA had been dismissed by the court, the agents sought to use a provision of the FTCA to have Susan Hallock's lawsuit dismissed. Under this provision, a judgment in an FTCA action "shall constitute a complete bar to any action by the claimant, by reason of the same subject matter, against the employee of the government whose act or omission gave rise to the claim." 28 U.S.C.A. § 2676. The district court denied the motion to dismiss, ruling that the dismissal of the FTCA claim was based only on a procedural ground and did not qualify as a "judgment bar" under the FTCA provision. The agents appealed this ruling to the Second **Circuit Court** of Appeals, which affirmed the lower court ruling. The Supreme Court agreed to hear the agents' appeal to resolve the judgment bar issue.

The Supreme Court, in a unanimous decision, declined to rule on the merits of the agents' appeals, concluding that the Second Circuit did not have jurisdiction to hear the appeal. Justice DAVID SOUTER, writing for the Court, noted that in the **federal courts**, most rulings made by the district court that do not resolve the case are not immediately appealable. Such "collateral order" appeals are reserved for a small number of issues and are the exception, not the rule. The rule, as mandated by Congress, grants jurisdiction to the circuit courts of appeals to review all "final decisions" of the district courts that are not immediately appealable to the Supreme Court. The Court established the "collateral order doctrine" to deal with a small class of rulings that do not conclude the litigation but conclusively resolve "claims of right separable from, and **collateral** to, rights asserted in the action." A collateral order appeal will be granted if it meets three conditions: (1) it conclusively determines the disputed question; (2) it resolves completely an important issue completely separate from the merits of the action; and (3) it would be effectively unreviewable on an appeal from a final judgment.

Justice Souter pointed out that orders rejecting absolute or qualified immunity of government officials are appealable under the collateral order doctrine, as our orders denying a state ELEVENTH AMENDMENT immunity. These are orders that deny "an asserted right to avoid the burdens of trial," and which cannot be reviewed effectively if the case proceeded to a conventional judgment. Justice Souter conceded that these examples "admittedly raise the lawyer's temptation to generalize" to a level where most orders would be immediately appealable, but it would leave the final order **statute** "in tatters." The proper way to look at the immunity exceptions was as the "avoidance of a trial that would imperil a substantial public interest," such as "honoring the separation of powers, [and] preserving the efficiency of government and the initiative of its officials."

The custom agents failed to show "such a weighty public objective" that would serve to invoke a collateral order appeal. The agents merely wanted to avoid "litigation for its own sake." The final decision requirement would "fade out whenever the government or an official lost an early round that could have stopped the fight." In addition, the agents could not have made their judgment bar claim if Susan Hallock had only filed the civil rights suit. This was different from an immunity claim, which can be invoked by a government official at the beginning of a lawsuit. Therefore, the appeal was dismissed. The agents could raise the judgment bar issue if they lost at the district court after a hearing on the merits by a judge or jury.

FIRST AMENDMENT

Beard v. Banks

In *Beard v. Banks*, No. 04–1739, 548 U.S. ___ (2006), the U.S. SUPREME COURT ruled that Pennsylvania prison officials did not violate FIRST AMENDMENT rights of a specific group of inmates by denying them access to newspapers and magazines. Although free speech and association issues under the U.S. Constitution were implicated, the Court held that state officials had shown legitimate reasons to justify the policy. The Court noted that, as mentioned in *Overton v. Bazzetta*, 539 U.S. 126, if faced with reviewing a *de facto* permanent ban involving a severe restriction on First Amendment rights, the Court might reach a different conclusion.

The Court's 6–2 majority opinion, delivered by Justice Breyer, reversed a ruling by the Third **Circuit Court** of Appeals. New Supreme Court Justice Samuel Alito, who had previously served on the Third Circuit **appellate court**, had written the lone dissent in the underlying opinion. Although his dissent was now validated by the Supreme Court decision, he had recused himself from participating in the high-court's decision. The high court's decision was based on a record consisting of a motion for **summary judgment**, rather than a trial verdict.

As background, the Pennsylvania state prison system houses its most dangerous inmates in a Long Term Segregation Unit (LTSU). At the time most relevant to this case, 40 inmates were housed there, divided into two groups. Inmates are first assigned to Level 2, which has the most severe restrictions; eventually, they may **advance** to the less restrictive Level 1, but their tenure in Level 2 is indefinite and premised on their behavior and attitude. All 40 inmates placed in the LTSU were deemed "incorrigible" and the most dangerous and recalcitrant.

Prisoners in the LTSU must remain in their cells 23 hours a day and are limited to one familial visit per month. They are prohibited from having televisions or radios, and, at issue here, are denied access to newspapers, magazines, and photographs.

Ronald Banks was one of the 40 prisoners confined to Level 2. On behalf of himself and other prisoners of the unit, Banks filed an action in federal **district court** against the Secretary of the Department of Corrections, alleging that the denial of access to magazines and newspapers violated the First Amendment to the U.S Constitution. During the discovery phase of the case, Banks took the deposition of the Deputy Prison Superintendent Dickson, and the parties introduced prison policy manuals and related documents into the record. Department of Corrections Secretary Beard then filed a motion for summary judgment, with a copy of the deposition and a statement of undisputed facts attached. Rather than filing a responsive brief or opposition to the motion, Banks, instead, filed his own cross-motion for summary judgment, relying on the same undisputed facts and deposition.

Pertinent to the outcome of this matter was a 1987 Supreme Court case, *Turner v. Safley*, 482 U.S. 78. In that case, the U.S. Supreme Court established a four-point test to determine whether prison regulations impermissibly violated constitutional rights, even though the Constitution sometimes permitted greater restrictions on such rights than that permitted elsewhere. Therefore, under *Turner*, restrictive prison regulations are permissible if they are "reasonably related to legitimate penological interests." 42 U.S. at 89. The remaining factors/considerations were whether alternative means of exercising that constitutional right remained open to prisoners; the impact that accommodating the asserted right would have on guards, other inmates, and prison resources; and, whether there were "ready alternatives" for furthering the government's interest. Importantly, the *Turner* Court also noted that deference must be accorded to prison authorities' views with respect to matters of professional judgment.

The Secretary's summary judgment motion created the record upon which the decisions of the district court, **appellate** court, and Supreme Court were based. For review of a motion for summary judgment, a Court examines the record to determine whether the moving party has demonstrated "the absence of a genuine issue of material fact," in which case, the moving party is entitled to summary judgment as a matter of law. If so, then the Court would determine whether Banks ("by affidavits or as otherwise provided") set forth specific facts showing a genuine issue for trial. Inferences about disputed facts would be drawn in Bank's favor, but deference would be accorded the views of prison authorities in matters of professional judgment.

For its part, the state prison justified the ban on newspapers and magazines as being for rehabilitative and security purposes. According to them, depriving inmates of these materials provided incentive for good behavior and transfer to Level 1, where such materials were permitted. For security purposes, it also eliminated the possibility that prisoners would use the materials to light cell fires, use the materials as weapons, or use as tools to fling feces at guards.

Using the test outlined in *Turner*, the district court adopted the decision of the **magistrate**, finding that prison officials had met the requisite standard, and ruling for summary judgment in their favor. Banks then appealed to the Third Circuit.

By a 2–1 vote, the Third Circuit reversed, noting that cutting prisoners off from news of the outside world only further undermined any genuine rehabilitation.

In June 2006, the U.S. Supreme Court again reversed, reinstating the original district court determination. Justice Breyer reasoned that the very first of the Secretary's justifications, i.e., the need to motivate better behavior on the part of particularly difficult and dangerous prisoners, sufficiently satisfied *Turner*'s requirements. According to him, the remaining factors added little to the first factor's logical rationale. But the important factor, noted the opinion, was not in balancing *Turner* factors, but rather, in determining whether the Secretary's supporting material for the summary judgment motion showed a reasonable, and not just logical, relation. The majority opinion found that the Third Circuit had placed too high an evidentiary burden on the Secretary, and afforded too little deference to the judgment of prison officials. Accordingly, because the challenged restrictions were placed only upon those prisoners with the most serious behavior problems, and only after prison authorities exercised their professional judgment in deeming such deprivation an effective tool, the state's burden was met.

Randall v. Sorrell

In three consolidated cases, captioned under *Randall v. Sorrell*, No. 04–1528, 548 U.S. ___(2006), the U.S. SUPREME COURT struck down several key provisions of Virginia's "Act 64," relating to mandatory limits on campaign expenditures and contributions. The Court essentially found expenditure limits too low, in that they impermissibly hindered the ability of candidates to raise money and speak to voters, and therefore, interfered with FIRST AMENDMENT rights. It also found some of the contribution limits as impermissible under the First Amendment, because of a disproportionate burden between protected interest and public purpose.

However, the very narrow decision was not easy to come by. Six separate opinions were filed (including two dissenting ones), and the 6–3 **plurality** opinion merely held that a state may not impose mandatory limitations on campaign expenditures under *Buckley v. Valeo*, 424 U.S. 1(1976). The Court did not categorically preclude the possibility that some form of mandatory spending limits might meet constitutional scrutiny. Moreover, the decision did not affect or preclude voluntary expenditure limitations contained in public finance systems. Finally, the plurality decision did not strike down limitations on campaign *contributions* as a general matter, but only limited the ruling to the Vermont law.

Prior to 1997, Vermont's campaign finance law did not impose limitations on expenditures, but did on contributions. In 1997, the state enacted a more stringent law, Pub. Act 64, codified as Vt. Stat. Ann., Tit. 17, §§2801 *et seq.* The new law imposed mandatory *expenditure* limits on the total amount a candidate for state office could spend during any two-year general election cycle, from $300,000 for governor, down to considerably smaller amounts for other offices. On the other end, mandatory *contribution* ceilings were as little as $200 per election cycle for state House races.

The new law was challenged by several individuals and groups, —primarily individuals running for state office, citizens who voted and contributed to campaigns, and political parties and committees. They filed suit against state officials tasked with enforcing the Act.

The **district court** found that Act 64's *expenditure* limits violated the First Amendment under *Buckley*. In that case, the U.S. Supreme Court had ruled that the government's stated interest (preventing corruption and the appearance of corruption) provided sufficient justification for limitations on *contributions* under the Federal Election Campaign Act of 1971, but the Act's limitation on campaign *expenditures* violated the First Amendment. Importantly, the Court explained the difference. Expenditure limits imposed significantly more severe restrictions on protected freedoms of political expression and association, than did contribution limits. Contribution limits were more generally "marginal restrictions" that nonetheless left a contributor free to discuss candidates and issues. Conversely, expenditure limitations directly restricted the amount of money a person or group could spend on political communication "by restricting the number of issues discussed, the depth of their exploration, and the size of the audience reached. . . ." (quoting *Buckley*, 424 US. at 20-21). The district court also found that Act 64's limitations on *contributions* from political parties was unconstitutional, but other contribution limits under the Act were constitutional.

The Second **Circuit Court** of Appeals found otherwise, holding that *all* of the Act's *contribution* limitations were constitutional, and that the *expenditure* limitations might also be constitutional because they were supported by compelling government interests. The **appellate court** remanded the matter to district court to determine whether the expenditure limits were narrowly tailored to those stated interests.

The U.S. Supreme Court reversed. It found that Vermont's *expenditure* limits violated the First Amendment under *Buckley*. Although state officials argued that Vermont's limitations should be distinguished (because *Buckley* did not consider that such limits might help to protect candidates from spending too much time raising money rather than devoting that time to campaigning), the majority found no significant basis for the distinction.

Regarding *contribution* limitations, the plurality opinion found that Vermont's low limit was excessively restrictive and also violated the First Amendment in its specific details. The effect was to burden protected interests in a manner disproportionate to the public purposes they were intended to **advance**, in other words, they were not narrowly tailored to suit the purpose. Moreover, it was virtually impossible to sever those impermissible ones from others in the Act without the Court having to rewrite the **statute** or leave gaping loopholes, which the Court will not do.

The plurality opinion cited five factors it found as indicative that Vermont's *contribution* limitations were not narrowly tailored: (1)the limits appeared to restrict the amount of money available to challengers to run competitive elections; (2)political parties were bound to the same low $200 to $400 contribution limit as individual contributors, thereby infringing on the right of association; (3) Act 64's treatment of volunteer services served to count a volunteer's expenses against the volunteer's contribution limit, disproportionately impinging on First Amendment rights of association; (4) the Act's limitations were not indexed for inflation; and (5)nowhere in the record was there an articulated justification for the low and restrictive limits.

The plurality opinion further explained that, while there was no magic number to precisely indicate an acceptable lower bound, the Court acknowledged that one does exist. Vermont's limitations were substantially lower than both the limits previously upheld by this Court, and also lower than comparable limits in other states.

Justices Thomas, Alito (in part), Kennedy, and Chief Justice Roberts concurred. Justices Thomas and Scalia wanted to overrule *Buckley*, saying that this case underscored the inability of the Court to apply it in any coherent and principled fashion. Justice Alito declined to reach the question of whether to overrule *Buckley*. Justices Souter and Ginsburg dissented; they would have followed the Second Circuit's approach and remanded for determination of whether sufficient reason existed to justify the limitations. Justice Stevens joined this dissent in part, but filed a separate dissent expressing his conviction that *Buckley* is wrong and it is time to overrule it.

Rumsfeld v. Forum for Academic and Institutional Rights, Inc.

Since 1993 the U.S. military has operated under a "Don't Ask, Don't Tell" policy concerning gays and lesbians serving in the armed services. This policy bars the military from asking members if they are homosexual. However, service members must be discharged if there is evidence of homosexual conduct or orientation. It has led to the discharge of thousands of service members over the years. As a result, many law schools imposed limited campus access to military recruiters who sought to interview potential military lawyers. Congress responded in turn by enacting a federal law known as the Solomon Amendment that withholds federal funds from colleges and universities that deny military recruiters the same access to students and campuses that they provide other employers. A group of law schools challenged the law on FIRST AMENDMENT grounds but the Supreme Court, in *Rumsfeld v. Forum for Academic and Institutional Rights, Inc.*, __U.S.__, 126 S.Ct. 1297, 164 L.Ed.2d 156 (2006), upheld its constitutionality.

In 1990, the American Association of Law Schools (AALS), which includes most U.S. law schools, amended its non-discrimination policy to bar employers from using their career placement facilities if they discriminated on the basis of sexual orientation. To implement this change, employers were required to sign a statement certifying compliance with the non-discrimination policy, which also barred discrimination on the basis of race or gender. The U.S. military refused to sign the compliance statements, contending that it conflicted with its "Don't ask, Don't tell" policy. Many law schools refused to allow recruiters to use their facilities to interview students for military lawyer positions. In 1994 Congress responded by passing the Solomon Amendment, named for Representative Gerald Solomon of New York. The amendment required that federal funding be withheld from any university that permitted its law school to deny military recruiters access to campus. Faced with the loss of federal funding, most law schools agreed to permit recruiters to talk with their students on campus, but they would not allow them to use the career services office. The military went along with this accommodation and the controversy disappeared.

The issue reappeared in 2002 when the Department of Defense demanded equal access to career placement services. An association of 30 law schools formed a group called the Forum for Academic and Institutional Rights (FAIR). This forum, which was concerned about the possible loss of federal funding, filed a lawsuit in 2003 that contended the Solomon Amendment violated the schools' First Amendment right of speech by forcing them to disseminate a viewpoint which they opposed. As the case proceeded in federal court, Congress amended the

Solomon Amendment in 2004 to make clear that the military must have equal access to career service facilities.

A federal **district court** denied FAIR's request for an injunction barring enforcement of the Solomon Amendment but in November 2004 the Third **Circuit Court** of Appeals overturned this decision. The appeals court concluded that the amendment imposed "unconstitutional conditions" on the law schools by threatening to withhold federal funds. Such conditions violated the schools' First Amendment rights. In addition, the right of "expressive association," which allows organizations and institutions to choose with whom they care to associate, gave the schools the right to bar military recruiters. The Department of Defense then appealed to the Supreme Court, which accepted review.

The Supreme Court, in an 8-0 vote, overturned the Third Circuit decision. Writing for the Court, Chief Justice John Roberts noted that although Congress has broad authority to pass laws governing military recruiting, it chose to give military recruiters campus access indirectly, using the Constitution's Spending Clause power. In other words, Congress could have passed a law that required equal access for military recruiters without tying it to funding. Despite Congress's indirect approach, the court still believed it must give deference to the legislative body in matters of military affairs. Therefore, placing a funding condition deserved as much respect as if Congress had "imposed a mandate on universities."

As to the legality of imposing funding conditions on the law schools, the Court pointed out that it found no First Amendment violation when a private college challenged a cut off of federal funds for gender discrimination under Title IX. There was no violation because the college was free to decline federal money if it wished to express its views on gender discrimination. As to the Third Circuit's belief that the Solomon Amendment imposed "unconstitutional conditions" on the law schools, Chief Justice Roberts found the conclusion misplaced. Such conditions did not apply because the condition in the present case could have been constitutionally imposed directly by Congress without any First Amendment considerations.

The Solomon Amendment did not limit the free speech rights of law schools. Law schools may express their views on the military's sexual orientation policies while continuing to receive federal aid. Viewed this way, the Solomon Amendment governed the conduct of the law schools, not speech. The law schools argued that they were compelled under the amendment to send e-mails and post announcement about military recruiting visits. Though the court agreed these aspects of compliance were subject to First Amendment scrutiny, it concluded that this compelled speech was "incidental" to the regulation of conduct. Sending an e-mail announcement was not equivalent to forcing a school child to recite the Pledge of Allegiance.

The law schools also claimed that if they allowed military recruiters equal access they would be sending a message that implied they endorsed the military's sexual orientation policies. The court rejected this argument as well, for nothing in the amendment forbid the law schools from criticizing the military policies. It was improbable that anyone would mistakenly believe the law schools endorsed these policies just because they were legally required to give equal access to military recruiters.

The Court also found no merit in the law schools' claim that the amendment violated the First Amendment's right to **freedom of association**. In a 2000 decision the court had recognized a First Amendment right of "expressive association" that allowed the Boy Scouts to exclude homosexuals. To allow a homosexual to become a scoutmaster would violate the right of the Boy Scouts to associate with whom they wished. The Solomon Amendment did not implicate a law school's associational rights because recruiters were not part of the law school; they were merely guests. The amendment did not force the law schools to accept members it did not desire, as in the Boy Scouts case. Instead, the schools merely had to grant military recruiters the same access they accorded civilian law firm recruiters. Therefore, the Solomon Amendment was constitutional and laws schools had to make a choice between equal access for military recruiters or the loss of federal aid.

FOURTH AMENDMENT

Brigham v. Utah

Over the years, the U.S. SUPREME COURT has rendered countless opinions addressing FOURTH AMENDMENT challenges to warrantless entries into private homes of citizens. It has carved out exceptions, clarified boundaries, defined terms, and justified circumstances. In *Brigham City, Utah v. Stuart* 547 U.S. ___, 126 S.Ct. 1943, ___ L.Ed.2d ___ (2006), the Court brought everyone back to the basics with respect to warrantless entries, and did so with an unanimous decision. It reminded courts that the Fourth Amendment has always accommodated entry into homes without a warrant when officers believe someone inside is seriously injured or imminently threatened with such an injury.

In the wee morning hours of July 23, 2000, Brigham City police received a call about a loud party at a private residence. When they arrived, they heard shouting inside, and also observed two juveniles drinking beer in the back yard. As police entered the yard, they could see through a screen door and window that an altercation was taking place inside the house's kitchen, where they observed four adults fighting with a juvenile. As the juvenile broke free from them, he struck one of the adults in the face, causing him to spit blood into the sink.

At that point, an officer opened the screen door and announced the presence of police. Amid the ongoing ruckus, his announcement was unheeded and apparently unnoticed. The officer then entered the kitchen and again cried out, after which time the fight eventually ceased. The officers then arrested the adults and charged them with contributing to the delinquency of a minor, **disorderly conduct**, and intoxication.

At the trial level, the defendants filed a motion to suppress all evidence obtained after the officers entered the house, arguing that the warrantless entry violated the Fourth Amendment.

The trial court granted their motion and the Utah Court of Appeals affirmed. The State Supreme Court also affirmed, but provided more detail in its ruling. It held that the injury caused by the juvenile's punch was insufficient to invoke the "emergency aid doctrine" (an exception to the requirement for a warrant to enter). The court found that the injury did not give rise to an objectionably reasonable belief that an unconscious, semiconscious, or missing person feared injured or dead was in the home. Second, the court found that the "exigent circumstances" exception also was likewise inapplicable, because the police needed **probable cause** *in addition* to a reasonable belief that the entry was necessary to prevent physical harm to the officers or other persons. (Notwithstanding, noted the court, under this exception, the injury need not be as serious as that required under the "emergency aid" exception.) The court acknowledged that this case involved a "close and difficult call."

The U.S. Supreme Court granted **certiorari**, noting differences among state courts and the courts of appeals "concerning the appropriate Fourth Amendment standard governing warrantless entry by law enforcement in an emergency situation."

In its ruling, the Court essentially revisited existing **case law** to delineate the parameters of the standard. For example, a basic principle of Fourth Amendment law is that searches and seizures inside a home without a warrant are presumptively unreasonable , *Groh v. Ramirez*, 540 U.S. 551, 124 S.Ct. 1284, 157 L.Ed.2d 1068 (2004). Notwithstanding, because the ultimate touchstone of the Fourth Amendment is "reasonableness," certain exceptions to the requirement for a warrant are acknowledged. *Flippo v. West Virginia*, 528 U.S. 11, 120 S.Ct. 7, 145 L.Ed.2d 16 (1999). The Court noted its decision in *Mincey v. Arizona*, 437 U.S. 385, 98 S.Ct. 2408, 57 L.Ed. 290 (1978), where it said, "[W]arrants are generally required to search a person's home or his person unless 'the exigencies of the situation' makes the needs of law enforcement so compelling that the warrantless search is objectively reasonable under the Fourth Amendment." The Court has repeatedly affirmed an *objective* standard for reasonableness, and repeatedly rejected (as in this case) the contention that, in assessing the reasonableness of an entry, consideration should be given to the subjective motivations of individual officers. Such subjective motivation is irrelevant.(See, e.g., *Bond v. United States*, 529 U.S. 334, 120 S.Ct. 1462, 146 L.Ed.2d 365 (2000).

Finally, the defendants had argued that, based on the Court's previous holding in *Welsh v. Wisconsin*, 466 U.S. 740, 104 S.Ct. 2091, 80 L.Ed.2d 732 (1984) "an important factor to be considered when determining whether any exigency exists is the gravity of the underlying offense for which the arrest is being made." However, the Court noted that such reliance was "misplaced." In *Welsh*, the only potential emergency was the need to preserve evidence of the suspect's blood alcohol level, an exigency that the Court held insufficient to justify a warrantless entry. But in the present case, the officers were confronted with ongoing violence inside the home, a situation hardly addressed in *Welsh*.

Therefore, in the present case, the Supreme Court held that the warrantless entry by officers was plainly reasonable under the circumstances. Given the state of ruckus inside the house, continued knocking at the door would have been futile. Once the announcement was made, the officers were free to enter. The role of a peace officer includes preventing violence and restoring order. Chief Justice Roberts, writing for the Court, noted, "Nothing in the Fourth Amendment required them to wait until another blow rendered someone 'unconscious' or 'semi-conscious' (quoting from the underlying opinion of the Utah Supreme Court) or worse before entering."

Georgia v. Randolph

The FOURTH AMENDMENT places restrictions on the police to conduct searches without a warrant. The Supreme Court, in *Georgia v. Randolph*, __U.S.__, 126 S.Ct. 1515, 164 L.Ed.2d 208 (2006), placed an additional restriction on searching a home. If two occupants are present at the time of the request to search the home and one occupant consent and the other objects, the police may not search the home.

In May 2001, Janet Randolph moved out of the house she shared with her son and husband Scott Randolph in Americus, Georgia. In July she moved back into the house but problems ensued. She called police on July 6 to say she and her husband had quarreled and that he had taken their son away. When police arrived Janet told them that Scott had been using cocaine and that his drug problem had caused financial difficulties. Scott returned during this interview and told the officers his son was at a neighbor's house. He denied he had a drug problem and said that Janet abused alcohol and drugs. Janet told the police that they would find evidence of drugs in the house. Police asked Scott permission to search the house, which he refused. However, Janet readily agreed to the search. She led police to Scott's bedroom where an officer found a drinking straw with a powdery residue that he suspected to be cocaine. The police took the evidence and then secured a search warrant. A later search turned up more evidence of drug use. Based on this evidence Scott Randolph was indicted for cocaine possession.

Scott Randolph asked the trial court to suppress the drug evidence found during the initial warrantless search, contending that the search was unauthorized. The trial court denied the motion, concluding that Janet Randolph's consent to search was sufficient to meet Fourth Amendment concerns. However, the Georgia Supreme Court agreed with Scott that the consent to search by Janet was not valid in the face of Scott's presence in the home and his refusal to grant consent.

The Georgia Supreme Court's ruling appeared to conflict with a 1984 U.S. SUPREME COURT decision, *U.S. v. Matlock* 415 U.S.164, 94 S.Ct. 988, 39 L.Ed.2d 242 (1984). In that case one occupant of a house consented to a warrantless search while the co-occupant was detained in a squad car parked nearby. The co-occupant later objected to the search but the Supreme Court ruled that the consent of a person who possesses common authority over a premises is valid as against the absent, nonconsenting person. The Georgia Supreme Court found *Matlock* inapplicable because the ruling dealt with an absent occupant. In this case Scott Randolph was present. The U.S. Supreme Court agreed to hear the state of Georgia's appeal to resolve the question of consent when a co-occupant is present and objects to a warrantless search.

The Supreme Court, in a 5–3 decision, upheld the state supreme court ruling. Justice DAVID SOUTER, writing for the majority, looked to the way a court must assess reasonableness in Fourth Amendment consent to search cases. The examination of reasonableness was shaped by "widely shared social expectations" about privacy. An occupant who was not present when police asked a co-occupant to search the premises did not have an expectation that the co-occupant must bar police. In that circumstance the absent occupant assumed a risk that the house might be searched based solely on the consent of another occupant. Such was the situation in *Matlock*. The court also left intact a 1990 decision, *Illinois v. Rodriquez*, 497 U.S.177, 110 S.Ct. 2793, 111 L.Ed.2d 148 (1990), which allowed a search with consent of one occupant while the person who would later object was asleep in the apartment. Justice Souter found that the separation of the sleeping occupant from the initial encounter with police was a crucial element.

The Court, having distinguished *Matlock* and *Rodriquez* examined the situation where two occupants were present and one objected to the search. The social expectations were much different-generally no "sensible person" would enter a shared premises where one occupant issues an invitation and the other occupants says to stay out unless there was a good reason. This is because when people who live together disagree over the use of their home a resolution of the issue must come through "voluntary accommodation" and not by appeals to authority. Therefore, a co-occupant has no authority in law or social practice to prevail over a present and objecting co-occupant on allowing someone to enter the premises. This conclusion held, whether a private citizen or a police officer was at the door. Justice Souter noted the long national tradition that regarded a man's home as his castle. Disputed permission to enter a home was "no match for this central value of the Fourth Amendment."

The Court admitted it was drawing a fine line between situations where objecting co-occupants were present and situations where they were absent to determine the constitutionality of a warrantless search. Justice Souter believed this distinction would make it easier to enforce in practice. Moreover, the court made clear that police may not remove a potentially objecting tenant from the home so as to make the search with the other occupant's consent.

Chief Justice John Roberts, in a dissenting opinion, contended that the majority's reasoning provided protection on a random and happenstance basis. The ruling protected an objecting co-occupant who happened to be at the front door when the police arrived but not a person who was asleep or watching television in another room. He believed that the ruling would hurt abused spouses who seek police entry into a home that they share with non-consenting abusers. As to differing social expectations, Roberts thought that the majority's basic assumption—that an invited guest encountering disagreeing co-occupants would leave—was no more than a hunch on how people would "typically act in an atypical situation." He argued that someone who chooses to share space with someone has agreed to share privacy and must assume the risk.

U.S. v. Grubbs

The FOURTH AMENDMENT requires law enforcement officials to obtain a search warrant from a judge that is based on **probable cause**. In addition, the amendment requires that the warrant include language "particularly describing the place to be searched, and the persons or things to be seized." In some situations the police will obtain an "anticipatory" search warrant, one which is based on a sworn affidavit that shows probable cause that at some future time certain evidence will be located at a particular place. The Supreme Court, in *U.S. v. Grubbs*, __U.S.__, 126 S.Ct. 1494, __L.Ed.2d __ (2006), upheld a constitutional challenge to anticipatory warrants and sustained a warrant that failed to include the supporting affidavit.

Jeffrey Grubbs, a California resident, purchased a videotape containing child pornography from an Internet web site in 2002. The site was operated by an undercover federal postal inspector. The Postal Inspection Service set up a controlled delivery of the videotape to Grubb's home and submitted a search warrant application to a federal **magistrate** judge. In the supporting affidavit, a postal inspector stated that the search warrant would not be executed until a person in the residence took delivery of the tape. At that time postal inspectors would execute the warrant and search for the tape and other child pornography. The affidavit also referred to two attachments, which described Grubbs' residence and the items the officers would seize. The magistrate judge issued this anticipatory warrant and the postal inspectors set their plan in motion. Two days later the package was delivered to the residence and Grubbs' wife signed for it and took it inside the home. When Grubbs left the home a few minutes afterwards, the inspectors detained him and searched the home. The inspectors did not give Grubbs a copy of the warrant for 30 minutes, which contained the two attachments but not the supporting affidavit. Grubbs agreed to be interrogated and admitted to ordering the tape. He was indicted on one count of receiving child pornography and pled guilty after his motion to suppress the evidence found in the search was denied. He contended that the warrant was defective because the affidavit, which described the triggering condition for the search (the delivery of the tape), was not attached to the warrant. Though he pled guilty, he reserved his right to appeal the denial of his motion.

The Ninth **Circuit Court** of Appeals sided with Grubbs, ruling that the anticipatory warrant was invalid because it did not meet the Fourth Amendment's particularity requirement. The warrant did not state the triggering condition for its execution nor was the affidavit that contained this information presented to Grubbs at the time of the search. Because the postal inspectors failed to present this affidavit to Grubbs or his wife, the warrant was invalid and the search was illegal. The government appealed to the Supreme Court, challenging the appeals court's reasoning.

The Court, in an 8–0 decision (newly confirmed Justice SAMUEL ALITO did not participate in the consideration of the case), reversed the Ninth Circuit ruling. Justice ANTONIN SCALIA, writing for the Court, first examined Grubbs' contention that anticipatory warrants were categorically unconstitutional. Scalia noted that an anticipatory warrant's execution is subject "to some condition precedent other than the mere passage of time—a so-called 'triggering condition.'" By definition the triggering condition that established probable cause "has not been satisfied when the warrant is issued." Grubbs argued that because there is no current probable cause when the warrant is issued, the warrant must be constitutionally defective. Justice Scalia rejected this reasoning because all search warrants were in sense anticipatory because the probable cause requirement "amounts to a prediction that the item will still be there when the warrant is executed." Therefore, anticipatory and regular warrants both require a magistrate or judge to determine that it is now probable that evidence of a crime will be on the described premises when the warrant is executed. The law enforcement official must convince the magistrate that the triggering condition will occur and that if it does, evidence of the crime will be found on the premises. In Grubbs' case the triggering condition was the delivery of the tape to his residence. It was sufficient to meet the probable cause requirement. The affidavit supported the belief that this triggering condition would occur.

Justice Scalia then turned to the Ninth Circuit's conclusion that the warrant failed to describe the triggering condition because of the missing affidavit. He dismissed the idea that the Fourth Amendment contained a general particularity requirement. The amendment only required that a warrant describe the place to be searched and the persons or things to be seized. There was no good reason for the Court to expand the scope of this provision by requiring the inclusion of the conditions precedent to the execution of the warrant. In addition, Scalia emphasized that the magistrate judge was not required to set out her basis for finding probable cause nor a description of a triggering condition. The Ninth Circuit also had found that the warrant needed to be more particular about the triggering condition so the property owner could effectively police the officer's conduct. Scalia rejected this claim as well, concluding that an executing officer does not have to give the property owner a copy of the warrant prior to beginning the search. The Fourth Amendment protected property owners by having a magistrate judge consider the strength of a warrant applications and by permitting the owner to seek suppression of the evidence that was improperly obtained. Therefore, the warrant was valid and the evidence could be used to prosecute Grubbs.

Justice DAVID SOUTER, in a concurring opinion joined by Justices JOHN PAUL STEVENS and RUTH BADER GINSBURG, agreed that anticipatory warrants were constitutional but cautioned the government to "beware of banking on the terms of a warrant without" the triggering condition to be sustained in all situations.

Hudson v. Michigan

The U.S. SUPREME COURT has imposed the **exclusionary rule** on evidence seized by state or federal law enforcement officers in violation of the FOURTH AMENDMENT. This remedy has prevented prosecutors from using valuable evidence in criminal prosecutions, yet the Court concluded a strict rule was needed to deter police from Fourth Amendment violations. This seemingly settled part of Fourth Amendment law was put into question by the Court in *Hudson v. Michigan*, __U.S.__, 126 S.Ct., __L.Ed.2d __ 2006 WL 1640577 (2006). The Court ruled that the exclusionary rule did not apply when police officers enter a home to execute a search warrant without following the "knock-and-announce" rule. This rule, which reaches back to medieval England, requires police to announce themselves and give the resident an opportunity to open the door. The 5–4 majority reasoned that the exclusionary rule did serve the purposes behind the knock and announce rule and that persons who alleged a Fourth Amendment violation could sue the police officers for damages under a federal civil rights law.

Detroit police obtained a warrant to search the home of Booker T. Hudson Jr. for illegal drugs and firearms. When the police arrived at his house they announced their presence but waited only three to five seconds before turning the knob of the unlocked door and entering his home. They soon discovered large quantities of drugs and a loaded gun. Hudson was charged with unlawful drug and firearm possession under Michigan law but he contested the constitutionality of the search, arguing that police had failed to knock on his front door and had entered his home precipitously. Though the Detroit police department admitted the officers had not waited long enough before entering the home, the state argued that the evidence should not be suppressed. The trial court granted Hudson's suppression motion but the Michigan Court of Appeals reversed, relying on Michigan Supreme Court cases that found suppression inappropriate in knock and announce cases. Hudson was then convicted of drug possession. He appealed, renewing his Fourth Amendment claim, but the appeals court and the state supreme court upheld the conviction. He then appealed to the U.S. Supreme Court.

The Court, in a 5–4 vote, upheld the Michigan decision. Justice ANTONIN SCALIA, writing for the majority, agreed that the knock-and-announce rule was a longstanding rule that deserved respect. However, he pointed out that the Court had carved out exceptions when police felt the threat of physical violence was real, if they believed that evidence would be destroyed if **advance** notice was given, or if they believed giving notice was futile. The difficulty in knock and announce cases was determining a reasonable waiting time on a case-by-case basis. In this case the police admitted they did not wait long enough, so the only question was the proper remedy for the violation.

Justice Scalia reasoned that the exclusionary rule was properly applied to warrantless searches that failed to protect the interests of the Fourth Amendment. The interests protected by the knock and announce requirement were "quite different and do not include the shielding of potential evidence from the government's eyes." The interests protected by knock and announce included the protection of human life and limb because an "unannounced entry may provoke violence in supposed self-defense by the surprised resident." The rule also gives individuals the chance to avoid the destruction of property that can occur with forcible and the opportunity to protect their privacy and dignity by assuring them "the opportunity to collect oneself before answering the door." The rule did not, however, protect a person's interest in preventing the government from seizing to taking evidence described in a warrant. Scalia concluded that the three interests behind the knock-and-announce rule had "nothing to do with the seizure of the evidence;" therefore, the exclusionary rule did not apply.

The Court also found that the social costs of applying the exclusionary rule in this case were "considerable." Allowing dangerous criminals to go free was one cost but another was the prospect of many criminal defendants claiming a knock and announce violation in hopes of suppressing incriminating evidence. Scalia stated that the "cost of entering this lottery would be small, but the jackpot enormous: suppression of all evidence, amounting in many cases to a get-out-of-jail-free card." He also was concerned that police officers would wait longer than the law required, leading to preventable attacks on officers and the destruction of evidence.

Justice Scalia told Hudson and others who have suffered a knock-and-announce violation that they could sue the police for damages under federal civil rights laws as a means of deterrence. In addition, he claimed that the quality of law enforcement had improved considerably in the 50 years since the application of the exclusionary rule to state violations of the Fourth Amendment. Police departments were now staffed with professionally trained officers who could held accountable through internal discipline processes and citizen review boards. There was no need in knock-and-announce violations to use the "massive remedy of suppressing evidence of guilt."

Justice ANTHONY KENNEDY concurred in the decision but filed a separate opinion in which he claimed the exclusionary rule was "not in doubt" and that the decision was limited to knock-and-announce cases. Justice STEPHEN BREYER, in a dissenting opinion joined by Justices JOHN PAUL STEVENS, DAVID SOUTER, and RUTH BADER GINSBURG, was not as sanguine as Justice Kennedy. Breyer was troubled by the Court's departure from its prior rulings and he feared that the decision "weakens, perhaps destroys, much of the practical value of the Constitution's knock-and-announce protection." He feared that the majority's argument was "an argument against the Fourth Amendment's exclusionary principle itself." Civil lawsuits were not a viable remedy for these violations. In addition, there were many cases throughout the country that showed police departments were violating the knock-and-announce requirement. Without the application of the exclusionary rule, law enforcement officers had little to worry about if they entered a home without giving notice.

FRAUD

A false representation of a matter of fact—whether by words or by conduct, by false or misleading allegations, or by concealment of what should have been disclosed—that deceives and is intended to deceive another so that the individual will act upon it to her or his legal injury.

Bank of China v. NBM

To establish a **common law** action for **fraud**, a plaintiff must prove, among other things, the ELEMENT of reasonable reliance by the injured party on the **fraudulent** statement or act, to his detriment. In *Bank of China v. NBM, et al.*, No. 03–1559, the U.S. SUPREME COURT initially granted **certiorari** limited to the following question: "Did the Court of Appeals for the Second Circuit err when it held that civil RICO plaintiffs alleging mail and wire fraud as predicate acts must establish 'reasonable reliance' under 18 U.S.C. §1964(c)?" However, before the case was argued, the Supreme Court dismissed the case without comment under Supreme Court Rule 46 (which generally covers party-initiated dismissals).

The dismissal resulted in the underlying (appealed) decision of the Second **Circuit Court** of Appeals being held as the **final decision** in the matter (359 F.3d 171 [2004]). However, holdings of the First, Third, Seventh, and Ninth Circuits have held to the contrary, making it likely that this issue may again come before the high court in another case.

In the underlying case, the Bank of China (Bank) filed charges in federal **district court** against numerous defendants, including John Chou and Sherry Liu, a married couple. According to the lawsuit, starting in 1991, Chou and Liu began an elaborate money-transferring scheme to defraud the Bank. Specifically, the suit alleged that the couple defaulted on loans (secured through misrepresentations and forged documents), converted borrowed funds into different currencies, then transferred them to other accounts (represented by Chou and Liu as independent third-party businesses, but in fact, alleged alter-egos and/or businesses controlled by Chou and Liu). The suit further alleged that Chou and Liu, by falsely representing the borrowed funds as "trade debts," falsely created the appearance that the third-party businesses (including defendant NBM, LLC) were thriving and had cash flows able to sustain the borrowing limits set by the Bank. The borrowed funds were also disguised as **collateral** for further loans. The suit claimed that additional funds were drawn against letters of credit secured through the presentation of false and forged documents for non-existent transactions. By the time of the scheme's collapse in 2000, the Bank estimated that it had more than $85 million in outstanding loans to defendants Chou and Liu and the businesses they controlled. The Bank ultimately recovered approximately $50 million in collateral, but was left with losses exceeding $34 million.

Finally, the Bank claimed that the defendants were able to succeed with their fraud by bribing a former bank deputy manager, Patrick Young, who was allegedly paid $120,000 to make false representations and submit false representations to Bank management. Young was separately convicted and served ten months in prison. (Chou and Liu were also independently prosecuted and convicted; both were sentenced to terms in prison.)

In conjunction with the district court civil trial, a jury returned a verdict finding that all defendants had been unjustly enriched at the Bank's expense; that they had committed fraud, breached loan contracts, and violated §§1962(c) and 1962(d) of the federal Racketeer Influenced and Corrupt Organizations Act (RICO). The court entered judgment in the amount of $106 million, constituting $35.4 million in **compensatory damages**, trebled (**punitive damages**) under RICO §1962(d). Defendants (excepting Young, the deputy bank manager) appealed.

On appeal, defendants argued that the jury instructions were erroneous. Specifically, at trial, defendants requested that the court charge the jury that "if senior Bank management knew of defendants' activities, that knowledge must be **imputed** to the Bank." (This would prove advantageous to defendants, as the Bank could not allege that it innocently relied on the fraudulent misrepresentations, because the Bank was imputedly aware of their falsehood.) But the trial court rejected this request, and instead instructed jurors in the context of common-law bank fraud, i.e., "I instruct you that an institution may be defrauded, even if its agents and employees permitted or participated in the fraud." In other words, the trial court told jurors that the Bank may have been defrauded even if high-ranking bank officers, such as Patrick Young, knew of the true nature of the transactions in question.

On appeal, defendants argued that this erroneous charge removed the Bank's need to prove that it had reasonably relied upon the misrepresentations, to its detriment. This essentially stripped defendants of their argument, at trial, that "the actions complained of were sanctioned and authorized by the Bank's officers, and that therefore the Bank could not have detrimentally relied on any of the defendant's [sic] representations."

In February 2004, the Second Circuit Court of Appeals unanimously agreed, vacating the lower court's judgment and remanding the case for a new trial; in light of the erroneous jury instruction and the award of treble damages under RICO, the court could not find the error harmless. The court noted that, to prevail in a RICO claim, a plaintiff must show that the alleged violation was the **proximate cause** of the injury. Therefore, in a RICO claim alleging predicate acts of mail, wire, and bank fraud (as in this case), a plaintiff must prove reliance upon the misrepresentations, and the reliance must be reasonable.

Finally, the court noted a narrow exception known as the "adverse interest exception." This

Michael Mastromarino (l), taken from court after arraignment on charges of forgery and theft in the Ney York City body parts scandal.
ARISTIDE ECONOMOPOULOS/ STAR LEDGER/CORBIS

might apply where an agent (e.g., Young) has totally abandoned his principal's (e.g., the Bank) interests. This would be an issue of material fact to be determined by the jury at retrial, and it would have been an appropriate instruction to give in conjunction with a "reasonable reliance" instruction for both common law fraud and civil RICO claims.

Illegal Harvesting of Body Parts Results in Fraud Cases

A November 2004 investigation into missing funeral prepayments led Brooklyn detective Patricia O'Brien to uncover a case of illegal human-tissue harvesting, potentially contaminated transplants, and fraud by former dental surgeon Michael Mastromarino and funeral-home owner Joseph Nicelli. O'Brien, with the help of Sergeant Timothy Breene and Detective Paul Courtney of the NYPD Major Case Squad, found evidence linking Mastromarino and Nicelli to more than 1,000 decedents whose tissue—skin, bones, tendons, ligaments, and heart valves—were allegedly harvested without their permission or the permission of their families. Many of those so harvested had died in old age or of diseases that made the tissue unusable to transplant patients. Forged consent papers, as well as altered death certificates, made the scheme appear legitimate.

Nicelli sold his Daniel George & Sons funeral home in Brooklyn to Robert Nelms and Debora Johnson, who called in Detective O'Brien about the missing funds. On a visit to the funeral home, O'Brien discovered a pristine operating room on the second floor, along with Federal Express labels listing the names of transplant companies. It also became evident that Nicelli had kept four keys to the property and was using the surgery after hours.

Mastromarino, whose drug abuse lost him his medical license in 2000, had previously partnered with Nicelli in a company called Bio Tissue Technologies of Brooklyn, a clearinghouse for transplant and research tissue. Mastromarino also owns Biomedical Tissue Services, Ltd., out of Fort Lee, New Jersey. Both companies allegedly facilitated the distribution of the tissue and were included in the investigation. The case became public in October 2005, at which time the FOOD AND DRUG ADMINISTRATION recalled transplant tissue that could be traced to customers of either biomedical firm. The recall reached to Florida, Georgia, Texas, and even Canada. Health officials asked hospitals that had already used the tissue to inform patients that they may be at risk for disease transmission, since the tissue was collected arbitrarily without consideration of the decedent's age or cause of death. Although transplant tissue is regularly sterilized prior to use and blood samples are supposed to accompany the tissue, the chance still existed for a patient to contract such illnesses as HIV, hepatitis, and syphilis, since it was impossible to know if the data sent with the tissue was legitimate. Officials said there is no way to tell how many transplant patients will ultimately be affected by the suspect tissue. Some patients wasted no time getting involved, and several class-action lawsuits have already resulted. The scandal has affected other related industries. Lifecell, Inc., a client of Biomedical Tissue Services, recalled three products made from body parts.

The FDA shut down Biomedical Tissue Services on February 3, 2006, for failing to screen the tissue for contamination. The investigation allegedly found death certificates in the company's files that were incongruous with those on record with the state as to the deceased's age, and time and cause of death.

On February 23, 2006, Mastromarino, Nicelli, Lee Crucetta, and Christopher Aldorasi were arraigned for defiling and selling human remains. Crucetta, a nurse, and Aldorasi are suspected assistants in the scheme. The four, who pleaded not guilty, were charged with 122 counts, including enterprise corruption, body stealing, opening graves, unlawful dissection, and forgery. Brooklyn District Attorney Charles J. Hynes told reporters at a press conference that, from 2001 to 2005, Nicelli allegedly received bodies from area funeral homes for embalming and then allowed Mastromarino and his assistants to harvest bones and tissue before preparing the bodies. Bones were sometimes replaced with PVC pipe to maintain the body's form. Most of the bodies Mastromarino allegedly dismembered were slated for cremation, a process that makes it difficult if not impossible to gather DNA evidence. Five funeral homes in New York City; eight in Rochester, New York; one in Philadelphia; and three in New Jersey were cited by New York City Police Commissioner Raymond Kelly as central players in the scheme, although as many as 40 funeral homes have been implicated. How much the employees of the homes knew is in question.

The investigation revealed that Nicelli received as much as $1000 for each body he delivered to the dissection surgery, while Mastromarino could make $7000 from the sale of tissue from each body. The indictment alleges that the defendants forged birth certificates to disguise the ages of the deceased, altered death certificates to change the cause of death to something acceptable for tissue harvest, and forged permission forms for the procedures, sometimes even resorting to the names of long-dead relatives for the documentation.

The lawyers for the accused maintain that their clients have done nothing illegal, denying the forgery and other claims. It is their intention to claim innocence to all charges in the indictment.

Current state and federal regulations focus more on the dissemination of transplant organs than on bodies donated for research uses. Under the National Organ Transplant Act of 1984, Congress established the Organ Procurement and Transplantation Network, which is overseen by the United Network for Organ Sharing. Only private, non-profit organizations with federal contracts can legally operate the network, which dictates the strictures for harvesting, transporting, and tracking organs for transplant. Transplant surgeons use harvested tissue to replace spinal disks, perform knee surgery, or make dental implants. Tissue banks not providing material for transplant are not required to register with any government agency. The sale of human tissue is illegal in the U.S., but agencies are allowed to set their own fees for handling various body parts for transplant.

The furor over the case has already brought about movement for changes to the laws affecting funeral homes and the disposition of human remains. Assemblywoman Valerie Vainieri Huttle (D-Englewood) and Dr. Herb Conaway (D-Burlington County) sponsored a bill to make it a first-degree crime to harvest body parts illegally. Offenders could face prison time and up to $200,000 in penalties. Forgery of consent forms or otherwise manipulating donor paperwork is a third-degree crime under the bill, as is selling a body part, although legitimate firms are still able to charge for their services.

FREEDOM OF RELIGION

Gonzales v. O Centro Espirita Beneficente Uniao Do Vegetal

Congress enacted the Religious Freedom Restoration Act of 1993 (RFRA), 42 U.S.C.A. § 2000bb *et seq.*, to reverse a 1990 Supreme Court ruling. The RFRA states that the federal government may not substantially burden a person's exercise of religion "even if the burden results from a rule of general applicability." The act grants an exception if the government can prove the burden is justified by a compelling government interest and is the least restrictive means of furthering the compelling interest. The Supreme Court, in *Gonzales v. O Centro Espirita Beneficente Uniao Do Vegetal*, __U.S.__, 126 S.Ct. 1211, 163 L.Ed.2d 1017 (2006), ruled that the federal government had failed to show a compelling interest in forbidding a small American branch of a Brazilian Christian Spiritist sect from using a sacramental tea that contained an illegal hallucinogen. In so ruling, the Court made clear that the mere invocation of the Controlled Substances Act, 21 U.S.C.A. § 801 *et seq.*, was not sufficient to prove a compelling government interest under the RFRA.

The O Centro Espirita Beneficente Uniao Do Vegetal (UDV) has approximately 130 members in the United States. Members receive communion through a sacramental tea called "hoasca," which is made from two plants found only in the Amazon region. One of the plants contains the hallucinogen dimethyltryptamine (DMT). When mixed with the other plant the hallucinogenic effect of the DMT is enhanced. Under the Controlled Substances Act DMT is a Schedule I substance that is illegal to possess and use. In 1999 U.S. Customs Service inspectors intercepted a shipment of hoasca and tracked down additional supplies at the home of a UDV member in Santa Fe, Mexico. Although no arrests were made, the church filed a federal lawsuit seeking an injunction that would permit the continued importation and sacramental use of the tea. The church alleged that applying the Controlled Substances Act to its religious use of tea violated the RFRA. At a hearing on the

Jeffrey Bronfman, president of the U.S. chapter of Espirita Beneficente Uniao Do Vegetal, speaks outside the U.S. SUPREME COURT, November 2005.
AP IMAGES

preliminary injunction the federal government admitted using the Controlled Substances would substantially burden the expression of the UDV faith. However, the government argued that this was permissible under the exception to the RFRA: the government had a compelling interest to protect the health and safety of UDV members, to keep the tea out of the hands of non-UDV members, and to comply with the 1971 UNITED NATIONS Convention on Psychotropic Substances, a treaty the U.S. signed in 1971.

The **district court** heard evidence on the safety and health risks of hoasca consumption from both sides and on the possible market for hoasca by persons who were not members of the church. The court concluded that the evidence on health risks and the diversion of the tea was "virtually balanced." In the face of this even showing the court concluded that the government had failed to prove that it had a compelling interest to place a substantial burden on the UDV's religious exercise. The granted the UDV a preliminary injunction that allowed the church to import the tea subject to federal permits and to limit access to church members. The Tenth **Circuit Court** of Appeals upheld the preliminary injunction.

The Supreme Court, in an 8-0 decision (newly confirmed Justice Samuel Alito did not participate in the consideration of the case), upheld the lower court decisions. Chief Justice John Roberts, writing for the Court, noted that the government did not challenge the district court's finding that the evidence was evenly balanced. Instead, the government argued that the evenly-balanced evidence was insufficient to justify a preliminary injunction against the enforcement of the Controlled Substances Act. Roberts disagreed, finding that the RFRA placed the burden on the government to show a compelling interest once the UDV established that it would be substantially burdened by the government's proposed action. The burden remained on the government whether at the preliminary injunction stage or at trial.

The government also contended that the description of Schedule I substances as a class in the Controlled Substances Act demonstrated that there could not be individualized exceptions like the one sought by the UDV. The prohibition on these substances was part of a comprehensive system that could not be sustained if courts handed out exemptions. The public would misread an exemption as meaning the substances was not harmful. Thus, the continued effectiveness of the Controlled Substances Act by itself justified the government's prohibition on the sacramental tea. Roberts rejected this line of argument, relying on the language of the RFRA that mandates that the compelling interest test must be satisfied through application of the challenged law :to the person." This meant that the "mere invocation of the general characteristics of Schedule I substances, as set forth in the Controlled Substances Act, cannot carry the day." Moreover, an exception had been made to the Schedule I ban for religious use, allowing the use of peyote by the Native American Church. This exemption, which goes back to the early 1970s, was extended in 1994 by Congress to all members of recognized Indian Tribes. Roberts stated that every risk and concern cited by the government against hoasca also applied to peyote, yet a religious exception had been made for peyote. It made no sense to worry about an exception for 130 hoasca users when "hundreds of thousands of Native Americans practicing their faith" had used peyote for many years.

Chief Justice Roberts rebuffed a third government argument that was based on "slippery-slope concerns" about opening the door for more religiously-based exceptions. He was unsympathetic, calling it the "classic **rejoinder** of bureaucrats throughout history: If I make an exception for you, I'll have to make one for everybody, so no exceptions." The RFRA required that exceptions be considered when a law substantially burdens a person's practice of religion.

FREEDOM OF SPEECH

Federal Courts Strike Down Video Game Laws

Federal district courts in three states during 2005 and 2006 struck down laws that prohibit the sale of violent or sexually explicit video games. These statutes were enacted to protect minors from possible dangers associated with playing these types of games. However, the **federal courts** that have reviewed these statutes found that none of them could survive scrutiny under the FIRST AMENDMENT's Free Speech Clause.

As video game technology has improved, the graphics in these video games has become increasingly more realistic. Several games allow users to simulate violent situations, such as gang wars and the like, and these games rely on graphic violence to entertain users. The popularity of these games has created a multi-billion dollar video game industry that markets its products to children and teenagers.

In addition to violence, these games have become more sexually explicit as well. One of the most popular video game series, entitled "Grand Theft Auto" (produced by Take Two Interactive), allows users to collect weapons, steal cars and money, kill victims, and the like. In 2005, a user modification to the most recent game in the series, "Grand Theft Auto: San Andreas," allowed PC users to access an explicit sex scene. The revelation of this hidden sex scene led the Electronic Software Ratings Board (ESRB) to change the game's rating from M (equivalent to an "R" movie rating) to AO (equivalent to NC-17). Several retailers, including Wal-Mart and Target, announced that they would pull the game off of the shelves.

Despite the presence of the ratings system, which is designed to warn parents of the contents of a game, even the violent and sexually explicit games are readily available in most instances to minors. Those who are opposed to the sale of these types of video games to minors point to studies tending to show that the exposure to violent video games can affect a user's behavior. These advocates also pushed for the approval of statutes that would limit sale of some of these games to minors.

Illinois Governor Rod Blagojevich has been one of the leading critics of the video games industry. He initially proposed to ban video game sales after hearing about the release of the game "JFK Reloaded," which allows users to simulate the assassination of President JOHN F. KENNEDY. In March 2005, he criticized the release of the game "NARC," which focuses on illegal drug use. At the time that Blagojevich made his statement, the Illinois General Assembly was considering proposed legislation that would create two criminal statutes, including the Violent Video Games Law (VVGL) and the Sexually Explicit Video Games Law (SEVGL). The General Assembly approved the laws on July 25, making Illinois the first state to enact such as **statute**.

Illinois Governor Rod Blagojevich speaks in his office, January 2005.
AP IMAGES

On the day that the statute was signed, several video industry trade associations brought a lawsuit in the U.S. **District Court** for the Northern District of Illinois. *Entertainment Software Association v. Blagojevich*, 404 F. Supp. 2d 1051 (N.D. Ill. 2005). These plaintiffs sought an INJUNCTION that would bar the application of the new statute. The plaintiffs' primary argument was that the statutes violated their rights to freedom of expression.

The court held a two-day hearing to investigate the effect that video games have on young people. One aspect of the hearing focused on whether playing video games increased aggressive thoughts and behavior. The second aspect focused on whether minors who play video games experience a decline in activity in the area of the brain controlling behavior. Neither study resulted in clear conclusions.

The court reviewed the plaintiff's First Amendment claims and found that neither the VVGL nor the SEVGL were narrowly tailored to serve a compelling governmental interest. Moreover, the court determined that the definitions of "violent video games" and "sexually explicit" contained in the statutes were unconstitutionally vague. Accordingly, the court permanently enjoined the enforcement of the statute on December 2, 2005.

California followed Illinois' lead by enacting a statute on October 7, 2005 that prohibited the sale of certain violent video games to minors. The Video Software Dealers Association and the Entertainment Software Association sued Governor Arnold Schwarzenegger and other officials, seeking to bar the enforcement of the statute. The statute in question provided several definitions related to the meaning of "violent video game," including definitions of the terms "cruel," "depraved," "heinous," "serious physical abuse," and "torture."

Unlike the Illinois court, the U.S. District Court for the Northern District of California did not believe that the California statute was unconstitutionally vague. However, the court concluded that the plaintiffs likely could prove that the statute's restriction on the sale of the games to minors as well as a labeling requirement in the statute violated the plaintiffs' First Amendment rights. The court thus granted the injunction on December 21. *Video Software Dealers Ass'n v. Schwarzenegger*, 401 F. Supp. 2d 1034 (N.D. Cal. 2005).

The third challenge to these video game laws took place in Michigan, which in September 2005 enacted a law regulating the distribution of both sexually explicit video games and "ultra violent" video games to minors. Under the statute, an "ultra violent" game is one that "continually and repetitively depicts extreme and loathsome violence." The Michigan Legislature made several conclusions related to the enactment of the statute, including conclusions regarding the harm and behavioral effects caused by a minor's exposure to video games.

The Entertainment Software Association, the Video Software Dealers Association, and the Michigan Retailers Association brought suit against officials in Michigan in the U.S. District Court for the Eastern District of Michigan. In November 2005, the court granted a **preliminary injunction** that temporarily barred enforcement of the statute, which originally was scheduled to take effect on December 1.

Despite legislative findings regarding the harm and effects of video games on children, the court determined that the state had not proven that the statute would materially advanced its goal of reducing aggressive behavior in children. The court determined that the statute was not narrowly tailored to further any compelling **state interest**. Moreover, the court found that the statute definition of "extreme and loathsome violence" was unconstitutionally vague. Thus, on March 31, 2006, the court permanently enjoined the enforcement of the statute. *Entertainment Software Ass'n v. Granholm*, No. 05-73634, 2006 WL 901711 (E.D. Mich. Mar. 31, 2006).

GAS

Members of Congress Question Increases in Gas Prices

Concerns regarding high gas prices coupled with record profits earned by major oil and natural gas companies led members of Congress to question actions taken by these companies to control costs. Although two Senate committees held a joint hearing in November to discuss the gas situation, gas prices during the spring of 2006 continued to escalate.

Since 2003, prices of gasoline and oil have escalated considerably. According to statistics from the U.S. DEPARTMENT OF ENERGY, the average price of gasoline per gallon (for all formulations) on December 29, 2003 was $1.478 cents per gallon. On September 5, 2005, this number reached $3.069, and although prices dropped during the winters of 2005 and 2006, the average price had risen back to $2.919 on May 1.

At the same time that the gas prices surged, so too did profits earned by major oil companies. During the third quarter of 2005, the top 21 energy companies operating in the U.S. reported a combined $26 billion in net income, representing a 69% profit increase from the third quarter of 2004. ExxonMobil saw the greatest dollar increase, with a $9.9 billion profit on $100 billion in revenue, representing a 75% increase from the previous year. ConocoPhillips' third-quarter profit in 2005 increased by 89% from the previous year. Other major companies, such as Shell and BP, also saw substantial increases.

Concerns about and damage caused by Hurricanes Katrina, Rita, and Wilma were partially to blame for the price increases. However, members of Congress expressed concerns about the possibility that gas companies engaged in price-gouging. House Speaker Dennis Hastert (R.-Ill.) publicly questioned the activities of these gas companies. "Oil and gas companies are enjoying record profits," he said. "That is fine. This is America. However, there have been allegations of price gouging in the wake of the hurricanes. This is unacceptable, and any company who does it will be prosecuted."

Shortages in the capacity of existing oil refineries have been blamed for part of the recent increases in gas prices. The last oil refinery in the U.S. was built nearly 30 years ago by Marathon Oil in Garyville, Indiana. Some Democrats in Congress have alleged that oil companies have refused to increase capacity of their refineries because this could reduce the gas prices. Samuel Bodman, Secretary of Energy, has also stated that oil companies should boost refinery capacity.

In addition to the rising prices in oil, the price of natural gas has escalated dramatically in recent years. One possible solution to controlling these prices focuses on the construction of a natural gas pipeline from Alaska's North Slope to the lower 48 states. According to estimates, this area holds 35 trillion cubic feet of natural gas and possibly 100 trillion cubic feet of undiscovered gas. Until a pipeline is constructed, though, this gas is considered to be "stranded."

The rising prices led Senate Majority Leader Bill Frist (R.-Tenn.) to call for a joint meeting of the Senate Committee on Energy and Natural Resources and the Committee on Commerce, Science, and Transportation. "At

Executives of five major oil companies are sworn in prior to their testimony before Congress in March 200.
JASON REED/REUTERS/CORBIS

the same time that oil companies are posting record profits, Americans are paying more than ever to fill up their cars and heat their homes," Frist said. "Whether it is fluctuating gas prices, disparities in gas prices at stations right next to each other, the sharp rise in natural gas costs, or the anticipated crunch for home heating oil, Americans are wondering what has happened to push costs through the roof."

On November 9, chief executive officers from the nation's five largest oil companies appeared at the joint hearing. Some members attacked the executives. Senator Barbara Boxer (D.-Cal.) said that the hearing was "about shared sacrifices in tough times versus oil company greed." Some senators suggested that the Congress should impose a tax on windfall profits, using the revenue of this tax to assist lower income families to pay for their energy bills. Others committee members focused on allegations of price-gouging, including a 24-cent per gallon increase in gas one day after Hurricane Katrina.

The CEOs defended the profits, noting that these companies invest their revenues in the development of new energy resources. According to Lee Raymond, Chairman and Chief Executive Officer of ExxonMobil, "Our numbers are huge because the scale of our industry is huge." Raymond also argued against the imposition of a windfall tax. "History teaches us that punitive measures hastily crafted in response to short-term rises in prices will have unintended consequences and disincentives to investment." Other executives represented Chevron, Conoco, BP, and Shell.

Senator Lamar Alexander (R.-Tenn.) focused his attention on the natural gas problem. "Natural gas prices are a bigger problem for our country," he said. "If gasoline prices had gone up recently as fast as natural gas prices, gasoline would be $6 or $7/gallon. At the moment, there are 50 new chemical plants being built in China and one new chemical plant being built in the United States." Other discussions focused on the construction of the Alaska pipeline.

Although the oil executives said that they favored the construction of the new Alaska pipeline, they noted that the issue was still being negotiated. Moreover, Raymond said that even if a pipeline deal were completed, the pipeline would not be operational for another decade.

The hearing had little or no impact on gas prices. Between April 1 and May 1 in 2006, the average price of a gallon of gasoline increased by about 40 cents. Democrats in late April blamed the policies of President GEORGE W. BUSH for the increase in prices. Senator Ron Wyden (D.-Ore.) said, "The same Bush administration that so tragically bungled the response to Hurricanes Katrina and Rita has now bungled its way to $3-per-gallon gasoline."

Hastert and Frist sent a letter to Bush to advise the president that the administration should take proactive steps to investigate whether price gouging by oil companies had occurred.

"Given the severity of the current situation regarding gas prices, we believe that the attorney general and the FEDERAL TRADE COMMISSION should devote all necessary resources to expedited review of complaints of price gouging against wholesalers or retailers of gasoline and other distillates," the letter said.

GAY AND LESBIAN RIGHTS

The goal of full legal and social equality for gay men and lesbians sought by the gay movement in the United States and other Western countries.

Limon v. Kansas

The U.S. SUPREME COURT's landmark decision in *Lawrence v. Texas*, 539 U.S. 558, 123 S.Ct. 2472, 156 L.Ed.2d 508 (2003) did more than strike down state **sodomy** laws as applied to gays and lesbians. The Court announced that homosexuals as well as heterosexuals enjoyed a fundamental right to conduct their intimate relations without interference by the state. In light of this decision other criminal laws that treated same-sex conduct differently from heterosexual sexual conduct came under judicial scrutiny. In *Limon v. Kansas*, 280 Kan. 275, 122 P.3d 22 (2005) the Kansas Supreme Court used *Lawrence* to strike down a "Romeo and Juliet" **statute** that punished consensual homosexual sex between teenagers more severely that consensual heterosexual sex. The court concluded that the less severe punishment meted out to heterosexual activity should apply to homosexual activity.

Matthew Limon was 18-years-old when he was sentenced to seventeen years in prison in 2000, for having had consensual oral sex with a 14-year-old boy. Had the boy been a girl, Limon's maximum sentence would have been 15 months under the Kansas law. Limon appealed his conviction to the U.S. Supreme Court, which remanded his case to the Kansas courts for reconsideration in light of the *Lawrence* decision.

Lawrence had declared a due process right to consensual, intimate conduct. In so ruling the majority rejected an alternate argument based on the **Equal Protection** Clause. That argument would have struck down the Texas sodomy law solely because it applied to acts committed by homosexual but not heterosexuals. The Court declined to employ this analysis because it might lead to the redrafting of the law to ban sodomy by "same-sex and different-sex participants." However, Justice SANDRA DAY O'CONNOR wrote a concurring opinion that argued the Texas law should have been struck down on equal protection grounds.

On remand a three-judge panel of the Kansas Court of Appeals concluded that the *Lawrence* decision did not invalidate the Kansas law. In *Limon v. Kansas*, 32 Kan.App.2d 369, 83 P.3d 229 (2004), the appeals court upheld the statute on a 2–1 vote. The two judges supporting the constitutionality of the law issued separate opinions. Judge Henry Green concluded that the legislature "could have rationally determined that heterosexual sodomy between a child and an adult could be put in a class by itself and could be dealt with differently than homosexual sodomy between a child and an adult." Judge Green presented four issues that he believed provided a rational basis for rejecting Limon's equal protection claim: protection of the normal sexual development of children, marriage and procreation, parental responsibility, and prevention of sexually transmitted diseases. With regard to sexual development, he wrote that the legislature "could well have concluded that homosexual sodomy between children and young adults could disturb the traditional sexual development of children."

In a concurring opinion for the appeals court, Judge Tom Malone noted that *Lawrence* was distinct from *Limon* in part because it involved adults. He noted that "if the only rational basis justifying the statute is the legislature's intention to protect children from increased health risk associated with homosexual activity until they are old enough to be more certain of their choice, it is within the legislature's prerogative to make that determination." Judge Joseph Pierron dissented, concluding that the law violated due process because it only sought to punish homosexuals more severely than heterosexuals. The disapproval of homosexuality was not enough to uphold the law.

Limon appealed this ruling to the Kansas Supreme Court, which reversed the appeals court decision in a unanimous 6–0 vote. The Supreme Court echoed Judge Pierron's dissent. Justice Marla J. Luckert, writing for the court, made clear that *Lawrence* controlled the court's analysis, undercutting the basis of the court of appeals reasoning. She rejected the notion that homosexual sex was more likely than heterosexual sex to transmit disease. She stated that the law was "over-inclusive because it increases penalties for sexual relations which are unlikely to transmit HIV and other sexually transmitted diseases." In addition, the Supreme Court ruled that state courts could not use laws to express "moral disapproval" of homosexuality.

The Kansas Supreme Court chose to use Justice O'Connor's equal protection argument from *Lawrence* that the law was unconstitutional because homosexuals were not treated the same as heterosexuals. The arguments put forward by Judges Green and Malone in the court of appeals had no merit and failed to sustain a rational basis for the differing criminal penalties. As to the appropriate remedy, the court could have ruled the statute unconstitutional as written and voided the bars against teenage sex. However, the court decided that the best course was to eliminate the phrase "and are members of the opposite sex" from the penalty portion of the statute. By doing so the criminal penalties would apply equally to homosexual and heterosexual conduct. The Court gave the state of Kansas the opportunity to charge Limon under this modified criminal statute. In November 2005 the prosecutor refiled charges against Limon, who had been discharged from prison after having served 4 years. The prosecutor acknowledged that under the law Limon would not serve anymore jail time but wanted him to be placed on probation for five years.

James D. Esseks, a lawyer for the Gay and Lesbian Rights Project of the AMERICAN CIVIL LIBERTIES UNION, stated that based on the *Limon* ruling, "not only this law, but a lot of other laws that treat gay people badly would fall."

Gay Marriage Update

Many states had the issue of gay marriage on their agendas in 2006. In Massachusetts, the only state that permitted same-sex marriage, the Supreme Judicial Court ruled that gay and lesbian couples who live in other states could not be legally married in Massachusetts unless same-sex marriage were to become legal in their home states. The majority opinion, written by Justice Francis X. Spina, stated that the court was upholding a 1913 **statute** that denies legal marriage to any non-Massachusetts residents for whom the marriage would be illegal in their home states, regardless of the reason. The opinion stated that the permission of same-sex marriage in Massachusetts should not allow couples who have no intention of living in Massachusetts the same right to a marriage license as state residents. The original lawsuit was filed by eight out-of-state same-sex couples who claimed that the 1913 statute was discriminatory and that it had become invalid when Massachusetts legalized same-sex marriage.

Massachusetts governor Mitt Romney was quoted as saying that each state should decide on its own how it defines marriage and that "Massachusetts should not become the Las Vegas of same-sex marriage."

In New Jersey, the State Supreme Court heard arguments about whether New Jersey should join Massachusetts and become the second state to permit same-sex marriage. New Jersey has extended domestic partner benefits, and the State Supreme Court is known to be among the more liberal-leaning state courts in the country, according to legal scholars.

Chief Justice Deborah T. Poritz was quoted as saying that marriage had already undergone dramatic changes in recent decades by allowing interracial marriage, despite lower courts' rulings that same-sex couples in New Jersey did not have the right to marry. A ruling was expected in the spring or summer of 2006.

The comparison to interracial marriage was echoed in Maryland, where **Circuit Court** Judge M. Brooke Murdock ruled in 2006 that the state law against same-sex marriage was discriminatory. Judge Murdock wrote, "Although traditions and values are important, they cannot be given so much weight that they alone will justify a discriminatory **statutory** classification." The Maryland Attorney General's office said that it plans to appeal, and same-sex couples were not yet eligible for legal marriage.

Hearings on a same-sex marriage case in New York were scheduled to begin at the end of May, and the California Supreme Court was expected to hear a similar case by the end of 2006. Lower courts in both New York and California ruled that same-sex marriage was constitutional, and the cases were scheduled to be heard by higher courts.

In addition, legislation to permit same-sex marriage was pending in Rhode Island, and Washington State was expected to rule on whether to uphold or overturn lower court rulings in favor of same-sex marriage.

As of spring 2006, legal efforts to seek permission for same-sex marriage were pending in ten states: California, Connecticut, Florida, Iowa, Maryland, Nebraska, New Jersey, New York, Oklahoma, and Washington. In 2005, Connecticut joined Vermont in allowing civil unions, but not marriages, for same-sex couples.

In 2005, voters in several states including Texas and Oregon, approved amendments to ban same-sex marriage. The Oregon Supreme

Court nullified approximately 3000 marriage licenses that had been issued in Multnomah County since 2004. The court said that a county could not act against the state's matrimonial law, which bans same-sex marriage. Several more states had scheduled votes on same-sex marriage bans in 2006, including Virginia, Wisconsin, Alabama, and Idaho.

In Georgia, Fulton County Superior Court Judge Constance C. Russell struck down an amendment to ban same-sex marriage that had been approved by a majority of Georgia voters in 2004. Judge Russell ruled that the amendment violated Georgia's single-subject rules for ballot questions by including several items in addition to same-sex marriage, namely, whether to allow civil unions and whether Georgia courts could rule on disputes that arose from same-sex relationships. State Governor Sonny Purdue said that he would convene a special legislative session to push the issue if the State Supreme Court had not ruled on the case by the end of the summer.

At the national level, Senate Majority Leader Bill Frist said that he would plan a vote in early June on a constitutional amendment to ban gay marriage, but members of both parties have privately admitted that they thought the ban would not receive enough votes to become an amendment. However, a U.S. Senate panel voted 10–8 along party lines to ban gay marriage, and Senate Judiciary Chairman Arlen Specter said that he had voted for the amendment because he believes that the full Senate should address the issue. The Senate was expected to address the bill in early June. If passed, the amendment would prevent any states from recognizing same-sex marriages.

GENEVA CONVENTION

Hamdan v. Rumsfeld

Salim Ahmed Hamdan, a Yemini national who once served as a driver for Osama bin Laden, has been a detainee at the U.S. military installation at Guantanamo Bay, Cuba, since the months following the September 11th attacks in 2001.

Hamdan and his legal team challenged President GEORGE W. BUSH on his use of presidential power to establish a separate justice system for detainees at Guantanamo Bay. The immediate issue is whether Hamdan can be declared an "enemy combatant" who then can be tried in a military **tribunal**, or whether he is entitled to a trial in a civilian court. The U.S. SUPREME COURT heard arguments in the case in March 2006, and a ruling was expected at the end of the session, in June or July. The case number is No.08–184.

Neal Katyal, attorney for Salim Ahmed Hamdan, speaks to reporters, April 2006; he is flanked by Lt. Commander Charles Swift, right, and David Remes, left.

AP IMAGES

Lawyers for the president stated that the commander-in-chief has the power to establish military commissions to try suspected terrorists. Although the commissions were established as part of the ongoing War on Terror, the Supreme Court may opt to check the power of the president to make new rules during wartime.

Hamdan was charged with conspiracy. His legal team argued that, since conspiracy is not a war crime, he could not be tried before a military commission.

In December 2005, Congress passed the Detainee Treatment Act (DTA) Pub. L. No. 109-148, 119 Stat. 2739, which supported the military commissions created by President Bush in November of 2001 to punish terrorists in the wake of the September 11 terrorist attacks. The DTA would suspend the ability of **federal courts**, including the Supreme Court, to hear future cases brought by detainees, essentially suspending the **writ** of **habeas corpus**. Habeas corpus, the means by which prisoners can legally challenge their imprisonment, has been suspended by Congress only four times in U.S. history.

Justice DAVID H. SOUTER was quoted as saying, "There are not two writs of habeas corpus, for some cases and for other cases. The rights that may be asserted, the rights that may be vindicated, will vary with the circumstances, but jurisdiction over habeas corpus is jurisdiction over habeas corpus."

Neal Kaytal, a Georgetown University law professor who serves as the lawyer for Mr. Hamdan, suggested that the Detainee Act be prospectively applied, in order to allow the Supreme Court to consider the Hamdan case.

In the fall of 2005, the U.S. military revised the rules for military tribunals. The changes included the ability to share classified information with defendants to some extent, and to bar classified information if it would impede a complete and fair trial. In addition, the new military tribunal rules place the presiding officer in a role similar to that of a judge, who would rule on all questions of law.

However, Hamdan still contends that military tribunals are unconstitutional because direct subordinates of the president not only define the nature of the crime but also choose the prosecutor and the judges who will act as the jury.

The case highlights several general issues, including the denial of Geneva Convention rights to Guantanamo Bay detainees. Under the Geneva Convention, each of the approximately five hundred detainees would be entitled to a hearing and access to federal courts through habeas corpus. Only ten of the detainees have been charged with crimes, and none of the cases has been decided.

The Supreme Court is aware of the far-reaching impact of the Hamdan case. As *Washington Post* reporter Charles Lane noted, "The court has been bombarded by friend-of-the-court briefs urging it to think about the impact of the Hamdan case on the image of the United States abroad."

Another angle on the case is the potential for a tied vote. In 2005, prior to his nomination and confirmation, Chief Justice John Roberts overruled a decision by the U.S. **District Court** in Washington, D.C., that had ruled in favor of Hamdan. Consequently, he will abstain from participating in the Supreme Court case.

GUN CONTROL

Government regulation of the manufacture, sale, and possession of firearms.

Congress Passes the Protection of Lawful Commerce in Arms Act

Due to concerns with large lawsuits brought against gun dealers and manufacturers for harm caused by their products, Congress in 2005 enacted the Protection of Lawful Commerce in Arms Act (PLCAA), Pub. L. No. 109-92, 119 Stat. 2095. The **statute** prohibits civil liability actions in any federal or state court against manufacturers, distributors, and importers of firearms and ammunition, except in cases that are outlined in the statute. The statute has been viewed as a major victory for the NATIONAL RIFLE ASSOCIATION but has been heavily criticized by gun control advocates.

In 1998, the cities of New Orleans and Chicago led an effort among several cities to sue gun manufacturers in order to recoup the cost of urban violence. The effort was modeled after successful litigation that was brought against tobacco companies. The harm to the manufacturers could come from a large judgment against them, or it could result from large legal fees generated from lengthy litigation.

Gun rights supporters later persuaded 33 states to enact legislation that would ban these types of lawsuits. However, action from Congress to enact a federal law that would provide immunity for gun makers took several years. In 1999, Republicans in Congress planned to move forward with federal legislation that would ban these suits, but the tragedy at Columbine High School effectively stalled this effort. Another bill was introduced in 2002, but a series of incidents in which two snipers terrorized residents in Washington, D.C. led lawmakers to shelve that proposal.

Senator Larry E. Craig (R.-Idaho) introduced the newest legislation on February 16, 2005. Craig said that the bill was designed to prevent trial lawyers from using lawsuits against manufacturers as a means to bankrupt the gun industry. The bill passed in the Senate on July 29 by a vote of 65 to 31. The House passed the bill on October 20 by a vote of 283 to 144. President GEORGE W. BUSH signed the bill into law on October 26.

Congress stated a number of findings about the need for this legislation. The legislation recognizes that litigation has been brought "against manufacturers, distributors, dealers, and importers of firearms that operate as designed and intended, which seek money damages and other relief for the harm caused by the misuse of firearms by third parties, including criminals." The statute explicitly states that these parties should not be liable for these actions. According to the findings, "The possibility of imposing liability on an entire industry for harm that is solely caused by others is an abuse of the legal system, erodes public confidence in our Nation's laws, threatens the diminution of a basic constitutional right and civil liberty, invites the disassembly and destabilization of other industries and economic sectors lawfully competing in the free enterprise system of the United States, and constitutes an unreasonable burden on interstate and foreign commerce of the United States."

The drafters of the bill also expressed concern that a "maverick judicial officer or **petit jury** would expand civil liability in a manner never contemplated by the framers of the Constitution, by Congress, or by the legislatures of the several States." Moreover, the drafters said that those who have initiated litigation against gun manufacturers and dealers effectively tried to use the judicial branch to circumvent the powers of the legislative branch, since judgments and judicial decrees place burdens on interstate and foreign commerce.

Congress stated several purposes behind the bill. One purpose was "[t]o prohibit causes of action against manufacturers, distributors, dealers, and importers of firearms or ammunition products, and their trade associations, for the harm solely caused by the criminal or unlawful misuse of firearm products or ammunition products by others when the product functioned as designed and intended." The statute was also enacted to preserve each citizen's right to access a supply of firearms and ammunition for lawful purposes.

The PLCAA forbids for a "qualified civil liability action" to be brought in either state or federal court. The statute defines this type of action as "a **civil action** or proceeding or an administrative proceeding brought by any person against a manufacturer or seller of a qualified product, or a trade association, for damages" or other remedies. Actions that were pending at the time of enactment were required to be dismissed.

The statute excludes several types of actions from its scope. A person who sells a firearm knowing that it will be used to commit a crime is not immune from liability. Similarly, a seller who negligently entrusts a firearm, who breaches a contract or warranty with respect to a firearm, or who sells a defective firearm can be held civilly liable.

President Bush applauded the legislation. "Our laws should punish criminals who use guns to commit crimes—not law-abiding manufacturers of lawful products," he said. "This legislation will further our efforts to stem frivolous lawsuits, which cause a logjam in America's courts, harm America's small businesses and benefit a handful of lawyers at the expense of victims and consumers."

Opponents of the legislation said that the statute's reach is "unprecedented." According to Robert Scheer, a columnist with the *L.A. Times*, "What [this statute] protects is irresponsible behavior on the part of gun manufacturers and sellers, such as allowing guns to be sold easily to individuals not allowed by law to own them." Some members of Congress echoed these concerns. "I just find it an absolute travesty that these people who are going to be killed [and] maimed by weapons that have been negligently handled [will] have no recourse," said Senator Dianne Feinstein (D.-Cal.). "And it's the only industry in America that's this way."

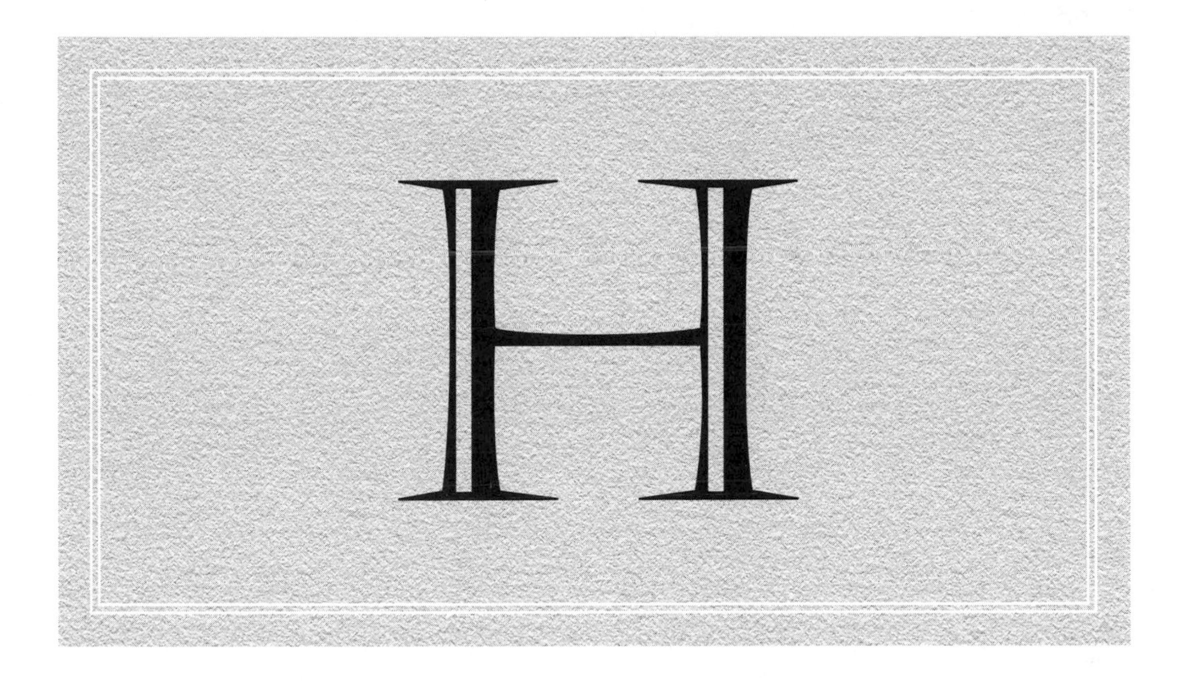

HABEAS CORPUS

[*Latin, You have the body.*] A writ (court order) that commands an individual or a government official who has restrained another to produce the prisoner at a designated time and place so that the court can determine the legality of custody and decide whether to order the prisoner's release.

Day v. McDonough

The Anti-Terrorism and Effective Death Penalty Act of 1996 (AEDPA), Pub. L. No. 104–132, imposed time limits on prisoners who sought to file petitions for writs of **habeas corpus**. If a prisoner waits too long, the statutes of limitations will bar a federal court from considering the action. Prosecutors routinely check the timing deadlines on newly filed habeas petitions and sometimes they mistakenly conclude petitions are timely. The Supreme Court, in *Day v. McDonough*, __U.S.__, 126 S.Ct. 1675, __L.Ed.2d __ (2006), was called on to decide if it was proper for a federal district judge to dismiss a habeas petition as untimely on his own initiative, even though the prosecutor had answered the petition and had not contested its timeliness. The Court ruled that courts are not required to dismiss on their own volition but are permitted to do so if they give the prisoner notice and a chance to prove the petition was timely.

Patrick Day was convicted of second-degree murder in Florida state court and sentenced to 55 years in prison. He appealed, unsuccessfully, to the Florida Court of Appeals, which entered its decision in December 1999. He waited almost one year before filing a petition for postconviction relief with the trial court. The court denied relief as did the appeals court in December 2002. In January 2003 he petitioned the federal **district court** for a **writ** of habeas corpus, citing ineffective assistance from his trial lawyer. The federal **magistrate** judge screened the petition and found it in proper form, notifying the prosecutor to file an answer. Under the AEDPA Day had one year to file the petition, running from "the date on which the judgment became final by the conclusion of direct review or the expiration of the time for seeking such review. However, the law also suspends the one-year clock during the time a prisoner properly files a state postconviction petition. The prosecutor miscalculated the limitations period, finding that the petition had been filed after 352 untolled days, beating the deadline by 13 days. In its answer, the state accepted the timeliness of the petition. The magistrate judge discovered the state's computational error; the petition had actually been filed 388 days after the state appeals court denied his petition.

The magistrate judge ordered Day to show why his petition should not be dismissed as untimely. Finding Day's answers unpersuasive, the magistrate recommended to the district court judge that the petition be dismissed. The judge agreed and dismissed Day's habeas petition. The Eleventh **Circuit Court** of Appeals allowed Day to appeal the dismissal but upheld the ruling. The appeals court found that the district court could on its own initiative dismiss the appeal as untimely, despite the fact that the state had failed to raise the issue in its answer to the petition. The Supreme Court agreed to hear Day's appeal because the circuit courts of appeals had disagreed over whether a district court could dismiss a habeas petition in such circumstances.

The Supreme Court, in a 5–4 decision, upheld the Eleventh Circuit ruling. Justice RUTH BADER GINSBURG, writing for the majority, stated that courts are not obligated to raise the **statute of limitations** issue on their own initiative. However, courts may, in appropriate circumstances and on their own initiative, raise procedural defaults made by petitioners. Day argued that under the federal rules governing habeas petitions the court may only raise AEDPA **statute** of limitations issues on its own initiative during the preanswer, initial screening stage. The magistrate judge in this case failed to do so, taking action only after the prosecutor filed an answer to the petition. Therefore, Day contended that the court lost its authority to rule the petition untimely on its own volition. In addition, the Federal Rules of **Civil Procedure**, which supplement the habeas rules, state that a defendant forfeits a statute of limitations defense if it is not asserted in its answer. The state countered that the purposes of the AEDPA counseled against an "excessively rigid or formal approach to the affirmative defenses" listed in the habeas rules. Instead, it proposed an "intermediate approach" in which the courts may exercise their discretion to decide whether "the administration of justice is better served by dismissing the case on statute of limitations grounds or by reaching the merits of the petition."

Justice Ginsburg concluded that the state's intermediate approach was the most workable solution. A district court was "not required to double-check the State's math," but "if a judge detects a clear computational error, no Rule, statute, or constitutional provision commands the judge to suppress that knowledge." A court that did detect such an error was obligated to give the parties notice and an opportunity to present their positions. In addition, the court must be sure that the petitioner is not "significantly prejudiced by the delayed focus on the limitation issue" and determine what is in the best interests of justice. In this case the court gave notice nine months after the state filed its answer. During that period there were no court hearings or any action on the case. Justice Ginsburg found that Day had not been prejudiced by this inadvertent error.

Justice JOHN PAUL STEVENS filed a dissent, arguing that another case the Court would hear in its next term would determine if the Ninth Circuit precedent on time calculations under the AEDPA was correct. Stevens thought it best to delay the decision for Day in the Supreme Court until this issue had been resolved. Justice ANTONIN SCALIA, in a dissenting opinion joined by Justices CLARENCE THOMAS and STEPHEN BREYER, accused the majority of ignoring the Federal Rules of Civil Procedure in habeas cases. Under these rules a party that fails to raise an **affirmative defense** in its answer to a complaint forfeits that defense. In his view the "rules are surely entitled to more respect than this apparent presumption that, when nothing substantial hangs on the point, they do *not* apply as written."

Evans v. Chavis

The **federal courts** have continued to struggle with the procedural rules governing petitions for writs of **habeas corpus** that Congress included in the Anti-Terrorism and Effective Death Penalty Act of 1996 (AEDPA), Pub. L. No. 104–132, 110 Stat. 1214. AEDPA sought to reduce the number of habeas filings by imposing strict timelines on petitions, but the federal courts must rely on state court determinations on whether a petition is timely. The state of California, unlike most other states, does not set firm time limits for the filing of state petitions for habeas corpus. This has produced confusing readings of time limits that the U.S. SUPREME COURT has tried to make understandable. In *Evans v. Chavis*, __U.S.__, 126 S.Ct. 846, 163 L.Ed.2d 684 (2006), the Court, in ruling that a federal habeas petition was untimely, chastised a federal appeals court for failing to follow a recent Court ruling and appealed for California legislators and judges to end timing uncertainties.

In 1991, Reginald Chavis was convicted of attempted murder by a California jury and sentenced to life in prison. After his conviction was upheld by the California Court of Appeals and his petition for review to the California Supreme Court was denied in 1992, Chavis sought a postconviction remedy by filing a state habeas corpus petition in 1993. The trial court denied the petition and he lost his appeal to the California Court of Appeals on September 29, 1994. Chavis waited more than three years to file a petition for review with the state supreme court, filing it on November 5, 1997. On April 29, 1998 the supreme court denied his petition, stating only that the **writ** for habeas corpus was denied. Chavis filed a federal habeas petition on August 30, 2000. The state of California asked the federal **district court** to dismiss the petition because it was untimely. Under AEDPA, prisoners have only one year to file their federal petitions. However, the act also included a tolling provision, which suspends the counting of the one-year time period while an application for a state habeas review is "pending." With Chavis, the federal court had to calculate how many days his state habeas review applications had been pending in the state courts and add these days to the AEDPA one-year limitation period. The district court performed the calculation and concluded that Chavis' petition must be dismissed as untimely.

The Ninth **Circuit Court** of Appeals disagreed with how the district court calculated the time and reversed its decision. The appeals court concluded that the California Supreme Court's 1998 order denying the petition for review was denied on the merits of Chavis' claim and not because it was untimely. Therefore, this petition was "pending" for AEDPA purposes during the interval between the 1994 Court of Appeals decision and the 1997 Supreme Court petition and the one-year federal filing period was tolled for that amount of time. By adding three years to the federal limitations period, Chavis' petition was timely by just two days.

The Supreme Court, in a unanimous decision, ruled that the Ninth Circuit had ignored or misread a recent Court habeas decision and must be reversed. Justice STEPHEN BREYER, writing for eight justices (Justice JOHN PAUL STEVENS issued a separate opinion agreeing with the outcome but differing on the reasoning), noted the importance of *Carey v. Saffold*, 536 U.S. 214, 122 S.Ct. 2134, 153 L.Ed.2d 260 (2002), to the present case. In that California habeas appeal, ruled on by the Ninth Circuit, the Court was confronted with the California rule that a petition is timely if filed within "a reasonable time." Because this timeline was "general rather than precise" the task of calculation of time by a federal court more difficult. The Court sent *Saffold* back to the Ninth Circuit to decide whether the prisoner had filed his California Supreme Court habeas petition within a "reasonable time." The Court also provided some guidelines to the appeals court, including one that stated the words "on the merits" did not prove that the California Supreme Court thought the petition was timely. The Court emphasized that the Ninth Circuit must not take words like "on the merits" as an "absolute bellwether" on the issue of timeliness. It also gave as an example of an incorrect approach by the Ninth Circuit a case in which the appeals court found a petition timely that had been file four years after the lower court reached its decision.

Justice Breyer agreed with California that the Ninth Circuit's ruling in favor of Chavis was inconsistent with the *Saffold* decision. The Ninth Circuit concluded that a denial on the merits of Chavis's petition meant the federal petition was timely, when the Court had clearly stated not to make that presumption. Moreover, the denial of the petition had not even stated that it had been based on the merits-the Ninth Circuits assumed this silence was equivalent to the phrase "on the merits." Justice Breyer thought it obvious that the absence of the phrase "makes it *less* likely, not *more* likely, that the California Supreme Court believed that Chavis' three-year delay was reasonable."

The frustration of the Court with California's reluctance to adopt firm time standards led Justice Breyer to ask the California courts to consider some helpful changes. The courts could clarify the scope of the words "reasonable time" or indicate on a petition denial order whether the petition had been timely. The Ninth Circuit could remove itself from the timeliness issue by certifying a question to the California Supreme Court asking whether a petition had been timely filed. Finally, Justice Breyer suggested the California state legislature could "impose more determinate time limits, conforming California law in this respect with the law of most other States."

As to the Chavis case, Justice Breyer rejected the prisoner's claims that he was delayed in filing because he had been denied access to the prison library and been held for long periods in his cell during prison lockdowns. Breyer pointed out that Chavis was able to gain more access to the library as time went on and that at least six months of the delay was unjustified. A six-month delay was much longer than the 30 to 60 days that most states provided for supreme court appeals, making Chavis' failure to file unreasonable. By cutting out the six months from the tolling period the federal habeas petition did not meet the federal filing deadline.

House v. Bell

Congress and the U.S. SUPREME COURT have put up many obstacles for a prisoner seeking **habeas corpus** review. One roadblock occurs when a prisoner fails to raise issues in a state court that he later wishes to argue in a federal petition for a **writ** of habeas corpus. The general rule is that the prisoner forfeits these claims in a federal habeas action. However, the Supreme Court has allowed an exception to this rule if the prisoner can make a plausible claim of innocence that is based on newly discovered evidence. This exception is exceedingly difficult to claim, but the Court allowed it in *House v. Bell*, __U.S.__, 126 S.Ct., __L.Ed.2d __ 2006 WL 1584475 (2006), basing it decision primarily on DNA evidence that was unavailable at the time of the criminal trial and which would have given reasonable jurors reasonable doubt as to the guilt of the defendant.

Paul House was convicted of murder for the killing of Carolyn Muncey in Union County, Tennessee in 1985 and sentenced to death. House, who was on parole for a sex offense in Utah, was convicted on the theory that he lured the young mother from her home by telling her that her husband, Hubert, had been injured in a car accident. Her body was discovered in an area where witnesses saw House. House lied about his whereabouts the night before and had discarded his shoes and other clothing before his arrest. Police found his pants, which the FBI expert witness at trial said contained traces of Muncey's blood. Semen was found on Muncey's nightgown and the expert concluded that it was House's. At **closing argument** of the guilt phase the prosecutor implied that House had sought to sexually assault Muncey. At the penalty phase the jury agreed that the murder was committed during an attempted rape and that this was an aggravating factor that justified the death penalty. House appealed his conviction to the Tennessee Supreme Court, which affirmed the decision. He then filed a petition for postconviction relief, arguing that he had received ineffective assistance of counsel. The Tennessee state courts denied relief, leading House to file a petition for habeas corpus in federal court based on his ineffective assistance of counsel claim and prosecutorial misconduct. The federal **district court** dismissed his petition after reviewing House's new evidence, which included challenges to the blood and semen evidence and the testimony of witnesses who claimed that Carolyn Muncey had been abused by her husband, and other witnesses who claimed that Hubert Muncey had confessed to them that he had murdered his wife. The Sixth **Circuit Court** of Appeals affirmed the dismissal but the Supreme Court agreed to hear House's appeal.

The Court, in a 5–3 decision (newly confirmed Justice Samuel Alito did not participate in the consideration of the case), reversed the Sixth Circuit and held that House was entitled to a hearing on his ineffective assistance of counsel claim. Justice ANTHONY KENNEDY, writing for the majority, acknowledged that as a general rule claims forfeited under state law cannot be considered by a federal court in a habeas action unless, as here, there was a miscarriage of justice. In *Schlup v. Delo*, 513 U.S. 298, 115 S.Ct. 851, 130 L.Ed.2d 808 (1995), the Court created a "gateway" for a prisoner such as House to get his defaulted claims before a federal court so as to prevent "manifest injustice." Under this ruling the prisoner must establish with the new evidence that "it is more likely than not that no reasonable juror would have found petitioner guilty beyond a reasonable doubt." Kennedy noted that the *Schlup* standard was demanding and that it was reserved for "extraordinary" cases. Despite this limitation, Kennedy concluded that district court had failed to correctly apply the *Schlup* reasonable juror standard and that the evidence House offered met the standard.

The DNA evidence undermined the prosecution case because it conclusively proved that the semen came from Hubert Muncey, not House. Kennedy stated that "When identity is in question, motive is the key." The prosecutor had implied at the guilt stage that House, a convicted sex offender, had sought to perpetrate an "indignity" on Mrs. Muncey. This was reinforced in the penalty phase when the jury concluded that the murder was committed in the course of a rape or kidnapping. A jury would have had to find another motive for House to have committed the crime if it had known the semen was not his. Kennedy was also troubled by the bloodstain evidence. The FBI lab had concluded that the blood on House's pants came from Mrs. Muncey. However, there was evidence to show that the blood samples from Mrs. Muncey leaked out the bottle while it was transported to the FBI lab. The pants were in the same box and House contended that the blood came from the autopsy samples and not from Mrs. Muncey's live or recently killed body. The assistant chief medical **examiner** for the Tennessee testified that the blood on the pants was chemically too degraded and similar to the blood collected at the autopsy to have come from Muncey's body on the night of the murder.

Justice Kennedy also found merit in the witnesses House's original lawyer failed to locate and put on the witness stand. Several neighbors testified that Mr. Muncey had struck his wife and that she had bruises and black eyes on several occasions. More importantly, two sisters came forward years after the trial to say that Mr. Muncey had confessed to them that he had struck his wife that night and that she had fallen, struck her head, and died. Kennedy pointed to other new evidence that contradicted Mr. Muncey's alibi the night of the crime and concluded that "no reasonable juror viewing the record as a whole would lack reasonable doubt." He made clear that this was not a "conclusive exoneration" and that decision only meant that House was entitled to a full hearing on his habeas claims. However, the Court's decision and reasoning will serve as a guide for the district court when it takes up House's case again.

Chief Justice John Roberts, in a dissenting opinion joined by Justices ANTONIN SCALIA and CLARENCE THOMAS, contended that the Court had failed to pay due deference to the federal district court's review of the new evidence. An **appellate court** does not hear testimony, so it made no sense to try to make credibility determinations. Roberts argued that unless the Court found the lower court's findings "clearly erroneous," it should not disturb the findings. In this case he believed the district court was not in error.

Rice v. Collins

One of the most difficult duties for an **appellate court** to perform is to make conclusions of fact based on trial court transcripts. Because it is very hard to make judgments about credibility and motives using a paper record, **appellate** courts generally refrain from these inquiries unless the trial court's ruling was irrational. In *Rice v. Collins*, __U.S.__, 126 S.Ct. 969, 163 L.Ed.2d 824 (2006), the Supreme Court reinforced this position, ruling that a federal **circuit court** of appeals improperly overruled a credibility determination made by a state trial judge examining whether the prosecutor challenged a juror because of her race. The Court made clear that in a federal **habeas corpus** proceeding, courts must defer to reasonable factual determinations made by state trial judges.

A California jury convicted Steven Collins on one count of cocaine possession with the intent to distribute. This was Collins' third conviction, subjecting him to a long prison sentence under the California three strike rule. Collins disputed the fairness of his trial, claiming that the prosecutor had improperly used a **peremptory challenge** to remove a black female from the jury. With a peremptory challenge, a prosecutor can remove a juror without giving a reason for cause for the challenge. However, the Supreme Court held in *Batson v. Kentucky*, 476 U.S.79, 106 S.Ct. 1712, 90 L.Ed.2d 69 (1986), that peremptory challenges based on race are prohibited. A defendant can challenge an allegedly race-based peremptory challenge through a three-step process. The trial court must first decide if the defendant has made a **prima facie** showing that the challenge by the prosecutor was exercised on the basis of race. If that showing is made the prosecutor must present a race-neutral explanation for striking the juror. The explanation does not need to be persuasive or even plausible; if the reason is not inherently discriminatory then the peremptory challenge must be allowed. The trial judge must evaluate the "persuasiveness of the justification" made by the prosecutor but the defendant has the ultimate **burden of persuasion** regarding racial motivation.

Collins met his prima facie burden because the juror in question was black. The prosecutor explained to the trial judge that Juror 16, as the woman was labeled, had rolled her eyes in response to a question from the judge. In addition, the juror was young and might be too tolerant of a drug crime. The prosecutor also noted that the Juror 16 was single and lacked ties to the community. Finally, the prosecutor mentioned the juror's gender. The judge rejected the gender explanation as improper under a later Supreme Court ruling banning peremptory challenges based on gender. The judge stated that he had not observed the demeanor of Juror 16 but found that the challenge was permissible based on the juror's youth.

Collins appealed his conviction to the California Court of Appeals, which upheld the verdict and the judge's peremptory challenge decision. The appeals found that youth was a legitimate reason as was the juror's demeanor. Moreover, the court concluded that the trial judge had conducted a full inquiry into the prosecutor's reasons for striking Juror 16. After the California Supreme Court rejected his petition for review, Collins filed a habeas corpus petition in federal **district court**. The district court denied his petition but the Ninth Circuit Court of Appeals reversed and remanded with instructions to grant the petition. The Ninth Circuit panel held that the state trial court judge had made an unreasonable factual determination by crediting the prosecutor with race-neutral reasons for removing Juror 16 from the case.

The U.S. SUPREME COURT, in a unanimous decision, reversed the Ninth Circuit ruling. Justice ANTHONY KENNEDY, writing for the Court, noted that on direct appeal a trial court's *Batson* determination is reviewed for clear error. However, under the Anti-Terrorism and Effective Death Penalty Act of 1996 (AEDPA), Pub. L. No. 104–132, 110 Stat. 1214, a federal habeas court must find the state-court conclusion "an unreasonable determination of the facts in light of the evidence presented in the State court proceeding." State court factual findings are presumed correct and a petitioner like Collins has the burden of rebutting this presumption by "clear and convincing evidence." The Ninth Circuit ruled that it was unreasonable for the trial court to accept the prosecutor's explanation but Justice Kennedy saw it much differently when examining the record.

The Ninth Circuit believed the focus on the juror's age was more complicated. Another prospective black juror, Juror 19, who was a grandmother, was referred to as "young" by the prosecutor. Justice Kennedy believed that it plausible that the prosecutor misspoke "with respect to a juror's numerical designation." It was at best a "tenuous inference" that this reference could undermine the prosecutor's credibility over Juror 16. Second, the appeals court found that the trial judge should have questioned the prosecutor's credibility when she raised the issue of gender. Kennedy pointed out that the trial court had immediately informed the prosecutor that it would not accept gender as a race-neutral explanation. Because the prosecutor provided other plausible race-neutral reasons, Collins could not prove that a "reasonable factfinder must conclude the prosecutor lied about the eye rolling and struck Juror 16 based on her race. Finally, the Ninth Circuit concluded the prosecutor's concerns about the juror's youth and her lack of ties to the community were pretextual. Juror 16 had stated during jury selection that she thought the crime that Collins was charged with should be illegal and that she could be impartial. However, Justice Kennedy held that it was not unreasonable for the prosecutor to worry that Juror 16 would have a harder time than an older person sentencing Collins to a lengthy prison term for a small amount of cocaine. In addition, the prosecutor used a peremptory challenge to remove a white male juror who was young and without strong ties to the community. Though "reasonable minds reviewing the record might disagree about the prosecutor's credibility," in a habeas review "that does not suffice to supersede the trial court's credibility determination." Therefore, the Ninth Circuit had failed to "satisfy AEDPA's requirements for granting a **writ** of habeas corpus."

HATE CRIME

A crime motivated by racial, religious, gender, sexual orientation, or other prejudice.

Alabama Church Arsonists Caught

Three college students were arrested in on March 8, 2006, for setting fire to nine rural Alabama churches. The fires damaged or destroyed five churches on February 3, and four more on February 7. All of the churches were Baptist. Four of the churches torched on February 3 were predominantly white congregations; the rest were predominantly black congregations. The first set of fires occurred in Bibb County, south of Birmingham. The latter four took place in counties in western Alabama.

Arrested were Matthew Lee Cloyd, 20; Benjamin Mosley, 19; and Russell DeBusk Jr., 19. All three are white. Moseley and DeBusk attended Birmingham-Southern College, a school affiliated with the United Methodist Church. Cloyd attended Birmingham-Southern, until transferring to the University of Alabama at Birmingham, in 2005. None of the defendants has a prior criminal record. DeBusk and Moseley were aspiring actors. The day they were arrested, a story about their work appeared in the campus newspaper. Cloyd reportedly planned to become a doctor, like his father.

Approximately 250 officers from state, local, and federal agencies conducted the investigation leading to the arrests. A spokesman for the Bureau of Alcohol, Tobacco, Firearms, and Explosives said the investigators tracked down about 1,000 leads, 500 vehicles, and 1,300 people.

Investigators had reports that a dark SUV with two men had been seen near some of the fires. Investigators made impressions of tire tracks found near six of the churches and discovered the matched a BF Goodrich all Terrain model. Agents scoured tire stores to find records for anyone who had purchased the tire in recent months. The search revealed that Cloyd's mother had purchased a set for her Toyota 4Runner. Mrs. Cloyd told investigators that her son was the main driver of the vehicle.

The defendants were initially arrested upon a complaint filed in U.S. District Court for the Northern District of Alabama. The complaint contained an affidavit of a Bureau of Alcohol, Tobacco, and Firearms agent. The complaint contended Matthew Cloyd told his parents that he knew who had set the fires. Cloyd also told his father that he was present. The complaint further alleged that Cloyd told another person that he and Moseley had done something stupid, as a joke that got out of hand. He told the person they had set a church on fire.

Tuscaloosa County Sheriff Ted Sexton speaks to press after arrests in the Alabama church burnings, March 2006.
AP IMAGES

According to the criminal complaint, Moseley admitted to investigators that he, Cloyd, and DeBusk had set the fires in Bibb County. After they torched the first two churches and saw fire trucks on the way, they burned the other three churches. Moseley told investigators that they burned the latter four churches in an attempt to throw investigators off their track.

DeBusk told investigators that he participated in the February 3 fires only. He told investigators that they were deer hunting the night of February 2, 2006, in Cloyd's Toyota 4Runner. DeBusk said he kicked in the door of two of the churches. He learned approximately two weeks later from Moseley that Moseley and Cloyd had set four more fires.

The three allegedly told investigators that they had been out night hunting, in violation of state law. They also admitted they shot a cow that night, and said that alcohol had been involved.

On March 29, 2006, a federal grand jury indicted the three on a ten-count indictment. Count 1 alleges a conspiracy to damage and destroy nine churches by fire. Counts 2 through 6 charge the defendants with the damage and destruction to the five churches in Bibb County. The remaining counts charge that Cloyd and Moseley damaged and destroyed four more churches in western Alabama, in Greene County, Sumter County, and Pickens County.

According to the Department of Justice, the minimum mandatory sentence for each count is imprisonment for at least seven years, and a fine of $250,000. Federal sentencing guidelines would permit the sentences for multiple counts to run concurrently.

In late May, Alabama Attorney General Troy King began to meet with members of the churches to discuss their feelings on possible penalties for the three defendants. The defendants also face state charges. The state charges each carries a maximum sentence of 20 years imprisonment and a $10,000 fine. A plea agreement would most likely cover all federal and state charges.

Cloyd, Moseley, and DeBusk are in jail pending trial. A trial date of November 13, 2006, has been set in federal district court.

After the arrests were announced, the president of Birmingham-Southern, David Pollick, said that the school would help rebuild the churches, both with money and labor. He also announced that Moseley and DeBusk were suspended and banned from entering campus.

HURRICANE KATRINA

Legal issues after Hurricane Katrina

Hurricane Katrina, the storm that destroyed many areas of the Gulf Coast by floodwaters in August 2005, left many legal issues in its wake.

Many people throughout the U.S. and abroad donated money to the American Red

An aerial shot of flooded neighborhoods in Louisiana after Hurricane Katrina.
AP IMAGES

Cross and other charities to be put toward relief efforts in the Gulf Coast region. However, legal limitations on the ways in which charities can use such donations raised issues that could prevent much of the donations to these two organizations (totalling more than one billion dollars), from being used for hurricane relief efforts.

When Hurricane Rita threatened the Gulf region shortly after Katrina, the question of diverting post-Katrina funds for relief from that disaster arose. In an interview with the *Washington Post*, Jill Manny, executive director of the National Center for Philanthropy and the Law at New York University, said that diverting funds to any cause other than the one for which the money was originally intended could expose charities to prosecution from state attorneys general.

In March 2006, the Humane Society of the United States and the American Red Cross came under investigation by the Louisiana attorney general's office on the suspicion that the organizations had diverted money and supplies from the relief effort, and that they had wasted and abused their donations.

Jerome Nickerson, a Baltimore-based lawyer who was asked by the Red Cross to investigate allegations of misuse of funds and supplies, reported in March 2006 on so-called "rogue warehouses" filled with supplies that they suspected were being sold. In addition, Nickerson and his team found that Red Cross volunteers were using multiple debit cards worth thousands of dollars, and that they were ordering conspicuously large amounts of supplies such as cooking oil, coffee, and canned goods for areas that did not need them. However, when Nickerson presented his findings to local Red Cross officials in Louisiana and stated his plan to investigate further, he was sent home.

In addition, the Humane Society has received complaints that, although the organization received millions of dollars in donations, not enough work has been done to reunite hurricane evacuees with their pets. The Humane Society's investigation is ongoing, but officials have not admitted to any wrongdoing or misuse of funds.

The possible manipulation of gasoline prices in response to the hurricane was another cause for concern. In May 2006, federal investigators issued a report in which they stated that they could find no evidence that oil companies had worked together to manipulate prices. *New York Times* reporter Stephen Labaton quoted a report from the FEDERAL TRADE COMMISSION as stating that, although some price gouging had occurred at the local level, regional or local trends appeared to justify the higher prices, and that these spikes were fairly short-lived. "Evidence gathered during our investigation indicated that the conduct of firms in response to the supply shocks caused by the hurricanes was consistent with competition," the report stated.

Insurance coverage remains another ongoing legal angle in the wake of Hurricane Katrina. In May 2006, 669 homeowners in the Gulf Coast region joined in a lawsuit against State Farm Insurance Co., in which they allege that the company refused to cover the costs of homes destroyed by the hurricane. The plaintiffs accused the company of using a "one-size-fits-all" engineering report to deny coverage, and of failing to investigate whether the damages were in fact due to Hurricane Katrina. The engineering report, which was prepared for State Farm by the Dallas, Texas based HAAG Engineering Co., stated that damage to homes on the Gulf Coast of Mississippi were due to "storm surge," which State Farm does not cover, rather than wind damage, which the company does cover.

Richard Scruggs, a lawyer who was suing several other insurance companies for denying post-Katrina insurance claims, alleged that State Farm had essentially blackmailed engineering firms by refusing to pay them if their reviews of the damages conflicted with State Farm's commissioned analysis. Scruggs has also accused State Farm of transferring or firing employees who did tell homeowners that their property had sustained wind damage before the storm surge occurred. Scruggs had lawsuits pending against Metropolitan Life Insurance Co., Nationwide Mutual Insurance Co., and the United Services Automobile Association.

In April 2006, a federal judge in Mississippi ruled that the policies of Allstate Insurance that exclude floodwater damage from Hurricane Katrina were valid.

The city of New Orleans, which was among the major metropolitan areas hardest-hit by Hurricane Katrina, was scheduled to re-open criminal trials at the end of May, although the lack of funds for public defenders for accused criminals who were awaiting trial had prompted some lawyers to file lawsuits demanding the release of jailed suspects.

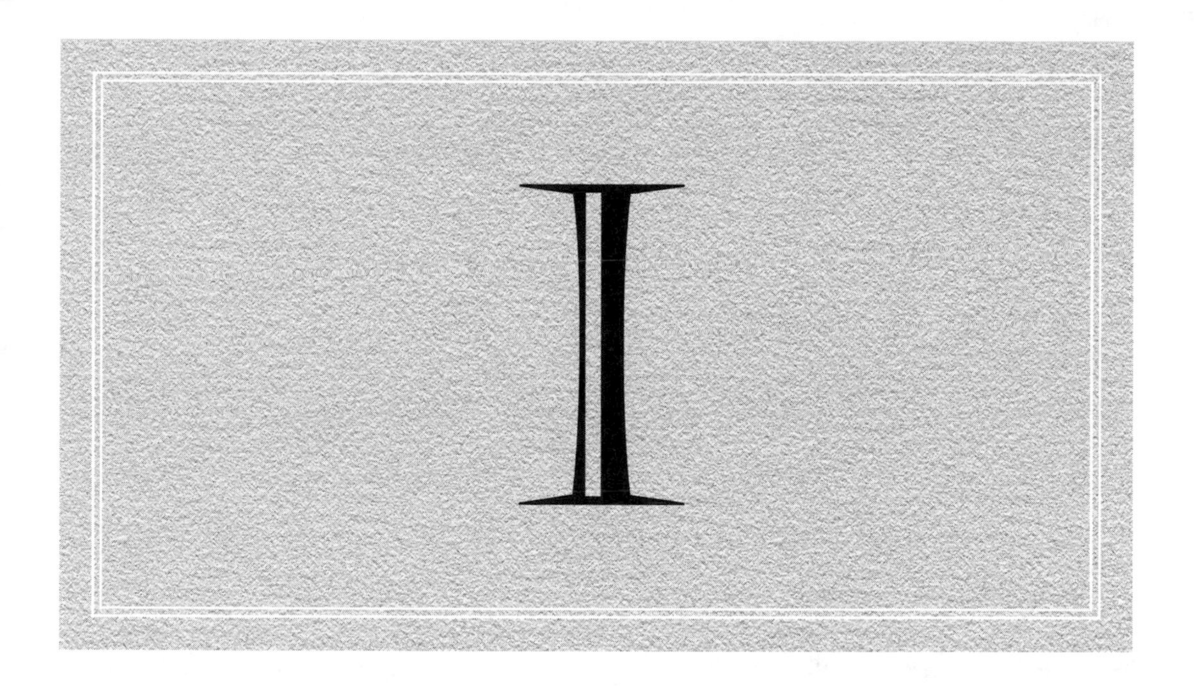

IDENTITY THEFT

The assumption of a person's identity in order, for instance, to obtain credit; to obtain credit cards from banks and retailers; to steal money from existing accounts; to rent apartments or storage units; to apply for loans; or to establish accounts using another's name.

United States v. Choicepoint

ChoicePoint, Inc., one of the largest purveyors of personal information in the United States, agreed in January 2006 to pay a federal fine of $10 million after security breaches exposed the personal information of more than 163,000 customers. In addition, the company required to pay $5 million that will be placed in a compensation fund for consumers. This represents the largest civil penalty in the history of the FEDERAL TRADE COMMISSION (FTC).

The number of cases of identity theft that have been directly linked to the ChoicePoint security failures remains uncertain, but the FTC has estimated that more than 800 cases are involved. Money from the compensation fund has been placed in an account and will be distributed to those individuals who can show real damages. Under the terms of the settlement, ChoicePoint did not admit to any of the charges filed against it by the FTC. However, the FTC voted unanimously to accept the terms.

The data-brokerage company, based in Alpharetta, Georgia, unwittingly delivered electronic information including names, addresses, Social Security numbers, financial details, and other personal information to Los Angeles-based con artists who were posing as officials in the debt collection, insurance, and check-cashing businesses.

ChoicePoint regularly sells information to intelligence officials, police officers, lawyers, and reporters via the Internet. The company's databases include records with information such as the criminal records and credit histories of almost every adult in the U.S. The tip of the iceberg for the insufficient security at ChoicePoint was discovered in late 2004, when ChoicePoint employees noticed that requests for information from several seemingly legitimate California-based companies were being sent by fax from public businesses, including Kinko's stores.

With help from Los Angeles authorities, ChoicePoint tricked a suspect, Olatunji Oluwatosin, into returning to one of the Kinko's stores, where he was arrested and charged with violating identity theft statutes.

The settlement between ChoicePoint and the FTC sends a message to other companies that deal in personal information that higher standards must be applied to protect consumers, and ChoicePoint has agreed to enact tougher measures to ensure consumer privacy. These measures include verifying the legitimacy of businesses or organizations that request consumer information, making site visits to business locations, and auditing the use of the information by the businesses.

In addition, the terms of the settlement require ChoicePoint to "establish, implement, and maintain a comprehensive information security program designed to protect the security, confidentiality, and integrity of the personal information it collects from or about consumers," according to an FTC statement. ChoicePoint must also obtain an audit for the security program from a qualified, independent professional every two years for the next twenty years.

The FTC stated that ChoicePoint had violated the FAIR CREDIT REPORTING ACT by providing consumer information to applicants without verifying who they were and how they intended to use the information. The FTC also charged ChoicePoint with violating the FTC Act by making misleading statements about its privacy policies, including such claims as, "Every ChoicePoint customer must successfully complete a rigorous credentialing process. ChoicePoint does not distribute information to the general public and monitors the use of its public record information to ensure appropriate use."

ChoicePoint had neglected to tighten security measures in the past, after receiving subpoenas from law enforcement officials relating to **fraudulent** activities as far back as 2001.

ChoicePoint chief executive Derek V. Smith said in a statement that the company had begun to implement the policy changes mandated by the terms of the settlement.

"Data security is critical to consumers, and protecting it is a priority for the FTC, as it should be to every business in America," FTC chairman Deborah Platt Majoras said in a statement.

The extent of the use or resale of the ChoicePoint information remains unknown, according to authorities investigating the case. However, the **fraud** appears to have involved multiple states.

The high-profile ChoicePoint case has increased public awareness of the potential for security breaches from data brokers and has raised concerns about the ease of buying and selling personal information online, and the ongoing risk of identity theft as a result.

IMMIGRATION

Congress Votes on Immigration Reform

Immigration reform took the spotlight in the spring of 2006, when Congress addressed the issue in response to President GEORGE W. BUSH's proposed plan to curb illegal immigration. One of the key components of the plan is a "guest worker program." This program would allow illegal immigrants who were already living and working in the U.S to register as temporary workers, which would permit them to remain in the country and begin the formal process of applying for U.S. citizenship. Bush had said that he does not support giving driver's licenses to illegal immigrants and that he does not support attempting to remove the illegal immigrants who are already in the U.S.

Bush had stated repeatedly that "guest worker" programs recognize the reality that the country needs some amount of immigrant workers to do the jobs that U.S. citizens are not willing to do.

In May 2006, Bush responded to pressure from the public and from Congress over the flood of illegal immigrants into the country across the Mexican border, and he promised to send as many as six thousand NATIONAL GUARD troops to reinforce the understaffed Border Patrol in the southwestern U.S.

Bush announced his plan to send National Guard troops to the border in a televised address from the Oval Office. "There is a rational middle ground between granting an automatic path to citizenship for every illegal immigrant and a program of mass deportation," he stated.

Some members of Congress had criticized the guest worker plan as thinly veiled amnesty for illegal immigrants, and other critics had argued that the show of force with the National Guard was simply a political move to **entice** Congressional conservatives to support the President's immigration bill.

The use of the National Guard would theoretically serve as a temporary support measure until the ranks of the Border Patrol are expanded as part of a larger immigration-reform plan. Immigration reform had been an issue for President Bush since his initial presidential campaign in 2000, but Congress has been unable to agree on specific legislation. The immigration bill under consideration in Congress this year includes a plan to substantially increase the number of border patrol officers along the Mexican border during the next five years. The National Guard, while on duty at the border, would assist with surveillance, intelligence-gathering, and administrative support, but the capturing and detaining of illegal immigrants would be left to the Border Patrol. California's governor, Arnold Schwarzenegger, had initially resisted sending National Guard troops to the border. However, he later said that although he opposes the use of National Guard troops for law enforcement, he was prepared to commit the state's National Guard to support Border Patrol operations, at least for the short-term.

In addition, immigration legislation in both houses of Congress called for the construction of a fence along the border with Mexico. In May 2006, the Senate approved a fence that would be three hundred seventy miles long; the House of Representatives had approved a fence of twice that length in December 2005. The Senate plan called for the fortification of seventy miles of existing fencing and the building of three hundred more miles of fencing in an area of the Arizona desert.

The Senate also voted in favor of a provision that called for immigrants who wished to obtain guest-worker permits to be sponsored by an employer and for tougher penalties on employers that hire illegal workers. An additional provision to the Senate plan, the Kyl-Cornyn amendment, would prohibit illegal immigrants who broke any U.S. laws, whether misdemeanors or felonies, from participating in the guest-worker program.

The Senate plan was more generous to illegal immigrants that the plan that was passed by the House of Representatives. In 2005, the House passed a bill that essentially ignored the citizenship aspect of illegal immigration and focused instead on increasing the penalties imposed on illegal immigrants and constructing a fence along the Mexican border.

Washington Post reporter Charles Babington noted that the Senate was likely to pass its version of an immigration reform bill and that negotiations with the House would begin in June 2006.

"The immigration issue fractures both parties, especially in the House, along unfamiliar lines, and it is far from clear whether House leaders can craft a compromise acceptable to majorities in both chambers," Babington wrote.

Spring 2006 was marked by a series of pro-immigration rallies in major cities across the U.S., including Washington, DC, New York, Dallas, Atlanta, and Los Angeles. The rallies showcased the strong feelings of the immigrants, both legal and illegal, in favor of legislation that would provide a path to citizenship. The size of the rallies and marches and the strong passions of the immigrant and non-immigrant participants (one event in Phoenix, Arizona drew 20,000 people) appeared to have captured the attention of Congress members and may have been a turning point for Latino political power in the U.S.

IMMUNITY

Exemption from performing duties that the law generally requires other citizens to perform, or from a penalty or burden that the law generally places on other citizens.

Hartman v. Moore

Under Supreme Court precedent, persons who believe that federal officers have violated their civil rights may file a claim for damages against these officers. The Court established this constitutional tort in *Bivens v. Six Unknown Named Agents of Federal Bureau of Narcotics*, 403 U.S. 388, 91 S.Ct. 1999, 29 L.Ed.2d 619 (1971). In the 35 year history of this **cause of action** the Court has been called upon to assess whether federal officers are entitled to absolute or qualified immunity from such lawsuits. The Court has also examined what elements must be shown to trigger *Bivens* liability. In *Hartman v. Moore*, __U.S.__, 126 S.Ct. 1695, __L.Ed.2d __ (2006), the Court held that in a retaliatory prosecution lawsuit, the plaintiff must plead and show the absence of **probable cause** for pressing the underlying criminal charges.

The underlying issues in the case reach back to the early 1980s, when the U.S. POSTAL SERVICE (USPS) introduced the four-number extension to the five-number zip code. William Moore, the chief executive office of Recognition Equipment, Inc.(REI), a company that made optical scanning technology, tried to interest the USPS in multi line character readers to read the new nine-digit zip codes. In 1983 the USPS announced it would continue to use its single-line character readers, which lead Moore to lobby the USPS board of governors and members of Congress to overturn this decision. The GENERAL ACCOUNTING OFFICE (GAO) and the Office of Technology Assessment issued reports that supported Moore's arguments for multi-line readers, pointing out the postal service was losing $1 million per day by using the single-line readers. In 1985 the board of governors reversed course and agreed to change to the multi-line readers. Despite this victory, Moore and REI did not benefit, for the postal service awarded the multi-million contracts for new readers to other firms. In addition, postal service inspectors opened investigations concerning purporting kickbacks by a public relations firm retained by REI to a postal service governor and REI's alleged improper role in selecting a new Postmaster General. Though the evidence against Moore and REI was very limited, the assistant U.S. attorney brought criminal charges against them in 1988. A federal **district court** judge acquitted the defendants on all charges after six weeks of trial after finding a "complete lack of evidence."

Moore then brought a *Bivens*action against the prosecuting attorney and the postal inspectors, alleging his prosecution was in retaliation for his criticism of the USPS, which was a violation of his FIRST AMENDMENT rights. The federal district court granted absolute immunity to the prosecutor but allowed the case against the inspectors to proceed. Over the course of ten years the case was litigated in the district and **appellate** courts without reaching trial. The inspectors argued that they should be granted qualified immunity because the underlying criminal charges had been supported by probable cause but failed to convince the Court of Appeals for the DISTRICT OF COLUMBIA. The Supreme Court agreed to hear the inspectors' appeal to resolve a split in the circuit courts of appeals over whether a plaintiff needed to provide evidence of lack of probable cause to prevail in a retaliatory prosecution *Bivens* action.

The Court, in a 5–2 decision, overturned the appeals court ruling and found that a lack of probable cause needed to be proven by the plaintiff. (Chief Justice John Roberts did not participate in the consideration of the case because he had recently served on the D.C. Circuit; Justice Samuel Alito did not participate because he had been confirmed after the case had been argued.) Justice DAVID SOUTER, writing for the majority, noted that the postal inspectors posited two main arguments for making the lack of probable cause an essential element. First, they claimed that without this requirement it would make it too easy for disgruntled criminal defendants to simply allege "a retaliatory **animus**, a subjective condition too easy to claim and too hard to defend against." An objective element, the lack of probable cause, was needed to filter out frivolous litigation. Second, the inspectors contended that the traditional tort of **malicious prosecution** was similar to a retaliatory prosecution action; in that tort the plaintiff was required to prove lack of probable cause. Though Justice Souter agreed with the idea of an objective fact requirement, he declined to adopt the **common law** parallel of malicious prosecution and he discounted the concern over frivolous litigation; fewer than two dozen retaliatory prosecutions had been filed under *Bivens* in the past 25 years.

Justice Souter instead based his reasoning on "the need to prove a chain of causation from animus to injury, with details specific to retaliatory-prosecution cases." If the plaintiff can demonstrate there was no probable cause for the criminal charge it will reinforce the retaliation evidence. If the plaintiff cannot show lack of probable cause it "will suggest that prosecution would have occurred even without a retaliatory motive." The need for this element was also imperative in a case such as this one, where the postal inspectors did not make the prosecutorial decision to bring charges. Moore needed to show that the inspectors acted in retaliation and also "induced the prosecutor to bring charges that would not have been initiated without his urging."

Justice RUTH BADER GINSBURG, in a dissenting opinion joined by Justice STEPHEN BREYER, argued that the burden of proving lack of probable cause should be placed with the postal inspectors. The Court's decision meant that "only *entirely* 'baseless prosecutions' would be checked." Evidence that was "barely sufficient" to support probable cause would allow federal officers to "accomplish their mission" of retaliatory prosecution.

INSANITY DEFENSE

A defense asserted by an accused in a criminal prosecution to avoid liability for the commission of a crime because, at the time of the crime, the person did not appreciate the nature or quality or wrongfulness of the acts.

Clark v. Arizona

There are no constitutional precedents regarding the use of the **insanity defense** in criminal trials, and since its inception in 18th century British **common law**, courts have left the consideration of a defendant's mental state to the courts and triers of fact. In the highly anticipated case of *Clark v. Arizona*, No. 05–5966, the U.S. SUPREME COURT upheld the State of Arizona's limited use of insanity evidence solely for the purpose of determining an ability to distinguish right from wrong. The Court found that this limitation did not violate a defendant's DUE PROCESS rights under the Fifth and Fourteenth Amendments to the U.S. Constitution.

The Court also found no violation in Arizona's restricted use of defense evidence of mental illness or incapacity solely for the purpose of proving an **affirmative defense** of insanity. In the present case, Arizona's narrow use of such evidence eliminated defendant Clark's ability to use evidence of his mental illness to counter prosecution's proof of MENS REA, or the mental element of criminal intent, needed to establish the crime of first degree murder.

The background facts showed that in the early morning hours of June 21, 2000, Officer Jeffrey Moritz of the Flagstaff, Arizona police responded in uniform to complaints that a pickup truck with blaring music was circling a residential block. When Officer Moritz spotted the truck, he turned on his emergency lights and siren on his marked patrol car. Seventeen-year-old Eric Clark pulled over. Officer Moritz got out of the patrol car and told Clark to stay where he was, but Clark shot the officer and ran away on foot. Officer Moritz was able to call for backup help before he died. Later that day, Clark was arrested with gunpowder residue still on his hands. A gun later traced to the one that killed the officer was found nearby, stuffed inside a knit cap.

Clark was charged with first-degree murder under Ariz. Rev. Stat. Ann. §§13–1105(A)(3), intentionally or knowingly killing a law enforcement officer in the line of duty. Clark waived his right to a jury and the case was heard by the state court.

At trial, Clark did not contest the shooting and death, but focused on his mental state. The defense tried to use evidence of Clark's undisputed paranoid schizophrenia in two contexts. First, it was introduced to support an affirmative defense of insanity. Second, it was used in an attempt to rebut evidence of the requisite criminal intent. Defense argued that Clark's mental illness at the time of the incident prevented him from having the specific intent to "intentionally and knowingly" kill a law enforcement officer.

Following this, prosecution rebutted with circumstantial evidence showing Clark's knowledge that Officer Moritz was a police officer, e.g., that Clark acknowledged the symbols of police authority and stopped and pulled over when Moritz sounded his sirens and activated his emergency lights behind Clark. Other testimony was offered which tended to show that Clark had intentionally lured a police officer to the area in order to kill him, having told several people a few weeks earlier that he wanted to shoot police officers.

The trial court refused to consider defense evidence bearing on the issue of mental illness for purposes of rebutting the element of *mens rea.* The court cited *State v. Mott*, 187 Ariz. 536, cert. denied, 520 U.S. 1234 (1997), in which that court refused to allow psychiatric testimony to negate specific intent, and held that "Arizona does not allow evidence of a defendant's mental disorder short of insanity . . . to negate the *mens rea* element of a crime." 187 Ariz. at 541.

Terry and Dave Clark, parents of Eric Clark, outside their Arizona home, April 2006.
AP IMAGES

At the close of Clark's trial, the judge issued a special verdict of first degree murder, expressly finding that Clark had shot and killed Officer Moritz **beyond a reasonable doubt**, and that Clark had failed to show that he was insane at the time. The judge further expressly noted that any mental illness from which Clark suffered did not distort his perception of reality so severely that he did not know his actions were wrong. Clark was sentenced to life imprisonment.

Clark moved to vacate the judgment and sentence, mainly arguing that Arizona's insanity test and its *Mott* rule each violated due process. The court denied the motion. The Court of Appeals of Arizona affirmed. The Supreme Court of Arizona denied further review, and the U.S. Supreme Court granted **certiorari** on the question of whether due process prohibited Arizona from narrowing its insanity test or excluding evidence of mental illness/incapacity to rebut evidence of criminal intent.

Justice Souter delivered the majority opinion of a divided Court. He was joined by Chief Justice Roberts and Justices Scalia, Thomas, and Alito. Justice Breyer concurred in part and in the ultimate **disposition**, but filed a separate opinion also dissenting in part. Justices Kennedy, Stevens, and Ginsburg dissented.

The Court discredited Clark's argument that Arizona's departure from the landmark English case that provided the foundation for considering mental state (*McNaghten's Case, 1843*) offended a basic principle of justice "so rooted in the traditions and conscience of our people as to be ranked as fundamental," (quoting *Patterson v. New York*, 432 U.S. 197). Neither did Arizona's abbreviated version of the *McNaghten* statement raise any claim that some constitutional minimum had been shortchanged. Cognitive incapacity is relevant under both the abbreviated and full statement, and evidence going to cognitive incapacity has the same significance under both.

Likewise, said the Court, the Arizona Supreme Court's *Mott* rule does not violate due process, and the reasons supporting the rule satisfy due process. They include Arizona's authority to define its presumption of sanity by choosing an insanity definition and placing the **burden of persuasion** on criminal defendants claiming incapacity as an excuse. Arizona's rule also serves to avoid juror confusion or misunderstanding.

The dissent argued that Clark should have been permitted to introduce "critical and reliable" evidence showing that he lacked intent or knowledge.

INTERNET

A worldwide telecommunications network of business, government, and personal computers.

Google Refuses to Give Search Engine Data to Government

Google Inc. refused to comply with a subpoena issued by the JUSTICE DEPARTMENT that sought the search terms that were entered into Google's system during one random week. The request was made as part of the government's case to defend its online pornography law. A federal judge in March 2006 said that he would require Google to turn over some records, but was hesitant to require the company to release the search queries.

Congress enacted the Child Online Protection Act, Pub. L. No. 105–277, 112 Stat. 2681 (1998), to deter Web sites from posting material that was harmful to minors. A series of court challenges ensued after the passage of the act, and the **statute** has never taken effect. These challenges have twice gone before the U.S. SUPREME COURT, which upheld injunctions that blocked the enforcement of the statute.

In *Ashcroft v. ACLU*, 542 U.S. 656, 124 S. Ct. 2783, 159 L. Ed. 2d 690 (2004), the Court remanded the case to the lower courts so that the courts could examine whether Internet-filtering technology could be a viable alternative to achieving the law's objectives. As part of its case in a U.S. **District Court** in San Jose, California, the Justice Department issued subpoenas to Google, American Online, the Microsoft Network, and Yahoo Inc. The government's subpoena did not include a request for information that could be used to identify the individuals who entered the various search queries.

The requests in the subpoenas became public in January 2006. Spokespersons for the companies other than Google said that they partially complied with the subpoenas but did not give up any personally identifiable data. Google, on the other hand, refused to comply and did not turn over any of the search queries. The government also asked Google to provide a random sample of one million Web pages that could be searched using Google's search engine. Google refused this request as well.

The news that the Justice Department had issued these subpoenas came during the same time that the government was being criticized for engaging in spying activities on U.S. soil. For instance, the Justice Department has reportedly relied on the USA PATRIOT Act, Pub. L. No. 107–56, 115 Stat. 272 (2001), to demand records regarding library patrons' use of the Internet.

The adult entertainment industry has long been the target of the federal government and state governments. The Internet has caused an explosion in the amount of pornographic and adult-oriented material that can be accessed. According to reports, more than 38 million people, representing about 25 percent of all Internet users in the U.S., accessed an adult Web site during the month of December in 2005. Whereas the entire adult entertainment industry recorded more than $12 billion in revenue in 2005, Web users spent an estimated $2.5 billion for adult entertainment available on the Internet.

Part of the growth in the online pornography business is due to the Internet's apparent anonymity. However, unbeknownst to many Web users, search engines retain information that can be used to identify those who enter the search terms. "Google has always been a kind of ticking time bomb because Google retains personally identifiable information," said Marc Rotenberg of the Electronic Privacy Information Center. "Even though Google may intend to protect online privacy, there will be circumstances beyond their control that will place Internet users at risk, and they include government warrants, as in this case, or future security breaches which have plagued the financial services sector over the past couple of years."

Several other privacy advocates and privacy law experts also expressed concerns over the government's requests. Aden J. Fine, a staff attorney with the AMERICAN CIVIL LIBERTIES UNION, said that the government had failed to show a need for the information. "The government's attitude, apparently, is that it's entitled to information without justification," Fine said.

Google's refusal was based on several grounds other than privacy concerns. First, the company maintained that the government had overreached in requesting the information, since Google was not a party to the lawsuit. Despite efforts on the part of the company to negotiate with the government, the Justice Department continued its effort to obtain the information.

Google also said that turning over the requested records could have chilling effect on its customers. According to a letter sent from the company to the Justice Department in October 2005, "Google's acceding to the request would suggest that it is willing to reveal information about those who use its services. This is not a perception Google can accept. And one can envision scenarios where queries could reveal identifying information about a specific Google user, which is another outcome that Google cannot accept."

In March, U.S. District Judge James Ware informed the parties that although he would require Google to submit some information, he was reluctant to require the company to submit the random search queries. Ware said that he would not want to create an impression that search engines could be used as tools for government surveillance. By the time that the hearing took place, the government had scaled down its requests, asking for a random sampling of 50,000 Web sites that Google indexes along with the text of 5,000 random search queries.

AOL Targets Phishers in Virginia Lawsuit

In February 2006, AOL became the first company to take advantage of a new anti-phishing law in Virginia. The company is seeking $18 million in damages from several organizations that engage in phishing, which is a practice where a perpetrator attempts to obtain personal information from a victim by luring the victim to an authentic-looking Web site. AOL said that it hopes to add several additional defendants to the suit in order to deter individuals and entities from engaging in this type of activity.

Phishing has become a pervasive and damaging aspect of the Internet. The scam usually involves the mass distribution of an email that appears to be from a legitimate company, such as PayPal, eBay, or a bank chain. The email is usually addressed to a generic customer, indicating that the company is having a problem with the customer's account. The email includes a link to a site that appears at first glance to be authentic. At this site, users are directed to enter personal information, including account numbers, credit card numbers, and passwords.

According to Symantec, a prominent computer security company, one out of every 125 emails sent in 2005 was part of a phishing scheme. One estimate indicated that 1.2 million people suffered losses as a result of phishing schemes between May 2004 and May 2005. Some states have taken the initiative to crack down on phishing scams by enacting legislation that either makes phishing a crime or imposes civil liability on those running the phishing scams.

During 2005, Virginia enacted several bills designed to crack down on computer and Internet crimes. Among these laws was the first law in the U.S. that made the act of phishing a crime. Scammers who are convicted under this **statute** could face $2,500 in fines and up to five years in prison. Many high-tech companies are located in Virginia, and about half of the world's emails are routed through the state.

AOL and other companies have relied on litigation in the past to attempt to deter online criminal activity. AOL, Microsoft, and other companies have relied on state and federal laws in the past to sue spammers that send unwanted advertisements through emails. The companies have had some success in court using this strategy. AOL relied on the federal Controlling the Assault on Non-Solicited Pornography and Marketing (CAN-SPAM) Act, 108–187, 117 Stat. 2699 (2003) to sue two spammers who were reportedly well known in the anti-spam community. In August 2005, the company announced that it had received a $13 million judgment.

In October 2005, AOL announced that it had entered into partnership agreements with some of the leading anti-phishing companies, including Cyota, MarkMonitor, and Cyveillance. These companies offer software that purportedly provides protection against phishing attacks for AOL members. AOL reported that it could block about eight million phishing attempts per day.

In February, AOL became the first major Internet service provider to cite Virginia's anti-phishing statute when the company filed three lawsuits in the U.S. **District Court** for the Eastern District of Virginia in Alexandria. The suit targets three major phishing "gangs," which the company alleges are responsible for victimizing many of the members of AOL and CompuServe. The suit alleges that 30 yet unnamed individuals violated the Virginia anti-phishing statute, as well as a federal computer **fraud** law and the federal trademark statute. Many of the alleged phishers are located in countries other than the U.S., including Germany and Romania. AOL is seeking $18 million in damages.

"Phishing scams have grown more sophisticated and more dangerous to consumers," said Curtis Lu, Senior Vice President and Deputy General Counsel at AOL. "The phishers targeted in our lawsuit spoof a variety of prominent Internet brands, including AOL." Another AOL spokesman, Nicholas Graham, said that the lawsuits were part of an ongoing effort to identify phishing operations. According to Graham, the number of defendants should grow as the lawsuit progresses. "Our intention is to bust them apart and put them out of business," he said.

The announcement of AOL's suit came at a time when phishing activity reportedly continued to increase. The Anti-Phishing Working Group (APWG), which is sponsored by several dozen major companies, received 18,480 unique phishing reports during the month of March in 2006. This was the most ever recorded by the group. The phishing attacks during that month hijacked 70 brand names in their attempts to lure customers to provide personal information. According to the report, the United States hosted the most phishing sites (35.13% of the total) during that month.

In addition to tactics where customers are lured to what appears to be legitimate Web sites, perpetrators are also relying more on other methods to steal information. One such method is to install malicious software, very similar to a virus, that tracks keystrokes entered by a user. These keyloggers can then be used by others to obtain user names and passwords, as well as other personal information. According to the APWG, the number of unique keylogger applications nearly tripled between April 2005 and March 2006.

The increase in phishing and related activities may suggest that litigation is only one possible solution to these problems. According to John R. Levine, chairperson of the Anti-Spam Research Group, it would take hundreds of high-profile cases against spammers to deter the practice.

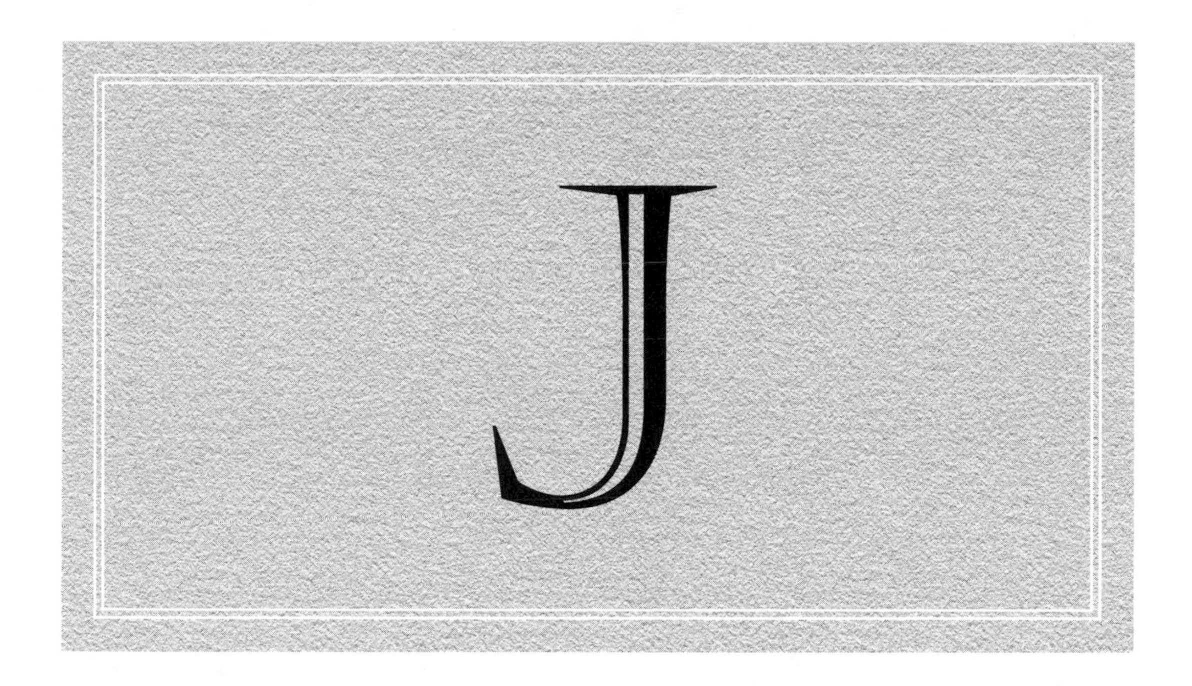

JURISDICTION

The geographic area over which authority extends; legal authority; the authority to hear and determine causes of action.

Empire Healthchoice v. McVeigh

In *Empire Healthchoice Assurance v. McVeigh*, No. 05-200, 547 U.S. ___ (2006), the U.S. SUPREME COURT was asked to decide whether FEDERAL QUESTION jurisdiction applied to reimbursement claims made by a federal healthcare contractor against proceeds from state-court litigation. Said the Court in the slim majority's opinion, "Federal courts should await a clear signal from Congress before treating such auxiliary claims as 'arising under' the laws of the United States."

Joseph McVeigh, a federal employee working for the ENVIRONMENTAL PROTECTION AGENCY (EPA), was seriously injured as a passenger in a 1997 car accident. Although, following surgery, he was able to return to work, he ultimately died in 2001 of a seizure related to head injuries suffered in the accident.

McVeigh's medical bills totaled somewhere between $100,000 and $157,000. (The disparity represented disagreement between the parties. An attorney for McVeigh's estate claimed the same $15,000 charge for brain surgery showed up three times on a charge summary statement, along with some other unrelated charges. In any event, the total amount owed was not part of the high court's ruling.)

As a federal employee, McVeigh's bills were paid under the Federal Employees Health Benefits Act (FEHBA), 5 USC 8901 *et seq.* Under FEHBA, the federal government pays for approximately 75 percent of premiums and federal employees pay the remainder. The combined premium payments are deposited in a special Treasury fund, from which **carriers** (such as Empire Healthchoice) draw to pay for covered benefits. The Act itself contains no provision that addresses carriers' **subrogation** or reimbursement rights or claims.

The federal Office of Personnel Management (OPM) negotiates and regulates health benefits plans for federal employees. OPM had contracted with the Blue Cross Blue Shield Association (BCBSA) to provide a nationwide fee-for-service health plan (the Plan), to be administered by local companies. Empire Healthchoice Assurance, Inc. (Empire) administered the BCBSA plan to federal employees in New York State. The Plan obligated Empire to make a "reasonable effort" to recover amounts paid for medical care. The "statement of benefits" distributed by Empire to its beneficiaries/enrollees notified them that monetary recoveries received by them must be used to reimburse Empire for benefits paid on their behalf.

After McVeigh's death, his widow, who was the administrator of his estate, filed a **wrongful death** suit in state court against those allegedly responsible for his death. Empire, as the health-care benefits provider, had notice of the state-court action, but took no part in it. Prior to trial, a large settlement was reached, and the parties agreed to the settlement. McVeigh's estate set aside $100,000 in **escrow** for reimbursement of benefits.

However, Empire instead filed suit against McVeigh's estate in federal **district court** for the Southern District of New York, seeking reimbursement for the $157,000 it allegedly paid for McVeigh's medical care. The district court dismissed Empire's suit for lack of federal jurisdiction, holding that the issue raised was a state, and not federal one.

For its part, Empire maintained that, since it was a federal contractor, its reimbursement claims implicated "uniquely federal interest[s]." (Empire quoted *Boyle v. United Technologies Corp.*, 487 U.S. 500, in which the appeals court held that courts may create federal **common law** only where state law would "significant[ly] conflict" with "uniquely federal interests.") Empire also argued that FEHBA contained a **preemption** provision that independently conferred federal jurisdiction.

The Second **Circuit Court** of Appeals affirmed the district court's dismissal of Empire's suit. It agreed that *Boyle* was controlling, but concluded that Empire had not met its burden of showing that there was "significant conflict" between federal law and New York state law.

Supreme Court Justice RUTH BADER GINSBURG, writing for the 5–4 slim majority, held that **federal courts** lacked jurisdiction over suits filed by a federal government contractor for reimbursement of benefits paid pursuant to a provision in a health benefits plan for federal employees. While the majority agreed that distinctly federal elements were involved, other considerations controlled. For example, the express language in the FEHBA's jurisdictional provision, §8912, created federal jurisdiction for civil actions "against the United States." Further, express language in OPM regulations channel disputes over *coverage or benefits* into federal court by designating OPM as the sole defendant, "and not against the carrier or carrier's subcontractors." 5 CFR 809.107(c). Nowhere in the Act or OPM regulations is there language that opens federal courts to *carriers* seeking reimbursement. Thus, the preemption provision cited by Empire did not apply to it as a carrier. Ultimately, the majority reasoned that state courts in which personal injury and wrongful death actions were more generally lodged were competent to apply federal law, and best suited to ascertain fair **apportionment** of tort recovery among co-parties. Accordingly, the majority opinion upheld both district court dismissal and the Second Circuit's affirming opinion.

However, the majority opinion was lengthy. Justice Breyer filed a dissenting opinion in which he was joined by Justices Kennedy, Souter, and Alito.

Lincoln Property Co. v. Roche

Defendants in a civil lawsuit filed in state court may ask a federal **district court** to remove the matter to federal court in that state if the defendants are not citizens of the state. This right to seek removal is part of federal diversity jurisdiction that is authorized by Congress in 28 U.S.C.A. § 1441. It is predicated on the belief that non-citizens of a state will receive a fairer hearing in federal court rather than state court. Section 1441 states that removal is permissible "only if none of the parties in interest properly joined as defendants is a citizen of the State in which [the] action [was] brought." The Supreme Court, in *Lincoln Property Co. v. Roche*, __U.S.__, 126 S.Ct. 606, 163 L.Ed.2d 415 (2005), ruled that named defendants do not have to an obligation to name some other **entity** that they are affiliated with and show that its **joinder** would not destroy diversity jurisdiction and send the case back to state court.

Christophe and Juanita Roche rented an apartment in Fairfax County, Virginia. The complex known as Westwood Village was managed by Lincoln Property Company. The Roches discovered toxic mold in the apartment, which can lead to serious health problems. Investigators concluded that the mold spores were airborne in the apartment and had contaminated carpeting and fabric-covered surfaces. The couple moved out of the unit while it was decontaminated, leaving their personal property in the care of Lincoln and the mold removal firm. The Roches later filed separate but similar civil lawsuits in Virginia state court against Lincoln and the State of Wisconsin Investment Board, which allegedly owned the apartment complex. They alleged that the mold had made them sick. They claimed memory loss, headaches, and respiratory problems as well as the alleged loss, theft, or destruction of their personal property during the period they had left the apartment. The couple sought damages for these alleged injuries.

Lincoln and the board removed the two cases to Virginia federal district court, citing diversity-of-citizenship jurisdiction under § 1441. The notice of removal stated that Lincoln was a Texas corporation with its principal headquarters in Texas. The board stated that it was an independent agency located in Wisconsin. This information had been contained in the Roches' state complaints and the Roches agreed in their federal complaints that the **federal courts** had jurisdiction to decide these matters. Lincoln answered the Roches' federal complaints, admitting that it managed the apartment complex in question. In addition, it did not try to avoid liability by claiming that some other entity was responsible for managing the complex. Though the Roches told the court that they would investigate to see if additional defendants needed to be joined to the lawsuit, they did not try to join any additional defendants. After discovery, the federal court granted Lincoln's motion to dismiss the case. Six days later the Roches moved the court to remand the case to state court, alleging for the first time that there was no diversity between Lincoln and them. They contended that Lincoln was not a Texas corporation but rather a partnership that had a partner residing in Virginia. The district court denied the motion after Lincoln presented documents that proved it was a Texas corporation.

The Fourth **Circuit Court** of Appeals reversed the district court and instructed it to remand the case to Virginia state court. The appeals court agreed that Lincoln was a Texas corporation and a proper party in the action but found that Lincoln operated under "many different structures." The court believed Lincoln was a nominal party and suspected that an unidentified Virginia subsidiary was the "real and substantial party in interest." Lincoln had failed to demonstrate the nonexistence of the Virginia entity and therefore had failed to meet is burden of establishing diversity. The Supreme Court agreed to hear Lincoln's appeal because the circuit courts of appeals were divided on whether an entity not named or joined as a defendant can still be considered a real party in interest whose presence would destroy diversity.

The Court, in a unanimous decision, reversed the Fourth Circuit ruling. Justice RUTH BADER GINSBURG, writing for the Court, noted that the Roches could have kept the case in state court if they had named and served as a defendant a party that resided in Virginia. Once removed to federal court, the Federal Rules of **Civil Procedure** reinforced the conclusion that no additional parties needed to be named for the action to proceed. As to Lincoln's status, Justice Ginsburg pointed out that Lincoln had accepted responsibility for managing the apartment complex. Therefore, a "named defendant who admits involvement in the controversy and would be liable to pay a resulting judgment is not 'nominal' in any sense except that it is named in the complaint." The Fourth Circuit had no authority to "inquire whether some other person might have been joined as an additional or substitute defendant." It was up to the plaintiff to deal with the consequences of selecting the named parties, and not the responsibility of a defendant to name additional defendants. As "masters of their complaint," the Roches had the duty to discover and then seek permission to join other parties that might defeat diversity.

Martin v. Franklin Capital Corporation

Under federal **statute** 28 U.S.C.A. § 1441 a defendant in a civil lawsuit that has been filed in state court may remove the case to a federal **district court** if the defendant is a citizen of another state. This diversity-of-citizenship jurisdiction is premised on the assumption that an out-of-state defendant will receive a fairer hearing in the federal court by avoiding local bias. However, diversity jurisdiction cannot be asserted if the plaintiff's claim for damages is less than $75,000. This provision prevents the **federal courts** from being overwhelmed by relatively minor disputes. Finally, if a defendant improperly removes the case to federal court and that court sends it back to state court, the plaintiff may recover attorney fees from the defendant under 28 U.S.C.A. § 1447(c). As to this last issue, the circuit courts of appeal were divided as to when attorney fees should be awarded under § 1447(c). The Supreme Court, in *Martin v. Franklin Capital Corp.*, __U.S.__, 126 S.Ct. 704, 163 L.Ed.2d 547 (2005), ruled that absent unusual circumstances, attorney's fees should not be awarded when the removing party "has an objectively reasonable basis for removal."

Gerald and Juana Martin filed a class-action lawsuit in New Mexico state court against Franklin Capital Corporation alleging that Franklin had improperly bought car insurance on their behalf to protect Franklin in case the car they had purchased on credit was involved in an accident. Franklin, which is a California corporation, removed the case to federal district court, as was its right under the federal removal statute. The **amount in controversy** was not clear when Franklin removed the case but it relied on legal precedent suggesting that **punitive damages** and attorney's fees could be included in a **class action** to meet the amount-in-controversy requirement. Fifteen months later the Martins filed a motion asking that the federal court send the case back to state court because their claims did not meet the amount-in-controversy requirement. The district denied their motion but the Tenth **Circuit Court** of Appeals reversed. The Tenth Circuit concluded that punitive damages and attorney's fees could not be aggregated to meet the **statutory** minimum for federal jurisdiction. The appeals court acknowledged that this ruling was based on decisions that had been made after the district court had rejected the Martin's motion to remand the case to state court.

Based on this ruling the Martins filed a motion in federal district court asking that Franklin pay their attorney's fees for the removal litigation under 28 U.S.C.A. § 1447(c). The district court rejected this motion as well, finding that Franklin had "objectively reasonable grounds" for believing its removal of the case to federal court was proper. The Martins appealed this ruling to the Tenth Circuit, arguing that attorney's fees must be awarded when a removed case is returned to state court. The Tenth Circuit declined to adopt this reasoning, ruling that under circuit precedent the trial judge had "wide discretion" to award fees based on the "propriety of defendant's removal." In this case Franklin had calculated the amount in controversy relying on court precedents; therefore its basis for removal was objectively reasonable. The Supreme Court agreed to hear the Martins' appeal because other circuit courts of appeal had developed different rules for awarding fees under 28 U.S.C.A. § 1447(c).

The Court, in a unanimous decision, affirmed the Tenth Circuit ruling. Chief Justice John Roberts, writing for the Court, found no merit in the Martins' claim that attorney's fees should be awarded automatically when a removed case is sent back to state court. The statute stated that the court "may" award attorney's fees, not "shall" or "should." The use of the word "may" clearly connoted discretion and the Court could not change the meaning of the text to make the awarding of feeds mandatory. Roberts pointed out that 28 U.S.C.A. § 1447(c) contained the word "shall" in enough places to indicate Congress knew what it was doing when it used the word "may" in dealing with attorney's fees. The Martins claimed that at minimum that there should be a strong presumption in favor of awarding attorney's fees. Roberts agree that the Martins were on "somewhat stronger ground" because the Court had created such a presumption involving a civil rights statute that permitted the discretionary award of attorney's fees. However, in the civil rights case the plaintiff had served as a "private attorney general" in trying to vindicate civil rights laws. Moreover, the defendant in that case had violated federal law. The Martins were not serving as private attorneys general when they convinced the court to remand the case to state court and Franklin had not violated federal law. Roberts emphasized that Franklin had the right to remove the case under the statute and its error in doing so was "not comparable to violating a substantive federal law."

The U.S. government had filed a brief in the case, urging the Court to limit attorney's fees to cases where the defendant's removal action was "frivolous, unreasonable, or without foundation." Chief Justice Roberts found no merit in this approach; Congress did not "tilt the exercise of discretion" either in favor or against fee awards. Judges had discretion to grant or deny awards, but they did not have unfettered discretion. They should balance Congress' desire to provide defendants with a right to remove as a general rule against the attempts by some defendants to use removal "for prolonging litigation and imposing costs on the opposing party." Judges may only award attorney's fees where "the removing party lacked an objectively reasonable basis for seeking removal." In this case the lower courts properly denied the request for fees because Franklin had an objectively reasonable grounds for removal, based on circuit precedent.

Wachovia Bank v. Schmidt

U.S. national banks are a special type of corporation, chartered to do business by the **Comptroller** of the Currency of the U.S. Treasury rather than by state governments. Congress has overseen the regulation of national banks since the Nineteenth Century and it has periodically passed legislation that deals with how courts of law will handle matters involving these banks. In *Wachovia Bank v. Schmidt*, __U.S.__, 126 S.Ct. 941, 163 L.Ed.2d 797 (2006), the U.S. SUPREME COURT had to decide whether a fair reading of these statutes precluded a national bank from asserting diversity jurisdiction and removing a state court lawsuit to federal court. The lower courts had found that because the national bank had a branch "located" in a state, that branch was a citizen of that state and must litigate the dispute in state court. The Supreme Court rejected this ruling, concluding that the text and legislative history of the **statute** allowed the national bank to claim citizenship in the place designated in its articles of association as the location of its main office.

Daniel Schmidt and other citizens of South Carolina filed suit in state court against Wachovia Bank, alleging that Wachovia had used **fraud** to induce them to buy tax shelters that were ruled illegal by the INTERNAL REVENUE SER-

VICE. Wachovia is a national bank with its designated main office in Charlotte, North Carolina. Wachovia filed a motion in the federal **district court** located in South Carolina, asking the court to compel arbitration to resolve the dispute. It based federal court jurisdiction for the matter on diversity-South Carolina plaintiffs and a North Carolina defendant. The district court denied Wachovia's motion and the bank appealed to the Fourth **Circuit Court** of Appeals. However, the Fourth Circuit declined to rule on the merits of the arbitration issue, finding that the district court lacked diversity jurisdiction over the matter. It directed that the lower court to dismiss the case.

Judge Michael Luttig of the Fourth Circuit, writing for the majority, noted that under 28 U.S.C.A. § 1348 national banks like Wachovia are, for diversity purposes, "deemed citizens of the States in which they are respectively located." Wachovia was "located" in every state in which it had a branch office and therefore it must be a "citizen" of these states as well. The Wachovia branch in South Carolina was a citizen of the state, thereby defeating federal diversity jurisdiction. The Supreme Court agreed to hear Wachovia's appeal, as the circuit courts of appeals had divided over the meaning of § 1348. Some agreed with the Fourth Circuit, while others believed national banks are citizens of their designate main offices.

The Supreme Court, in an 8-0 decision (Justice CLARENCE THOMAS did not participate in the consideration of the case), reversed the Fourth Circuit ruling. Justice RUTH BADER GINSBURG, writing for the Court, reviewed the legislative history of national banks, which were first specifically authorized by Congress in 1863. This law granted **federal courts** jurisdiction to hear proceedings for and against national banks, without regard to diversity, the **amount in controversy**, or the existence of a **federal question**. This stood in contrast to state-chartered banks, which like any state-incorporated business organization could pursue a federal lawsuit only on the basis of diversity or the federal question jurisdiction. However, in 1882 Congress reversed course and removed national banks' automatic federal jurisdiction. This amendment placed national banks on the same footing as the banks of the state where they were located. In 1887 Congress returned to the issue, replacing the 1882 provision and using the "located" language now found in § 1348. Congress still sought to place national and state banks on the same jurisdictional plane. Almost 25 years passed before Congress recodified the national bank jurisdiction language in 1911. The phrase "citizens of the States in which they are respectively located" was retained and in 1948 Congress enacted § 1348 in its present form. The law states that federal districts have **original jurisdiction** to hear national bank cases "established in the district for which the court is held," as well as the "located" provision.

Justice Ginsburg rejected the three major reasons advanced by the Fourth Circuit. First, the word "located" did not have a fixed, plain meaning as claimed by the appeals court. In some provisions the word "unquestionably refers to a single place: the site of the banking association's designated main office." In other provisions the word seemed to refer to or include branch offices. Second, Congress may have intended the words "located" and established" as synonymous or alternative terms. When Congress addressed this issue (1863, 1882, 1887, 1911 and 1948), national banks "were almost always 'located' in the State in which they were 'established.'" With few exceptions a national bank was not permitted to operate branches outside its home state. It was not until 1994 that Congress gave national banks the authority to establish branches in other states. Justice Ginsburg surmised that "Congress' use of the two terms may be best explained as a coincidence of **statutory** codification." Third, a 1977 Court ruling relied on by the Fourth Circuit was not applicable. The Court had interpreted the word "located" in a now-repealed **venue** statute for national banks to include any county in which a bank maintained a branch office. Justice Ginsburg held that venue and subject-matter jurisdiction were "not concepts of the same order." Venue is "largely a matter of litigational convenience" (where is the best place to hear a case for the convenience of the parties), while subject-matter jurisdiction "concerns a court's competence to adjudicate a particular category of cases" (what can a court hear). Therefore, the Court did not need to honor this case precedent. The Fourth Circuit decision would have meant that national banks would rarely, if ever, be able to claim diversity jurisdiction. The best course was to locate a national bank in the state designated by its articles of association as its main office.

LABOR LAW

An area of the law that deals with the rights of employers, employees, and labor organizations.

Whitman v. Department of Transportation

Labor relations involving the federal government and its employees are governed by **collective bargaining agreement** and federal statutes that impose certain procedures for dealing with employees' grievances. The 1978 Civil Service Reform Act (CSRA), 49 U.S.C.A. § 40122(g)(2)(C), provides rules for grievances, but Congress has authorized the FEDERAL AVIATION ADMINISTRATION (FAA) to develop its own procedures, which incorporate parts of the CSRA. The FAA implemented the CSRA grievance provision that requires employees to exhaust administrative grievance proceedings before they are allowed to sue in federal court. However, in 1995 Congress amended the CSRA to state that grievance proceedings are the "exclusive administrative procedures" for resolving disputes. The insertion of the word "administrative" into this phrase suggested that employees could sue before exhausting administrative procedures. The Supreme Court, in *Whitman v. Department of Transportation*, __U.S.__, 126 S.Ct. 2014, __L.Ed.2d __ (2006), decided not to resolve a conflict among the federal circuit courts of appeals, remanding the case to the Ninth **Circuit Court** of Appeals. However, the Court did give directions to the appeals court that may resolve the conflict.

Terry Whitman was a 13-year air traffic assistant at the Anchorage, Alaska Air Route Traffic Control Center. Federal law requires that the FAA conduct random substance-abuse tests of employees whose jobs include "safety-sensitive functions." FAA regulations provided detailed requirements for the random selection of employees for testing, yet Whitman found that he had been tested 10 times more than two other traffic assistants who had worked as long as he had in the Anchorage center. Whitman tested negatively each time. Whitman first filed a grievance with the Federal Labor Relations Board, which refused to consider it because it was outside the board's jurisdiction. It only dealt with issues relating to an employee's union activity. Whitman then filed a lawsuit in federal court, alleging that the FAA had violated the law governing drug tests and the FIRST AMENDMENT by subjecting him to a disproportionate number of tests.

The Alaska federal **district court** dismissed Whitman's lawsuit, agreeing with the government that the CSRA governed his grievance and that the CSRA did not expressly confer federal court jurisdiction over such claims. The court stated that his sole remedy was to use the negotiated grievance procedures detailed in the collective bargaining agreement between the FAA and the National Association of Government Employees. Whitman appealed to the Ninth Circuit Court of Appeals, which upheld the district court ruling. Judge Kim Wardlow, writing for the three-judge panel, 382 F.3d 938 (2004), noted that that the FAA Personnel Management System was an "integrated scheme of administrative and judicial review." The FAA System incorporated the grievance provisions of the CSRA, which defined "grievance" to include an employee's complaint "concerning any matter relating to the employment of the employee" and "any claimed violation, misinterpretation, or misapplication of any law, rule, or regulation affecting conditions of employment." Wardlow concluded that this broad definition included the allegations that Whitman had made against the FAA. In addition, the CSRA required all collective bargaining agreements to have negotiated procedures for the resolution of employee grievances. The FAA had negotiated such procedures with Whitman's association, thereby satisfying the **statutory** requirement.

The Ninth Circuit acknowledged that the 1994 CSRA amendment changed the grievance provision to make it the "exclusive administrative procedures for resolving grievances which fall within its coverage." Moreover, the Eleventh and Federal Circuits had interpreted this amendment to mean that Congress had given federal employees the right to seek a judicial remedy for their grievances. Judge Wardlow stated that the Ninth Circuit precedent went the other way and the law of the circuit barred grievances from **federal courts**. Apart from precedent, a reading of the amendment demonstrated that it did not expressly grant federal courts jurisdiction; all the amendment did was establish an exclusive administrative remedy. Because the amendment did not confer federal court jurisdiction, Whitman had to press his claims through the grievance process negotiated in the collective bargaining agreement." Whitman also asserted that the his claims about the drug and alcohol testing was not an "employee" grievance but a "prohibited personnel practice." Using this characterization, Whitman would have had to pursue corrective action under the CSRA through the Office of Special Counsel. Though this too was an administrative process, Whitman argued that it was a dead end because the FAA was immune from such an investigation. Therefore, he was entitled to file a federal lawsuit. Judge Wardlow disagreed, finding that the Office of Special Counsel could investigate the FAA System.

The Supreme Court agreed to hear the case to resolve the conflict among the three circuit courts. However, in a unanimous decision, the Court issued a *per curiam* opinion (one in which no judge is identified as the author), vacating the Ninth Circuit decision and returning it to that circuit for reconsideration based on the Court's ruling. The Court agreed with the Ninth Circuit that the 1994 amendment did not confer jurisdiction on the federal courts but stated that the issue was whether the amendment removed federal court jurisdiction. Before the Court could determine whether the amendment precluded jurisdiction, it needed to "ascertain where Whitman's claims fit within the statutory scheme, as the CSRA provides different treatment for grievances depending on the nature of the claim. The Court of Appeals had failed to do this, as it did not determine if the FAA's actions constituted a "prohibited personnel practice." Therefore, the court sent the case back to the Ninth Circuit to resolve this issue as well as the preclusion issue. The Court also said the appeals court was free to analyze a host of other issues that could help resolve the matter.

MALPRACTICE

Improper, unskilled, or negligent treatment of a patient by a physician, dentist, nurse, pharmacist, or other health care professional.

Wisconsin Supreme Court Strikes Down Caps on Damages

Many states have attempted to limit medical malpractice damages awards, fearing that large awards drive up the cost of malpractice insurance premiums, increase medical costs, and discourage doctors from working in their states. Wisconsin addressed this problem by placing a cap, adjusted for inflation, on non-economic damages (pain and suffering) for medical malpractice awards. However, the Wisconsin Supreme Court, in *Ferdon v. Wisconsin Patients Compensation Fund*, 701 N.W.2d 440 (2005), ruled that the cap violated the state constitution's **equal protection** clause. Therefore, a child who had been injured at birth was entitled to the $700,000 jury award for past and future noneconomic damages.

Under Wisconsin law prior to this case, a person who brought a claim for medical malpractice against a health care provider could recover both economic and non-economic damages. Non-economic damages include compensation for pain and suffering, mental distress, loss of enjoyment of normal activity, and loss of society and companionship. When this **statute** was originally enacted in 1995, the legislature established a $350,000 limit on non-economic damages, though this amount was adjusted annually to take inflation into account. By 2005, the limit was established at $445,775. Economic damages are not capped.

The case centered on Matthew Ferdon, who was injured at birth during his delivery in 1997. The doctor pulled on Ferdon's head and caused an injury that partially paralyzed and deformed the boy's right arm; the arm will never function normally. Ferdon underwent surgeries and occupational therapy and he will need to undergo further surgery and therapy in the future.

Ferdon, through a **guardian ad litem**, sued the doctor who delivered him and the hospital where he was delivered. Also joined in the suit, as required, was the Wisconsin Patients Compensation Fund. The Fund was responsible for paying medical malpractice awards that exceeded primary insurance coverage. A jury in the case awarded Ferdon $403,000 for future medical expenses and $700,000 in non-economic damages. The trial court reduced this amount of non-economic damages to $410,322, which was the maximum allowed in 2002 when the verdict was reached.

After a state **appellate court** affirmed the trial court's decision to reduce the damage awards, the case was appealed to the state supreme court. Counsel for the child argued that the state's system was unconstitutional under the Equal Protection Clause of the FOURTEENTH AMENDMENT. According to this argument, the state statute created two classes of individuals: (1) those who sustained damages greater than $350,000 and who were only able to recover a fraction of these damages; and (2) those who sustained damages of $350,000 or less and who were fully compensated for their non-economic damages.

The Wisconsin Supreme Court had previously ruled on the constitutionality of different provisions of the statute authorizing the Patient Compensation Fund. In a 1978 case the court had upheld the constitutionality of a review panel process and in a 2001 case the court deadlocked 3–3 over a court of appeals case that upheld the cap on non-economic damages. In *Ferdon* the court, in a 5–4 decision, first rejected the defendants' argument that the court was bound by these precedents to uphold the constitutionality of the cap amount. Chief Justice Shirley Abrahamson, in her majority opinion, noted that neither case addressed Ferdon's argument that the **statutory** cap violated the equal protection clause of the state constitution. Because the prior decisions were not squarely on point the court was free to determine whether the cap on non-economic damages was unconstitutional.

The court first determined the appropriate standard of review to review an equal protection challenge. There are three types of standards: **strict scrutiny**, intermediate scrutiny, and rational basis. Strict scrutiny places a very high burden on the government to justify the constitutionality of a law while intermediate scrutiny places a lesser burden on the government. The rational basis standard of review is much more generous to the government, requiring only that the government show that the law is rationally related to a legitimate government interest. The court opted to use the rational basis standard but stated that its review was "rational basis with teeth." Under this modified standard the court had to determine whether the law had "more than a speculative tendency as the means of furthering a valid legislative purpose."

The court concluded that the cap divided people who were injured as a result of medical negligence into two classes: severely injured persons and less severely injured persons. Those severely injured persons received only a part of their damages, while less severely injured persons (those with non-economic damages below the statutory cap) were able to receive full compensation. The statutory cap also created a second classification scheme: those injured people who were single, those who are married and who have children, and those who are single who have children.

The rational basis for the cap on non-economic damages was based on a number of objectives: to insure adequate compensation for victims with legitimate injury claims, to reduce malpractice awards and malpractice insurance premiums, to protect the fund's financial integrity, to reduce overall healthcare costs, to encourage healthcare providers to practice in Wisconsin, to reduce the use of defensive medicine, and to retain malpractice insurers in the state. The court rejected the conclusion that these objectives sustained the constitutionality of the statute. It found that the cap was not reasonably related to compensating injured persons because the most severely injured persons were treated less favorably than less severely injured persons. To allow the cap would create an undue hardship on a small group of plaintiffs. In addition, the court ruled that the cap had not significantly reduced malpractice insurance premiums nor had the fund demonstrated that it needed the cap to protect its financial integrity. Since its creation in 1975 the fund had only paid 609 claims out of almost 5000 filed. As to reducing overall healthcare costs the court ruled that malpractice premiums were only a very small part of the costs. Finally, the court pointed to a study by the federal government that the caps on non-economic damages did not cause doctors to move in or out of states. Therefore, the proclaimed purposes of the act were not rationally related to legitimate state interests and the cap on non-economic damages violated equal protection. In short, all persons injured by medical malpractice were entitled to their full damages and Ferdon was entitled to the full $700,000 award.

The dissenting justices contended that the legislative purposes rejected by the majority did, in fact, have merit. A substantial portion of very large medical negligence awards was non-economic damages. Moreover, the cap served as an effective means of discouraging some claims from being filed. As to the effectiveness of the cap on overall healthcare costs, the dissenters cited a 2003 congressional report that indicated that malpractice reform could save the federal government anywhere from $12 to $19 billion a year.

The decision set off a firestorm among state legislators. "This is another example of an activist court overstepping its authority," said John Gard, speaker of the state's assembly. "Fixing this ruling will be a top priority." Several politicians, specifically Republicans, along with those in the health care industry warned that this decision could cause residents to lose access to medical care due to rising medical costs.

The legislature spent much of the fall working to reinstate the damage caps. The legislature approved a bill that raised the damage caps to $550,000 for malpractice victims who are younger than 18, and $450,000 for adults. However, Governor Jim Doyle vetoed this bill because the awards were too close to the previous statute. In January 2006, a jury in Dane County, Wisconsin awarded a plaintiff $8.4 million, of which about half was for pain and suffering. The decision energized the debate about the need for damage caps.

In March, the legislature agreed to a proposal that increased the cap on non-economic damages to $750,000. Doyle signed the bill into law. At the time of the signing, Doyle said that he thought the new legislation represented a "reasonable compromise" between the old statute and the court's decision. However, shortly after the bill was enacted, the Wisconsin Academy of Trial Lawyers said that it would challenge the new law in court.

MANSLAUGHTER

The unjustifiable, inexcusable, and intentional killing of a human being without deliberation, premeditation, and malice. The unlawful killing of a human being without any deliberation, which may be involuntary, in the commission of a lawful act without due caution and circumspection.

Hawaii Reverses Manslaughter Conviction for Newborn's Death from Prenatal Substance Abuse

In a state precedent-setting decision, the Hawaii Supreme Court ruled that women cannot be prosecuted for the death of their children caused by detrimental conduct during pregnancy. *State v. Aiwohi*, No. 26838 (November 2005). In so ruling, the state high court overturned the **manslaughter** conviction of 32-year-old Tayshea Aiwohi for the death of her two-day-old son. Medical evidence at trial had linked his death to Aiwohi's drug use during the latter days of pregnancy. The case drew nationwide attention from drug rehabilitation groups and health professionals who feared that such prosecutions might discourage pregnant drug users from seeking treatment and adequate prenatal care.

As background, Aiwohi gave birth to son Treyson on July 15, 2001. At the time of Treyson's birth, Aiwohi was the mother of four other children and had a lengthy and well-documented history of substance abuse for which she had received various treatments. Although she had been tested for drug use during various intervals of her pregnancy, it appeared that she had not been tested in the weeks just prior to Treyson's delivery. Following his birth at a local hospital, she was permitted to breastfeed the baby several times on July 15 and 16. She was discharged from the hospital at approximately 7:00 p.m. on July 16. She reported that she breastfed the baby once more at approximately 1:30 a.m. on July 17; the family then went to sleep, apparently newborn with parents. She further reported that her husband later awakened her and told her that the baby was not breathing. They called 911, and an ambulance transported the baby to Castle Medical Center, where Treyson was pronounced dead at 6:32 a.m. on July 17.

The city medical examiner's office testified before a **grand jury** that high levels of methamphetamine and amphetamine were found in the baby's body. The autopsy report indicated that death was caused by these drugs, consistent with exclusive prenatal exposure through the mother. The medical **examiner** further testified that there was no evidence of disease or disorder, or any evidence of accidental death by suffocation caused by an adult sleeping in the same bed as the baby.

On August 29, 2001, the chief investigator for the Department of the Medical Examiner telephoned Aiwohi and specifically queried her about her use of crystal methamphetamine during her pregnancy. Aiwohi began to cry and admitted to smoking crystal methamphetamine on July 12, 13 and 14, as well as one "hit" on July 15, the morning of Treyson's birth.

Aiwohi waived trial and pleaded no contest to manslaughter under Hawaii Revised Statute §§707-702(1)(a)(which is part of the Hawaii Penal Code) on condition that she could appeal the circuit court's refusal to dismiss the charges based on defense counsel's Motion to Dismiss Indictment, which was denied. The case was appealed directly to the Hawaii Supreme Court from the First **Circuit Court** (FC-CR. No. 03-1-0036)

On appeal, Aiwohi raised several constitutional issues, including that (1) HRS §§707-702(1)(a) was vague and failed to provide fair notice (of proscribed conduct), in violation of Hawaii's and the U.S. Constitution, 14th Amendment; (2) prosecution for manslaughter interfered with an expectant mother's fundamental right to procreate; (3)the prosecution was an unconstitutional expansion of §§707-702(1)(a); and (4)Aiwohi was unconstitutionally denied her right to present a defense when the circuit court rejected her common-law defense of immunity for an expectant mother's prenatal conduct.

In its 38-page opinion, the Hawaii Supreme Court first discussed whether Aiwohi's prosecution for manslaughter was consistent with the plain meaning of HRS §§707-702(1)(a). That provision holds a person guilty of manslaughter if that person "recklessly causes the death of another person." In order to be guilty of manslaughter, said the court, Aiwohi must have "acted . . . recklessly . . . with respect to each element of the offense." HRS §§707-704.

After a lengthy discussion of "attendant circumstances," the court went on to note that the MODEL PENAL CODE (from which the Hawaii Penal Code was substantially derived) requires that a defendant's conduct must occur at a time when the victim is within the class contemplated by the legislature.

Although Aiwohi's prenatal conduct may have proximately caused the newborn's death, her conduct occurred at the time when Treyson was a fetus within her womb. The Hawaii Penal Code (HPC) §§707-700 defines a "person" as "[a] human being who has been born and is alive." "According to the plain language of the HPC," concluded the court, "a fetus is not included within the definition of 'person,'" and therefore, not within the class contemplated by the legislature.

The court concluded that, as a result of that classification, Aiwohi could not have had the requisite state of mind because she could not contemplate causing the death of another "person." The court noted that the provisions of the HPC "cannot be extended by analogy so as to create crimes not provided for herein." Moreover, resolution of this first issue disposed of the entire case, concluded the court. Therefore, the court did not address the other challenges raised by Aiwohi in her appeal.

In conclusion, the court held that a mother's prosecution for her own prenatal conduct, which caused the death of a baby subsequently born alive, was not within the clear meaning of HRS §§707-702(1)(a). Therefore, the circuit court erred in denying defense's Motion to Dismiss, and the "Amended Judgment Guilty Conviction and Probation Sentence, filed on October 4, 2005, was reversed.

MEDICAID

A joint federal-state program that provides health care insurance to low-income persons.

Arkansas Department of Health and Human Services v. Ahlborn

When states agree to participate in the **Medicaid** program they receive reimbursement of patient care from the federal government that ranges from 50% to 83% of their costs. In return states must comply with the requirement of the federal Medicaid **statute** for eligibility rules, collecting and maintaining information, and administering the program. One provision of the law mandates that the state agency in charge of the Medicaid program "take all reasonable measures to ascertain the legal liability of third parties . . . to pay for care and services available under the plan." The law further declares that if a Medicaid recipient receives compensation from a **third party** the state must be assigned a portion of the compensation to reimburse itself for medical expenses. In *Arkansas Department of Health and Human Services v. Ahlborn*, __U.S.__, 126 S.Ct. 1752, __L.Ed.2d __ (2006), the Supreme Court was called on to decide whether a state could lay claim to a substantial portion of a personal injury settlement to reimburse Medicaid. The Court held that the state could only claim the portion of the settlement that was allocated to medical expenses.

Heidi Ahlborn was a 19-year-old college student in 1996 when she became a victim of a car accident. The accident left her with permanent and severe brain injuries and medical bills she could not pay. The Arkansas Department of Health and Human Services (ADHHS) deemed her eligible for medical assistance and paid over $215,000 to medical providers. Ahlborn retained a lawyer to seek compensation for her injuries. ADHHS sent letters to the lawyer, which stated that under state law the agency had a claim of reimbursement from any settlement or award that Ahlborn obtained from a third party. Ahlborn had assigned this right to ADHHS when she applied for benefits. The lawyer filed suit in 1997, asking that Ahlborn be compensated for past medical costs, permanent physical injury, future medical expenses, pain and suffering, lost earnings, and **mental anguish**. In 2002 the case was settled out of court for $550,000. The parties did not allocate the settlement between the various categories of damages. ADHHS then asserted a **lien** against the settlement proceeds for the $215,000 it had paid in medical care expenses for Ahlborn.

Ahlborn filed a lawsuit in Arkansas federal **district court**, asking the court to declare that the lien violated federal Medicaid laws because the state sought money from the settlement that did not address past medical expenses. ADHHS and Ahlborn stipulated that her entire claim was valued at over $3 million, that the settlement was approximately one-sixth of this amount, and that, if Ahlborn's interpretation of federal law was correct, ADHHS would be entitled only to $35,000, the portion of the settlement that applied to reimbursement for medical payments. The district ruled in favor of ADHHS, finding that Ahlborn had assigned to ADHHS her right to any recovery to the full extent of the Medicaid payments made on her behalf. The Eighth **Circuit Court** of Appeals reversed, holding that ADHHS was only entitled to that part of the settlement that represented payments for medical care.

The Supreme Court, in a unanimous decision, upheld the appeals court ruling. Justice JOHN PAUL STEVENS, writing for the Court, noted that the federal Medicaid law provision requires Medicaid recipients to assign to the state any rights "to payment for medical care from any third party." This limitation on the assignment of payments was reinforced by another provision that third parties who paid Medicaid recipients for their injuries had legal liability "to pay for care and services available under the plan." In Ahlborn's case the third parties accepted liability for one-sixth of her overall damages and ADHHS agreed that only $35,000 (one-sixth) of that sum represented compensation for medical expenses. The agency pointed to other Medicaid law provisions that suggested it could demand full reimbursement of its costs from Ahlborn's settlement but Justice Stevens concluded that these provisions referred not to the entire settlement but only that part allocated for medical expenses.

Justice Stevens also noted another Medicaid law provision that prohibited states from placing liens against or seeking recovery of benefits from a Medicaid recipient. Read literally it would ban a lien for the recovery of medical payments, yet even Ahlborn did not make that argument. Instead, she contended that this anti-lien provision precluded "attachment or encumbrance of the remainder of the settlement." Justice Stevens agreed with this interpretation, rejecting the agency's claim that the anti-lien provision did not apply because Ahlborn lost her property rights the moment she applied for Medicaid. Stevens found this illogical, for why would ADHHS "need a lien on its own property?" The agency called the lien an "assignment" but that did not change the Court's analysis. Arkansas was entitled to recover that part of the settlement allocated to medical expenses but it could claim other parts of the settlement to full reimburse itself for all medical expenses paid on behalf of Ahlborn because the anti-lien provision "affirmatively prohibits it from doing so."

MEXICO AND THE UNITED STATES

Civilian Patrols Policing the U.S.-Mexico Border Cause Nationwide Controversy

While civilian patrols have policed the U.S.-Mexico border for years, more attention has focused on the area since the terrorist attacks of 2001. In early 2005, deputy secretary of the HOMELAND SECURITY DEPARTMENT James Loy reported that intelligence indicated al-Qaida members would be likely to enter the United States at the southern border. A changing political climate regarding illegal immigration has also stirred people to action.

The 370-mile Arizona-Mexico border sees more than its share of illegal immigrants. Of the 1.1 million people captured by the U.S. Border Patrol in 2004, more than 50 percent were along this stretch. Citing these statistics, decorated VIETNAM WAR veteran and retired accountant Jim Gilchrist formed the Minuteman Project in April 2005 to assist Border Patrol officers in monitoring the territory. Gilchrist's Minutemen began patrolling 40 miles of the Arizona border in April 2005, reporting any illegal immigrants to a central member, who then relayed the information to the Border Patrol. Organizer Chris Simcox claims their assistance helped in apprehending 335 immigrants. Other than offering food, water, and medical care, the Minutemen refrained from interacting with those crossing the border. Gilchrist wanted media attention to jumpstart legislative changes and hoped to prove that the solution is increased personnel.

Although it began in Arizona, the Minuteman Project has gathered more members by going online. Its membership includes those from across the nation who have joined the patrols along the southern border, as well as some who monitor the border with Canada. Project members have proceeded relatively unhampered in Arizona, but they received little welcome when they expanded operations to include the Texas border with Mexico. Most of that land is privately owned, more urban, and has a large Hispanic population. In a resolution, State Senator Juan "Chuy" Hinojosa (D) urged Texas Governor Rick Perry to oppose the Minuteman Project in the state. In addition to the border patrols, the Minuteman Project employs a Minuteman Caravan, which travels across the country to drum up support for the cause. A Washington, D.C., rally on May 12, 2006, was deemed a success by the group.

U.S. Representative Sheila Jackson Lee (D) agreed with the need for better funding for bor-

Ed Whitbread, member of the Minutemen, sits atop his mobile home watching for illegal aliens.
ANDREW HOLBROOK/CORBIS

der security, but expressed concern that members of the Minuteman Project might prove a catalyst for outbreaks of violence. She called for the group to disband, saying it had served its purpose in drawing national attention to the issue. But members of the Minuteman Project and other civilian patrols claim to be doing the work neglected by their government.

Feuding within the original group created different factions. In California, former Minuteman Jim Chase created the California Border Watch, which patrolled a 26-mile area in July and August 2005. Like some members of the Minuteman Project, Chase and his people carry guns while patrolling. Though he claims the weapons are strictly for self-defense, authorities are concerned about the potential for violence. Gilchrist has stated that any member of the Minuteman Project who steps outside of the law will be prosecuted. Also in California is Friends of the Border Patrol, which monitored the San Diego sector from June to November 2005.

In all three states, protestors have harried the civilian patrollers. Many fear the groups are stirring up racism, especially since the majority of volunteers are retired white men. President GEORGE W. BUSH called the Minutemen vigilantes in a press conference in May 2005. Despite the labels and concerns, the civilian patrollers have not broken the law.

Border Patrol officials object to the civilian patrols for a number of reasons, not the least of which is that these are untrained people. The patrols blunder into border sensors and inadvertently obscure traces of immigrant activity. Rather than assisting the U.S. Border Patrol, officials say they are more likely to hamper operations.

In February 2005, roughly 10000 federal agents were patrol officers; a number that Customs and Border Protection Commissioner Robert C. Bonner expected at the time would be increased. At the end of 2005, Minuteman Project members, whose own numbers have topped 1,000, were calling for a tripling of border patrol officers and wanted a wall to be built along the entire U.S.-Mexico border.

In early 2006, reports revealed that the U.S. Border Patrol was tipping off Mexico officials as to the whereabouts of Minuteman and other civilian patrol members. Minuteman Project members were outraged at this perceived betrayal by their own government, while a U.S. Customs and Border Protection official called it a standard procedure to protect migrants' rights and an effort to allay the Mexican government's perception of the civilian patrols as vigilantes. The Minutemen deplored the cooperation for destroying their effectiveness and potentially endangering their lives. Other detractors saw the agreement as evidence of the Mexican consulate's influence over the National Border Patrol Council, a union that represents more than 10000 agents.

Evidence points to U.S. economy as a key factor in the number of illegal immigrants entering the country. As the economy takes a downturn, immigration rises to meet the demand for cheap labor. Approximately two-thirds of illegal immigrants arrived illegally in the United States, while the remaining one-third overstayed their visa expirations.

MIRANDA RIGHTS

Maryland v. Blake

In November 2005, a few days after oral arguments, the U.S. SUPREME COURT dismissed its previously-granted **writ** of **certiorari** as improvidently granted in the case of *Maryland v. Blake*, 546 U.S. ___, 126 S.Ct. 602 . The dismissal effectively let stand the underlying (appealed) decision in the matter by the Maryland Court of Appeals, which is the state's highest court.

The case involved the suppression of incriminating statements from a juvenile, Leeander Blake, while in police custody, who had participated in a 2002 murder. The 17-year-old Blake initially told a police detective that he did not want to talk without an attorney, and questioning immediately stopped. Shortly thereafter, Blake was given a printed statement of the charges against him. The charging statement also indicated that a conviction for the charged crimes could result in a death sentence (in fact, as a juvenile, he could not be sentenced to death). One of the officer's then stated, "I bet you want to talk now, huh!" The officer was quickly corrected by the original officer, who said, "No, he doesn't want to talk to us. He already asked for a lawyer. We cannot talk to him."

About a half hour later, the detective returned with some clothes for Blake. At that time, Blake said "I can still talk to you?" The detective asked, "Are you saying you want to talk to me now?" Blake said yes. He was then led into an interrogation room and advised of his Miranda rights for a second time. He waived his right to remain silent and discussed the crimes, incriminating himself; he also agreed to a polygraph exam, during which he made additional incriminating statements. (Blake later testified at an evidentiary hearing that it was the police who re-initiated the conversation, and he denied that he first asked the detective if he could talk to him.)

At trial, Blake's attorney argued that it was the officer who had re-initiated conversation by asking Blake first, "Do you wish to still talk to me?" Counsel then filed a motion to suppress all the incriminating statements on the grounds that the police had violated *Miranda v. Arizona*, 86 S.Ct. 1602, 16 L.Ed.2d 694 (1966), and *Edwards v. Arizona* 451 U.S. 477, 101 S.Ct. 1880, 68 L.Ed.2d 378 (1981).

The trial court agreed and granted defendant's motion. But in an unpublished opinion, Maryland's Court of Special Appeals reversed. Blake then appealed to Maryland's highest court, called the Court of Appeals. The single question on appeal was whether the police actions constituted the functional equivalent of interrogation, following Blake's initial request to be silent until he could see a lawyer, thereby violating his rights against compelled self-incrimination. The Maryland Court of appeals held that the police actions constituted the equivalent of interrogation, thereby violating Blake's rights, and under the circumstances presented, the trial court had properly suppressed Blake's statements. It was this opinion that was appealed to the U.S. Supreme Court and initially granted certiorari.

The Maryland Court of Appeals explained its conclusion by revisiting the relevant precedent in *Miranda* and *Edwards*. The court first reiterated that under *Miranda*, a suspect taken into custody is entitled to certain procedural safeguards before law enforcement personnel may interrogate. If the suspect requests to speak with an attorney, that person may not be interrogated until either counsel has been made available or the suspect validly waives the earlier request for an attorney. Said the court,

> . . . *Miranda* and *Edwards* mean exactly what they say: once the accused requests the presence **of counsel** at a **custodial interrogation**, the FIFTH AMENDMENT to the Constitution of the United States of America and Article 22 of the Maryland Declaration of Rights are *ipso facto* invoked, and *all questioning must cease.*"

(quoting from *Bryant v. State*, 49 Md. App. 272 [1981]).

The court next reminded that under *Edwards*, an accused who has invoked his desire to deal with the police only through counsel cannot be further interrogated until counsel has been made available to him, "unless the accused himself initiates further communication, exchanges, or conversations with the police." 451 U.S. at 484–485. A valid waiver of that right (once a suspect has requested counsel) cannot be established by merely showing that the accused responded to further police-initiated interrogation. 451 U.S. at 484. Instead, the burden is on the state to show that the accused, after invoking his right to counsel, initiated further discussion with the police. Importantly, if a court finds that a suspect did not initiate further discussions with police, there is no need to consider whether he subsequently waived his right to counsel.

After noting that "Interrogation means more than direct, explicit questioning and includes the functional equivalent of interrogation," the Maryland high court agreed with the conclusion of the circuit (trial) court. The court stated in its opinion,

> "Petitioner had requested counsel; he had been given a document that told him he was subject to the death penalty, when legally he was not; he was seventeen years of age; he had not consulted with counsel; he was in a cold holding cell with little clothing; an officer had suggested in a confrontational tone that petitioner might want to talk; and the misstatement as to the potential penalty as one of "DEATH" had never been corrected. There was no break in custody or adequate lapse in time sufficient to **vitiate** the coercive effect of the impermissive interrogation. . . . We hold that all statements made by petitioner after he invoked his *Miranda* rights are inadmissible and the motion to suppress the statements was properly granted."

MURDER

The unlawful killing of another human being without justification or excuse.

DNA, Additional Testimony among Key Evidence in Fourth Appeal for Fatal Vision Case

On February 17, 1970, police received a call from former Green Beret and U.S. Army doctor Jeffrey MacDonald, who told them his family had been attacked in their Fort Bragg, North Carolina, home by a group of crazed hippies. MacDonald's pregnant wife Colette, 26, and his daughters Kimberley, 5, and Kirsten, 2, had been beaten and stabbed to death. MacDonald was beaten and stabbed multiple times. Because the crime occurred on a U.S. Army base, the military had jurisdiction. They found there was insufficient evidence to prosecute MacDonald for the murders. A non-military trial, however, convicted MacDonald and sentenced him to serve three consecutive life terms.

MacDonald has maintained his innocence in the slayings, sticking by his story of an attack by outsiders, including a woman in a wig, whom his defense attorneys contend was drug addict Helena Stoeckley. An early suspect in the investigation because of her resemblance to MacDonald's description of one of the alleged intruders, Stoeckley testified in the 1979 trial that she could not recall the events of the night in question. Only later, in a 1982 interview with a former FBI official hired by MacDonald, did she claim to have been with a group of Charles Manson-worshipping hippies in the MacDonald home during the murders.

Stoeckley died in 1983, but the discrepancy between her testimony and later statements are a factor in MacDonald's fourth appeal to overturn the conviction. Late in 2005, retired deputy federal marshal Jimmy B. Britt, a member of MacDonald's security detail during the 1979 trial, stepped forward to claim he heard lead prosecutor Jim Blackburn threaten to charge Stoeckley with the murders if she testified to being in the MacDonald home during the attacks. Britt, stating under oath that Blackburn lied to the judge and intimidated a key defense witness, said he is trying to clear his conscience. MacDonald's lawyers contend that, had trial judge Franklin Dupree, Jr., known of Stoeckley's alleged confession, he may have permitted testimony from others to whom Stoeckley had made the same statements. Dupree ruled against the proposed testimony because Stoeckley was a known drug user whose story did not match the murder evidence.

Blackburn, who entered private practice shortly after the trial, strongly contests the allegation, saying that Stoeckley never claimed to be in the MacDonald home. Britt has countered by saying that Stoeckley repeated her story as he drove her to the 1979 trial, even describing some details of the MacDonald home. The issue is complicated by Blackburn's disbarment upon his conviction and three-and-a-half-year prison term on charges of forgery, **fraud embezzlement**, and obstruction of justice in an unrelated case. He currently works as a motivational speaker.

Britt's statements led MacDonald's attorneys to request permission from a federal **appellate court** in mid-December 2005 to present new evidence to the U.S. **District Court** in Raleigh. Government lawyers dismissed Britt's claims and asked the federal court to reject the appeal, arguing that Britt's recollections are unlikely to be accurate so long after the events and should not affect the conviction. A similar claim, they also argued, was raised by MacDonald in 1984 and rejected by the **federal courts**.

On January 13, 2006, a federal appeals court granted MacDonald's request for a fourth appeal based on Britt's testimony. The defense may argue that the ruling lends credence to the appeal, since approving a hearing for a lower trial court requires the appeals court to rule that the evidence presented was not available during the initial trial, and therefore the jurors might not have found MacDonald guilty.

The physical evidence of the murders has also come under scrutiny as **forensic** technology has progressed since the 1979 trial. MacDonald's third appeal, made in 1997, concerned blood and hair evidence from the crime scene, which a judge ordered to be DNA tested by the Armed Forces DNA Identification Laboratory, one of the foremost investigators of DNA evidence in the country.

The lab released its findings in early 2006, more than eight years after the appeal. Tests determined that a hair found in Colette MacDonald's left hand matched MacDonald's DNA, but there was no genetic match available for hair found under Kristen MacDonald's fingernail. DNA from three test hairs from the scene did not match that of MacDonald family members or anyone considered a suspect, including Stoeckley or her boyfriend, Gregory Mitchell.

Focusing on the DNA match for the hair in Colette's hand, federal prosecutors announced on March 10, 2006, that the DNA results did not support MacDonald's claims of a home invasion. The defense, however, contends that the lack of a match for the other tested hairs supports MacDonald's story. Whether or not this evidence, coupled with Britt's testimony, is enough to vacate MacDonald's conviction will be the focus of the as yet unscheduled fourth appeal and any subsequent legal action. MacDonald remarried in 2002.

NATIVE AMERICAN RIGHTS

Wagnon v. Prairie Band Potawatomi Nation

American Indian tribes are recognized as sovereign entities by the U.S. government, yet the federal government has made many exceptions to tribal sovereignty. One thorny issue involves the taxation by state governments of goods sold on tribal property. The Supreme Court has wrestled with the proper standards for evaluating the legality of these taxes, most recently in *Wagnon v. Prairie Band Potawatomi Nation*, __U.S.__, 126 S.Ct. 676, 163 L.Ed.2d 429 (2005). In this case the Court ruled that a motor fuel tax imposed on a distributor of gasoline residing within the state could be passed on to a gas station located on an Indian reservation.

The Prairie Band Potawatomi Nation in Kansas has a large gambling casino on its reservation. The casino's employees are overwhelmingly members of the Nation and the profits earned by the casino are used to improve the standard of living for tribal members. A state highway is the only way for the public to access the casino. The Nation established a gas station that sells fuel to customers who visit the casino (73 per cent of the station's customers) and it imposed an **excise** tax on the fuel as a way to maintain the portion of the highway that is on tribal land. In 1995 the state of Kansas imposed a tax on the distributors of motor fuels residing within the state. The distributors passed along the tax as a cost of business to gas station owners. When the fuel distributors passed along the tax to the Nation's gas station, the Nation objected, claiming that by paying the additional amount for fuel it was, in effect, paying a tax to the state of Kansas. The nation argued that this was a violation of tribal sovereignty and filed suit in federal **district court**.

The federal district court dismissed the lawsuit, reasoning that on balance the interests of the state trumped those of the Nation. The "legal incidence of the tax" was directed to off-reservation fuel distributors and most of the purchasers of the fuel were non-Indian casino patrons who received most of their governmental services from the state of Kansas. The Nation could not block the tax merely because it imposed its own fuel tax. The Tenth **Circuit Court** of Appeals disagreed, finding that the balancing of interests favored the Nation. The appeals court concluded that the Nation's fuel revenues were "derived from the value generated primarily on its reservation" through the presence of the casino. The Nation's desire to tax this reservation-created value to help with maintaining the highway outweighed the state's interest in raising revenues. The state then appealed to the Supreme Court, which granted review to determine whether a tax on the off-reservation receipt of fuel was subject to the balancing test used by the lower courts.

The Court, in a 7–2 decision, overruled the Tenth Circuit, finding that the balancing test did not apply in this situation because the motor fuel tax was a nondiscriminatory tax imposed on an off-reservation transaction that involved non-Indians. Justice CLARENCE THOMAS, in his majority opinion, noted that under the Court's Indian tax immunity decisions the "'who' and the 'where' of the challenged tax have significant consequences." A state may not place an excise tax on a tribe or tribal members for sales made within a reservation without congressional approval. Likewise, when a state imposes a tax on a non-Indian seller on a transaction that takes place on the reservation, it may be prohibited under a balancing of interests test. The Nation argued that the legal incidence of the tax occurred on tribal land but Justice Thomas concluded that the Nation had failed both the "who" and "where" test. In this case Kansas imposed the tax on fuel distributors who did business within the state's boundaries. The distributor, not the retailer, was liable to pay the motor fuel tax. Therefore, the legal incidence of the tax fell on the distributor (the "who") rather than the tribal retailer. As to the "where" of the tax, Thomas found that it occurred off tribal land.

The Court declined to extend the balancing of interest test to this type of tax. Justice Thomas stated that this test must be limited to on-reservation transactions "between a nontribal **entity** and a tribe or tribal member." Prior decisions by the Court had ignored the balancing test when the state asserted taxing authority outside of tribal lands. For example, a state was permitted to tax the gross receipts of an off-reservation Indian-owned ski resort. If a state was permitted to tax Indian tribes for their off-reservation activities, "it follows that it may apply a nondiscriminatory tax where, as here, the tax is imposed on non-Indians as a result of an off-reservation transaction." The Court refused to expand the interest balancing test to any off-reservation tax for goods imported by the Nation. It made not difference that the state tax interfered with the tribal gas tax. The Nation sold gas at the prevailing market rates, so "its decision to impose a tax should have no effect on net revenues from the operation of the station." If the tax had been struck down the Nation would have increased those revenues by purchasing untaxed fuel. Therefore, the state was entitled to pass the tax onto to Nation through the prices charged by the distributors.

Justice RUTH BADER GINSBURG, in a dissenting opinion joined by Justice ANTHONY KENNEDY, noted that Kansas had provided many exemptions to the collection of the motor fuel tax yet it had not made one for the Nation. The effect of the state tax meant that if the Nation continued to impose its tax "scarcely anyone will fill up at its pumps." Because of this double taxation the Nation would either have to cut prices and operate the station at a loss or close the station. The balancing of interests test should be applied in such circumstances. If applied, the Nation should prevail because the operation of the gas station and the collection of the tribal tax was needed to fund reservation road-building programs.

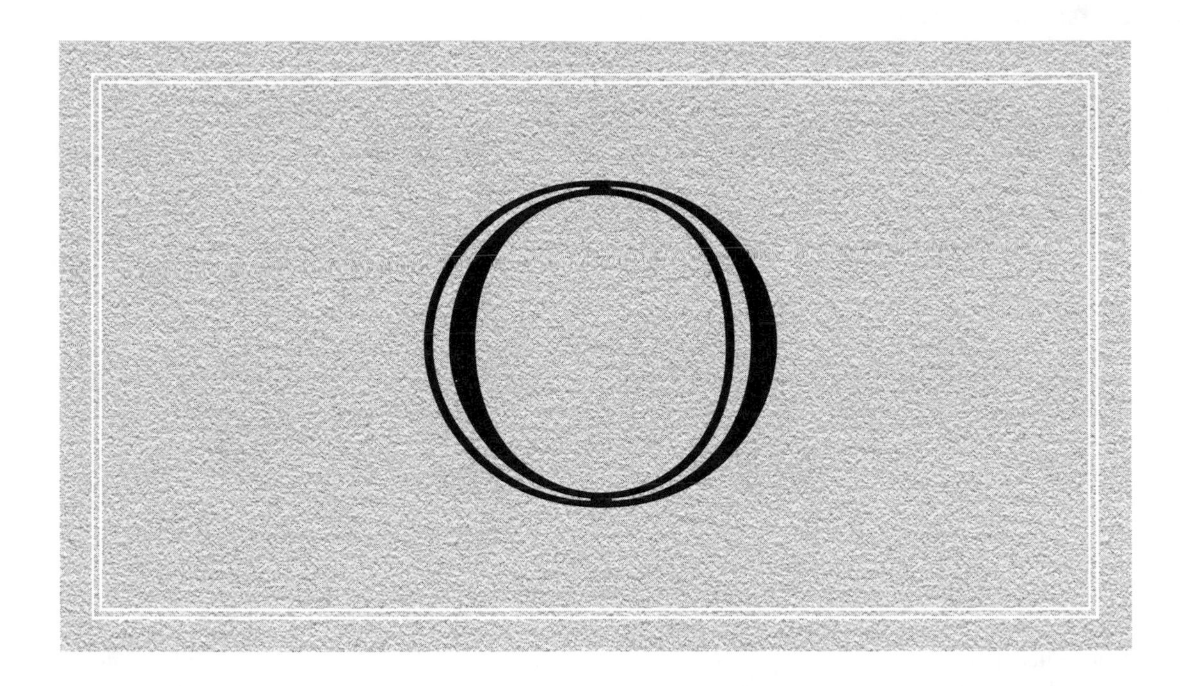

OBSCENITY

The character or quality of being obscene; an act, utterance, or item tending to corrupt the public morals by its indecency or lewdness.

Nitke v. Gonzales

The Communications Decency Act of 1996 (CDA), 110 Stat. 133, makes it a crime to transmit obscenity by means of the Internet to person under 18 years of age. Individuals and organizations that display erotic subject matter on their Web sites challenged the constitutionality of the CDA, arguing that the law was overbroad and violated the FIRST AMENDMENT's right to freedom of expression. Under the CDA, challenges to the act must be heard by a special panel of three judges. In *Nitke v. Gonzales*, 413 F. Supp.2d 262 (2005), the special panel dismissed the First Amendment challenge, concluding that the plaintiffs had failed to demonstrate that the CDA was overbroad. The panel issued its decision in July 2005 and the U.S. SUPREME COURT allowed the ruling to stand when it denied review in 2006.

Plaintiff Barbara Nitke is an art photographer who specializes in sexually explicit subjects, including couples engaged in sadomasochistic acts and other hardcore activities. Nitke, who is on the faculty of a visual arts school and president of the Camera Club of New York, challenged the CDA because she maintained a Web site that displayed her photographs, which she claimed had artistic merit. Another plaintiff in the litigation was the National Coalition for Sexual Freedom (NCSF), a not-for-profit organization that sought to fight discrimination against non-mainstream sexual practices. Some of NCSF's members maintained Web sites that contained sexually explicit content. Nitke and NCSF filed the lawsuit in 2001, which did not come to trial until October 2004 before **Circuit Court** Judge Robert Sack and **District Court** Judes Richard Berman and Gerard Lynch.

The panel issued a *per curiam* decision, which meant that the author of the opinion was not identified. The panel agreed that the plaintiffs had standing to bring the federal lawsuit, for they had an actual and well-founded fear that the CDA would be enforced against them. As to the legal standards governing review, the panel noted that the CDA incorporated the legal definition of obscenity created by the Supreme Court in *Miller v. California*, 413 U.S.15, 93 S.Ct. 2607, 37 L.Ed.2d 419 (1973). Under the *Miller* three-part test a communication is obscene if (1) "the average person, applying contemporary community standards would find that the work, taken as a whole, appeals to the prurient interest;" (2) "the work depicts or describes, in a patently offensive way, sexual conduct" when judged by contemporary community standards; and, (3) "the work, taken as a whole, lacks serious literary, artistic, political, or scientific value." The first two parts of the test are determined by the standards of the particular locality where the allegedly obscene material is challenged, while the third element is based on a national standard for establishing serious artistic value. The CDA provided two affirmative defenses for publishing obscene content on the Web: (1) the defendant in **good faith** took reasonable, effective and appropriate actions to restrict or prevent access by minors, or (2) restricted access by requiring a visitor to use a verified credit card, debit card, adult access code, or adult personal identification number. The Supreme Court has ruled that obscene speech is not protected by the First Amendment. Speech that is not obscene, including sexually explicit material categorized as "indecent" is protected by the First Amendment.

The plaintiffs had the burden of showing that the CDA was substantially overbroad because it reached obscene and non-obscene speech. They claimed that applying the *Miller* test to the Internet captured too much protected speech. Moreover, they could not control where their Internet content was received, leading to an outcome where their materials were obscene if one or more communities, but not in others. The court noted in its decision that the plaintiffs had failed to meet two evidentiary thresholds. The plaintiffs could not show the total amount of speech that was implicated by the CDA. Second, the plaintiffs failed to show the amount of protected speech that might be considered obscene in some communities but not in others. The panel concluded that the plaintiffs had not offered sufficient evidence to show "the extent to which standards vary from community to community or the degree to which these standards vary with respect to the types of works in question." Moreover, the plaintiffs' expert witness was unable to determine obscenity standards in "any given region." Therefore, the facial challenge of the CDA's constitutionality was unsuccessful. However, lawsuits could be filed in the future challenging the CDA if a plaintiff sought to prove that the law had, in practice, restricted the plaintiff's First Amendment rights. The heavy evidentiary burden placed on Nitke's facial challenge would not be present in an action based on concrete facts alleging infringement of freedom of expression.

ORGANIZED CRIME

Criminal activity carried out by an organized enterprise.

Two Mistrials for Reputed Gambino Crime Family Leader

John A. (Junior) Gotti, reputed head of the Gambino organized crime family, managed to escape conviction in two trials in 2005 and 2006. Gotti stood trial on charges that he ordered a violent kidnapping of Curtis Sliwa, founder of the Guardian Angels crime-fighting group and outspoken radio talk-show host. Prosecutors said they would retry Gotti a third time. Gotti is the son of the late John Gotti, who was known as "Dapper Don." The elder Gotti died in prison in 2002 while serving a life sentence on murder and racketeering charges.

In the first trial, in September 2005, a federal jury acquitted Gotti, 41, of securities **fraud** charges under 18 U.S.C. §. 371. However, the jury could not agree to a verdict on two alleged racketeering counts under the Racketeer Influenced and Corrupt Organizations Act ("RICO"), 18 U.S.C. §. 1962. The RICO charges alleged that Gotti has participated in the conduct of the affairs of a racketeering organization. For a RICO conviction, the **statute** requires a finding that a defendant has engaged in "at least two acts of racketeering activity." The indictment against Gotti alleged several acts of racketeering activity. The alleged RICO activity included conspiring to kidnap, and the kidnapping of Curtis Sliwa; conspiring to commit securities fraud; conspiring to commit extortion in the construction industry; loansharking; and conspiracy to commit loansharking.

After eight days of juror deliberations, U.S. District Judge Shira Scheindlin declared a mistrial on the RICO counts. Gotti asked that an acquittal be entered instead. He alleged that the prosecution had failed to prove two racketeering acts, and that under the **Double Jeopardy** Clause, the U.S. Constitution prohibited retrial on the charges. Judge Scheindlin disagreed and ruled that Gotti could be retried. However, she granted his request to be released from jail pending a retrial. Secured by a $7 million bond, Gotti was placed on house arrest following the 2005 mistrial.

Gotti appealed the mistrial ruling. On February 9, 2006, a panel of three judges from the Second **Circuit Court** of Appeals issued a summary order upholding Judge Scheindlin's decision. The **appellate court** issued a detailed opinion on May 25, 2006. The summary order paved the way for Gotti's second trial, which began in mid-February. On March 10, 2006, after one and a half days of deliberation, the judge again declared a mistrial after jurors said they could not come to an agreement.

To support the charges of extortion and loansharking, the prosecution introduced evidence that in February 1997, a police search of a basement uncovered more than $350,000 in a gym bag that belonged to Gotti. Gotti's lawyers contended the money was simply cash wedding gifts that Gotti and his wife had received. The prosecution also presented evidence that a gun equipped with a silencer was found in the basement.

The attempted abduction of Sliwa took place in 1992. Prosecutors alleged that Gotti arranged the kidnapping of Sliwa as retaliation for on-air rants against Dapper Don Gotti; Gotti denied that he ordered Sliwa's attacks. In one instance, Sliwa was beaten with a baseball bat. Several weeks later, Sliwa and a masked hit man struggled in a taxi. During the struggle, Sliwa was shot. He dived out of the moving taxi, recovered, and testified at both trials. Convicted mobsters also testified against Gotti.

Gotti did not testify on his own behalf. However, his lawyers contended that he left the crime family in 1999 or even earlier, for the sake of his wife and children. Sliwa's radio co-host, Ronald L. Kuby, testified as a defense witness. Kuby said that Gotti told him in 1998 that he was "sick of this life."

Prosecutors contended Gotti continued his criminal activity after 1999, including issuing orders and collecting kickbacks. This issue was crucial to the trial. If jurors believed Gotti, the five-year **statute of limitations** on the RICO charges would have expired.

At one point, Gotti turned down a plea agreement that would have landed him in prison for seven years, on a 10-year sentence. A conviction carried the possibility of a 30-year sentence. Gotti pleaded guilty to unrelated racketeering charges in 1999, for which he was sentenced to six and a half years.

On May 22, 2006, a rewritten federal indictment was issued. It charges that Gotti has continued his mob-related activities, including alleged witness tampering in 2005. It also alleges that he used illegally **earned income** to create and operate real estate holding companies for buying real estate and collecting rent, and that he used racketeering money to establish and operate a brokerage company. According to the indictment, Gotti promoted crime family members if they committed murders.

John Gotti Jr., leaves Federal Court in Manhattan after a mistrial in his trial on accusations of leading the Gambino crime family.
MIKE SEGAR/REUTERS/CORBIS

Gotti's third trial was set to begin on July 5, 2006. With the issuance of the rewritten indictment, Judge Scheindlin postponed the opening until August 28, to give lawyers adequate preparation time.

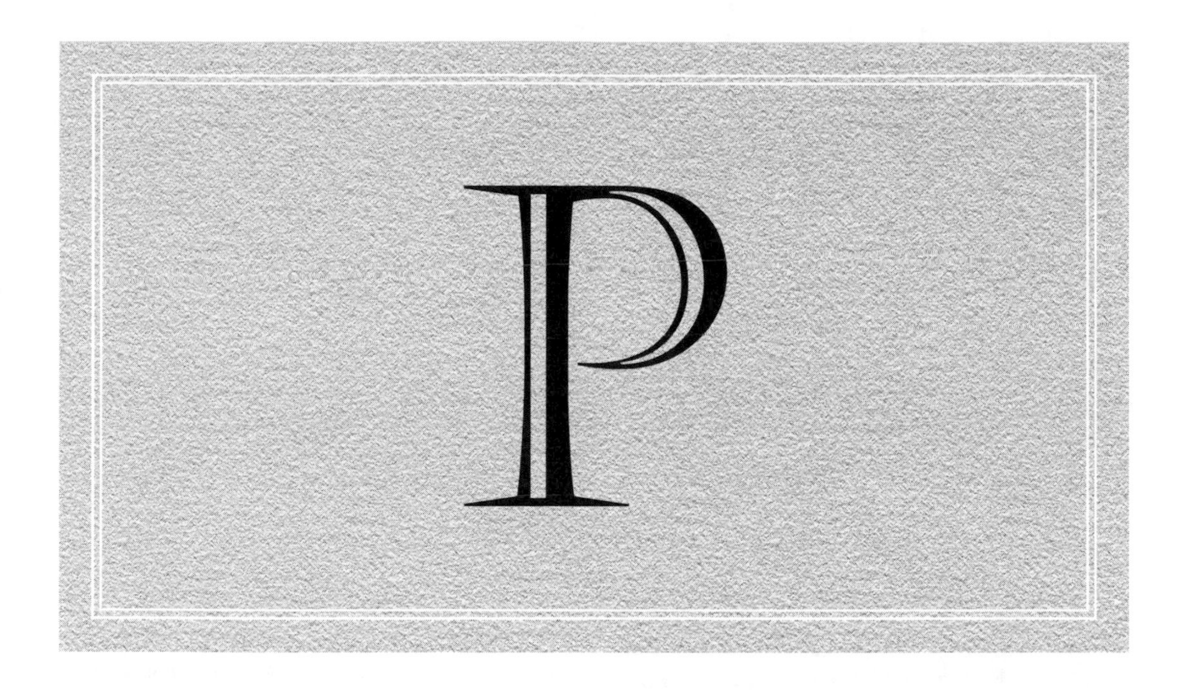

PATENTS

Rights, granted to inventors by the federal government, pursuant to its power under Article I, Section 8, Clause 8, of the U.S. Constitution, that permit them to exclude others from making, using, or selling an invention for a definite, or restricted, period of time.

BlackBerry Case Settles

Research in Motion (RIM), maker of BlackBerry, the ubiquitous wireless e-mail device, escaped a shutdown of its services after the company agreed to pay $612.5 million to settle a patent dispute with NTP, a company based in Arlington, Virginia, which holds several patents related to wireless e-mail technology.

As a result of the settlement, the Canadian-based RIM will license the BlackBerry technology and will allow the wireless services to remain operational, to the relief of BlackBerry users in business, government, emergency services, and other professional fields who have come to rely on the technology in order to be accessible at all times.

Thomas Campana, Jr., a co-founder of NTP, developed a wireless communications system for his pager company, which he patented. Campana and co-founder Donald Stout incorporated NTP to hold these patents. The company does not provide services or create products. However, NTP argued that the wireless technology of the BlackBerry device infringed its patents.

Lawyers for RIM argued that the NTP wireless system only allows users to read and print e-mail, while the BlackBerry allows them to reply to messages and to forward e-mail on a handheld wireless device. RIM's brief stated that the Virginia court had misunderstood the functions of the devices and that the products and services did not infringe the NTP patents.

During a hearing in 2006, U.S. District Court Judge James R. Spencer suggested that if the companies failed to reach a settlement, he would uphold a 2002 decision in which a jury in the U.S. District Court for the Eastern District of Virginia found that RIM had infringed patents held by NTP. Enforcement of the 2002 decision would have led to the total shutdown of the BlackBerry system.

In 2004, the U.S. Court of Appeals for the Federal Circuit upheld the ruling from the lower court, which raised the possibility of a shutdown of the BlackBerry service.

In an interesting twist, the Department of Justice filed a brief late in 2005 in which it requested a delay of any shutdown of BlackBerry service because of the widespread use of BlackBerries among federal employees. It asked for 90 days to compile a list of essential government personnel whose BlackBerry service should not be cut off in the event that the companies did not reach a settlement. However, the companies took the threat of injunction seriously and reached an agreement.

NTP wanted to protect the right to license its patents to other companies, and RIM wanted to ensure that wireless carriers would be protected from future litigation. James Balsilllie, a co-chief executive of RIM, said that the settlement amounted to "taking one for the team" to protect its partners from litigation.

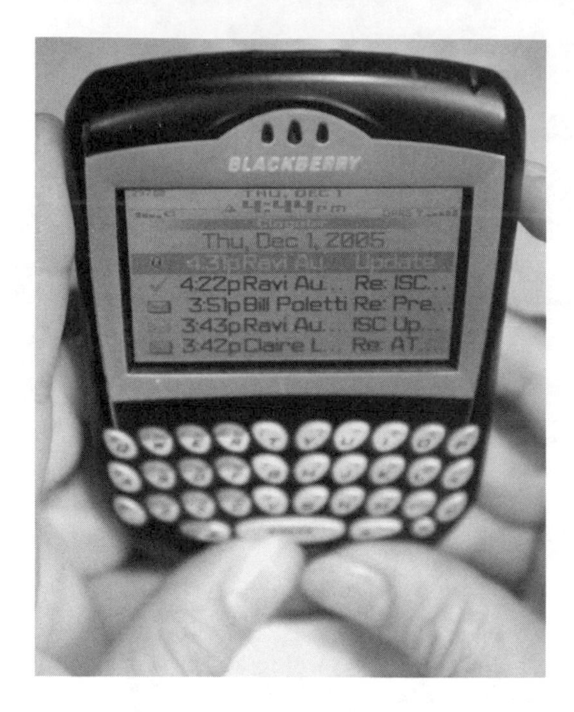

A BlackBerry device in use.
JUSTIN LANE/EPA/CORBIS

Investors and businesses viewed the issue as a litmus test for ways in which the patent system adapts to the digital world. In a *Washington Post* article, intellectual property attorney Donald R. Steinberg explained that a settlement is often desirable in patent cases because it limits risk to both companies. "There was some risk to NTP that the patents would ultimately be invalidated and then they wouldn't get anything," he said. He added that the risk to RIM was that the patents would be upheld and they would be enjoined, "and in essence they would have to pay more money to get out of the injunction."

Attorneys for RIM argued against the possible injunction by stressing that it was in the public interest to keep the BlackBerry service operational.

The companies said in a joint statement that all terms have been finalized, and that litigation by NTP had been dismissed. Although Campana died in 2004, Stout said in a written statement that "NTP is pleased that the issue has been resolved and looks forward to enhancing its businesses."

BlackBerry may not be out of the woods yet, however. In May 2006, Visto, a wireless e-mail software company owned in part by NTP, filed a patent infringement lawsuit against RIM in which it seeks to shut down BlackBerry services. Although NTP owns an undisclosed stake in Visto, NTP is not involved in the Visto lawsuit, which seeks an injunction rather than royalties. Visto alleges that RIM was aware of the Visto patents but that it had made no attempt to license them. RIM states that the Visto patents are invalid and is considering suing Visto for infringing the RIM BlackBerry patents.

Supreme Court Rejects Mandatory Patent Infringement Injunctions

When a patent is infringed, the holder of the patent may sue the infringer for damages and may seek an injunction barring further infringement. The **federal courts** have developed a general rule that an injunction must be granted to the patent-holder once infringement has been proven. This rule came under attack in *eBay Inc. v. MercExchange, L.L.C.*, __U.S.__, 126 S.Ct. 1837, __L.Ed.2d __ (2006). The Supreme Court rejected a categorical rule and held that the decision to issue an injunction must be made on a case-by-case basis using traditional equitable principles.

The infringement case involved the Internet auction site run by eBay Inc., which has become enormously popular and profitable. MercExchange, a small, Virginia-based network engineering firm, claimed in 2001 that eBay had infringed on the patents held by its founder Thomas Woolston for a method of selling fixed-price goods online that included an automatic payment system. The specific patent involved the "Buy It Now" feature on eBay that processes transactions for fixed-price purchasing on the web site. MercExchange filed an infringement lawsuit in federal court, alleging that after it had failed to negotiate a licensing fee from eBay to use its patents, eBay proceeded to use an automatic payment system based on the Woolston patents.

In 2003, a federal **district court** in Virginia found that eBay had infringed two patents held by Woolston, and ordered the company to pay MercExchange approximately $5.5 million in damages. However, the court refused to issue an injunction that would have prevented eBay from continuing to use the "Buy It Now" feature. The court concluded that because MercExchange had failed to engage in commercial activity to market its patent, there was no pressing need to issue the injunction. It was in business to license and enforce its patents.

In 2005, the United States Court of Appeals for the Federal Circuit overturned the lower court decision, ruling that MercExchange was entitled to an injunction. The appeals court stated that injunctions were the rule, rather than the exception, in patent infringement cases, and that an injunction should be granted in this case.

The Supreme Court agreed to hear eBay's appeal to determine whether this general rule mandating patent infringement injunctions was correct.

The Court, in an 8-0 decision (newly-confirmed Justice Samuel Alito did not participate in the consideration of the case), overturned the Federal Circuit's decision and the general rule. However, the Court did not resolve the dispute between the parties, returning the case to the lower courts for reconsideration based on the Court's reasoning. Justice CLARENCE THOMAS, writing for the Court, concluded that the district court and the appeals court used different, but incorrect, reasons to support their decisions. Both courts had failed to apply the basic four-part test used to assess whether a permanent injunction is merited. Under this test, the party seeking the injunction must convince the court that it has suffered **irreparable injury**, that monetary damages were inadequate, that a balancing of the hardships between the parties favored the plaintiff, and that the public interest "would not be disserved by a permanent injunction."

Justice Thomas found that this test applied "with equal force" to patent disputes and that nothing in the U.S. Patent Act indicated that Congress intended to depart from these principles. Therefore, the court of appeals judgment was vacated and the case was remanded so the four-part test could be applied under the equitable discretion of the district court.

Chief Justice John Roberts, in a concurring opinion joined by Justices ANTONIN SCALIA and RUTH BADER GINSBURG, noted that "from at least the early 19th century, courts have granted injunctive relief upon a finding of infringement in the vast majority of patent cases." Therefore, federal courts were not "writing on an entirely clean slate." Roberts implied that this historical precedent should guide judges when they apply the four-part test.

Justice ANTHONY KENNEDY also wrote a concurring opinion, which was joined by Justices JOHN PAUL STEVENS, DAVID SOUTER, and STEPHEN BREYER. This group of justices argued that while history may be instructive, new economic and technological circumstances may argue against an almost automatic granting of patent injunctions. Kennedy noted that "An industry has developed in which firms use patents not as a basis for producing and selling goods but, instead, primarily for obtaining licensing fees." For these firms an injunction could be used "as a bargaining tool to charge exorbitant fees to companies that seek to buy licenses to practice the patent." In this situation an injunction might not serve the public interest.

eBay offices in San Jose, California.
AP IMAGES

Whether an injunction would cripple eBay was uncertain. An eBay spokesman was quoted in *The New York Times* as saying that the company had made changes to the "Buy It Now" feature following the 2003 ruling, and that an injunction, if it were granted, would have little effect on the day-to-day function of the web site. MercExchange argued that it did in fact actively practice its patent by licensing technology to companies that compete with eBay, such as Ubid.com and Autotrader.com., suggesting that the company was not the type cited by Justice Kennedy. More troubling for MercExchange was the fact that the PATENT AND TRADEMARK OFFICE had begun reconsidering the validity of the patents in question. This process could take year to resolve and would likely produce more litigation.

Laboratory Corporation of America v. Metabolite

In *Laboratory Corporation of America Holdings v. Metabolite*, No. 04-607, 548 U.S. ___ (2006), the U.S. SUPREME COURT initially granted **certiorari** on the question of whether a patent that instructed parties/users to "correlate test results" between elevated levels of homocysteine in the body and certain vitamin deficiencies, could validly claim a **monopoly** over a basic scientific relationship. The Supreme Court had, **sua sponte**, requested an amicus brief from the **Solicitor General**, expressing the government's opinion on whether the patent was invalid, since "laws of nature, natural phenomena and abstract ideas" are not patentable. The Solicitor General recommended denying certiorari, noting that the issue of natural phenomenon had not even been raised in the lower courts or in the petition for certiorari. The Solicitor General did not opine as to whether the patent was valid on its merits.

Notwithstanding, the Supreme Court granted certiorari in September 2005. Nine months later, in June 2006, the Court dismissed the certiorari as "improvidently granted," without explanation. However, see below, Metabolite had raised the threshold matter (in its responding brief to the Court) that Laboratory Corporation of America Holdings (LabCorp) did not properly raise the objection of non-patentable subject matter, i.e., the issue of natural phenomenon, at trial, or preserve it on appeal. Metabolite contended that LabCorp did not even contemplate such an argument until the Supreme Court had requested opinion on this issue from the Solicitor General.

The dismissal of certiorari left standing, then, the underlying decision of the U.S. Court of Appeals for the Federal Circuit, No. 03-1120, 370 F.3d 1354 (2004). That decision affirmed the trial court's finding of patent infringement against LabCorp.

Initially at the heart of this patent infringement case was a "method" patent (sometimes called a "process patent") to detect medical conditions in warm-blooded animals, specifically, humans. As early as the 1980s, researchers at University Patents Inc. (UPI) had discovered a relationship between elevated levels of an amino acid, homocysteine, and decreased levels of certain vitamins in the body, namely folate and cobalamin (components of Vitamin B12). Elevated levels of homocysteine have been linked to several medical problems, including arthritis, lupus, heart disease, renal disease, and Alzheimer's disease.

The research professors then developed an assay (test) to determine homocysteine levels in blood. The two-step test consisted of (1) assaying a body fluid for elevated levels of homocysteine (the homocysteine test), and (2)correlating elevated levels of homocysteine with a deficiency of cobalamin or folate (by conducting a second test using methylmalonic acid, to identify which vitamin was deficient) The patent claim contemplated protection for both tests as a two-step process.

The U.S. PATENT AND TRADEMARK OFFICE (PTO) initially rejected the application, instructing that it needed to "distinctly claim the subject matter . . . regard[ed] as the invention." After the professors amended the application to reflect their two-step process, it was accepted and awarded Patent No. 4,940,658 (the '658 patent). Subsequent to that, the patent was assigned to Competitive Technologies, Inc. (CTI), a company that licenses academic technological advancements to private industry. CTI, in turn, licensed the process to Metabolite Laboratories, Inc. Metabolite granted a sublicense to LabCorp to use the process, in return for patent royalties paid to Metabolite and CTI. Royalties were to be paid each time the two-step assay and correlation process was utilized.

All was well until LabCorp discovered that Abbott Industries had come up with a more efficient and faster test. LabCorp reasoned that if it used Abbott's process, it would no longer have to pay royalties to Metabolite.

When Metabolite and CTI learned of LabCorp's switch, they sued in federal **district court** for breach of contract (licensing agreement), patent infringement, inducing infringement of a patent, and contributory infringement of a patent. The complaint argued that LabCorp was using the patented assay test for homocysteine levels and reporting results to physicians. The physicians, in turn, would correlate the test results (level of homocysteines found) with estimated deficiencies of the B vitamins. According to the complaint, each time a physician did this, Metabolite was entitled to royalty paymet.

In the November 2001 trial, the jury awarded Metabolite nearly $5 million in damages, finding that LabCorp had breached its contract/licensing agreement and had willfully infringed Metabolite's '658 patent. The district court, in light of the jury's finding of willfulness, doubled the jury's infringement award.

LabCorp filed a post-judgment Motion for Judgment as a Matter of Law (JMOL) on the issues of infringement, breach of contract, invalidity, and willfulness of infringement. The motion was denied. The Federal **Circuit Court** of Appeals, using a standard of review for substantial evidence (to support the jury's finding) found that the record supported the jury's verdicts and the trial court's decisions, and affirmed.

Despite the ultimate dismissal of certiorari previously granted by the U.S. Supreme Court, Justices Breyer, Stevens, and Souter filed a lengthy dissent. They disagreed with the dismissal. Said Justice Breyer,

> "The question presented is not unusually difficult. We have the authority to decide it. We said we would do so. The

parties and the *amici* have fully briefed the question. And those who engage in medical research, who practice medicine, and who as patients depend upon proper health care, might well benefit from this Court's authoritative answer."

PERJURY

A crime that occurs when an individual willfully makes a false statement during a judicial proceeding, after he or she has taken an oath to speak the truth.

Cheney's Chief of Staff Indicted

A two-year long investigation into allegations that a top government official had leaked the identity of a operative of the CENTRAL INTELLIGENCE AGENCY led to the indictment in November 2005 of I. Lewis "Scooter" Libby, chief of staff to Vice President Dick Cheney. Libby has been charged on five counts, including obstruction of justice, false statements, and perjury.

At his State of the Union address in 2003, President GEORGE W. BUSH attempted to garner support for an invasion of Iraq. During his speech, he made the following statement: "The British government has learned that Saddam Hussein recently sought significant quantities of uranium from Africa." These sixteen words became the subject of extensive debate after reporters learned that the statement contradicted the findings of former ambassador Joseph C. Wilson, who had visited Niger in February 2002.

In May 2003, *New York Times* columnist Nicholas Kristof wrote an article questioning the so-called "sixteen words" in Bush's speech. Throughout much of the summer of 2003, journalists focused considerable attention on the alleged source of the information in the speech, which turned out to be Wilson. On July 6, Wilson wrote an op-ed piece entitled "What I Didn't Find in Africa," in which he said that "some of the intelligence related to Iraq's nuclear weapons program was twisted to exaggerate the Iraqi threat."

During July of 2003, journalists covering this story continued to focus their attention on Wilson. By that time, some reporters knew that Wilson's wife, Valerie Plame, was a CIA operative and that she was involved in sending her husband on the trip to Africa. On July 14, syndicated columnist Robert Novak revealed Plame's identity as an intelligence agent, attributing the information to two "senior administration officials." Three days later, three reporters for *Time* wrote that government officials had disclosed Plame's identity to them.

Lewis "Scooter" Libby leaves federal court in Washington, DC, February 3, 2006.
JIM YOUNG/REUTERS/CORBIS

Some members of the press suspected that the source of the leak was presidential advisor Karl Rove. In September 2003, the JUSTICE DEPARTMENT called for a full investigation into the source of the leak. U.S. Attorney Patrick J. Fitzgerald ran the investigation after former attorney general JOHN ASHCROFT recused himself. Agents of the FEDERAL BUREAU OF INVESTIGATION interview several officials of the Bush administration, including Rove, press secretary Scott McClellan, and former White House Counsel (and current attorney general) Alberto R. Gonzales. Some of these individuals, along with other officials, were called to testify about the case before a **grand jury** convened for the U.S. **District Court** for the DISTRICT OF COLUMBIA.

In August 2004, journalists Judith Miller of the *New York Times* and Matthew Cooper of *Time* both refused to reveal the sources of their information. Cooper was one of the *Time* reporters who said that officials had told him of Plame's identity. Miller, on the other hand, had not written a story about the leak. For refusing to testify, both Cooper and Miller were held in contempt of court. The reporters, along with their employers, challenged the contempt charges, but the U.S. SUPREME COURT in June 2005 refused to hear their appeals.

Cooper and *Time* on July 6 agreed to cooperate with the government's investigation. On July 10, *Newsweek* reported that Cooper's source was

Rove. According to Rove's attorney, Rove had appeared before the grand jury but was not a target of the investigation. Cooper later said that Rove never referred to Plame by name, but Rove did inform the reporter that Wilson's wife was a CIA agent who was involved with issues related to weapons of mass destruction.

Miller was jailed on July 6 for refusing to reveal her own sources. Nearly three months later, she was released from a detention center in Virginia after agreeing to testify. The editors of the *New York Times* said that her source offered her assurances that he wanted her to testify. On September 30, the *Times* reported that Miller's source was Libby.

Libby was obligated under 18 U.S.C. § 793 (2000) and by executive orders issued by presidents Bush and BILL CLINTON not to disclose classified information to unauthorized persons. He was also required to exercise the proper care in safeguarding classified information against authorized disclosure. Moreover, in his testimony before the grand jury in March 2004, Libby stated that he learned of Plame's identity from journalists.

Miller wrote an article for the *New York Times* on October 16, stating that she and Libby had discussed Plame's CIA position, though Libby did not mention Plame by name. On October 25, the *Times* reported that according to Libby's notes, he became aware of Plame's identity through a conversation with Cheney weeks before her identity became public. This revelation contradicted his testimony that he had learned of her identity through journalists.

Libby was indicted on October 28 and charged with one count of obstruction of justice, two counts of making false statements, and two counts of perjury. He resigned his position as Cheney's chief of staff and pleaded not guilty to the charges on November 3. Fitzgerald said that Libby had intentionally deceived authorities. "Mr. Libby's story that he was at the tail end of a chain of phone calls, passing on from one reporter what he heard from another, was not true," Fitzgerald said. "He was at the beginning of the chain of the phone calls, the first official to disclose this information outside the government to a reporter. And he lied about it afterwards, under oath and repeatedly."

On November 15, 2005, Bob Woodward of the *Washington Post* testified that a "senior administration official" had told him about Plame nearly a month before Novak had referred to her in his column. Although Woodward did not disclose the source of the information, he said that it was not Libby. As of May 2006, no other official had been charged with a crime for the leak.

PIRACY

Companies Look For Legal Downloading Solutions

In the wake of the June 2005 decision handed down by the U.S. SUPREME COURT, Grokster Ltd., a company whose file-sharing software had been used to illegally download music and movies via the Internet, agreed in November 2005 to shut down its operations as part of the settlement of the case with the Recording Industry Association of America and the National Music Publishers' Association.

Grokster changed its web site to say that it no longer offered software for free downloads of music and movies, and it referred potential customers to other sites. In a *Washington Post* article, Marty Lafferty, head of the Distributed Computing Industry Association, a trade group that includes some file-sharing services, said that the settlement is a sign that the file-sharing industry is moving toward making itself legal and that the Grokster action is "part of the conversion from open peer-to-peers to industry-acceptable, sanctioned business methods."

The Grokster brand may survive in the form of a fee-based version of the software that allows users to download files legally, but the status of such a product remains uncertain while the sale of Grokster's assets is pending. However, the cessation of Grokster's file-sharing operations will not prevent customers who have already downloaded the software from using it.

The Supreme Court's unanimous decision in *Metro-Goldwyn-Meyer Studios v. Grokster* stated that distributors of file-sharing software were liable for secondary copyright infringement associated with the direct copyright infringement demonstrated by the individuals who used the software to illegally download and share music and video files.

In September 2005, several other online file-sharing companies in addition to Grokster reacted to the Grokster ruling by seeking agreements with the recording industry. Grokster has negotiated a tentative agreement with Mash-Boxx, a company sponsored by Sony that is trying to establish itself as a legal file-sharing service. *New York Times* reporter Saul Hansell wrote that, according to an anonymous source involved in the negotiations, "Mashboxx would make a nominal payment for Grokser, but would share future revenue."

Several file-sharing services, including LimeWire, eDonkey, and BearShare, received letters from the Recording Industry Association of America in the fall of 2005, buoyed by the Grokster decision, demanding that the companies prohibit users of their services from trading copyrighted files. The companies were invited to discuss possible settlements in **advance** of litigation.

The file-sharing service known as iMesh, which reached a settlement with the recording industry in 2004, has made overtures to purchase other file-sharing services if they would settle their own claims with the recording industry. In the iMesh settlement, the company paid four million dollars in damages and converted to a paid, legal service that will block the trading of copyrighted files without the owner's permission. The goal is less about making money than about helping other file-sharing services avoid litigation, said iMesh executive chairman Robert E. Summer in the *New York Times*. Summer was quoted as saying that iMesh's potential acquisition of other file-sharing companies would be "good for iMesh and good for the industry."

Although iMesh spent the better part of a year developing itself as a paid service, the recording industry expects an end to free file-sharing as soon as the software is developed. Spokespersons from Mashboxx and iMesh have stated that the companies intend to use technology that reviews downloaded files and compares them with a master list of copyrighted songs from the recording industry. If someone tries to download a copyrighted file, the download will simply be blocked, or the downloader will be asked for a fee, in the manner of the iTunes Music Store established by Apple.

Another twist on the file-sharing issue involves a lawsuit by StreamCast Networks, the company named along with Grokster in the Supreme Court case. StreamCast has sued the online auction company eBay over its use of StreamCast's Morpheus file-sharing technology that allows customers to make phone calls over the Internet. Ebay owns Skype, an online telephone service.

StreamCast is seeking more than four billion dollars in damages, and has asked the court to force compliance. The lawsuit stated that eBay and twenty-one other companies have taken advantage of the technology in "an attempt to steal and wrongfully profit from technology that rightfully belongs to StreamCast." An eBay spokesperson expressed awareness of the lawsuit and declined to comment.

PRIVACY

In constitutional law, the right of people to make personal decisions regarding intimate matters; under the common law, the right of people to lead their lives in a manner that is reasonably secluded from public scrutiny, whether such scrutiny comes from a neighbor's prying eyes, an investigator's eavesdropping ears, or a news photographer's intrusive camera; and in statutory law, the right of people to be free from unwarranted drug testing and electronic surveillance.

Wisconsin Governor Vetoes Cloning Ban Proposal

In November 2005, Wisconsin Governor Jim Doyle vetoed a bill that would have forbidden all forms of human cloning in the state. The bill drew strong opposition from members of the scientific and biotechnology communities, but nevertheless the Wisconsin State Assembly passed the bill. Doyle vowed to allow Wisconsin to "remain at the forefront of stem cell research" through his veto.

Embryonic stem cell research has been at the center of an ongoing debate in the United States for much of the past decade. The essential question in this debate is whether a scientist should destroy human embryos for the sake of research. Many oppose such research due to religious, moral, or other beliefs regarding the sanctity of human life, even when that life is in the form of an undeveloped embryo. Supporters of this research generally believe that stem cell research could result in major medical breakthroughs that could save lives and improve the quality of medical science.

A related debate concerns the cloning of human embryos. In May 2005, scientists in Newcastle of Great Britain announced that they had successfully cloned a human embryo. Besides the Newcastle researchers, only a team of scientists in South Korea had perfected this technique. The Newcastle team completed its cloning as part of a research project that has focused on treatments for diabetes. Scientists in South Korea have announced that they will study means by which specific medical conditions could be addressed through the creation of specialized stem cells.

Using the science being developed in Britain and South Korea could allow researchers to extract stem cells from cloned embryos. This process has been heavily criticized in some circles because the process of harvesting stem cells would kill the cloned embryo. Many of those who opposed both stem cell research and human cloning are also pro-life activists in the debate over abortion.

Twenty representatives in the Wisconsin State Assembly sponsored Assembly Bill 499, which was introduced on June 16, 2005. A related bill was also introduced in the state senate. Immediately after its introduction, members of the scientific and biotechnology communities announced their opposition to the bill. Ron Kuehn, vice president of government relations for the Wisconsin Biotechnology and Medical Device Association, said that embryonic stem cell research "could be the technology of the future," and that if the ban were in place, "then the future may be denied us in research." Wisconsin is generally considered to be an international leader in stem cell research.

Others who opposed the bill said that the real impact of the bill would have been to divert research money elsewhere. According to Tom Still, president of the Wisconsin Technology Council, the majority of states are competing for biotechnology investments, and that a statewide ban would harm researchers in Wisconsin. "It's counterproductive for our policy makers to take steps that could make Wisconsin less attractive," he said. "There are other places that would gladly welcome the kind of research that we do, and especially if some of our policy makers are intent on pushing it out the door."

Supporters, including those in the state legislature, said that they hoped that the state should not want the money from this type of research. "If we're chasing dollars with the intention of cloning embryos, all I can say is the public would say shame on us," said state representative Steve Kestell, one of the bill's sponsors. "Can we control what's going to happen all over the world? Absolutely not. I thing we do have a right, even a responsibility, to chart our own course and to control what we do." Pro-life supporters echoed these types of statements.

The Wisconsin proposal banned cloning not only for reproductive purposes, but also for therapeutic and research. The bill defined "human cloning" as "asexual reproduction accomplished by introducing nuclear material from one or more human somatic cells into an enucleated oocyte so as to produce a living organism having genetic material that is virtually identical to the genetic material of an existing or previously existing human organism." In addition to human cloning, the bill also would have banned human parthenogenesis, which is "the process of manipulating the genetic material of a human oocyte, without introducing into the oocyte the genetic material from any other cell, in a way that causes the oocyte to become a human embryo."

The bill would have forbidden anyone in the state from performing or attempting to perform human cloning or human parthenogenesis. An individual who violated this **statute** would have faced a fine of up to $250,000. An **entity** other than an individual would have faced a fine of up to $500,000. If an individual or entity had made a **pecuniary** gain from the research, the fines could increase up to $1 million. The bill established a violation of this statute as a Class G **felony**, and a person who violated the statute could have faced up to 10 years in prison in addition to the fine.

Biotechnology associations attempted to compromise with the bill's supporters by suggesting an amendment that would allow therapeutic cloning but not reproductive cloning. Unlike reproductive cloning, therapeutic cloning does not result in the formation of an embryo that would become a fully formed human being upon maturity. Therapeutic cloning can be used to harvest stem cells, but this recommendation met with resistance because some view any form of human cloning to be immoral. The proposed amendment was rejected in the State Assembly.

The bill passed in the State Assembly by a vote of 59 to 38, thus short of the two-third majority that would be needed to override the governor's veto. The debate continued in September, when the state senate considered the proposal. Researchers and others in the scientific community continued to oppose the bill, but the senate approved the measure by a vote of 21 to 12.

Even as the bill was being considered by the senate, Doyle had vowed to veto it, calling the proposal "ill advised" and "extreme." On November 3, 2005, Doyle formally vetoed the bill. "The real purpose of this bill is to restrict stem cell research, which holds enormous potential for our state as well as the promise of curing juvenile diabetes, spinal cord injuries, and Parkinson's disease," he said in a letter to the State Assembly. "Allowing our scientists to search for cures to diseases isn't about being liberal or conservative. It's about being compassionate. And respect for human life means you don't turn your back on cures that can save lives."

Doyle symbolically announced the veto at the University of Wisconsin-Madison's Biotechnology Center. Supporters of the bill expressed disappointment, saying that researchers have no guidelines regarding the type of research that they can conduct in the state.

PROBATE

The court process by which a will is proved valid or invalid. The legal process wherein the estate of a decedent is administered.

Marshall v. Marshall a.k.a Anna Nicole Smith

After years of convoluted federal and state litigation with accompanying **appellate** review, the U.S. SUPREME COURT decided, in *Marshall v. Marshall*, 547 U.S. ___, 126 S.Ct. 1735, ___ L.Ed.2d ___ (2006), that Vickie Lynn Marshall, a.k.a. Anna Nicole Smith, could pursue her probate-related claims (involving her deceased husband's estate) in federal court. The unanimous high court reached its decision on a very narrow issue that clarified the right of a federal judge to intervene in a state **probate** matter. Writing for the Court, Justice RUTH BADER GINSBURG explained that while the "probate exception" to federal jurisdiction generally means that state probate courts adjudicate matters involving wills and estate administration, the present case included additional claims that made federal jurisdiction appropriate. The high court's ruling reversed a Ninth **Circuit Court** of Appeals decision that had overruled both federal bankruptcy and federal **district court** decisions.

In 1994, billionaire J. Howard Marshall II was approaching the age of 90 when he married 26-year-old Anna Nicole Smith (1992 Playmate of the Year and model for jeans commercials) in 1994. One year later, in 1995, he died without naming his new widow (whose real name is Vickie Lynn) in the will or accompanying trust instrument. His son, E. Pierce Marshall (Pierce), was the sole named heir in the estate plan.

In ongoing Texas probate court proceedings, Vickie argued that her deceased husband had intended to provide for her through a "catch-all" trust. While probate was still pending, Vickie filed for bankruptcy under Chapter 11 of the federal Bankruptcy Code in a California federal bankruptcy court. Pierce Marshall then filed a proof of claim in the bankruptcy court, alleging that Vickie had defamed him in her contacts with the media, accusing him of forgery, **fraud**, and overreaching to gain control of his father's assets. Pierce petitioned for a declaration that his claim was not dischargeable in bankruptcy. In her **responsive pleading**, Vickie raised counterclaims, including one alleging that Pierce tortiously interfered with her husband's intended gift to her in a scheme to deny her an inheritance.

Anna Nicole Smith arrives at the U.S. Supreme Court for a hearing on her probate case. February 25, 2006.
CHRIS KLEPONIS/REUTERS/CORBIS

The federal bankruptcy court held that Vickie's **tortious** interference counterclaim turned her responsive pleading into an "adversary proceeding" under Fed. Rule Bkrtcy. Proc. 3007. Accordingly, it ruled on the merits of the claim and counterclaims. It further ruled that both Vickie's objection to Pierce's claim as well as her own counterclaim qualified as "core proceedings" under 28 U.S.C. § 157, giving the court authority to enter a final judgment disposing of those claims. It then granted **summary judgment** for Vickie on Pierce's claim and awarded her several million dollars (in both compensatory and **punitive damages**) for her counterclaim. Pierce next filed a post-trial motion to dismiss for lack of subject-matter jurisdiction, arguing that Vickie's counterclaim related to a probate matter reserved for the Texas probate court proceedings. The bankruptcy court dismissed his motion, holding that **federal courts** have jurisdiction to adjudicate rights in probate matters, barring any final judgment that would interfere with a state court's possession of the property.

Meanwhile, a Texas probate court declared that J. Howard Marshall's estate plan, naming only Pierce as beneficiary, was valid.

Next, Pierce appealed the bankruptcy court's ruling in federal district court. While the district court agreed with the bankruptcy court that there was federal jurisdiction over the matter unless such jurisdiction interfered with probate proceedings, it disagreed that Vickie's counterclaim qualified as a "core proceeding" over which a bankruptcy court could exercise plenary power, 28 U.S.C. § 157(b), (c). Therefore, the federal district court treated the bankruptcy court's decision as a proposed rather than final ruling, and undertook its own review **de novo**. Ultimately, it adopted and supplemented the bankruptcy court's findings that Pierce had tortiously interfered with Vickie's expectancy by conspiring to suppress or destroy an **inter vivos** trust inter vivos trust that J. Howard had directed his lawyers to prepare for Vickie. The court also found that Pierce had tried to divest his father of assets by **backdating**, altering, and otherwise falsifying documents that he presented to his father under **false pretenses**. The court awarded Vickie some $44.3 million in **compensatory damages**, and based on "overwhelming" evidence of willful fraud and **malice** on the part of Pierce, an equal amount in punitive damages.

The Ninth Circuit Court of Appeals reversed. It held that the probate exception barred federal jurisdiction in this case. It further explained that a State's vesting of exclusive jurisdiction over probate matters stripped federal courts of jurisdiction over any probate matter. Finding Vickie's counterclaim fell within a probate court's determination of validity of a decedent's estate planning instrument, whether involving questions of fraud, undue influence, or tortious interference, the Ninth Circuit struck both federal decisions.

Not so, said the U.S. Supreme Court. It unanimously held that the Ninth Circuit had no warrant from Congress or from previous Supreme Court decisions for its sweeping extension of the probate exception. (The so-called probate exception is not found in text of either federal **statute** or Constitution, but rather, devolves from longstanding English legal history and subsequent case law.) According to the Supreme Court, Vickie's counterclaim, provoked by Pierce's claim in the bankruptcy proceedings, did not involve the administration of an estate, the probate of a will, or any other purely probate matter. Instead, it was grounded in common **tort law** as a claim of tortious interference. The only connection with probate matters was the fact that the subject matter of Pierce's tortious interference was an intended gift of inheritance. The remedy remedy for such a claim is an **in personam** judgment (in personam jurisdiction) against Pierce personally, and not the probate or annulment of any will or estate instrument.

Moreover, said the Court, while it is clear, under ***Erie R. Co. v. Tompkins***, 58 S.Ct. 817, 82 L.Ed.2d 1188 (1938), that Texas state law governs the substantive elements of Vickie's counterclaim, "[I]t is also clear . . . that Texas may not reserve to its probate courts the exclusive right to adjudicate a transitory tort."

Justice Stevens filed a separate opinion, concurring in part and concurring in the judgment. The reasoning in his opinion went further than that of the majority, in that he doubted there is any "probate exception" whatever that ousts a federal court of jurisdiction it otherwise possesses.

PROPERTY LAW

Alaska v. United States

In the January 2006 matter of *Alaska v. United States*, 126 S.Ct. 1014, 163 L.Ed.2d 995 (2006); the U.S. SUPREME COURT entered its final decree and order relating to its earlier 2005 decision, *Alaska v. United States*, 545 U.S. ___; 125 S.Ct. 2137, 163 L.Ed.2d 57. It is the latter 2005 case that adjudicated the substantive merits of the controversy, which involved disputed ownership of certain submerged lands in Southeast Alaska.

The high court had previously decided a similar dispute (in 1997) in *United States v. Alaska*, 521 U.S. 1, 117 S.Ct. 1888, 138 L.Ed.2d 231 (1997). Both that case and the present case involved the Submerged Lands Act of 1953, 43 U.S.C. § 1301(c). In the earlier decision, the Court noted that states are generally entitled "under both the equal footing doctrine and the Submerged Lands Act to submerged lands beneath tidal and inland navigable waters, and under the Submerged Act alone to submerged lands extending three miles seaward of [their] coastline" (521 U.S. 1 at 6,9). But in the 1997 case, the Court ruled against Alaska and declared that the United States owned disputed lands along Alaska's Arctic Coast that were adjacent to the federal Arctic National Wildlife Refuge and the National Petroleum Reserve. Despite the protections of the cited Act and related doctrine, the Court held that the United States could overcome such a presumption of title (vesting in Alaska) by setting submerged lands aside before statehood in a way that shows an intent to retain title (as was held in this case).

The Equal Footing doctrine provides that new states entering the Union have the same sovereign powers and jurisdiction as the original 13 states. Accordingly, new states generally acquire title to the beds of inland navigable waters. Under the Submerged Lands Act of 1953, states have title to submerged lands beneath inland navigable waters and beneath offshore marine waters within three miles from the coastline.

The underlying controversy for the present case started in 2000, when the Supreme Court granted leave to the State of Alaska (still at odds with the 1997 decision) to file a complaint to quiet title relating to two other areas of submerged lands in Southeast Alaska. Specifically, the first consisted of pockets of submerged lands underlying waters in the Alexander Archipelago that are located more than three nautical miles offshore. (Alaska could claim these only if the archipelago waters qualified as inland waters.) The second area involved submerged lands beneath the inland waters of Glacial Bay. The United States needed to rebut the presumption of title to Alaska.

In March 2001, the Supreme Court referred Alaska's amended complaint and the United States' answer to a Special Master. From 2001 to 2004, the Special Master oversaw voluminous filings and briefings of motions for **summary judgment** from both sides. In 2004, the Court received and filed the Report of the Special Master.

The recommendation of the Special Master was that summary judgment be granted to the United States with respect to both geographic areas. In particular, the report concluded that the Alexander Archipelago waters did not qualify as "inland waters," either under an historic inland waters theory, or under a "juridical" (relating to laws and their administration) bay theory. The report also concluded that the United States had successfully rebutted any presumption that title to submerged lands beneath the Glacial Bay area passed to Alaska at statehood. Alaska then filed "exceptions" to these conclusions.

Alaska first contended that the plain language in the Alaska Statehood Act did not express the unambiguous intent of Congress to reserve title to the subject submerged lands within the boundaries of the Glacier Bay National Monument. Alaska also argued that the undisputed historical record showed that the United States continuously exercised sovereignty over the waters of the Alexander Archipelago *with the* ***acquiescence*** *of foreign nations.* Further, argued Alaska, the undisputed record demonstrated that the areas qualified as **juridical** bays under Article 7 of the Convention on the Territorial Sea and Contiguous Zone, thereby invoking assimilation principles applied in *United States v. Maine,* 469 U.S. 504, 105 S.Ct. 992, 83 L.Ed.2d 998 (1986).

The Supreme Court, in an opinion delivered by Justice Kennedy, unanimously rejected Alaska's arguments and agreed with the Special Master in its June 2005 decision, 545 U.S. 75, 125 S.Ct. 2137, 163 L.Ed.2d 57. First, the Court found that the Archipelago's waters were not historic inland waters. To make such a claim, Alaska needed to show that the United States, in its exercise of sovereignty with the acquiescence of foreign nations, asserted such power as to exclude all foreign vessels and navigation. The Special Master examined records going back to 1821 and found that the United States had not exerted the requisite authority over such waters.

Nor did the Alexander Archipelago waters qualify as inland waters under the juridical bay theory, said the Court. Such juridical bays would exist only if, at a minimum, four of the area's islands formed a constructive peninsula, dividing the waters in two. Then, assuming **arguendo**, the resulting two bodies of water would have to constitute such well-marked indentations with physical features that would allow a mariner (without such markings on a navigational chart) to nonetheless be able to perceive the bays' limits in order to avoid illegal **encroachment** into inland waters.

Finally, said the Court, the United States had rebutted Alaska's presumptive title to the submerged lands underlying the Glacial Bay area. Even though there was no express language in the statehood act, the United States could still defeat a future state's title by setting aside lands as part of a federal reservation, such as a wildlife refuge. Under the Alaska Statehood Act, Alaska retained all property previously belonging to the Territory of Alaska, and the United States retained title to its property located within Alaska's borders. Although a proviso in the statehood act directed a transfer to Alaska of any U.S. property used "for the sole purpose of conservation and protection of [Alaska's] fisheries and wildlife," that clause did not apply to "lands withdrawn or otherwise set apart as refuges or reservations for [wildlife] protection." In the

1997 case, the Supreme Court held that Congress had indeed intended to retain title to such reservations as the Alaska National Wildlife Refuge, sufficiently defeating any presumptive state title under both the equal footing doctrine and the Submerged Lands Act.

After overruling Alaska's exceptions, the Court directed the parties to prepare and submit a proposed decree to the Special Master for the Court's consideration. In the January 2006 case, the decree was entered as the Court's final judgment and order.

REHNQUIST, WILLIAM HUBBS

Although some Supreme Court justices have not shared Rehnquist's staunchly conservative views, they generally respected his efficiency, quiet humor, and fairness. He served on the Supreme Court for more than 30 memorable years.

The son of a paper salesman, Rehnquist grew up in suburban Shorewood, Wisconsin. Since his family worshipped Republican President Herbert Hoover, William had little affection for Democratic President Franklin Delano Roosevelt, who was president for much of his childhood. When one of William's elementary school teachers inquired about his career goals, he answered that he wanted to change the government.

After completing high school in Milwaukee, Rehnquist served in the United States Army Air Force in the middle 1940s. Like many other American men who fought in World War II, Rehnquist used the GI Bill to attend college. He enrolled in Stanford University and graduated with both a bachelor of arts (Phi Beta Kappa) and master of arts in political science in 1948. Two years later, Harvard University conferred upon him another master of arts in government. He returned to Stanford University to study law. In 1952, he received a law degree and graduated first in his class. Considered brilliant by his instructors and classmates, Rehnquist also acquired a reputation as an conservative student.

One of Rehnquist's Stanford professors arranged for Supreme Court Justice Robert H. Jackson to interview Rehnquist for a clerkship, and he clerked for Jackson in 1952 and 1953. After his clerkship ended, Rehnquist married Natalie Cornell. The couple moved to Phoenix, Arizona, where he worked in the law firm of Evans, Kitchel & Jenckes from 1953 to 1956. Subsequently, he formed a law partnership with Keith Ragan. Gradually, Rehnquist allied himself with many conservative Republican politicians in Arizona. He often criticized the Supreme Court's liberalism, attributing it partly to the leftist tendencies of the justices' law clerks. He particularly disliked the reasoning of Justices William O. Douglas, Earl Warren, and Hugo L. Black for what he perceived as their interpreting the U.S. Constitution too loosely to reflect their own biases.

After dissolving his partnership with Ragan, Rehnquist became a partner in the law firm of Cunningham, Carson, & Messenger. In 1958, he also became a special Arizona state prosecutor, and part of his work involved charging many state officials with highway frauds.

Rehnquist's friendship with conservative Richard Kleindienst, the national field director of the presidential campaigns of Barry Goldwater in 1964 and Richard Nixon in 1968, proved important. In February 1969, soon after Kleindienst was appointed deputy attorney general in President Nixon's administration, Kleindienst arranged for Rehnquist to become assistant attorney general in charge of the office of legal counsel.

In October 1971, President Nixon nominated Rehnquist to fill one of two vacancies on the Supreme Court. Democratic Senators Birch Bayh and Edward M. Kennedy were initially suspicious of Rehnquist's conservatism. Many labor leaders and liberal spokespersons also op-

WILLIAM HUBBS REHNQUIST

1952 Graduated from Stanford University Law School

1952 Clerked for Supreme Court Justice Robert H. Jackson

1953-1956 Practiced private law in Arizona

1958 Became a special Arizona state prosecutor

1969 Became assistant attorney general in charge of the office of legal counsel

1971 Richard Nixon appoints Rehnquist to the Supreme Court

1986 Ronald Reagan nominates Rehnquist to replace retiring Chief Justice Warren Burger

2005 Rehnquist dies at age 80 from thyroid cancer

posed him for what they perceived as his lack of concern for civil rights. A Rehnquist memorandum in favor of continuing the *separate but equal* doctrine for public schools was discovered, written when he clerked for Justice Jackson. In effect, Rehnquist's memo endorsed the racial segregation of public schools. Rehnquist's opponents also learned that in 1964 he had taken a stand against public accommodations legislation in Phoenix, and in 1967 Rehnquist had disputed an integration plan for the Phoenix high schools.

Rehnquist confronted these accusations in testimony before the Senate Judiciary Committee in November 1971. He said he now endorsed the public accommodations law that he had formerly contested. Rehnquist denied that he had ever supported school segregation by saying his memorandum on the topic reflected Justice Jackson's beliefs, not his own. Along those lines, Rehnquist argued that several of his former positions reflected his status as a government advocate; personally, he had not always agreed with those views. Although Rehnquist's critics still opposed his nomination for the Supreme Court, the Senate in December 1971 voted 68 to 26 to confirm it. Nearly every Republican in the Senate voted for him, and even some of the Democrats that did not agree with his opinions thought he was qualified to serve on the Supreme Court.

In his first years on the Court, Rehnquist often disagreed with the other justices. Unlike the others, he did not believe the Equal Protection Clause of the Fourteenth Amendment generally pertained to state-sponsored discrimination of children born out of wedlock, resident aliens, and women; he believed the Equal Protection Clause concerned predominantly racial discrimination. Rehnquist dissented on *Roe v. Wade*, a landmark 1973 decision permitting women the right to have abortions. He also disagreed with the majority opinion in *United Steel Workers of America v. Weber* (1979), in which the Supreme Court declared that discrimination against whites was not prohibited by the Civil Rights Act of 1964.

In the middle 1970s, Rehnquist wrote many majority opinions that undermined the power of the federal government in favor of states' rights. One of the most memorable of these decisions evolved out of *National League of Cities v. Usery*, in which Rehnquist interpreted the Tenth Amendment to void a federal statute that controlled state government employees' earnings and hours.

When Chief Justice Warren Burger declared his resignation in 1986, President Reagan nominated Rehnquist to replace him. Senator Edward Kennedy and other liberals opposed his nomination for many of the same reasons that they had opposed Rehnquist's nomination to the Supreme Court in 1971. Many of them criticized his record on civil rights and race and considered him a right-wing fanatic. However, no significant charges of misconduct were brought against Rehnquist in his term as an associate justice. After much debate, the Senate confirmed him as chief justice in September 1986, by a vote of 65 to 33.

After Rehnquist became chief justice, the Court often supported the powers of the states over the federal government. Another Supreme Court trend was a smaller caseload; in 1986, 175 cases were argued before the Court; in 1995, that number had declined to 90. Chief Justice Rehnquist advocated similar views to the ones he expressed as an associate justice, although his image as the lone dissenter of the Court was mostly gone. While Rehnquist's vision impacted on the direction of the Supreme Court, his vote was usually not the pivotal one in close decisions.

In the 1990s, Rehnquist voted against the majority opinion in two extremely significant

Court decisions. The first was *Planned Parenthood v. Casey*, which reaffirmed *Roe v. Wade*, thus protecting women's right to abortions. The second was *Romer v. Evans*, in which the Court voided an antigay Colorado state constitutional amendment. In 1996, Rehnquist clashed openly with Republicans over their criticism of President Clinton's judicial appointments. In the early months of 1999, Rehnquist presided over the impeachment trial of President Bill Clinton in the U. S. Senate.

In January 2001, without addressing the Supreme Court's election ruling (5-4 in favor of Bush after the Supreme Court had to step in after George W. Bush contested the Florida court's ruling), Rehnquist wrote, "Despite the seesaw aftermath of the presidential election, we are once again witnessing an orderly transition of power from one presidential administration to another. . . . This presidential election, however, tested our constitutional system in ways it has never been tested before. The Florida state courts, the lower federal courts and the Supreme Court of the United States became involved in a way that one hopes will seldom, if ever, be necessary in the future."

Though many speculated for years as to when he would retire, he continued to work at home up until a few days before his death from thyroid cancer in September 2005. He was 80 years old.

RELIGION

Debate Over Teaching Evolution and Intelligent Design Continues

The national debate over the teaching of evolution versus other alternative theories continued in 2005 and 2006. Supporters of a theory known as intelligent design have attempted to integrate its teachings with those of evolution. These proposals, however, have been rebuked by many members of the scientific community, who view intelligent design as theology rather than science. The dispute reached something of a climax in December 2005, when a judge in Pennsylvania ruled that public schools in that state could not teach intelligent design because the concept is really creationism in disguise.

The argument over the teaching of evolution in public schools extended through much of the 20th century. In one of the century's most famous trials, John Scopes, a biology teacher in Tennessee, was charged with violating the state's Butler Act, which prohibited the teaching of evolution in the public schools. Scopes was prosecuted by William Jennings Bryan and defended by CLARENCE DARROW. The trial, dubbed the "Scopes Monkey Trial," has long been remembered for the interactions between Bryan and Darrow, as well as for certain assertions made about the creation of life.

The Scopes trial did not resolve constitutional questions regarding the teaching of evolution in schools. The U.S. SUPREME COURT finally addressed this issue in 1968 by invalidating a state **statute** that prohibited the teaching of evolution. *Epperson v. Arkansas*, 393 U.S. 97, 89 S. Ct. 266, 21 L. Ed. 2d 228 (1968). By the latter part of the 20th century, scientists had largely accepted evolution, even though many aspects of evolution are in apparent contradiction with Biblical stories. Some states attempted to balance teaching of evolution and the Bible by requiring schools to teach both creationism and evolution. The Court invalidated one of these types of laws in 1987. *Edwards v. Aguillard*, 482 U.S. 578, 107 S. Ct. 2573, 96 L. Ed. 2d 510 (1987).

During the 1980s, some individuals, largely associated with academia, began to develop new theories on the creation of life. These theorists strategically separated themselves from specific references to creationism. They instead focused their arguments on assertions that life on Earth is too complex to have been developed as a random occurrence. According to their arguments, an intelligent being must have designed the system that created life on this planet.

Proponents of intelligent design direct much of their attention on discrediting evolution. Ostensibly, their goal is to allow schools to teach intelligent design as an equally viable alternative to the theory of evolution. This argument, however, depends largely on the characterization of intelligent design as science. Although defenders of this movement say that they do not need to identify a specific "designer" in order to prove their theory, many who oppose this movement say that the theory is really based on religious beliefs rather than science.

Some scientists have taken firm positions in opposition to the intelligent design movement. In October 2005, for instance, six Nobel laureates joined other scientists and religious leaders in opposing the teaching of intelligent design in schools. According to a letter sent by these laureates to all 50 governors in the U.S., teaching intelligent design in the classroom could cause American students to fall behind students abroad. "We certainly will not be able to close this gap if we substitute ideology for fact in our science classrooms," the letter said.

Intelligent design advocates secured what they viewed as a victory in November, when the Kansas Board of Education approved new science standards that cast doubt on the theory of evolution. According to supporters, the decision would allow local schools to broaden the scope of their science classes by offering not only natural explanations for phenomena, but also supernatural explanations for these occurrences. In contrast, opponents of the proposals said that the state would become a "laughingstock" of the nation because of how the Kansas standards define science.

Boards in several other states have considered and approved other challenges to evolution. In Alabama, for instance, biology textbooks must bear disclaimers that read, "Evolution is a controversial theory." According to reports, states that have boards of education consisting of elected members are more likely to have standards that challenge evolution than states where board members are appointed. Polls have indicated that the American public is split on the treatment of evolution and alternative theories of creation in schools.

A local school board in Dover, Pennsylvania in October 2004 initiated a requirement that ninth-grade biology teachers read a statement introducing intelligent design to their classes. It represented the **first instance** in which intelligent design was formally included as part of a curriculum. A group of 11 parents sued the school board to prevent this policy from taking effect. The case drew national attention.

In December 2005, U.S. District Judge John E. Jones III struck down the policy. His opinion discredited intelligent design as "a religious view, a mere re-labeling of creationism, and not a scientific theory." Moreover, the judge said that the board hid its true motive, which was to "promote religion in the public school classroom." According to the judge, "This case came to us as the result of the activism of an ill-informed faction on a school board, aided by a national public interest law firm eager to find a constitutional **test case** on [intelligent design], who in combination drove the Board to adopt an imprudent and ultimately unconstitutional policy. The breathtaking inanity of the Board's decision is evident when considered against the factual backdrop which has now been fully revealed through this trial. The students, parents, and teachers of the Dover Area School District deserved better than to be dragged into this legal maelstrom, with its resulting utter waste of monetary and personal resources." *Kitzmiller v. Dover Area Sch. Dist.*, 400 F. Supp. 2d 707 (M.D. Penn. 2005).

About a month after the Pennsylvania decision, a rural school district in California cancelled an elective intelligent design course. Schools in several others states continued to consider whether to attempt to teach the theory as a challenge to evolution in light of the *Kitzmiller* opinion. The National Center for Science Education, along with other organizations, has said that it will continue to challenge the teaching of intelligent design in the schools.

Florida Supreme Court Strikes Down Voucher Program

The Florida Supreme Court in 2006 struck down a **statute** that authorized a program that provided vouchers for children at failing schools. The decision was based on an interpretation of the state's constitution and cannot be appealed to the U.S. SUPREME COURT. The statute in question was considered to be one of Florida Governor Jeb Bush's chief accomplishments.

In 1999, Florida became the first state to offer a statewide **voucher** program to children from kindergarten to grade 12. The voucher program consisted of three parts. First, the Opportunity Scholarship Program (OSP) provided $3,900 to children who attended a school that failed Florida's Comprehensive Assessment Test (FCAT) two years in a row. The vouchers would allow a child to attend a religiously affiliated school. Second, the McKay Scholarship, instituted in 2001, provides funding for children with disabilities. Third, the Corporate Tax Credit, also begun in 2001, provides tax incentives for businesses that provide scholarships for private schooling to low-income students.

In creating the OSP, the Florida Legislature expressed the collective belief that students should not be forced to remain in a failing school against the wishes of the students' parents. The program was designed "to provide enhanced opportunity for students in this state to gain the knowledge and skills necessary for postsecondary education, a career education, or the world of work." The scholarship would give students at failing schools the opportunity to attend a better public school or to attend a private school that may provide superior education.

Shortly after its establishment, various parents of children who attended public schools in Florida, as well as several organizations, filed complaints alleging that the voucher program was unconstitutional under both the Florida and U.S. constitutions. A trial court originally held that the OSP violated the state constitution, but this decision was reversed by the First **District Court** of Appeals. *Bush v. Holmes*, 767 So. 2d 668, 675 (Fla. App. 2000). Two years after the case, the U.S. Supreme Court ruled that school voucher programs were constitutional under the Establishment Clause to the federal constitution. *Zelman v. Simmons-Harris*, 536 U.S. 639, 122 S. Ct. 2460, 153 L. Ed. 2d 604 (2002). Thus, the plaintiffs' claims under the Establishment Clause were dropped from the case.

Article I, Section 3 of the Florida Constitution provides, "No revenue of the state or any political subdivision or agency thereof shall ever be taken from the public treasury directly or indirectly in aid of any church, sect, or religious denomination or in aid of sectarian institution." The trial court found that the OCP violated this provision, and the court of appeals agreed. *Bush v. Holmes*, 886 So. 2d 340 (Fla. App. 2004). Under state law, the Florida Supreme Court was required to hear the appeal because the **appellate court** had rule a state statute unconstitutional.

Opponents of the voucher program noted that simply because a school is a private school does not mean that a student will receive a superior education. The FCAT scores of private schools are not made available to the public, which means that parents cannot be assured that a private school's performance is better than that of a failing public school. Critics of the program said that the OCP and the voucher system in general does little or nothing to improve education. Instead, these critics charged that using tax dollars to fund vouchers to private schools allowed the state legislature to "move itself out of the costly education business."

In addition to Florida's constitution, 36 other state constitutions have similar bans on funding of religious institutions. Few states have voucher programs in place, although several have considered them after the *Zelman* decision. The case drew attention on a national basis because it could provide guidance to those states that are considering such a program.

In a five-to-two ruling, the Florida Supreme Court held that the OCP violated the Florida Constitution. Instead of Article I, Section 3, the court focused its attention on a second constitutional provision. Under Article IX, Section 1(a), the state constitution requires the state to provide a "uniform, efficient, safe, secure, and high quality system of free public schools." The court determined that this provision not only mandates that the state provide for children's education, but it also restricts the means by which the state can offer this education. The court also concluded that private schools are not uniform because they are exempted from many requirements imposed on public schools.

The court directly addressed its view of the voucher programs in general. "We do not question the basic right of parents to educate their children as they see fit," wrote Chief Justice Barbara J. Pariente. "We recognize that the proponents of vouchers have a strongly held view that students should have choices. Our decision does not deny parents recourse to either public or private school alternatives to a failing school. Only when the private school option depends upon public funding is the choice limited."

Bush immediately criticized the ruling, calling it a "blow to educational reform." According to Bush, "It temporarily removes a critical tool for improving Florida's public schools and it also challenges the power of the Florida Legislature to decide as a matter of **public policy** the best way to improve our educational system." Bush also indicated that he would explore amendments to the Florida Constitution in response to the decision. Other supporters of the voucher program expressed concern that the decision could bring an end to the McKay Scholarship Program and to other voucher programs.

The plaintiffs in the case were supported by several organizations, including the NATIONAL EDUCATION ASSOCIATION, the American Federation of Teachers, the AMERICAN CIVIL LIBERTIES UNION, and the NATIONAL ASSOCIATION FOR THE ADVANCEMENT OF COLORED PEOPLE (NAACP).

RICO

A set of federal laws (18 U.S.C.A. § 1961 et seq. [1970]) specifically designed to punish criminal activity by business enterprises.

Anza v. Ideal Steel Supply Corporation

In June 2006, the U.S. SUPREME COURT held that New York company Ideal Steel Supply (Ideal) could not maintain its RICO (Racketeer Influenced and Corrupt Organizations Act) claims against its competitor, National Steel Supply (National), and its owners, the Anzas. *Anza v. Ideal Steel Supply Corp.*, 126 S. Ct. 1991 (2006). The high court premised its decision on insufficient PROXIMATE CAUSE, i.e., the remoteness of Ideal's alleged damages to the alleged illegal conduct: National's filing of false or **fraudulent** tax returns and its failure to pay certain taxes. In ruling on the present case, the Court reiterated its holding in *Holmes v. Securities Investor Protection Corporation*, 503 U.S. 258, 268 (1992) to wit, that only a plaintiff whose injury is "proximately caused" by an alleged RICO violation (18 USC §1962) could bring a civil suit. In the present case, ruled the Court, Ideal's alleged damages of lost market share and lost sales were too remote, indirect, and speculative.

Ideal, a supplier of steel milled products, operated two stores in Queens and the Bronx in New York. Its principal competitor, National, owned by Joseph and Vincent Anza, also operated two stores, one in Queens and one in the Bronx, New York. Ideal sued National and the Anzas in federal **district court**, claiming that National failed to charge New York sales tax to its cash-paying customers, thus allowing it to offer products similar to Ideal's at an artificially-reduced price without affecting its profit margin. Ideal also alleged that National submitted fraudulent state tax returns to conceal its conduct. This allegedly involved committing mail and wire **fraud**, —proscribed forms of "racketeering activity" under RICO, which also provides for a private **cause of action** to "[a]ny person injured in his business or property by reason of a violation." (18 USC §1962)

Ideal was specific in alleging that the Anzas violated §1962(c) by "conducting or participating in the conduct" of an enterprise's affairs through a pattern of racketeering activity. Second, the complaint alleged that the defendants violated §1962(a) for using or investing income derived from a pattern of racketeering activity in an enterprise engaged in or affecting interstate or foreign commerce. Specifically, the complaint alleged, defendants used funds generated by the fraudulent tax scheme to pay for National's Bronx location. The damages suffered, according to the complaint, were Ideal's loss of business and market share.

The federal district court granted defendants' motion to dismiss for failure to state a claim under which relief could be granted. It found that Ideal had not shown proximate cause because there was no specific reliance by Ideal on defendants' alleged fraudulent misrepresentations, as required in RICO mail and wire fraud claims.

On Ideal's appeal, the Second **Circuit Court** of Appeals vacated the judgment of the district court. The **appellate court** held that where a complaint alleges a pattern of racketeering activity "that was intended to and did give the defendant a competitive advantage over the plaintiff, the complaint adequately pleads proximate cause, and the plaintiff has standing to pursue a civil RICO claim." 373 F.3d 251 at 263. The **appellate** court opined that the district court had erroneously relied on other cases generally alleging fraudulent transactions, but that RICO did not require the fraudulent communications to be specifically directed at plaintiff. Finally, the appellate court found that Ideal had articulated a cognizable claim by alleging injury resulting from National's use and investment of racketeering proceeds "as distinct from injury traceable simply to the predicate acts of racketeering alone or to the conduct of the business of the enterprise." 373 F.3d 251 at 264. The Supreme Court granted **certiorari**.

Justice Kennedy delivered the opinion of the Court, which found the issue resolved through a straightforward application of its *Holmes* requirement that there be a direct relation between the injury asserted and the injurious conduct alleged. According to the Supreme Court, Ideal did not establish that link. The Court concluded that New York, not Ideal, was the direct victim of defendants' alleged tax fraud scheme. Moreover, defendant National's lower prices do not directly prove fraud, and fraud would not necessarily lead to lower prices. Even assuming that National's goal was to take market share away from Ideal, the means chosen to achieve that end would more directly injure New York, not Ideal.

Contrary to the rationale employed by the Second Circuit, said the Court, a RICO plaintiff cannot avoid the proximate cause requirement simply by claiming the defendants' aim was to increase market share at the expense of plaintiff.

Justice Scalia filed a separate concurring opinion, noting that it was "inconceivable" that the type of injury alleged in the complaint was within the zone of contemplated interests protected by RICO. Justice Breyer concurred in part, but dissented in the remand, opining that he believed RICO did not cover injuries by one competitor engaging in legal pro-competitive activities that may cause injury to another competitor. Justice Thomas took the opposite view. He concurred in the remand of the §1962(a) claim, but filed a lengthy dissent arguing that the injury alleged by Ideal was sufficiently direct under RICO because it was neither duplicative nor derivative of New York's interest.

The case was remanded to the Second Circuit for determination as to whether plaintiff's alleged injuries were proximately caused by defendants' alleged §1962(a) violations.

Mohawk v. Williams

In June 2006, the U.S. SUPREME COURT dismissed (as "improvidently granted") the previously-granted **writ** of **certiorari** in *Mohawk Industries v. Williams*, 126 S. Ct. 2016; 164 L. Ed. 2d 776 (2006) and remanded the matter to the 11th **Circuit Court** of Appeals. It did this in connection with another decision issued that same day, *Anza v. Ideal Steel Supply Corp.*, No.04–433, 547 U.S. ___ (2006). The high court vacated the previous judgment of the 11th Circuit in *Mohawk* (411 F.2d 1252, 2005) and instructed the **appellate court** to further consider the merits in light of *Anza*.

Mohawk Industries, located in Georgia, is the second largest manufacturer of rugs and carpeting in the country, and has been in business for 120 years. It employs over 30,000 people.

In 2004, plaintiff Shirley Williams and several coworkers filed a CLASS ACTION law suit in federal court against their employer, Mohawk Industries, Inc. The suit alleged that Mohawk hired illegal/undocumented immigrants, causing plaintiffs' wages to be depressed and costing them thousands of dollars in workers' compensation. Importantly (at least, as later deemed under *Anza*, which was not yet decided), Williams and her fellow employees alleged that Mohawk's improper hiring practices reduced the number of available jobs for legal employees, and put significant pressure on them to work for similarly low wages. They also claimed that the hiring of undocumented workers caused plaintiffs to avoid reporting work-related injuries or filing workers' compensation claims, for fear of losing their jobs to other undocumented immigrants.

Included in the complaint was the claim that Mohawk had violated both state and federal racketeering (RICO) laws (see below) when it colluded with a hiring agency in Brownsville, Texas to hire the undocumented workers and arrange for them to be housed with legal Mohawk employees. These undocumented workers were hired at a reduced hourly pay rate. The complaint alleged that Mohawk hid evidence by destroying several documents and records along the way.

Specifically, the complaint alleged that (1) Mohawk entered into contracts with outside recruiters with the purpose of violating the Immigration and Nationality Act; (2) Mohawk and the recruiters together constitute a RICO "enterprise" as an "association-in-fact" (see below); and (3) Mohawk participated in the affairs of the enterprise.

The definition of enterprise under the federal Racketeer Influenced and Corrupt Organizations Act (RICO), 18 USC 1961-1968, "includes any individual, partnership, corporation, association or other legal **entity**, and any union or group of individuals associated in fact, though not a legal entity." It is well settled law (not at issue here) that a RICO defendant must have conducted or participated in the affairs of some larger enterprise and not just its own.

For its part, Mohawk defended that (1) a corporation cannot be part of an association-in-fact enterprise under RICO; (2) there was no separate enterprise because it was simply engaged in internal functions (hiring) through an external agent (the recruiting agency); and (3) it was conducting and participating in its own affairs, and not that of some larger enterprise.

The **district court** held that Mohawk's collaboration with the recruiters constituted an "enterprise" and denied Mohawk's motion to dismiss. The 11th Circuit Court of Appeals affirmed, calling the relationship between Mohawk and the recruiters an "association-in-fact" functioning as a separate enterprise. *Mohawk Industries v. Williams*, 411 F.3d 1252 (11th Cir. 2005).

Legal scholars and case-watchers assumed that the Supreme Court would affirm or reverse that holding, as, in fact, this was the question upon which the writ of certiorari had been granted. Moreover, there was conflict with another **appellate** decision *Baker v. IBP, Inc.*, 357 F.3d 685, in which the Seventh Circuit Court of Appeals ruled to the contrary in a similar case.

But the Supreme Court side-swept this issue altogether. The remand, predicated upon the Court's decision in *Anza*, addressed an issue of **proximate cause** for plaintiffs' injuries. In *Anza*, (decided the same day), the Court held that a RICO plaintiff must prove that the alleged RICO violation was the proximate cause of the plaintiff's injury, which required "some direct relation between the injury asserted and the injurious conduct alleged" (citing *Holmes v. Securities Investor Protection Corporation*, 503 U.S. 258 at 268).

Scheidler v. National Organization For Women, Inc.

The NATIONAL ORGANIZATION FOR WOMEN (NOW) engaged in a 20-year effort to use federal criminal and civil laws to curtail the alleged efforts of abortion opponents to disrupt through violence and other illegal activities health care clinics that performed abortions.

The Supreme Court examined the case in 1994 and 2003. In its 2003 decision it returned the case to the lower courts with a strong suggestion that it be dismissed. However, the Seventh **Circuit Court** of Appeals did not order the **district court** to end the case but instead directed it to examine new legal grounds proposed by NOW. The Supreme Court, in *Scheidler v. National Organization For Women, Inc.*, __U.S.__, 126 S.Ct. 1264, 164 L.Ed.2d 10 (2006), overturned this ruling, finding that the language of the federal **statute** in question did not apply to the anti-abortion activities in question.

NOW filed its lawsuit in Illinois federal district court in 1986, alleging that certain individuals and organizations had violated the Hobbs Act, 18 U.S.C.A. § 1851, a federal **criminal law** that outlaws extortion, as well as the Racketeer Influenced and Corrupt Organizations Act (RICO), 18 U.S.C.A. § 1962. NOW contended that the defendants' clinic-related protests amounted to extortion; that these acts of extortion created a pattern of racketeering activity banned by RICO. It sought a permanent nationwide injunction as well as damages. Ultimately the Supreme Court ruled that NOW could use RICO to pursue its claims because the law did not require a defendant to have an economic motive for its actions. The case went to trial and NOW was awarded damages and was granted a nationwide injunction forbidding the activities. However, in 2003 the Court reversed the verdict, finding that the Hobbs Act required as an element of extortion the improper "obtaining of property from another." The claimed property rights of women seeking services from a clinic and the doctors and staff performing the services could not be used to characterize the defendants' actions as the obtaining of property from them. Therefore, the defendants did not commit extortion under the Hobbs Act and the RICO violation was reversed. The Court concluded that without the RICO violation "the injunction issued by the District Court must necessarily be vacated."

On remand, NOW argued to the Seventh Circuit that the jury's RICO verdict had been based not only on incidents of extortion but also four instances or threats of physical violence unrelated to extortion. The appeals court found that the Supreme Court had not considered this Hobbs Act theory, so it remanded the cases to the district court for examination. The defendants appealed to the Supreme Court and the Court agreed to hear the case for a third time.

The Court, in an 8–0 decision (newly confirmed Justice Samuel Alito did not participate in the consideration of the case), reversed the Seventh Circuit ruling. Justice STEPHEN BREYER, writing for the Court, reviewed the language of the Hobbs Act makes it a crime to affect, obstruct, or delay interstate commerce by **robbery**, extortion, or "commit[ting] or threaten[ing] physical violence to any person or property in furtherance of a plan or purpose to do anything in violation of this section." The core of the dispute was the meaning of "in furtherance of a plan or purpose to do anything in violation of this section." Did it refer to violence committed to aid in the furtherance of robbery or extortion or did it refer to violence committed to assist the purposes that affect interstate commerce in general? The former interpretation would limit the statute to behavior only associated with robbery or extortion, while the latter interpretation would allow the statute to govern "a far broader range of human activity, namely, all violent actions (against persons or property) that affect interstate commerce." The Court opted to take the former, more restrictive reading of the Hobbs Act.

Justice Breyer based this conclusion on a review of the statute's language as well as the legislative history of the Hobbs Act. A reading of the text confirmed that the violence committed or threatened "in furtherance of a plan or purpose" referred to a plan or purpose to engage in robbery or extortion. Moreover, the term "affecting commerce" should not be read to broaden reach of the act because Congress often intended this to be read as a **term of art** "connecting the congressional exercise of legislative authority with the constitutional provision (here, the **Commerce Clause**) that grants Congress that authority." This type of jurisdictional language could limit but not define the "behavior that the statute calls a 'violation' of federal law."

The Court also noted the history of the Hobbs Act. Its predecessor was enacted in 1934 and barred coercion and extortion connected to interstate commerce. In another provision it introduced the "furtherance of a plan or purpose" clause but it explicitly linked it to the clauses dealing with coercion and extortion. In 1946, Congress passed the Hobbs Act, which modified the 1934 criminal law. The Hobbs Act added robbery and deleted coercion as crimes. It also linked the "furtherance" clause to the section that made it a **felony** to commit robbery or extortion. Nowhere in the legislative history was it suggested that Congress intended to make physical violence "a freestanding crime." The current Hobbs Act language was written in 1948 as part of a general revision of the federal criminal code. The 1948 revision was not meant to create any new crimes but merely to recodify those in existence. Therefore, the 1948 revision, while less clear than the 1946 version, did not change the substance of the crimes covered by the Hobbs Act. The linguistic changes were, according to the Reviser's Notes, "changes in phraseology and arrangement necessary to effect consolidation."

Justice Breyer rejected the broadening of the Hobbs Act urged by NOW because it would make federal crimes out of ordinary criminal behavior that is subject to state prosecution. Congress would not have intended to give the Hobbs Act an expansive reading. Finally, Congress addressed the issue of abortion clinic violence in the 1994 Freedom of Access to Clinic Entrances Act, 18 U.S.C.A. § 248(a)(3). If Congress had believed the Hobbs Act would cover the actions addressed in the NOW litigation, it would not have found it necessary to pass this legislation.

SEARCH AND SEIZURE

In international law, the right of ships of war, as regulated by treaties, to examine a merchant vessel during war in order to determine whether the ship or its cargo is liable to seizure.

A hunt by law enforcement officials for property or communications believed to be evidence of crime, and the act of taking possession of this property.

Court Upholds Raid of Congressional Office of U.S. Representative William Jefferson

In July 2006, the United States **District Court** for the DISTRICT OF COLUMBIA issued a 28-page opinion upholding the FBI raid of the congressional office of U.S. Representative William Jefferson, in conjunction with an ongoing criminal investigation. *In re: Search of the Rayburn House Office Building, Room Number 2113, Washington, D.C. 20515*, Case. No. 06–1231 M-01 (July 10, 2006). The execution of a search warrant upon the office of a sitting Congressman is apparently the first in the 200-year history of the Constitution.

The seizure of materials followed the government's application for a search warrant, supported by an 83-page affidavit outlining the evidence against Jefferson thus obtained over the course of the investigation. The application also set forth "special search procedures" to minimize the chance that any politically-sensitive materials or documents that "may fall within the **purview** of the SPEECH OR DEBATE CLAUSE . . . or any other pertinent privilege" would be affected. *Affidavit, para.136.*

Shortly after the raid, President GEORGE W. BUSH ordered all seized materials sealed, hoping that the Department of Justice (DOJ) and House negotiators could resolve their disagreement over the constitutional legality of the seizure. Several House leaders from both political parties had objected to the seizure as unnecessary to **advance** the federal corruption investigation of the eight-term New Orleans Democrat. They also objected that it violated the separation of powers between executive and legislative branches, and violated the Speech or Debate Clause (Article I, §6) of the U.S. Constitution. Even though the 45-day seal expired the day before the court's decision, the seal was extended. Upon the release of the court's decision, prosecutors were free to immediately review all material seized during May-20-21, 2006, including all documents and computer hard drives seized from the congressman and his staff.

The major allegation against Jefferson was that he accepted payments in return for using his position in Congress to help secure equipment and service contracts in several African countries for a small Kentucky telecommunications company, iGate Inc. The CEO of iGate, Vernon Jackson pleaded guilty to bribery and conspiring to bribe Jefferson. (One of Jefferson's former congressional staffers also pleaded guilty to the same charges and was sentenced to eight years of imprisonment.) Jackson told officials that he paid more than $400,000 to a company controlled by Jefferson's family. An iGate investor, who cooperated with the FBI and wore a wire during meetings and telephone conversations with Jefferson, was videotaped handing a briefcase containing $100,000 to Jefferson, reportedly to be used as a bribe for the vice president of Nigeria. All but $10,000 of that money was later found in the freezer of Jefferson's Washington home. Jefferson has publicly stated that he has an honorable explanation for the allegations against him.

Pending before the district court was Jefferson's Motion for Return of Property. (His Motion for Interim Relief was rendered moot by President Bush's order for the custody and seal of all seized materials).

The district court rejected each of Jefferson's arguments. The court noted that the Speech or Debate Clause offered broad protections in support of the independence of the legislature, including absolute immunity from prosecution or suit for legislative acts and freedom from being "questioned" about those acts. But, "The Court declines to extend those protections further, holding that the Speech or Debate Clause does not shield Members of Congress from the execution of valid search warrants." The court then quoted from *United States v. Brewster*, 408 U.S. 501 at 516, that the Speech or Debate Clause did not "make Members of Congress super-citizens, immune from criminal responsibility." Said the court,

> "Congressman Jefferson's interpretation of the Speech or Debate privilege would have the effect of converting every congressional office into a taxpayer-subsidized sanctuary for crime. Such a result is not supported by the Constitution or judicial precedent and will not be adopted here."

The court noted that no one argued that the warrant was not properly administered, so there was no impermissible intrusion on the legislature. According to the opinion, the fact that some privileged material may have been incidentally captured did not render the search unconstitutional as an unlawful intrusion.

As to separation of powers, the court noted that the power to determine the scope of one's own privilege is not available to any person, including congressmen, judges, or the President of the United States. The court rejected Jefferson's arguments that the search was unnecessary because DOJ had not exhausted less intrusive measures, and that the FBI had taken privileged material. The court stated:

> "While the search here entailed an invasion somewhat greater than usual because it took place in a congressional office certain to contained privileged legislative material, the Government has demonstrated a compelling need to conduct the search in relation to a criminal investigation involving very serious crimes, and has been unable to obtain the evidence sought through any other reasonable means. Therefore, the search conducted of Congressman Jefferson's congressional office was reasonable under the FOURTH AMENDMENT."

Samson v. California

The Supreme Court has permitted police officers in certain circumstances to search a criminal suspect without a search warrant. However, officers must either have **probable cause** or a reasonable suspicion to justify the waiver of the terms contained in the FOURTH AMENDMENT. In a prior case, *United States v. Knights*, 534 U.S.112, 122 S.Ct. 587, 151 L.Ed.2d 497 (2002), the Court ruled that police may search a person on probation who has signed an agreement that permits such searches if the police have reasonable suspicion of a crime. Questions lingered after this ruling as to whether police could search a person on probation or a parolee who had signed agreement permitting searches without reasonable suspicion. The Court answered these questions in *Samson v. California*, __U.S.__, 126 S.Ct., __L.Ed.2d __ 2006 WL 1666974 (2006), holding that parolees may be searched without reasonable suspicion because the interests of society outweigh their privacy interests.

The state of California paroled Donald C. Samson in September 2002 after serving time for possession of a firearm. A few days later a San Bruno police officer saw Samson walking down the street with a woman and a child. The officer knew Samson was on parole and believed that there was a warrant out on him. The officer stopped Samson, questioned him about his parole status, and then confirmed via his radio that Samson was telling the truth. Nevertheless, the officer search Samson based on his parolee status. He found a plastic bag that contained methamphetamine in a cigarette box that was in Samson's shirt pocket. Samson was charged and convicted of drug possession and sentenced to seven years in prison. Samson appealed his conviction to the California Court of Appeals, arguing that the seized drugs should be suppressed because the search had been illegal. The appeals court upheld the search and the conviction, ruling that suspicionless searches of parolees were lawful under California law. The search in Samson's case was not arbitrary, capricious, or harassing. Samson then took his case to the U.S. SUPREME COURT.

The Court, in a 6–3 decision, upheld the California Court of Appeals ruling. Justice CLARENCE THOMAS, writing for the majority, reviewed the *United States v. Knights* decision, in which Knights had signed a probation agreement that permitted searches of his person and property without the need for reasonable cause. However, the police searched Knights' apartment based on the reasonable suspicion that he had committed arson and vandalism. Justice Thomas noted that in *Knights* the Court had found that Knights' probationary status lessened his expectation of privacy. By agreeing to probation, Knights had surrendered part of his liberty. In the Court's view the probation agreement's search provision enhanced the goal of rehabilitation and the protection of society. Moreover, the government had a legitimate concern that Knights might break the law again, as statistics revealed that probationers have a "significantly higher" **recidivism** rate than the general crime rate. Because probationers have "even more of an incentive to conceal their criminal activities" because they face prison if their probation is revoked, the police must be able to act quickly if they have reasonable suspicion. Justice Thomas concluded that these interests had even great weight when applied to a person paroled from prison. Recent California statistics indicated that 70 per cent of paroled inmates reoffended within 18 months of release. However, the *Knights* opinion state that "nothing in the condition of probation suggests that it was confined to searches bearing upon probationary status and nothing more." Therefore, in the current case the majority needed to find a different legal footing to justify its conclusions.

Justice Thomas found that footing in prior cases that held that prison inmates have no expectations of privacy. Parolees had fewer expectations of privacy than probationers because "parole is more akin to imprisonment than probation is to imprisonment." The "essence" of parole was the release from prison, before the completion of sentence, on the condition that the parolee follows the rules laid down in the parole agreement. In California a parolee could be required to report to a parole officer within 72 hours of any change in employment status, request permission to travel more than 50 miles from home, and refrain from possessing firearms or consuming drugs and alcohol. These and other conditions, including the right of police to search the parolee without reasonable cause, proved that parolees had "severely diminished expectations of privacy by virtue of their status alone." Therefore, the Court concluded that Samson did not have a legitimate expectation of privacy that would requires reasonable suspicion for a search.

Justice JOHN PAUL STEVENS, in a dissent joined by Justices DAVID SOUTER and STEPHEN BREYER, agreed that the privacy interests and expectations of probationers and parolees are not as "robust" as ordinary citizens. However, Stevens contended that the Court's approval of suspicionless searches of parolees was "an unprecedented curtailment of liberty." He pointed out that suspicionless searches were the "very evil the Fourth Amendment was intended to stamp out." In prior decisions the court had identified "special needs" that justified suspicionless searches but *Knights*did not support "a blanket grant of discretion untethered by any procedural safeguards." A parolee's status was not the equivalent of a prisoner but rather was much like that of a **probationer**. Therefore, the same standard of reasonable suspicion announced in *Knights* should have been applied to parolees.

SENTENCING

The postconviction stage of the criminal justice process, in which the defendant is brought before the court for the imposition of a penalty.

Washington v. Recuenco

The U.S. SUPREME COURT held, in *Washington v. Recuenco*, No. 05-83, 548 U.S. ___ (2006) that the failure to submit an enhanced sentencing factor to a jury was not a "structural error" requiring automatic reversal. The substantive ruling reversed a decision of the Washington Supreme Court, after first addressing a secondary argument that the high court did not have the power to reverse. The decision involved reliance upon, and discussion of, several previous U.S. Supreme Court cases.

In September 1999, Arturo Recuenco engaged in a fight with his wife, ultimately threatening her with a handgun. Evidence of his use of a handgun during the assault was copious at the trial level. The State of Washington charged him with assault in the second degree, i.e., "intentiona[l] assault . . . with a deadly weapon, to-wit: a handgun." At trial, a special verdict form asked the jury to determine whether Recuenco was "armed with a deadly weapon at the time of the commission of the crime [the assault]." Under Washington law, a "firearm" qualifies as a deadly weapon. However, the special verdict form did not expressly require the jury to find that Recuenco had engaged in the assault with a "firearm" as distinguished from any other type of deadly weapon. In any event, the jury found Recuenco guilty of the assault and answered the special verdict question in the affirmative.

At the sentencing phase, the State requested a 3-year sentence enhancement based on Washington Rev. Code §9.94A533(3)(b) (commission of a crime while armed with a firearm), rather than requesting the 1-year sentence enhancement under Washington Rev. Code §9.94A533(4)(b) (commission of a crime while armed with a deadly weapon). Although the jury had not been asked that specific question, the state trial court concluded that evidence at trial had satisfied the condition for a firearm enhancement, and then enhanced Recuendo's assault sentence with an additional 3-year sentence.

Meanwhile, before the appeals reached the Washington Supreme Court, the U.S. Supreme Court had decided two pertinent cases. In *Apprendi v. New Jersey*, 530 U.S. 466 the Court held that "[o]ther than the fact of a prior conviction, any fact that increases the penalty for a crime beyond the prescribed **statutory** maximum must be submitted to a jury, and proved beyond a reasonable doubt." In *Blakely v. Washington*, 542 U.S. 296, the Court clarified that the 'statutory maximum,' for purposes of *Apprendi*, meant the maximum sentence a judge could impose *solely on the basis of the facts reflected in the jury verdict or admitted by the defendant.*

When Recuenco's case finally reached the Washington Supreme Court, the state had already conceded, under the newly-decided *Blakely* case, that a SIXTH AMENDMENT violation had occurred (a "*Blakely* violation"). However, the state urged the Washington Supreme Court to find that the *Blakely* violation was **harmless error** in Recuendo's case, and therefore affirm the sentence.

But the Washington Supreme Court vacated his sentence and remanded the matter for sentencing based solely on the deadly weapon enhancement. On the very same day that it rendered its decision, it also decided *Washington v. Hughes*, in which it declared any *Blakely* violation to be "'structural' erro[r]" which "will always invalidate the conviction." In support of that holding, the Washington Supreme Court quoted from the U.S. Supreme Court's decision in yet another case, *Sullivan v. Louisiana*, 508 U.S. 275. (In *Sullivan*, the Court held that where a jury is not instructed of a prosecutor's burden to prove all elements of an offense, the entire framework upon which the prosecutor's case moved forward was undermined, and therefore constituted "structural" reversible error.) **Certiorari** to the U.S. Supreme Court for Recuenco's case was based on the Washington high court's interpretation and use of these precedents.

However, the Supreme Court first needed to dispose of a challenge that it lacked power to review the decision of the Washington Supreme Court. Recuenco had argued that the state high court's judgment was based on adequate and independent state law grounds. Recuendo argued that at the time of his conviction, Washington law provided no procedure by which a jury could determine whether a defendant was armed with a firearm. Therefore, reviewing the matter under *Apprendi* or *Blakely* for harmless error analysis was inappropriate.

After noting that Recuendo's interpretation of Washington law may not be correct (citing, e.g., *Washington v. Pharr*, 131 Wn. App. 119 [2006], affirming a trial court's imposition of an enhanced firearm sentence) the Court then noted that the correctness of Recuenco's interpretation was not determinative of the issue before the Court anyway. This Court's review was of the state high court's conclusion that a *Blakely* error could never be deemed harmless error. Therefore, the Court need not resolve that open question of Washington law.

Justice Thomas, writing the 7–2 majority opinion for the Court, continued to the substantive matter before the Court. He first noted that the Court has repeatedly recognized that constitutional errors at trial do not, alone, entitle a defendant to automatic reversal. Instead, most constitutional errors could be harmless. In fact, "if the defendant had counsel and was tried by an impartial adjudicator, there is a strong presumption that any other [constitutional] errors that may have occurred are subject to harmless-error analysis." *Neder v. United States*, 527 U.S. 1. Only in rare cases has the Court ruled an error "structural," requiring reversal.

The Court next found that Recuenco's case was constitutionally indistinguishable from *Neder*, in which a harmless error analysis was used to determine the effect of a failure to submit an element of an offense to the jury. (In a harmless error analysis, **appellate** review determines whether a jury would have reached the same conclusion despite the error, thus making the error "harmless.")

The Court further noted that it has treated sentencing factors, like elements, as facts that have to be tried to the jury and proved **beyond a reasonable doubt**. The only difference between Recuenco's case and *Neder* was that one involved a sentencing factor, and the other involved an element. Therefore, under *Neder*, the error in Recuenco's case was not structural in nature, mandating reversal.

SEX OFFENSES

A class of sexual conduct prohibited by the law.

California Bill Bans State-Funded Viagra for Sex Offenders

California Governor Arnold Schwarzenegger approved a bill on October 4, 2005, excluding registered sex offenders from receiving state funds for erectile-dysfunction drugs through the California health insurance program. The bill, introduced by assemblyman George Plescia (R-San Diego), amends a current California law designed to help the poor.

Schwarzenegger's decision was part of a nationwide reassessment based on an Associated Press survey in early 2005 that revealed that nearly 800 convicted sex offenders in 14 states were receiving government-funded prescriptions for Viagra and other impotence drugs. The majority of cases were found in Florida, New York, and Texas, and resulted from a broad interpretation of a 1998 letter from the Clinton Administration as a basis for providing coverage. The instructions in the letter made suggestions on how to curb abuse, requiring **Medicaid** to cover all FDA-approved drugs, with certain exceptions such as weight control, cosmetic, and fertility drugs. Some states did decline to provide impotence-drug coverage prior to the AP survey, exercising their right to determine which treatments were medically necessary. South Dakota, for instance, considered impotence drugs to fall under the umbrella of fertility drugs.

Federal legislation with 29 co-sponsors was introduced in the House in February 2005. It specified excluding Viagra coverage under the **Medicare** prescription drug benefit. The Centers for Medicare and Medicaid Services estimation that Medicaid spends approximately $38 million per year on ED drugs, all but $2 million on Viagra, precipitated legislation to eliminate all Medicare and Medicaid for these drugs. Introduced by Senator Charles Grassley (R-Iowa), the bill was co-sponsored by Republican Senators Trent Lott of Mississippi, Rick Santorum of Pennsylvania, and John Ensign of Nevada. While lawmakers moved on May 24, 2005, to eliminate federal payments for Viagra and other impotence drugs for convicted sex offenders, the Prescription Drug Coverage Stewardship Act of 2005 would not prevent the government from paying for ED drugs prescribed for treatments unrelated to sexual performance. The House approved the amendment on June 24, 2005.

As each state administers Medicaid differently, legislation in individual states regarding funding of ED drugs for felons was also addressed in many cases in 2005, as evidenced by the California bill. Director of the Center for Medicaid and State Operations Dennis Smith informed states that providing ED drugs to convicted sex offenders could be considered **fraud**, abuse, or misappropriation of Medicaid funds, adding that each state should review its drug-coverage procedures to avoid government sanctions.

The first to make changes was New York, where it was first uncovered that Medicaid had paid for sex offenders' Viagra prescriptions. It was the New York report that prompted the federal government and other states to take action. With 198 cases revealed in the AP survey, only Florida had more prescriptions subsidized with state funds. Governor George Pataki (R) issued a temporary ban on public funding for ED drug coverage for convicted sex offenders to give the New York Legislature time to enact a permanent preventative measure.

Virginia Governor Mark Warner (D) issued an emergency order on May 26, 2005, to stop ED drug payments for sex offenders. The state, which had 52 cases of subsidization, has one year to make the order permanent, and the medical assistance program will determine whether to drop coverage for all beneficiaries.

The New Jersey Department of Human Services proposed on May 27 that pharmacists stop dispensing all ED drugs to sex offenders. The state had 55 cases reported by the Associated Press.

Also in May, Texas Legislature passed bills to prohibit state payments for ED prescriptions for any registered sex offenders. With 191 cases of subsidized impotence drugs for registered sex offenders, Texas was number three in the AP survey.

The other states mentioned in the survey were Florida, with 218 cases; Missouri, 26; Kansas, 14; Ohio, 13; Michigan, seven; Maine, five;

Georgia and Montana, with three each; Alabama, two; and North Dakota, one.

In addition to the ED drugs bill, Governor Schwarzenegger approved bills to extend an existing crime-prevention program for rural communities in the Central Valley; allow state and local officials to monitor parolees with GPS; permit children to testify in sexual assault cases via closed-circuit television, facing their assailants from outside the courtroom; denying parent custody of a child if that parent lives with a registered sex offender; block the California Department of Mental Health from placing sexually violent patients near schools after release from treatment; and increase boat registration and renewal fees to help fund waterway safety and law-enforcement programs. He vetoed a bill that would create a sexual-offender board to help advise the Legislature and the governor on management of adult offenders, stating that such a law would not protect citizens, but would instead increase government; and a bill to provide a prison-diversion program for veterans who suffer from post-traumatic stress disorder, with the explanation that such a program would jeopardize public safety.

SEXUAL HARASSMENT

Unwelcome sexual advances, requests for sexual favors, and other verbal or physical conduct of a sexual nature that tends to create a hostile or offensive work environment.

Arbaugh v. Y & H Corporation

Title VII of the Civil Rights Act of 1964 makes it unlawful for an employer to discriminate on the basis of sex. 42 U.S.C.A. § 2000e-2(a)(1). When Congress passed Title VII it was concerned about subjecting small employers to it reach, so it made the law applicable to employers who have fifteen or more employees. 42 U.S.C.A. § 2000e(b). Since its enactment the lower **federal courts** have divided over whether the numerical qualification affects federal subject-matter jurisdiction or sets out a substantive element of a Title VII claim. If the fifteen-employee provision was jurisdictional, then a court could not hear the Title VII action. If the provision is a element of the case that must be considered by the jury, however, then the plaintiff will have her day in court. The Supreme Court, in *Arbaugh v. Y & H Corporation*, __U.S.__, 126 S.Ct. 1235, __L.Ed.2d __ (2006), concluded that the provision was not jurisdictional.

Jennifer Arbaugh worked as a waitress and bartender at the Moonlight Café, located in New Orleans, from May 2000 to February 2001. Arbaugh left her job after one of the owners allegedly made lewd comments about her body and groped her. She filed a Title VII sexual harassment suit against Y & H Corporation, the owner of the café, alleging that her employer had created a hostile work environment on the basis of sex. A jury awarded Arbaugh $5,000 in back pay, $5,000 in **compensatory damages** and $30,000 in **punitive damages**. In a pretrial order signed by the parties, Y & H did not dispute that the court had jurisdiction to hear the case nor did it list the number of employees as a contested issue of fact or a contested legal issue. At trial Y & H did not raise an objection to the fact that the business met the definition of a qualified employer-having at least 15 employees for 20 or more weeks during the time in question. However, two weeks after judgment was entered in the case, Y & H moved to dismiss the entire action for lack of subject-matter jurisdiction. It now claimed that it had fewer than 15 employees at the time Arbaugh was employed.

The **district court** permitted discovery on this issue, which centered on the employee status of eight delivery drivers and the company's four owners, which included the café's two managers and their spouses. The district court concluded that the 12 individuals did not qualify as employees, which reduced the employee count below 15. Therefore, the court vacated the judgment and dismissed Arbaugh's Title VII claim. The Fifth **Circuit Court** of Appeals upheld the decision, using its prior decisions to conclude that the failure to meet the minimum employee standard deprived the district court of subject-matter jurisdiction. Because the circuit courts of appeals were divided on this issue, the Supreme Court agreed to hear Arbaugh's appeal.

The Supreme Court, in an 8-0 decision (newly confirmed Justice Samuel Alito did not participate in the consideration of the case), reversed the Fifth Circuit. Justice RUTH BADER GINSBURG, writing for the Court, agreed that if the Court agreed that if the employee numerosity requirement was jurisdictional, then the district court properly dismissed the case. However, if the requirement was just one element of Arbaugh's case, then Y & H had raised the issue too late. Its pretrial stipulations and its failure to raise the issue during trial would preclude it from having the judgment vacated in its favor. Justice Ginsburg admitted that the Court had not always been clear in defining the parameters of subject-matter jurisdiction and that some Title VII cases on different definitional issues suggested that the Fifth Circuit interpretation was correct. However, Ginsburg that these cases did not apply.

The Court found that nothing in the provisions of Title VII indicated that Congress "intended courts, on their own motion, to assure that the employee-numerosity requirement is met." Justice Ginsburg stated that if "an essential element of a **claim for relief** is at issue," the jury is the "proper trier of contested facts." Congress had the power to make this Title VII requirement jurisdictional, but the employee requirement was not located in the jurisdictional section of the **statute**. Instead, it appeared in a separate provision that did not "speak in jurisdictional terms." Ginsburg said the Court would "leave the ball in Congress' court" if it wanted to make the number of employees a threshold jurisdictional issue. Absent such an explicit **statutory** limitation, "courts should treat the restriction as nonjurisdictional in character." Therefore, the threshold number of employees was an element of a plaintiff's claim for relief that could be proven or disproven at trial.

SIXTH AMENDMENT

United States v. Gonzalez-Lopez

In *United States v. Gonzalez-Lopez*, No.05–352, 548 U.S. ___, a 5–4 divided U.S. SUPREME COURT ruled that a defendant's SIXTH AMENDMENT right to a fair trial could be violated if he was blocked from being represented by paid counsel of his choosing. The decision affirmed the Eighth **Circuit Court** of Appeals, which had reversed the trial court. As a result of this ruling, the conviction of defendant Gonzalez-Lopez was overturned and the matter remanded to the trial court.

Cuauhtemoc Gonzalez-Lopez was charged in federal **district court** (in Missouri) with conspiracy to distribute more than 100 kilograms of marijuana. His family hired attorney John Fahle to represent him. However, following his arraignment, Gonzalez-Lopez contacted an attorney in California, Joseph Low to discuss whether Low could represent him, either in addition to, or in substitution of, Fahle.

Some time later, both attorneys appeared and represented Gonzalez-Lopez at an evidentiary hearing. The **magistrate** accepted Low's provisional appearance on the condition that he immediately file a motion for admission **pro hac vice**, (for this matter only). However, during the evidentiary hearing and while attorney Fahle was cross-examining a witness, attorney Low passed notes to him. The magistrate immediately revoked his provisional acceptance of Low's appearance, stating that Low had violated a court rule that limited cross-examination of witnesses to one examining attorney.

The following week, Gonzalez-Lopez informed Fahle that he wanted Low to be his only attorney. Low filed a motion for admission but the district court denied his application without comment. One month later, Low again filed a second motion for admission, which the district court again denied without explanation. Low appealed to the Eighth Circuit Court of Appeals, in the form of a **writ** of **mandamus**, (petitioning a higher court to compel a lower court to take action owed to the petitioner), which also was denied.

Attorney Fahle then filed a motion to withdraw and for sanctions against attorney Low, arguing that Low had violated Mo. Rule of Prof. Conduct 4–4.2, which prohibits a lawyer, "[i]n representing a client," from "communicat[ing] about the subject [matter] of the representation with a party . . . represented by another lawyer" without that lawyer's consent. Low filed a motion to strike Fahle's motion, but the court granted in part Fahle's motion to withdraw. Fahle withdrew as counsel, and the court granted a continuance to give Gonzalez-Lopez time to find another attorney. He retained a local attorney, Karl Dickhaus, for the trial. At that point, the district court formally denied Low's motion to strike, and, for the first time, explained that its denial of admission was premised on another case before it, in which Low had violated Rule 4–4.2 by communicating with a represented party.

Dickhaus represented Gonzalez-Lopez at trial, at which time Low made one last move for admission, but was denied. The court also denied Dickhaus's request to have Low join him at counsel's table during trial, and ordered Low to sit in the audience at trial and have no contact with Dickhaus. A U.S. Marshal stayed between Low and Dickhaus at trial.

Gonzalez-Lopez was found guilty by the jury. Following trial, the district court granted Fahle's motion for sanctions against Low, by reading Rule 4–4.2 as prohibiting Low's conduct in this case as well as the separate case upon which the court had based its denial for admission.

The Eighth Circuit Court of Appeals held that the district court's denials of Low's motions were erroneous, based on error in the district court's interpretation of Rule 4–4.2. Accordingly, the district court had violated Gonzalez-Lopez's Sixth Amendment right to paid counsel of his choosing. Further finding that the violation was not subject to harmless-error review, the **appellate court** vacated Gonzalez-Lopez's guilty conviction. 399 F.3d 924. The U.S. Supreme Court granted **certiorari**.

The Sixth Amendment to the U.S. Constitution provides that in all criminal prosecutions, "the accused shall enjoy the right . . . to have the Assistance **of Counsel** for his defence." The Supreme Court has previously held that an element of this right is the right of a defendant who does not require appointed counsel to choose who will represent him. *Wheat v. United States*, 486 U.S. 153 (1988).

For its part, the government did not dispute that the district court erroneously deprived Gonzalez-Lopez of his counsel of choice. Rather, the government argued that there is no Sixth Amendment violation unless the defendant can show that substitute counsel was ineffective within the meaning of *Strickland v. Washington*, 466 U.S. 668 (1984). This meant a showing that the substitute counsel's performance was deficient and that it prejudiced the defendant. In the alternative, the government argued that defendant must at least show that his chosen counsel would have pursued a different strategy creating a reasonable possibility that the results of the proceedings would have been different.

Writing for the majority, Justice Scalia balked at this interpretation, noting that, "Stated as broadly as this, the Government's argument in effect reads the Sixth Amendment as a more detailed version of the Due Process Clause-and then proceeds to give no effect to the details." Instead, said the majority opinion, the Sixth Amendment . . . "commands, not that a trial be fair, but that a particular guarantee of fairness be provided-to wit, that the accused be defended by the counsel he believes to be best." Accordingly, a trial court's erroneous denial of a criminal defendant's choice of counsel entitles him to reversal of his conviction.

Nor, continued the Court, is such a Sixth Amendment violation subject to **harmless error** review. Such an error as this qualifies as "structural error" because it affects the very framework within which the trial proceeds, and not simply an error during the trial itself. *Sullivan v. Louisiana*, 508 U.S. 275.

Justice Alito filed a dissenting opinion, joined by Chief Justice Roberts and Justices Kennedy and Thomas. In his first written dissent, Justice Alito believed the majority had made "a subtle but important mistake." According to the dissent, the focus of the Sixth Amendment right is the quality of representation, not the identity of the attorney who provides the representation.

Davis v. Washington

The U.S. SUPREME COURT in June 2006 resolved a dispute over what constitutes a "testimonial statement" in the context of the Confrontation Clause of the SIXTH AMENDMENT. The Court reviewed two separate cases that involved the admission of witness statements in trials where those witnesses were not available. In one case, the Court determined that a victim's statements made to a 911 operator were admissible even though the victim did not testify at the trial. In the second case, however, the Court ruled that a victim's written statements made to police officers after a domestic dispute were not admissible.

The Confrontation Clause of the Sixth Amendment to the U.S. Constitution provides, "In all criminal prosecutions, the accused shall enjoy the right . . . to be confronted with the witnesses against him." In *Crawford v. Washington*, 541 U.S. 36, 124 S. Ct. 1354, 158 L. Ed. 2d 177 (2004), the Court concluded that this clause bars "admission of testimonial statements of a witness who did not appear at trial unless he was available to testify, and the defendant had a prior opportunity for cross-examination." Although the Court attempted to provide some guidance as to what statements are considered testimonial, it did not provide a clear definition of the term.

The case of *State v. Washington*, 111 P.3d 844 (Wash. 2005) focused on the admission of statements made by Michelle McCottry during a 911 call in 2001. McCottry called 911 after a former boyfriend, Adrian Davis, had entered her house and assaulted her. Davis was the subject of a domestic no-contact order and violated that order by entering McCottry's house. During the call, McCottry identified Davis to the 911 operator and said that Davis had struck her with his fists. Officers arrived at McCottry's house within minutes of the call and observed the McCottry had been injured on her face and forearms.

Davis was charged with violation of the no-contact order, which constitutes a **felony**. McCottry did not testify at trial. The state called only two witnesses, which were the officers who arrived at the scene. Neither officer could testify regarding the cause of McCottry's injuries. In order to prove the case, the state presented a recording of McCottry's exchange with the 911 operator. Against Davis's objection, the court admitted the tape and convicted Davis for the offense.

Davis appealed his conviction to the Washington Court of Appeals, which affirmed the trial court's ruling. *Davis v. State*, 64 P.3d 661 (Wash. App. 2003). He then sought to appeal the decision to the Washington Supreme Court. During interim between the decision from the intermediate **appellate court** and the state's high court, the U.S. Supreme Court issued its ruling in *Crawford* which altered the analysis of the admissibility of testimonial statements. The Washington Supreme Court determined that the portion of the statement in which McCottry identified Davis was not testimonial in nature. Moreover, the court ruled that even if portions of the conversation were testimonial, their admission was harmless. *Davis v. Washington*, 111 P.3d 844 (Wash. 2005).

A separate case that was consolidated with *Davis* arose when police officers responded to a domestic disturbance at the home of Hershel and Amy Hammon in Peru, Indiana. When the officers arrived, they found Amy sitting outside of the house by herself, appearing "somewhat frightened." During the course of their investigation, the officers kept Amy and Hershel separated and eventually convinced Amy to sign a **battery** affidavit. Upon this evidence, Hershel was convicted of domestic battery and for violating his probation. Although Amy did not testify at Hershel's trial, the court admitted her affidavit as evidence.

The case eventually reached the Indiana Supreme Court, which reviewed the admissibility of Amy's statement under *Crawford* The state court determined that Amy's written statement was testimonial and that her oral statement to officers was non-testimonial in nature. Nevertheless, the court affirmed Hershel's conviction because if found that admission of the Amy's testimonial statement constituted **harmless error**. *Hammon v. State*, 829 N.W.2d 444 (Ind. 2005).

The U.S. Supreme Court, in an opinion by Justice ANTONIN SCALIA, sought to clarify the definition of a testimonial statement. According to the Court, "[s]tatements are nontestimonial when made in the course of a police interrogation under circumstances objectively indicating that the primary purpose of the interrogation is to enable police assistance to meet an ongoing emergency." By comparison, the Court considers a statement to be testimonial "when the circumstances objectively indicate that there is no such ongoing emergency, and that the primary purpose of the interrogation is to establish or prove past events potentially relevant to later criminal prosecution."

In the case involving McCottry, the victim spoke of the events as they occurred, as opposed to a statement that was made hours after the events took place. McCottry's statements were necessary to allow officers to resolve the emergency, rather than to ascertain what happened in the past. Amy Hammon's statements, by comparison, were given some time after the events related to the domestic disturbance. Police in that case questioned the victim in order investigate past events to determine whether a crime had been committed. The Court unanimously ruled that Davis' statement was admissible because it was nontestimonial. However, Hammon's statement was inadmissible because it was testimonial and the defendant did not have an opportunity to cross-examine her. The Court decided the portion of the decision related to Hammon by an 8–1 vote, with Justice CLARENCE THOMAS dissenting.

Critics of the decision argued that the Court has made prosecution of domestic violence cases more difficult. Because victims of domestic violence are often reluctant to testify against their assailants, officers began to rely more heavily on victims' statements made in crime reports or interviews. Under *Crawford* and *Davis* such a statement may not be admitted to court unless the victim makes a nontestimonial statement, such as the 911 call, or testifies in court.

Holmes v. South Carolina

Under the SIXTH AMENDMENT a criminal defendant is provided with constitutional guarantees for a fair trial. The defendant is entitled to present a full defense and evidence offered by the defendant must be admitted by the trial court unless it violates evidentiary rules. However, some state supreme courts have established rules that limit a defendant's right to introduce certain types of evidence. The U.S. SUPREME COURT has reviewed these rules and has struck rules it concluded served no useful purpose or were disproportionate to the ends they sought to promote. Such was the case in *Holmes v. South Carolina*, __U.S.__, 126 S.Ct. 1727, __L.Ed.2d __ (2006), where the Court struck down a South Carolina Supreme Court precedent that barred the defendant from introducing proof that another person committed the crime when there is strong evidence of the defendant's guilt.

Bobby Lee Holmes was convicted of raping, robbing, and killing an 86-year-old woman and sentenced to death. The South Carolina Supreme Court granted a new trial to Holmes because of trial errors. At the second trial the prosecution relied on **forensic** evidence that included Holmes' palm print on the door of the victim's home, fibers from his sweatshirt, his DNA, and a mixture of his blood and the victim's. The prosecution also produced evidence that Holmes had been seen near the victim's home within an hour of the attack. Holmes' defense relied mainly on the contention that the forensic evidence had been contaminated and that the police had plotted to frame him. In addition, Holmes sought to introduce the testimony of several people who claimed that another man, Jimmy McCaw White, had been in the victim's neighborhood on the morning of the crime and had bragged to them that he had assaulted the victim. At a pretrial hearing the judge heard the witnesses' testimony; White testified as well, denying that he had many any incriminating statements. The trial judge excluded Holmes' third-party guilt evidence because under state supreme court precedent it cast a "bare suspicion upon another" and it raised "a conjectural inference as to the commission of the crime by another." The South Carolina Supreme Court upheld this ruling, finding that where there was strong evidence of guilt based on forensics, the evidence of a third-party's alleged guilt did not raise a reasonable inference of the defendant's innocence.

The U.S. Supreme Court, in a unanimous decision, overturned the state supreme court's ruling. Justice Samuel Alito, writing for the Court, noted that state and federal rulemakers had broad discretion to establish rules that excluded evidence from criminal trials but there were limits to this authority. Under the Sixth Amendment and the Due Process Clause of the FOURTEENTH AMENDMENT criminal defendants had the right to present a "complete defense." This right was curtailed when evidence rules were arbitrary or disproportionate to the purposes they were meant to serve. Justice Alito pointed out that the Court had struck down arbitrary rules that excluded important defense evidence without serving any legitimate interests. In a Texas case the Court struck down a rule that barred a person charged as a participant in the crime from testifying unless the person had been acquitted of the charge. In a Mississippi case the Court ruled that the state could not bar a defendant from impeaching his own witness when the witness had made self-incriminating statements about the crime. In a Kentucky case a defendant was not permitted to show that his confession was unreliable because of the way police had obtained it. The Court threw out this prohibition as well.

Justice Alito contrasted these unconstitutional rules with rules of evidence that allowed trial judges to exclude evidence "if its **probative** value is outweighed by certain other factors such as unfair prejudice, confusion of the issues, or potential to mislead the jury." In the matter at hand, trial courts have the discretion to exclude evidence by the defendant that someone else committed the crime if the evidence is "so remote and lack[s] such connection with the crime." This widely accepted rule was not, however, at issue in this case. Justice Alito concluded that the South Carolina Supreme Court had "radically changed and extended" this evidentiary rule by adding a new factor: the strength of the evidence showing the defendant's guilt. The problem with this approach was that the trial judge did not focus on "the probative value or the potential adverse effects of admitting the defense evidence of third-party guilt but instead looked to the strength of the prosecution's case. If the prosecution's case is strong, then evidence of third-party guilt would be excluded even if, viewed independently, that evidence had merit and would not confuse the issues before the court.

The Holmes case showed why the state rule was unconstitutional. The state supreme court did not evaluate the credibility of the prosecution witnesses or the reliability of the **state's evidence**, yet it concluded that the forensic evidence was strong enough to exclude the defense evidence. The state supreme court's ruling was based on an assumption of the state's evidence rather than on a searching examination. Justice Alito found that "by evaluating the strength of only one party's evidence, no logical conclusion can be reached regarding the strength of contrary evidence offered by the other side to rebut or cast doubt." Therefore, the rule as arbitrary and served no legitimate purpose.

SOCIAL SECURITY

Lockhart v. United States

The federal government has become very active in collecting debts on unpaid federally reinsured student loans. Its practice of withholding a portion of a debtor's Social Security payments to payback the loan has come under legal attack. The Supreme Court, in *Lockhart v. United States*, __U.S.__, 126 S.Ct. 699, 163 L.Ed.2d 557 (2005), ruled that this practice was legal and did not violate a set of federal laws governing Social Security and the collection of student loan debt.

James Lockhart, a Washington resident, was laid off of his job in the early 1980s, when he was in his early 40s. He enrolled in four different higher education institutions and accumulated more than $80,000 in student loan debts. Lockhart was never able to find a steady job and his health declined to the point where he could not work. He received $874 in monthly Social Security disability benefits until he reached age 65. At that point he began to receive Social Security old age benefits. In 2002 the federal government began withholding a portion of these benefits to offset his debt. Lockhart filed a lawsuit in federal **district court**, alleging that the Debt Collection Act of 1982, 31 U.S.C.A. §3716(e)(1), barred the collection of debts more than ten years old. The district court dismissed his action and the Ninth **Circuit Court** of Appeals upheld this ruling. The Supreme Court accepted Lockhart's appeal to resolve a conflict in the law between the Ninth and Eighth Circuits.

The Supreme Court, in a unanimous decision, upheld the Ninth Circuit ruling. Justice SANDRA DAY O'CONNOR, writing for the Court, examined the interplay of various provisions from the Debt Collection Act, the Social Security Act, 49 Stat. 620, and the 1991 Higher Education Technical Amendments, 105 Stat. 123. Under the Debt Collection Act the use by federal agencies of administrative offsets to collect outstanding debt was recognized as a valid tool. However, the Social Security Act states that Social Security benefits generally are not "subject to execution, levy, attachment, **garnishment**, or other legal process." 42 U.S.C.A. § 407(a). In addition, the act also purported to protect this section from change through the use of language that barred any past or future law from being construed "to limit, supersede, or otherwise modify the provisions of this section except to the extent that it does so by express reference to this section. 42 U.S.C.A. § 407(b). Though the Debt Collection Act did not authorize the collection of claims more than ten years old, the Higher Education Technical Amendments eliminated time limitations on a number of federal loans. One of the provisions stated that there was no time limitation on the use of offset for the repayment of student loans. 20 U.S.C.A. § 1091a(a)(2)(D). However, this provision did not eliminate the Social Security anti-attachment rule. It was not until 1996 that Congress passed an amendment to the Debt Collection Act that explicitly allowed the use of offset of Social Security benefits to collect federal debts.

Justice O'Connor concluded that the Social Security provision banning the use of benefits for collection efforts, known as express-reference provisions, did not need to be considered in deciding the case because the 1996 amendment provided "exactly the sort of express reference that the Social Security Act say is necessary to supersede the anti-attachment provision." As to the ten-year limit on collecting debt, O'Connor found that the 1991 Higher Education Technical Amendments removed this bar on Social Security benefits. Lockhart had argued that Congress could not have intended this result because it did not allow debt collection by Social Security offset until 1996. The Court rejected this claim, finding that the fact Congress had not foreseen all of the consequences in 1991 was not "a sufficient reason for refusing to give effect to its plain meaning." Though the 1996 amendments retained the 10-year bar on offset authority found in the original Debt Collection Act, the 1991 technical amendments lawfully abrogated this bar "as a limited exception to the Debt Collection Act time bar in the student loan context." Finally, Justice O'Connor declined to consider a failed 2004 effort by some members of Congress to amend the Debt Collection Act to explicitly authorize offset of debts over 10 years old. The courts are wary of interpreting a **statute** using failed legislative proposals and it was "unclear what meaning we could read into this effort even if we were inclined to do so." Therefore, the Court upheld the debt collection practice.

Justice ANTONIN SCALIA, in a concurring opinion, agreed with the outcome of the case but wished the Court had ruled that the Social Security express-reference provision was not binding; in effect, the debt collection could have been upheld even if Congress had not made the express exception in the 1991 amendments. It was long-held precedent that one legislature cannot limit the powers of a succeeding legislature. In other cases the Court had made clear that an "express-reference or express-statement provision cannot nullify the unambiguous import of a subsequent statute." Scalia urged Congress to refrain from including such provisions in future legislation, as they are ineffective.

SOVEREIGN IMMUNITY

The legal protection that prevents a sovereign state or person from being sued without consent.

Dolan v. United States Postal Service

The FEDERAL TORT CLAIMS ACT (FTCA), 28 U.S.C.A. § 1346(b), provides a limited waiver of the sovereignty of the U.S. government when government employees are negligent within the scope of their employment. However, the FTCA qualifies this waiver of immunity for 13 types of claims. If one of these 13 exceptions applies, the government remains immune to a civil damages lawsuit. One of the 13 categories, § 2680(b), pertains to postal operations. It states that the FTCA will not apply to any "claim arising out of the loss, miscarriage, or negligent transmission of letters or postal matter." The Supreme Court was called upon in *Dolan v. United States Postal Service*, __U.S.__, 126 S.Ct. 1252, 163 L.Ed.2d 1079 (2006), to determine whether a woman who was injured by tripping over a bundle of mail left on her porch could sue the U.S. POSTAL SERVICE (USPS) for damages under the FTCA. The Court decided she could, overturning lower court rulings that found that the bundle of mail constituted a "negligent transmission" which barred the lawsuit.

In 2001 a postal worker left a bundle of letters, magazines, and packages on the porch of Barbara Dolan's Pennsylvania home. Dolan allegedly tripped over the bundle and fell, causing injuries. After her administrative complaint with the USPS was denied in 2002, she filed a complaint under the FTCA in federal **district court**. The government asked the court to dismiss her suit, citing the immunity exception in § 2680(b). The district court agreed and dismissed the case. The Third **Circuit Court** of Appeals upheld the lower court ruling, finding that the **statutory** exception for the postal service applied.

The Supreme Court, in a 7–1 decision (newly confirmed Justice Samuel Alito did not participate in the consideration of the case), overturned the Third Circuit ruling. Justice ANTHONY KENNEDY, writing for the majority, noted that the USPS enjoys federal **sovereign immunity** unless specifically waived by **statute**. The FTCA waives sovereign immunity by conferring federal-court jurisdiction in a defined category of case involving negligent acts by government workers. The statute also make the United States liable in these categories "in the same manner and to the same extent as a private individual under like circumstances," though a plaintiff cannot collect pre-judgment interest or **punitive damages**. Justice Kennedy agreed that § 2680(b) does not waive immunity for the loss, miscarriage, or negligent transmission of letters or postal matter," but it was the job of the Court to determine whether this exception applied to a slip and fall case caused by a postal worker.

The meaning of the phrase "negligent transmission" was at the center of the argument. Justice Kennedy agreed that the phrase, when viewed in isolation, could embrace a large group of negligent acts committed by postal workers, including slip and fall cases like Dolan's. However, he said it was a mistake to look at phrase in isolation. The interpretation of the phrase depended "upon reading the whole statutory text, considering the purpose and context of the statute, and consulting any precedents or authorities that inform our analysis." Using these sources it became clear that "negligent transmission" had a narrower meaning and did not "comprehend all negligence occurring in the course of mail delivery." The phrase followed the terms "loss" and "miscarriage," indicating that it referred to the "failings in the postal obligation to deliver mail in a timely manner to the right address." This reading of the phrase was reinforced by a 1984 case in which the Court stated that the negligent operation of a motor vehicle did not come under the "negligent transmission" exception. Therefore, Justice Kennedy concluded that the Court could not now use § 2680(b) "to cover all negligence in the course of mail delivery. Postal trucks might be transmitting mail when they collide with other vehicles, yet that did confer immunity on the government.

Justice Kennedy also thought it more likely that Congress only intended to retain immunity for injuries connected to mail either failing to arrive or arriving late. For example, the government is immune from a lawsuit that alleges personal or financial harms that resulted from the non-delivery of a financial document or from the negligent handling of a mailed parcel whose contents arrived broken. If Congress had intended to make a broad exception to preserve immunity, it would not have limited the provision to a "subset of postal wrongdoing." Moreover, the losses that can result from negligent transmission of letters "are at to some degree avoidable or compensable through postal registration and insurance."

The USPS claimed that waiving immunity for slip and fall cases would result in a torrent of frivolous litigation. Justice Kennedy countered that this type of liability was, under state tort laws, a risk of business shared by any business that makes home deliveries. In addition, the granting of a wide exception would undercut the "central purpose" of the FTCA. Therefore, Dolan was free to pursue her claim on the merits in federal district court.

Justice CLARENCE THOMAS, in a dissenting opinion, disagreed with the meaning assigned to "negligent transmission." He argued that the postal exception exempted the USPS from any claim involving the negligent delivery of the mail.

United States v. Olson

Individuals who wish to sue the federal government for damages must use the FEDERAL TORT CLAIMS ACT (FTCA), 28 U.S.C.A. § 1346, which waives the federal government's **sovereign immunity**. The **statute** has been widely litigated to determine which types of government actions come under the FTCA. The law authorizes private tort actions "under circumstances where the United States, if a private person, would be liable to the claimant in accordance with the law of the place where the act or omission occurred." 28 U.S.C.A. § 1346(b)(1). The Supreme Court, in *United States v. Olson*, __U.S.__, 126 S.Ct. 510, 163 L.Ed.2d 306 (2005), ruled that this provision could not be interpreted to permit a lawsuit where local law would make state or municipal government entities liable.

Joseph Olson, an Arizona mine worker, along with his wife and another miner, sued the federal government after the two miners were injured in a mine ceiling collapse. They argued that the government was liable because inspectors from the Mine Safety and Health Administration had been negligent in not inspecting the mine thoroughly. A DEPARTMENT OF LABOR investigation confirmed this allegation, finding that the company had not adequately supported the ceiling. The federal government asked the federal **district court** to dismiss the case, contending that the FTCA did not apply in this situation. The court agreed, dismissing the case because plaintiffs had failed to show that Arizona law would impose liability on a private person in similar circumstances.

The Ninth **Circuit Court** of Appeals reversed the district court decision. The appeals court grounded its decision on two points. First, where "unique governmental functions" were at issue, the FTCA waived sovereign immunity if a "state or municipal **entity** would be [subject to liability] under the law" of the state where the activity occurred. Second, federal mining inspection was a "unique governmental function" with no private sector equivalent and Arizona law would make a state or municipal entity liable for the actions alleged by the plaintiffs. Therefore, the lawsuit could be pursued under the FTCA.

The Supreme Court, in a unanimous decision, reversed the Ninth Circuit. Justice STEPHEN BREYER, writing for the Court, disagreed with both of the Ninth Circuit's reasons. The first premise of the Ninth Circuit, which waived immunity if a state or local entity could be sued for the alleged negligence, was too broad. Justice Breyer pointed out that § 1346(b)(1 referred to a "private person" for establishing liability, not state or local government units. A 1955 Supreme Court case had made clear that an assessment of federal government liability required a court "to look to the state-law liability of private entities, not to that of public entities." A 1957 Court decision rejected the claim that liability for a "uniquely governmental function" depended on whether state law made local governments liable for the negligence of their agents in similar circumstances. Justice Breyer concluded there was nothing in the "context, history, or objectives" of the FTCA or in the Court's opinions that implied a waiver of sovereign immunity on this theory.

Justice Breyer found the Ninth Circuit's second premise was too narrow, as it read the FTCA too restrictively. Under 28 U.S.C.A. § 2674, the federal government is liable "in the same manner and to the same extent as a private individual under like circumstances." The phrase "like circumstances" did not mean the court was limited to looking for the "same circumstances. The Court had ruled in a prior case that the Coast Guard was liable for the negligent operation of a lighthouse that resulted in damage to a ship that relied upon its signal. The Court concluded that this negligence was analogous to misconduct by a private person "who undertakes to warn the public of danger and thereby induces reliance." This "Good Samaritan" theory applied to the Arizona mines, for there are private persons in "like circumstances" to federal mine inspectors: private mine inspectors. The Ninth Circuit should have conducted a search for an analogy similar to the lighthouse example, as it could have established grounds for waiving immunity under the FTCA.

Though the federal government conceded that a private person analogy existed in this case, the Court noted that the parties disagreed over which Arizona **tort law** doctrine applied. Therefore, it remanded the case to the lower courts for a determination of this issue, leaving the ultimate outcome dependant on state law.

George Mitchell and baseball commissioner Bud Selig discuss baseball's upcoming steroid investigation, March 2006.
AP IMAGES

SPORTS LAW

Allegations of Steroid Use in Baseball Continue

Allegations of rampant steroid use by Major League Baseball (MLB) players continued in 2005 and 2006. In March 2006, about a year after the House Government Reform Committee held hearings about the use of steroids in professional sports, a book was released that detailed steroid usage by Barry Bonds and several other star players. These allegations came during a time when Bonds was on the verge of surpassing Babe Ruth in career home runs.

The House committee called a number of well-known baseball stars to a hearing in March 2005. Among the players called were Mark McGuire, Sammy Sosa, Rafael Palmeiro, and Curt Schilling. A book written by former star Jose Canseco alleged that several players, including McGuire, Palmeiro, and Jason Giambi, had used steroids in the past. These players either denied using steroids or declined to address the subject.

At the time of the hearings, Victor Conte, Jr., former head of Bay Area Laboratory Cooperative (BALCO) faced several charges related to illegal steroid production. The investigation into BALCO produced allegations that athletes in a number of sports had been guilty of using steroids. At his State of the Union Address in 2004, President GEORGE W. BUSH even referred to the steroid problem in sports and called for an end to the use of these drugs.

Major League Baseball Commissioner Bud Selig announced a zero-tolerance policy in the sport. Under a new policy, a player who tests positive for steroid use faces suspension. Much of the attention in 2005 focused on Bonds due to his connection with BALCO through a personal trainer. Bonds, who admitted to a **grand jury** that he had taken a substance but did not knowingly use steroids, broke the single season home run mark in 2001 by hitting 73 home runs. Entering the 2005 season, Bonds needed 12 home runs to surpass Ruth for the second most home runs in history. Henry "Hank" Aaron holds the career record with 755.

Bonds sat out much of the 2005 season due to an injury. In May 2005, an MLB spokesperson said that baseball was not investigating allegations that Bonds had used steroids. About two months later, Conte pleaded guilty to charges of conspiracy to distribute steroids and **money laundering**. Bonds' personal trainer, Greg Anderson, also pleaded guilty to those charges. The result of this case meant that Bonds and other athletes, such as Giambi and track star Marion Jones, would not have to testify about steroid use.

In August, Palmeiro became the first high-profile baseball player to be suspended for steroid use. He had expressly denied having ever used steroids when he testified before the House committee in March that year, leading to speculation as to whether he would be indicated for perjury. The suspension came just two weeks after he became only the fourth player in history to amass 3,000 hits and 500 home runs. Also well known for his role as a pitch man for Viagra, Palmeiro denied that he had knowingly ingested steroids. The suspension lasted a period of 10 days.

Bonds returned near the end of the 2005 season, hitting five home runs over the last 18 games. Even though he was not charged in the case, the result of the BALCO trial left a number of questions surrounding Bonds unanswered. Several critics said that Bonds should be prevented from surpassing Ruth's record due to the steroid allegations. Just weeks after the season ended, Conte, Anderson, and other BALCO executives were sentenced to short prison terms.

Baseball was not the only sport involved in the House committee investigation in 2005. In April, committee members criticized the steroid policy of the National Football League, with some members of Congress suggesting the implementation of uniform drug testing for all sports. NFL officials argued against this proposal, saying that was unnecessary. The BALCO scandal led several professional sports to adopt more rigorous steroid policies. For instance, at the 2006 Winter Olympics at Turin, Italy, officials exercised more vigilance than in previous years due largely to the focus on steroid caused by the BALCO trial.

In the weeks leading up to the 2006 MLB season, a new book led to additional allegations about steroid use by Bonds and other baseball players. The book, entitled "Game of Shadows: Barry Bonds, BALCO, and the Steroids Scandal that Rocked Professional Sports," was written by Mark Fainaru-Wada and Lance Williams of the *San Francisco Chronicle*. These authors had previously written stories about Bonds' alleged steroid use for the Chronicle, and the book expands upon this coverage by relying on grand jury testimony, documents, and interviews. Sports Illustrated also published an excerpt from the book a few weeks before its release.

According to the book, Bonds began using steroids after McGuire and Sosa had engaged in a well-publicized home run race during the 1998 season. Though Bonds had won three most valuable player awards prior to that season, he had never hit more than 46 home runs in a season. During the 1998 season, a 34-year-old Bonds hit 34 homers, well behind McGuire's record 70 that year. After that season, Bonds hired Anderson as his personal trainer, and the book alleges that Anderson later introduced Bonds to steroids.

BALCO allegedly produced several types of steroids that could not be detected through tests available prior to about 2003. Among the products that Bonds allegedly used were "the clear," a substance that contained the steroid THG; "the cream," which contained testosterone; and human growth hormone. Bonds said that he thought that Anderson had given him flaxseed oil and an arthritis salve, but the book counters that Bonds had adhered to a regimen when taking the steroids. Statements by Kimberly Bell, Bonds' ex-girlfriend, corroborated other evidence of Bonds' drug use.

Between 2000 and 2004, Bonds never hit fewer than 45 home runs, including the record-setting 73 homers during the 2001 season. By hitting more than 260 home runs after the age of 35, Bonds put himself in position to challenge the all-time career record. Due to the scandal, MLB announced that it would not celebrate when Bonds surpassed Ruth's record, indeed did not do so when Bonds passed Ruth on May 28, 2006.

SUPREME COURT

Supreme Court Sees First Major Changes in More Than a Decade

After years of speculation about possible nominees for positions on the U.S. SUPREME COURT that would likely become vacant, President GEORGE W. BUSH in 2005 and 2006 appointed two new members, including a new chief justice. These appointments, which became necessary due to the retirement of Justice SANDRA DAY O'CONNOR and the death of Chief Justice WILLIAM H. REHNQUIST, left many questioning whether the Court would head in a new direction philosophically.

On July 1, 2005, O'Connor announced that she would step down after serving 24 years on the bench. Appointed by President RONALD REAGAN in 1981 as the first woman justice, O'Connor had long been considered to be the key swing vote between conservative and liberal factions on the Court. Most significantly, she voted to uphold abortion rights in several key decisions in the 1990s and 2000s. She remained on the Court for part of the 2005–2006 term. O'Connor penned her final opinion in another abortion case, *Ayotte v. Planned Parenthood of Northern New England*, ___ U.S. ___, 126 S. Ct. 961, 163 L. Ed. 2d 812 (2006), where the Court unanimously invalidated a New Hampshire law requiring minors seeking abortions to notify their parents.

Almost two months after O'Connor's announcement, Rehnquist died at his home in Virginia. Rehnquist, who was 80 when he died, was the second oldest justice in history to lead the Court. Since assuming the position of chief justice in 1986, Rehnquist oversaw the Court's conservative shift. He also reduced the number of cases that the Court heard and demanded clearer and more strongly reasoned opinions. Rehnquist often aligned himself with Justices ANTHONY KENNEDY, ANTONIN SCALIA, and CLARENCE THOMAS as part of the Court's conservative voting bloc.

After O'Connor's retirement announcement, about 10 names surfaced as possible replacements. Most of the potential nominees served as judges at federal **appellate** courts, with U.S. Attorney General Alberto Gonzales being the exception. The name that rose to the top of this list was JOHN ROBERTS, a judge with the U.S. Court of Appeals for the D.C. Circuit. Roberts received his law degree from Harvard Law School in 1979. After clerking at a federal appeals court, he became a clerk for Rehnquist, who then served as an **associate justice**. He argued before the Supreme Court on numerous occasions, both as a deputy **solicitor general** and as a private practitioner.

Roberts became the leading candidate to become the new chief justice after Rehnquist's death. During confirmation hearings held in September, members of the SENATE JUDICIARY COMMITTEE asked Roberts a number of questions about how he would vote on certain issues. He repeatedly declined, saying that he could not comment on potential issues or questions that might come before the Court. Although some Democrats complained that he did not answer their questions adequately, the Senate confirmed his nomination by a vote of 78 to 22. He was sworn in on September 29.

Naming O'Connor's replacement proved to be more challenging for Bush. Many commentators expected Bush to replace O'Connor with another female, possibly a minority woman. During the first week of October, Bush surprised many by announcing the nomination of presidential counsel Harriet Miers. The decision was reportedly based in large part to Miers' loyalty to the president, as well as to her conservative views. Although some officials nodded their approval informally, her nomination met significant resistance from others. Critics accused Bush of cronyism, while some Republicans said that they wanted assurances that the nominee would remain true to their conservative ideologies.

Many questioned Miers background for the position as a justice on the Court. She spent much of her career as a corporate lawyer, and critics doubted that she could perform nearly as well as Roberts during the public confirmation process. She also had no experience as a judge, and while this type of experience is not an absolute requirement, commentators noted that she would have difficulty answering some questions during the hearings. The last Supreme Court justice to be appointed without prior judicial experience was LEWIS F. POWELL JR., who was appointed by President RICHARD NIXON in 1972.

In less than a month, Miers withdrew as a nominee. Members of the Senate said that they intended to request documents about Miers' service in the White House in order to ascertain her judicial philosophy. Miers cited these requests as part of her reasons for her withdrawal. "Repeatedly in the courts of the process of confirmation for nominees for other positions, I have steadfastly maintained that the independence of the Executive Branch be preserved and its confidential documents and information not be released to further a confirmation process," she wrote in her letter of withdrawal to Bush. "I feel compelled to adhere to this position, especially related to my own nomination. Protection of the prerogatives of the Executive Branch and continued pursuit of my conformation are in tension. I have decided that seeking my confirmation should yield."

Bush next turned to SAMUEL A. ALITO JR., who served as a judge with the U.S. Court of Appeals for the Third Circuit since 1990. A graduate of Yale Law School, Alito drew comparisons with Scalia, not only because both are Italian-American, but also because Alito has often voted conservatively in the past. Although analysis of opinions written by Scalia and Alito showed a number of differences in their judicial approaches, many liberals expressed concerns about the nomination's potential to shift the focus on the Court even further to the right.

Some Democrats threatened to **filibuster** Alito's nomination, due largely to objections to the judge's position on abortion. Many pro-choice advocates believed that Alito's appointment would signify the end to abortion rights under *Roe v. Wade*. Although the effort to filibuster the vote fell through, the final vote in the Senate was clearly partisan, with Alito receiving the confirmation by a vote of 58 to 42.

After Alito was sworn in, several Democrats said that Bush's nominations would haunt him in the November elections in 2006. The Court's three youngest members, including Roberts, Alito, and Thomas, are conservatives. The two oldest judges, RUTH BADER GINSBURG (72) and JOHN PAUL STEVENS (85), are both liberals. Conservative groups applauded the appointments and said that they were historic victories for their causes.

Commentators noted that the appointments of two conservatives likely meant that Kennedy's vote would become the most crucial. In the past, the Court was generally viewed to have four liberals and three conservatives, with two swing votes of O'Connor and Kennedy. With Alito joining the Court, commentators expect that Kennedy will remain the only moderate member on the bench.

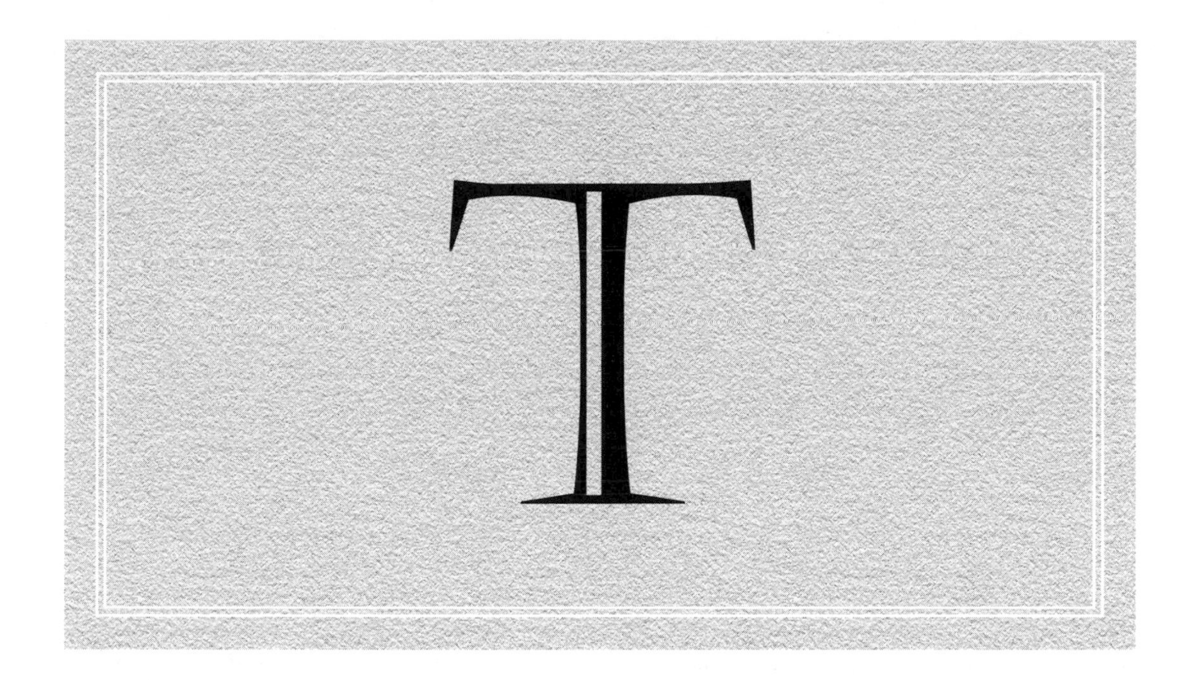

TAXATION

The process whereby charges are imposed on individuals or property by the legislative branch of the federal government and by many state governments to raise funds for public purposes.

President's Panel Recommends Major Tax Reform

An advisory panel established by President GEORGE W. BUSH in 2005 concluded that the U.S. needs to reform its entire tax system. A report issued by the panel on November 1, 2005 concluded that the tax code needs to be simplified and constructed in a manner that ensures efficiency and fairness. The proposal drew criticism because some of the proposed reforms would eliminate or change some popular deductions, credits, and other tax breaks.

The INTERNAL REVENUE CODE (IRC), codified as title 26 of the United States Code, has been criticized due to its complexity. The last major reform of this code occurred in 1986, but it has been the subject of more than 14,000 revisions since that time. Commentators have noted that these revisions are often made for the purpose of stimulating the national economy, but the changes can also have unintended consequences in later years. In his State of the Union Address in 2005, Bush pledged to reform what he called an "archaic, incoherent" code.

Bush created the panel by way of executive order on January 7, 2005. This order said that the purpose of the panel was "to submit to the Secretary of Treasury . . . a report with revenue neutral policy option for reforming the [IRC]." The order required the panel to review three options, including the following: (1) a simplification of federal tax laws that would reduce the costs and administrative burdens of complying with these laws; (2) a sharing of the "burdens and benefits of the Federal tax structure in an appropriately progressive manner," while also taking into account "the importance of homeownership and charity in American society;" and (3) promotion of long-term economic grown and job creation, along with better encouragement of work effort, savings, and investment, in order to "strengthen the competitiveness of the United States in the global marketplace."

The panel was chaired by former senator Connie Mack III, now senior advisor at King & Spaulding LLP. Other members of the committee included former senator John Breaux; former representative William Eldridge Frenzel; Elizabeth Garrett, professor of public interest law, legal ethics, and political science at the University of Southern California; Edward P. Lazear, a senior fellow of the Hoover Institution and professor of human resources, management and economics at Stanford University; Timothy J. Muris, a professor at George Mason School of Law; James Michael Poterba, a professor of economics at the Massachusetts Institute of Technology; Charles O. Rossotti, senior advisor at the Carlyle Group; and Liz Ann Sonders, chief investment strategist for Charles Schwab.

The panel began hearing public testimony in February 2005. Discussion of reform efforts met with skepticism, with several commentators noting that any meaningful change was unlikely. One major reason for their doubt was that the budget deficit has continually grown larger throughout Bush's presidency. Other commentators noted that meaningful changes will take several years to implement.

After conducting the hearings during the spring of 2005, the panel already recognized the need for tax reform. The panel issued a statement in April 2005 that summarized its findings from those hearings. "For millions of Americans, the annual rite of filing taxes has become a headache of burdensome record-keeping, lengthy instructions, and complicated schedules, worksheets and forms—often requiring multiple computations that are neither logical nor intuitive," the statement said. "Not only is our tax system maddeningly complex, it penalizes work, discourages saving and investment, and hinders the competitiveness of American businesses. The tax code is riddled with tax provisions that treat similarly situated taxpayers differently and create perceptions of unfairness."

The panel echoed many of the concerns raised during the public hearing process when the panel issued its report on November 1, 2005. Among its conclusions, the panel determined that objectives of simplicity, fairness, and economic growth are often at odds with each other, and that when policymakers make choices among these objectives, the policymakers much sacrifice simplification. The panel also concluded that the frequent changes to the IRC help to cause the tax system in the U.S. to be unstable and unpredictable.

The Panel developed two possible tax reform plans. These were entitled the Simplified Income Tax Plan and the Growth and Investment Tax Plan. Both plans share goals of "providing simple and straightforward ways for Americans to save free of tax and lower the tax burden on productivity-enhancing investment by businesses." The primary difference between the two plans is the taxation of businesses and capital income.

Both plans aim to reduce the complexity of the tax system. For instance, taxpayers would use a simple tax form that is only half the length of the current 1040. These plans are also designed to improve fairness in the system by ensuring that many of the tax breaks and benefits that are available now to a few taxpayers are available to all taxpayers. The plans additionally promote economic growth in a variety of ways, such as reducing double taxation of corporations and reducing paperwork burdens for small businesses.

One of the major concerns that the panel had related to the Alternative Minimum Tax (AMT). The AMT is a tax that must be paid on top of the regular income tax. Although it was originally designed to ensure that those with very high income could not avoid taxes through special benefits, a growing number of Americans, including those in lower tax brackets, are required to pay the AMT. The panel noted that these numbers could reach 21 million in 2006 and 52 million by 2015. Both of the panel's plans call for the **repeal** of the AMT.

After the White House received the report, Treasury Secretary John Snow referred to the proposals as "bold recommendations," but Bush would not embrace any part of the proposal until Snow had an opportunity to make his own suggestions. The members of the panel recognized that some of its own recommendations would meet resistance. "The effort to reform the tax code is noble in its purpose, but it requires political willpower," wrote the group in a letter to Snow. "Many stand waiting to defend their breaks, deductions and loopholes, and to defeat our efforts."

TERRORISM

The unlawful use of force or violence against persons or property in order to coerce or intimate a government or the civilian population in furtherance of political or social objectives.

Guantanamo Bay Developments

In May 2006, the Pentagon released a list of individuals who are being held in a detention center at Guantanamo Bay, Cuba, under suspicion of terrorist activities. This list was allegedly the first complete list of Guantanamo detainees released to the public since the detention center was established more than four years ago, after the September 11th attacks in 2001.

The Associated Press had requested the names, photos, and other details of current and former detainees under the FREEDOM OF INFORMATION ACT in January 2006, and had filed a lawsuit in March after the Pentagon had not responded to the request.

A Pentagon spokesman said that the names had been kept classified because of the security operations and intelligence operations that occur at Guantanamo Bay, but he did not comment on why the Pentagon chose not to contest the Associated Press's request.

Although the list of names will help lawyers and human rights advocates track down detainees in order to investigate allegations of abuse at Guantanamo, the list did not include

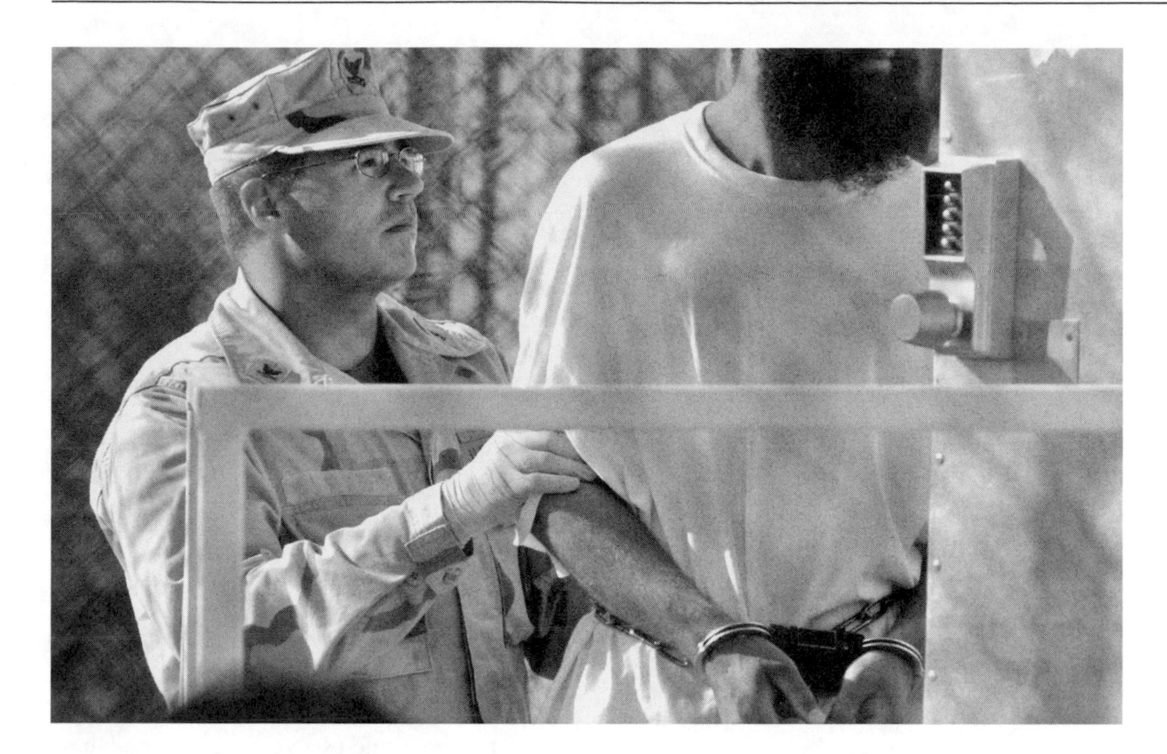

Military solider with detainee (identity hidden) at Guantanamo Bay naval base prison.
AP IMAGES

the names of some top terrorists in custody, including Khalid Shaikh Mohammed and Ramzi Binalshibh, who have been accused of plotting the attacks of September 11, 2001. Although the most recent list included more than 200 names that had not previously been disclosed by the Department of Defense, questions persist about the existence of a "secret prison" at Guantanamo Bay. A spokesperson from the Department of Defense has denied the existence of other detention facilities at Guantanamo Bay, however.

The Pentagon had released a list of more than 500 names to the Associated Press in April 2006, when ordered to do so by a federal judge in response the Freedom of Information Act request, but the list was not complete.

"This list takes us one step closer to our goal of fully reporting who has been swept into U.S. military custody in Guantanamo, and how they and their cases are being handled," said David Tomlin, the assistant general counsel for the Associated Press.

The interest in contacting detainees stems in part from allegations of prisoner abuse that surfaced in late 2004, when agents with the FEDERAL BUREAU OF INVESTIGATION reported the use of loud music, bright lights, and growling dogs to disorient and intimidate prisoners. The agents also reported having seen prisoners chained to the floor. An ongoing, high-level military investigation was initiated once the Pentagon became aware of the reports.

Secretary of State Condoleezza Rice denied the allegations of torture at Guantanamo during a television interview in Liverpool, England, in April 2006.

"We don't want to be the world's jailer, and we certainly want to try people or release them," Rice said in the interview. "One of the misunderstandings about Guantanamo is the sense that somehow hundreds and hundreds and hundreds of people have been there forever with no prospect of release. Indeed, we have released hundreds of people from Guantanamo either because we've deemed them not as dangerous as thought or because we've released them to their governments, as we did with Great Britain."

The U.S. SUPREME COURT addressed the question of how to manage the legal rights of the Guantanamo detainees in 2006. President Bush had used his prerogative as commander in chief during times of war and mandated that military tribunals would try the detainees, rather than civilian courts. In 2004, the Court ruled that the president could not indefinitely detain prisoners without filing charges. Later in 2004, U.S. District Judge James Robertson found that Guantanamo Bay detainees should be considered prisoners of war and therefore entitled to certain protections under the Geneva Conventions, including the right to hear the charges against them.

Many detainees have challenged their imprisonment. In 2006, the U.S. Supreme Court was scheduled to rule on whether the detainees would be tried in military or civilian courts. Without a Supreme Court ruling, "it will be difficult for military commissions and status-review panels to decide fairly whether a detainee is a prisoner of war, after top Executive Branch and military leaders have declared all of them enemy combatants, not POWs," said Eugene R. Fidell, a Washington, DC-based lawyer specializing in military justice, in an interview with the Washington Post in 2004.

In an interesting twist, four British citizens who had been held at Guantanamo Bay for three years and then released to Great Britain won the right in 2006 to sue Donald Rumsfeld, the U.S. Secretary of Defense, for damages. The former detainees have stated that they will seek $10 million in damages from Rumsfeld and ten other military commanders for violating their religious rights by forcing them to shave their beards, harassing them during their worship activities, and forcing them to watch a Guantanamo guard flush a copy of the Muslim holy book, the Koran, down a toilet.

Cases Against Padilla and Moussaoui Continue

During 2005 and 2006, two terrorist suspects continued their legal disputes. Jose Padilla, who was designated by President GEORGE W. BUSH as an "enemy combatant" in 2002, petitioned a federal **district court** in South Carolina for a **writ** of **habeas corpus** in an effort to force the U.S. government either to charge him with a crime or release him. Although the trial court agreed with Padilla, the Fourth **Circuit Court** of Appeals reversed the trial court's decision. In a second criminal case, Zacarias Moussaoui, the only person charged for the SEPTEMBER 11TH ATTACKS in 2001, received a life sentence by a federal court in Virginia.

According to court records, Padilla, a U.S. citizen and native of Brooklyn, received training from al Qaeda in Afghanistan in 2000 and 2001. After the terrorist attacks in 2001, Padilla was present as U.S. forces fought Taliban forces in Afghanistan. He eventually escaped to Pakistan, where he continued to communicate with al Qaeda operatives. One senior planner for the terrorist organization, Khalid Sheikh Mohammad, directed Padilla to travel to the United States in order to conduct terrorist activities. Officials accused Padilla of leading a plot to set off a radioactive "dirty" bomb and of planning to blow up apartment buildings.

When Padilla arrived at O'Hare International Airport in Chicago, agents of the FEDERAL BUREAU OF INVESTIGATION immediately arrested him pursuant to a warrant issued by the U.S. District Court for the Southern District of New York. Federal agents transported him to New York, where he was held at a civilian correctional facility. On June 9, 2002, Bush designated Padilla as an enemy combatant pursuant to a federal **statute** enacted shortly after the terrorist attacks took place. Under this directive, Padilla was held at a naval brig in South Carolina without being formally charged with a crime.

Shortly after Bush issued the directive, Padilla filed a petition for writ of habeas corpus in the Southern District of New York. Later in 2002, Padilla's attorney, Donna Newman, successfully argued before the New York court that Padilla was entitled to speak with her. *Padilla ex rel. Newman v. Bush*, 233 F. Supp. 2d 564 (S.D.N.Y. 2002). The government had maintained that he would use Newman as a conduit to transmit information to terrorists. Two years later, the U.S. SUPREME COURT dismissed Padilla's petition, ruling that he had improperly filed them in New York. *Rumsfeld v. Padilla*, 542 U.S. 426, 124 S. Ct. 2711, 159 L. Ed. 2d 513 (2004). Padilla then filed a petition with the U.S. District Court for the District of South Carolina.

Bush issued his directive based on the Authorization for Use of Military Force Joint Resolution (AUMF), which was approved by Congress on September 18, 2001. Pub. L. No. 107–40, 115 Stat. 224 (2001). This **joint resolution** provides as follows: "[T]he President is authorized to sue all necessary and appropriate force against those nations, organizations, or persons he determines planned, authorized, committed, or aided the terrorist attacks that occurred on September 11, 2001, or harbored such organizations or persons, in order to prevent any future attacks of international terrorism against the United States by such nations, organizations, or persons."

In a decision issued on February 28, 2005, U.S. District Judge Henry F. Floyd Jr. determined that neither the AUMF by Congress nor powers inherently possessed by the president allowed Bush to hold Padilla. Accordingly, the judge ruled that the government must either charge Padilla with a crime or release him. *Padilla v. Hanft*, 389 F. Supp. 2d 678 (D.S.C. 2005). The government appealed the decision to the Fourth Circuit Court of Appeals, which reversed the district court's decision in an opinion issued on September 9. *Padilla v. Hanft*, 423 F.3d 386 (4th Cir. 2005).

The **appellate court** reviewed the holding of *Hamdi v. Rumsfeld*, 542 U.S. 507, 124 S. Ct. 2633, 159 L. Ed. 2d 578 (2004), where the U.S. Supreme Court upheld the detention of a U.S. citizen who fought with Taliban forces in Afghanistan. The Court in a **plurality** opinion in *Hamdi* determined that the AUMF authorized the detention of the citizen because the citizen was a combatant of war. The Fourth Circuit decided that like the citizen in *Hamdi*, Padilla was an enemy combatant and that the result should be the same.

About two months later, the government submitted a motion to the Fourth Circuit, asking the court to allow the government to transfer Padilla to a civilian facility. Padilla had filed a petition for writ of **certiorari** with the Supreme Court, and the apparent purpose behind the government's motion was to avoid consideration of the issues in the case by the Court. The Fourth Circuit on December 21 denied the government's motion, deciding that the Supreme Court was the appropriate body to decide whether to approve the government's request. *Padilla v. Hanft*, 432 F.3d 582 (4th Cir. 2005). Early in January, however, the Supreme Court issued an order that granted the government's request to transfer custody to civilian authorities. Padilla was transferred to a federal detention facility in January 2006.

Like Padilla, Moussaoui's criminal case has extended over several years, with a number of delays during the process. A self-proclaimed al Qaeda operative, the government alleged that Moussaoui was part of the original September 11th plot. Had he not been arrested weeks before the attacks on an immigration violation, he would have been the twentieth hijacker, according to the government's case. Much of the prosecution's case was based on evidence from other suspected terrorists who were in the custody of the government. In 2004, the Fourth Circuit issued a complicated ruling about which witnesses that Moussaoui's counsel could depose. *United States v. Moussaoui* 382 F.3d 453 (4th Cir. 2004).

Moussaoui in April 2005 pleaded guilty to six charges of conspiracy related to his alleged terrorist activities. His trial began in February 2006. Government prosecutors sought the death penalty despite reports that the government had in its possession evidence suggesting that Moussaoui was not part of the September 11th plot. On May 3, 2006, a jury rejected the imposition of the death penalty on Moussaoui, and the court sentenced him to life in prison on the following day.

Two days after he was sentenced, Moussaoui's attorneys filed a motion to withdraw his guilty plea and request a new trial on the question of whether he was guilty as to the charges. The motion said that Moussaoui "did not have any knowledge of and was not a member of the plot to hijack planes and crash them into buildings on September 11." Because the motion was filed after he was sentenced, the court summarily denied the motion on May 8.

Renewal of PATRIOT Act Delayed but Finally Approved

After months of debate and negotiations, Congress in March 2006 authorized the renewal of the USA PATRIOT ACT, which was originally passed in 2001 at the urging of President GEORGE W. BUSH and then-Attorney General JOHN ASHCROFT. Many Democrats charged that the **statute** had been used to allow the government to infringe upon civil liberties of Americans. These concerns caused Congress to delay the act's reauthorization by several months.

In response to the SEPTEMBER 11TH ATTACKS in 2001, Congress approved the Uniting and Strengthening America by Providing Tools Required to Intercept and Obstruct Terrorism Act of 2001, Pub. L. No. 107–56, 115 Stat. 272. The statute, which was more than 100 pages long, enhanced security and surveillance procedures and authorized the use of a number of tools that the government could use to combat terrorists. Congress approved the act by overwhelming majorities in both the House and Senate in October 2001.

The AMERICAN CIVIL LIBERTIES UNION (ACLU) criticized the statute from the time of its enactment. As the government continued implementing programs to combat terrorism, the ACLU became increasingly vocal about the potential for abuse by law enforcement. By 2005, even some conservative groups, such as the American Conservative Union, had begun to question whether the act went too far in terms of impeding individual rights.

Several of the PATRIOT Act's provisions were set to expire on December 31, 2005. Representatives of the Bush administration, including Attorney General Alberto Gonzales and FEDERAL BUREAU OF INVESTIGATION Director Robert Mueller, advocated for renewal of the statute throughout much of 2005. In April, Gonzales and Mueller testified before the SENATE JUDICIARY COMMITTEE. Gonzales testified that the statute "has been an integral part of the federal government's successful prosecution of the war against terrorism" and that "now is not the time to relinquish some of our most effective tools in the fight."

Just days after one of several bombing incidents in London in July 2005, the House approved a bill that made 14 of the Act's 16 provision permanent. The bill would have extended the other two provisions for an additional 10 years. The bill passed by a vote of 257 to 171, with 14 Republicans voting against it and 43 Democrats voting in favor of it. Although support for the bill was largely partisan, several top Democrats, including Minority Whip Steny Hoyer, voted for the legislation.

While the House was considering its proposed legislation in July, the Senate was also considering its own proposal. As the Act's expiration date neared, members of the House and Senate judiciary committees met in joint session to attempt to negotiate. On December 9, the negotiators announced that they had reached a tentative deal, though other members of Congress immediately attacked the new proposal, saying that it still did not adequately protect civil rights. The House approved the conference committee's version on December 15.

Shortly after the conference committee made its announcement, news reports indicated that Bush had secretly authorized the National Security Agency to eavesdrop on American citizens in the months that followed the attacks in 2001. For some members of the Senate, this news signified that the government could not be trusted with all of the powers included in the PATRIOT Act. On December 16, members of the Senate successfully filibustered the bill when only 52 senators voted to cut off debate, eight fewer than necessary to end the **filibuster**.

The Senate blocking of the proposal left Republicans scrambling to save the act prior to December 31. Senators who opposed passage of the act said that they were willing to compromise. Those who supported the bill, however, said that they were more willing to let the statute expire than to agree to a version that they might view as less effective. After the debate continued for several more days, the Senate agreed to a six-month extension of the PATRIOT Act.

Members of the House did not agree with the length of the extension. Representative James Sensenbrenner, Jr. (R.-Wis.), the chair of the House Judiciary Committee, said that the extension "would have simply allowed the Senate to duck the issue until the last week in June." In a nearly empty chamber on December 22, the House agreed through a voice vote to extend the act until February 3. The Senate approved this extension shortly thereafter.

Negotiation continued during January and February in 2006. Most of the debate centered on the protection of certain civil liberties. At a minimum, critics wanted to limit the government's access to library and business records. Unable to reach a compromise by the February 3 deadline, the House and Senate again agreed to an extension, this time through March 10. In both chambers, negotiators attempted to add procedural safeguards that would protect civil liberties, including the allowance of court challenges to some requests for information by the government.

On March 1, the Senate approved an amended bill that included many of these procedural safeguards by a vote of 89 to 10. About a week later, the House agreed to the proposals by a vote of 280 to 138. Supporters for the final legislation noted that negotiators had added several provisions that were designed to ensure that civil liberties would not be abused. Critics, on the other hand, continued to question whether the government could be trusted with the tools provided for in the statute. Bush signed the bill on March 9.

Millennium Bomber Sentenced

Ahmed Ressam, the Algerian man who was convicted of attempting to blow up the Los Angeles airport at the turn of the millennium, was sentenced in July 2005 to 22 years in prison.

Ressam, who came to be referred to as the "Millennium Bomber," received a lighter sentence than the prosecutors had hoped for because he had helped the federal government as an informant during the years since his arrest. However, Ressam became less cooperative in 2003, and his reluctance to talk to investigators has hamstrung cases against two individuals who have been accused of conspiring with him in the Los Angeles airport bombing plot. The sentencing for Ressam had been scheduled for April of 2005, but it was postponed in the hope of eliciting further cooperation. U.S. District Judge John C. Coughenour said he had hoped that Ressam would testify against Samir Ait Mohamed and Abu Doha, who were waiting to be extradited from Canada and Britain, respectively, and who had also been charged in the airport bombing plot.

Among other useful information, Ressam supplied details that led to the capture of potential bomber Richard Reid, who attempted to blow up an American Airlines flight in 2001 with a bomb secreted in his shoe.

The Associated Press quoted public defender Thomas Hillier as saying that the government sentence did not sufficiently account for Ressam's cooperation. "It is a flat fact that law enforcement, the public, and public safety have benefited in countless ways" as a result of Ressam's cooperation with federal investigators, he said.

Ressam has reportedly provided detailed information about al-Qaeda terrorist training camps in Afghanistan and has helped U.S. authorities identify more than 100 individuals with suspected links to al-Qaeda.

U.S. customs agents arrested Ressam in 1999, when he was driving a car filled with bomb-making materials off a ferry that had arrived in Port Angeles from British Columbia.

The prosecutors had asked for a 35-year sentence, and lawyers for Ressam had asked for 12 and a half years. The attorneys for Ressam have said that he is willing to cooperate again and that his valuable help in the past justifies a "substantial reduction" in his sentence.

The government had offered a 27-year sentence, which Ressam accepted in exchange for cooperation. Although defense lawyers have said that the defense felt manipulated by the twenty-seven-year offer, government prosecutors said that Ressam knew that he would be unlikely to receive a shorter sentence, given that had been convicted of nine federal counts related to the Los Angeles airport bombing attempt. In August 2005, the government appealed and requested a longer prison term, but the sentence had not been changed by early 2006. The prosecutors justified their request by arguing that when Ressam stopped cooperating, he became eligible for a harsher sentence that would start at 65 years.

TOBACCO

Boeken v. Philip Morris Incorporated

Smokers of cigarettes have filed many civil lawsuits against tobacco companies seeking damages for injuries caused by tobacco. These lawsuits typically allege negligence, strict **product liability**, and **fraudulent** misrepresentation. A California case, *Boeken v. Philip Morris Incorporated*, 127 Cal.App.4th 1640, 26 Cal.Rptr.3d 638 (2005), drew national attention when the California **Court of Appeals** ruled that the plaintiff

Accused millennium bomber Ahmed Ressam.
CORBIS SYGMA

could use a "consumer expectations test" to show that "light" cigarettes were a defective product. In addition, the court reduced the $100 million **punitive damages** award to $50 million, signaling the need to follow a U.S. SUPREME COURT case that sought to curtail excessive punitive damages awards.

Richard Boeken started smoking cigarettes when he was 10-years old and continued to smoke until his death at age 57 from lung cancer in 2002. Boeken and his heirs sued Philip Morris Incorporated, the maker of Marlboro and Marlboro Light cigarettes, which Boeken smoked throughout his life. A California jury awarded Boeken over $5 million in **compensatory damages** and $5 billion in punitive damages. Punitive damages are a quasi-criminal remedy that seeks to punish the defendant for offensive and reprehensible conduct. The trial court reduced the punitive damages award to $100 million but Philip Morris appealed the verdict.

The California Court of Appeals for the Second District upheld the findings of negligence, product liability, and **fraud**. Justice J. Gary Hastings, writing for the court, traced the growing rate of lung cancer in the United States from the early twentieth century to the present. Lung cancer was a rare disease until the introduction of pre-rolled cigarettes in 1913. By the 1930s there was a sharp increase in the number of diagnosed lung cancer cases, a number that increased 20-fold by 1945. In the late 1940s scientists started to make statistical connections between smoking and cancer. In the 1950s the

Boeken attorney Michael Piuze speaks to media, June 2001.
AP IMAGES

tobacco companies started a public relations campaign that tried to create public doubt about the linkage between smoking and cancer, though they did not issue actual denials. In 1969 Congress enacted a law that required cigarette manufacturers to place a health warning on every cigarette package but the manufacturers continued to question the linkage between smoking and cancer. For example, in 1994 a group of tobacco executives denied under oath that smoking was addictive or that it caused cancer. Boeken testified that he seen part of these 1994 hearings and he believed they would not lie to Congress under oath. Boeken also testified to his unsuccessful attempts to quit smoking. Though he was able to end both a heroin and an alcohol addiction, he never stopped smoking for more than 30 or 40 days. In 1981 Boeken began to smoke Marlboro Light cigarettes, because they were lower in tar and nicotine. He later switched to Marlboro Ultralights. He did not find out until much later in his life that these new brands contained accelerants, additives, or chemicals that were added to increase their addictiveness. At trial Boeken testified that if Philip Morris had made clear in the 1960s, 1970s or 1980s that cigarettes caused lung cancer he would have quit smoking or made an "honest effort" to quit. In addition, he claimed he would have stopped smoking if the company had revealed it had added ingredients to increase their addictiveness.

Justice Hastings rejected the company's claim that there was not sufficient evidence to support the jury's finding that Marlboro Lights were a defective product under the consumer expectation test. This test is met when the evidence shows that "the product failed to perform as safely as an ordinary consumer would expect when used in an intended or reasonably foreseeable manner." A medical expert had testified that Marlboro Lights and Ultralights were not light at all because they delivered nicotine and tar to smokers in a way that led smokers to "compensate." Smokers compensate when they adjust the way they smoke to get a "satisfying amount of nicotine, by covering the holes in the filter, sucking harder, drawing the smoke further into the lungs, and keeping it in longer." Most smokers thought that light cigarettes were safer and did not know they compensated. As a consequence, these smokers drew carcinogens further into their lungs, which is more likely to produce a more aggressive form of lung cancer than those "more prevalent among smokers of regular cigarettes." Philip Morris argued that this test was based on a failure to warn, which was preempted by the federal Public Health Cigarettes Smoking Act of 1969. The appeals court agreed that a failure-to-warn claim would be preempted by the law but concluded that the consumer expectations test was a different **cause of action** that was not preempted.

The appeals court agreed with Philip Morris that the punitive damages award of $100 million was too high. The U.S. Supreme Court, in *State Farm Mutual Automobile Insurance Co. v. Campbell*, 538 U.S. 408, 123 S.Ct. 1513, 155 L.Ed.2d 585 (2003), sought to curtail excessive punitive damages awards by setting out several factors for courts to help determine the degree of reprehensibility. The appeals court found that these factors supported the jury's conclusion "that a substantial punitive damages award was appropriate in this case." The *State Farm* decision also stated that the computation of punitive damages should be calculated by multiplying the compensatory award by a single-digit multiplier. The appeals court ruled that despite the company's "40 years of fraud", a multiplier of 9 was justified. Multiplying the compensatory award by 9 and rounding it off led to a $50 million punitive damages award.

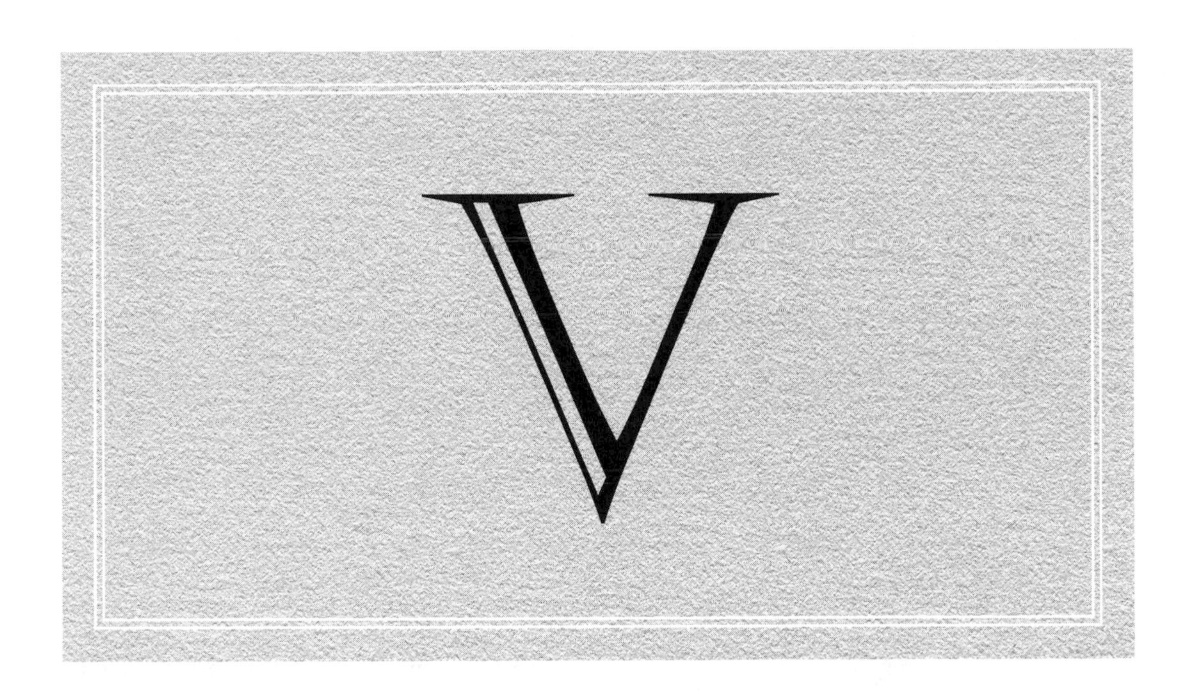

VOTING

Illinois Democrats Convicted in Vote-Buying Scheme

In June 2005, five Democrats from East St. Louis, Illinois, were found guilty in federal court for their participation in a vote-buying scheme. The charges stemmed from activity during the November 2004 election. Three committeemen and an election worker had already entered guilty pleas to charges relating to the same investigation. It is perhaps the biggest voter **fraud** conviction in the city's history.

Prosecutors contended that the purpose of the scheme was to maximize the turnout for Democrats, including Barack Obama of Chicago and U.S. Senator John Kerry, the Democratic presidential nominee. Obama was an Illinois state senator who was elected to the U.S. Senate in the November election. In the November election, Belleville, Illinois mayor Mark Kern, a Democrat, prevailed in a close race over Republican Steve Reeb, to capture the chair of the St. Clair County Board. Kern's win was spurred by his 83 percent win in East St. Louis.

Jurors deliberated more than five hours to reach a decision. The defendants were found guilty on all counts. East St. Louis DEMOCRATIC PARTY leader, Charles Powell, Jr., age 61, was convicted of conspiracy to commit fraud. Jurors listened to a recording of Powell telling committeemen to calculate their budget request based on $5 per vote. In fact, they listened to hours of secret recordings involving the defendants and FBI informers. Other evidence showed that some voters were paid $10 each.

Four others were convicted of conspiracy and aiding and **abetting** voter fraud. Sheila Thomas, 31, was the party secretary for the city's Democratic Party. Also convicted were Kelvin Ellis, age 55; Yvette Johnson, 46, an election worker; and Jesse Lewis, 56, a precinct committeeman for the 42nd Precinct in East St. Louis.

Witnesses testified that East St. Louis has had a long tradition of vote buying. For example, in 1931, paid voters typically received $2 for a vote. Five voters were convicted of accepting money in exchange for their votes. In the 2005 trial, prosecutors presented evidence about a $79,000 transfer from the county Democratic Party to many of the precinct committeemen days before the election. The defendants allegedly received a total of $7,900 two days before the election.

Defense attorneys worked to discredit government witnesses, and brought out a number of inconsistencies. However, after the verdict, one juror remarked that although the prosecution's witnesses had some credibility issues, the secret recordings provided persuasive evidence of wrongdoing.

Jesse Lewis was sentenced to 15 months in prison, a $200 fine, a $200 **special assessment**, and a two-year term of supervised release following his release. Thomas, the Democratic Precinct Committeeman for the 17th Precinct in East St. Louis, was sentenced to 18 months, plus a $200 fine and $200 special assessment. She was also ordered to a two-year supervised release term following her incarceration. Johnson was sentenced to two years' probation, with

Charles Powell, Jr. leaves federal court in East St Louis, Illinois, after sentencing on vote fraud charges.
AP IMAGES

the first five months to be served as home confinement.

Charles Powell, Jr., received a sentence of 21 months' imprisonment. He was also ordered to pay a fine of $2500, a $100 special assessment, and two years of supervised release following his incarceration.

At the time of his indictment, Kelvin Ellis was the Director of Regulatory Affairs for East St. Louis. He was terminated in April 2005, after his indictment. Ellis received a sentence of 54 months imprisonment. In addition, he was ordered to pay a fine of $2500, a $200 special assessment, and serve a three-year term of supervised release following his incarceration.

Prior to his indictment in the vote-fraud scheme, Ellis had been indicted on charges of income tax evasion and obstruction of justice in January 2005. He pleaded guilty to those charges after the guilty verdict on the voting fraud charges. He received a 21-month sentence on the tax evasion charge. The vote-buying sentence and the tax evasion sentence will run concurrently.

The obstruction of justice charges stemmed from events during late 2004. Ellis learned that an individual had become a cooperating government witness in the federal **grand jury** investigation regarding election fraud and vote buying. Ellis and a government informant planned to discredit the individual by planting drugs on her, and then to have her arrested and jailed. The indictment also alleged that he later schemed to have the woman killed to prevent her ongoing cooperation.

Several States Fail to Comply with Election Reform Law

Electionline.org, a nonpartisan group that studies the implementation of election laws, reported that many states are not compliant with a 2002 federal election law. The report noted that among the problems with implementation of the requirements were controversies regarding the need for paper trails and the legality of voter identification requirements.

Congress enacted the Help American Vote Act of 2002 (HAVA), Pub. L. No. 107–252, 116 Stat. 1666, in order to provide funding for states to update voting systems and to establish minimum election administration standards for states and local governments. The enactment of HAVA was largely the result of the 2000 presidential election. The **statute** established the Election Assistance Commission to assist in the administration of federal elections. The statute established January 1, 2006 as a deadline for several of its deadlines.

Electionline.org has advocated election reform since the 2000 elections. After Congress set forth requirements by enacting HAVA in 2002, the organization began publishing *Election Reform: What's Changed, What Hasn't, and Why*, which summarizes the effort among the states of implementing the statute's requirements. The report is available for free download on the organization's Web site, at http://www.electionline.org.

The organization's director, Doug Chapin, has noted the changes in voting procedures since the debacle of the 2000 presidential election. "The issue of election reform has matured rapidly in the past few years," Chapin said. "Two years ago, few people had ever heard of voter-verified paper audit trails; now, states are deciding whether to use them in recounts. In many states, the debate over whether voter ID should be required has evolved into whether voters should be provided IDs free of charge. In those states and others, fears about a lack of federal funding for HAVA mandates have subsided, leaving new concerns about state legislatures' ability (and willingness) to make funds available to maintain federally-funded improvements."

One of the major concerns addressed by the 2002 legislation was the replacement of the punch card and lever voting machines used by many states. It first appeared that paperless electronic voting machines would replace these older systems. However, electronic machines that were used in such states as Florida, North Carolina, Indiana, Maryland, and California have had problems with certification questions, security concerns, and questions about reliability and accuracy. In one election in North Carolina, an electronic voting machine did not accurately count the votes for a statewide election due to a programming error. Electionline.org referred to this as a "nightmarish scenario."

One solution to the problems caused by paperless voting machines has been the implementation of voter-verified paper audit trails (VVPATs), which produce a printed record of each vote. These records can be used to conduct an **independent audit** of a paperless vote. The states of Florida, Maryland, and Georgia first implemented requirements of electronic voting with independent paper trails in 2003. As of 2006, 25 states require VVPATs.

People with disabilities have raised concerns with the newer voting methods, however. Many machines have been designed to be convenient for voters, but do not take into account all of the needs of disabled persons. For instance, some machines require the voter to handle marked ballots in order to vote. A disabled person who is unable to handle paper must rely on a non-disabled person to submit a vote. Electionline.org estimates that more than one-third of the states fail to meet requirements that every polling place have at least one machine available for use by those with disabilities.

HAVA included a somewhat unpopular provision that required voters to show IDs at polling locations. Prior to 2002, only 11 states had ID requirements. The issue of voter IDs has been a partisan one, with Republicans generally favoring their use and Democrats generally opposing them. In 2005, the Commission on Federal Election Reform, chaired by former President JIMMY CARTER, endorsed a universal ID system. Despite Carter's presence on the commission, Democrats immediately argued against the proposal.

The major concern over the requirement of IDs has been that many voters, especially those who are poor, elderly, or members of minorities, could effectively become disenfranchised as a result of ID requirements. The reason for this concern is that citizens that fall into those categories are less likely to have a driver's license or another form of a government-issued photo ID and would be less likely to obtain one. Supporters of the ID requirement say that the ID proposal would actually add citizens to the voter rolls.

The statute also requires the development of a uniform voter registration database in each state. Electionline.org's report found that more than 20 percent of the states did not have compliant databases. The report noted additionally that Congress approved $3.9 billion to upgrade the election system across the country but has only allotted $3 billion since the statute's enactment.

According to the JUSTICE DEPARTMENT, the state of New York lags behind all others in updating their election system. It is one of the states that does not have a HAVA-compliant database, and several proposals to upgrade voting machines have stalled in the state's legislature. The concern over New York's failure to upgrade its election procedures and equipment led the Justice Department to threaten to sue the state. State officials said that they were working with the department to avoid intervention by the courts.

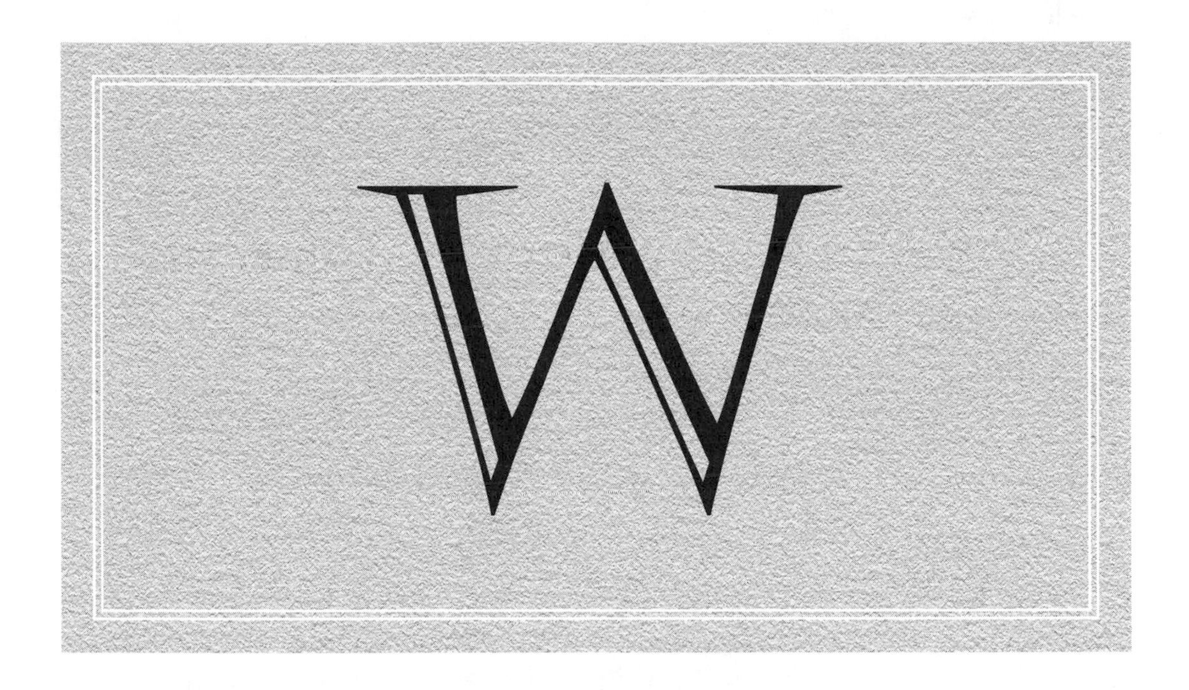

WAIVER

The voluntary surrender of a known right; conduct supporting an inference that a particular right has been relinquished.

Zedner v. United States

The Speedy Trial Act of 1974, 18 USC 3161 *et seq.*, generally requires a federal criminal trial to begin within 70 days after a defendant is charged or makes an initial appearance. In recognition of valid reasons why extra time may be needed, the Act includes a lengthy list of periods of delay that are excluded in computing the time within which trial must commence. To promote compliance, the Act requires dismissal of pending charges if a trial does not start on time and the defendant files a motion to dismiss prior to the start of trial or entry of a guilty plea. In *Zedner v. United States*, No.05–5992, 547 U.S. ___ (2006), the U.S. SUPREME COURT dismissed a criminal defendant's waiver "for all time" of his right to a speedy trial under the Act, as ineffective, because a defendant may not prospectively waive the application of the Act.

In March 1996, Jacob Zedner attempted to open an account at several financial institutions by depositing a counterfeit $10 million dollar bond issued by the fictitious "Ministry of Finance of U.S.A." Several mistakes in the bond caused each institution to refrain from opening an account for Zedner, and one alerted the United States SECRET SERVICE. Shortly thereafter, Zedner was arrested, and several more counterfeit bonds were found in his briefcase. A **grand jury** later indicted him on several counts of attempting to defraud a financial institution under 18 USC 1344, and one count of knowingly possessing counterfeit bonds, under 18 USC 472.

Zedner's attorney did not appear at the first status conference, and in accordance with the Speedy Trial Act, the **district court** excluded the time delay until a second scheduled conference under one of the Act's exclusionary exceptions. This was but the beginning of a convoluted series of delays and exclusionary orders issued by the court, based on a myriad of reasons. It was undisputed that Zedner and/or his counsel caused or contributed to many of the delays.

One of the enumerated exclusionary provisions under the Act is for "ends-of-justice" continuances under §3161(h)(8). This permits a district court to grant continuances and exclude the delay if it makes findings on the record that the ends of justice served by granting the continuance outweigh the public's and defendant's interests in a speedy trial. The district court granted two of these, citing on the record the complexity of the case as reason. However, at the November 8, 1996 status conference, Zedner requested yet a further adjournment until January 1997 (unopposed by the government), and the district court noted on the record its concerns. Then the court instructed Zedner and his attorney that if such a lengthy adjournment were granted, the court would have to take a waiver for all time. Defense counsel responded that defense would "waive for all time. That will not be a problem. That will not be an issue in this case." The record on appeal reflected that the court then attempted to explain to Zedner the operation of §3162(a)(2) of the Act, under which a defendant waives his right to move for dismissal based on a trial that does not start on time, unless he or she files a motion prior to trial or entry of a guilty plea. The Court then produced a pre-printed form, captioned "Waiver of Speedy Trial Rights," and both Zedner and defense counsel signed it.

Four years of proceedings, delays, competency hearings, and continuances followed, but no trial. Even though the district court admonished defense counsel for some of the delays, it made no mention of the Act and did not make any findings on the record to support exclusion of a 91-day period between January 31 and May 2, 1997 (the 1997 continuance).

In March 2001, Zedner filed a motion to dismiss the indictment, citing failure to comply with the Act. The district court denied the motion on the grounds of Zedner's waiver "for all time" and the complexity of the case. In April 2003, trial began, and Zedner was ultimately convicted and sentenced to prison.

The Second **Circuit Court** of Appeals affirmed the conviction. Although it acknowledged that a defendant's waiver of rights under the Act may be ineffective because of the public interest served by compliance with the Act, it found that an exception could be found for situations "when defendant's conduct causes or contributes to a period of delay." 401 F.3d at 43–44 (quoting *United States v. Gambino*, 59 F.3d 353). The **appellate court** also suggested that the district court's failure to place findings on the record for the 1997 continuance might be harmless, because the court could just as well have properly excluded that period under the "ends-of-justice" exception, given the case complexity and defense's request for additional preparatory time.

The U.S. Supreme Court granted **certiorari** on three related questions: whether the waiver was effective; whether Zedner was estopped from challenging the validity of the waiver; and whether the trial judge's failure to make the findings required to exclude a period of delay under §3161(h)(8) of the Act constituted **harmless error**. A nearly unanimous Court ultimately reversed and remanded.

The Court held that a defendant could not prospectively waive the application of the Act because the Act does not allow a defendant to opt out. Instead, it demands any continuance to fit within one of its specific exclusions. If a defendant could simply waive the Act's application in order to secure more time, no defendant would ever need to articulate reasons before the court to justify qualification for one of the enumerated exceptions.

Next, the Court held that Zedner was not estopped from challenging the excludability of the 1997 continuance. An **estoppel** based on Zedner's promise not to move for dismissal would entirely swallow the Act's no-waiver policy.

Finally, the Court held that when a district court makes no findings on the record to support a §3161(h)(8) continuance, harmless error review is not available or appropriate.

WHISTLEBLOWING

The disclosure by a person, usually an employee, in a government agency or private enterprise; to the public or to those in authority, of mismanagement, corruption, illegality, or some other wrongdoing.

Garcetti v. Ceballos

The Supreme Court has examined a number of cased involving the FIRST AMENDMENT rights of public employees. The Court has allowed an employee to speak out "as a citizen upon matters of public concern" and has stated that a public employee does not surrender all First Amendment rights upon government employment. However, the Court withdrew First Amendment protection from public employees when they speak out in the course of their official duties. The decision in *Garcetti v. Ceballos*, __U.S.__, 126 S.Ct., __L.Ed.2d __ 2006 WL 1458026 (2006), affects millions of public employees and suggests that employees may be protected if they write a letter to the editor but not an internal memorandum.

Richard Ceballos was a long-time employee of the Los Angeles County District Attorney's Office, serving as a deputy district attorney. In 2000 he was a calendar deputy in the office's Pomona branch, where he supervised other lawyers. He was contacted by a defense lawyer who complained that an affidavit supporting a search warrant included inaccurate information. Ceballos investigated the affidavit and contacted a deputy sheriff who did not give him a satisfactory explanation. He then wrote a memorandum to his supervisors, outlining his findings and recommending dismissal of the case. Ceballos wrote a second memorandum, which led to a meeting with his supervisors and employees of the sheriff's department. The meeting became heated and Ceballos was criticized by an police officer. Despite his objections, his supervisors allowed the case to proceed. The defense lawyer called him as a witness in hearing that challenged the warrant. The judge sustained the warrant. Ceballos alleged that he was subjected to retaliatory actions because of memo in the warrant dispute. He was reassigned to a trial deputy position in another courthouse and was denied promotion. After failing to win an employee grievance proceeding, he filed a federal civil rights lawsuit in federal **district court**, alleging that his supervisors had violated the First Amendment by retaliating against him based on the original memorandum. The district court dismissed his action, finding that the memo was not protected by the First Amendment because the memo had been written as part of his job duties. The Ninth **Circuit Court** of Appeals reversed this decision, holding that Ceballos's memo constituted protected speech under the First Amendment. The court concluded that the memo raised matters of "public concern" that required it to balance Ceballos's interest in his speech against his supervisors' interests in responding to it. The court came down on Ceballos's side, finding that the memo did not disrupt the office or cause any inefficiencies.

The Supreme Court, in a 5–4 decision, overruled the Ninth Circuit. Justice ANTHONY KENNEDY, writing for the majority, held that "when public employees make statements pursuant to their official duties, the employees are not speaking as citizens for First Amendment purposes, and the Constitution does not insulate their communications from employer discipline." The "controlling factor" in the case was that Ceballos's expressions were made pursuant to his duties as calendar deputy. It was part of his job to write the memo and it was "immaterial whether he experienced some personal gratification" in writing it. Restricting employee free speech rights reflected the "exercise of employer control over what the employer itself has commissioned or created."

Justice Kennedy reasoned that employers had a strong interest in controlling the speech of employees, for "official communications have official consequences." In Ceballos's case, his supervisors had the authority to take corrective action if they believed his memo was inflammatory or wrong. To rule otherwise would draw state and **federal courts** into the oversight of internal government speech controversies between supervisors and employees. This "displacement of managerial discretion by judicial supervision" was not supported by prior cases. However, Justice Kennedy made clear that public employees could be protected by the First Amendment if they communicated their concerns in a public forum. In addition, employers could not seek to restrict employees' rights by crafting broad job descriptions that would cover a broad range of professional duties. Kennedy noted that public employees still have access to whistle-blower protection laws to expose wrongdoing. Finally, he declined to extend this holding to academic scholarship or classroom instruction, leaving that issue for another day.

Justice JOHN PAUL STEVENS, in a dissenting opinion, found it "perverse to fashion a new rule that provides employees with an incentive to voice their concerns publicly before talking frankly to their superiors." Justice DAVID SOUTER, in a dissent joined by Justices Stevens and RUTH BADER GINSBURG, argued that the balancing test used by the Ninth Circuit was the proper course of action. This case-by-case approach was superior to a bright line rule. The government employer had substantial interests in implementing its "chosen policy and objectives," yet the "private and public interests in addressing official wrongdoing and threat to health and safety can outweigh the government stake" in implementing its policy. Public employees should be eligible to claim First Amendment protections when they "speak on matters in the course of their duties."

WIRETAPPING

A form of electronic eavesdropping accomplished by seizing or overhearing communications by means of a concealed recording or listening device connected to the transmission line.

Government Tracks Foreign and Domestic Communications

In spring 2006, the facts came to light to suggest that the National Security Agency had amassed a massive database of domestic phone records totaling billions of calls within the U.S. Allegedly, the agency does not possess the content of the calls, but it does have records of when calls were made and to which numbers. President GEORGE W. BUSH told the press, "We are not trolling through the personal lives of innocent Americans."

After the September 11th attacks in 2001, President Bush wanted to take action, and although he believed that the public would support measures that would help identify terrorists and prevent another attack, he kept the phone and Internet surveillance a secret from the public, although members of Congress from both parties were briefed on the plan.

In December 2005, the *New York Times* broke the story that the NSA had been monitoring the international phone calls and Internet messages of people inside the U.S. without obtaining warrants. Former NSA director General Michael Hayden, who at the time of writing was the likely candidate to take over leadership of the CENTRAL INTELLIGENCE AGENCY, had said in public statements that the NSA only monitored international calls, not domestic calls.

A senior Bush administration official who asked to remain anonymous was quoted in a *Newsweek* article as saying that the NSA's eavesdropping on international calls had, in fact, identified and foiled terrorist operations, although the official declined to be more specific.

Although legal experts have been quoted as saying that the government could collect a database of phone records without infringing the privacy of U.S. citizens, the three phone companies that cooperated with the NSA's request for records, BellSouth, Verizon, and AT&T, could be sued by their customers for violating the restrictions imposed by seemingly arcane communications laws. The NSA was allegedly banned from domestic spying in the 1970s in the wake of the WATERGATE scandal, when the story emerged that the government had been conducting domestic espionage activities such as opening the mail and tapping the phones of perceived enemies of the state.

Once the government has the phone records, the next step is to "data-mine" or look for patterns in the endless flow of electronic traffic that might identify a terrorist before he or she acts. However, data mining is a work in progress, and savvy terrorists may avoid phones for that reason, opting to hide messages on web sites, for example. With no record of any e-mail or phone call, the NSA has no way of intercepting such messages, which calls the value of wiretapping into question.

The NSA's activities since September 11, 2001, including eavesdropping on international calls and collecting records of domestic calls, could threaten citizens' rights to privacy. The risk of invading someone's privacy must be balanced with the probability that broad-based phone surveillance will result in the early capture of terrorists. The details as to whether the government monitors the personal phone and Internet communications of ordinary citizens who have not been convicted of a crime in the interest of national security remain uncertain.

Another layer of intrigue surfaced in 2006 when the FEDERAL BUREAU OF INVESTIGATION admitted to seeking news reporters' phone records in order to investigate leaked information on such subjects as secret prisons in Europe and wiretapping of U.S. citizens' phones without a warrant.

Although some members of Congress defended the NSA's activities as an important aspect of national security, others said that they found the report of domestic surveillance disturbing, and 52 members of Congress asked the president to appoint a special counsel to investigate the matter.

The New York Times reported that the NSA may have eavesdropped on the international phone calls between U.S. residents and thousands of people overseas since September 11, 2001, and the *Washington Post* reported that almost all of the 5000 U.S. citizens who had been subject to eavesdropping had been cleared of any suspicion.

President Bush emphasized that domestic call-tracing was not the same as eavesdropping on calls while they are taking place. The administration has remained circumspect on the subject and has maintained that domestic calls are only being logged into a database and not monitored.

Statements from AT&T, Verizon, and BellSouth said that the companies had protected customers' privacy. The companies refrained from discussing details.

The AMERICAN CIVIL LIBERTIES UNION (ACLU)launched campaigns in 20 states in May 2006 to attempt to stop the NSA from eavesdropping on calls and from acquiring information from phone companies. The FEDERAL COMMUNICATIONS COMMISSION has said that it will not pursue complaints against the NSA at this time because it is unable to obtain classified material, and this lack of action prompted the ACLU to take the issue to the states.

Attorney General Alberto R. Gonzales defended the data collection by citing a 1979 case heard by the U.S. SUPREME COURT, *Smith v. Maryland* 442 U.S. 735, 99 S.Ct. 2577, 61 L.Ed.2d 220, in which police officers installed a surveillance device at its central office in order to monitor the numbers called by a **robbery** suspect. Since the device was not installed at the person's home, his privacy was not violated, and since the numbers called appeared on a monthly phone bill, there should have been no expectation of privacy with regard to the locations of the calls.

Gonzales was quoted in a *Washington Post* article as saying, "There is no reasonable expectation of privacy in those kinds of records," and his reference to the 1979 case hints that similar devices may be in use as part of the current NSA operation.

BIBLIOGRAPHY

ABORTION

AYOTTE V. PLANNED PARENTHOOD OF NORTHERN NEW ENGLAND

Greenhouse, Linda. "Court in Transition." *New York Times.* February 22, 2006.

Greenhouse, Linda. "Justices Reaffirm Abortion Access For Emergencies." *New York Times.* January 19, 2006.

Holland, Gina. "Supreme Court Gives New Hampshire A Chance To Save Its Abortion Limits." *Boston Globe.* January 19. 2006.

INDIANA, MISSOURI SUPREME COURTS UPHOLD WAITING PERIODS FOR ABORTIONS

Franck, Matt, "24-Hour Wait for Abortion Is Upheld in Missouri," *St. Louis Post-Dispatch*, Feb. 28, 2006.

Martin, Deanna, "Ind. Court Upholds Abortion Waiting Period," ABCNews.com, Nov. 23, 2005, <http://abcnews.go.com/US/LegalCenter/wireStory?id=1340666&CMP=OTC-RSSFeeds0312>.

COURTS STRIKE DOWN PARTIAL BIRTH ABORTION BAN ACT

Henderson, Stephen, "Justices Take Key Case on Abortion," *Philadelphia Inquirer*, February 22, 2006, at A1.

Savage, David G., "Major Abortion Case Goes to Justices," *L.A. Times*, February 22, 2006, at 1.

SOUTH DAKOTA LAW BANS MOST ABORTIONS

Davey, Monica, "Ripples from Law Banning Abortion Spread Through South Dakota," *New York Times*, April 16, 2006, at 114.

Davey, Monica, "South Dakota's Governor Says He Favors Abortion Ban Bill," *New York Times*, February 25, 2006.

Haga, Chuck, "Abortion Test," *Star-Tribune*, April 2, 2006, at 1A.

Nieves, Evelyn, "S.D. Abortion Bill Takes Aim at 'Roe'," *Washington Post*, February 23, 2006, at A01.

ALIENS

FERNANDEZ-VARGAS V. GONZALES

Fernandez-Vargas v. Gonzales, No. 04-1376, 548 U.S. ___ (2006), Available at www.supremecourtus.gov/opinions

"Fernandez-Vargas v. Gonzales." Summary available at http://law.duke.edu./archives

Lane, Charles. "Ruling Opens Doors to Deportations." *Washington Post*, 23 June 2006. Page A16.

Shawl, Jeannie. "Supreme Court Rules on Deportation, . . ." *Jurist*, 22 June 2006. Available at http://www.jurist.law.pitt.edu/paperchase/2006/06/supreme-court-rules-on-deportation.php

"Samuel A. Alito, Jr." *Biography Resource Center Online.* Gale, 2005.

AMERICANS WITH DISABILITIES ACT

U.S. V. GEORGIA

Greenhouse, Linda. "Supreme Court Allows Disabled Georgia Inmate to Proceed With Suit Against State." *New York Times.* January 11, 2006.

Lane, Charles. "Court Hears Paraplegic Inmate's Case." *Washington Post.* November 10, 2005.

Holland, Gina. "Supreme Court Backs Disabled Ga. Inmate. *Boston Globe.* January 11, 2006.

ANTITRUST LAW

ILLINOIS TOOL WORKS INC. V. INDEPENDENT INK, INC.

Mauro, Tony. "High Court Patent Ruling a Victory for Big Business." *www.law.com* March 1, 2006.

Gellhorn, Ernset. *Antitrust Law And Economics In A Nutshell.* Saint Paul, MN.: West Group. Fifth Edition, 2004.

American Bar Association. *Market Power Handbook: Competition Law and Economic Foundation.* Chicago, Ill.: 2006.

TEXACO INC.V. DAGHER

Holland, Gina. "Supreme Court Throws Out Gas Prices Suit. *Seattle Post-Intelligencer.* February 28, 2006.

Gellhorn, Ernset. *Antitrust Law And Economics In A Nutshell.* Saint Paul, MN.: West Group. Fifth Edition, 2004.

American Bar Association. *Market Power Handbook: Competition Law and Economic Foundation.* Chicago, Ill.: 2006.

VOLVO TRUCKS NORTH AMERICA, INC. V. REEDER-SIMCO GMC, INC.

American Bar Association. *Market Power Handbook: Competition Law and Economic Foundation.* Chicago, Ill.: 2006.

Gellhorn, Ernset. *Antitrust Law And Economics In A Nutshell.* Saint Paul, MN.: West Group. Fifth Edition, 2004.

Macavoy, Christopher. *A Primer on the Federal Price Discrimination Laws: A General Review of the Robinson-Patman Act for Business Managers.* Chicago, Ill.: American Bar Associaton. 1999.

Volvo Trucks North America, Inc. v. Reeder-Simco GMC, Inc., __U.S.__, 126 S.Ct. 860, 163 L.Ed.2d 663 (2006)

ARBITRATION

BUCKEYE CHECK CASHING, INC. V. CARDEGNA

Nolan-Haley, Jaqueline. *Alternative Dispute Resolution In A Nutshell.* Saint Paul, MN: Westgroup. Second Edition. 2001.

Barett, Jerome. *A History of Alternative Dispute Resolution: The Story of a Political, Social, and Cultural Movement.* Hoboken, N.J.: Jossey-Bass. 2004.

Ware, Stephen. *Alternative Dispute Resolution.* Saint Paul, MN: Westgroup. 2001.

ASSISTED SUICIDE

GONZALES V. OREGON

Barnett, Jim, "Given Ruling, Smith Says He Won't Fight Assisted Suicide," *The Oregonian*, January 18, 2006, A1.

McCall, William, "Little Change in Suicide Since Ruling," *Seattle Times*, March 10, 2006.

ATTORNEY

RISE IN INTERNET LEGAL SERVICES RAISES QUESTIONS

Averitt, James J., "Legal Ethics and the Internet: Defining a Lawyer's Responsibility in a New Frontier," *Journal of the Legal Profession*, 2004–2005, at 171.

Levin, John, "Unauthorized Practice: Who Brings a Claim? And Who Pays?" *CBA Record*, May 2005, at 47.

McCauley, James M., "Legal Ethics in Cyberspace," Virginia Lawyer Register, December 2000.

BANKRUPTCY

CENTRAL VIRGINIA COMMUNITY COLLEGE V. KATZ

Epstein, David. *Bankruptcy and Related Law in a Nutshell.* St. Paul, MN: West. 2004. Seventh Edition.

Skeel, David. *Debt's Dominion: A History of Bankruptcy Law in America.* Princteon, NJ: Princeton University Press. 2003.

Mann, Bruce. *Republic of Debtors: Bankruptcy in the Age of American Independence.* Cambridge, MA: Harvard University Press. 2003.

HOWARD DELIVERY SERVICE V. ZURICH

Bennett, Brian. "Howard Delivery Service v.Zurich American Insurance Co." *On the Docket*, 15 June 2006. Available at http://docket.medill.northwestern.edu/archives.

Gudsnuk, Sarah and Nathan Burgess. "Venable Appellate Team Secures Major Win in U.S. Supreme Court Resolving Circuit Split on Priority of Unsecured Creditors in Bankruptcy." Venable Press Release, 19 June 2006. Available at http://www.venable.com/news.

Howard Delivery Service v. Zurich American Insurance Co., No.05–128U.S. ___ (2006). Available at www.supremecourtus.gov/opinions.

UNIFORM DEBT MANAGEMENT SERVICES ACT

"#6: Consumer Credit Counseling Organizations." Panel on the Nonprofit Sector, 22 September 2005. Available at http://www.nonprofitpanel.org/supplemental/6_credit

"ABA Approves New State Law that Regulates the Credit Counseling Industry." NCCUSL News Display, 13 February 2006. Available at http://www.nccusl.org

"Comments on the NCCUSL's Uniform Debt Management Service Act." National Consumer Law Center, Inc., March 2006. Available at http://www.consumerlaw.org/action

"The New Uniform Debt-Management Services Act." ABA Newsletter, undated Available at http://www.abanet.org/bus/law/newsletter/0044/materials/pp2.pdf

"Uniform Debt-Management Services Act." 10 November 2005. Available at http://www.law.upenn.edu/bll/ulc/UCDC/2005Final.htm

BIRTH CONTROL

WAL-MART SUED FOR FAILING TO STOCK EMERGENCY CONTRACEPTIVES

Banks, Margaret Moffett, "Druggist Refusals Gaining Exposure," *News & Record*, April 24, 2005, A1.

Belluck, Pam, "Massachusetts Veto Seeks to Curb Morning-After Pill," *New York Times*, July 26, 2005.

Coleman-Lochner, Lauren, "Under Pressure, Wal-Mart Will Sell the Morning-After Pill," *Philadelphia Inquirer*, March 4, 2006, A6.

Greenberger, Scott S., "Lawmakers Override Governor's Contraception Veto," *Boston Globe*, Sept. 16, 2005.

Mohl, Bruce, "Suit Aims to Force Wal-Mart to Sell Pill," *Boston Globe*, Feb. 1, 2006, E1.

Thottam, Jyoti, "A Big Win for Plan B," *Time*, March 13, 2006, 41.

"Wal-Mart Urged to Stock 'Morning-After' Pills," *New Jersey Record*, Feb. 4, 2006, A9.

CAPITAL PUNISHMENT

BROWN V. SANDERS

Bedau, Hugo and Cassell, Paul. *Debating the Death Penalty.* New York: Oxford Univ. Press. 2004.

Banner, Stuart. *The Death Penalty: An American History.* Cambridge, Mass.: Harvard Univ. Press. 2003.

Cohen, Stanley. *The Wrong Men: America's Epidemic of Wrongful Death Row Convictions.* New York: Carroll and Graf. 2003.

ABA RECOMMENDS MORATORIUM ON DEATH PENALTY IN GEORGIA

American Bar Association, "Death Penalty Moratorium Implementation Project: Georgia. Available at www.abanet.org/moratorium/assessmentproject/georgia.html

Associated Press, "Report: Georgia Should Have Moratorium on Seeking Death Penalty," Macon.com, Jan. 29, 2006. Available at www.macon.com/mld/macon/news/politics/13742929.htm.

Press Release, "Georgia Cannot Ensure Fairness, Accuracy in Death Penalty Cases, Says State Legal Team in ABA Project," American Bar Association. Available at http://www.abanet.org/media/releases/news013006.html.

HILL V. MCDONOUGH

Hill v. McDonough No. 05-8794, 547 U.S. ___ (2006), Available at <www.supremecourtus.gov/opinions>

"Hill v. McDonough." *Duke Law*,. Available at <www.law.duke.edu/publiclaw/supremecourtonline/cergrants/2005/hilvcro.html>

KANSAS V. MARSH

Lane, Charles. "Justices Clash Over Death Penalty Case." *Washington Post.* June 27, 2006.

Greenhouse, Linda. "Supreme Court Roundup." *New York Times.* June 26, 2006.

Bedau, Hugo, and Paul Cassell. *Debating the Death Penalty.* New York: Oxford Univ. Press. 2004.

NEW JERSEY SUSPENDS EXECUTIONS, PENDING STUDY

Chen, David W., "Suspension of the Death Penalty Is All but Assured in New Jersey," *New York Times*, Jan. 6, 2006.

McHugh, Margaret, "Moratorium on Executions Puts Murder Trial Status in Question," *Star-Ledger*, Mar. 24, 2006, at 37.

"New Jersey Legislature Suspends Death Penalty," MSNBC.com, Jan. 9, 2006. Available at www.msnbc.msn.com/id/10779872/.

OREGON V. GUZEK

Bedau, Hugo and Cassell, Paul. *Debating the Death Penalty.* New York: Oxford Univ. Press. 2004.

Banner, Stuart. *The Death Penalty: An American History.* Cambridge, Mass.: Harvard Univ. Press. 2003.

Cohen, Stanley. *The Wrong Men: America's Epidemic of Wrongful Death Row Convictions.* New York: Carroll and Graf. 2003.

CENSUS

LEAGUE OF UNITED LATIN AMERICAN CITIZENS V. PERRY

League of United Latin American Citizens v. Perry, No.05–204, 548 U.S. ___ (2006). Available at www.supremecourtus.gov/opinions.

Kitte, Damian. "League of United Latin American Citizens v. Perry." *Election Law Litigation*, 29 June 2006. Available at moritzlaw.osu.edu/electionlaw/litigation/LULACdecisionchart.php.

Shawl, Jeannie. "Supreme Court Leaves Texas Redistricting Map Largely Intact." *Jurist*, 28 June 2006. Available at www.jurist.law.pitt.edu/paperchase/2006/06/supreme-court-leaves-texas.php.

CIVIL PROCEDURE

UNITHERM FOOD SYSTEMS, INC. V. SWIFT-ECKRICH, INC.

Baicker-McKee, Steven. *Student's Guide to the Federal Rules of Civil Procedure.* St. Paul,MN: West. 2005.

Kane, Mary Kay. *Civil Procedure in a Nutshell.* St. Paul, MN: West. 2003.

Wright, Charles Alan. *Law of Federal Courts.* Saint Paul, MN: West Group. 2002. Sixth Edition.

CIVIL RIGHTS

BURLINGTON NORTHERN & SANTA FE RAILWAY CO. V. WHITE

Burlington Northern & Santa Fe Railway Co. v. White, No. 05–259, 548 U.S. ___ (2006), Available at www.supremecourtus.gov/opinions

Savage, David G. "Justices Define Employer Reprisal Liberally." *Los Angeles Times*, 23 June 2006.

DOMINO'S PIZZA, INC. V. MCDONALD

Lewis, Jr., Harold and Norman, Elizabeth. *Civil Rights Law and Practice.* St. Paul, MN: West Group. 2004.

Vieira, Norman. *Constitutional Civil Rights in a Nutshell.* St. Paul, MN.: West Group. 1998.

Rohwer, Claude D., and Anthony M. Skroki. *Contracts in a Nutshell.* St. Paul, MN.: West Group. 2000.

CLASS ACTION

KIRCHER V. PUTNAM FUNDS TRUST

Kircher v. Putnam Funds Trust, No. 05–409, 547 U.S. ___ (2006), Available at www.supremecourtus.gov/opinions

Settles, William. "Kircher Decided." *The 10B-5 Daily*, 16 June 2006. Available at http://www.the10b-5daily.com/archives/000721.html

"Kircher v. Putnam Funds." Summary available at http://law.duke.edu./archives

MERRILL LYNCH, PIERCE, FENNER & SMITH V. DABIT

Masters, Brooke, "Ruling Limits Investors' Legal Options." *Washington Post.* March 22, 2006.

"Justices Limit Jurisdiction of States in Investor Suits." *New York Times.* March 22, 2006.

Holland, Gina. "Supreme Court Blocks State Investor Class-Action Suits. *Boston Glove* March 22, 2206.

CLEAN WATER ACT

RAPANOS V. UNITED STATES

Savage, David. "Divided Supreme Court Upholds Federal Protections for Wetlands." *Los Angeles Times.* June 20, 2006.

Lane, Charles. "Justices Rein in Clean Water Act." *Washington Post.* June 20, 2006.

Greenhouse, Linda. "Justices Divided on Protections Over Wetlands." *New York Times.* June 20, 2006.

S.D. WARREN COMPANY V. MAINE BOARD OF ENVIRONMENTAL PROTECTION

Findley, Roger. *Environmental Law in Nutshell.* St. Paul, MN: West Group. 2004. Sixth Edition.

Getches. David. *Water Law in a Nutshell.* St. Paul, MN: West Group. 1997. Third Edition.

Shiva, Vandana. *Water Wars: Privatization, Pollution, and Profit.* Cambridge, MA: South End Press. 2002.

COMMERCE CLAUSE

DAIMLERCHRYSLER CORP. V. CUNO

"Supreme Court Throws Out Ohio Tax Incentive Case," *Cincinnati Business Courier* , May 15, 2006.

Yost, Pete, "High Court Blocks Tax Incentive Suit," *Cincinnati Post*, May 16, 2006.

CONSPIRACY

TOM DELAY INDICTED, RESIGNS SEAT IN CONGRESS

Shenon, Philip and Carl Hulse, "Delay is Indicted in Texas Case and Forfeits G.O.P. House Post," *New York Times*, Sept. 29, 2005.

Smith, R. Jeffrey, "DeLay Indicted in Texas Finance Probe," *Washington Post*, Sept. 29, 2005, A1.

Smith, R. Jeffrey and Jonathan Weisman, "DeLay Departing on Own Terms," *Washington Post*, April 5, 2006, A1.

CONVICTION OF FORMER ALABAMA GOVERNOR DON SIEGELMAN

Bank of China v. NBM, LLC, et al No. 02-9267, Available at www.lawprofessors.typepad.com

Curran, Eddie; Barrow, Bill; and Sallie Owen. "Siegelman, Scrushy Found Guilty: Hamrick, Roberts Acquitted." *Alabama Press-Register*, 30 June 2006.

Lowry, Bob. "Siegelman, Scrushy Vow to Win Appeal." *Montgomery Advertiser*, 30 June 2006.

Rawls, Phillip. "Convictions Spotlight History of Corruptions." *Montgomery Advertiser*, 11 July 2006.

U.S. Dept. of Justice. "Former Alabama Governor Don Siegelman, Others Indicted in Racketeering, Bribery and Extortion Conspiracy." *DOJ News Release*, 26 October 2005. Available at http://www.usdoj.gov/opa/pr/2005/October/05crm_568.html

Whitmire, Kyle. "Ex-Governor and Executive Convicted of Bribery." *New York Times*, 30 June 2006.

CONSULS

SANCHEZ-LLAMAS V. OREGON

Sanchez-Llamas v. Oregon, No.04–10566, 548 U.S. ___ (2006). Available at www.supremecourtus.gov/opinions

Nelson, Samantha. "Sanchez-Llamas v. Oregon." Medill News Service, 28 June 2006. Available at http://docket.medill.northwestern.edu/archives

Rushford, Michael. "Supreme Court Denies Claim to Suppress Confession." Press Release, Criminal Justice Legal Foundation (CJLF), 17 June 2006. Available at http://www.cljf.org/releases/06–17.htm

CORPORATE FRAUD

TOP ENRON EXECUTIVES CONVICTED

Babineck, Mark, "Lawyers Who Saw Lay Testify Say Abrasive Way is Ill-Advised," *Houston Chronicle*, May 3, 2006.

Flood, Mary, "Lay Defends Lavish Habits and Big Cash Withdrawals," *Houston Chronicle*, May 2, 2006.

Flood, Mary, "Lay Gets Loud and Angry with Prosecutor," *Houston Chronicle*, April 27, 2006.

Barton, Jill. "Perelman Wins Round in Suit Against Morgan Stanley." *Associated Press*, May 17, 2005.

Beck, Susan. "Recipe for Disaster." *The American Lawyer*, April 1, 2006.

Craig, Susanne. "How Morgan Stanley botched a big case by fumbling e-mails." *The Wall Street Journal*, Monday, May 16, 2005.

WORLDCOM CEO CONVICTED OF CORPORATE FRAUD

Belson, Ken. "WorldCom's Audacious Failure and Its Toll On An Industry." *The New York Times*, January 18, 2005.

Crawford, Krysten. "Ex-WorldCom CEO Ebbers is Guilty," *CNNMoney.com*, March 15, 2005.

Neumeister, Larry. *Associated Press*, Monday, January 30, 2006.

Solomon, Deborah. "Called to Account." *NewsHour with Jim Lehrer*, March 2, 2004.

CHRISTOPHER COX

"Christopher Cox." *Carroll's Federal Directory* Carroll Publishing, 2006. Reproduced in Biography Resource Center. Farmington Hills, Mich.: Thomson Gale. 2006.

CRIMINAL PROCEDURE

MEDINA V. PEOPLE OF THE STATE OF COLORADO

Hethcock, Bill. "Lawyers Glad Jurors May Query Witnesses." *Colorado Springs Gazette*, 3 January 2006.

Medina v. People, No. 04SC167 (2005) Available at www.courts.state.co.us/supct/supctcaseannctsindex.htm

Sarche, Jon. "Court: Colorado Jurors May Question Witnesses." 27 June 2005. Associated Press release.

DNA

KOHLER V. ENGLADE

www.aclunc.org/aclunews/news0410/forum.html

Black, Jane. "Whose DNA is it, Anyway?" *Business-Week Online* June 26, 2003.

Halbfinger, David M. "Police Dragnets for DNA Tests Draw Criticism." *The New York Times* January 4, 2003.

Wilson, Glynn. "In Louisiana, debate over a DNA Dragnet." *Christian Science Monitor*, February 21, 2003.

DRUGS AND NARCOTICS

FDA APPROVES VACCINE FOR HUMAN PAPILLOMA VIRUS

Bridges, Andrew. "FDA Panel Endorses Cervical Cancer Vaccine." *Associated Press.* May 19, 2006.

"FDA Approves Cervical Cancer Vaccine." *CBS2Chicago.com.* http://cbs2chicago.com/health/local_story_159161716.html (accessed June 9, 2006).

Focus on the Family Position Statement: Human Papillomavirus Vaccines. http://www.family.org/cforum/fosi/abstinence/parents/a0039250.cfm (accessed June 6, 2006).

Graham, Judith. "FDA Panel Backs Key STD Vaccine." *Chicago Tribune.* May 18, 2006.

"HPV Questions and Answers." *Centers for Disease Control and Prevention.* http://www.cdc.gov/std/hpv/STDFact-HPV-vaccine.htm#vaccine (accessed June 6, 2006).

Merck's Investigational Vaccine GARDASIL Prevented 100 Percent of Cervical Pre-cancers and Non-invasive Cervical Cancers Associated with HPV Types 16 and 18 in New Clinical Study. http://www.merck.com/newsroom/press_releases/research_and_development/2005_1006_print.html (accessed June 6, 2006)

Panel Urges U.S. to OK Cervical Cancer Vaccine. *The Associated Press.* May 18, 2006.

CITIES, STATES DEBATE LEGALIZING MARIJUANA

Johnson, M.L., "New Medical Marijuana Law Doesn't Say Where Patients Will Get Pot," Boston.com, Jan. 15, 2006. Available at <http://www.boston.com/news/local/rhode_island/articles/2006/01/15/new_medical_marijuana_law_doesnt_say_where_patients_will_get_pot/>

O'Driscoll, Patrick, "Denver Voters to Legalize Marijuana Possession," *USA Today*, Nov. 3, 2005.

Richman, Josh, "House Bill Could End Pot Legal Confusions, Advocates Say," *Alameda Times-Star*, April 28, 2006.

Washinton, April M., "Pot Law Makes Ballot," *Denver Rocky Mountain News*, August 25, 2005, at 5A.

DUE PROCESS

JONES V. FLOWERS

Greenhouse, Linda. "Court Puts Teeth in 'Notice' Needed to Seize Property." *New York Times.* April 27, 2006.

Savage, David. "High Court Rules Against State's Seizure of House." *Los Angeles Times.* April 27, 2006.

Orth, John. *Due Process of Law: A Brief History.* Lawrence, KS: University of Kansas Press. 2003.

EDUCATION

ARLINGTON CENTRAL SCHOOL DISTRICT BOARD OF EDUCATION V. MURPHY

Arlington Central School District Board of Education v. Murphy, No. 05-18, 548 U.S. ___ (2006), Available at www.supremecourtus.gov/opinions

Smith, Gerry. "Arlington Central School District Board of Education v. Murphy." *On the Docket*, 26 June 2006. Available at http://www.docket.medill.northwestern.edu/archives

BUSH V. HOLMES

Moe, Terry. *Schools, Vouchers, and the American Public.* Washington D.C.: Brookings Institution. 2002.

Kahlenberg, Richard. *Public School Choice Vs. Private School Vouchers./emphasis]Washingoton, D.C.: Century Foundation Press. 2003.*

Hacsi, Timothy. *Children as Pawns: The Politics of Educational Reform.* Cambridge, MA: Harvard University Press. 2003.

SCHAFFER V. WEAST

Lane, Charles and Aratini, Lori. "High Court to Hear Md. Special-Ed Case." *Washington Post.* October 5, 2005.

Greenhouse, Linda. "Parents Carry Burden of Proof in School Cases, Court Rules." *New York Times.* November 14, 2005.

Lane, Charles and Aratini, Lori. "D.C. Schools See Opportunity to Pare Back." *Washington Post.* November 15, 2005.

ELECTIONS

WISCONSIN RIGHT TO LIFE V. FEDERAL ELECTION COMMISSION

Kriva, Christopher. "Wisconsin Right to Life v. FEC." *On the Docket*, Medill News Service, 23 January 2006.

Wisconsin Right to Life v. FEC, No. 04–1581 126 S.Ct. 1016; 163 L.Ed.2d 990. Available at www.supremecourtus.gov/opinions

ELEVENTH AMENDMENT

NORTHERN INSURANCE COMPANY OF NEW YORK V. CHATHAM COUNTY, GEORGIA

Chemerinsky, Erwin. *Federal Jurisdiction.* New York: Aspen Publishers. 2003. Fourth Edition.

Currie, David. *Federal Jurisdiction in a Nutshell.* Saint Paul, MN: West Group. 1999.

Wright, Charles Alan. *Law of Federal Courts.* Saint Paul, MN: West Group. 2002. Sixth Edition.

EMINENT DOMAIN

SUPREME COURT'S EMINENT DOMAIN CASE LEADS TO FALLOUT

Associated Press, "Congress Works to Blunt Court Decision," MSNBC.com, June 30, 2005. Available at http://www.msnbc.msn.com/id/8422790.

Mehren, Elizabeth, "States Working to Fine-Tune Court Ruling on Property," *Chicago Tribune*, April 22, 2006, at 17.

Roberts, Paul Craig, "The Kelo Calamity," *Washington Times*, August 7, 2005, at B4.

ENVIRONMENTAL LAW

STATES OF CALIFORNIA, NEW MEXICO, AND OREGON SUE BUSH ADMINISTRATION FOR DISMANTLING ENVIRONMENTAL RESTRICTIONS

"California Attorney General Lockyer Challenges Repeal of Forest 'Roadless Rule.'" *Capitol Reports.* www.caprep.com/0905001.htm (accessed July 1, 2005.)

"Complaint for Declaratory and Injunctive Relief." *State of California Office of the Attorney General.* ag.ca.gov/newsalerts/cms05/05-072_0a.pdf (accessed July 1, 2005.)

ERISA

SEREBOFF V. MID ATLANTIC MEDICAL SERVICES., INC.

Conison, Jay. *Employee Benefit Plans in a Nutshell.* St. Paul. MN: West Group. 2003. Third Edition.

Ziesenhiem, Ken. *Understanding ERISA: A Compact Guide to the Landmark Act.* New York: Marketplace Books. 2002.

Covington, Robert, and Kurt Decker. *Employment Law in a Nutshell.* St. Paul, MN: West Group. 2002. 2nd Edition.

ESTABLISHMENT CLAUSE

FEDERAL JUDGE STRIKES DOWN IOWA FAITH-BASED PRISON PROGRAM

Banerjee, Neela "Court Rejects Evangelical Prison Plan Over State Aid," *N.Y. Times*, June 3, 2006, at A8.

Cooperman, Alan, "Judge Rules Colson Prison Program Unconstitutional," *Washington Post*, June 3, 2006.

EXHAUSTION OF REMEDIES

WOODFORD V. NGO

Bertner, Jaclyn. "Woodford, Jeanne, et al. v. Ngo, Viet Mike." *On the Docket*, Medill News Service, 22 June 2006. Available at http://docket.medill.northwestern.edu/archives

Woodford v. Ngo, No. 05–416, 548 U.S. ___ (2006) Available at www.supremecourtus.gov/opinions

"Woodford v. Ngo." Summary available at http://law.duke.edu./archives

FAIR LABOR STANDARDS ACT

IBP, INC. V. ALVAREZ

Leslie, Douglas. *Labor Law in a Nutshell.* Saint Paul, MN: West Group. 2000. Fourth Edition.

Covington, Robert and Decker, Kurt. *Employment Law in a Nutshell.* Saint Paul, MN: West Group. 2002. Second Edition.

Gould, William. *A Primer on American Labor Law. Cambridge, MA: MIT Press. 2004. Fourth Edition.*

FEDERAL TORT CLAIMS ACT

WILL V. HALLOCK

Chemerinsky, Erwin. *Federal Jurisdiction.* New York: Aspen Publishers. 2003. Fourth Edition.

Currie, David. *Federal Jurisdiction in a Nutshell.* Saint Paul, MN: West Group. 1999.

Wright, Charles Alan. *Law of Federal Courts.* Saint Paul, MN: West Group. 2002. Sixth Edition.

FIRST AMENDMENT

BEARD V. BANKS

Beard v. Banks, No. 04–1739, 548 U.S. ___ (2006), Available at www.supremecourtus.gov/opinions

"Beard v. Banks." Case summary available at www.law.duke.edu/publiclaw/supremecourtonline/certgrants/2004/alavuni.html

"Prisons Can Restrict Inmates' Reading Matter." Associated Press News Release, 28 June 2006. Available at http://www.firstamendmentcenter.org/news.aspx?id=17081

Royko, Kevin. "Beard, Jeffrey (PA Dept. of Corrections) v. Banks, Ronald." *On the Docket*, 28 June 2006. Available at http://docket.medill.northwestern.edu/archives

RANDALL V. SORRELL

"High Court Rejects Vt. Campaign-Finance Limits." Associated Press News Story, 26 June 2006. Available at http://www.firstamendmentcenter.org/news.aspx?id=17064.

Randall v. Sorrell, No. 04–1528, (2006) (Available at www.supremecourtus.gov/opinions

"Randall v. Sorrell." Brennan Center for Justice at NYU School of Law. Undated. Available at www.brennancenter.org/programsdem_cfr_lit_randall.html

RUMSFELD V. FORUM FOR ACADEMIC AND INSTITUTIONAL RIGHTS, INC.

Greenhouse. Linda. "U.S. Wins Ruling Over Recruiting at Universities." *New York Times.* March 7, 2006.

Barbash, Fred. "Victory for Military Recruiters." *Washington Post.* March 7, 2006.

Holland, Gina. "Supreme Court Upholds College Military Recruiting Law." *Seattle Times.* March 6, 2006.

FOURTH AMENDMENT

BRIGHAM V. UTAH

Brigham City, Utah v. Stuart No. 05–502, 547 U.S. ___ (2006), Available at www.supremecourtus.gov/opinions

Goldstein, Seth. "Brigham City, Utah v. Stuart, Charles, et al." *On the Docket*, 22 May 2006. Available at http://docket.medill.northwestern.edu/archives

"Recent Case Report: Brigham City v. Stuart." Alameda County District Attorney's Office. Available at http://www.acgov.org/da/pov/documents/BrighamCity.pdf.

GEORGIA V. RANDOLPH

Greenhouse, Linda. "Roberts Dissent Reveals Strain Beneath Court's Placid Surface." *New York Times.* March 23, 2006.

Lane, Charles. "High Court Trims Police Power to Search Homes." *Washington Post.* March 23, 2006.

Holland, Gina. "Supreme Court Splits in Limiting Police Searches." *Boston Globe.* March 22, 2006.

U.S. V. GRUBBS

Dash, Samuel. *The Intruders: Unreasonable Searches and Seizures from King John to John Ashcroft.* Rutgers, NJ: Rutgers University Press. 2004.

Long, Carolyn. *Mapp V. Ohio: Guarding Against Unreasonable Searches And Seizures.* Lawrence, KS: University Press of Kansas. 2006.

Cammack, Mark and Garland, Norman. *Advanced Criminal Procedure in a Nutshell.* St. Paul, MN: West Publishing Co. 2001.

HUDSON V. MICHIGAN

Greenhouse, Linda. "Court Limits Protection Against Improper Entry." *New York Times.* June 16, 2006.

Barbash, Fred. "High Court Backs Police No-Knock Searches."

Savage, David. "Supreme Court Weakens Police 'Knock and Announce' Rule." *Los Angeles Times.* June 16, 2006.

FRAUD

BANK OF CHINA V. NBM

Bank of China v. NBM, LLC, et al., (Dismissal) No. 03–1559, Available at www.supremecourtus.gov/qp/03–1559qp.pdf

Bank of China v. NBM, LLC, et al No. 02-9267, Available at www.lawprofessors.typepad.com

Bennett, Brian. "Bank of China NY Branch v. NBM, L.L.C., et al." *On the Docket*, 1 September 2005. Available at http://docket.medill.northwestern.edu/archives

Chaitman, Helen Davis. "Foreign Bank Finds That It's Not So Easy to Keep an American Run-away Jury Verdict." *LAWorld*, 7 April 2005. Available at http://www.laworld.com/news_articledetail.asp?idNews=25.

ILLEGAL HARVESTING OF BODY PARTS RESULTS IN FRAUD CASES

Armour, Stephanie. "Illegal Trade in Bodies Shakes Loved Ones." *USA TODAY.* April 28, 2006.

"As Scandal Widens, Many Who Received Stolen Body Parts and Human Tissue Claim to Have Been Infected with Deadly Viruses." *Newsinferno.* www.newsinferno.com/archives/1129 May 1, 2006.

"Body Parts Thefts May Extend Beyond N.Y. Funeral Homes." *The Toledo Blade.* December 24, 2005.

Calder, Rich and Andy Geller. "'Ghoul and the Gang' in Cadaver Scam: DA." *New York Post.* February 24, 2006.

Destefano, Anthony M. "DA: Alleged Body Parts Harvests Were 'Medical Terrorism'." *Newsday.com.* February 24, 2006.

Hays, Tom. "Body-Parts Case 'Like Horror Movie'." *The Toronto Star.* February 23, 2006.

Sherman, William. "Body Snatchers." *New York Daily News.* October 7, 2005.

Troncone, Tom. "Body Parts Case to Yield New Charges, Source Says." *North Jersey Media Group, Inc.* March 9, 2006.

Troncone, Tom. "Bill Sets Jail Term for Body Parts Thieves." *North Jersey Media Group, Inc.* May 17, 2006.

FREEDOM OF RELIGION

GONZALES V. O CENTRO ESPIRITA BENEFICENTE UNIAO DO VEGETAL

Greenhouse, Linda. "Sect Allowed to Import Its Hallucinogenic Tea." *New York Times.* February 22, 2006.

Lane, Charles. "Supreme Court to Decide Whether Church Can Import Drug." *Washington Post.* April 19, 2005.

Holland, Gina. "High Court Hears Hallucinogenic Tea Case." *Boston Globe.* November 1, 2005.

FREEDOM OF SPEECH

FEDERAL COURTS STRIKE DOWN VIDEO GAME LAWS

Associated Press, "Federal Court Strikes Down Illinois Video Game Law," *USA Today*, December 3, 2005.

Associated Press, "Michigan Video Game Ban Struck Down, MSNBC.com, April 4, 2006. Available at www.msnbc.msn.com/id/12151797.

GAS

MEMBERS OF CONGRESS QUESTION INCREASES IN GAS PRICES

"GOP Jawbones Gas Industry as Profits Soar," *Inside FERC*, October 31, 2005, at 1.

Hurt, Charles, "Democrats Blaming Bush for Gas Prices," *Washington Times*, April 25, 2006, at A4.

Isidore, Chris, "Big Oil CEOs Under Fire in Congress," CNN.com, November 9, 2005. Available at money.cnn.com/2005/11/09/news/economy/oil_hearing/?cnn=yes

"Producer Execs Defend Soaring Profits as Senators Probe Prices, Alaska Pipe Project," *inside FERC*, November 14, 2005, at 1.

GAY AND LESBIAN RIGHTS

LIMON V. KANSAS

Lane Charles. "Bias Ruled in Law on Same-Sex Rape." *The Washington Post* , October 22, 2005.

Liptak, Adam. "Kansas Law on Gay Sex by Teenagers Is Overturned." *The New York Times*, October 22, 2005.

State of Kansas v. Matthew R. Limon

John Geddes Lawrence and Tyron Garner v. State of Texas

GAY MARRIAGE UPDATE

Belluck, Pam. "Massachusetts Court Limits Same-Sex Marriages." *The New York Times*, March 30, 2006.

Chen, David W. "N.J. State Court Deliberates Issue of Gay Marriage." *The New York Times*, February 16, 2006.

Gurney, Kaitlin. "Same-sex Marriage Goes to Top Court." *The Philadelphia Inquirer*, February 12, 2006.

Henry, Ed. "Frist Plans June Vote on Gay Marriage." *CNN*, February 13, 2006. Online at http://www.conn.com/2006/POLITICS/02/13/gay.marriage/index.html.

Mosk, Matthew and John Wagner. "Judge Strikes Down Md. Ban on Gay Marriage." *The Washington Post*, January 21, 2006.

Peterson, Kavan. "Washington Gay Marriage Ruling Looms." *Stateline.org*, March 30, 2006.

Sullivan, Andy. "Senate Panel OKs Gay-Marriage Ban." *Reuters*, May 18, 2006.

GENEVA CONVENTION

HAMDAN V. RUMSFELD

Greenhouse, Linda. "Justices Hint That They'll Rule on Challenge Filed by Detainee." *The New York Times* March 29, 2006.

"Guantanamo Trial Should Proceed, U.S. Tells Justices." *Associated Press.*

Lane, Charles. "Court Case Challenges Power of President." *The Washington Post*, March 26, 2006.

Savage, David G. "High Court to Review Guantanamo Case." *Los Angeles Times* March 28, 2006.

GUN CONTROL

CONGRESS PASSES THE PROTECTION OF LAWFUL COMMERCE IN ARMS ACT

"Congress Agrees to Rule Out Gun Suits," *Richmond Times Dispatch*, Oct. 21, 2005, at A3.

Sandler, Michael and Seth Stern, "Liability Measure Represents Years of Maneuvering by Gun Rights Supporters," *CQ Today*, October 19, 2005.

Scheer, Robert, "Congress Caves on Gun Liability," *The Record*, October 26, 2005, at L11.

HABEAS CORPUS

DAY V. MCDONOUGH

Freedman, Eric. *Habeas Corpus: Rethinking the Great Writ of Liberty.* New York: New York Univ. Press. 2003.

Federman, Cary. *The Body And the State: Habeas Corpus And American Jurisprudence.* New York, NY: State University of New York Press. 2006.

Frank, Jerome. *Courts on Trial.* Princeton, NJ: Princeton University Press. 1973.

EVANS V. CHAVIS

Freedman, Eric. *Habeas Corpus: Rethinking the Great Writ of Liberty.* New York: New York Univ. Press. 2003.

Federman, Cary. *The Body And the State: Habeas Corpus And American Jurisprudence.* New York, NY: State University of New York Press. 2006.

Frank, Jerome. *Courts on Trial.* Princeton, NJ: Princeton University Press. 1973.

HOUSE V. BELL

Greenhouse, Linda. "Justices Grant Death Row Inmate a New Hearing in 1985 Tennessee Murder." *New York Times.* June 13, 2006.

Locy, Tony. "High Court: Tenn. Inmate May Use DNA Tests." *Los Angeles Times.* June 12, 2006.

Lane, Charles. "Justices Open Door for Injection Case." *Washington Post.* June 13, 2006.

RICE V. COLLINS

Freedman, Eric. *Habeas Corpus: Rethinking the Great Writ of Liberty.* New York: New York Univ. Press. 2003.

Federman, Cary. *The Body And the State: Habeas Corpus And American Jurisprudence.* New York, NY: State University of New York Press. 2006.

Frank, Jerome. *Courts on Trial.* Princeton, NJ: Princeton University Press. 1973.

HATE CRIME

ALABAMA CHURCH ARSONISTS CAUGHT

Department of Justice Press Release. "Three Indicted for Arson of Nine Churches." March 29, 2006.

Indictment. U.S. v. Matthew Lee Cloyd, Benjamin Nathan Moseley, Russell Lee DeBusk. U.S. District Court for the Northern District of Alabama, Western Division (March 29, 2006).

Reeves, Jay. "King Meets With Arson Victims." *The Associated Press.* May 29, 2006.

Reeves, Jay. "Three College Students Charged With A String Of Alabama Church Arsons." *The Associated Press.* March 9, 2006.

Robinson, Carol. "Church Fires Fueled by Alcohol, Night Hunting." *Newhouse News Service.* March 9, 2006.

"Students Charged with Alabama Church Fires." *Newhouse News Service.* March 23, 2006, pg. 216B3.

"Suspect: Church Fires started as 'joke.'" *CNN.com.* March 9, 2006, pg. 216B3.

HURRICANE KATRINA

LEGAL ISSUES AFTER HURRICANE KATRINA

Epstein, Edward. "Feds: No Evidence Post-Katrina Gas Prices Were Manipulated." *San Francisco Chronicle*, May 22, 2006.

Kunzelman, Michael. "669 Sue State Farm Over Katrina Claims." *The Associated Press*, May 9, 2006.

Labaton, Stephen. "Report on Gas Prices Finds No Collusion." *The New York Times*, May 22, 2006.

Parker, Laura. "New Orleans Plans First Criminal Trials Since Katrina." *USA Today*, May 23, 2006.

Salmon, Jacqueline. "Red Cross, Humane Society Under Investigation." *The Washington Post*, March 26, 2006.

Salmon, Jacqueline and Elizabeth Williamson. "Charities Wary on Use of Katrina Donations." *The Washington Post*, September 23, 2005.

IDENTITY THEFT

UNITED STATES V. CHOICEPOINT

Federal Trade Commission. "ChoicePoint Settles Data Security Breach Charges; to Pay $10 Million in Civil Penalties, $5 Million for Consumer Redress." www.ftc.gov/opa/2006/01/choicepoint.html, January 26, 2006.

O'Harrow, Robert, Jr. "ID Data Conned From Firm." *The Washington Post*, February 17, 2005.

Mohammed, Arshad. "Record Fine for Data Breach." *The Washington Post* January 27, 2006.

Zeller, Tom, Jr. "U.S. Settles With Company on Leak of Consumers' Data." *The New York Times* January 27, 2006.

IMMIGRATION

CONGRESS VOTES ON IMMIGRATION REFORM

Babington, Charles. "Bush Seen As Key to Accord on Immigration." *The Washington Post*, May 24, 2006.

Balz, Dan and Darryl Fears. "We Decided Not to Be Invisible Anymore." *The Washington Post*, April 11, 2006.

Gamboa, Suzanne. "Senate to Vote on Immigration Overhaul." *The Associated Press*, May 25, 2006.

Fletcher, Michael. "Bush Immigration Plan Meets GOP Opposition." *The Washington Post*, January 2, 2005.

Murray, Shailagh. "Conservatives Split in Debate on Curbing Illegal Immigration." *The Washington Post*, March 25, 2005.

Pickler, Nedra. "Bush to Send up to 6,000 Troops to Border." *The Associated Press*, May 15, 2006.

"Schwarzenegger Set to Send Guard to Border." *Reuters*, May 24, 2006.

Weisman, Jonathan. "Senate Backs Fence, Guest-Worker Curbs." *The Washington Post*, May 18, 2006.

IMMUNITY

HARTMAN V. MOORE

Lewis, Jr., Harold and Norman, Elizabeth. *Civil Rights Law and Practice.* Saint Paul, MN: West Group. 2004.

Vieira, Norman. *Constitutional Civil Rights in a Nutshell.* Saint Paul, MN.: West Group. 1998.

Currie, David. *Federal Jurisdiction in a Nutshell.* Saint Paul, MN: West Group. 1999.

INSANITY DEFENSE

CLARK V. ARIZONA

Clark v. Arizona, No. 05–5966, Available at www.supremecourtus.gov/opinions

"Supreme Court Considers Insanity Defense . . ." *Jurist*, 19 April 2006. Available at http://www.jurist.law.pitt.edu/paperchase/2006/04/supreme-court-considers-insanity.php

"Supreme Court Upholds Arizona Law on Insanity Defense." *Jurist*, 29 June 2006. Available at http://www.jurist.law.pitt.edu/paperchase/2006/06/supreme-court-upholds-arizona-law-on.php

INTERNET

GOOGLE REFUSES TO GIVE SEARCH ENGINE DATA TO GOVERNMENT

Hafner, Katie and Matt Richtel, "Google Resists U.S. Subpoena of Search Data," *New York Times*, January 20, 2006, at A1.

Liedtke, Michael, "Judge to Order Google to Give Up Some Data," *Charleston Gazette*, March 15, 2006, at 10A.

Mohammed, Arshad, "Google Refuses Demand for Search Information," *Washington Post*, January 20, 2006, at A1.

AOL TARGETS PHISHERS IN VIRGINIA LAWSUIT

Brulliard, Karin, "Va. Lawmakers Aim to Hook Cyberscammers," *Washington Post*, April 10, 2005, at C8.

Gross, Grant, "Update: AOL Sues Big Phishing Organizations," *InfoWorld Daily*, February 28, 2006.

Musgrove, Mike, "AOL Wins Judgment Against Spammers," *Washinton Post*, August 11, 2005, at D5.

JURISDICTION

EMPIRE HEALTHCHOICE V. MCVEIGH

Empire Healthchoice Assurance v. McVeigh, No. 05–200, 547 U.S. ___ (2006), Available at www.supremecourtus.gov/opinions

Sachs, Peter. "Empire Healthchoice Assurance v. McVeigh." Medill News Service, 15 June 2006. Available at http://docket.medill.northwestern.edu/archives

LINCOLN PROPERTY CO. V. ROCHE

Chemerinsky, Erwin. *Federal Jurisdiction.* New York: Aspen Publishers. 2003. Fourth Edition.

Currie, David. *Federal Jurisdiction in a Nutshell.* Saint Paul, MN: West Group. 1999.

Wright, Charles Alan. *Law of Federal Courts.* Saint Paul, MN: West Group. 2002. Sixth Edition.

MARTIN V. FRANKLIN CAPITAL CORPORATION

Chemerinsky, Erwin. *Federal Jurisdiction.* New York: Aspen Publishers. 2003. Fourth Edition.

Currie, David. *Federal Jurisdiction in a Nutshell.* Saint Paul, MN: West Group. 1999.

Wright, Charles Alan. *Law of Federal Courts.* Saint Paul, MN: West Group. 2002. Sixth Edition.

WACHOVIA BANK V. SCHMIDT

Chemerinsky, Erwin. *Federal Jurisdiction.* New York: Aspen Publishers. 2003. Fourth Edition.

Currie, David. *Federal Jurisdiction in a Nutshell.* Saint Paul, MN: West Group. 1999.

Wright, Charles Alan. *Law of Federal Courts.* Saint Paul, MN: West Group. 2002. Sixth Edition.

LABOR LAW

WHITMAN V. DEPARTMENT OF TRANSPORTATION

Leslie. David. *Labor Law in a Nutshell.* Saint Paul, MN: West Law School. 2000. Fourth Edition.

Covington, Robert, and Decker, Kurt. *Employment Law in a Nutshell.* Saint Paul, MN: West Law School. 2002. Second Edition.

Currie, David. *Federal Jurisdiction in a Nutshell.* Saint Paul, MN: West Law School. 1999. Fourth Edition.

MALPRACTICE

WISCONSIN SUPREME COURT STRIKES DOWN CAPS ON DAMAGES

Callender, David, "GOP Promises to Reverse Court's Malpractice Ruling," *Capital Times*, July 15, 2006, at 1A.

Pribek, Jane, "Wisconsin Gov. Jim Doyle Signs Medical Malpractice Cap Bill," *Wisconsin Law Journal*, March 29, 2006.

Ziemer, David, "Discussion of Medical Malpractice Caps Intensifies in Wisconsin," *Wisconsin Law Journal*, February 22, 2006.

MANSLAUGHTER

HAWAII REVERSES MANSLAUGHTER CONVICTION FOR NEWBORN'S DEATH FROM PRENATAL SUBSTANCE ABUSE

Kobayashi, Ken. "Meth Mother's Conviction Overturned." *The Honolulu Adviser*, 30 November 2005.

State v. Aiwohi, No. 26838 (November 29, 2005), Available at www.courts.state.hi.us.

MEDICAID

ARKANSAS DEPARTMENT OF HEALTH AND HUMAN SERVICES V. AHLBORN

Hacker, Jacob. *The Divided Welfare State: The Battle over Public and Private Social Benefits in the United States.* New York: Cambridge Univ. Press. 2002.

Weissert, Carol. *Governing Health: The Politics of Health Policy.* Baltimore,MD: Johns Hopkins Univ. Press. 2002. 2nd Edition.

Hackey Robert. *The New Politics of State Health Policy.* Lawrence, KS: University of Kansas Press. 2001.

MEXICO AND THE UNITED STATES

CIVILIAN PATROLS POLICING THE U.S.-MEXICO BORDER CAUSE NATIONWIDE CONTROVERSY

"California Group Launches Civilian Patrol of U.S.-Mexico Border." *Associated Press.* www.kvoa.com/global/story.asp?s=3603895&ClientType=Printable July 17, 2005.

Carter, Sara A. "U.S. Tipping Mexico to Minuteman Patrols." *Inland Valley Daily Bulletin.* May 9, 2006.

"Civilian Patrol Group That Monitors U.S.-Mexico Border Not So Welcome in Texas." *Associated Press.* June 2, 2005.

Hendricks, Tyche. "On the Border." *San Francisco Chronicle.* December 5, 2005.

Jordan, Lara Jakes. "Civilian Border Patrol Forming in Arizona." *Pittsburgh Tribune-Review.* February 22, 2005.

Schleicher, Annie. "Civilian Militia Patrol U.S.-Mexico Border." *MacNeil/Lehrer Productions.* April 6, 2005.

MIRANDA RIGHTS

MARYLAND V. BLAKE

Maryland v. Blake, No. 04–373, 546 U.S.___ (2005), Available at www.supremecourtus.gov/opinions

Tagliavia, Tony. "Maryland v. Blake, Leeander" *On the Docket*, 1 September 2005. Available at http://docket.medill.northwestern.edu/archives/003.307.php

Rushford, Michael. "High Court to Review Blocking Incriminating Evidence." Pres Release from the Criminal Justice Legal Foundation, 27 October 2005. Available at http://www.cjlf.org/releases/05–24.htm

MURDER

DNA, ADDITIONAL TESTIMONY AMONG KEY EVIDENCE IN FOURTH APPEAL FOR FATAL VISION CASE

Eisley, Matthew. "'Fatal Vision' Appeal Rebutted." *The News & Observer* December 30, 2005.

Eisley, Matthew. "MacDonald Gets Fourth Appeal." *The News & Observer* January 14, 2006.

"New Evidence in 'Fatal Vision' Case." *ABC News*. December 15, 2005.

Ovaska, Sarah. "MacDonald Gets DNA Answer." *The News & Observer* March 11, 2006.

NATIVE AMERICAN RIGHTS

WAGNON V. PRAIRIE BAND POTAWATOMI NATION

Canby, William. *American Indian Law in a Nutshell.* St. Paul, MN: West. 2004 Fourth Edition.

Wilkins, David. *Uneven Ground: American Indian Sovereignty and Federal Law.* Norman, OK: University of Oklahoma Press. 2002.

Wilkins, David. *American Indian Sovereignty and the U.S. Supreme Court.* Austin, TX: University of Texas Press. 1997.

OBSCENITY

NITKE V. GONZALES

Barron, Jerome. *The First Amendment in a Nutshell.* St. Paul, MN: West Group. 2004. Third Edition.

Saunders, Kevin. *Saving Our Children from the First Amendment.* New YorK: New York University Press. 2004.

Nelson, Samulel. *Beyond the First Amendment: The Politics of Free Speech and Pluralism.* Baltimore, MD: Johns Hopkins University Press. 2005.

ORGANIZED CRIME

TWO MISTRIALS FOR REPUTED GAMBINO CRIME FAMILY LEADER

Hartocollis, Anemona. "For a Second Time, a Jury Fails to Reach a Verdict on Gotti." *The New York Times.* March 11, 2006.

Hartocollis, Anemona. "One Side Depicts Gotti as Disillusioned Son, the Other as Stony Avenger." *The New York Times.* February 22, 2006.

Hays, Tom. "Judge Declares Mistrial in Gotti Case." *The Associated Press.* September 20, 2005.

Hays, Tom. "Judge Declares Mistrial on Most Serious Counts in Gotti Mafia Trial." *The Associated Press.* September 20, 2005.

"'Junior' Gotti indicted . . . again." *CNN.com.* http://www.cnn.com/2006/LAW/05/22/gotti.indictment.ap/index.html. May 22, 2006.

Neumeister, Larry. "Gotti Jr. Begins Racketeering Retrial." *Associated Press Online.* February 14, 2006.

Neumeister, Larry. "Judge Criticizes Government's New Indictment in Gotti Trial." http://www.news.findlaw.com. May 25, 2006.

"Second Mistrial for John Gotti." *UPI.* March 11, 2006.

U.S. v. Gotti, Docket No. 05-6872-cr (2nd Cir., May 26, 2006).

PATENTS

BLACKBERRY CASE SETTLES

Austen, Ian. "New Patent Case Filed Over BlackBerry." *The New York Times*, May 2, 2006.

Eckert, Barton. "BlackBerry Patent Case Settled." *Washington Business Journal*, March 3, 2006.

Krazit, Tom. "RIM Fights For Its BlackBerry Rights." *IDG News Service*, June 8, 2004.

Noguchi, Yuki. "BlackBerry Patent Dispute Is Settled." *The Washington Post*, March 4, 2006.

Noguchi, Yuki. "Government Enters Fray Over BlackBerry Patents." *The Washington Post*, November 12, 2005.

Svensson, Peter. "Settlement Reached in BlackBerry Dispute." *The Associated Press*, March 3, 2006.

SUPREME COURT REJECTS MANDATORY PATENT INFRINGEMENT INJUNCTIONS

Noguchi, Yuki. "Government Sides Against Ebay in Patent Dispute." *The Washington Post*, March 11, 2006.

eBay, Inc. "eBay Statement on Supreme Court Oral Argument and MercExchange Patent Reexamination." http://investor.ebay.com.

Hafner, Katie. "Justices Will Hear Patent Case Against eBay." *The New York Times*, March 27, 2006.

Noguchi, Yuki and Charles Lane. "High Court Considers Ebay Case on Patent." *The Washington Post*, March 30, 2006.

LABORATORY CORPORATION OF AMERICA V. METABOLITE

Chadhuri, Arnab and Nina Jenkins-Johnston. "Supreme Court Collection: Oral Argument Previews." *Legal Information Institute bulletin*, 21 March 2006. Available at http://www.law.cornell.edu/supct/cert/04-607.html

Laboratory Corporation of America Holdings v. Metabolite, No. 04-607, 548 U.S. ___ (2006), Available at www.supremecourtus.gov/opinions

Metabolite Laboratories, Inc. v. Laboratory Corporation of America Holdings, No. 03–1120, 370 F.3d 1354 (2nd Cir. 2004). Available at www.findlaw.com.

PERJURY

Cheney's Chief of Staff Indicted

Ballard, Tanya N. and Kevin Dumouchelle, "Key Players in the Plame Affair," *Washington Post*, October 20, 2005.

Brune, Tom, "Indictment—The Overview," *Newsday*, October 29, 2005, A2.

National Public Radio, "Timeline: The CIA Leak Case. Available at www.npr.org/templates/story/story.php?storyId=4764919.

PIRACY

Companies Look For Legal Downloading Solutions

"Grokster Goes Down." *The Associated Press*, November 8, 2005.

Hansell, Saul. "File-Sharing Services Seek Pact with Record Studios." *The New York Times*, September 20, 2005.

Krim, Jonathan and Frank Ahrens. "Legal Pressure Shutters Grokster." *The Washington Post*, November 8, 2005.

Veiga, Alex. "File-Sharing Firm Sues eBay, 21 Others." *The Associated Press*, May 23, 2006.

Yegyazarian, Anush. "File Sharing and the Supreme Court: The Fallout." *PCWorld*, July 7, 2005.

PRIVACY

Wisconsin Governor Vetoes Cloning Ban Proposal

Forster, Stacy, "Doyle Vetoes Ban on Human Cloning," *Milwaukee Journal Sentinel*, November 4, 2005.

Johnston, Josephine, "Stem Cell Research: New Frontiers in Science and Ethics," *Amyloid*, December 1, 2005, at 263.

Yeung, Patrick Jr., "When Does Human Life Begin?," *Ethics & Medicine*, July 1, 2005, at 69.

PROBATE

Marshall v. Marshall a.k.a Anna Nicole Smith

Marshall v. Marshall, No. 04–1544, 547 U.S. ___ (2006) Slip Opinion available at www.supremecourtus.gov/opinions

Stout, David. "Anna Nicole Smith Wins Supreme Court Case." *New York Times*, 1 May 2006.

PROPERTY LAW

Alaska v. United States

Alaska v. United States, No. 128, 546 U.S. ___. Available at www.supremecourtus.gov/opinions

Alaska v. United States, No. 128, 546 U.S. ___. Syllabus available at www.law.cornell.edu/supct/html/128ORIG.ZS.html

"State of Alaska v. United States." Case summary available at www.law.duke.edu/publiclaw/supremecourtonline/certgrants/2004/alavuni.html

RELIGION

Debate Over Teaching Evolution and Intelligent Design Continues

Goodstein, Laurie, "Issuing Rebuke, Judge Rejects Teaching of Intelligent Design," *New York Times*, December 21, 2005, at A1.

Lieberman, Bruce, "Designed to Create Controversy," *San Diego Union-Tribune*, February 16, 2006, at A1.

Florida Supreme Court Strikes Down Voucher Program

Dillon, Sam, "Florida Supreme Court Blocks School Vouchers," *New York Times*, January 6, 2006, at A16.

Postal, Leslie and John Kennedy, "Florida's Top Court Bars Vouchers for F Schools," *Orlando Sentinel*, January 6, 2006, at A1.

RICO

Anza v. Ideal Steel Supply Corporation

Anza v. Ideal Steel Supply Corp., 126 S. Ct. 1991 (2006). Available at www.supremecourtus.gov/opinions

Wiggin and Dana. "Supreme Court Update." *Publications*, 6 June 2006. Available at http://www.wiggin.com/pubs/scupdate_template.asp?ID=103021672006&groudid=5

"Abstract: Anza v. Ideal Steel Supply Corporation." 5 June 2006. Available at http://www.law.duke.edu/

Mohawk v. Williams

Anza v. Ideal Steel Supply Corp., No. 04–433, 546 U.S. ___ (2006), Slip Opinion Syllabus available at www.supremecourtus.gov/opinions

Mohawk Industries v. Williams, No. 05–465, 547 U.S. ___ (2006), Available at www.supremecourtus.gov/opinions

"Mohawk Industries v. Williams (Docket No. 05–465) Employee vs. Employer Civil RICO Case Remanded to the 11th Circuit." *Employment Law Memo*, 5 June 2006. Available at http://www.lawmemo.com/docs/us/mohawk.

Scheidler v. National Organization For Women, Inc.

Greenhouse. Linda. "Abortion Opponents Win Dispute." *New York Times.* March 1, 2006.

Lane, Charles. "Court Backs Anti-Abortion Protesters." *Washington Post.* February 28, 2006.

Korn, Peter. *Lovejoy: A Year in the Life of an Abortion Clinic.* New York: Atlantic Monthly Press. 1996.

SEARCH AND SEIZURE

COURT UPHOLDS RAID OF CONGRESSIONAL OFFICE OF U.S. REPRESENTATIVE WILLIAM JEFFERSON

Alpert, Bruce. "But It Will Remain in Effect for Awhile." *The Times-Picayune*, 9 July 2006.

Alpert, Bruce. "Judge Upholds Jefferson Raid." *The Times-Picayune*, 10 July 2006.

In re: Search of the Rayburn House Office Building Room Number 2113 Washington. D.C. 20515, Case. No. 06–1231 M-01 (July 10, 2006). Available at http://www.dcd.uscourts.gov/opinions/2006/Hogan/2006-MS-231

Locy, Toni. "Judge: FBI Raid on Lawmaker's Office Legal." *WTOP* 10 July 2006. Available at http://www.wtopnews.com

SAMSON V. CALIFORNIA

Spano, John. "Supreme Court Upholds Spot Searches of Parolees." *Los Angeles Times.* June 20, 2006.

Mears, Bill. "Court OKs Random Searches of Parolees." *cnn.com.* June 20, 2006.

Richey, Warren. "Supreme Court Upholds California's Searches of Parolees. *Christian Science Monitor.* June 20, 2006.

SENTENCING

WASHINGTON V. RECUENCO

Washington v. Recuenco, No. 05-83, 548 U.S. ___ (2006) Available at www.supremecourtus.gov/opinions

Welch, Dan. "Washington v. Recuenco." *On the Docket*, 26 June 2006. Available at http://www.docket.medill.northwestern.edu/archives

Berman, Professor Douglas A, editor. "Resources on Sentencing Law." Available at http://moritzlaw.osu.edu/faculty/berman/states/washington.html

SEX OFFENSES

CALIFORNIA BILL BANS STATE-FUNDED VIAGRA FOR SEX OFFENDERS

Chorneau, Tom. "California Governor Signs Ban on Subsidized Viagra for Sex Offenders." *Law & Court Decision News.* October 4, 2005.

"House Excludes Viagra from Coverage." *Daily News Central.* health.dailynewscentral.com/content/view/857/62 June 24, 2005.

"Legislation Cuts Off Impotence-Drug Payments for Sex Offenders." *Daily News Central.* health.dailynewscentral.com/content/view/1137/0 May 26, 2005.

"States Ban Medicaid Coverage of Erectile Dysfunction Treatments for Sex Offenders." *California Healthline.* May 31, 2005.

SEXUAL HARASSMENT

ARBAUGH V. Y & H CORPORATION

Lewis, Jr., Harold and Norman, Elizabeth. *Civil Rights Law and Practice.* Saint Paul, MN: West Group. 2004.

Vieira, Norman. *Constitutional Civil Rights in a Nutshell.* Saint Paul, MN.: West Group. 1998.

Covington, Robert and Decker, Kurt. *Employment Law in a Nutshell.* Saint Paul, MN: West Group. 2002. Second Edition.

SIXTH AMENDMENT

UNITED STATES V. GONZALEZ-LOPEZ

United States v. Gonzalez-Lopez, No.05–352, 548 U.S. ___, (Available at www.supremecourtus.gov/opinions

"Justices: Judge Erred in Barring Attorney." *Arkansas Democrat Gazette*, 27 June 2006.

DAVIS V. WASHINGTON

Biskupic, Joan, "Justices Draw a Line on What Evidence is Admissible," *USA Today*, June 20, 2006, at 4A.

Locy, Toni, "Justices Consider Barring Victims' Statements to 911," *St. Louis Post-Dispatch*, March 21, 2006, at A3.

Savage, David G., "Court Makes Domestic Prosecutions Harder," *Los Angeles Times*, June 20, 2006.

HOLMES V. SOUTH CAROLINA

Greenhouse, Linda. "In Death Row Case, Justices Order Retrial Over Evidence." *New York Times.* May 2. 2006.

Rothstein, Paul. *Evidence in a Nutshell.* St. Paul, MN: West Group. 2003. Fourth Edition.

Graham, Michael. *Federal Rules of Evidence in a Nutshell.* St. Paul, MN: West Group. 2003. Sixth Edition.

SOCIAL SECURITY

LOCKHART V. UNITED STATES

Greenhouse, Linda. "Student Debt Collectible by Social Security." *New York Times.* December 8, 2005.

Holland, Gina. "Supreme Court: Social Security Not Off Limits For Old Student Loan Debt." *AP Online.* December 7, 2005.

Lane, Charles. "Justices to Review Loan Offsets." *Washington Post.* April 26, 2005.

SOVEREIGN IMMUNITY

DOLAN V. UNITED STATES POSTAL SERVICE

Chemerinsky, Erwin. *Federal Jurisdiction.* New York: Aspen Publishers. 2003. Fourth Edition.

Currie, David. *Federal Jurisdiction in a Nutshell.* Saint Paul, MN: West Group. 1999.

Wright, Charles Alan. *Law of Federal Courts.* Saint Paul, MN: West Group. 2002. Sixth Edition.

UNITED STATES V. OLSON

Chemerinsky, Erwin. *Federal Jurisdiction.* New York: Aspen Publishers. 2003. Fourth Edition.

Currie, David. *Federal Jurisdiction in a Nutshell.* Saint Paul, MN: West Group. 1999.

Wright, Charles Alan. *Law of Federal Courts.* Saint Paul, MN: West Group. 2002. Sixth Edition.

SPORTS LAW

ALLEGATIONS OF STEROID USE IN BASEBALL CONTINUE

Kroichick, Ron, "Book Traces Bonds' Steroid Use to HR Race Season," *Monterey County Herald*, March 7, 2006.

Sandomir, Richard, "Sheffield and Giambi Linked to BALCO in Book," *New York Times*, March 23, 2006, at D2.

SUPREME COURT

SUPREME COURT SEES FIRST MAJOR CHANGES IN MORE THAN A DECADE

"Alito Likely to Solidify Right Bloc," *Richmond Times Dispatch*, February 1, 2006, at A1.

Kirkpatrick, David D., "Alito Sworn in as Justice After Senate Gives Approval," *New York Times*, February 1, 2006.

Taylor, Stuart Jr. and Evan Thomas, "Keeping It Real," *Newsweek*, November 14, 2005, at 22.

TAXATION

PRESIDENT'S PANEL RECOMMENDS MAJOR TAX REFORM

Associated Press, "Reform Panel's Plan Erases Most Tax Breaks," *Washington Times*, October 19, 2005.

"Tax Panel Urges Huge Overhaul," CBS News, November 1, 2005. Available at www.cbsnews.com/stories/2005/11/01/national/main999400.shtml

TERRORISM

GUANTANAMO BAY DEVELOPMENTS

"British Guantanamo Detainees Sue U.S. for $10 Million." *Times Online.* Online at http://www.timesonline.co.uk/printFriendly/0,,1-61-2175790-61,00.html.

"Concerns About Guantanamo Based on Misunderstandings, Rice Says." Transcript from interview with Jonathan Dimbleby Programme ITV1, April 2, 2006. Online at http://usinfo.state.gov/dhr/Archive/2006/Apr/03-725937.html.

Leonnig, Carol D. and John Mintz. "Judge Says Detainees' Trials Are Unlawful." *The Washington Post.* November 9, 2004.

Lewis, Neal A. and Eric Schmitt. "Inquiry Finds Abuses at Guantanamo Bay." *The New York Times.* May 1, 2005.

"List of Guantanamo Detainee Names Released." *The Associated Press.* April 19, 2006.

Selsky, Andrew. "Pentagon Releases Gitmo Detainees' Names." *The Associated Press.* May 15, 2006.

CASES AGAINST PADILLA AND MOUSSAOUI CONTINUE

Cole, David. "The Security Sham." *Philadelphia Inquirer.* May 7, 2006, D7.

Savage, David G. "Analysis: Moussaoui Verdict Raises Questions." *Los Angeles Times.* May 4, 2006.

Zajac, Andrew. "Legal Front Mostly Quiet in Terror War." *Chicago Tribune.* April 20, 2006.

RENEWAL OF PATRIOT ACT DELAYED BUT FINALLY APPROVED

Jackson, David, "Bush, Prosecutors Push Patriot Act," *USA Today*, January 4, 2006, 5A.

Schmitt, Richard B., "Senate Stalls Patriot Act Renewal," *Orlando Sentinel*, December 17, 2005, A19.

MILLENNIUM BOMBER SENTENCED

Harden, Blaine. "U.S. Contests Terrorist's Request for Reduced Sentence." *The Washington Post*, April 27, 2005.

"'Millennium Bomber' Gets 22 Years." *BBC News*, http://news.bbc.co.uk, July 27, 2005.

Penaloza, David Carillo. "Washington: Longer Sentence Sought for Bomber." *The New York Times*, August 27, 2005.

"22 Years for Millennium Bomb Plot." *The Associated Press*, July 27, 2005.

TOBACCO

BOEKEN V. PHILIP MORRIS INCORPORATED

Holland, Gina. "Supreme Court Won't Review Tobacco Award." *www.abcnews.com* March 20, 2006.

Kluger, Richard. *Ashes to Ashes: America's Hundred-Year Cigarette War, the Public Health, and the Unabashed Triumph of Philip Morris.* New York: Vintage Books. 1997.

Kessler, David. *A Question of Intent: A Great American Battle With a Deadly Industry.* New York: Public Affairs. 2002.

VOTING

ILLINOIS DEMOCRATS CONVICTED IN VOTE-BUYING SCHEME

Gonzalez, Steve. "East St. Louis Politico Pleads Guilty in Election Fraud Case." *The Madison Record.* October 12, 2005.

Press Release, Office of the U.S. Attorney, Southern District of Illinois. "Former East St. Louis Precinct Committeeman Sentenced in Vote-Buying Conspiracy." February 28, 2006.

Press Release, Office of the U.S. Attorney, Southern District of Illinois. "Two More Sentenced For Roles in East St. Louis Vote-Buying Conspiracy." February 6, 2006.

Shaw, Michael, Doug Moore, and Paul Hampel. "All Are Guilty in Vote Fraud Trial." *St. Louis Post-Dispatch* June 30, 2005, p. A1.

SEVERAL STATES FAIL TO COMPLY WITH ELECTION REFORM LAW

Cooper, Michael, "U.S. Threatens to Sue Albany Over Voting," *New York Times*, January 12, 2006.

Electionline.org, *Election Reform: What's Changed, What Hasn't, and Why, 2000–2006*. Available at www.electionline.org/Portals/1/Publications/2006.annual.report.Final.pdf.

WAIVER

ZEDNER V. UNITED STATES

Zedner v. United States, No.05–5992, (Available at www.supremecourtus.gov/opinions

"Zedner v. United States (05–5992)." *Supreme Court Collection*, 27 June 2006. Available at www.law.cornell.edu/supct/cert/05–5992.html

WHISTLEBLOWING

GARCETTI V. CEBALLOS

Richey, Warren. "From High Court, Warning to Whistle-Blowers." *Christian Science Monitor*. May 31, 2006.

Stout, David. "Justices Set Limits on Public Employees' Speech Rights." *New York Times*. May 31, 2006.

Holland, Gina. "High Court Limits Whistleblower Rights." *Los Angeles Times*. May 31, 2006.

WIRETAPPING

GOVERNMENT TRACKS FOREIGN AND DOMESTIC COMMUNICATIONS

Eggen, Dan. "Negroponte Had Denied Domestic Call Monitoring." *The Washington Post*, May 15, 2006.

Gellman, Barton and Arshad Mohammed. "Data on Phone Calls Monitored." *The Washington Post*, May 12, 2006.

Hosenball, Mark and Evan Thomas. "Hold the Phone." *Newsweek*, May 22, 2006.

Lichtblau, Eric and Scott Shane. "Bush Is Pressed Over New Report on Surveillance." *The New York Times*, May 12, 2006.

Pincus, Walter. "Gonzales Defends Phone-Data Collection." *The Washington Post*, May 24, 2006.

Regan, Tom. "FBI Checking Reporters' Phone Rrecords." *The Christian Science Monitor*, Online at www.csmonitor.com/2006/0516/dailyUpdate.html.

"Rights Group Requests Wiretapping Probe." *Reuters*, May 24, 2006.

Risen, James and Eric Lichtblau. "Bush Lets U.S. Spy on Callers Without Courts." *The New York Times*, December 16, 2005.

Svensson, Peter. "Verizon Denies Giving NSA Phone Records." *The Associated Press*, May 16, 2006.

APPENDIX

ABORTION

South Dakota 2006 Anti-Abortion Law

ENTITLED, An Act to establish certain legislative findings, to reinstate the prohibition against certain acts causing the termination of an unborn human life, to prescribe a penalty therefor, and to provide for the implementation of such provisions under certain circumstances. BE IT ENACTED BY THE LEGISLATURE OF THE STATE OF SOUTH DAKOTA:

Section 1. The Legislature accepts and concurs with the conclusion of the South Dakota Task Force to Study Abortion, based upon written materials, scientific studies, and testimony of witnesses presented to the task force, that life begins at the time of conception, a conclusion confirmed by scientific advances since the 1973 decision of Roe v. Wade, including the fact that each human being is totally unique immediately at fertilization. Moreover, the Legislature finds, based upon the conclusions of the South Dakota Task Force to Study Abortion, and in recognition of the technological advances and medical experience and body of knowledge about abortions produced and made available since the 1973 decision of Roe v. Wade, that to fully protect the rights, interests, and health of the pregnant mother, the rights, interest, and life of her unborn child, and the mother's fundamental natural intrinsic right to a relationship with her child, abortions in South Dakota should be prohibited. Moreover, the Legislature finds that the guarantee of due process of law under the Constitution of South Dakota applies equally to born and unborn human beings, and that under the Constitution of South Dakota, a pregnant mother and her unborn child, each possess a natural and inalienable right to life.

Section 2. That chapter 22-17 be amended by adding thereto a NEW SECTION to read as follows:

No person may knowingly administer to, prescribe for, or procure for, or sell to any pregnant woman any medicine, drug, or other substance with the specific intent of causing or abetting the termination of the life of an unborn human being. No person may knowingly use or employ any instrument or procedure upon a pregnant woman with the specific intent of causing or abetting the termination of the life of an unborn human being.

Any violation of this section is a Class 5 felony.

Section 3. That chapter 22-17 be amended by adding thereto a NEW SECTION to read as follows:

Nothing in section 2 of this Act may be construed to prohibit the sale, use, prescription, or administration of a contraceptive measure, drug or chemical, if it is administered prior to the time when a pregnancy could be determined through conventional medical testing and if the contraceptive measure is sold, used, prescribed, or administered in accordance with manufacturer instructions.

Section 4. That chapter 22-17 be amended by adding thereto a NEW SECTION to read as follows:

No licensed physician who performs a medical procedure designed or intended to prevent the death of a pregnant mother is guilty of violating section 2 of this Act. However, the physician shall make reasonable medical efforts under the circumstances to preserve both the life of the mother and the life of her unborn child in a manner consistent with conventional medical practice.

Medical treatment provided to the mother by a licensed physician which results in the accidental or unintentional injury or death to the unborn child is not a violation of this statute.

Nothing in this Act may be construed to subject the pregnant mother upon whom any abortion is performed or attempted to any criminal conviction and penalty.

Section 5. That chapter 22-17 be amended by adding thereto a NEW SECTION to read as follows:

Terms used in this Act mean:

(1) "Pregnant," the human female reproductive condition, of having a living unborn human being within her body throughout the entire embryonic and fetal ages of the unborn child from fertilization to full gestation and child birth;

(2) "Unborn human being," an individual living member of the species, homo sapiens, throughout the entire embryonic and fetal ages of the unborn child from fertilization to full gestation and childbirth;

(3) "Fertilization," that point in time when a male human sperm penetrates the zona pellucida of a female human ovum.

Section 6. That § 34-23A-2 be repealed.

Section 7. That § 34-23A-3 be repealed.

Section 8. That § 34-23A-4 be repealed.

Section 9. That § 34-23A-5 be repealed.

Section 10. If any court of law enjoins, suspends, or delays the implementation of a provision of this Act, the provisions of sections 6 to 9, inclusive, of this Act are similarly enjoined, suspended, or delayed during such injunction, suspension, or delayed implementation.

Section 11. If any court of law finds any provision of this Act to be unconstitutional, the other provisions of this Act are severable. If any court of law finds the provisions of this Act to be entirely or substantially unconstitutional, the provisions of § § 34-23A-2, 34-23A-3, 34-23A-4, and 34-23A-5, as of June 30, 2006, are immediately reeffective.

Section 12. This Act shall be known, and may be cited, as the Women's Health and Human Life Protection Act.

DRUGS AND NARCOTICS

Denver's Alcohol-Marijuana Equalization Initiative

WHEREAS, according to the National Institutes of Health, an average of 317 Americans die annually as the result of alcohol overdoses; and

WHEREAS, there has never been even a single fatal marijuana overdose recorded in the medical literature, as noted by the British Medical Journal in September 2003; and

WHEREAS, according to U.S. Department of Justice, "About 3 million crimes occur each year in which victims perceive the offender to have been drinking at the time of the offense. Among those victims who provided information about the offender's use of alcohol, about 35% of the victimizations involved an offender who had been drinking"; and

WHEREAS, extensive research, documented in official reports by the British government's Advisory Council on the Misuse of Drugs and the Canadian Senate Special Committee on Illegal Drugs, among others, shows that — unlike alcohol — marijuana use is not generally a cause of violence or aggressive behavior and in fact tends to reduce violence and aggression;

WHEREAS, it is the intent of this ordinance to have the private adult use and possession of marijuana treated in the same manner as the private adult use and possession of alcohol;

NOW, THEREFORE, BE IT ENACTED BY THE COUNCIL OF THE CITY AND COUNTY OF DENVER

TEXT OF PROPOSED INITIATIVE

(proposed addition in all caps, underlined)

Amend Art. 5, Div. 3, Sec. 38-175 (Revised Municipal Code)

(a) It shall be unlawful for any person UNDER THE AGE OF TWENTY-ONE (21) to possess one (1) ounce or less of marihuana. If such person is under the age of eighteen (18) years of age at the time of the offense, no jail sentence shall be imposed and any fine imposed may be supplanted by treatment as required by the court.

INTERNET

Child Online Protection Act

SEC. 1401. SHORT TITLE.

This title may be cited as the Child Online Protection Act.

SEC. 1402. CONGRESSIONAL FINDINGS.

The Congress finds that—

(1) while custody, care, and nurture of the child resides first with the parent, the widespread availability of the Internet presents opportunities for minors to access materials through the World Wide Web in a manner that can frustrate parental supervision or control;

(2) the protection of the physical and psychological well-being of minors by shielding them from materials that are harmful to them is a compelling governmental interest;

(3) to date, while the industry has developed innovative ways to help parents and educators restrict material that is harmful to minors through parental control protections and self-regulation, such efforts have not provided a national solution to the problem of minors accessing harmful material on the World Wide Web;

(4) a prohibition on the distribution of material harmful to minors, combined with legitimate defenses, is currently the most effective and least restrictive means by which to satisfy the compelling government interest; and

(5) notwithstanding the existence of protections that limit the distribution over the World Wide Web of material that is harmful to minors, parents, educators, and industry must continue efforts to find ways to protect children from being exposed to harmful material found on the Internet.

SEC. 231. RESTRICTION OF ACCESS BY MINORS TO MATERIALS COMMERCIALLY DISTRIBUTED BY MEANS OF WORLD WIDE WEB THAT ARE HARMFUL TO MINORS.

(a) Requirement To Restrict Access.—

(1) Prohibited conduct.—Whoever knowingly and with knowledge of the character of the material, in interstate or foreign commerce by means of the World Wide Web, makes any communication for commercial purposes that is available to any minor and that includes any material that is harmful to minors shall be fined not more than $50,000, imprisoned not more than 6 months, or both.

(2) Intentional violations.—In addition to the penalties under paragraph (1), whoever intentionally violates such paragraph shall be subject to a fine of not more than $50,000 for each violation. For purposes of this paragraph, each day of violation shall constitute a separate violation.

(3) Civil penalty.—In addition to the penalties under paragraphs (1) and (2), whoever violates paragraph (1) shall be subject to a civil penalty of not more than $50,000 for each violation. For purposes of this paragraph, each day of violation shall constitute a separate violation.

(b) Inapplicability of Carriers and Other Service Providers.—For purposes of subsection (a), a person shall not be considered to make any communication for commercial purposes to the extent that such person is—

(1) a telecommunications carrier engaged in the provision of a telecommunications service;

(2) a person engaged in the business of providing an Internet access service;

(3) a person engaged in the business of providing an Internet information location tool; or

(4) similarly engaged in the transmission, storage, retrieval, hosting, formatting, or translation (or any combination thereof) of a communication made by another person, without selection or alteration of the content of the communication, except that such person's deletion of a particular communication or material made by another person in a manner consistent with subsection (c) or section 230 shall not constitute such selection or alteration of the content of the communication.

(c) Affirmative Defense.—

(1) Defense.—It is an affirmative defense to prosecution under this section that the defendant, in good faith, has restricted access by minors to material that is harmful to minors—

(A) by requiring use of a credit card, debit account, adult access code, or adult personal identification number;

(B) by accepting a digital certificate that verifies age; or

(C) by any other reasonable measures that are feasible under available technology.

(2) Protection for use of defenses.—No cause of action may be brought in any court or administrative agency against any person on account of any activity that is not in violation of any law punishable by criminal or civil penalty,

and that the person has taken in good faith to implement a defense authorized under this subsection or otherwise to restrict or prevent the transmission of, or access to, a communication specified in this section.

(d) Privacy Protection Requirements.—

(1) Disclosure of information limited.—A person making a communication described in subsection (a)—

(A) shall not disclose any information collected for the purposes of restricting access to such communications to individuals 17 years of age or older without the prior written or electronic consent of—

(i) the individual concerned, if the individual is an adult; or

(ii) the individual's parent or guardian, if the individual is under 17 years of age; and

(B) shall take such actions as are necessary to prevent unauthorized access to such information by a person other than the person making such communication and the recipient of such communication.

(2) Exceptions.—A person making a communication described in subsection (a) may disclose such information if the disclosure is—

(A) necessary to make the communication or conduct a legitimate business activity related to making the communication; or

(B) made pursuant to a court order authorizing such disclosure.

(e) Definitions.—For purposes of this subsection, the following definitions shall apply:

(1) By means of the world wide web.—The term 'by means of the World Wide Web' means by placement of material in a computer server-based file archive so that it is publicly accessible, over the Internet, using hypertext transfer protocol or any successor protocol.

(2) Commercial purposes; engaged in the business.—

(A) Commercial purposes.—A person shall be considered to make a communication for commercial purposes only if such person is engaged in the business of making such communications.

(B) Engaged in the business.—The term 'engaged in the business' means that the person who makes a communication, or offers to make a communication, by means of the World Wide Web, that includes any material that is harmful to minors, devotes time, attention, or labor to such activities, as a regular course of such person's trade or business, with the objective of earning a profit as a result of such activities (although it is not necessary that the person make a profit or that the making or offering to make such communications be the person's sole or principal business or source of income). A person may be considered to be engaged in the business of making, by means of the World Wide Web, communications for commercial purposes that include material that is harmful to minors, only if the person knowingly causes the material that is harmful to minors to be posted on the World Wide Web or knowingly solicits such material to be posted on the World Wide Web.

(3) Internet.—The term 'Internet' means the combination of computer facilities and electromagnetic transmission media, and related equipment and software, comprising the interconnected worldwide network of computer networks that employ the Transmission Control Protocol/Internet Protocol or any successor protocol to transmit information.

(4) Internet access service.—The term 'Internet access service' means a service that enables users to access content, information, electronic mail, or other services offered over the Internet, and may also include access to proprietary content, information, and other services as part of a package of services offered to consumers. Such term does not include telecommunications services.

(5) Internet information location tool.—The term 'Internet information location tool' means a service that refers or links users to an online location on the World Wide Web. Such term includes directories, indices, references, pointers, and hypertext links.

(6) Material that is harmful to minors.—The term 'material that is harmful to minors' means any communication, picture, image, graphic image file, article, recording, writing, or other matter of any kind that is obscene or that—

(A) the average person, applying contemporary community standards, would find, taking the material as a whole and with respect to minors, is designed to appeal to, or is designed to pander to, the prurient interest;

(B) depicts, describes, or represents, in a manner patently offensive with respect to minors, an actual or simulated sexual act or sexual contact, an actual or simulated normal or perverted sexual act, or a lewd exhibition of the genitals or post-pubescent female breast; and

(C) taken as a whole, lacks serious literary, artistic, political, or scientific value for minors.

(7) Minor.—The term 'minor' means any person under 17 years of age.

PRIVACY

Wisconsin's Anti-Cloning Law

SECTION 1. 146.347 of the statutes is created to read:

146.347 Human cloning and parthenogenesis. (1) In this section:

(a) "Asexual reproduction" means reproduction not initiated by the union of an oocyte and a sperm.

(b) "Enucleated oocyte" means a fertilized or unfertilized oocyte, the nuclear material of which has been removed or inactivated.

(c) "Human cloning" means asexual reproduction accomplished by introducing nuclear material from one or more human somatic cells into an enucleated oocyte so as to produce a living organism having genetic material that is virtually identical to the genetic material of an existing or previously existing human organism.

(d) "Human embryo" means a human organism derived by fertilization, parthenogenesis, cloning, or any other means from one or more human gametes or human diploid cells. "Human embryo" includes a zygote but does not include a human organism at or beyond the stage of development at which the major body structures are present.

(e) "Human parthenogenesis" means the process of manipulating the genetic material of a human oocyte, without introducing into the oocyte the genetic material from any other cell, in a way that causes the oocyte to become a human embryo.

(f) "Living organism" includes a human embryo.

(g) "Somatic cell" means a cell that has a complete set of chromosomes and that is obtained or derived from a living or dead human organism at any stage of development.

(2) No person may knowingly do any of the following:

(a) Perform or attempt to perform human cloning or human parthenogenesis.

(b) Transfer or acquire for any purpose a human embryo produced by human cloning or human parthenogenesis or any embryo, cell, tissue, or product derived from a human embryo produced by human cloning or human parthenogenesis.

(3) (a) Any person who violates sub. (2) is guilty of a Class G felony, except that, notwithstanding the maximum fine specified in s. 939.50 (3) (g), the person may be fined under par. (b).

(b) 1. The maximum fine for a person other than an individual who violates sub.

(2) is $500,000 or, if the person derives a pecuniary gain from the violation, an amount equal to twice the gross amount of the person's pecuniary gain, whichever is greater.

2. The maximum fine for an individual who violates sub. (2) is $250,000 or, if the individual derives a pecuniary gain from the violation, an amount equal to twice the gross amount of the individual's pecuniary gain, whichever is greater.

GLOSSARY OF LEGAL TERMS

This section includes difficult or uncommon legal terms (**bolded** in the essays) *and their definitions from* West's Encyclopedia of American Law *(WEAL). Simple or common legal terms such as "lawsuit" and "plaintiff" are not* **bolded** *in the text and do not appear in this glossary; they do, however, have full entries in WEAL. Furthermore, terms that appear in* SMALL CAPS *within the essays—such as acts, cases, events, organizations, and persons—also appear in WEAL.*

A

Abet: To encourage or incite another to commit a crime. This word is usually applied to aiding in the commission of a crime. To abet another to commit a murder is to command, procure, counsel, encourage, induce, or assist. To facilitate the commission of a crime, promote its accomplishment, or help in advancing or bringing it about.

In relation to charge of aiding and abetting, term includes knowledge of the perpetrator's wrongful purpose, and encouragement, promotion or counsel of another in the commission of the criminal offense.

A French word, *abeter*—to bait or excite an animal.

Abrogation: The destruction or annulling of a former law by an act of the legislative power, by constitutional authority, or by usage. It stands opposed to *rogation;* and is distinguished from derogation, which implies the taking away of only some part of a law; from subrogation, which denotes the substitution of a clause; from *dispensation,* which only sets it aside in a particular instance; and from *antiquation,* which is the refusing to pass a law.

Acquiescence: Conduct recognizing the existence of a transaction and intended to permit the transaction to be carried into effect; a tacit agreement; consent inferred from silence.

Actual notice: Conveying facts to a person with the intention to apprise that person of a proceeding in which his or her interests are involved, or informing a person of some fact that he or she has a right to know and which the informer has a legal duty to communicate.

Adjudication: The legal process of resolving a dispute. The formal giving or pronouncing of a judgment or decree in a court proceeding; also the judgment or decision given. The entry of a decree by a court in respect to the parties in a case. It implies a hearing by a court, after notice, of legal evidence on the factual issue(s) involved. The equivalent of a determination. It indicates that the claims of all the parties thereto have been considered and set at rest.

Administrative Agency: An official governmental body empowered with the authority to direct and supervise the implementation of particular legislative acts. In addition to *agency,* such governmental bodies may be called commissions, corporations (e.g., FDIC), boards, departments, or divisions.

Advance: To pay money or give something of value before the date designated to do so; to provide capital to help a planned enterprise, expecting a return from it; to give someone an item before payment has been made for it.

Affirmative defense: A new fact or set of facts that operates to defeat a claim even if the facts supporting that claim are true.

Allocation: The apportionment or designation of an item for a specific purpose or to a particular place.

Amount in controversy: The value of the relief demanded or the amount of monetary damages claimed in a lawsuit.

Animus: [*Latin, Mind, soul, or intention.*] A tendency or an inclination toward a definite, sometimes unavoidable, goal; an aim, objective, or purpose.

Antitrust Law: Legislation enacted by the federal and various state governments to regulate trade and commerce by preventing unlawful restraints, price-fixing, and monopolies, to promote competition, and to encourage the production of quality goods and services at the lowest prices, with the primary goal of safeguarding public welfare by ensuring that consumer demands will be met by the manufacture and sale of goods at reasonable prices.

Appellate: Relating to appeals; reviews by superior courts of decisions of inferior courts or administrative agencies and other proceedings.

Appellate Court: A court having jurisdiction to review decisions of a trial-level or other lower court.

Apportionment: The process by which legislative seats are distributed among units entitled to representation. Determination of the number of representatives that a state, county, or other subdivision may send to a legislative body. The U.S. Constitution provides for a census every ten years, on the basis of which Congress apportions representatives according to population; but each state must have at least one representative. *Districting* is the establishment of the precise geographical boundaries of each such unit or constituency. Apportionment by state statute that denies the rule of one-person, one-vote is violative of equal protection of laws.

Also, the allocation of a charge or cost such as real estate taxes between two parties, often in the same ratio as the respective times that the parties are in possession or ownership of property during the fiscal period for which the charge is made or assessed.

Arguendo: In the course of the argument.

Associate justice: The designation given to a judge who is not the chief or presiding justice of the court on which he or she sits.

B

Backdating: Predating a document or instrument prior to the date it was actually drawn. The negotiability of an instrument is not affected by the fact that it is backdated.

Battery: At common law, an intentional unpermitted act causing harmful or offensive contact with the person of another.

Beyond a Reasonable Doubt: The standard that must be met by the prosecution's evidence in a criminal prosecution: that no other logical explanation can be derived from the facts except that the defendant committed the crime, thereby over-coming the presumption that a person is innocent until proven guilty.

Burden of Persuasion: The onus on the party with the burden of proof to convince the trier of fact of all elements of his or her case. In a criminal case the burden of the government to produce evidence of all the necessary elements of the crime beyond a reasonable doubt.

Burglary: The criminal offense of breaking and entering a building illegally for the purpose of committing a crime therein.

Carriers: Individuals or businesses that are employed to deliver people or property to an agreed destination.

Case Law: Legal principles enunciated and embodied in judicial decisions that are derived from the application of particular areas of law to the facts of individual cases.

Cause of Action: The fact or combination of facts that gives a person the right to seek judicial redress or relief against another. Also, the legal theory forming the basis of a lawsuit.

Certiorari: [*Latin, To be informed of.*] At common law, an original writ or order issued by the Chancery of King's Bench, commanding officers of inferior courts to submit the record of a cause pending before them to give the party more certain and speedy justice.

A writ that a superior appellate court issues on its discretion to an inferior court, ordering it to produce a certified record of a particular case it has tried, in order to determine whether any irregularities or errors occurred that justify review of the case.

A device by which the Supreme Court of the United States exercises its discretion in selecting the cases it will review.

Circuit Court: A specific tribunal that possesses the legal authority to hear cases within its own geographical territory.

Civil Action: A lawsuit brought to enforce, redress, or protect rights of private litigants (the plaintiffs and the defendants); not a criminal proceeding.

Civil Law: Legal system derived from the Roman *Corpus Juris Civilus* of Emperor Justinian I; differs from a common-law system, which relies on prior decisions to determine the outcome of a lawsuit. Most European and South American countries have a civil law system. England and most of the countries it dominated or colonized, including Canada and the United States, have a common-law system. However, within these countries, Louisiana, Quebec, and Puerto Rick exhibit the influence of French and Spanish settlers in their use of civil law systems.

A body of rules that delineate private rights and remedies and govern disputes between individuals in such areas as contracts, property, and family law; distinct from criminal or public law.

Civil Procedure: The methods, procedures, and practices used in civil cases.

Claim for Relief: The section of a modern complaint that states the redress sought from a court by a person who initiates a lawsuit.

Class Action: A lawsuit that allows a large number of people with a common interest in a matter to sue or be sued as a group.

Clemency: Leniency or mercy. A power given to a public official, such as a governor or the president, to in some way lower or moderate the harshness of punishment imposed upon a prisoner.

Closing argument: The final factual and legal argument made by each attorney on all sides of a case in a trial prior to a verdict or judgment.

Collateral: Related; indirect; not bearing immediately upon an issue. The property pledged or given as a security interest, or a guarantee for payment of a debt, that will be taken or kept by the creditor in case of a default on the original debt.

Collective Bargaining Agreement: The contractual agreement between an employer and a labor union that governs wages, hours, and working conditions for employees and which can be enforced against both the employer and the union for failure to comply with its terms.

Color of Law: The appearance of a legal right.

Commerce Clause: The provision of the U.S. Constitution that gives Congress exclusive power over trade activities between the states and with foreign countries and Indian tribes.

Common Law: The ancient law of England based upon societal customs and recognized and enforced by the judgments and decrees of the courts. The general body of statutes and case law that governed England and the American colonies prior to the American Revolution.

The principles and rules of action, embodied in case law rather than legislative enactments, applicable to the government and protection of persons and property that derive their authority from the community customs and traditions that evolved over the centuries as interpreted by judicial tribunals.

A designation used to denote the opposite of statutory, equitable, or civil; for example, a common-law action.

Compensatory Damages: A sum of money awarded in a civil action by a court to indemnify a person for the particular loss, detriment, or injury suffered as a result of the unlawful conduct of another.

Comptroller: An officer who conducts the fiscal affairs of a state or municipal corporation.

Consumer credit: Short-term loans made to enable people to purchase goods or services primarily for personal, family, or household purposes.

Criminal Law: A body of rules and statutes that defines conduct prohibited by the government because it threatens and harms public safety and welfare and that establishes punishment to be imposed for the commission of such acts.

Criminal Procedure: The framework of laws and rules that govern the administration of justice in cases involving an individual who has been accused of a crime, beginning with the initial investigation of the crime and concluding either with the unconditional release of the accused by virture of acquittal (a judgment of not guilty) or by the imposition of a term of punishment pursuant to a conviction for the crime.

Cruel and Unusual Punishment: Such punishment as would amount to torture or barbarity, and cruel and degrading punishment not known to the common law, or any fine, penalty, confinement, or treatment so disproportionate to the offense as to shock the moral sense of the community.

Custodial interrogation: Questioning initiated by law enforcement officers after a person is taken into custody or otherwise deprived of his or her freedom in any significant way, thus requiring that the person be advised of his or her constitutional rights.

D

Death warrant: An order from the executive, the governor of a state, or the president directing the warden of a prison or a sheriff or other appropriate officer to carry into execution a sentence of death; an order commanding that a named person be put to death in a specified manner at a specific time.

De Novo: [*Latin, Anew.*] A second time; afresh. A trial or a hearing that is ordered by an appellate court that has reviewed the record of a hearing in a lower court and sent the matter back to the original court for a new trial, as if it had not been previously heard nor decided.

Directed verdict: A procedural device whereby the decision in a case is taken out of the hands of the jury by the judge.

Disorderly Conduct: A broad term describing conduct that disturbs the peace or endangers the morals, health, or safety of a community.

Disposition: Act of disposing; transferring to the care or possession of another. The parting with, alienation of, or giving up of property. The final settlement of a matter and, with reference to decisions announced by a court, a judge's ruling is commonly referred to as disposition, regardless of level of resolution. In criminal procedure, the sentencing or other final settlement of a criminal case. With respect to a mental state, denotes an attitude, prevailing tendency, or inclination.

District Court: A designation of an inferior state court that exercises general jurisdiction that it has been granted by the constitution or statute which created it. A U.S. judicial tribunal with original jurisdiction to try cases or controversies that fall within its limited jurisdiction.

Doing business: A qualification imposed in state long-arm statutes governing the service of process, the method by which a lawsuit is commenced, which requires nonresident corporations to engage in commercial transactions within state borders in order to be subject to the personal jurisdiction of state courts.

Double Jeopardy: A second prosecution for the same offense after acquittal or conviction or multiple punishments for same offense. The evil sought to be avoided by prohibiting double jeopardy is double trial and double conviction, not necessarily double punishment.

Due Process of Law: A fundamental, constitutional guarantee that all legal proceedings will be fair and that one will be given notice of the proceedings and an opportunity to be heard before the government acts to take away one's life, liberty, or property. Also, a constitutional guarantee that a law shall not be unreasonable, arbitrary, or capricious.

E

Earned income: Sources of money derived from the labor, professional service, or entrepreneurship of an individual taxpayer as opposed to funds generated by investments, dividends, and interest.

Embezzlement: The fraudulent conversion of another's property by a person who is in a position of trust, such as an agent or employee.

Eminent Domain: The power to take private property for public use by a state, municipality, or private person or corporation authorized to exercise functions of public character, following the payment of just compensation to the owner of that property.

En banc: [*Latin, French. In the bench.*] Full bench. Refers to a session where the entire membership of the court will participate in the decision rather than the regular quorum. In other countries, it is common for a court to have more members than are usually necessary to hear an appeal. In the United States, the Circuit Courts of Appeal usually sit in panels of judges but for important cases may expand the bench to a larger number, when the judges are said to be sitting *en banc.* Similarly, only one of the judges of the U.S. Tax Court will typically hear and decide on a tax controversy. However, when the issues involved are unusually novel or of wide impact, the case will be heard and decided by the full court sitting *en banc.*

Encroachment: An illegal intrusion in a highway or navigable river, with or without obstruction. An encroachment upon a street or highway is a fixture, such as a wall or fence, which illegally intrudes into or invades the highway or encloses a portion of it, diminishing its width or area, but without closing it to public travel.

Entice: To wrongfully solicit, persuade, procure, allure, attract, draw by blandishment, coax, or seduce. To lure, induce, tempt, incite, or persuade a person to do a thing. Enticement of a child is inviting, persuading, or attempting to persuade a child to enter any vehicle, building, room, or secluded place with intent to commit an unlawful sexual act upon or with the person of said child.

Entity: A real being; existence. An organization or being that possesses separate existence for tax purposes. Examples would be corporations, partnerships, estates, and trusts. The accounting entity for which accounting statements are prepared may not be the same as the entity defined by law.

Entity includes corporation and foreign corporation; not-for-profit corporation; profit and not-for-profit unincorporated association; business trust, estate, partnership, trust, and two or more persons having a joint or common economic interest; and state, U.S., and foreign governments.

An existence apart, such as a corporation in relation to its stockholders.

Entity includes person, estate, trust, governmental unit.

Equal Protection: The constitutional guarantee that no person or class of persons shall be denied the same protection of the laws that is enjoyed by other persons or other classes in like circumstances in their lives, liberty, property, and pursuit of happiness.

Escrow: Something of value, such as a deed, stock, money, or written instrument, that is put into the custody of a third person by its owner, a grantor, an obligor, or a promisor, to be retained until the occurrence of a contingency or performance of a condition.

Estoppel: A legal principle that precludes a party from denying or alleging a certain fact owing to that party's previous conduct, allegation, or denial.

Et seq.: "An abbreviation for the Latin *et sequentes* or *et sequentia*, meaning 'and the following.'"

Examiner: An official or other person empowered by another—whether an individual, business, or government agency—to investigate and review specified documents for accuracy and truthfulness.

A court-appointed officer, such as a master or referee, who inspects evidence presented to resolve controverted matters and records statements made by witnesses in the particular proceeding pending before that court.

A government employee in the Patent and Trademark Office whose duty it is to scrutinize the application made for a patent by an inventor to determine whether the invention meets the statutory requirements of patentability.

A federal employee of the Internal Revenue Service who reviews income tax returns for accuracy and truthfulness.

Excise: A tax imposed on the performance of an act, the engaging in an occupation, or the enjoyment of a privilege. A tax on the manufacture, sale, or use of goods or on the carrying on of an occupation or activity, or a tax on the transfer of property. In current usage the term has been extended to include various license fees and practically every internal revenue tax except the income tax (e.g., federal alcohol and tobacco excise taxes).

Exclusionary rule: The principle based on federal constitutional law that evidence illegally seized by law enforcement officers in violation of a suspect's right to be free from unreasonable searches and seizures cannot be used against the suspect in a criminal prosecution.

F

Fair market value: The amount for which real property or personal property would be sold in a voluntary transaction between a buyer and seller, neither of whom is under any obligation to buy or sell.

False pretenses: False representations of past or present material facts, known by the wrongdoer to be false, made with the intent to defraud a victim into passing title in property to the wrongdoer.

Federal Courts: The U.S. judicial tribunals created by Article III of the Constitution, or by Congress, to hear and determine justiciable controversies.

Federal question: An issue directly involving the U.S. Constitution, federal statutes, or treaties between the United States and a foreign country.

Felonious: Done with an intent to commit a serious crime or a felony; done with an evil heart or purpose; malicious; wicked; villainous.

Felony: A serious crime, characterized under federal law and many state statutes as any offense punishable by death or imprisonment in excess of one year.

Fiduciary: An individual in whom another has placed the utmost trust and confidence to manage and protect property or money. The relationship wherein one person has an obligation to act for another's benefit.

Filibuster: A tactic used by a LEGISLATIVE representative to hinder and delay consideration of an action to be taken on a proposed bill through prolonged, irrelevant, and procrastinating speeches on the floor of the House, Senate, or other legislative body.

Final Decision: The resolution of a controversy by a court or series of courts from which no appeal may be taken and that precludes further action. The last act by a lower court that is required for the completion of a lawsuit, such as the handing down of a final judgment upon which an appeal to a higher court may be brought.

Finance charge: The amount owed to a lender by a purchaser-debtor to be allowed to pay for goods purchased over a series of installments, as opposed to one lump sum at the time of the sale or billing.

First Instance: The initial trial court where an action is brought.

Fiscal: Relating to finance or financial matters, such as money, taxes, or public or private revenues.

Forensic: Belonging to courts of justice.

Forfeiture: The involuntary relinquishment of money or property without compensation as a consequence of a breach or nonperformance of some legal obligation or the commission of a crime. The loss of a corporate charter or franchise as a result of illegality, malfeasance, or nonfeasance. The surrender by an owner of her or his entire interest in real property mandated by law as a punishment for illegal conduct or negligence. In old English law, the release of land by a tenant to the tenant's lord due to some breach of conduct, or the loss of goods or chattels (articles of personal property) assessed as a penalty against the perpetrator of some crime or offense and as a recompense to the injured party.

Fraud: A false representation of a matter of fact—whether by words or by conduct, by false or misleading allegations, or by concealment of what should have been disclosed—that deceives and is intended to deceive another so that the individual will act upon it to her or his legal injury.

Fraudulent: The description of a willful act commenced with the specific intent to deceive or cheat, in order to cause some financial detriment to another and to engender personal financial gain.

Freedom of Association: The right to associate with others for the purpose of engaging in constitutionally protected activities.

G

Garnishment: A legal procedure by which a creditor can collect what a debtor owes by reaching the debtor's property when it is in the hands of someone other than the debtor.

Gerrymander: The process of dividing a particular state or territory into election districts in such a manner as to accomplish an unlawful purpose, such as to give one party a greater advantage.

Good Faith: Honesty; a sincere intention to deal fairly with others.

Grand Jury: A panel of citizens that is convened by a court to decide whether it is appropriate for the government to indict (proceed with a prosecution against) someone suspected of a crime.

Guardian: A person lawfully invested with the power, and charged with the obligation, of taking care of and managing the property and rights of a person who, because of age, understanding, or self-control, is considered incapable of administering his or her own affairs.

Guardian Ad Litem: A guardian appointed by the court to represent the interests of infants, the unborn, or incompetent persons in legal actions.

H

Habeas Corpus: [*Latin, You have the body.*] A writ (court order) that commands an individual or a government official who has restrained another to produce the prisoner at a designated time and place so that the court can determine the legality of custody and decide whether to order the prisoner's release.

Harmless Error: "A legal doctrine in criminal law that allows verdicts to stand without new trials being ordered despite errors of law at trial as long as all errors were insufficient to affect the final outcome. Rule 52(a) of the Federal Code of Criminal Procedure explains it as, "'Any error, defect, irregularity or variance which does not affect substantial rights shall be disregarded.'"

Husband and Wife: A man and woman who are legally married to one another and are thereby given by law specific rights and duties resulting from that relationship.

I

Imputed: Attributed vicariously.

Independent audit: A systematic review of the accuracy and truthfulness of the accounting records of a particular individual, business, or organization by a person or firm skilled in the necessary accounting methods and not related in any way to the person or firm undergoing the audit.

Informed Consent: Assent to permit an occurrence, such as surgery, that is based on a complete disclosure of facts needed to make the decision intelligently, such as knowledge of the risks entailed or alternatives.

The name for a fundamental principle of law that a physician has a duty to reveal what a reasonably prudent physician in the medical community employing reasonable care would reveal to a patient as to whatever reasonably foreseeable risks of harm might result from a proposed course of treatment. This disclosure must be afforded so that a patient—exercising ordinary care for his or her own welfare and confronted with a choice of undergoing the proposed treatment, alternative treatment, or none at all—can intelligently exercise judgment by reasonably balancing the probable risks against the probable benefits.

In personam: [*Latin, Against the person.*] A lawsuit seeking a judgment to be enforceable specifically against an individual person.

Insanity Defense: A defense asserted by an accused in a criminal prosecution to avoid liability for the commission of a crime because, at the time of the crime, the person did not appreciate the nature or quality or wrongfulness of the acts.

Inter vivos: [*Latin, Between the living.*] A phrase used to describe a gift that is made during the donor's lifetime.

Irreparable injury: Any harm or loss that is not easily repaired, restored, or compensated by monetary damages. A serious wrong, generally of a repeated and continuing nature, that has an equitable remedy of injunctive relief.

J

Joinder: The union in one lawsuit of multiple parties who have the same rights or against whom rights are claimed as coplaintiffs or codefendants. The combination in one lawsuit of two or more causes of action, or grounds for relief. At common law the acceptance by opposing parties that a particular issue is in dispute.

Joint resolution: A type of measure that Congress may consider and act upon, the other types being bills, concurrent resolutions, and simple resolutions, in addition to treaties in the Senate.

Joint Venture: An association of two or more individuals or companies engaged in a solitary business enterprise for profit without actual partnership or incorporation; also called a joint adventure.

Juridical: Pertaining to the administration of justice or to the office of a judge.

Jurisprudence: "From the Latin term *juris prudentia,* which means 'the study, knowledge, or science of law'; in the United States, more broadly associated with the philosophy of law."

L

Lien: A right given to another by the owner of property to secure a debt, or one created by law in favor of certain creditors.

M

Magistrate: Any individual who has the power of a public civil officer or inferior judicial officer, such as a justice of the peace.

Mail Fraud: A crime in which the perpetrator develops a scheme using the mails to defraud another of money or property. This crime specifically requires the intent to defraud, and is a federal offense governed by section 1341 of title 18 of the U.S. Code. The mail fraud statute was first enacted in 1872 to prohibit illicit mailings with the Postal Service (formerly the Post Office) for the purpose of executing a fraudulent scheme.

Malice: The intentional commission of a wrongful act, absent justification, with the intent to cause harm to others; conscious violation of the law that injures another individual; a mental state indicating a disposition in disregard of social duty and a tendency toward malfeasance.

Malicious Prosecution: An action for damages brought by one against whom a civil suit or criminal proceeding has been unsuccessfully commenced without probable cause and for a purpose other than that of bringing the alleged offender to justice.

Mandamus: [*Latin, We command.*] A writ or order that is issued from a court of superior jurisdiction that commands an inferior tribunal, corporation, municipal corporation, or individual to perform, or refrain from performing, a particular act, the performance or omission of which is required by law as an obligation.

Manslaughter: The unjustifiable, inexcusable, and intentional killing of a human being without deliberation, premeditation, and malice. The unlawful killing of a human being without any deliberation, which may be involuntary, in the commission of a lawful act without due caution and circumspection.

Medicaid: A joint federal-state program that provides health care insurance to low-income persons.

Medicare: A federally funded system of health and hospital insurance for persons age sixty-five and older and for disabled persons.

Mental anguish: When connected with a physical injury, includes both the resultant mental sensation of pain and also the accompanying feelings of distress, fright, and anxiety. As an element of damages implies a relatively high degree of mental pain and distress; it is more than mere disappointment, anger, worry, resentment, or embarrassment, although it may include all of these, and it includes mental sensation of pain resulting from such painful emotions as grief, severe disappointment, indignation, wounded pride, shame, despair, and/or public humiliation. In other connections, and as a ground for divorce or for compensable damages or an element of damages, it includes the mental suffering resulting from the excitation of the more poignant and painful emotions, such as grief, severe disappointment, indignation, wounded pride, shame, public humiliation, despair, etc.

Mitigating Circumstances: Circumstances that may be considered by a court in determining culpability of a defendant or the extent of damages to be awarded to a plaintiff. Mitigating circumstances do not justify or excuse an offense but may reduce the severity of a charge. Similarly, a recognition of mitigating circumstances to reduce a damage award does not imply that the damages were not suffered but that they have been partially ameliorated.

Money Laundering: The process of taking the proceeds of criminal activity and making them appear legal.

Monopoly: An economic advantage held by one or more persons or companies deriving from the exclusive power to carry on a particular business or trade or to manufacture and sell a particular item, thereby suppressing competition and allowing such persons or companies to raise the price of a product or service substantially above the price that would be established by a free market.

Mutual fund: A fund, in the form of an investment company, in which shareholders combine their money to invest in a variety of stocks, bonds, and money-market investments such as U.S. Treasury bills and bank certificates of deposit.

Of counsel: A term commonly applied in the practice of law to an attorney who has been employed to aid in the preparation and management of a particular case but who is not the principal attorney in the action.

Original Jurisdiction: The authority of a tribunal to entertain a lawsuit, try it, and set forth a judgment on the law and facts.

Pecuniary: Monetary; relating to money; financial; consisting of money or that which can be valued in money.

Pension: A benefit, usually money, paid regularly to retired employees or their survivors by private business and federal, state, and local governments. Employers are not required to establish pension benefits but do so to attract qualified employees.

Per curiam: [*Latin, By the court.*] A phrase used to distinguish an opinion of the whole court from an opinion written by any one judge.

Peremptory Challenge: The right to challenge a juror without assigning, or being required to assign, a reason for the challenge.

Petit jury: The ordinary panel of twelve persons called to issue a verdict in a civil action or a criminal prosecution.

Plurality: The opinion of an appellate court in which more justices join than in any concurring opinion.

The excess of votes cast for one candidate over those votes cast for any other candidate.

Preemption: A doctrine based on the Supremacy Clause of the U.S. Constitution that holds that certain matters are of such a national, as opposed to local, character that federal laws preempt or take precedence over state laws. As such, a state may not pass a law inconsistent with the federal law.

A doctrine of state law that holds that a state law displaces a local law or regulation that is in the same field and is in conflict or inconsistent with the state law.

Preliminary Injunction: A temporary order made by a court at the request of one party that prevents the other party from pursuing a particular course of conduct until the conclusion of a trial on the merits.

Prima Facie: [*Latin, On the first appearance.*] A fact presumed to be true unless it is disproved.

Primary authority: Law, in various forms, that a court must follow in deciding a case.

Privileges and Immunities: Concepts contained in the U.S. Constitution that place the citizens of each state on an equal basis with citizens of other states in respect to advantages resulting from citizenship in those states and citizenship in the United States.

Probable Cause: Apparent facts discovered through logical inquiry that would lead a reasonably intelligent and prudent person to believe that an accused person has committed a crime, thereby warranting his or her prosecution, or that a cause of action has accrued, justifying a civil lawsuit.

Probate: The court process by which a will is proved valid or invalid. The legal process wherein the estate of a decedent is administered.

Probationer: A convict who is released from prison provided he or she maintains good behavior. One who is on probation whereby he or she is given some freedom to reenter society subject to the condition that for a specified period the individual conduct him or herself in a manner approved by a special officer to whom the probationer must report.

Probative: Having the effect of proof, tending to prove, or actually proving.

Product Liability: The responsibility of a manufacturer or vendor of goods to compensate for injury caused by a defective good that it has provided for sale.

Pro hac vice: For this turn; for this one particular occasion. For example, an out-of-state lawyer may be admitted to practice in a local jurisdiction for a particular case only.

Proprietary: As a noun, a proprietor or owner; one who has the exclusive title to a thing; one who possesses or holds the title to a thing in his or her own right; one who possesses the dominion or ownership of a thing in his or her own right.

As an adjective, belonging to ownership; owned by a particular person; belonging or pertaining to a proprietor; relating to a certain owner or proprietor.

Proximate Cause: An act from which an injury results as a natural, direct, uninterrupted consequence and without which the injury would not have occurred.

Public Policy: A principle that no person or government official can legally perform an act that tends to injure the public.

Punitive Damages: Monetary compensation awarded to an injured party that goes beyond that which is necessary to compensate the individual for losses and that is intended to punish the wrongdoer.

Purview: The part of a statute or a law that delineates its purpose and scope.

Q

Quasi-judicial: The action taken and discretion exercised by public administrative agencies or bodies that are obliged to investigate or ascertain facts and draw conclusions from them as the foundation for official actions.

R

Ratification: The confirmation or adoption of an act that has already been performed.

Rebuttable presumption: A conclusion as to the existence or nonexistence of a fact that a judge or jury must draw when certain evidence has been introduced and admitted as true in a lawsuit but that can be contracted by evidence to the contrary.

Recidivism: The behavior of a repeat or habitual criminal. A measurement of the rate at which offenders commit other crimes, either by arrest or conviction baselines, after being released from incarceration.

Redress: Compensation for injuries sustained; recovery or restitution for harm or injury; damages or equitable relief. Access to the courts to gain reparation for a wrong.

Rejoinder: The answer made by a defendant in the second stage of common-law pleading that rebuts or denies the assertions made in the plaintiff's replication.

Repeal: The annulment or abrogation of a previously existing statute by the enactment of a later law that revokes the former law.

Rescind: To declare a contract void—of no legal force or binding effect—from its inception and thereby restore the parties to the positions they would have occupied had no contract ever been made.

Responsive pleading: A formal declaration by a party in reply to a prior declaration by an opponent.

Restitution: In the context of criminal law, state programs under which an offender is required, as a condition of his or her sentence, to repay money or donate services to the victim or society; with respect to maritime law, the restoration of articles lost by jettison, done when the remainder of the cargo has been saved, at the general charge of the owners of the cargo; in the law of torts, or civil wrongs, a measure of damages; in regard to contract law, the restoration of a party injured by a breach of contract to the position that party occupied before she or he entered the contract.

Restraint of trade: Contracts or combinations that tend, or are designed, to eliminate or stifle competition, create a monopoly, artificially maintain prices, or otherwise hamper or obstruct the course of trade as it would be carried on if it were left to the control of natural economic forces.

Robbery: The taking of money or goods in the possession of another, from his or her person or immediate presence, by force or intimidation.

S

Sodomy: Anal or oral intercourse between human beings, or any sexual relations between a human being and an animal, the act of which may be punishable as a criminal offense.

Solicitor General: An officer of the U.S. Department of Justice who represents the U.S. government in cases before the U.S. Supreme Court.

Sovereign Immunity: The legal protection that prevents a sovereign state or person from being sued without consent.

Special assessment: A real property tax proportionately levied on homeowners and landowners to cover the costs of improvements that will be for the benefit of all upon whom it is imposed.

State interest: A broad term for any matter of public concern that is addressed by a government in law or policy.

State's Evidence: A colloquial term for testimony given by an accomplice or joint participant in the commission of a crime, subject to an agreement that the person will be granted immunity from prosecution if she voluntarily, completely, and fairly discloses her own guilt as well as that of the other participants.

Statute: An act of a legislature that declares, proscribes, or commands something; a specific law, expressed in writing.

Statute of Limitations: A type of federal or state law that restricts the time within which legal proceedings may be brought.

Statutory: Created, defined, or relating to a statute; required by statute; conforming to a statute.

Strict scrutiny: A standard of judicial review for a challenged policy in which the court presumes the policy to be invalid unless the government can demonstrate a compelling interest to justify the policy.

Sua sponte: [*Latin, Of his or her or its own will; voluntarily.*]

Subject matter jurisdiction: The power of a court to hear and determine cases of the general class to which the proceedings in question belong.

Subrogation: The substitution of one person in the place of another with reference to a lawful claim, demand, or right, so that he or she who is substituted succeeds to the rights of the other in relation to the debt or claim, and its rights, remedies, or securities.

Summary Judgment: A procedural device used during civil litigation to promptly and expeditiously dispose of a case without a trial. It is used when there is no dispute as to the material facts of the case and a party is entitled to judgment as a matter of law.

T

Tax Sale: A transfer of real property in exchange for money to satisfy charges imposed thereupon by the government that have remained unpaid after the legal period for their payment has expired.

Term of art: A word or phrase that has special meaning in a particular context.

Test case: A suit brought specifically for the establishment of an important legal right or principle.

Third party: A generic legal term for any individual who does not have a direct connection with a legal transaction but who might be affected by it.

Tortious: Wrongful; conduct of such character as to subject the actor to civil liability under tort law.

Tort Law: A body of rights, obligations, and remedies that is applied by courts in civil proceedings to provide relief for persons who have suffered harm from the wrongful acts of others. The person who sustains injury or suffers pecuniary damage as the result of tortious conduct is known as the plaintiff, and the person who is responsible for inflicting the injury and incurs liability for the damage is known as the defendant or tortfeasor.

Tribunal: A general term for a court, or the seat of a judge.

Trustee: An individual or corporation named by an individual, who sets aside property to be used for the benefit of another person, to manage the property as provided by the terms of the document that created the arrangement.

Tying arrangement: An agreement in which a vendor conditions the sale of a particular product on a vendee's promise to purchase an additional, unrelated product.

U

U.S. Code: A multivolume publication of the text of statutes enacted by Congress.

Usurious: Characterized by an unconscionable or exorbitant rate of interest.

Usury: The crime of charging higher interest on a loan than the law permits.

V

Venue: A place, such as the territory from which residents are selected to serve as jurors.

A proper place, such as the correct court to hear a case because it has authority over events that have occurred within a certain geographical area.

Vitiate: To impair or make void; to destroy or annul, either completely or partially, the force and effect of an act or instrument.

Voucher: A receipt or release which provides evidence of payment or other discharge of a debt, often for purposes of reimbursement, or attests to the accuracy of the accounts.

W

Writ: An order issued by a court requiring that something be done or giving authority to do a specified act.

Wrongful Death: The taking of the life of an individual resulting from the willful or negligent act of another person or persons.

Z

Zoning: The separation or division of a municipality into districts, the regulation of buildings and structures in such districts in accordance with their construction and the nature and extent of their use, and the dedication of such districts to particular uses designed to serve the general welfare.

ABBREVIATIONS

A.	Atlantic Reporter
A. 2d	Atlantic Reporter, Second Series
AA	Alcoholics Anonymous
AAA	American Arbitration Association; Agricultural Adjustment Act of 1933
AALS	Association of American Law Schools
AAPRP	All African People's Revolutionary Party
AARP	American Association of Retired Persons
AAS	American Anti-Slavery Society
ABA	American Bar Association; Architectural Barriers Act of 1968; American Bankers Association
ABC	American Broadcasting Companies, Inc. (formerly American Broadcasting Corporation)
ABM	Antiballistic missile
ABM Treaty	Anti-Ballistic Missile Treaty of 1972
ABVP	Anti-Biased Violence Project
A/C	Account
A.C.	Appeal cases
ACAA	Air Carrier Access Act
ACCA	Armed Career Criminal Act of 1984
ACF	Administration for Children and Families
ACLU	American Civil Liberties Union
ACRS	Accelerated Cost Recovery System
ACS	Agricultural Cooperative Service
ACT	American College Test
Act'g Legal Adv.	Acting Legal Advisor
ACUS	Administrative Conference of the United States
ACYF	Administration on Children, Youth, and Families
A.D. 2d	Appellate Division, Second Series, N.Y.
ADA	Americans with Disabilities Act of 1990
ADAMHA	Alcohol, Drug Abuse, and Mental Health Administration
ADC	Aid to Dependent Children
ADD	Administration on Developmental Disabilities
ADEA	Age Discrimination in Employment Act of 1967
ADL	Anti-Defamation League
ADR	Alternative dispute resolution
AEC	Atomic Energy Commission

AECB	Arms Export Control Board
AEDPA	Antiterrorism and Effective Death Penalty Act
A.E.R.	All England Law Reports
AFA	American Family Association; Alabama Freethought Association
AFB	American Farm Bureau
AFBF	American Farm Bureau Federation
AFDC	Aid to Families with Dependent Children
aff'd per cur.	Affirmed by the court
AFIS	Automated fingerprint identification system
AFL	American Federation of Labor
AFL-CIO	American Federation of Labor and Congress of Industrial Organizations
AFRes	Air Force Reserve
AFSC	American Friends Service Committee
AFSCME	American Federation of State, County, and Municipal Employees
AGRICOLA	Agricultural Online Access
AIA	Association of Insurance Attorneys
AIB	American Institute for Banking
AID	Artificial insemination using a third-party donor's sperm; Agency for International Development
AIDS	Acquired immune deficiency syndrome
AIH	Artificial insemination using the husband's sperm
AIM	American Indian Movement
AIPAC	American Israel Public Affairs Committee
AIUSA	Amnesty International, U.S.A. Affiliate
AJS	American Judicature Society
ALA	American Library Association
Alcoa	Aluminum Company of America
ALEC	American Legislative Exchange Council
ALF	Animal Liberation Front
ALI	American Law Institute
ALJ	Administrative law judge
All E.R.	All England Law Reports
ALO	Agency Liaison
A.L.R.	American Law Reports
ALY	*American Law Yearbook*
AMA	American Medical Association
AMAA	Agricultural Marketing Agreement Act
Am. Dec.	American Decisions
amdt.	Amendment
Amer. St. Papers, For. Rels.	American State Papers, Legislative and Executive Documents of the Congress of the U.S., Class I, Foreign Relations, 1832–1859
AMS	Agricultural Marketing Service
AMVETS	American Veterans (of World War II)
ANA	Administration for Native Americans
Ann. Dig.	Annual Digest of Public International Law Cases
ANRA	American Newspaper Publishers Association
ANSCA	Alaska Native Claims Act
ANZUS	Australia-New Zealand-United States Security Treaty Organization
AOA	Administration on Aging
AOE	Arizonans for Official English
AOL	America Online
AP	Associated Press
APA	Administrative Procedure Act of 1946
APHIS	Animal and Plant Health Inspection Service
App. Div.	Appellate Division Reports, N.Y. Supreme Court

Arb. Trib., U.S.-British	Arbitration Tribunal, Claim Convention of 1853, United States and Great Britain Convention of 1853
Ardcor	American Roller Die Corporation
ARPA	Advanced Research Projects Agency
ARPANET	Advanced Research Projects Agency Network
ARS	Advanced Record System
Art.	Article
ARU	American Railway Union
ASCME	American Federation of State, County, and Municipal Employees
ASCS	Agriculture Stabilization and Conservation Service
ASM	Available Seatmile
ASPCA	American Society for the Prevention of Cruelty to Animals
Asst. Att. Gen.	Assistant Attorney General
AT&T	American Telephone and Telegraph
ATFD	Alcohol, Tobacco and Firearms Division
ATLA	Association of Trial Lawyers of America
ATO	Alpha Tau Omega
ATTD	Alcohol and Tobacco Tax Division
ATU	Alcohol Tax Unit
AUAM	American Union against Militarism
AUM	Animal Unit Month
AZT	Azidothymidine
BAC	Blood alcohol concentration
BALSA	Black-American Law Student Association
BATF	Bureau of Alcohol, Tobacco and Firearms
BBS	Bulletin Board System
BCCI	Bank of Credit and Commerce International
BEA	Bureau of Economic Analysis
Bell's Cr. C.	Bell's English Crown Cases
Bevans	United States Treaties, etc. *Treaties and Other International Agreements of the United States of America, 1776–1949* (compiled under the direction of Charles I. Bevans, 1968–76)
BFOQ	Bona fide occupational qualification
BI	Bureau of Investigation
BIA	Bureau of Indian Affairs; Board of Immigration Appeals
BID	Business improvement district
BJS	Bureau of Justice Statistics
Black.	Black's United States Supreme Court Reports
Blatchf.	Blatchford's United States Circuit Court Reports
BLM	Bureau of Land Management
BLS	Bureau of Labor Statistics
BMD	Ballistic missile defense
BNA	Bureau of National Affairs
BOCA	Building Officials and Code Administrators International
BOP	Bureau of Prisons
BPP	Black Panther Party for Self-defense
Brit. and For.	British and Foreign State Papers
BSA	Boy Scouts of America
BTP	Beta Theta Pi
Burr.	James Burrows, *Report of Cases Argued and Determined in the Court of King's Bench during the Time of Lord Mansfield* (1766–1780)
BVA	Board of Veterans Appeals
c.	Chapter
C^3I	Command, Control, Communications, and Intelligence
C.A.	Court of Appeals
CAA	Clean Air Act
CAB	Civil Aeronautics Board; Corporation for American Banking

CAFE	Corporate average fuel economy
Cal. 2d	California Reports, Second Series
Cal. 3d	California Reports, Third Series
CALR	Computer-assisted legal research
Cal. Rptr.	California Reporter
CAP	Common Agricultural Policy
CARA	Classification and Ratings Administration
CATV	Community antenna television
CBO	Congressional Budget Office
CBS	Columbia Broadcasting System
CBOEC	Chicago Board of Election Commissioners
CCC	Commodity Credit Corporation
CCDBG	Child Care and Development Block Grant of 1990
C.C.D. Pa.	Circuit Court Decisions, Pennsylvania
C.C.D. Va.	Circuit Court Decisions, Virginia
CCEA	Cabinet Council on Economic Affairs
CCP	Chinese Communist Party
CCR	Center for Constitutional Rights
C.C.R.I.	Circuit Court, Rhode Island
CD	Certificate of deposit; compact disc
CDA	Communications Decency Act
CDBG	Community Development Block Grant Program
CDC	Centers for Disease Control and Prevention; Community Development Corporation
CDF	Children's Defense Fund
CDL	Citizens for Decency through Law
CD-ROM	Compact disc read-only memory
CDS	Community Dispute Services
CDW	Collision damage waiver
CENTO	Central Treaty Organization
CEO	Chief executive officer
CEQ	Council on Environmental Quality
CERCLA	Comprehensive Environmental Response, Compensation, and Liability Act of 1980
cert.	*Certiorari*
CETA	Comprehensive Employment and Training Act
C & F	Cost and freight
CFC	Chlorofluorocarbon
CFE Treaty	Conventional Forces in Europe Treaty of 1990
C.F. & I.	Cost, freight, and insurance
C.F.R	Code of Federal Regulations
CFNP	Community Food and Nutrition Program
CFTA	Canadian Free Trade Agreement
CFTC	Commodity Futures Trading Commission
Ch.	Chancery Division, English Law Reports
CHAMPVA	Civilian Health and Medical Program at the Veterans Administration
CHEP	Cuban/Haitian Entrant Program
CHINS	Children in need of supervision
CHIPS	Child in need of protective services
Ch.N.Y.	Chancery Reports, New York
Chr. Rob.	Christopher Robinson, *Reports of Cases Argued and Determined in the High Court of Admiralty* (1801–1808)
CIA	Central Intelligence Agency
CID	Commercial Item Descriptions
C.I.F.	Cost, insurance, and freight
CINCNORAD	Commander in Chief, North American Air Defense Command
C.I.O.	Congress of Industrial Organizations

CIPE	Center for International Private Enterprise
C.J.	Chief justice
CJIS	Criminal Justice Information Services
C.J.S.	Corpus Juris Secundum
Claims Arb. under Spec. Conv., Nielsen's Rept.	Frederick Kenelm Nielsen, *American and British Claims Arbitration under the Special Agreement Concluded between the United States and Great Britain, August 18, 1910* (1926)
CLASP	Center for Law and Social Policy
CLE	Center for Law and Education; Continuing Legal Education
CLEO	Council on Legal Education Opportunity; Chief Law Enforcement Officer
CLP	Communist Labor Party of America
CLS	Christian Legal Society; critical legal studies (movement); Critical Legal Studies (membership organization)
C.M.A.	Court of Military Appeals
CMEA	Council for Mutual Economic Assistance
CMHS	Center for Mental Health Services
C.M.R.	Court of Military Review
CNN	Cable News Network
CNO	Chief of Naval Operations
CNOL	Consolidated net operating loss
CNR	Chicago and Northwestern Railway
CO	Conscientious Objector
C.O.D.	Cash on delivery
COGP	Commission on Government Procurement
COINTELPRO	Counterintelligence Program
Coke Rep.	Coke's English King's Bench Reports
COLA	Cost-of-living adjustment
COMCEN	Federal Communications Center
Comp.	Compilation
Conn.	Connecticut Reports
CONTU	National Commission on New Technological Uses of Copyrighted Works
Conv.	Convention
COPA	Child Online Protection Act (1998)
COPS	Community Oriented Policing Services
Corbin	Arthur L. Corbin, *Corbin on Contracts: A Comprehensive Treatise on the Rules of Contract Law* (1950)
CORE	Congress on Racial Equality
Cox's Crim. Cases	Cox's Criminal Cases (England)
COYOTE	Call Off Your Old Tired Ethics
CPA	Certified public accountant
CPB	Corporation for Public Broadcasting, the
CPI	Consumer Price Index
CPPA	Child Pornography Prevention Act
CPSC	Consumer Product Safety Commission
Cranch	Cranch's United States Supreme Court Reports
CRF	Constitutional Rights Foundation
CRR	Center for Constitutional Rights
CRS	Congressional Research Service; Community Relations Service
CRT	Critical race theory
CSA	Community Services Administration
CSAP	Center for Substance Abuse Prevention
CSAT	Center for Substance Abuse Treatment
CSC	Civil Service Commission
CSCE	Conference on Security and Cooperation in Europe
CSG	Council of State Governments

CSO	Community Service Organization
CSP	Center for the Study of the Presidency
C-SPAN	Cable-Satellite Public Affairs Network
CSRS	Cooperative State Research Service
CSWPL	Center on Social Welfare Policy and Law
CTA	*Cum testamento annexo* (with the will attached)
Ct. Ap. D.C.	Court of Appeals, District of Columbia
Ct. App. No. Ireland	Court of Appeals, Northern Ireland
Ct. Cl.	Court of Claims, United States
Ct. Crim. Apps.	Court of Criminal Appeals (England)
Ct. of Sess., Scot.	Court of Sessions, Scotland
CTI	Consolidated taxable income
CU	Credit union
CUNY	City University of New York
Cush.	Cushing's Massachusetts Reports
CWA	Civil Works Administration; Clean Water Act
DACORB	Department of the Army Conscientious Objector Review Board
Dall.	Dallas's Pennsylvania and United States Reports
DAR	Daughters of the American Revolution
DARPA	Defense Advanced Research Projects Agency
DAVA	Defense Audiovisual Agency
D.C.	United States District Court; District of Columbia
D.C. Del.	United States District Court, Delaware
D.C. Mass.	United States District Court, Massachusetts
D.C. Md.	United States District Court, Maryland
D.C.N.D.Cal.	United States District Court, Northern District, California
D.C.N.Y.	United States District Court, New York
D.C.Pa.	United States District Court, Pennsylvania
DCS	Deputy Chiefs of Staff
DCZ	District of the Canal Zone
DDT	Dichlorodiphenyltricloroethane
DEA	Drug Enforcement Administration
Decl. Lond.	Declaration of London, February 26, 1909
Dev. & B.	Devereux & Battle's North Carolina Reports
DFL	Minnesota Democratic-Farmer-Labor
DFTA	Department for the Aging
Dig. U.S. Practice in Intl. Law	Digest of U.S. Practice in International Law
Dist. Ct.	D.C. United States District Court, District of Columbia
D.L.R.	Dominion Law Reports (Canada)
DMCA	Digital Millennium Copyright Act
DNA	Deoxyribonucleic acid
Dnase	Deoxyribonuclease
DNC	Democratic National Committee
DOC	Department of Commerce
DOD	Department of Defense
DODEA	Department of Defense Education Activity
Dodson	Dodson's Reports, English Admiralty Courts
DOE	Department of Energy
DOER	Department of Employee Relations
DOJ	Department of Justice
DOL	Department of Labor
DOMA	Defense of Marriage Act of 1996
DOS	Disk operating system
DOT	Department of Transportation
DPT	Diphtheria, pertussis, and tetanus
DRI	Defense Research Institute

DSAA	Defense Security Assistance Agency
DUI	Driving under the influence; driving under intoxication
DVD	Digital versatile disc
DWI	Driving while intoxicated
EAHCA	Education for All Handicapped Children Act of 1975
EBT	Examination before trial
E.coli	Escherichia coli
ECPA	Electronic Communications Privacy Act of 1986
ECSC	Treaty of the European Coal and Steel Community
EDA	Economic Development Administration
EDF	Environmental Defense Fund
E.D.N.Y.	Eastern District, New York
EDP	Electronic data processing
E.D. Pa.	Eastern-District, Pennsylvania
EDSC	Eastern District, South Carolina
EDT	Eastern daylight time
E.D. Va.	Eastern District, Virginia
EEC	European Economic Community; European Economic Community Treaty
EEOC	Equal Employment Opportunity Commission
EFF	Electronic Frontier Foundation
EFT	Electronic funds transfer
Eliz.	Queen Elizabeth (Great Britain)
Em. App.	Temporary Emergency Court of Appeals
ENE	Early neutral evaluation
Eng. Rep.	English Reports
EOP	Executive Office of the President
EPA	Environmental Protection Agency; Equal Pay Act of 1963
ERA	Equal Rights Amendment
ERDC	Energy Research and Development Commission
ERISA	Employee Retirement Income Security Act of 1974
ERS	Economic Research Service
ERTA	Economic Recovery Tax Act of 1981
ESA	Endangered Species Act of 1973
ESF	Emergency support function; Economic Support Fund
ESRD	End-Stage Renal Disease Program
ETA	Employment and Training Administration
ETS	Environmental tobacco smoke
et seq.	*Et sequentes* or *et sequentia* ("and the following")
EU	European Union
Euratom	European Atomic Energy Community
Eur. Ct. H.R.	European Court of Human Rights
Ex.	English Exchequer Reports, Welsby, Hurlstone & Gordon
Exch.	Exchequer Reports (Welsby, Hurlstone & Gordon)
Ex Com	Executive Committee of the National Security Council
Eximbank	Export-Import Bank of the United States
F.	Federal Reporter
F. 2d	Federal Reporter, Second Series
FAA	Federal Aviation Administration; Federal Arbitration Act
FAAA	Federal Alcohol Administration Act
FACE	Freedom of Access to Clinic Entrances Act of 1994
FACT	Feminist Anti-Censorship Task Force
FAIRA	Federal Agriculture Improvement and Reform Act of 1996
FAMLA	Family and Medical Leave Act of 1993
Fannie Mae	Federal National Mortgage Association
FAO	Food and Agriculture Organization of the United Nations
FAR	Federal Acquisition Regulations

FAS	Foreign Agricultural Service
FBA	Federal Bar Association
FBI	Federal Bureau of Investigation
FCA	Farm Credit Administration
F. Cas.	Federal Cases
FCC	Federal Communications Commission
FCIA	Foreign Credit Insurance Association
FCIC	Federal Crop Insurance Corporation
FCLAA	Federal Cigarette Labeling and Advertising Act
FCRA	Fair Credit Reporting Act
FCU	Federal credit unions
FCUA	Federal Credit Union Act
FCZ	Fishery Conservation Zone
FDA	Food and Drug Administration
FDIC	Federal Deposit Insurance Corporation
FDPC	Federal Data Processing Center
FEC	Federal Election Commission
FECA	Federal Election Campaign Act of 1971
Fed. Cas.	Federal Cases
FEHA	Fair Employment and Housing Act
FEHBA	Federal Employees Health Benefit Act
FEMA	Federal Emergency Management Agency
FERC	Federal Energy Regulatory Commission
FFB	Federal Financing Bank
FFDC	Federal Food, Drug, and Cosmetics Act
FGIS	Federal Grain Inspection Service
FHA	Federal Housing Administration
FHAA	Fair Housing Amendments Act of 1998
FHWA	Federal Highway Administration
FIA	Federal Insurance Administration
FIC	Federal Information Centers; Federation of Insurance Counsel
FICA	Federal Insurance Contributions Act
FIFRA	Federal Insecticide, Fungicide, and Rodenticide Act
FIP	Forestry Incentives Program
FIRREA	Financial Institutions Reform, Recovery, and Enforcement Act of 1989
FISA	Foreign Intelligence Surveillance Act of 1978
FISC	Foreign Intelligence Surveillance Court of Review
FJC	Federal Judicial Center
FLSA	Fair Labor Standards Act
FMC	Federal Maritime Commission
FMCS	Federal Mediation and Conciliation Service
FmHA	Farmers Home Administration
FMLA	Family and Medical Leave Act of 1993
FNMA	Federal National Mortgage Association, "Fannie Mae"
F.O.B.	Free on board
FOIA	Freedom of Information Act
FOMC	Federal Open Market Committee
FPA	Federal Power Act of 1935
FPC	Federal Power Commission
FPMR	Federal Property Management Regulations
FPRS	Federal Property Resources Service
FR	Federal Register
FRA	Federal Railroad Administration
FRB	Federal Reserve Board
FRC	Federal Radio Commission
F.R.D.	Federal Rules Decisions

FSA	Family Support Act
FSB	Federal'naya Sluzhba Bezopasnosti (the Federal Security Service of Russia)
FSLIC	Federal Savings and Loan Insurance Corporation
FSQS	Food Safety and Quality Service
FSS	Federal Supply Service
F. Supp.	Federal Supplement
FTA	U.S.-Canada Free Trade Agreement of 1988
FTC	Federal Trade Commission
FTCA	Federal Tort Claims Act
FTS	Federal Telecommunications System
FTS2000	Federal Telecommunications System 2000
FUCA	Federal Unemployment Compensation Act of 1988
FUTA	Federal Unemployment Tax Act
FWPCA	Federal Water Pollution Control Act of 1948
FWS	Fish and Wildlife Service
GAL	Guardian ad litem
GAO	General Accounting Office; Governmental Affairs Office
GAOR	General Assembly Official Records, United Nations
GAAP	Generally accepted accounting principles
GA Res.	General Assembly Resolution (United Nations)
GATT	General Agreement on Tariffs and Trade
GCA	Gun Control Act
Gen. Cls. Comm.	General Claims Commission, United States and Panama; General Claims United States and Mexico
Geo. II	King George II (Great Britain)
Geo. III	King George III (Great Britain)
GHB	Gamma-hydroxybutrate
GI	Government Issue
GID	General Intelligence Division
GM	General Motors
GNMA	Government National Mortgage Association, "Ginnie Mae"
GNP	Gross national product
GOP	Grand Old Party (Republican Party)
GOPAC	Grand Old Party Action Committee
GPA	Office of Governmental and Public Affairs
GPO	Government Printing Office
GRAS	Generally recognized as safe
Gr. Br., Crim. Ct. App.	Great Britain, Court of Criminal Appeals
GRNL	Gay Rights-National Lobby
GSA	General Services Administration
Hackworth	Green Haywood Hackworth, *Digest of International Law* (1940–1944)
Hay and Marriott	Great Britain. High Court of Admiralty, *Decisions in the High Court of Admiralty during the Time of Sir George Hay and of Sir James Marriott, Late Judges of That Court* (1801)
HBO	Home Box Office
HCFA	Health Care Financing Administration
H.Ct.	High Court
HDS	Office of Human Development Services
Hen. & M.	Hening & Munford's Virginia Reports
HEW	Department of Health, Education, and Welfare
HFCA	Health Care Financing Administration
HGI	Handgun Control, Incorporated
HHS	Department of Health and Human Services
Hill	Hill's New York Reports
HIRE	Help through Industry Retraining and Employment
HIV	Human immunodeficiency virus

H.L.	House of Lords Cases (England)
H. Lords	House of Lords (England)
HMO	Health Maintenance Organization
HNIS	Human Nutrition Information Service
Hong Kong L.R.	Hong Kong Law Reports
How.	Howard's United States Supreme Court Reports
How. St. Trials	Howell's English State Trials
HUAC	House Un-American Activities Committee
HUD	Department of Housing and Urban Development
Hudson, Internatl. Legis.	Manley Ottmer Hudson, ed., *International Legislation: A Collection of the Texts of Multipartite International Instruments of General Interest Beginning with the Covenant of the League of Nations* (1931)
Hudson, World Court Reps.	Manley Ottmer Hudson, ea., *World Court Reports* (1934–)
Hun	Hun's New York Supreme Court Reports
Hunt's Rept.	Bert L. Hunt, *Report of the American and Panamanian General Claims Arbitration* (1934)
IAEA	International Atomic Energy Agency
IALL	International Association of Law Libraries
IBA	International Bar Association
IBM	International Business Machines
ICA	Interstate Commerce Act
ICBM	Intercontinental ballistic missile
ICC	Interstate Commerce Commission; International Criminal Court
ICJ	International Court of Justice
ICM	Institute for Court Management
IDEA	Individuals with Disabilities Education Act of 1975
IDOP	International Dolphin Conservation Program
IEP	Individualized educational program
IFC	International Finance Corporation
IGRA	Indian Gaming Regulatory Act of 1988
IJA	Institute of Judicial Administration
IJC	International Joint Commission
ILC	International Law Commission
ILD	International Labor Defense
Ill. Dec.	Illinois Decisions
ILO	International Labor Organization
IMF	International Monetary Fund
INA	Immigration and Nationality Act
IND	Investigational new drug
INF Treaty	Intermediate-Range Nuclear Forces Treaty of 1987
INS	Immigration and Naturalization Service
INTELSAT	International Telecommunications Satellite Organization
Interpol	International Criminal Police Organization
Int'l. Law Reps.	International Law Reports
Intl. Legal Mats.	International Legal Materials
IOC	International Olympic Committee
IPDC	International Program for the Development of Communication
IPO	Intellectual Property Owners
IPP	Independent power producer
IQ	Intelligence quotient
I.R.	Irish Reports
IRA	Individual retirement account; Irish Republican Army
IRC	Internal Revenue Code
IRCA	Immigration Reform and Control Act of 1986
IRS	Internal Revenue Service
ISO	Independent service organization

ISP	Internet service provider
ISSN	International Standard Serial Numbers
ITA	International Trade Administration
ITI	Information Technology Integration
ITO	International Trade Organization
ITS	Information Technology Service
ITT	International Telephone and Telegraph Corporation
ITU	International Telecommunication Union
IUD	Intrauterine device
IWC	International Whaling Commission
IWW	Industrial Workers of the World
JAGC	Judge Advocate General's Corps
JCS	Joint Chiefs of Staff
JDL	Jewish Defense League
JNOV	Judgment *non obstante veredicto* ("judgment nothing to recommend it" or "judgment notwithstanding the verdict")
JOBS	Jobs Opportunity and Basic Skills
John. Ch.	Johnson's New York Chancery Reports
Johns.	Johnson's Reports (New York)
JP	Justice of the peace
K.B.	King's Bench Reports (England)
KFC	Kentucky Fried Chicken
KGB	Komitet Gosudarstvennoi Bezopasnosti (the State Security Committee for countries in the former Soviet Union)
KKK	Ku Klux Klan
KMT	Kuomintang (Chinese, "national people's party")
LAD	Law Against Discrimination
LAPD	Los Angeles Police Department
LC	Library of Congress
LCHA	Longshoremen's and Harbor Workers Compensation Act of 1927
LD50	Lethal dose 50
LDEF	Legal Defense and Education Fund (NOW)
LDF	Legal Defense Fund, Legal Defense and Educational Fund of the NAACP
LEAA	Law Enforcement Assistance Administration
L.Ed.	Lawyers' Edition Supreme Court Reports
LI	Letter of interpretation
LLC	Limited Liability Company
LLP	Limited Liability Partnership
LMSA	Labor-Management Services Administration
LNTS	League of Nations Treaty Series
Lofft's Rep.	Lofft's English King's Bench Reports
L.R.	Law Reports (English)
LSAC	Law School Admission Council
LSAS	Law School Admission Service
LSAT	Law School Aptitude Test
LSC	Legal Services Corporation; Legal Services for Children
LSD	Lysergic acid diethylamide
LSDAS	Law School Data Assembly Service
LTBT	Limited Test Ban Treaty
LTC	Long Term Care
MAD	Mutual assured destruction
MADD	Mothers against Drunk Driving
MALDEF	Mexican American Legal Defense and Educational Fund
Malloy	William M. Malloy, ed., *Treaties, Conventions International Acts, Protocols, and Agreements between the United States of America and Other Powers* (1910–1938)

Martens	Georg Friedrich von Martens, ea., *Noveau recueil général de traités et autres actes relatifs aux rapports de droit international* (Series I, 20 vols. [1843–1875]; Series II, 35 vols. [1876–1908]; Series III [1909–])
Mass.	Massachusetts Reports
MCC	Metropolitan Correctional Center
MCCA	Medicare Catastrophic Coverage Act of 1988
MCH	Maternal and Child Health Bureau
MCRA	Medical Care Recovery Act of 1962
MDA	Medical Devices Amendments of 1976
Md. App.	Maryland, Appeal Cases
M.D. Ga.	Middle District, Georgia
Mercy	Movement Ensuring the Right to Choose for Yourself
Metc.	Metcalf's Massachusetts Reports
MFDP	Mississippi Freedom Democratic party
MGT	Management
MHSS	Military Health Services System
Miller	David Hunter Miller, ea., *Treaties and Other International Acts of the United States of America* (1931–1948)
Minn.	Minnesota Reports
MINS	Minors in need of supervision
MIRV	Multiple independently targetable reentry vehicle
MIRVed ICBM	Multiple independently targetable reentry vehicled intercontinental ballistic missile
Misc.	Miscellaneous Reports, New York
Mixed Claims Comm., Report of Decs	Mixed Claims Commission, United States and Germany, Report of Decisions
M.J.	Military Justice Reporter
MLAP	Migrant Legal Action Program
MLB	Major League Baseball
MLDP	Mississippi Loyalist Democratic Party
MMI	Moslem Mosque, Incorporated
MMPA	Marine Mammal Protection Act of 1972
Mo.	Missouri Reports
MOD	Masters of Deception
Mod.	Modern Reports, English King's Bench, etc.
Moore, Dig. Intl. Law	John Bassett Moore, *A Digest of International Law*, 8 vols. (1906)
Moore, Intl. Arbs.	John Bassett Moore, *History and Digest of the International Arbitrations to Which United States Has Been a Party*, 6 vols. (1898)
Morison	William Maxwell Morison, *The Scots Revised Report: Morison's Dictionary of Decisions* (1908–09)
M.P.	Member of Parliament
MP3	MPEG Audio Layer 3
MPAA	Motion Picture Association of America
MPAS	Michigan Protection and Advocacy Service
MPEG	Motion Picture Experts Group
mpg	Miles per gallon
MPPDA	Motion Picture Producers and Distributors of America
MPRSA	Marine Protection, Research, and Sanctuaries Act of 1972
M.R.	Master of the Rolls
MS-DOS	Microsoft Disk Operating System
MSHA	Mine Safety and Health Administration
MSPB	Merit Systems Protection Board
MSSA	Military Selective Service Act
N/A	Not Available
NAACP	National Association for the Advancement of Colored People
NAAQS	National Ambient Air Quality Standards

NAB	National Association of Broadcasters
NABSW	National Association of Black Social Workers
NACDL	National Association of Criminal Defense Lawyers
NAFTA	North American Free Trade Agreement of 1993
NAGHSR	National Association of Governors' Highway Safety Representatives
NALA	National Association of Legal Assistants
NAM	National Association of Manufacturers
NAR	National Association of Realtors
NARAL	National Abortion and Reproductive Rights Action League
NARF	Native American Rights Fund
NARS	National Archives and Record Service
NASA	National Aeronautics and Space Administration
NASD	National Association of Securities Dealers
NATO	North Atlantic Treaty Organization
NAVINFO	Navy Information Offices
NAWSA	National American Woman's Suffrage Association
NBA	National Bar Association; National Basketball Association
NBC	National Broadcasting Company
NBLSA	National Black Law Student Association
NBS	National Bureau of Standards
NCA	Noise Control Act; National Command Authorities
NCAA	National Collegiate Athletic Association
NCAC	National Coalition against Censorship
NCCB	National Consumer Cooperative Bank
NCE	Northwest Community Exchange
NCF	National Chamber Foundation
NCIP	National Crime Insurance Program
NCJA	National Criminal Justice Association
NCLB	National Civil Liberties Bureau
NCP	National contingency plan
NCSC	National Center for State Courts
NCUA	National Credit Union Administration
NDA	New drug application
N.D. Ill.	Northern District, Illinois
NDU	National Defense University
N.D. Wash.	Northern District, Washington
N.E.	North Eastern Reporter
N.E. 2d	North Eastern Reporter, Second Series
NEA	National Endowment for the Arts; National Education Association
NEH	National Endowment for the Humanities
NEPA	National Environmental Protection Act; National Endowment Policy Act
NET Act	No Electronic Theft Act
NFIB	National Federation of Independent Businesses
NFIP	National Flood Insurance Program
NFL	National Football League
NFPA	National Federation of Paralegal Associations
NGLTF	National Gay and Lesbian Task Force
NHL	National Hockey League
NHRA	Nursing Home Reform Act of 1987
NHTSA	National Highway Traffic Safety Administration
Nielsen's Rept.	Frederick Kenelm Nielsen, *American and British Claims Arbitration under the Special Agreement Concluded between the United States and Great Britain, August 18, 1910* (1926)
NIEO	New International Economic Order
NIGC	National Indian Gaming Commission
NIH	National Institutes of Health

NIJ	National Institute of Justice
NIRA	National Industrial Recovery Act of 1933; National Industrial Recovery Administration
NIST	National Institute of Standards and Technology
NITA	National Telecommunications and Information Administration
N.J.	New Jersey Reports
N.J. Super.	New Jersey Superior Court Reports
NLEA	Nutrition Labeling and Education Act of 1990
NLRA	National Labor Relations Act
NLRB	National Labor Relations Board
NMFS	National Marine Fisheries Service
No.	Number
NOAA	National Oceanic and Atmospheric Administration
NOC	National Olympic Committee
NOI	Nation of Islam
NOL	Net operating loss
NORML	National Organization for the Reform of Marijuana Laws
NOW	National Organization for Women
NOW LDEF	National Organization for Women Legal Defense and Education Fund
NOW/PAC	National Organization for Women Political Action Committee
NPDES	National Pollutant Discharge Elimination System
NPL	National priorities list
NPR	National Public Radio
NPT	Nuclear Non-Proliferation Treaty of 1970
NRA	National Rifle Association; National Recovery Act
NRC	Nuclear Regulatory Commission
NRLC	National Right to Life Committee
NRTA	National Retired Teachers Association
NSA	National Security Agency
NSC	National Security Council
NSCLC	National Senior Citizens Law Center
NSF	National Science Foundation
NSFNET	National Science Foundation Network
NSI	Network Solutions, Inc.
NTIA	National Telecommunications and Information Administration
NTID	National Technical Institute for the Deaf
NTIS	National Technical Information Service
NTS	Naval Telecommunications System
NTSB	National Transportation Safety Board
NVRA	National Voter Registration Act
N.W.	North Western Reporter
N.W. 2d	North Western Reporter, Second Series
NWSA	National Woman Suffrage Association
N.Y.	New York Court of Appeals Reports
N.Y. 2d	New York Court of Appeals Reports, Second Series
N.Y.S.	New York Supplement Reporter
N.Y.S. 2d	New York Supplement Reporter, Second Series
NYSE	New York Stock Exchange
NYSLA	New York State Liquor Authority
N.Y. Sup.	New York Supreme Court Reports
NYU	New York University
OAAU	Organization of Afro American Unity
OAP	Office of Administrative Procedure
OAS	Organization of American States
OASDI	Old-age, Survivors, and Disability Insurance Benefits
OASHDS	Office of the Assistant Secretary for Human Development Services

OCC	Office of Comptroller of the Currency
OCED	Office of Comprehensive Employment Development
OCHAMPUS	Office of Civilian Health and Medical Program of the Uniformed Services
OCSE	Office of Child Support Enforcement
OEA	Organización de los Estados Americanos
OEM	Original Equipment Manufacturer
OFCCP	Office of Federal Contract Compliance Programs
OFPP	Office of Federal Procurement Policy
OIC	Office of the Independent Counsel
OICD	Office of International Cooperation and Development
OIG	Office of the Inspector General
OJARS	Office of Justice Assistance, Research, and Statistics
OMB	Office of Management and Budget
OMPC	Office of Management, Planning, and Communications
ONP	Office of National Programs
OPD	Office of Policy Development
OPEC	Organization of Petroleum Exporting Countries
OPIC	Overseas Private Investment Corporation
Ops. Atts. Gen.	Opinions of the Attorneys-General of the United States
Ops. Comms.	Opinions of the Commissioners
OPSP	Office of Product Standards Policy
O.R.	Ontario Reports
OR	Official Records
OSHA	Occupational Safety and Health Act
OSHRC	Occupational Safety and Health Review Commission
OSM	Office of Surface Mining
OSS	Office of Strategic Services
OST	Office of the Secretary
OT	Office of Transportation
OTA	Office of Technology Assessment
OTC	Over-the-counter
OTS	Office of Thrift Supervisors
OUI	Operating under the influence
OVCI	Offshore Voluntary Compliance Initiative
OWBPA	Older Workers Benefit Protection Act
OWRT	Office of Water Research and Technology
P.	Pacific Reporter
P. 2d	Pacific Reporter, Second Series
PAC	Political action committee
Pa. Oyer and Terminer	Pennsylvania Oyer and Terminer Reports
PATCO	Professional Air Traffic Controllers Organization
PBGC	Pension Benefit Guaranty Corporation
PBS	Public Broadcasting Service; Public Buildings Service
P.C.	Privy Council (English Law Reports)
PC	Personal computer; politically correct
PCBs	Polychlorinated biphenyls
PCIJ	Permanent Court of International Justice Series A-Judgments and Orders (1922–30) Series B-Advisory Opinions (1922–30) Series A/B-Judgments, Orders, and Advisory Opinions (1931–40) Series C-Pleadings, Oral Statements, and Documents relating to Judgments and Advisory Opinions (1923–42) Series D-Acts and Documents concerning the Organization of the World Court (1922 –47) Series E-Annual Reports (1925–45)
PCP	Phencyclidine

P.D.	Probate Division, English Law Reports (1876–1890)
PDA	Pregnancy Discrimination Act of 1978
PD & R	Policy Development and Research
Pepco	Potomac Electric Power Company
Perm. Ct. of Arb.	Permanent Court of Arbitration
PES	Post-Enumeration Survey
Pet.	Peters' United States Supreme Court Reports
PETA	People for the Ethical Treatment of Animals
PGA	Professional Golfers Association
PGM	Program
PHA	Public Housing Agency
Phila. Ct. of Oyer and Terminer	Philadelphia Court of Oyer and Terminer
PhRMA	Pharmaceutical Research and Manufacturers of America
PHS	Public Health Service
PIC	Private Industry Council
PICJ	Permanent International Court of Justice
Pick.	Pickering's Massachusetts Reports
PIK	Payment in Kind
PINS	Persons in need of supervision
PIRG	Public Interest Research Group
P.L.	Public Laws
PLAN	Pro-Life Action Network
PLC	Plaintiffs' Legal Committee
PLE	Product liability expenses
PLI	Practicing Law Institute
PLL	Product liability loss
PLLP	Professional Limited Liability Partnership
PLO	Palestine Liberation Organization
PLRA	Prison Litigation Reform Act of 1995
PNET	Peaceful Nuclear Explosions Treaty
PONY	Prostitutes of New York
POW-MIA	Prisoner of war-missing in action
Pratt	Frederic Thomas Pratt, *Law of Contraband of War, with a Selection of Cases from Papers of the Right Honourable Sir George Lee* (1856)
PRIDE	Prostitution to Independence, Dignity, and Equality
Proc.	Proceedings
PRP	Potentially responsible party
PSRO	Professional Standards Review Organization
PTO	Patents and Trademark Office
PURPA	Public Utilities Regulatory Policies Act
PUSH	People United to Serve Humanity
PUSH-Excel	PUSH for Excellence
PWA	Public Works Administration
PWSA	Ports and Waterways Safety Act of 1972
Q.B.	Queen's Bench (England)
QTIP	Qualified Terminable Interest Property
Ralston's Rept.	Jackson Harvey Ralston, ed., *Venezuelan Arbitrations of 1903* (1904)
RC	Regional Commissioner
RCRA	Resource Conservation and Recovery Act
RCWP	Rural Clean Water Program
RDA	Rural Development Administration
REA	Rural Electrification Administration
Rec. des Decs. des Trib. Arb. Mixtes	G. Gidel, ed., *Recueil des décisions des tribunaux arbitraux mixtes, institués par les traités de paix* (1922–30)

Redmond	Vol. 3 of Charles I. Bevans, *Treaties and Other International Agreements of the United States of America, 1776–1949* (compiled by C. F. Redmond) (1969)
RESPA	Real Estate Settlement Procedure Act of 1974
RFC	Reconstruction Finance Corporation
RFRA	Religious Freedom Restoration Act of 1993
RIAA	Recording Industry Association of America
RICO	Racketeer Influenced and Corrupt Organizations
RLUIPA	Religious Land Use and Institutionalized Persons Act
RNC	Republican National Committee
Roscoe	Edward Stanley Roscoe, ed., *Reports of Prize Cases Determined in the High Court Admiralty before the Lords Commissioners of Appeals in Prize Causes and before the judicial Committee of the Privy Council from 1745 to 1859* (1905)
ROTC	Reserve Officers' Training Corps
RPP	Representative Payee Program
R.S.	Revised Statutes
RTC	Resolution Trust Corp.
RUDs	Reservations, understandings, and declarations
Ryan White CARE Act	Ryan White Comprehensive AIDS Research Emergency Act of 1990
SAC	Strategic Air Command
SACB	Subversive Activities Control Board
SADD	Students against Drunk Driving
SAF	Student Activities Fund
SAIF	Savings Association Insurance Fund
SALT	Strategic Arms Limitation Talks
SALT I	Strategic Arms Limitation Talks of 1969–72
SAMHSA	Substance Abuse and Mental Health Services Administration
Sandf.	Sandford's New York Superior Court Reports
S and L	Savings and loan
SARA	Superfund Amendment and Reauthorization Act
SAT	Scholastic Aptitude Test
Sawy.	Sawyer's United States Circuit Court Reports
SBA	Small Business Administration
SBI	Small Business Institute
SCCC	South Central Correctional Center
SCLC	Southern Christian Leadership Conference
Scott's Repts.	James Brown Scott, ed., *The Hague Court Reports*, 2 vols. (1916–32)
SCS	Soil Conservation Service; Social Conservative Service
SCSEP	Senior Community Service Employment Program
S.Ct.	Supreme Court Reporter
S.D. Cal.	Southern District, California
S.D. Fla.	Southern District, Florida
S.D. Ga.	Southern District, Georgia
SDI	Strategic Defense Initiative
S.D. Me.	Southern District, Maine
S.D.N.Y.	Southern District, New York
SDS	Students for a Democratic Society
S.E.	South Eastern Reporter
S.E. 2d	South Eastern Reporter, Second Series
SEA	Science and Education Administration
SEATO	Southeast Asia Treaty Organization
SEC	Securities and Exchange Commission
Sec.	Section
SEEK	Search for Elevation, Education and Knowledge
SEOO	State Economic Opportunity Office
SEP	Simplified employee pension plan

Ser.	Series
Sess.	Session
SGLI	Servicemen's Group Life Insurance
SIP	State implementation plan
SLA	Symbionese Liberation Army
SLAPPs	Strategic Lawsuits Against Public Participation
SLBM	Submarine-launched ballistic missile
SNCC	Student Nonviolent Coordinating Committee
So.	Southern Reporter
So. 2d	Southern Reporter, Second Series
SPA	Software Publisher's Association
Spec. Sess.	Special Session
SPLC	Southern Poverty Law Center
SRA	Sentencing Reform Act of 1984
SS	*Schutzstaffel* (German, "Protection Echelon")
SSA	Social Security Administration
SSI	Supplemental Security Income
START I	Strategic Arms Reduction Treaty of 1991
START II	Strategic Arms Reduction Treaty of 1993
Stat.	United States Statutes at Large
STS	Space Transportation Systems
St. Tr.	State Trials, English
STURAA	Surface Transportation and Uniform Relocation Assistance Act of 1987
Sup. Ct. of Justice, Mexico	Supreme Court of Justice, Mexico
Supp.	Supplement
S.W.	South Western Reporter
S.W. 2d	South Western Reporter, Second Series
SWAPO	South-West Africa People's Organization
SWAT	Special Weapons and Tactics
SWP	Socialist Workers Party
TDP	Trade and Development Program
Tex. Sup.	Texas Supreme Court Reports
THAAD	Theater High-Altitude Area Defense System
THC	Tetrahydrocannabinol
TI	Tobacco Institute
TIA	Trust Indenture Act of 1939
TIAS	Treaties and Other International Acts Series (United States)
TNT	Trinitrotoluene
TOP	Targeted Outreach Program
TPUS	Transportation and Public Utilities Service
TQM	Total Quality Management
Tripartite Claims Comm., Decs. and Ops.	Tripartite Claims Commission (United States, Austria, and Hungary), Decisions and Opinions
TRI-TAC	Joint Tactical Communications
TRO	Temporary restraining order
TS	Treaty Series, United States
TSCA	Toxic Substance Control Act
TSDs	Transporters, storers, and disposers
TSU	Texas Southern University
TTBT	Threshold Test Ban Treaty
TV	Television
TVA	Tennessee Valley Authority
TWA	Trans World Airlines

UAW	United Auto Workers; United Automobile, Aerospace, and Agricultural Implements Workers of America
U.C.C.	Uniform Commercial Code; Universal Copyright Convention
U.C.C.C.	Uniform Consumer Credit Code
UCCJA	Uniform Child Custody Jurisdiction Act
UCMJ	Uniform Code of Military Justice
UCPP	Urban Crime Prevention Program
UCS	United Counseling Service
UDC	United Daughters of the Confederacy
UFW	United Farm Workers
UHF	Ultrahigh frequency
UIFSA	Uniform Interstate Family Support Act
UIS	Unemployment Insurance Service
UMDA	Uniform Marriage and Divorce Act
UMTA	Urban Mass Transportation Administration
U.N.	United Nations
UNCITRAL	United Nations Commission on International Trade Law
UNCTAD	United Nations Conference on Trade and Development
UN Doc.	United Nations Documents
UNDP	United Nations Development Program
UNEF	United Nations Emergency Force
UNESCO	United Nations Educational, Scientific, and Cultural Organization
UNICEF	United Nations Children's Fund (formerly United Nations International Children's Emergency Fund)
UNIDO	United Nations Industrial and Development Organization
Unif. L. Ann.	Uniform Laws Annotated
UN Repts. Intl. Arb. Awards	United Nations Reports of International Arbitral Awards
UNTS	United Nations Treaty Series
UPI	United Press International
URESA	Uniform Reciprocal Enforcement of Support Act
U.S.	United States Reports
U.S.A.	United States of America
USAF	United States Air Force
USA PATRIOT Act	Uniting and Strengthening America by Providing Appropriate Tools Required to Intercept and Obstruct Terrorism Act
USF	U.S. Forestry Service
U.S. App. D.C.	United States Court of Appeals for the District of Columbia
U.S.C.	United States Code; University of Southern California
U.S.C.A.	United States Code Annotated
U.S.C.C.A.N.	United States Code Congressional and Administrative News
USCMA	United States Court of Military Appeals
USDA	U.S. Department of Agriculture
USES	United States Employment Service
USFA	United States Fire Administration
USGA	United States Golf Association
USICA	International Communication Agency, United States
USMS	U.S. Marshals Service
USOC	U.S. Olympic Committee
USSC	U.S. Sentencing Commission
USSG	United States Sentencing Guidelines
U.S.S.R.	Union of Soviet Socialist Republics
UST	United States Treaties
USTS	United States Travel Service
v.	*Versus*
VA	Veterans Administration
VAR	Veterans Affairs and Rehabilitation Commission

VAWA	Violence against Women Act
VFW	Veterans of Foreign Wars
VGLI	Veterans Group Life Insurance
Vict.	Queen Victoria (Great Britain)
VIN	Vehicle identification number
VISTA	Volunteers in Service to America
VJRA	Veterans Judicial Review Act of 1988
V.L.A.	Volunteer Lawyers for the Arts
VMI	Virginia Military Institute
VMLI	Veterans Mortgage Life Insurance
VOCAL	Victims of Child Abuse Laws
VRA	Voting Rights Act
WAC	Women's Army Corps
Wall.	Wallace's United States Supreme Court Reports
Wash. 2d	Washington Reports, Second Series
WAVES	Women Accepted for Volunteer Service
WCTU	Women's Christian Temperance Union
W.D. Wash.	Western District, Washington
W.D. Wis.	Western District, Wisconsin
WEAL	*West's Encyclopedia of American Law;* Women's Equity Action League
Wend.	Wendell's New York Reports
WFSE	Washington Federation of State Employees
Wheat.	Wheaton's United States Supreme Court Reports
Wheel. Cr. Cases	Wheeler's New York Criminal Cases
WHISPER	Women Hurt in Systems of Prostitution Engaged in Revolt
Whiteman	Marjorie Millace Whiteman, *Digest of International Law*, 15 vols. (1963–73)
WHO	World Health Organization
WIC	Women, Infants, and Children program
Will. and Mar.	King William and Queen Mary (Great Britain)
WIN	WESTLAW Is Natural; Whip Inflation Now; Work Incentive Program
WIPO	World Intellectual Property Organization
WIU	Workers' Industrial Union
W.L.R.	Weekly Law Reports, England
WPA	Works Progress Administration
WPPDA	Welfare and Pension Plans Disclosure Act
WTO	World Trade Organization
WWI	World War I
WWII	World War II
Yates Sel. Cas.	Yates's New York Select Cases
YMCA	Young Men's Christian Association
YWCA	Young Women's Christian Association

Table of Cases Cited By Name

A

Alaska v. United States, 152–154
Americans United for Separation of Church & State v. Prison Fellowship Ministries, 72
Anza v. Ideal Steel Supply Corp., 159–161
Apprendi v. New Jersey, 168
Arbaugh v. Y & H Corporation, 170–171
Arkansas Department of Health and Human Services v. Ahlborn, 130–131
Arlington Central School District Board of Education v. Murphy, 61–62
Arthur Anderson, L.L.P. v. United States, 48
Ashcroft v. ACLU, 116
A Woman's Choice-East Side Women's Clinic v. Newman, 3
Ayotte v. Planned Parenthood of Northern New England, 1–2, 179

B

Baker v. IBP, Inc., 161
Bank of China v. NBM, et al., 86–88
Batson v. Kentucky, 105
Beard v. Banks, 77–79
Birbrower, Montalbano, Condon, & Frank, P.C. v. Superior Court, 17
Bivens v. Six Unknown Named Agents of Federal Bureau of Narcotics, 113, 114
Blakely v. Washington, 168
Boeken v. Philip Morris Inc., 187–188
Bond v. United States, 82
Boyle v. United Technologies Corp., 120
Breard v. Greene, 48
Brigham City, Utah v. Stuart, 81–83
Brown v. Sanders, 25–26
Bryant v. State, 133
Buckeye Check Cashing, Inc. v. Cardegna, 13–14
Buckley v. Valeo, 79, 80
Burlington Northern & Santa Fe Railway Co. v. White, 35–36
Bush v. Holmes, 62–64, 159
Bustillo v. Johnson, Virginia Department of Corrections, 47

C

Carey v. Saffold, 103
Carhart v. Ashcroft 331 F. Supp. 2d 805 (D. Neb. 2004)., 4
Carhart v. Gonzales 413 F.3d 791 (8th Cir. 2005)., 4
Cathcart v. State Farm Insurance,, 54
Central Virginia Community College v. Katz, 19–20
ChoicePoint, Inc., United States v., 111–112
Clark v. Arizona, 114–116
Clinic for Women, Inc. v. Brizzi, 3
Complete Auto Transit, Inc. v. Brady, 43
Cone v. West Virginia Pulp & Paper Co., 34
Crawford Fitting Co. v. J.T. Gibbons, 62
Crawford v. Washington, 172, 173
Cuno v. DaimlerChrysler, 43

D

DaimlerChrysler Corp. v. Cuno, 42–44
Davis v. State, 173
Davis v. Washington, 172–173
Day v. McDonough, 101–102
Dolan v. United States Postal Service, 176–177
Domino's Pizza, Inc. v. McDonald, 36–37

E

eBay Inc. v. MercExchange, L.L.C., 144–145
Edwards v. Aguillard, 157
Edwards v. Arizona, 133
Empire Healthchoice Assurance v. McVeigh, 119–120
Entertainment Software Ass'n v. Granholm, 92
Entertainment Software Association v. Blagojevich, 91
Epperson v. Arkansas, 157
Erie R. Co. v. Tompkins, 152
Evans v. Chavis, 102–103

F

Ferdon v. Wisconsin Patients Compensation Fund, 127–129
Fernandez-Vargas v. Gonzales, 6
Flippo v. West Virginia, 82
Franklin v. Lynaugh, 32
Furman v. Georgia, 30

G

Garcetti v. Ceballos, 194–195
Georgia, United States v., 8–9
Georgia v. Randolph, 83–84
Gonzales v. O Centro Espirita Beneficente Uniao Do Vegetal, 89–90
Gonzales v. Oregon, 14–16
Gonzales v. Raich, 57
Gonzalez-Lopez, United States v., 171–172
Great-West Life & Annuity Insurance Company v. Knudson, 71
Groh v. Ramirez, 82
Grubbs, United States v., 84–85

H

Hamdan v. Rumsfeld, 97–98
Hamdi v. Rumsfeld, 185
Hammon v. State, 173
Hartman v. Moore, 113–114
Hill v. McDonough, 27–28
Hill v. State, 28
Holmes v. Securities Investor Protection Corporation, 160, 161
Holmes v. South Carolina, 173–174
House v. Bell, 103–105
Howard Delivery Service v. Zurich American Insurance Co., 20–21
Hudson v. Michigan, 85–86

I

IBP, Inc. v. Alvarez, 75–76
Illinois Tool Works Inc. v. Independent Ink, Inc., 9–11
Illinois v. Rodriquez, 83

J

Jones v. Flowers, 58–59

K

Kansas v. Marsh, 28–30
Kelo v. City of New London, 67–69
Kircher v. Putnam Funds Trust, 37–38
Kitzmiller v. Dover Area Sch. Dist., 158
Knights, United States v., 167
Kohler v. Englade, 55–56

L

Laboratory Corporation of America Holdings v. Metabolite, 145–147
Landgraf v. USI Film Products, 7
Lawrence v. Texas, 95, 96
League of United Latin American Citizens v. Perry, 32–33
Lemon v. Kurtzman, 72
Limon v. Kansas, 95–96
Lincoln Property Co. v. Roche, 120–121
Lockhart v. United States, 174–175

M

Marshall v. Marshall, aka Anna Nicole Smith, 151–152
Martin v. Franklin Capital Corporation, 121–122
Maryland v. Blake, 133–134
Matlock, United States v., 83
McConnell v. Federal Election Commission, 66
Medina v. People, 53
Merrill Lynch, Pierce, Fenner & Smith v. Dabit, 38–40
Metro-Goldwyn-Meyer Studios v. Grokster, 148
Miller v. California, 139, 140
Mincey v. Arizona, 82
Miranda v. Arizona, 133–134
Mohawk Industries v. Williams, 161
Moses v. People, 53
Moussaoui, United States v., 185

N

National Abortion Federation v. Gonzales, 4
Neder v. United States, 168, 169
Nelson v. Campbell, 28
Nitke v. Gonzales, 139–140

Northern Insurance Company of New York v. Chatham County, Georgia, 66–67

O

Olson, United States v., 177
Oregon v. Ashcroft, 15
Oregon v. Guzek, 31–32
Overton v. Bazzetta, 77

P

Padilla ex rel. Newman v. Bush, 184
Padilla v. Hanft, 184, 185
Patterson v. New York, 116
People v. LaValle, 30
Planned Parenthood Federation of America v. Ashcroft, 320 F. Supp. 2d 957 (N.D. Cal. 2004)., 4
Planned Parenthood Federation of America v. Gonzales, 4
Planned Parenthood v. Casey, 2, 3, 6
Prima Paint Corp. v. Flood & Conklin Mfg. Co., 13, 14, 15

R

Raich v. Ashcroft, 57
Randall v. Sorrell, 79–80
Rapanos v. United States, 40–41
Reproductive Health Services of Planned Parenthood of the St. Louis Region v. Nixon, 3
Rice v. Collins, 105–106
Richard F. Mallen & Assoc., Ltd. v. Myinjuryclaim.com, Corp., 16
Rochon v. Gonzales, 36
Roe v. Wade, 2, 4, 5, 6, 180
Rumsfeld v. Forum for Academic and Institutional Rights, Inc., 80–81
Rumsfeld v. Padilla, 184

S

Samson v. California, 166–167
Sanchez-Llamas v. Oregon, 47–48
Schaffer v. Weast, 64–65
Scheidler v. National Organization For Women, Inc., 161–163
Schlup v. Delo, 104
S.D. Warren Company v. Maine Board of Environmental Protection, 41–42
Search of the Rayburn House Office Building Room Number 2113, Washington, D.C. 20515, In re, 165–166
Sereboff v. Mid Atlantic Medical Services., Inc., 70–71
Sims v. State, 28
Smith v. Maryland, 196
Society for the Propagation of the Gospel v. Wheeler, 7
South Florida Water Management District v. Miccosukee Tribe of Indians, 42
State Farm Mutual Automobile Insurance Co. v. Campbell, 188
State v. Aiwohi, 129–130
State v. Doleszny, 54
State v. Mott, 115
State v. Washington, 172
Stenberg v. Carhart 530 U.S. 914, 120 S.Ct. 2597, 147 L.Ed.2d 743 (2000)., 4
Strickland v. Washington, 172
Sullivan v. Louisiana, 168, 172

T

Texaco Inc. v. Dagher, 11–12
Thornburg v. Gingles, 33
Turner v. Safley, 78, 79

U

United States v. Alaska, 152
United States v. Brewster, 166
United States v. Gambino, 194
United States v. Maine, 153
United States v. Reorganized CF&I Fabricators of Utah, Inc., 21
Unitherm Food Systems, Inc. v. Swift-Eckrich, Inc., 33–35

V

Video Software Dealers Ass'n v. Schwarzenegger, 92
Vieth v. Jubelirer, 33
Volvo Trucks North America, Inc. v. Reeder-Simco GMC, Inc., 12–13

W

Wachovia Bank v. Schmidt, 122–123
Wagnon v. Prairie Band Potawatomi Nation, 137–138
Walton v. Arizona, 29
Washington v. Glucksberg, 14
Washington v. Hughes, 168
Washington v. Pharr, 168
Washington v. Recuenco, 167–169
Welsh v. Wisconsin, 82
West Virginia Univ. Hospitals v. Casey, 62
Wheat v. United States, 172
Whitman v. Department of Transportation, 125–126

Will v. Hallock, 76–77
Wisconsin Right to Life v. FEDERAL ELECTION COMMISSION, 65–66
Woodford v. Ngo, 73–74

Z

Zedner v. United States, 193–194
Zelman v. Simmons-Harris, 62, 63, 159

INDEX
BY NAME AND SUBJECT

Page numbers appearing in boldface indicate major treatment of entries. Italicized page numbers refer to photos.

A

AALS (American Association of Law Schools), 80
ABA (American Bar Association)
  Georgia death penalty moratorium recommendation, 26–27
  Task Force on the Model Definition of the Practice of Law, 16
Abortion, **1–6**
  emergency contraceptives, 22
  RICO and abortion clinic protests, 161–163
Abrahamson, Shirley, 128
Abramoff, Jack, 45
Abrogation of sovereign immunity, 8–9
ACLU (American Civil Liberties Union)
  National Security Administration, wiretapping by the, 196
  USA PATRIOT Act, 185
Act 64 (Virginia), 79–80
ADA (American with Disabilities Act), **8–9**
Administrative Procedure Act (APA), 69–70
Adverse inference order, 51
Advisory Committee on Immunization Practices, 57
Affirmative defense in marijuana possession cases, 58
Aggravating factors in capital punishment cases, 25, 28–30, 31–32
Ahlborn, Heidi, 130–131
Aiwohi, Tayshea, 129–130
al Qaeda, 184, 185, 187
Alabama
  church arsons, 106–107
  Siegelman conspiracy charges, 45–46
Alaska, 152–154
Alexander, Lamar, 94
Alexander Archipelago, 153
Alibi evidence, 31–32
Aliens, **6–7**
  See also Immigration
Alito, Samuel Anthony, Jr., *7*, **7–8**
  abortion, 4
  exclusion of evidence, 174
  exhaustion of remedies under the Prison Litigation Reform Act, 73–74
  right to fair trial, 172
  Supreme Court, appointment to the, 180
Allstate Insurance Co., 109
Alternative Minimum Tax (AMT), 182
America Online, 117–118
American Association of Law Schools (AALS), 80
American Bar Association (ABA)
  Georgia death penalty moratorium recommendation, 26–27
  Task Force on the Model Definition of the Practice of Law, 16
American Center for Law and Justice, 4
American Civil Liberties Union (ACLU)
  National Security Administration, wiretapping by the, 196
  USA PATRIOT Act, 185
American Conservative Union, 185
American Red Cross, 107–108
Americans United For Separation of Church and State, 72
Americans with Disabilities Act, **8–9**
Amount-in-controversy requirements, 121–122
AMT (Alternative Minimum Tax), 182
Anti-Phishing Working Group (APWG), 118
Anti-retaliatory provision of Title VII, Civil Rights Act of 1964, 35–36

Anti-Terrorism and Effective Death Penalty Act, 101–103
Anticipatory warrants, 84–85
Antitrust law, **9–13**
Anza, Joseph and Vincent, 160
AOL, 117–118
APA. *See* Administrative Procedure Act (APA)
Appeals process
  civil procedure rules, 34–35
  "collateral order doctrine," 77
APWG (Anti-Phishing Working Group), 118
Arbaugh, Jennifer, 170
Arbitration, **13–14**
Arizona, 115–116
Arkansas, 58–59
Arkansas Department of Health and Human Services, 130–131
Arlington Central School District, 61–62
Arthur Anderson, 48
Article 36, Vienna Convention, 47
Ashcroft, John
  assisted suicide ruling, 14–15
  USA PATRIOT Act, renewal of the, 185
"Ashcroft Directive," 14–15
Assisted suicide, **14–16**
Athletes, 178–179
AT&T, 196
Attorneys, **16–17**
Attorneys' fees, 61, 122
Authorization for Use of Military Force (AUMF) Joint Resolution, 184–185
Ayotte, Kelly, *2*

B

Bailey, Nick, 46
Baker, Thurbert, 27
Balancing of interest test, 137–138
BALCO (Bay Area Laboratory Cooperative), 178–179
Balsillie, James, 143
Bank of China, 87
Bankruptcy, **19–22,** 151–152
Bankruptcy Abuse Prevention and Consumer Protection Act of 2005, 22
Banks, 123
Barber Foods, Inc., 75
Battel, *23*
Bay Area Laboratory Cooperative (BALCO), 178–179
Bayh, Birch, 155
Bell, Kenneth, 64
Bell, Kimberly, 179
Bell-South, 196
Berman, Richard, 139
Bidding and price concessions, 12–13
Binalshibh, Ramzi, 183
Bio Tissue Technologies, 88
Biomedical Tissue Services, Ltd., 88
Bipartisan Campaign Reform Act of 2002, 65
Birth control, **22–24**
BlackBerry, 143–144, *144*
Blackburn, Jim, 134
Blagojevich, Rod, 91, *91*
Blake, Leeander, 133
Blunt, Roy, 45
Body parts, harvesting of, 88–89
Boeken, Richard, 187–188
Bonds, Barry, 178, 179
Border patrol, 112, 131–133
Boxer, Barbara, 94
Breaux, John, 181
Breene, Timothy, 88
Breyer, Stephen
  burden of persuasion in Individualized Education Program hearings, 65
  consular notification and suppression of evidence, 48
  "costs" in the Individuals with Disabilities Education Act, 62
  habeas corpus, statute of limitations for, 103
  Hobbs Act, 162–163
  jurisdiction, 120
  new evidence in sentencing phase of capital punishment cases, 31–32
  prisoners' access to media, denial of, 78–79
  retaliatory discrimination, 36
  RICO violations and proximate cause, 160
  sovereign immunity, 177
Britt, Jimmy B., 134–135
Bronfman, Jeffrey, *90*
Brown, Marvin, 35
Bryan, William Jennings, 157
Buckeye Check Cashing, Inc., 13
Burger, Warren, 156
Burlington Northern & Santa Fe Railway, 35
Bush, George W.
  Alito, Samuel Anthony, Jr., appointment of, 8
  Guantanamo Bay detainees, 97, 183
  immigration policy, 112–113
  Minuteman Project, 132
  Padilla, Jose, case of, 184
  Protection of Lawful Commerce in Arms Act, 98, 99
  search and seizure, 165
  Supreme Court appointees, 6, 179–180
  tax reform panel, 181–182
  USA PATRIOT Act, renewal of the, 185
  wiretapping, 195–197
Bush, Jeb, 62, 158, 159

C

California
  capital punishment, 25–26
  habeas corpus, statute of limitations for, 102–103
  medical use of marijuana, 57
  Roadless Repeal, 69–70
  sex offenders, 169–170
  suspicionless searches of parolees, 166–167
  video games statute, 92
California Border Watch, 132
Campaign spending and contribution limits, 79–80
Campana, Thomas, Jr., 143–144
Cannabis clubs, 57
Canseco, Jose, 178
Capital punishment, **25–32**
Carabell, Keith, *41*
Cardegna, John, 13
Carter, Jimmy, 191
Causey, Richard, 48–49
CDA (Communications Decency Act), 139–140
Ceballos, Richard, 194–195
Census, **32–33**
Central Intelligence Agency, 147–148
Certiorari, 145–147
Cervical cancer, 56–57
CFA (Consumer Federation of America), 22
Chapin, Doug, 190
Charities, 107–108
Chase, Jim, 132
Chatham County, Georgia, 66–67
Chavis, Reginald, 102–103
Cheney, Dick, 147, 148
Child Online Protection Act, 116
ChoicePoint, 111–112
Chou, John, 87
Choy, Herbert, 52
Church arsons, 106–107
Civil actions
  constitutionality of execution method, 27–28
  state *vs.* federal court jurisdiction in securities class actions, 37–38
Civil liability of gun manufacturers, 98–99
Civil liberties, 185–186
Civil procedure, **33–35**
Civil rights, **35–37,** 185–186
Civil Rights Act of 1964, Title VII, 35–36, 170
Civil Service Reform Act (CSRA), 125–126
Civilian border patrols, 131–132
Clark, Terry and Dave, *115*
Class action, **37–40**
Classified information, 147–148
Clayton Act, 10
Clean Water Act, **40–42**
Clinton, Bill
  impeachment trial, 157
  partial birth abortion ban bills, veto of, 4
Cloning, 149–151
Cloyd, Matthew Lee, 106–107
Codey, Richard, 31
Collective bargaining, 125–126
Collins, Steven, 105–106
Colorado, 53–54
Colorado Jury Reform Pilot Project Subcommittee, 53
Colson, Charles W., 72
Commerce Clause, **42–44**
Commission on Federal Election Reform, 191
Communications Decency Act (CDA), 139–140
Compensable work time, 75–76
"Competing harms" laws, 1–2
Competitive bidding, 12––13
Competitive Technologies, Inc. (CTI), 145
ConAgra, 34
Conaway, Herb, 89
Condemnation of property, 67–69
Confrontation Clause, 172–173
Congressional redistricting plans, 32–33
Conspiracy, **44–46**
Constitution, U.S., 19–20
Consuls, **46–48**
Consumer credit counseling industry, 21–22
Consumer Federation of America (CFA), 22
Consumer protection, 21–22
Conte, Victor, Jr., 178
Contracts
  arbitration *vs.* courts, 13–14
  discrimination, contractual rights to sue for, 36–37
Controlled Substances Act, 14–16, 57, 89–90
Copyright infringement, 148–149
Corporate fraud, **48–52**
Corporations
  discrimination, 36–37
  fraud, 48–52
Corruption, 46
Coughenour, John C., 186
Courtney, Paul, 88
Cox, Christopher, *52,* **52**
Craig, Larry E., 98
Creationism, 157
Credit/debt counseling industry, 21–22
Creditors' claims, 20–21
Criminal procedure, **52–54**
Cruel and unusual punishment
  aggravating and mitigating circumstances in capital punishment sentencing, 29
  Title II, Americans with Disabilities Act, 9
CSRA (Civil Service Reform Act), 125–126

CTI (Competitive Technologies, Inc.), 145
Cunningham, Carson, & Messenger, 155

D

Dabit, Shadi, 39
DaimlerChrysler Corporation, 42–44, *43*
Damages, 70–71, 127–129
Dams, 41–42
Darrow, Clarence, 157
Data brokers, 111–112
Databases, DNA, 55–56
Daughtrey, Martha Craig, 43
Davis, Adrian, 172–173
Day, Patrick, 101–102
Death Penalty Moratorium Implementation Project, 26–27
Debt Collection Act, 175
Debt management industry, 21–22
DeBusk, Russell, Jr., 106–107
DeLay, Tom, 44–45, *45*, 67–68
Democratic Party, 189–190
Demonstrations and rallies, *15*, *63*, 113
Deportation, 6–7
Detainee Treatment Act (DTA), 97–98
Detainees, 182–184, *183*
Detention, 97–98
Detention-of-goods exception, 77
Dickhaus, Karl, 171
Diegelman, Don, 45–46
Dimethyltryptamine (DMT), 89
Directed verdicts, 34–35
Disabled persons
  Americans with Disabilities Act, 8–9
  Individuals with Disabilities Education Act (IDEA), 61–62, 64–65
  voting methods, 191
Discovery misconduct, 50–51
Discrimination
  congressional redistricting plans, 32–33
  disabled persons, 8–9
  retaliatory, 35–36
Diversity-of-citizenship jurisdiction, 120–121
DNA, **55–56,** 104–105, 135
Doha, Abu, 186
Dolan, Barbara, 176–177
Domestic violence cases, 173
Domino's Pizza, 36–37
"Don't ask, Don't tell" policy, 80
Dover Area School District, 158
Doyle, Jim, 128, 149–151
Drugs and narcotics, **56–58**
  erectile-dysfunction drugs for sex offenders, ban on state funding of, 169–170
  manslaughter charges for prenatal drug abuse, 129–130
  religious ceremonies, 89–90
  steroid use by professional athletes, 178–179
  substance-abuse tests, 125–126
DTA (Detainee Treatment Act), 97–98
Due process, **58–59**
  Title II, Americans with Disabilities Act, 9
  unborn children, 5
Dupree, Franklin, Jr., 134

E

Earle, Ronnie, 45
Earley, Mark, 73
East St. Louis, Illinois, 189–190
Eavesdropping, 186, 196
eBay, 144–145, *145*, 149
Ebbers, Bernard, *51*, 51–52
Economic development, 67–69
Education, **61–65**
  evolution/intelligent design debate, 157–158
  school vouchers, 158–159
EEOC (Equal Employment Opportunity Commission), 35
Eighth Amendment
  aggravating and mitigating circumstances in capital punishment sentencing, weight of, 29
  lethal injection, 27, 28
  new evidence in sentencing phase of capital punishment cases, 31–32
  Title II, Americans with Disabilities Act, 9
Electionline.org, 190–191
Elections, **65–66**
  campaign spending and contribution limits, 79–80
  DeLay, Tom, 44–45
  presidential election of 2000, 157
  reform, 190–191
  See also Voting
Electronic voting machines, 190–191
Eleventh Amendment, 20, 66–67
Eligibility factors in capital punishment, 25–26, 27, 28–30, 31–32
Ellis, Kelvin, 189, 190
Embryos, cloning of, 149–151
Emergency contraceptives, 22–24
Eminent domain, **67–69**
Empire Healthchoice Assurance, Inc., 119–120
Employee benefit plans, 20–21
Employee Retirement Income Security Act (ERISA), **70–71**
Endangered species, 70
Enemy combatants, 97, 184–185
Energy prices, 93–95, 108
Enron, 48–49

Ensign, John, 169
Environmental law, 40–42, **69–70**
Equal Employment Opportunity Commission (EEOC), 35
Equal Footing doctrine, 153
Equal Protection Clause
congressional redistricting plans, 33
medical malpractice damages limits, 127–128
Title II, Americans with Disabilities Act, 9
Equilon, 11–12
Equitable relief, 70–71
Erectile-dysfunction drugs, 169–170
ERISA, **70–71**
Esseks, James D., 96
Establishment Clause, 62–64, **71–73**
Ethics
Internet legal services, 16–17
U.S. House of Representatives rules, 45
Evans, Kitchel & Jenckes, 155
Evidence
exclusionary rule, 47–48, 85–86
right to a fair trial, 174
sentencing phase of capital punishment cases, 31–32
Evolution, 157–158
Excessive punitive damages, 188
Exclusionary rule, 47–48, 85–86
Execution methods, 27–28
Exhaustion of remedies, **73–74**
Exoneration, 56
Experts' fees in IDEA litigation, 61–62

F

FAA (Federal Aviation Administration), 125–126
Fahle, John, 171
Failure-to-warn, 188
Fainaru-Wada, Mark, 179
FAIR (Forum for Academic and Institutional Rights), 80–81
Fair Labor Standards Act, **75–76**
Fastow, Andrew, 48, 49
Fastow, Lea, 48
FBI (Federal Bureau of Investigation), 165–166
FCAT (Florida's Comprehensive Assessment Test), 158–159
FCC (Federal Communications Commission), 196
FEC. *See* Federal Elections Commission (FEC)
FEC (Federal Elections Commission), 65–66
Federal Arbitration Act, 13–14
Federal Aviation Administration (FAA), 125–126
Federal Bureau of Investigation (FBI), 165–166, 196
Federal Communications Commission (FCC), 196
Federal courts
exhaustion of remedies doctrine, 73–74
Federal Arbitration Act, 14
state *vs.* federal court jurisdiction in class actions, 37–38
Federal Elections Commission (FEC), 65–66
Federal Employees Health Benefits Act (FEHBA), 119–120
Federal Energy Regulatory Commission (FERC), 41
Federal question
Federal Employees Health Benefits Act, 119–120
state investment tax credits, 43–44
Federal Rules of Civil Procedure, 33–34, 102
Federal Tort Claims Act, **76–77,** 176–177
Federal Trade Commission Act, 10
Federal Trade Commission (FTC), 111–112
Fee-shifting provisions, 61–62
FEHBA (Federal Employees Health Benefits Act), 119–120
Feinstein, Dianne, 99
FERC (Federal Energy Regulatory Commission), 41
Ferdon, Matthew, 127–128
Fernandez-Vargas, Humberto, 6–7
Fidell, Eugene R., 184
File-sharing software, 148–149
Final Environmental Impact Statement (FEIS), 69–70
First Amendment, **77–81**
faith-based prison programs, 72–73
school voucher programs, 62–64
whistleblowing, 194–195
See also Freedom of speech
Fitzgerald, Patrick J., 147–148
Florida
civil actions on constitutionality of execution methods, 27–28
school voucher programs, 62–64, 158–159
Florida's Comprehensive Assessment Test (FCAT), 158–159
Flowers, Linda, 58
Floyd, Henry F., Jr., 184
Focus on the Family, 57
Foreign nationals, 47–48
Forest Service. *See* U.S. Forest Service
"Forest Service Roadless Area Conservation," 69–70
Forum for Academic and Institutional Rights (FAIR), 80–81
Fourteenth Amendment, 9
Fourth Amendment, **81–86**

Franklin Capital Corporation, 121–122
Fraud, **86–89**
  arbitration agreements, 14
  vote buying, 189–190
Freedom of association, 81
Freedom of Information Act, 182
Freedom of religion, **89–90**
Freedom of speech
  campaign spending and contribution limits, 79–80
  prisoners' access to media, denial of, 77–79
  Solomon Amendment, 80–81
  video games statutes, 91–92
  whistleblowing, 194–195
  See also First Amendment
Frenzel, William Eldridge, 181
Friends of the Border Patrol, 132
Frist, Bill, 93–94, 97
FTCA (Federal Tort Claims Act), 176–177

G

G. H. Construction Company, 46
Gambino crime family, 140–141
Game laws, 91–92
Gard, John, 128
Gardasil, 56–57
Garrett, Elizabeth, 181
Garrett, Scott, 68
Garth, Leonard I., 7
Gas, **93–95,** 108
Gay and lesbian rights, **95–97**
Gee, Rebekah, *23*
Geneva Convention, **97–98**
Georgia
  American Bar Association death penalty moratorium recommendation, 26–27
  Fourteenth Amendment violations, 8–9
  same-sex marriage, 96–97
Gerrymandering, 32–33
GI Forum of Texas, 33
Giambi, Jason, 178
Gilchrist, Jim, 131
Ginsburg, Ruth Bader
  burden of persuasion in Individualized Education Program hearings, 65
  competitive bidding, 12––13
  habeas corpus, statute of limitations for, 102
  jurisdiction, 120, 121, 123
  malicious prosecution, 114
  sexual harassment cases, 170–171
  Spending Clause, 62
  state probate matters, 151–152
  taxes on goods sold on tribal property, 137–138
  unpaid workers' compensation premiums and the Bankruptcy Code, 21
Glacial Bay area, 153–154
Glisan, Ben, 48
Gonzales, Alberto R.
  Fitzgerald investigation, 147
  Partial Birth Abortion Ban Act of 2003, 4
  USA PATRIOT Act, 185–186
  wiretapping, 196–197
Gonzalez-Lopez, Cuauhtemoc, 171–172
Goodman, Tony, 8–9, *9*
Google Inc., 116–117
Gotti, John, Jr., 140–141, *141*
Government employees, 194–195
Graham, Nicholas, 118
Grassley, Charles, 169
Great-West Life & Annuity Insurance Company, 71
Green, Henry, 95, 96
Grokster Ltd., 148–149
Growth and Investment Tax Plan, 182
Grubbs, Jeffrey, 84
Guantanamo Bay detainees, 97–98, 182–184, *183*
Guest worker programs, 112–113
Gun control, **98–99**
Guzek, Randy Lee, 31

H

HAAG Engineering Co., 109
Habeas corpus, **101–106**
  Bankruptcy Act of 1800, 20
  capital punishment cases, 27–28
Hallock, Susan, 76–77
Hamdan, Salim Ahmed, 97
Hamilton, Phyllis J., 4
Hammon, Hershel and Amy, 173
Hamrick, Paul Michael, 46
Harmless error analysis, 167–169
Hastert, Dennis, 45, 94
Hastings, J. Gary, 187–188
Hate crime, **106–107**
HAVA (Help American Vote Act), 190–191
Hawaii, 129–130
Hayden, Michael, 196
Health and medical issues
  human papillomavirus (HPV) vaccine, 56–57
  medical use for marijuana, 57–58
"Health of the mother" exceptions to parental notification law, 2
Help American Vote Act (HAVA), 190–191
Higher Education Technical Amendments, 175
Hill, Clarence, 28
Hinojosa, Juan "Chuy," 131

Hispanic Americans, 33
Hobbs Act, 162
Hodges, Ken, 27
Holden, Bob, 3
Holding claims, securities, 38–40
Holmes, Bobby Lee, 174
Horizontal price fixing, 11–12
House, Paul, 104
House Government Reform Committee, 178–179
Howard Delivery Service, 20
Hoyer, Steny, 186
HPV (human papillomavirus) vaccine, 56–57
Hudson, Booker T., Jr., 85–86
Hueston, John, 49
Human embryo cloning, 149–151
Human papillomavirus (HPV) vaccine, 56–57
Humane Society of the United States, 108
Hurricane Katrina, **107–109,** *108*
Huttle, Valerie Vainieri, 89
Hynes, Charles J., 88

I

IBP, Inc., 75
IDEA (Individuals with Disabilities Education Act), 61–62, 64–65
Ideal Steel Supply, 159–161
Identity theft, 76–77, **111–112**
IEPs (Individualized Education Programs), 61, 64–65
iGate, 165–166
IIRIRA (Illegal Immigration Reform and Immigrant Responsibility Act), 6–7
Illegal immigrants. *See* Immigration
Illegal Immigration Reform and Immigrant Responsibility Act (IIRIRA), 6–7
Illinois, 91–92
Illinois Tool Works, Inc., 10–11
iMesh, 149
Immigration, **112–113,** 131–133
  See also Aliens
Immigration and Naturalization Act (INA), 6–7
Immunity, **113–114**
In rem actions, 19–20
INA (Immigration and Naturalization Act), 6–7
Income tax reform, 181–182
Independent Ink Inc., 10–11
Indiana, 2–3
Individualized Education Programs (IEPs), 61, 64–65
Individuals with Disabilities Education Act (IDEA), 61–62, 64–65
Informed consent, 2–3
Injunctions, 144–145
InnerChange Freedom Initiative, 72
Innocence Project, 56
Insanity defense, **114–116**
Institute for Justice, 68
Insurance
  Hurricane Katrina, 109
  Medicaid, 130–131
  reimbursement of benefits paid, 70–71, 119–120
Intelligent design, 157–158
Internal Revenue Code, 181–182
International treaties, 47–48
Internet, **116–118**
  eBay, injunction against, 144–145
  legal services, 16–17
  obscenity, 139–140
  piracy, 148–149
Interrogation, 133–134
Investigations, 147–148
Investment tax credits, 42–44
Iowa, 71–73

J

Jackson, Robert H., 155, 156
Jackson, Vernon, 165
Jeep plant, *43*
Jefferson, Wallace B., 45
Jefferson, William, 165–166
Johnson, Bruce, 44
Johnson, Debora, 88
Johnson, Yvette, 189
Joiner, Bill, 35
Jones, Gary, 58
Jones, John E., III, 158
Jones, Robert E., 15
Judgment bar claims, 77
Jurisdiction, **119–123**
  bankruptcy proceedings, 19–20
  "collateral order doctrine," 77
  sexual harassment cases, 170–171
  state probate matters, 151–152
Juror questions, 53–54
JWM Investments, Inc., 36–37

K

Kansas
  capital punishment sentencing, 28–30
  evolution/intelligent design debate, 158
  gay and lesbian rights, 95–96
  taxation, 137–138
Katyal, Neal, *97*
Katz, Bernard, 19
Katz, David A., 43
Kautzky, Walter "Kip," 72
Kaytal, Neal, 98

Kelo, Susette, 69
Kennedy, Anthony
  "Ashcroft Directive," 15
  exclusionary rule in "knock-and-announce" cases, 86
  habeas corpus review, 103–106
  mandatory patent infringement injunctions, 145
  public employees and the freedom of speech, 195
  RICO violations and proximate cause, 160
  "significant nexus" test for wetlands classification, 40–41
  submerged lands ownership dispute, 153
  unpaid workers' compensation premiums and the Bankruptcy Code, 21
  U.S. Postal Service and sovereign immunity, 176–177
Kennedy, Edward, 155, 156
Kern, Mark, 189
Kerry, John, 189
Kestell, Steve, 150
King, Troy, 107
Kirsch, William Curtis, 46
Kleindienst, Richard, 155
"Knock-and-announce" rule, 85–86
Kohler, Shannon, 55
Kopf, Richard G., 4
Kristof, Nicholas, 147
Kuby, Ronald L., 141
Kuehn, Ron, 150

L

LabCorp., 146
Labor law, **125–126**
Lafferty, Marty, 148
Lake, Sim, 49
Law schools, 80–81
Lay, Kenneth, 48–49, *49*
Lazear, Edward P., 181
League of United Latin American Citizens (LULAC), 32–33
Leaks, classified information, 147–148
Lee, Sheila Jackson, 131–132
Lending practices, 13–14
Lethal injection, 28
Levine, John R., 118
Lewis, Jesse, 189
Liability of gun manufacturers, 98–99
Libby, Lewis "Scooter," *147*, 147–148
Light cigarettes, 187–188
Limon, Matthew, 95
Lincoln Property Company, 120–121
Liu, Sherry, 87
Local government, 66–67
Location of banks, 123
Lochyer, Bill, 57
Lockhart, James, 175
Los Angeles airport bombing attempt, 186–187
Los Angeles County District Attorney's Office, 194–195
Lott, Trent, 169
Louisiana, 55
Low, Joseph, 171–172
Loy, James, 131
Lu, Curtis, 118
Luckert, Marla J., 95
Ludwig, James, 66
LULAC (League of United Latin American Citizens), 32–33
Lung cancer, 187–188
Luttig, Michael, 123
Lynch, Gerard, 139
Lynn, Barry, 72

M

Maass, Elizabeth, 50–51
MacDonald, Jeffrey, 134
Mack, Connie, III, 181
Major League Baseball, 178–179
Malicious prosecution, 114
Malone, Tom, 95, 96
Malpractice, **127–129**
Mandatory patent infringement injunctions, 144–145
Manny, Jill, 108
Manslaughter, **129–130**
Marijuana legalization, 57–58
Market power in tying arrangements, 10–11
Marlboro Lights, 187–188
Marsh, Michael, 29
Marshall, E. Pierce, 151–152
Marshall, J. Howard, II, 151–152
Marshall, Vickie Lynn. *See* Smith, Anna Nicole
Martin, Gerald and Juana, 121–122
Maryland, 96
Mashboxx, 148–149
Massachusetts
  emergency contraceptives, 22, 23
  gay marriage, 96
Mastromarino, Michael, 88, *88*, 89
McCain-Feingold Act, 65
McCarty, Katrina, *23*
McClellan, Scott, 147
McCottry, Michelle, 172
McDonald, John W., 36–37
McGuire, Mark, 178
McVeigh, Joseph, 119
Media, prisoners' access to, 77–79
Medicaid, **130–131,** 169

Medical use of marijuana, 57–58
Medicare, 169
Medina, Yvonne, 53
Mentally retarded persons, 27
MercExchange, 144
Merck and Co., 56
Merrill Lynch, 39
Metabolite, 146
Method patents, 145–146
Mexico and the United States, 112–113, **131–133**
Michigan, 92
Mid Atlantic Medical Services, Inc., 70–71
Miers, Harriet E., 7, 8, 180
Military recruiters, 80–81
Military tribunals, 97–98, 183
"Millennium Bomber," 186–187
Miller, Judith, 147
Miller test, 139–140
Minorities, 32–33
Minuteman Project, 131–132
Miranda rights, 47, **133–134**
Missouri, 3
Mitchell, George, *178*
Mitigating factors in capital punishment cases, 25, 27, 28–30, 31–32
Mohamed, Samir Ait, 186
Mohammed, Khalid Sheikh, 183, 184
Mohawk Industries, 161
Money laundering, 45
Monson, Diane, 57
Montgomery County Public School System, 64–65
Moore, William, 113–114
Morgan Stanley & Co., Inc., 50–51
Moritz, Jeffrey, 115
"Morning after pill," 22–24
Mosley, Benjamin, 106–107
Motion for Return of Property, 166
Moussaoui, Zacarias, 184, 185
Mueller, Robert, 46, 185
Muncey Hubert, 104–105
Murder, **134–135**
  Bobby Lee Holmes case, 174
  Clarence Hill case, 28
  Eric Clark case, 115–116
  Michael Marsh case, 29
  Patrick Day case, 101–102
  Paul House case, 104–105
  Randy Lee Guzek case, 31–32
  Reginald Chavis case, 102–103
  Robert Sanders case, 25–26
  Viet Mike Ngo case, 73
Murdock, M. Brooke, 96
Muris, Timothy J., 181
Murphy, Pearl and Theodore, 61

N

Nachtigal, Allison, 50
Narcotics. *See* Drugs and narcotics
National Center for Science Education, 158
National Coalition for Sexual Freedom (NCSF), 139
National Conference of Commissioners on Uniform State Laws (NCCLUSL), 22
National Environmental Policy Act (NEPA), 69–70
National Football League, 178–179
National Guard, 112–113
National Organ Transplant Act, 89
National Organization for Women (NOW), 161–163
National Security Agency, 186, 195–197
National Steel Supply, 159–161
Native American rights, **137–138**
Natural gas prices, 93, 94
NCCUSL (National Conference of Commissioners on Uniform State Laws), 22
NCSF (National Coalition for Sexual Freedom), 139
"Negligent transmission," 176–177
Nelms, Robert, 88
NEPA (National Environmental Policy Act), 69–70
New evidence
  habeas corpus review, 103–105
  Jeffrey MacDonald case, 134–135
  in sentencing phase of capital punishment cases, 31–32
New Hampshire
  eminent domain, 68
  Parental Notification Prior to Abortion Act, 1
New Jersey
  death penalty moratorium, 30–31
  same-sex marriage, 96
  sex offenders, 169
New Jersey Death Penalty Study Commission, 30–31
New London, Connecticut, 67–69
New Mexico, 69–70
New York
  election reform, 191
  sex offenders, 169
The New York Times, 147–148, 196
Ngo, Viet Mike, 73
Nicelli, Joseph, 88, 89
Nickerson, Jerome, 108
Nitke, Barbara, 139–140
Nixon, Richard, 155
Northern Insurance Company, 66–67
Notice, 58–59
Novak, Robert, 147, 148

NOW (National Organization for Women), 161–163
NTP, 143–144

O

O Centro Espirita Beneficente Uniao Do Vegetal (UDV), 89–90
Obama, Barack, 189
Obituaries, 155–157
O'Brien, Patricia, 88
Obscenity, **139–140**
O'Connor, Sandra Day
  burden of persuasion in Individualized Education Program hearings, 64–65
  garnishment of Social Security payments for student loan debts, 175
  gay and lesbian rights, 95
  parental notification for abortion, 1–2
  replacement of, 8
  retirement, 179–180
Office of Personnel Management (OPM), 119–120
Ohio, 42–44
Oil companies, *94*, 108
Olson, Joseph, 177
Oluwatosin, Olatunji, 111
OPM (Office of Personnel Management), 119–120
Opportunity Scholarship Program (OSP), 62–64, 158–159
Oregon
  Oregon Death with Dignity Act, 14–16
  Roadless Repeal, 69–70
  same-sex marriage, 96–97
Organized crime, **140–141**
OSP (Opportunity Scholarship Program), 158–159
Out-of-state attorneys, 17

P

Padilla, Jose, 184–185
Palmeiro, Rafael, 178
Parental notification, 1
Pariente, Barbara J., 63, 159
Parolees, 166–167
Partial birth abortion, 3–4
Partisan gerrymandering, 32–33
Pataki, George, 169
Patents, 9–11, 34, **143–147**
Pear, Debbie, 36
Pennsylvania, 157, 158
Per se rule, 11
Perdue, Sonny, 27
Perelman, Ronald, *50*
Peremptory challenges, 105–106
Perjury, **147–148**
Perkins, Bob, 45
Perry, Rick, 131
Personal property tax exemption, 42–44
Personhood, 5
Pharmacists for Life, 23
Philip Morris Incorporated, 187–188
Phishing, 117–118
Pierron, Joseph, 95
Piracy, **148–149**
Piuze, Michael, *188*
Plame, Valerie, 147–148
Plan B (contraceptive), 22–24
Planned Parenthood of Northern New England, 1–2
Planned Parenthood v. Casey, 2
PLCAA (Protection of Lawful Commerce in Arms Act), 98–99
Plescia, George, 169
PLRA (Prison Litigation Reform Act), 73–74
Poritz, Deborah T., 96
Pornography, online, 116–117
Portal-to-Portal Act, 75–76
Possession of marijuana laws, 57–58
Poterba, James Michael, 181
Powell, Charles, Jr., 189, 190, *190*
Practice of law, 16–17
Prairie Band Potowatomi Nation, 137–138
Pratt, Robert W., 71–72
Preclusion issues, 38
Preferential transfer proceedings, 19–20
Prenatal drug abuse, 129–130
Presidential powers, 97–98
Price concessions, 12–13
Price fixing, 11–12, 12–13
Price gouging, 93, 94, 108
Priest, Pat, 45
Priority status in bankruptcy claims, 20–21
Prison Fellowship Ministries, 72
Prison Litigation Reform Act (PLRA), 73–74
Prisoners of war, 183–184
Prisons
  denial of media access, 77–79
  faith-based programs, 71–73
  Prison Litigation Reform Act, 73–74
Privacy, 116–117, **149–151**
Private schools, 62–64
Privileges and Immunities Clauses, 9
Probable cause
  DNA testing, 55
  retaliatory prosecution lawsuits, 113–114
  search warrants, 84–85
Probate, **151–152**
Procedure, civil. *See* Civil procedure

Profiteering in a Non-Profit Industry: Abusive Practices in Credit Counseling (Permanent Subcommittee on Investigations of the Committee on Homeland Security), 22
Property law, 152–154
Protection of Lawful Commerce in Arms Act (PLCAA), 98–99
Proximate cause, 160–161
Public employees, 194–195
Public Health Cigarettes Smoking Act, 188
Public schools. *See* Education
Punitive damages, 188

R

Race
- church arsons, 106–107
- discrimination, 36–37
- Georgia death penalty implementation, 27
- peremptory challenges based on, 105–106

Racketeer Influenced and Corrupt Organizations (RICO) Act, 86–88, 140, **159–163**
Ragan, Keith, 155
Raich, Angel McClary, 57
Randolph, Janet, 81
Randolph, Scott, 81
Rapanos, John, 40–41
Raymond, Lee, 94
Reagan, Ronald, 156
"Reasonable reliance" element, 86–88
Reassignment of duties as retaliatory discrimination, 35–36
Reauthorization of the USA PATRIOT Act, 185–186
Rebuttable presumption of market power, 10–11
Recognition Equipment, Inc. (REI), 113–114
Recording Industry of America, 148–149
Recuenco, Arturo, 167–169
Redistricting plans, 32–33
Reeder-Simco GMC Inc., 12–13
Reentry of aliens, 6–7
Rehnquist, William Hubbs, **155–157,** 179–180
REI (Recognition Equipment, Inc.), 113–114
Reid, Richard, 187
Reimbursement of benefits paid, 130–131
Religion, 62–64, 71–73, **89–90, 157–159**
Religious Freedom Restoration Act (RFRA), 89–91
Republican National State Elections Committee (RNSEC), 44–45
Research in Motion (RIM), 143–144
Residual-doubt evidence, 31–32
Ressam, Ahmed, 186–187, *187*
Retaliatory discrimination, 35–36
Retaliatory prosecution lawsuits, 113–114
Retroactivity, 6–7
RFRA (Religious Freedom Restoration Act), 89–91
Rhode Island, 57
Rice, Condoleezza, 183
RICO (Racketeer Influenced and Corrupt Organizations) Act, 86–88, 140, **159–163**
Riel, Arthur, 50
Right to a fair trial, 53–54, 171–174
Right to a speedy trial, 193–194
Right to counsel, 133–134, 171–172
Riley, Bob, *68*
RIM (Research in Motion), 143–144
RNSEC. *See* Republican National State Elections Committee (RNSEC)
Roadless Repeal, 70
Roadless Rule, 69–70
Roberts, John
- abortion, 4
- consular notification and suppression of evidence, 47–48
- equitable relief under ERISA, 71
- Guantanamo Bay detainees, 98
- habeas corpus review for newly discovered evidence, 105
- jurisdiction, 122
- mandatory patent infringement injunctions, 145
- religious use of controlled substances, 90
- Solomon Amendment, 81
- Supreme Court, appointment to the, 179–180
- tax forfeiture sales notice, 59
- taxpayers' standing in Commerce Clause suit, 44
- warrantless entry, 83
- warrantless searches, 84

Robertson, James, 183
Robinson-Patman Price Discrimination Act, 12–13
Roche, Christophe and Juanita, 120–121
Roe v. Wade, 2
Romney, Mitt, 23, 96
Rosenthal, Ed, 58
Rossotti, Charles O., 181
Rotenberg, Marc, 116
Rounds, Mike, *5*, 6
Rove, Karl, 147–148
Rule of reason, 11
Rules 50(a) and 50(b), Federal Rules of Civil Procedure, 34–35
Rumsfeld, Donald, 184

S

S. D. Warren Company, 41–42
Sack, Robert, 139
Safer Alternative for Enjoyable Recreation, 57–58
Same-sex marriage, 96–97
Samson, Donald C., 166–167
Sanders, Ronald, 25, *26*
Santorum, Rick, 169
Scalia, Antonin
  anticipatory warrants, 84–85
  arbitration agreements, 13–14
  "Ashcroft Directive," 15–16
  capital punishment eligibility factors, 25–26
  discrimination, contractual rights to sue for, 37
  exclusionary rule in "knock-and-announce" cases, 85–86
  Fourteenth Amendment violations, 9
  garnishment of Social Security payments for student loan debts, 175
  RICO violations and proximate cause, 160
  right to fair trial, 172
  testimonial statements, 173
  wetlands classification, 40
Scanlon, Michael, 45
Schaffer, Brian, 64–65
Scheindlin, Shira, 140–141
Schilling, Curt, 178
Schmidt, Daniel, 122–123
School vouchers, 62–64, 158–159
Schwarzenegger, Arnold, 112, 169
Scopes, John, 157
"Scopes Monkey Trial," 157
Scruggs, Richard, 109
Scrushy, Richard M., 46
Search and seizure, 83–85, **165–167**
Secrest, George "Mac," 49
Securities, 37–38, 51
Securities and Exchange Commission, 52
Securities Litigation Uniform Standards Act of 1998 (SLUSA), 37–40
Segregation, 156
Selig, Bud, *178*, 178–179
Sensenbrenner, James, Jr., 186
Sentencing, 27–32, **167–169**
Separation of powers, 166
September 11th terrorist attacks, 184, 185
Sereboff, Marlene and Joel, 71
Severability rule, 14
Sex offenses, **169–170**
Sexton, Ted, *107*
Sexual harassment, **170–171**
Sexually Explicit Video Games Law (Illinois), 91–92
Shareholders, 36–37
Sharkey, Percy, 35
Shell Oil, 11
Sherman Act
  horizontal price fixing, 11–12
  tying arrangements, 10
"Significant nexus" test for wetlands classification, 40–41
Simcox, Chris, 131
Simplified Income Tax Plan, 182
Sixth Amendment, **171–174**
Skilling, Jeffrey, 48–49
Sliwa, Curtis, 140–141
SLUSA. *See* Securities Litigation Uniform Standards Act of 1998 (SLUSA)
Smith, Anna Nicole, *151*, 151–152
Smith, Dennis, 169
Smith, Derek V., 112
Smoking. *See* Tobacco
Snow, John, 182
Social Security, **174–175**
Solomon, Gerald, 80
Solomon Amendment, 80–81
Sonders, Liz Ann, 181
Sosa, Sammy, 178
Souter, David
  aggravating and mitigating circumstances in capital punishment sentencing, 30
  anticipatory warrants, 85
  "collateral order doctrine," 77
  "discharge" definition and the Clean Water Act, 41–42
  habeas corpus, 97
  Illegal Immigration Reform and Immigrant Responsibility Act of 1996, 7
  insanity defense, 115–116
  malicious prosecution, 114
  public employees and the freedom of speech, 195
  state *vs.* federal court jurisdiction in securities class actions, 37–38
  warrantless searches, 83–84
South Dakota, 4–6
South Dakota Task Force to Study Abortion, 4–5
Sovereign immunity, **176–177**
  Americans with Disabilities Act, Title II, 8–9
  Bankruptcy Code, 19
  local governments, 66–67
Spamming, 117–118
Specter, Arlen, 97
Speech or Debate Clause, 165–166
Speedy Trial Act, 193–194
Spencer, James R., 143
Spending Clause, 62
Spitzer, Eliot, 39
Sports law, **178–179**

Standards of proof
  aggravating and mitigating circumstances in capital punishment sentencing, weight of, 29
  death penalty sentencing, 27
  Individualized Education Program hearings, 64–65
Standing, taxpayers', 44
State courts
  Federal Arbitration Act applicability, 14
  jurisdiction issues, 37–38, 120–123
State Farm Insurance Co., 109
States
  "Ashcroft Directive," 15–16
  Fourteenth Amendment violations, 8–9
  securities class action suits, 37–40
Statutes of limitations, 102–103
Stem cell research, 150
Steroid use, 178–179
Stevens, John Paul
  compensable work time, 76
  competitive bidding, 13
  exhaustion of remedies under the Prison Litigation Reform Act, 73–74
  federal court jurisdiction, 152
  habeas corpus, statute of limitations for, 102
  Illegal Immigration Reform and Immigrant Responsibility Act of 1996, 7
  Medicaid benefits paid, reimbursement for, 131
  public employees and the freedom of speech, 195
  securities class action suits, 39–40
  "significant nexus" test for wetlands classification, 41
  sovereign immunity in bankruptcy proceedings, 19–20
  suspicionless searches of parolees, 167
  tying arrangements, 10
  "weighing" and "unweighing" in capital punishment sentencing, 26
Stoeckley, Helena, 134
Stout, Donald, 143, 144
StreamCast Networks, 149
Strong, William, 50
Student loan debt, 174–175
Submerged Lands Act, 152–154
Sullivan, Scott, 51
Summer, Robert E., 149
Sunbeam Corporation, 50
Supreme Court, United States, **179–180**
  abortion cases, 1–2
  Americans with Disabilities Act, Title II, 9
  anticipatory warrants, 84–85
  antitrust cases, 10–13
  arbitration, 13–14
  assisted suicide cases, 15–16
  bankruptcy cases, 19–21
  Bipartisan Campaign Reform Act, 65, 66
  capital punishment cases, 25–26, 27–28, 29–30, 31–32
  civil rights cases, 35–37
  Clean Water Act, 40–42
  Commerce Clause, 44
  compensable work time, 76
  congressional redistricting, 32–33
  consular notification and suppression of evidence, 47–48
  eminent domain cases, 67
  equitable relief under ERISA, 71
  exclusion of evidence, 174
  exclusionary rule in "knock-and-announce" cases, 85–86
  exhaustion of remedies under the Prison Litigation Reform Act, 73–74
  Federal Tort Claims Act, 76–77
  garnishment of Social Security payments for student loan debts, 175
  Guantanamo Bay detainees, 183–184
  habeas corpus review, 102–106
  Hobbs Act, 162–163
  Illegal Immigration Reform and Immigrant Responsibility Act, 7
  Individuals with Disabilities Education Act, 62, 64–65
  insanity defense, 115–116
  jurisdiction issues, 120–123, 151–152
  malicious prosecution, 114
  mandatory patent infringement injunctions, 145
  Medicaid benefits paid, reimbursement for, 131
  prisoners' access to media, denial of, 78–79
  public employees and the freedom of speech, 195
  religious use of controlled substances, 90
  RICO violations and proximate cause, 160–161
  right to fair trial, 172
  rules of civil procedure, 34–35
  securities class action lawsuits, 38–40
  sentencing and harmless error analysis, 168–169
  sexual harassment cases, 170–171
  Solomon Amendment, 81
  sovereign immunity, 66–67, 176–177
  submerged lands ownership dispute, 153–154
  suspicionless searches of parolees, 167
  tax forfeiture sales notice, 59
  taxes on goods sold on tribal property, 137–138
  testimonial statements, 173

Supreme Court, United States *(cont'd)*
waiver of speedy trial, 194
warrantless entry, 82–83
warrantless searches, 83–84
See also Specific justices
Symantec, 117

T

Tallman, Richard C., 15
Task Force on the Model Definition of the Practice of Law, ABA, 16
Tax forfeiture sales notice, 58–59
Taxation, 137–138, **181–182**
Terrorism, 97–98, **182–187**, 195–197
Texaco, 11
Texans for a Republican Majority PAC, 44–45
Texas
congressional redistricting plans, 32–33
elections law, 44–45
sex offenders, 169
Third-party compensation, 70–71, 119–120, 130–131
Thomas, Clarence
aggravating and mitigating circumstances in capital punishment sentencing, 29
civil procedure rules, 34–35
Federal Arbitration Act applicability to state courts, 14
horizontal price fixing, 11–12
mandatory patent infringement injunctions, 145
"negligent transmission," 176–177
RICO violations and proximate cause, 160
sentencing and harmless error analysis, 168–169
sovereign immunity, 67
suspicionless searches of parolees, 167
tax forfeiture sales notice, 59
taxes on goods sold on tribal property, 137–138
Thomas, Sheila, 189
Time, 147–148
Title II, Americans with Disabilities Act, 8–9
Title VII, Civil Rights Act of 1964, 170
Tobacco, **187–188**
Tomlin, David, 183
Trident Industrial Inkjet, 10
TRMPAC (Texans for a Republican Majority), 44–45
Tying arrangements, 10–11

U

UDMSA (Uniform Debt-Management Services Act), 21–22
UDV (O Centro Espirita Beneficente Uniao Do Vegetal), 89–90
Unauthorized practice of law, 16–17
Uniform Debt-Management Services Act (UDMSA), 21–22
United Network for Organ Sharing, 89
Unitherm Food Systems, Inc., 34
Uniting and Strengthening America by Providing Tools Required to Intercept and Obstruct Terrorism Act, 185–186
University Patents Inc. (UPI), 146
U.S. Army Corps of Engineers, 40
U.S. Border Patrol, 112, 132
U.S. Department of Defense, 80–81
U.S. Department of Justice, 143, 191
U.S. Food and Drug Administration
emergency contraceptives, 22
human papillomavirus (HPV) vaccine, 56–57
transplant tissue recall, 88
U.S. Forest Service, 69–70
U.S. House of Representatives
Cox, Christopher, 52
ethics rules, 45
search and seizure, 165–166
U.S. Postal Service, 113–114, 176–177
USA PATRIOT Act, 185–186
Usury, 13

V

Vaccines, 56–57
Verizon, 196
Vermont, 79–80
Viagra, 169–170
Video games, 91–92
Vienna Convention on Consular Relations, 47–48
Violent Video Games Law (Illinois), 91–92
Virginia
anti-phishing law, 117–118
campaign spending limits, 79
sex offenders, 169
Visto, 144
Volvo Trucks North America Inc., 12–13
Voter ID, 190, 191
Voter-verified paper audit trails (VVPATs), 191
Voting, **189–191**
See also Elections
Vouchers, school. *See* School vouchers
VVPATs (voter-verified paper audit trails), 191

W

Wachovia Bank, 122–123

Waiting periods for abortion, 2–3
Waiver, **193–194**
Wal-Mart, 22–24
Wallace Bookstores, Inc., 19
Wardlow, Kim, 125–126
Ware, James, 117
Warner, Mark, 169
Warrantless entry, 81–83
Warrantless searches, 83–84, 166–167
Washington Post, 196–197
"Weighing" and "unweighing" in capital punishment sentencing, 26
Wetlands, 40–41
Whistleblowing, **194–195**
Whitbread, Ed, *132*
White, Sheila, 35–36
Whitman, Terry, 125
Williams, Lance, 179
Williams, Shirley, 161
Wilson, Joseph C., 147
Wiretapping, **195–197**
Wisconsin
  cloning ban proposal, 149–151
  medical malpractice damages, 127–129
Wisconsin Biotechnology and Medical Device Association, 150
Wisconsin Right to Life (WTRL), 65–66
Women's Health and Human Life Protection Act (South Dakota), 6
Woodward, Bob, 148
Woolston, Thomas, 144
Worker's compensation, 20–21
WorldCom, 51–52
Wright, Scott O., 3
WTRL (Wisconsin Right to Life), 65–66
Wyden, Ron, 94
Wynne, Michael, 49

Y

Y & H Corporation, 170
Young, Clayton, 46

Z

Zedner, Jacob, 193–194
Zurich American Insurance, 20

ISBN-13: 978-0-7876-9029-8
ISBN-10: 0-7876-9029-5